I0816677

Gene Kelly

Gene Kelly

The Making of a Creative Legend

Earl J. Hess and Pratibha A. Dabholkar

University Press of Kansas

Published by the University Press of Kansas (Lawrence, Kansas 66045), which was organized by the Kansas Board of Regents and is operated and funded by Emporia State University, Fort Hays State University, Kansas State University, Pittsburg State University, the University of Kansas, and Wichita State University.

Library of Congress Cataloging-in-Publication Data
Names: Hess, Earl J., author. | Dabholkar, Pratibha A., author.
Title: Gene Kelly : the making of a creative legend / Earl J. Hess, Pratibha A. Dabholkar.
Description: Lawrence : University Press of Kansas, 2020. | Includes bibliographical references and index.
Identifiers: LCCN 2020011789
ISBN 9780700630172 (cloth)
ISBN 9780700630189 (epub)
Subjects: LCSH: Kelly, Gene, 1912–1996. | Motion picture actors and actresses—United States—Biography. | Dancers—United States—Biography. Classification: LCC PN2287.K64 H47 2020 |
DDC 791.4302/8092 [B]—dc23
LC record available at https://lccn.loc.gov/2020011789.

British Library Cataloguing-in-Publication Data is available.

Printed in the United States of America

10 9 8 7 6 5 4 3 2 1

The paper used in this publication is acid free and meets the minimum requirements of the American National Standard for Permanence of Paper for Printed Library Materials Z39.48-1992.

To Julie and all our Angels
With eternal love

Contents

Illustrations

Maps

Figures

Preface

Gene Kelly was a multifaceted entertainer—dancer, choreographer, actor, singer, director—whose large fan following mostly views him as a dancer of vigor, inventiveness, and style on the big screen. Most people fail to realize that Kelly was a renaissance man of entertainment whose career stretched from Broadway musicals in the late 1930s, through his domination of the Golden Age of the Hollywood musical in the 1940s and 1950s, to television and radio. Only when advancing age caught up with him did Kelly wind down his active work by the late 1980s.

Kelly is an unusually good subject for a thoroughly researched, detailed, and competently analyzed account of his life and career. He was a college-educated intellectual deeply interested in every aspect of his profession. He had an active political life that got him graylisted in the Red Scare. His rejection of ethnic and racial prejudice is evidenced not only in his personal life but in his dances, in ways atypical of film musicals of the era. He was driven to excel in his own career and often pursued his goals with an aggressive sharpness that rubbed some people the wrong way. Yet, he also found fulfillment in mentoring colleagues and helped several of them greatly.

The length and breadth of Kelly's show-business career is unmatched even by Fred Astaire, especially when considering the wide variety of work that interested Kelly and in which he excelled. Along with Astaire, Kelly was at the top of the pyramid in dance films. But, unlike Astaire, Kelly not only incorporated a mélange of dance styles including ballet into his performances but made significant contributions to directing, choreography, and many other aspects of entertainment. Fans, interested students of film history, and entertainment historians need a biography of him that mixes the best of academic research and analysis with an accessible writing style and a keen sense of explaining the how and why of this show-business phenomenon.

This is exactly what we hope to achieve with our book. It is primarily a career biography of Gene Kelly. After all, his first wife Betsy Blair said that even though Gene was a very loving husband and father, "his work was the most important part of his life."[1] We do, however, examine his personal life when we see connections between it and his career that are important in understanding him.

Kelly's career, unique as it is, has never been given the treatment it deserves by those who have written of him. His previous biographers have produced generic narratives about his life and work based on limited research, relying heavily on secondary sources and interviews while ignoring archival material. None of them explain why he became the kind of person he was or evaluate how and why his career developed as it did. All of them merely chronicle his life and career with little analysis or explanation, and they often even get the details wrong.

The first book on Kelly was written by film historian Tony Thomas and published in 1974. It is in coffee-table format, titled *Films of Gene Kelly*, and contains some unique photographs. It also has a succinct, twenty-eight-page biography and is dedicated to Jeanne Coyne, Kelly's second wife, who died the previous year of leukemia. At roughly the same time, British journalist Clive Hirschhorn wrote a biography of Kelly (published in Great Britain in 1974 and in the United States in 1975). On the plus side, it contains information from many interviews, including conversations with Gene, his former wife Betsy Blair, and his adult daughter Kerry Novick and also has some analysis. Unfortunately, it has several errors including Gene's birthdate, the location of the scar on his face, and the dates and circumstances for some of his stage work and Navy experience. Also, the book severely shortchanges Kelly's contributions after *Singin' in the Rain*. Hirschhorn produced a second edition in 1984, which contained the unmodified earlier version (including the errors) but with an eight-page addendum, updating to the early 1980s.

On Kelly's passing in 1996, authors Sheridan Morley and Ruth Leon published a pictorial book about him, but the material, including the incorrect birthdate, is taken mostly from Hirschhorn. In the same year appeared a biography of Kelly by documentary filmmaker Alvin Yudkoff. Although he thanked people at various archives and indicated he used material provided by Lois McClelland, Gene's longtime secretary, Yudkoff provided no notes to document how he used any of this material. On reading his book, it is evident that most of it came from Hirschhorn. Worse, Yudkoff wrote in a fanciful way to re-create Kelly's thoughts and musings at key points in his life. For example, he put thoughts into Gene's head while he was being honored by the American Film Institute in 1985. Yudkoff also provided quotes from private conversations between Gene and Betsy Blair without explaining how he had access to this information. As a result, much of his book is palpably unreliable.

The next Kelly biography was by sisters Cynthia and Sara Brideson in 2017. It is based on wider research than any previous book and is packed with details about his personal life and work. A lot of the material is obtained from the website of Sue Cadman, a devoted Gene Kelly fan, and adds new information. But most of it is left undigested rather than woven into analysis. Although many secondary sources are cited, much of this information is reported inaccurately. For example, they claim that Kelly took over the direction of *For Me and My Gal* when actually this was his first film and he was just beginning to learn how to act for the camera. They cite Hirschhorn for this even though that author made no such claim. This sort of thing happens in literally hundreds of instances, some minor, but even so it creates a distorted picture of reality. Based on Yudkoff, they claim that Kelly never went to Washington, DC, to support the Hollywood Nineteen, even though they cite Blair's book, which confirms he was part of the entourage in Washington. They repeat the incorrect dates from Hirschhorn for Gene's birth, stage work, and Navy projects, even though they cite a source that actually has the correct dates for the stage work. Their book includes a lot of text with no footnotes even though it is obvious that the information is taken from secondary sources. Even where cites are used, the Bridesons very often embellish the details of incidents beyond what their sources allow in terms of veracity. And sadly, they frequently make up quotes not in the sources they cite. As a result, what appears on the surface to be a promising biography of Kelly also leaves a lot to be desired.

There is still a need for a completely different kind of biography than has been produced thus far—one that is based on thorough research, attempts to chart and analyze the trajectories in Kelly's life and career, and assesses his accomplishments within the wider context of American culture.

Our book is based on more than a decade of thorough research in the primary literature concerning Kelly. He gave literally dozens of interviews that offer rich insights into his thoughts and experiences. Many of those interviews were published in newspapers and magazines, but just as many of them were never published. Conducted as lengthy oral histories, each one was transcribed and deposited in one of several archives across the country. These oral histories of Kelly, which constitute a major category of primary source material in our study, have not been used by previous biographers.

His personal papers and the papers of several people who worked with him also have never been utilized by previous biographers. These too constitute an important resource base for this book. We believe that only through seeking out every source of information (including unpublished archival material and published primary material) can it be possible to truly understand the life of a complex person like Gene Kelly. We do include secondary sources as well and also have conducted interviews with several people who worked with Kelly or knew him personally.

As film historians and Kelly researchers for the last fifteen years, we have done extensive archival research in many special collections including the Academy of Motion Picture Arts and Sciences, the Howard Gotlieb Archival Research Center, Columbia University, the New York Public Library, the Pittsburgh Regional History Center, the University of Pittsburgh, the University of California Film and Television Archives, the Arthur Freed Collection at the University of Southern California, and the Harry Ransom Center at the University of Texas. These rich sources of unpublished material, along with an extensive survey of published primary sources (especially interviews and newspaper commentary), provide the foundation for our book. Our two previous studies of Kelly films (*Singin' in the Rain: The Making of an American Masterpiece*, University Press of Kansas, 2009, and *The Cinematic Voyage of the Pirate: Kelly, Garland, and Minnelli at Work*, University of Missouri Press, 2014) and our third study (*Gene Kelly's Invitation to the Dance: A Misguided Dream*, in progress) similarly draw on extensive archival research to provide comprehensive coverage.

Our book explains how Kelly was deeply influenced by his family life and hometown environment. Born in Pittsburgh, he lived there until leaving for New York in 1938. Those first twenty-six years of his life taught him many things that are important in understanding his career. Inspired by his father and uncle, the young Gene developed an abiding love of sports. His mother exposed him to the arts and insisted he take both dance and violin lessons. Taunted by local boys for being a sissy, Gene developed a fierce desire to prove that dance and sports were intimately linked as manly endeavors. Growing up in a conservative Irish Catholic family, he developed a strong sense of family devotion, a thriving work ethic, and a rejection of conservative political values when he saw the hardships endured by his family during the Great Depression. Dancing in the local dives of Pittsburgh to make money to help his family, Gene learned from the ground up how to entertain the masses. Taking ballet lessons in Chicago, Kelly incorporated it into his popular dance style while in college, laying the groundwork for the interesting mix of styles he would develop as a professional dancer. Gene thrived as a teacher in his family's two dance studios, at the Beth Shalom Synagogue, and in the Cap and Gown student productions at the University of Pittsburgh. He became the dance master of his hometown after graduation from college, gaining wide-ranging experience as performer, choreographer, and impresario as he staged entire amateur shows on a regular basis.

We discuss how Kelly's Pittsburgh preparation helped him to quickly conquer Broadway after arriving in New York in 1938. We explain how he learned to create a character through dance in *The Time of Your Life* and to entertain a higher class, smarter, and more sophisticated audience. We narrate how Gene took New York by storm when he starred in *Pal Joey*, choreographing his dances and achieving the difficult task of playing a likable heel. We chronicle how he came to choreograph *Best Foot Forward*, becoming a triple threat in professional productions on Broadway.

We reveal the complex machinations that eventually lured Kelly to California in 1941. Once there, Gene became fascinated with the biggest professional challenge of his career—how to film dance effectively for the screen. No one was then working on that question and Kelly took it on, creating a lifelong career for himself in the movie industry. He was a major player in the development of cine-dance—the effort to craft choreography and camera technique to portray dance on film in exciting and unique ways. We also discuss Kelly's important role in the creation of film ballet—an extended dance that often explored the inner life of key characters in the plot. Kelly always had a keen sense of making movies for mass audiences, but he also experimented with new techniques, fresh choreographic moves, and blending many dance styles into his screen performances. He considered his dance films something of a true art form and enjoyed the challenge of making them better than musicals of the past.

Along with Fred Astaire, Kelly came to dominate the Golden Age of the Hollywood musical during the 1940s and 1950s, shaping the history of that musical form. Many writers have compared Kelly and Astaire as dancers, and we do the same. But, in addition, we think it is important to compare their personal lives, their politics, and their attitudes toward their work. We also think it is informative to study their joint mastery of the dance musical. They were an interesting and important pair of entertainers whose lives often intersected.

We discuss how the Golden Age offered Kelly opportunities to do much more than dance on screen. He developed his acting talents, choreographed extensively for his own dances and that of others, became a director, and wrote scenarios for movies. No other film star excelled in so many different areas of moviemaking as did Kelly.

We examine how even his service in the Navy during World War II came to play an important role in his career. He worked for one and a half years making films for the government, learning how to shoot scenes on location, how to edit, and how to convey a particular message to a designated audience with minimal resources and little time.

Previous biographers have skimmed lightly over Kelly's political life, but it was vitally important to him. New York exposed him to left-wing political views that he found intriguing. Gene was a solid New Deal Democrat, a liberal in the eyes of those conservatives who pushed the hunt for communism in Hollywood after World War II. His outspoken stand in favor of freedom of speech branded him as a fellow traveler. It is impossible to understand Kelly's political life and his experience during the Red Scare without consulting his FBI file, which we obtained through the Freedom of Information Act. Why he spoke out and how he survived the Red Scare are important and previously unknown aspects of his life and career.

No biographer has discussed Kelly's role as auteur. But in fact Kelly's multifaceted career opened the door to many important issues concerning his achievement and his legacy. He was an auteur in different ways; one way was by placing his unique style on many pictures, which film scholars regard as an indication of an auteur.[2] In addition, Kelly wrote, casted, directed, starred in, choreographed, and coproduced *Invitation to the Dance*, achieving a kind of total authorship over one film, something rarely if ever duplicated in an industry that relied heavily on the collaboration of dozens of artists.

Of all his roles in moviemaking, none is more controversial lately than Kelly's work as a film director. Based on meticulous research, we analyze his achievement in that area much more positively than any previous authors. Kelly was the leader in his collaboration with Stanley Donen as codirectors early in their careers, despite the exaggerated claims of Donen biographers and supporters. In his later solo directorial work Kelly also produced innovative and noteworthy effects praised by many critics.

We also argue that, contrary to the idea started by Hirschhorn without careful analysis and latched on to by other writers, Kelly's career did not take a nosedive after 1952. He had achieved an unusually high level of accomplishment by the time he made *Singin' in the Rain*, the pinnacle of his film career.

Everyone experiences a career decline after reaching their peak, but strangely only Kelly is branded as "failing" after that. We see his career as branching off in different and successful directions for decades to come after that peak rather than as failing and we fully discuss those paths. For example, he began to direct and produce films and acted extensively on television where his talents shone. He also became an acknowledged expert on the history of dance in American culture, an advocate for dance education, and a cultural ambassador for the State Department.

Our book takes Kelly's work on television and radio more seriously than do previous biographers. Television gave Gene a venue for exploring important themes in his life and career, and he elevated the quality of television programming in creative and entertaining ways. The small screen was good for Kelly and he was good for it. Radio allowed him to act with his voice alone, something impossible to do on the stage or screen. He turned in many fine performances and stretched himself as an actor on radio. He also supported his political ideals and worked for social causes through radio.

We also stress something Kelly himself admitted—that he thought of himself as a teacher. He not only taught hundreds of young people how to dance in the family's Pittsburgh and Johnstown schools, but he helped colleagues in his stage and film projects to improve their dancing and acting styles. Gene was also a mentor to his assistants. He significantly helped build career paths for Leslie Caron, Vera-Ellen, Cyd Charisse, Stanley Donen, and Debbie Reynolds, among others. Our book examines Kelly's unique impact as a teacher and mentor to people of all ages.

As a complicated person, Kelly is a wonderful subject for any biographer. He held a college degree, loved to read, was an intellectual, and developed a deep interest in Europe and its culture. His passion for dance (performing it, choreographing it, studying it, and understanding it within its culture) was a lifelong joy for him. All of this made Gene almost unique among his contemporaries on Broadway and in Hollywood. Yet, he saw himself as a middle-class American. When columnist Hedda Hopper asked him what he missed about his own country after coming back from an extended stay in Europe, he said, "I discovered that I am a middle class American who likes suburban life—the life we live in Beverly Hills—I like a back yard, a dog—the corny things we all kid about—I like it and I missed it."[3]

In both his life and his work, Kelly blended seemingly contradictory elements with success. He was cosmopolitan but valued the elements of middle-class life in America. He was a free thinker and yet held on to Catholic traditions. He was a Hollywood star but felt so connected with his roots that he danced as a "common man." He found ballet exciting but excelled at popular dancing for the multitude with balletic elements worked into his performance.

In chapter 19 we sum up Kelly's life work, assess his impact on everything he touched, and stress the remarkable versatility of this dynamo of entertainment. Our appendix has a more thorough list of Kelly's work than has been previously published. It includes his major television appearances and his radio roles along with a more complete list of his stage work, as well as all his films. In addition to stills from his stage and screen appearances tied to discussions in the text, this book includes many photographs never before published. Several maps help to define where Kelly lived, studied, worked, and played in Pittsburgh.

Kelly had always been interested in history, and late in life was keen to have his story told. "Historically speaking," he said in 1994, two years before his death, "I'm one of the last ones left who can correct inaccuracies about MGM musicals in show biz books these days."[4] But he did not excel at writing long pieces, and his own efforts to pen his memoirs failed.

"I hope a strong revealing look at this man will be written," asserted director of photography Roy Wagner, who worked with and admired Gene. "Everything has made him so one dimensional."[5] We agree with Wagner and have tried to correct that inadequate view of Kelly in this book.

We owe a debt of gratitude to the staff at all the archival institutions listed in the bibliography. In particular we thank Ned Comstock at the University of Southern California for going out of his way to help us gain access to the rich storehouse of material in the Arthur Freed Collection under his charge. Ned also pointed us to important archival material at other institutions.

We thank Michelle Brannen and Eric Arnold at the University of Tennessee Studio for making the maps in this book. We appreciate comments from Rick Altman and Beth Genné on an earlier draft of this book. We thank Lois Elias for permission to use material from the Samuel and Bella Spewack Papers at Columbia University and Joseph McBride for permission to use his notes from an interview with Kelly in the Joseph McBride Papers at the Wisconsin Center for Film and Theater Research.

We enjoyed our contacts with several people who worked with or knew Gene Kelly. Claude Bessy, principal dancer of the Paris Opera Ballet who danced for Kelly in the film *Invitation to the Dance*, on one of his Pontiac television specials, and in the stage ballet *Pas de Dieux*, was in touch with us through an email interview. Lois Elias, a student of Gene's in Pittsburgh as a young girl, spoke with us by telephone at age eighty about the impact Kelly had on her life. As a boy, David Kasday appeared briefly in *An American in Paris* and *Singin' in the Rain* and danced with Kelly in "Sinbad the Sailor" from *Invitation to the Dance*. He expressed his memories about his work with Kelly in an email exchange with us. Ruth Zekaria Levy and her brother Ike Zekaria wrote emails to us about their experiences as next-door neighbors to Gene in Beverly Hills from the late 1960s to the 1980s. Bobby Riha danced with Kelly as a boy in the television special *Jack and the Beanstalk*. He shared his memories with us over the telephone. Cinematographer Roy Wagner shared his views about Kelly and his contributions to filmmaking with us by email. We are grateful to all these people for taking the time and trouble to share their memories and thoughts.

CHAPTER 1

Son of Pittsburgh, 1912–1929

Gene Kelly was born on August 23, 1912, in a house at the corner of Portland and Bryant in Pittsburgh's Highland Park neighborhood. His parents, James and Harriet Kelly, had rented the house in 1906 soon after getting married, and Gene's two older siblings were also born here.[1]

The authors' field research showed that this house, at 1161 Portland Street, was substantial—with five bedrooms and nearly 2,700 square feet—almost too large for a newly married couple in 1906. But it appears they had planned a large family, so it was perfect for them. Highland Park, in northeast Pittsburgh, is situated on high ground, and from the corner of Portland and Bryant one can enjoy an expansive view of the city that shaped Gene Kelly's life.

FAMILY HERITAGE

James Patrick Joseph Kelly, Gene's father, was just as proud of his Irish heritage as Gene would be later in life. James's grandfather had immigrated to the new world after the potato famine of the 1840s and worked as a blacksmith in Peterborough, Ontario. James was born in that city in 1875 and left Peterborough at age twenty-eight for the United States. He became an American citizen and lived in Buffalo, St. Louis, and Philadelphia, making a living by selling phonographs and records, the new means of mass entertainment. Eventually James found himself in Pittsburgh working for the Edison Phonograph Company and later for the Columbia Phonograph Company.[2]

Harriet Curran, Gene's mother, came from a large Irish American family of thirteen children. Harriet's father had immigrated to the United States from Londonderry by way of Scotland in 1845. He became manager of Sterling Mines in northern Pennsylvania, making enough money to leave $50,000 to each of his nine surviving children when he died of pneumonia. Ironically, all of them lost it fairly quickly.[3] Harriet lost her inheritance when the recession

Figure 1.1 This house, at 1161 Portland Street in Highland Park, was rebuilt in 1925 in the same style and size as the original house on this site, where Gene was born and lived until age two. It is the last building on the right. (Photo by authors)

of 1907 dropped the bottom out of the real estate she had purchased. This was only one year after her marriage to James Kelly. The two had met backstage at an amateur concert where Harriet had performed in 1905. After marrying in 1906, the couple honeymooned in Ontario and then rented their first home in Highland Park. Their first three children were Harriet (called Jay by the family), James, and Eugene (Gene). Harriet came from a family of so-called black Irish—people of Irish descent who had dark hair and eyes. Gene's first wife Betsy Blair noted that her husband inherited his looks from his mother and his charm from "Pop Kelly." The father was "loving and gentle with wit in his blue eyes and the Irish gift of the gab," Blair recalled in her memoirs. "He was like an old wood-burning stove, radiating warmth at the heart of the family." Gene seconded these feelings, referring to his father as "a doll man" and "an angel" in a 1953 interview.[4]

In 1914, when Gene was two years old, the Kellys rented their second home at 722 Mellon Street in East Liberty. It represented, in many ways, a decline in the family's lifestyle because the house was smaller and the family continued to grow, with Louise born on July 6, 1914 and Fred on June 29, 1916. Decades later, Gene half-jokingly said that his mother would be hurt if he heard him call the Mellon Street area "ghetto-type housing, but that's what it was." To make ends meet, the family boarded an aunt and uncle in a back room, four kids shared another bedroom, and the baby slept in the parents' room. "It wasn't luxury living," Gene recalled.[5]

COPING WITH A TOUGH TOWN

The city that Gene Kelly grew up in was enormously important in shaping his character, his outlook on life, and his future prospects as a man. Pittsburgh and its suburbs, in many ways, reflected an unusual history and culture. It was located at the confluence of the Allegheny River coming in from the northeast with the Monongahela River coming up from the southeast. Where they met—the famous Forks of the Ohio—was the beginning of the Ohio River, which ran 981 miles southwest to join the Mississippi River. England and France fought for possession of these forks in the French and Indian War, with the British winning and planting Fort Pitt to protect their holdings. Out of that military conquest grew a civilian town called Pittsburgh.

Industry began to develop even before the Civil War offered the town opportunities for supplying the Union army. When journalist James Parton visited Pittsburgh in December 1866, he was impressed by all the manufacturing establishments, the nonstop business activity, and the terrible pollution that already was beginning to characterize the city. There were so many open furnace fires that the place looked like "hell with the lid taken off," when viewed from the highlands at night.[6]

By the time of Gene Kelly's birth, Pittsburgh was reaching the height of its industrial history. The many factories crammed along the narrow bottomlands of the Allegheny and the Monongahela produced a pall of smoke that often hung like a shroud over downtown, located where the forks join. But Highland Park and East Liberty are located on higher ground, so the Kelly family was relatively unaffected by the dense smoke on the bottomlands of Pittsburgh.

When the Kellys moved to 722 Mellon Street, World War I broke out in Europe only a few weeks later. The United States entered the war in April 1917, and this provided yet another boost to city industries. But after the war ended in November 1918, the local economy slowed. By the onset of the Great Depression in 1929, iron and steel production was only a bit higher in Pittsburgh than it had been in 1916. In fact, overall manufacturing experienced a real decline in the area by the end of the 1920s.[7]

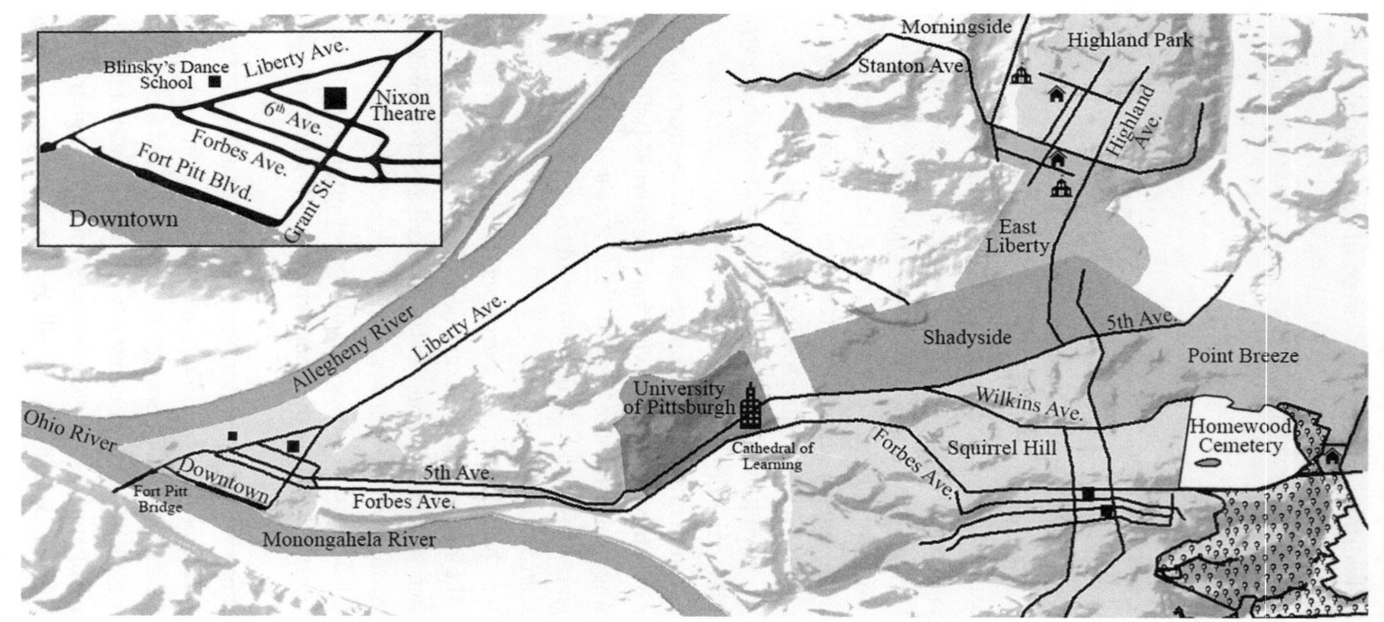

Map 1.1 Map of Pittsburgh, showing places relevant to Gene Kelly, including his three homes, two of the three schools he attended, and the University of Pittsburgh, where he studied from 1930 to 1933. The Cathedral of Learning, a Pittsburgh landmark, was under construction while Gene was attending the university. The Inset of Downtown shows the Nixon Theatre (see Figure 1.2) and Blinsky's Dance School that the Kelly boys attended. (All three maps are made with GPS and precisely show roads, topographical features, suburbs, and the locations of places of interest.)

Biographers and commentators have always pointed out that Gene Kelly grew up in a tough, working-class environment, and there is no doubt that a lot of that toughness rubbed off on the young boy. But the Kelly family was by no means a working-class family. James's sales career placed him squarely in the middle class, not in the lower middle (or working) class. The descent from Portland Street to Mellon Street was temporary, brought on by a rapidly growing family and sales receipts that were not yet keeping up with the expenses.

Furthermore, the Mellon Street neighborhood was not a ghetto or a slum. Our field research showed that the lots were a bit smaller than on Portland Street and the houses were smaller too. But the style of the houses and the appearance of the lots were similar to those in the previous neighborhood. In fact, the second house was only seven blocks south of the first, on the northern fringe of East Liberty. It was the much smaller house at 722 Mellon, with an area of about 1,400 square feet, and the crowding of the family (including the aunt and uncle) within, that led to Gene's recalling it as ghetto-type housing. But that phrase by no means implies that it was actually a ghetto as previous biographers have assumed. There were many other neighborhoods in Pittsburgh at the time that better fit that description.

Pittsburgh also had a rich heritage of ethnic and racial diversity, and the Kellys were part of it. The city's population had grown fast—by more than one-third every ten years—from 1865 to 1900. It leveled off at about 670,000 residents from 1930 to 1940 and then declined. The largest racial minority was African American. Pittsburgh had more Polish, Italian, and German residents than Irish, but the children of immigrants (as Gene was) constituted more than one-third of the city's entire population in the 1930s.[8]

In the fall of 1930, when Gene was a college student, *Harper's Magazine* published an article with the provocative title "Is Pittsburgh Civilized?" Written by Robert Luther Duffus, it described the "Smoky City" in blunt terms: "From whatever direction one approaches the once lovely conjunction of the Allegheny and the Monongahela the devastation of progress is apparent. Quiet valleys have been inundated with slag, defaced with refuse, marred by hideous buildings. Streams have been polluted with sewage and waste from the mills. Life for the majority of the population has been rendered unspeakably pinched and dingy."[9] This may be a good description of parts of Pittsburgh, but not all of it.

James spared his family the misery of a life in the worst parts of Pittsburgh. He chose decent neighborhoods to raise his family, avoiding the dirtiest,

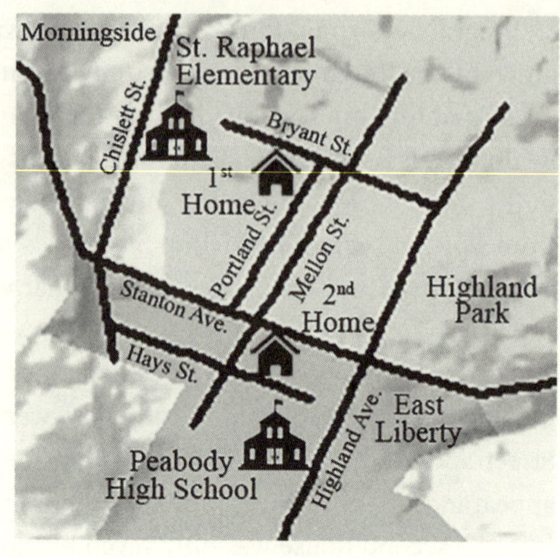

Map 1.2 This map (enlarged from the northeastern section of Map 1.1) shows the location of Gene's first home at 1161 Portland Street in Highland Park (from birth to two years, 1912–1914; see Figure 1.1). It also shows the location of his second home at 722 Mellon Street in East Liberty (age two to thirteen, 1914–1925), which was replaced in 2000. The schools Gene attended—St. Raphael Elementary (see Figure 1.3) and Peabody High—are also located on the map. A photo of Peabody High is not included because the building has been completely renovated.

industrial parts of Pittsburgh as well as the densely packed ethnic neighborhoods. Moreover, all five children not only finished high school but also went on to earn a college degree, an astounding achievement in a society nearly wrecked by the Great Depression. The Kelly family was not mired down in the worst aspects of Pittsburgh. And until the Depression, James provided the money necessary for the family to maintain its middle-class status.

HARRIET'S INFLUENCE

Harriet was the driving force to get the kids interested in art and entertainment. She always felt passionately about both, but had no opportunity to continue dabbling in such things after her marriage, except by working through her five children. From the earliest memory of the family, Harriet encouraged, pushed, and cajoled the kids to learn a musical instrument and dancing. She took the family to numerous shows, including at the Nixon Theatre on Sixth Avenue in downtown, one of the upper-class theatrical venues in Pittsburgh (see Map 1.1). Gene remembered his mother as "a frustrated actress," but she "always managed to find artistic talent of some kind in all of the kids." Harriet was aware of this important theme in her life. "I guess I transferred my stage ambitions to my five children," she admitted to a newspaper reporter in 1940.

Figure 1.2 The Nixon Theatre, ca. 1910–1920, on Sixth Avenue in downtown Pittsburgh. It is the third building from the right (with the dome), and no longer exists today. The Kelly children and their mother, Harriet, saw touring shows here. Gene's high-school play was performed in this theater, as were the Cap and Gown shows (staged by the University of Pittsburgh) in which Gene participated. (Library of Congress)

Fred Kelly had a different take on this subject. He thought Uncle Gus, one of Harriet's brothers, had put the entertainment bug in the family.[10]

Harriet insisted that her sons take dance lessons. Fred needed no encouragement. He was a natural dancer who had enjoyed performing since he was a little boy. But James and Gene rebelled. Gene recalled years later that his first exposure to dance was anything but auspicious. When he was four, Harriet took him to see Pavlova perform in Pittsburgh. "I fell asleep," he recalled. "It's her favorite story." That was about 1916. Now it was 1919; Gene was seven years old and could voice his objection. Nevertheless Harriet insisted, and the three trouped off to Blinsky's Dancing School at the corner of 6th Street and Penn Street downtown (see Map 1.1). It was a long way from 722 Mellon Street. At first Harriet took her sons on the streetcar and into the school to make sure they did not play hooky. They were the only boys in the class, which made it even more unappealing to James and Gene. Also, Harriet insisted on dressing the three in Buster Brown collars, gloves, and little socks, which only increased the cringing self-awareness James and Gene felt. In 1975, Gene remembered a bit of what they learned during these lessons: "It was some ballet positions, a little bit of dancing with a girl, a mélange of many things."[11]

After a while, Harriet trusted the boys and stopped escorting them. But then the worst part of the experience happened. On their way to the streetcar, they went through some tough neighborhoods where the local boys mercilessly taunted the three coming and going. Dance lessons were bad enough, but dressing in Buster Brown outfits was worse. The Kelly boys were mocked for being sissies and fights broke out. "Jim was very tough and he'd fight," Fred recalled. "Or Gene would start the fight and Jim would finish it. Jim was our protector. But it was sort of our daily routine. Fighting, that was the style in Pittsburgh in those days."[12]

The troubling experience left its mark on Gene. For the rest of his life he cringed at the thought of being called a sissy because he came to embrace dancing not only as an art form but for the sheer joy it later brought to his life. Out of this seed grew his desire to craft a dance style adapted to prevailing concepts of manliness in American culture. He argued strenuously that a man's role as dancer was different from a woman's. Gene was not unique in this. As discussed later, other dance artists were aware that American culture had branded the male dancer as suspect in terms of manliness and sexual orientation. Pittsburgh was not unique in its tough judgment of the male dancer; it was a nearly universal assumption in early twentieth-century America and still persists today.

As the dance lessons continued, Gene joined with James in defending their collective honor. "I don't know if Gene enjoyed the dancing or the fighting the most," Fred half-jokingly said. "I'm happy to tell you," Gene told an interviewer in 1959, "we beat the hell out of 'em."[13]

James and Gene put up with the lessons for a year and a half, a time of "great duress, stress and strain." They complained so much that even the iron-willed Harriet allowed them to stop. The lessons apparently did not help Gene in his later career. By the late 1950s, after a string of phenomenally successful dance films, Kelly admitted, "I guess I hated it." But he quickly added that with the passage of several decades it was easier for him to see that Harriet had been "far-sighted." He had thought it was "sissy stuff" then, but "I bless her for it now."[14]

Soon after the lessons ended, Harriet insisted Gene learn to play the violin. Again, he thought his mother's wish was "a sissy thing," but this time he did not rebel. Harriet and James paid for private violin lessons with two teachers across town and finally with a nun at his school, St. Raphael Elementary in Morningside (see Maps 1.1 and 1.2). Harriet also urged Gene to play for the nuns while he was there. He had to go through a couple of rough neighborhoods to reach the school, located a dozen blocks northwest of their home. Merely the sight of him carrying a violin case through those neighborhoods brought on more fights with the local toughs. At least Gene was not alone in the violin story; Harriet made Jay, James, and Louise learn how to play the piano while assigning Fred to the drums. Only Fred enjoyed his lessons; the other children disliked the whole experience. Harriet also made them perform for visitors to the house. Despite his reluctance to play, Gene persisted for his mother's sake and became fairly proficient with the violin until he broke his arm in a football game in high school and Harriet allowed him to stop his lessons.[15]

THE FIVE KELLYS

Long before that football injury, Harriet achieved a coup in her ambitions for the children by forming a group called The Five Kellys. This was in 1920 when Gene was eight years old. Harriet was the manager, bookkeeper, and chaperone for what sometimes was billed as the Five Dancing Kellys. She even talked some dancers who toured through Pittsburgh into giving her group dance instruction to sharpen their skills. She booked the kids into benefit performances, and shows for churches and hospitals. Fred, the youngest, was only four when this started and brought the house down when the group sang their last name. Jay began with a "K," followed by James with an "E," Gene with an "L," and Louise with another "L." When Fred sang his "Y" the audience loved it. "I remember the orchestra cracked up," Fred testified later, "laughing even at rehearsals. . . . I wasn't at all with the music. I just took a great big break and yelled Y!"[16]

Figure 1.3 St. Raphael Elementary School, which Gene attended and where he took his violin lessons. The school, at 1154 Chislett Street, is still there today. (Photo by authors)

Figure 1.4 The Five Kellys performing in local venues. They even performed at the Nixon Theatre once. *From left*: Harriet (Jay), James, Eugene (Gene), Louise, and Fred. (Still from *Anatomy of a Dancer*, 2002)

The Seven Little Foys, who served as a model for Harriet, inadvertently gave The Five Kellys their biggest break. Scheduled to perform in Pittsburgh in 1921, the Foys had to cancel the engagement and left the theater manager in the lurch. He contacted Harriet, who filled the bill. The Kellys "became very popular" in town after that, according to Fred. Even if all five kids could not make it, two or three performed whenever they were asked. "Every show in Pittsburgh had to have a Kelly in it," Fred claimed years later. "And boy, did I love it."[17]

Harriet's influence on Gene's development was enormous. He remained in awe of her energy, authority, foresight, and maternal devotion for the rest of his life. But he was a boy with strong feelings and interests of his own.

OTHER INFLUENCES

Art, music, dancing, and performance were things Gene had to do for his mother. But his own enjoyment came first and foremost from sports. This interest he in part inherited from James, for his father was a fervent sportsman as well. James worked out with dumbbells and Indian clubs at home and reportedly was a fair amateur boxer. He flooded the backyard at 722 Mellon Street during cold spells in western Pennsylvania and taught Gene how to ice-skate when he was five. In Gene's own words, he could skate "like a wizard" by age six. Gene also became a good swimmer and lacrosse player.[18] Virtually any sport was his game, and he had the physical skills and the mental concentration to be good at all of them.

Boxing became the trigger for why we call him "Gene" instead of "Eugene." He had been named after St. Eugene by Harriet and James, and for his first ten years the family called him Eugene. But then Gene Tunney won the light heavyweight title in 1923, and from that point Kelly preferred to be known as Gene. Ironically, the Kelly boys received some boxing lessons from Harry Greb, another lightweight champ who had fought five bouts with Tunney.[19] Known as "The Pittsburgh Windmill," Greb hailed from Pittsburgh and had adopted a strategy of pummeling his opponents with a blizzard of hard knocks.

There is little wonder that the young Gene Kelly enjoyed learning to box. He grew up believing that fighting was necessary to survive. As he explained: "Because I was so small, I felt that I always had to prove myself, and the best way to do this was with my fists. I wasn't going to be pushed around by anyone." He played football with older boys whose toughness he tried to duplicate. Gene later believed he must have really rubbed those older boys the wrong way "with my insistence that I was just as good as they were. But I had this obsession to prove to them I was."[20] This fierce sense of proving himself never left Gene, and it was especially strong for the first half of his life.

Even when he played by himself, Gene was always daring and challenging life. At age five, he rode a tricycle without handlebars along the street, fell forward, and dashed his face on a bit of cast iron. A neighbor took him home, but when the gash would not stop bleeding, a doctor was called to stitch the wound. This left a "small, half-moon scar" on his left cheek for life. Later, as a star, Kelly refused to use makeup to cover the scar. In another incident, Gene rode on a makeshift sled on an icy street and was soon out of control. He rolled under a passing truck but was totally unhurt simply by missing the moving truck's wheels by inches.[21]

Summer vacations allowed Gene to escape the tough town temporarily and revel in the open space and clean air. Until 1916, the family went to Ripley on Lake Erie and from 1916 to 1924, to Conneaut Lake in western Pennsylvania. Harriet took the kids out of school two weeks before the spring term ended and brought them back two weeks after the fall term began. James continued to travel during the summer but always joined the family for weekends. Gene could run free in the countryside, swim, row a canoe, and play tennis. He greatly enjoyed these physical activities. Sometimes, the Kelly children put on shows for other kids they met at the lake, and this too was a lot of fun.[22] Both places are fairly close to Pittsburgh. Ripley is only 150 miles almost due north of the city, while Conneaut Lake is a mere 90 miles north.

Back in Pittsburgh, James was most particular about how he dressed at home, always wishing to impress if anyone happened to drop by the house. He insisted that the kids also dress formally at home and Gene hated it.[23] As a reaction to this strict rule, Gene developed a much more informal attitude about home life that carried over into the dance style he created for himself as an adult. One of the enduring themes of his career was to dress casually for his dances.

James and Harriet also took religion seriously. In an interview with a Franciscan priest in 1980, Gene called them an "old-fashioned Irish" family. "We would celebrate Lent and Advent by going to Mass every morning. The whole family said the rosary together every night on our knees. It was the old-time Roman Catholic religion. The Lenten rules of fast and abstinence were carried out strictly and with no dispensations. No meat on Fridays—or mortal sin!" As a boy Gene attended Sacred Heart Church in East Liberty.[24] But as he grew into his teen years and with the influence of a nonparochial high school, Gene experimented with agnosticism, as discussed later.

THE ARTSY SIDE OF PITTSBURGH

Kelly was exposed to a good deal of art, entertainment, and culture while growing up in Pittsburgh, beyond his mother's insistence that he learn how to dance and play the violin. The city had a surprisingly vibrant and varied cultural life despite its heavy investment in industrial production. It took a while, however, for the city to develop its artistic side.

By the time of Gene's birth, Pittsburgh had a dozen stage theaters located in the metropolitan area, five of them downtown. The Nixon Theatre was the premier venue, a high-end theater that normally hosted dramatic and musical productions. In addition to stage theatres, Pittsburgh boasted 200 movie theaters, many of them nickelodeons—small theaters set up in converted storefronts—that projected movies on a screen and charged a nickel for admission. By 1923, when Gene was eleven, Pittsburgh had ten main vaudeville houses that drew audiences of up to 30,000 people each day. The city also began developing a more elitist culture in Oakland, a suburb two miles east of downtown where the University of Pittsburgh was located. Oakland was the home of the Pittsburgh Symphony Orchestra and the Carnegie Music Hall, where Shakespeare as well as opera were performed.[25]

Ironically, Pittsburgh became as important for culture as for heavy industry. It had a thriving theater life and participated in the development of the movie industry. The list of film stars and celebrities who grew up in Pittsburgh is by no means limited to Gene Kelly. In fact, IMDb (the Internet Movie Database) lists no fewer than 1,134 professionals in the film industry who were born and raised in Pittsburgh. They include Dick Powell, William Powell, Charles Grodin, F. Murray Abraham, Regis Toomey, Frank Gorshin, Burt Mustin, Ted Cassidy, Adolph Menjou, Oscar Levant, Fritz Weaver, and David Selznick.

When Gene was a boy, the price of a movie ticket had gone up only to a dime. The Kelly family had no difficulty in paying for the kids' many movie outings. Gene especially liked adventure films. His overwhelming favorite was Douglas Fairbanks's *The Three Musketeers*, which came out in 1921. "I admired Douglas Fairbanks Sr. very much because of the way he moved. I've always loved movement." He admired Lon Chaney Sr. for the same reason. Gene thought that great silent screen stars were "complete dancers. They were balletic, and they moved like dancers."[26] Silent movies impelled these actors to learn how to convey emotions through movement, and that intrigued Gene even as a kid.

The great comedians of the silent era also impressed Gene. He enjoyed films by Charlie Chaplin and Buster Keaton, especially the latter. "Keaton had a great influence on me," Kelly admitted in 1979. "A lot of his moves I certainly intuitively copied in doing certain numbers," for example the squeaky board dance in *Summer Stock* (1950). "I didn't look like him, but I often wish I did. He was a complete genius, and there was a lot of dance inherent in his movements."[27]

Live theater had a great attraction for Gene. He often attended plays at the Nixon Theatre. "We'd sit way up in peanut heaven, but we'd enjoy it," he recalled in 1981. Staged musical productions also tugged at Gene's attention. Unlike the movies, he could relate more readily to a live performance. He remembered seeing Dancing Dotson, an obscure black performer who appeared at Loew's Penn Theatre in Pittsburgh. Dotson specialized in tap, and Gene attended the show repeatedly so he could pick up the unusual steps Dotson used. He also saw George M. Cohan in *Little Nellie Kelly*, a 1922 stage musical that Cohan wrote, performed in, produced, and directed. Gene liked Cohan's cockiness and the fact that he seemed to wear his Irish heritage on his sleeve.[28] Kelly himself used this style later in the Irish number of *Take Me Out to the Ball Game* (1949) and in part of the ballet in *An American in Paris* (1951).

ELEMENTARY SCHOOL YEARS

Pittsburgh's blend of parochial and public schools offered the Kelly family choices in the children's education. Gene initially attended Fulton Elementary School at the corner of Mellon and Hampton in East Liberty. The school was only six blocks from home, but Gene later shifted to St. Raphael Elementary. Even though it was twice the distance from home as Fulton, Gene completed the rest of his elementary education at St. Raphael, graduating in spring 1925. Gene also was an altar boy at services of the St. Raphael Church for a time. He became at least partially interested in school plays by about age twelve. The nuns made everyone participate, which "took the onus off it," as Kelly remembered. "I found that dancing was easy for me. It tied in with the sports I loved, it was using my body, and it was sort of fun to be in the plays." He was in *Babes in Toyland* in the fall of 1924 during his final year at the school. He played the role of Tom-Tom, the oldest son of a widow with fourteen children, and performed a tap dance to the title song "Toyland."[29]

Soon after, James Kelly purchased a home at 7514 Kensington.[30] The reason James was able to purchase a house in 1925 (rather than rent as he had done so far) was that the national economy boomed in 1924 and people had more disposable income to spend on luxuries such as phonographs and records. As a result, James Kelly's career soared, and he was able to move the family out of Mellon Street and to a different suburb called Point Breeze, two miles away in the southeastern part of the Pittsburgh metropolitan area. The new home was many steps up the social ladder in a clearly middle-class neighborhood.

This is the house where Gene lived for the next thirteen years—the remainder of his life in Pittsburgh. Our field research showed that the house still stands today. At nearly 2,000 square feet with four bedrooms, two and a half baths, two porches, an attic, and a basement, it was a substantial home by the standards of 1925 when it was built. It is the third house from an entrance to the northern part of Frick Park. The park is still there today, with beautiful old forests and a peaceful sense of being far away from city life. There is no doubt that Gene enjoyed the park, given his penchant for running through woods for miles on end.

In winter months, the Kelly kids ice-skated. "There was this huge lake," Gene recalled decades later, "which froze over in winter—and we'd skate ourselves into a state of perfection."[31] Our field research showed that immediately west of Frick Park lies the expansive Homewood Cemetery. Encompassing 205 hilly acres, its grounds are sculpted with ponds and trees. The "huge lake" Gene referred to was a large pond on these grounds close to their home.

The Kelly family, like other Pittsburghers, benefited from the economic boom in the 1920s. By 1930, about 40 percent of households owned their homes. As a native of Canada, James Kelly was among the 52 percent of foreign-born whites who owned their homes. Foreign-born residents such as James constituted about 16 percent of the city's population of 670,000 people. James's sales career placed him in the lower white-collar ranks, which represented nearly 22 percent of the city's work force by 1930.[32]

In true Irish fashion, James boasted about his sales exploits. Fred admitted later that "I never believed my dad. I always thought it was the blarney." He referred to James's claims that he had been responsible for opening up the

Figure 1.5 Gene's third home at 7514 Kensington Street in Point Breeze, where he lived from age thirteen to twenty-six (1925–1938). The original house is still there. It is the third house from an entrance to Frick Park and overlooks the gorgeous park from its upper floors. (Photo by authors)

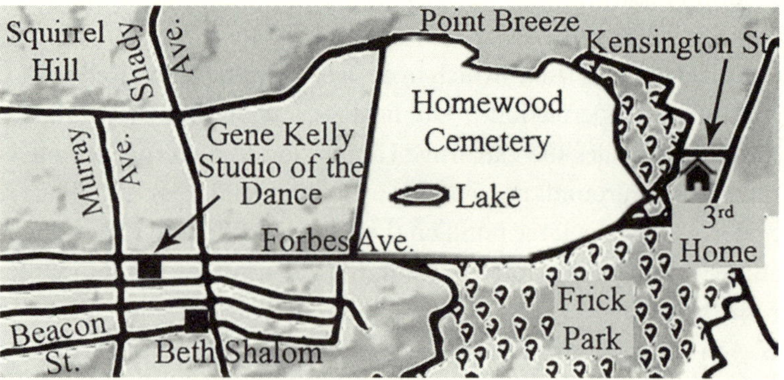

Map 1.3 This map (enlarged from the southeastern section of Map 1.1) shows the location of Gene's third home at 7514 Kensington Street in Point Breeze (age thirteen to twenty-six, 1925–1938; see Figure 1.5). The map also shows the location of the pond where Gene skated (see Figure 1.6), the Gene Kelly Studio of the Dance (see Figure 2.1), and Beth Shalom, which Kelly was associated with from 1931 to 1938. The dance studio and Beth Shalom buildings are in Squirrel Hill.

Figure 1.6 The large pond in Homewood Cemetery, where Gene enjoyed perfecting his skating skills. It is now filled with lotuses and is overgrown with vegetation along the borders, but its shape and size are still clearly visible. (Photo by authors)

market for phonographs west of the Mississippi River, and that he had sold machines to the governors of Missouri, Nebraska, and Kansas. But eventually Fred believed him. "My dad sold a hundred trains loaded with phonographs and records," Fred told an interviewer in 1989 after he saw an old newspaper article confirming this. "My dad was the top salesman for Columbia Phonograph," he proudly claimed.[33]

HIGH SCHOOL

It was from the new home on Kensington Street that Gene started his high school career in the fall of 1925. Initially he attended Sacred Heart High School in its two-year-old building on Sheridan Avenue in Shadyside. At least one lasting influence on his life took hold there. Gene recalled many years later that "some very good Dominican priest" explained to him how it was possible to reconcile the evolutionary science of Charles Darwin with the Bible.[34]

After only one year at Sacred Heart, Gene transferred to a public school in the fall of 1926. Peabody High School, located at 515 North Highland Avenue, had been created the year before he was born. It was only a block west of Sacred Heart but a world apart from that small, Catholic institution. Peabody was a large public school that drew students from many different families in the larger area. Chalmers M. Roberts, the son of a Shadyside dentist, came from a Protestant Republican family but he wanted to attend Peabody. "The sons of the rich and of the more ambitious social climbers went to the private Shadyside Academy," he later wrote. Roberts, an aspiring journalist, became a classmate of Gene Kelly at the more egalitarian Peabody High.[35]

Gene threw himself into the student life at Peabody with enthusiasm. He participated in its dramatic clubs, played football, and competed in track, tennis, gymnastics, and volleyball. He also became the associate editor of the school newspaper and joined the Toreadors, "a Literary Society and Discussion Group," as Gene's classmate Emerson Venable described it. The Toreadors met weekly to discuss poetry, literature, philosophy, and current events. They engaged in debates on "some very serious social topics," as Venable put it. Membership in the Toreadors prepared Gene for a spirited classroom debate in which Mel Evans argued for the election of Republican candidate Herbert Hoover in 1928 while Gene argued for Democrat Al Smith—the first Catholic to run for the presidency.[36]

Gene wrote several poems that appeared in *The Civitan*, a literary magazine published by the student body at Peabody. One of them, titled "Streets," creates an analogy between different kinds of city streets and people. "One street I know climbs roughly up a rugged hill," Gene wrote, "and then slopes gently down the other side" into a beautiful valley. "A man I know is like that street," who struggles mightily with life until he can lay his burden down, and "allow the cool, damp mist to cover him / And he will sleep."[37]

"Streets" demonstrates that the tough Pittsburgh milieu had not destroyed the sensitive, creative side of the teenager's personality. In fact, Gene was only just beginning to explore that softer side of himself as he began to mature at Peabody. The school and its opportunities opened him to a variety of experiences he could not have easily found elsewhere, ranging from debates to poetic expression.

His interest in sports also intensified at Peabody. He became a substitute halfback on the football team and won his letter. "I was one of the best school hockey players you could find," he later boasted. Gene won medals for his work on the parallel bars in high school gymnastics. He felt he was good on the mats, "fair on the horizontal bar," but "very poor on the side-horse." His excellence on the parallel bars stemmed from his innate love of body

Figure 1.7 Peabody High sports team with Gene at the far right, front row. Despite his insecurities about being short, it is easy to see that Gene is the same height as the others on the team and in fact slightly taller than his teammates in the front row. (Still from *Anatomy of a Dancer*, 2002)

movement mixed with style. "Like ballet," he later said, "you must cultivate a long line" to do well on the parallel bars. Uncle Gus, even at age sixty, was excellent on the parallel bars as well. Sixty years after he graduated, Kelly was thankful to receive from Emerson Venable a copy of the 1929 Peabody yearbook with a photograph of the gym team in it.[38] It is clear that Gene's early gymnastic training greatly influenced the athletic aspect of his dancing.

Gene's high school years brought dancing back to his life. His teacher convinced him to take tap dancing lessons for a school show, which he did. But he refused when the teacher wanted him to continue taking lessons. Looking back on it with the benefit of hindsight, Gene admitted in 1975 that his "poor little tap dance" was "really very bad." But it was the best any student of his cohort could do, and the performance made him a hero at Peabody. "They thought I was some kind of young dancing genius," Kelly recalled, also confessing, "I thrived on this kind of attention."[39] Finally, he was bitten by the show business bug in a way that began to change his life.

Gene realized from his first year at Peabody that "girls just adored young men who could dance." So dancing became a strategy that worked for a guy who was self-conscious about his height. "I worked my way into a lot of affections," he told Ron Haver in a 1984 interview. "It was a sesame into the social life. As embarrassing as this is to admit, that's what really got me hooked on dancing."[40] In many of his interviews over the years, Kelly acknowledged that much of his motivation to dance in high school was that it helped in meeting girls and dating.

As part of our research we examined about two hundred song sheets that Kelly donated to Boston University in the mid-1980s. Before he released them to the university, he penned short comments on many of them that tell us of his connections with these songs. "Shine on Harvest Moon" was an extremely popular song in America during this period, but for Gene it held a special place in his memory. "This was our high school 'HIT'!," he wrote on the cover. "The trio of Ralston, Davidson & Kelly—real hot shots at Peabody High, Psb., Pa."[41]

Gene's attitude toward religion changed drastically in high school. During his sophomore year at Peabody he became an agnostic and by his junior year seriously considered atheism. It was an extreme reaction to the high level of religiosity at 7514 Kensington Street. The family went to mass every Sunday. For the rest of that day James insisted on no play or unusual noise. After years of this kind of Catholicism, Gene was ready to rebel. He read H. G. Wells's *Outline of History* and rejected religion as a whole. But by his senior year at Peabody, he had reconciled himself to the family's conservative take on Catholicism.[42]

This high school flirtation with agnosticism and atheism had been a needed release for Gene before he came back to his religious roots. For the rest of his life, he mostly enjoyed a nonreligious lifestyle, only to revert later to his conservative Catholic upbringing in Pittsburgh. The church had an enduring influence on him.

Later in life Gene remembered a priest named Father Tynan who was tough, played baseball, and had a way with children. Gene admired him for all these attributes.[43] Tynan undoubtedly influenced Gene when he created the role of Father O'Malley in the television series *Going My Way* in 1962.

When Gene was a junior at Peabody, Harriet enrolled Fred in Lou Bolton's School of Dancing at 5826 Forbes Avenue (moved a few years later to 5858 Forbes Avenue on the same block). She began to work for Bolton as a receptionist in exchange for Fred's lessons, still hoping that Fred would be a professional dancer someday.[44] Because she became involved in helping Bolton, it eventually led the whole family, including Gene, to become more engaged in dance. Moreover, it was convenient for the Kellys because the studio was located in Squirrel Hill, a suburb just west of Homewood Cemetery, not far from home (see Map 1.3).

Squirrel Hill was the most affluent community in the county. Forbes Avenue was the major thoroughfare, dividing it into northern and southern sections. Upper-class families moved into the northern half while middle-level managers in the steel companies spread out through the neighborhood.[45] Bolton had planted his dance school right in the middle of Squirrel Hill's main commercial block, along Forbes Avenue between Shady Avenue and Murray Avenue. This was the heart of Squirrel Hill. There could be no better place to have a dance academy.

In 1929, the Great Depression forced a life change on James by taking away his job. He never held another one after that. The same year, Harriet took over management of the studio with Bolton's approval. Gene agreed to be the main teacher even while he was in his final year of high school. He took the job seriously, developing eight basic dance routines, graded from easy to difficult. Louise pitched in to work up the curriculum on paper. Twelve-year-old Fred's job was to work with students who had missed a lesson and catch them up with the rest. "I think we were the only dance studio in the world that did this," Fred recalled. His other job was to act as a shill to encourage boys to sign up for lessons, pretending to be just another neighborhood kid enthusiastic about taking lessons.[46]

Before leaving Peabody, Gene performed in the biggest stage production thus far of his life. Mrs. Yeamans selected the cast for the senior class production of *A Successful Calamity*. She chose Gene to play the former fiancé of the daughter of the main character. The production was staged at the Nixon Theatre on May 24, 1929. A review in *The Peabody*, the school newspaper, described Gene's character as "the efficient, self-possessed, wise-cracking suitor of Marguerite Wilton." It sounds like *Pal Joey* to come. The reviewer praised Gene by writing that he "had no difficulty in making [his] acting a real success."[47] Even though the reviewer praised other performers as well, some more highly than Gene, there is ample evidence here to conclude that performing on stage in a convincing way came easily for the young Kelly.

Because Gene had received credits from his first year at Sacred Heart High School, he graduated from Peabody after three years in the spring of 1929. He graduated with honors and was listed as a member of several societies, committees, and sports teams. He had also served as associate editor of *The Civitan* and assistant editor of the student handbook. Page five of the 1929 issue of *The Peabody*, which was also the name of the student yearbook, contained the "Peabody Questionnaire" in which Gene appears several times. He tied with Bob Scott and Dick Darrah for best male dancer and placed second as "The Wittiest." When it came to who *thought* they were the wittiest, Gene won hands down.[48]

The 1929 graduating class at Peabody placed 429 students into the world. Eleven of them were African Americans. Peabody was the largest high school in the Pittsburgh metropolitan area, and there was no legalized segregation. "I have no recollection of race problems" at the school, recalled Chalmers Roberts, who went on to work for the *Washington Post*.[49] In his interviews over the years, Gene does not specifically mention the black students in his high school; he gave no indication that, at this time of his life, he was aware of racial issues of any kind. That would change in the years to come. But at this stage, attending college was the only thing on his mind.

CHAPTER 2

Dancing through College, 1929–1933

In planning to attend college, Gene Kelly placed himself within a small group of young people in America. Higher-level education was still an elitist endeavor in the early twentieth century. According to government statistics, only 7.2 percent of the national population between eighteen and twenty-four years of age enrolled in college during the academic year 1929–1930.[1]

In view of these statistics, it is remarkable that all five Kelly children went to college. Harriet ("Jay") graduated from the University of Pittsburgh in 1932, became a schoolteacher in the city, and earned a graduate degree in Education in 1939. James studied at Carnegie Tech (today Carnegie Mellon University) in Pittsburgh, graduating with a Bachelor of Arts degree. He went on to work as a commercial artist and later as an aeronautical designer. Both Jay and James likely relied on their father for tuition until the Depression, as Gene did for his first year of college at Penn State. After that, Gene worked his way through the University of Pittsburgh, as did his two younger siblings. Louise graduated from the University of Pittsburgh in 1936, became a teacher in the city, and later earned a Master's degree in Education. Fred completed a degree in Economics at the University of Pittsburgh in 1939.[2]

PENN STATE

Gene differed from Jay and James by opting to attend Pennsylvania State University rather than a hometown institution. Located about 130 miles east of Pittsburgh at College Station, his choice indicates a desire to experience the world away from the family home. In that sense he seems to have been more adventurous than his older siblings.

In Gene's first year at Penn State, dance continued to be important to him.

He befriended Jim Barry, a tap dancer and drummer, who was five years older. Soon the two performed at college functions and traded dance routines. Gene began to create new dance steps, taking his first dip into choreography. Just as at Peabody, he found that dancing struck a chord with the girls. He also grew a bit taller.[3] This must surely have eased his self-consciousness about being short.

But his first year at Penn State also produced a new thought for Gene that he would take seriously for the rest of his life. He became conscious of social prejudice. When trying to join a fraternity that his Protestant friends from high school belonged to, he discovered there were different fraternities for different religions at Penn State. "I found the whole thing degrading and disgusting," he said, "including the sadistic initiation ceremonies." It "made a terrific impression on me, probably because I'd come from a family where the word prejudice was never mentioned."[4]

That last quote has, in fact, a double meaning. It indicates that the Kelly family did not practice prejudice, but it also ignored the prejudice that obviously took place in Pittsburgh. Only when he left the family setting for a while did Gene learn an important fact of American life. But, once awakened in him, a revulsion against prejudice and discrimination of any kind became a hallmark of his life to come. He became a champion of tolerance and fair play.

While making *The Pirate* (1948), Kelly insisted on including the Nicholas Brothers, a black dancing team, as an integral part of the film. By then he had achieved enough clout as a star to influence such decisions. Gene did not care if the movie would be banned in the segregated South.[5] He fought against racial or ethnic prejudice whenever possible.

The Depression intervened to end Gene's short term as a student at Penn State. Fred Kelly remembered that his father's sales had already begun to slacken by the late 1920s because the expansion of radio had cut into the phonograph and record business. Then the Depression put an end to his work. On average, 40 percent of all employable people in Pittsburgh could not find a job. Charming and bighearted as he was, James had never trained for a career. He was successful at selling only because of his personality and perseverance. When the bottom dropped out of the phonograph business, he had nothing to fall back on and essentially remained jobless the rest of his life. By the spring of 1930, it was apparent that Gene would have to return home and help the family survive. He was amazed years later that despite his traumatic experience, his father continued to be a Republican even though ultraconservative Republican policies had contributed heavily to the Depression.[6]

SUMMER OF 1930

Gene felt a bit guilty about his one year at Penn State, spending his father's money without much awareness of the financial problems produced by the Depression. "I joined a fraternity and spent so much money that I wish my father had kicked me," he told an interviewer. But a new sense of urgency and family responsibility awakened in him. He spent the summer of 1930 in Pittsburgh doing a variety of odd, poorly paid jobs not only to help the family but also to earn some funds to continue his college career at the University of Pittsburgh.[7]

His most rewarding employment, both in terms of learning and salary, was in working as a counselor at YMCA Camp Porter on Lake Erie during the summer of 1930. Harriet steered him toward this opportunity. It paid him $150, enough to cover his tuition at Pitt for the next academic year. Gene worked with boys aged seven to sixteen, staging shows on Saturday night. It was his first chance to mount an amateur production, to choreograph dances, and to coach young people for stage performances. Gene performed in the shows and encouraged other counselors to join in as well. He especially wanted the athletic counselors to participate, stressing the link between dance and sports to begin a lifelong theme to combat the "sissy" image of the male dancer.[8]

Although he had resisted when his mother wanted him to learn dancing, Gene had come a long way toward a career in entertainment by the time he entered the University of Pittsburgh in the fall of 1930. In fact, it was because of his mother that he was able to salvage his college career. Camp Porter and the $150 sent him to college during the Depression, with a father out of work.

UNIVERSITY OF PITTSBURGH

The University of Pittsburgh had its origins in the Pittsburgh Academy of 1787. With the rapid growth of the city it moved to a new 43-acre campus at Oakland in 1908, only four years before Gene's birth. To celebrate the growth of the institution, university leaders initiated the construction of the Cathedral of Learning, a tower of offices and classrooms soaring 40 stories high (see Map 1.1). It was begun in 1926, but completion of the landmark was slowed by the Depression. Described as "the most brilliant structure in the city," it was still slowly being built when Gene enrolled for classes in 1930 and was finally completed seven years later.[9] The Oakland campus was two miles east of downtown and three miles west of the Kelly home on Kensington Street. A good city bus and trolley system provided Gene with transportation to the university.

Initially, Gene wanted to be a writer but soon realized he was not right for the role. "I found that writing was beyond me," he told an interviewer years later. "Going to Pitt I decided I had better find another way than writing to earn a living."[10] What that would be was yet to be discovered.

Once again, Gene flirted with agnosticism as the influence of the college environment sank in. This happened in his sophomore year, the first year at Pitt. According to some accounts, the agnosticism deepened once again into atheism. "What did jolt me was the discovery that some fellows could not believe in God and still be just as nice, if not nicer, than those of us who went to church," he later said.[11] But Gene came back to the Catholic fold pretty soon.

At least one of his friends had some difficulty taking his agnosticism or atheism seriously. Jules Steinberg, who became a favorite drinking buddy of Gene's during his college days in Pittsburgh, knew that Gene often attended early morning mass after a night at a speakeasy called Bakey's. In fact, Steinberg recalled that one night Gene was ready to fight a newspaperman he met at Bakey's because the reporter spoke of Catholic priests as ordinary men with normal urges, also claiming that most priests he knew of in Italy visited brothels. Gene had to be restrained from hitting the reporter for these remarks.[12] Apparently, Gene was ready to defend Catholicism despite his need to question the very foundation of his religion.

ODD JOBS

Unlike young men from more affluent families, Gene could not afford to be idle. He pursued his college studies with intensity but also knew that his family needed him as the Depression worsened. "Like every other boy from a large family," he said, "I decided I had to help my parents get me through college." He mentioned different jobs including pumping gas, jerking sodas, digging ditches, boxing tires at a factory, and working as a concrete mixer, as well as a carpenter's helper and a bricklayer. Kelly continued working at these jobs while taking a full load of classes from fall to spring and also during the summer of 1931. He never made much money at these odd jobs, taking home up to $20 per week.[13] But it surely helped when added to the income that other family members managed to bring in.

Gene's academic transcript at Pitt is not open to public inspection, so we do not know how this rigorous work schedule affected his grades. But the odd jobs illustrate Gene's commitment to his family, his self-discipline, and his determination to go to school and fulfill his family obligations at the same time.

Betsy Blair readily saw this side of Gene when she got to know him a few years later. "He had been forced to take over and be the 'man' in his family at an early age," she wrote. "His older brother James was more like Pop Kelly and not inclined toward being in charge of anyone. But Gene was a natural carer and a smart, creative, and benevolent boss type. He didn't want to be the center of attention, he wanted to quietly control the whole thing. I don't think for a moment that he was aware of this."[14] Still, he had set a hectic pace for himself, attending classes and then working the equivalent of a full-time job in the evenings and taking home what was at best a modest amount of money for the effort. His jobs could not have brought him any degree of fulfillment, making the grind even worse.

Meanwhile, Fred was doing what he truly enjoyed—dancing and making money performing at various venues such as amateur nights and shows. To Gene, it looked like his younger brother was reaping a better return for less work. "Back in those days when I was jerking sodas and pumping gas for 25 cents an hour, it wasn't hard for my brother, Fred, to get me to do a dance act for $5 a night for two hours work," he recalled. "I began to find out that for my whole week's work, he could match it in a few nights with about one-twentieth of the time."[15]

TEAMING WITH FRED

Gene agreed to work up an act with his brother. In fact, he admitted that Fred taught him many tap dance steps at this time. Then, together they developed a handful of routines and began to perform in the evenings while Gene studied prelaw during the day. By now he had bowed to his mother's wish that he become a lawyer. At the same time, Gene began teaching dancing to students in the basement of the Kensington home, charging 50 cents an hour for the lessons.[16] Dancing was slowly becoming more important to him.

The brothers initially called their act Gene and Fred Kay, "which we thought was very dashing." They chose popular songs, pitching their act to a low common denominator. "The Daughter of Rosie O'Grady" became "a standard in my early nightclub repertoire," Gene recalled in 1992. The brothers also relied on "I Want to be Happy," a popular song from *No, No, Nanette*, a musical show that opened in Chicago in 1924 and in New York the following year. In addition to songs and tap dancing, the act included acrobatics and roller-skating. Fred was particularly good at dancing with roller skates strapped to his shoes, even performing backflips with them.[17]

Gene always gave Fred full credit for his role in developing routines and for teaching him many of the basics of popular dance. Fred was not interested in the more artistic forms such as ballet, but he thrived on "the rougher dancing and he loved folk dancing of any kind." The brothers drew on their gymnastic work in high school, and Gene especially noted that playing hockey was a big help in their ability to handle tap dancing on roller skates.[18]

Another person who taught Gene many dance steps was Frank Harrington, an African American dancer from New York who worked at the Bolton School for one season. With all their exposure to dancing, the team of Gene and Fred Kay worked up interesting and entertaining routines, but they mostly played in low-class dives around Pittsburgh beginning in the fall of 1931. The brothers called these places "cloops," a contraction of the words "club" and "chicken coop," which described how they felt toward the clientele and the atmosphere in them. They could earn up to $10 a night at these places. But they also entertained at better establishments such as amateur evenings held in movie theaters, where they earned $12–15 per night. They even performed in tuxedos if the venue called for it. Fred worked up a few minutes of magic tricks to lengthen their act so that it could run as long as twenty minutes.[19]

In many ways this act with Fred was one of the most formative experiences of Gene's early life. It brought him into close contact with average Americans from a working-class environment. It taught him a great deal about how to relate to an audience of differing sorts of people from those he was used to dealing with in high school or college.

Looking back at playing the cloops, Gene recalled the low expectations of the audience. They were happy if someone told a few off-color jokes and then sang a song. He tried to give them what he considered pretty smart dance moves, but they often missed it because they were too busy drinking or chatting with friends. Worse than that, drunken patrons occasionally yelled insults at him. "Sometimes I belted them," he admitted in an interview years later. "One night a guy called me a fag, and I jumped off the stage and hit him. But I had to make a run for it, because the owner of the place and his brother took after me with a couple of baseball bats."[20] Such interactions only increased Gene's sensitivity about the male dancer in working-class American culture.

But Gene's most prominent memory of playing the cloops was that he usually was ignored by an audience that failed to appreciate what he thought was a classy act. The fact that he often followed acts involving stripteasers did not help. Another thing that embarrassed Gene was the crass reaction of the audience even when they did appreciate the boys' act. Sometimes they threw coins onto the stage as a tip. Gene was ready to go out and punch the first man who did this, but when others followed he knew he could not fight the entire audience. "I just had to grin and bear it," he recalled. Fred, however, loved it. He picked up the coins and kept dancing for more. "But I was mortified, shocked and ashamed. . . . I was just ready to die of humiliation."[21]

It is easy to sympathize with Gene, who obviously held himself to a high standard and tried to lift his audience a bit out of the gutter. But in the world of the cloops that was a hopeless dream. He wanted to be noticed, appreciated for his skill at dancing and entertaining, and to aspire to higher things than offering a bawdy time to an audience.

Along the way, he also learned to be tolerant of less skilled performers. When he and Fred competed in an amateur night at the Butler Theatre in Butler, Pennsylvania, the pianist played their song too fast. "Where d'you think you're going? To a fire?" he asked her loud enough to be heard by the audience. She heard him but deliberately continued to play at a fast speed. The audience did not like Gene for that remark, and he could feel it in their reaction to the routine. He always felt he and Fred had lost the $10 prize that night because of his intemperate remark. Instead, they received only a dollar for showing up. He realized that if he had asked her politely to slow down the tempo and blown her a kiss, that "would have been classy."[22]

Gene and Fred broke racial stereotypes when they performed with Cab Callaway at Altoona, Pennsylvania. Calloway was only twenty-three at the time but already a big star with his hit "Minnie the Moocher." He was on his way to Philadelphia and stopped at the Sunset in Altoona for a performance on August 12, 1931, billed as "Red Hot from Harlem" with his Cotton Club Orchestra. Actually, the Altoona audience was not told that Callaway's Cotton Club Orchestra was still in Harlem. Instead, he played with his former backup band led by Nappy Harvey, which was on a tour of Pennsylvania and New York and invited Callaway to join them. But his scheduled dancers, the Nicholas Brothers, dropped out suddenly to perform in a film. Calloway asked the William Morris Agency to round up a couple of black dancers, and the agency called its contacts in Pittsburgh. Told that the Kelly brothers were a class act, Calloway agreed without realizing they were not black. Gene and Fred took the train to Altoona, 100 miles due east from Pittsburgh, and arrived at 10 A.M. on a Sunday when Calloway and his band already were rehearsing. The theater manager was stunned and stopped the rehearsal to introduce the new act to Calloway. Fred recalled what happened next. "Somebody done make a *big* mistake!" Calloway shouted in an imitation of Amos 'n' Andy. He asked the brothers if they knew they were being asked to perform with a black band, and they said yes. In fact, both assured Calloway they liked his music very much and were eager to do the show.[23]

In rehearsal, Calloway asked which of the two danced faster. Fred answered that he did and wanted to dance to "Star Dust." When Calloway pointed out that this was not a fast song, Fred said he would start at half-time, then segue to full-time, then to double-time, and end at quadruple-time. "This is something I want to see!" said Calloway, and both Gene and Fred did exactly as Fred promised. The entire band was impressed, according to Fred, and gave them a standing ovation.[24]

After the rehearsal, Calloway told the pair to get a meal at the restaurant across the street; he had already reserved a table for them. Gene and Fred were sitting at the window table when the theater across the street changed the marquee for that night's show. "Extra-Special added Attraction," it read, "Gene and Fred Kelly—The Kelly Brothers." It was a rush for both young men. "Now we knew we had made it!" Fred exulted as late as 1989. "What a time that was: just kids, and having the time of our lives."[25] The experience also seems to have given the brothers the confidence to bill themselves as "Kelly" for future engagements.

But the name "Kay" stuck with Gene for a short while. When he had a chance to perform at a country club in Johnstown, about sixty miles east of Pittsburgh, he chose his elder sister Jay to dance with him. She already had graduated from Pitt and was a schoolteacher by this time. But Gene thought she was a better dancer than his younger sister Louise. She also had more bravado when performing before an audience. The siblings worked up a ballroom number and a jazz ballet and wowed the audience, earning $150 in one night. They pretended not to be related but instead a professional dancing duo billed as Joe and Kay. They especially enjoyed dancing to a song called "Will You Remember," from the Broadway musical *Maytime*, with music by

Sigmund Romberg. Gene and Jay had seen it in a film short called *Will You Remember?* (1927) at the Regent Theatre in East Liberty. The song was performed by Vivienne Segal and John Charles Thomas in the film. "We imitated them for months," Gene recalled.[26] Ironically, Segal would costar with Gene in *Pal Joey* fourteen years after the short was released.

BETH SHALOM

As if he was not busy enough, Gene took on another rewarding job as manager of the annual Kirmess, a show sponsored by the Beth Shalom Synagogue as a fundraising event. Lou Bolton had originally agreed to do this but left town before the event, and the Sisterhood of the Beth Shalom had to find a replacement. Harriet recommended Gene. Anne Greenberg, a member of the Sisterhood, remembered that the committee in charge of the event agreed to hire him for a salary of $15 per week. Gene had put together a show called *Main Street to Broadway* for Lou Bolton's students at the Alvin Theatre on June 22, 1931. He had written the book and starred in the performance, which proved to be valuable experience for the Kirmess. In September 1931, Gene began working with a large number of kids, holding classes every Sunday from 2 to 4 P.M. He held separate sports lessons for the boys so they could see the connection between dance and their favorite sports. Greenberg was awed by his work and remembered years later that Gene "worked so fantastically well with children. You could tell at a glance he was a star. He had this incredible magnetism, and he could somehow get children to do anything he wanted them to do."[27]

Months of hard work, planning routines, teaching a variety of dance steps to kids of all ages, and putting it all together into a respectable show paid off. On April 13, 1932, the first Kirmess staged by Gene, called *Revue of Revues*, opened to a packed and highly appreciative audience at Taylor Allderdice High School. The furnishings were sparse, with only one backdrop sufficing for all acts, and costumes were made by the mothers of the performers. Not only did the children do well but Gene also danced, causing explosive rounds of applause according to an admiring Anne Greenberg. Even though ticket prices were only 25 cents for children and 50 cents for adults, the event brought in $1,100. It was such a success that Gene was asked to continue indefinitely, managing the event for a total of seven years until he left for New York.[28] It brought in a steady income for the family.

The Beth Shalom experience was very important for Gene. "I got my first real acclaim locally as a dancing teacher" from it, he later recalled.[29] The experience was an opportunity not only to teach children, which he increasingly loved to do, but also in learning how to meld amateur performers into a cohesive group that could work on the stage. His latent skills as a choreographer, stage manager, mentor, and teacher were brought out more forcefully and developed more carefully at Beth Shalom than they would be in any other endeavor he undertook in Pittsburgh.

By the time his first Kirmess took place, Gene entered upon an incredibly intense period of work involving the development of his entertainment and teaching skills. As a result, 1932 proved to be a pivotal year in his life. He was only nineteen, a sophomore and then a junior in college, but he acted like a mature man in the way he professionalized all his activities relating to dance, teaching, and entertainment. His motivation was to a large extent a driving need to take care of his family with increased income. But it was more than that as well—without realizing it, Gene was preparing himself for a life in show business.

DANCE STUDIOS

The family had already expanded its business interests by opening another dance school in Johnstown. Harriet's brother Gus was the impetus for this. He told Harriet there was no good dance studio in this working-class town of 70,000 inhabitants. Harriet convinced a reluctant Lou Bolton to partner the creation of this studio with her by agreeing to manage it. They rented a room on the third floor of the American Legion Hall and called it the Lou Bolton School of Dancing to match the Pittsburgh location's name. Bolton and an assistant taught classes there Saturday morning, but Gene filled in for Bolton whenever he could not make it, which was often. Bolton soon found the Johnstown school not worth his trouble, so Harriet took it over completely. When Bolton left Pittsburgh in 1931, the Kellys were now in charge of both schools.[30] The transition appears to have been fairly seamless. After all, there was no capital investment, only the monthly rent and minor expenses to manage the schools.

At first the Johnstown venture did not do well. A competitor tried to ruin their business by spreading the word that the Kellys did not belong to the dance teachers' union. Also, Gene had developed a serious curriculum instead of just teaching simple steps to please the parents. He insisted that his pupils learn a variety of steps even if it took them some time to do so. The price was not exorbitant—only 50 cents per lesson—but even so many parents could not afford to pay cash. They offered food to the Kellys or cleaned the studio in lieu of payment.[31]

Gene thought that a better location would help the Johnstown studio and urged the family to locate a building with more room. They found one on Main Street and moved there in 1932. The grand opening of the new location was heralded with ads and a celebration that offered refreshments, but the family was stunned when virtually no one came except two former students. The Kellys never discovered why the grand opening bombed. Harriet cried and was ready to give up, but Gene refused. His fighting blood was up, and he mounted a major campaign to make not only the Johnstown studio but the Pittsburgh location a success.[32]

The first thing they did was to rename both institutions the Gene Kelly Studio of the Dance. It was a smart move. Not only was Lou Bolton no longer associated with the schools, but Gene was a rising star among the small group of dance instructors in both towns. Maybe there was magic in that name, or maybe it was that Gene notched up his energy and charisma. Whatever the reason, both schools began to prosper from 1932 onward—the Pittsburgh studio on Forbes Avenue and the Johnstown studio on Main Street. Old students and new began to arrive at the Main Street location in a steady stream. By 1933 there were 150 students at Johnstown. Gene had to hire some dance instructors because he and his siblings could not handle such a crowd by themselves. The family bought a Chevrolet and hired a driver to take them from Pittsburgh to Johnstown on Fridays, staying overnight at a boarding house. The next day they taught these 150 children all day until 10 P.M. and then motored back that night.[33]

The Kellys worked together as a family to make the two studios a success. Gene talked his out-of-work father into taking care of accounts at both locations, and Harriet continued to be the manager for the two ventures. The move rehabilitated James Kelly, and Gene recalled that "he was very grateful." Fred remembered that his father had experienced "abject humiliation" because he could not find a job after the Depression. James had given up trying for work after a year of fruitless searching and had formed a habit of spending time drinking with his friends. Harriet and Jay were critical of his attitude, but Gene seemed to understand, stating that it was as if his father "had had a stroke." However, James had not been so traumatized as to completely forget

Figure 2.1 This three-story building, located at 5858 Forbes Avenue, was the second home of the Gene Kelly Studio of the Dance. It had previously been located a few doors away at 5826 Forbes Avenue, and would later be moved about four blocks southwest to the Beacon Apartments near the junction of Beacon Street and Munhall Road. The studio was operated by the Kelly family for more than twenty-five years. The two Forbes Avenue locations were in the heart of the Squirrel Hill shopping district. Today there is still a dance studio here, as seen by the promotional artwork on the building. (Photo by authors)

his family responsibilities. Gene discovered that James had borrowed "on his insurance to keep up the monthly payments" on the Kensington Street house.[34]

Gene's role as the primary instructor of the Pittsburgh and Johnstown studios was a difficult and responsible position. "The teacher was *King*" in dance schools of the 1930s, Fred remembered years later. Each class lasted one hour "and you danced, you didn't sit down." The Johnstown classes were bigger and the students more ambitious about crafting a career in show business, even if only in vaudeville. Gene admitted that often he was "only one step ahead of my pupils; I'd go to a night club, watch the routines, pick up a couple and teach them the next day in class." He never forgot the sensitivity boys felt when attending dance classes. He often gave them a quick lesson in basketball, so they could realize that body movement was the same for sports and dancing.[35]

"I loved it," Gene reminisced about those days in 1958. "I loved teaching children." He disdained a curriculum built around social dancing and insisted that his students be exposed to a wide variety of dance styles. While the classes emphasized tap and ballet, they also included "modern, acrobatic, ethnic dances, national dances, folk dances," he remembered. "I was quite a scholar, quite a student of the dance all this time, studying every summer."[36] His enthusiasm, rapport with the young students, and charisma made attendance at the Gene Kelly Studio of the Dance, whether in Johnstown or Pittsburgh, a special event.

Gene used the ambitious Johnstown students to stage summer events in area towns in order to showcase their talent and drum up new business for the studio. These shows had titles such as *Johnstown on Parade*, or *Gene Kelly's Kiddie's Vodvil*, or *The Talk of the Town Revue*. The shows became so popular that Gene was able to hire a full orchestra and use elaborate scenery. Just as he was doing with the Beth Shalom students, Gene crafted a variety of skits and dances for his Johnstown students (aged four to eighteen) for these gala events.[37]

The two studios at Johnstown and Pittsburgh did so well that the family could weather what was left of the Depression. His mother gave him spending money rather than a salary. She did not even tell Gene how much income the schools drew in. Harriet made sure the family's monthly expenses were covered and eventually hired a full-time maid for the Kensington Street house. Still, Gene continued to think of becoming a lawyer or a journalist, not an entertainer. "I considered dancing a means to an end," he recalled later, "and so did my brothers and sisters."[38]

CAP AND GOWN

Eventually Gene also got involved in the Cap and Gown Club at the University of Pittsburgh. Created in 1908, Cap and Gown was an all-male club that mounted a large musical stage show every spring semester. It grew so popular that only Pitt sports drew more attention. Something like 300 college men tried out for it, and mostly alumni wrote the shows for them. G. Norman Reis, a Pitt grad of 1916, wrote the libretto for nine different shows and also filmed parts of them with a small movie camera. Dr. Benjamin Levant, a 1919 graduate, wrote the music for many shows.[39] His younger brother Oscar became a popular concert pianist and would costar with Gene in *An American in Paris*.

Altogether, Cap and Gown staged thirty-six shows until 1947. The performances were held in Pittsburgh's best playhouse, the Nixon Theatre on Sixth Avenue in downtown. With 2,183 seats, it was hailed as "The World's Perfect Playhouse" when completed for $1.2 million in 1903 for the "carriage trade" (patrons who were wealthy enough to ride to the theater in their own carriage). Virtually every kind of upper-end entertainment came to the Nixon, from recent Broadway shows to international ballet and opera productions.[40] The Nixon's reputation lent a great deal of credibility to these amateur college productions.

Gene was a student at Pitt when he participated in his first Cap and Gown show, *What's Up—A Musical Take-off in Two Ascents and Twelve Landings*, written by Reis. Gene appeared in two musical numbers of this revue, "Hot Steps" in Act One and "Happy Rhythm" in Act Two. He was correctly credited as Eugene Kelly for the two numbers, but in a group photo of the cast his last name was misspelled as Kelley. The show played for a week at the Nixon in April 1931 to glowing reviews.[41] It was the twenty-fourth annual production for Cap and Gown, but to many it seemed the best yet and approached a real Broadway show rather than an amateur effort in Pittsburgh.

Cap and Gown's twenty-fifth anniversary was celebrated with *The Silver Domino* in the spring of 1932. It contained two acts, eight scenes, and twenty-three dances. There were nineteen principal actors and forty chorus members. Florence Parry mentioned that Gene and his dance partner William Pillich had pulled off "a tricky tap" and further praised Gene, saying he "danced beautifully." The program included a caricature of Kelly in a tuxedo doing his "tricky tap." "Gene has a personality that coaxes the smiles to the audiences' faces," wrote an anonymous reviewer for *Pitt Weekly*.[42] All of the performers were males and thus many dressed as women, as was true of every show.

Notable for its elaborate ambition, *The Silver Domino* was a travelogue packed with dancing. Kelly donned "a complete body make-up" for the "Barbarian Dance" set in Borneo, which was called the highlight of the show by several reviewers. Horace Hubbard also had a full body make-up to play Mahatma Gandhi in another number, so he and Gene shared a dressing room at the Nixon that had a bathtub. Unusually for Gene, he agreed to dress as a woman, and William Schindel performed the male part in "The Glass

Figure 2.2 Caricatures of some of the major players (including Kelly) in the 1932 Cap and Gown Program of *The Silver Domino*. His name is misspelled as "Kelley." (Cap and Gown Records, University of Pittsburgh)

Figures" set in Venice.[43] The program included a photograph of the pair in costume. It is the only time that Gene Kelly performed in drag. The program misspelled his name as "Engene Kelley" for the "Barbarian Dance" as well as for "The Glass Figures," but they at least got his first name right for another number called "Hot Spot."

All to the Point—A Musical Romance of Early Pittsburgh, the third Cap and Gown show that Gene took part in, was staged in the spring of 1933. It was a historical play in eighteenth-century costume, and Gene performed in two numbers—"Sand Dance" and "Old King Cole." Israel Goldberg's review

Figure 2.3 Gene (in drag) in a Cap and Gown performance with William Schindel. The dance, called "The Glass Figures," was in Act Two, Scene One (Venice), of *The Silver Domino*, performed at the Nixon Theatre in 1932. (Cap and Gown Records, University of Pittsburgh)

singled out Gene and William Pillich for their dancing. The program continued to add an extra "e" to Kelly but got his first name right. G. Norman Reis, who wrote the libretto, also filmed many of the performances of this show, including Gene's dance in period costume.[44]

The clip of Gene's dance is only seventeen seconds long but it is important because this is the first time his performance was captured on film and reveals how he danced at that age. In his solo dance, the choreography is simple with a lot of high leg kicks and a bit of jumping about. Actually he does not really dance much better than the other amateurs who appear by the dozens in large ensemble numbers of *All to the Point*. But the difference between Gene and the rest is his huge smile and his presence on the stage. He did not yet have the dancing technique that would set him apart later in life, but he had the charisma, the self-confidence, and the ability to appeal to the audience in an immediate, certain way. And he was only twenty years old.

Gene already was an accomplished entertainer. That came from his personality, his drive, and his interest in people. But he needed to become a better dancer. What he was able to do worked fine for Cap and Gown and

Figure 2.4 Gene dancing in *All to the Point*, the Cap and Gown show of 1933. These images were taken with a small home movie camera in 1933, and this is the reason they are a bit blurry. But they are unique because they reveal that Gene did not at this point have the grace that he developed after learning ballet, but his charm and charisma are very much present even at this early stage. (Stills from *Anatomy of a Dancer*, 2002)

for the cloops, but it was small-town dancing nevertheless. The thing that raised Gene's dancing to the next level was ballet. It offered him the self-discipline to coordinate all parts of his body, and to think of the steps holistically rather than just kicking about. In addition, ballet taught him the importance of holding himself so the audience could see and appreciate the long line of his body and its movement.

BALLET

Gene took his first "rudimentary ballet lessons" in 1930 from a Pittsburgh dance instructor. They do not seem to have helped much. But in the spring of 1932 he saw the Ballet Russe de Monte Carlo perform at the Shrine Auditorium in Pittsburgh. This legendary company had just been organized the previous January and was at the beginning of its impact on America. Its first night's performance was *Les Sylphides*. On the second night he was treated to *La Concurrence* and on the third night it was *L'Apres-midi d'Un Faune*. Gene was enthralled and decided to make a study of ballet as a result. In the summer of that year, with both dance studios in recess, Gene and Fred drove to Chicago so Gene could immerse himself in ballet. They supported themselves by dancing in local clubs. "I still consider Chicago the place where I really learned my basic dancing," he recalled in 1983.[45] The ballet lessons changed Gene's attitude toward dance.

Gene also became a member of the Chicago National Association of Dance Masters in 1932. He had applied for admission the previous year, but his competitor in Johnstown had written to the association claiming that Kelly did not deserve membership. That competitor left Johnstown when Gene's studio took off, so now there was no opposition to his joining the Dance Masters.[46]

REVELATION

After three years of hard work at the University of Pittsburgh, Gene graduated in the spring of 1933. He earned a bachelor's degree in economics with a minor in French. The commencement ceremony was held outdoors under a "broiling sun," as his friend Horace J. Hubbard reported years later. Hubbard recalled that he sat next to Gene for the ceremony and was proud that his friend had a thriving dance studio in Johnstown, Hubbard's hometown.[47] At this point Gene had no idea that his future would be in entertainment, even though everything indicated that it was his consuming interest.

Soon after commencement, Gene drove back to Chicago for the summer of 1933 and studied ballet more intently than he had the previous year. The Chicago National Association of Dance Masters offered master classes every summer. Gene stayed at a cheap hotel, paid the admission fee, and could attend any class he wanted. Some of the best and most influential dance instructors in the country were in Chicago at this time, and Gene learned from many of them. Russian dance master Alexander Kotchetovsky and Hispanic performer Angel Cansino (Rita Hayworth's uncle, who taught Gene Spanish dancing) were special favorites of Gene's. They were "down-to-earth, even tough guys" who pursued dance as a profession. "They taught me a lot," Gene said. He recalled drinking with them in Chicago bars and having the best time of his life. To him, they gave the lie to the sissy image of the male dancer. Gene supplemented his classes with self-directed study in the Chicago Public Library. "I even read the ones that were in French, and that was strictly labor because my French is just school French," he told an interviewer a few years later.[48]

Two incidents that summer in Chicago illustrate aspects of Gene's character. He continued to work wherever possible to fund his stay in the city. The Chicago World's Fair, which celebrated the centennial of the city's founding, offered many opportunities for performers. An agent sent Gene and Fred to dance two shows at a venue at the fair, but the owner forced them to do four shows. When Gene complained to the agent, the man refused to give him more money but instead demanded his commission of 50 cents. Gene was furious and hit the man "so hard I broke a finger in my hand, and had to spend the money getting it fixed in a hospital." By the 1970s Gene had mellowed enough to admit that in those days "I hadn't learned to control my temper—and I didn't really get to control it until years after I'd been in Hollywood." On another occasion that summer, while performing at the La Salle Hotel, Gene stumbled and broke his arm. Despite the shock and pain, he had the physical strength and the presence of mind to take a bow before leaving the stage.[49]

Gene survived this hard summer in Chicago and prepared to enter Pitt's law school in the fall of 1933. Despite the fact that he had become more intensely interested in dance than at any previous time of his life, he was still going along with Harriet's wishes. But with each passing week in law school his plan to become a lawyer weakened. After two months of classes he finally faced reality. He was taking a class on torts when the absurdity of it all really sank in. "What am I doing?" he asked himself. "I *know* I'm a good dancer,'" but he had no confidence that he could become a good lawyer.[50] More importantly, he had no real interest in law, whereas dancing filled his imagination and made him happy.

More than forty years later, Gene felt that his exposure to the art of ballet had quietly prepared him to take this step. The performance of those three ballets by the Ballet Russe de Monte Carlo in 1932 "changed my whole life. I think if I hadn't seen them that maybe I would have continued and gone through law school, been a lawyer, and just earned money."[51] If he was reading the course of his life correctly, then ballet certainly played a key role in his development.

It took Gene a surprisingly long time to reach this important point, but he finally chose a life in entertainment rather than law. His natural talent, his ability to deliver what the audience wanted, and his love of teaching dance and creating routines won out over parental direction.

CHAPTER 3

Dance Master of Pittsburgh, 1933–1938

Gene was not only a boy of the Depression, he was also a young man of President Franklin D. Roosevelt's New Deal. The Depression started only two months after Gene entered college in 1929. Roosevelt initiated the New Deal to combat the effects of that economic catastrophe only two months before Gene graduated in 1933. Roosevelt's experimentation with government intervention in the national economy, his support for the common man, and his encouragement of labor unions had a decisive effect on Kelly's political views for life. But for now he had to focus on his own future. As the economy slowly improved, Gene struggled to find his own way. He knew now that dancing was the key, but exactly how to make that the basis of a career was not clear.

BALLET

Gene understood instinctively that continuing to learn was important. He already had two summers of ballet training in Chicago (in 1932 and 1933) and would have three more (in 1934, 1935, and 1936). In 1933, he took instruction under Bernice Holmes and was the only man in her classes. Holmes loomed large in Gene's preparation as a professional. He thought he had gained the most intense understanding of ballet technique from her. Gene was impressed that Holmes had studied with Adolph Bolm, "a great Russian dancer and a very, very masculine fellow," he recalled. Fred Kelly later claimed that his brother had to learn ballet in Chicago to avoid ostracism in Pittsburgh, but a more important reason was the higher level of training available there. The ballet classes he had taken in Pittsburgh had not helped much. Gene knew that New York and Los Angeles had good teachers, but Chicago was "the dance capital of the United States" at that time. He took several other master classes sponsored by the Chicago National Association of Dance Masters as well.[1] The master classes in Chicago exposed Gene to the glories of dance as art rather than as mere entertainment. They opened a new world to him.

Ironically, he was presented with an opportunity to make that art world his home—if he wanted it. The Ballet Russe de Monte Carlo came back to Pittsburgh not long after he dropped out of law school. Gene asked for an audition, and principal dancer David Lichine agreed to see him the next day. But when Gene arrived he found that Lichine was not there. The ballet master, however, was impressed enough with Gene's technique to offer him a job in the chorus once the company reached Chicago two weeks later.[2]

The offer presented a life-changing decision for Gene. The pay was minimal at $35 per week. It was difficult for him to imagine living on such a low salary after making "a couple of hundred" a week for a while now. Moreover, he already knew that his dance style had been weaned on popular music played for the most part before a middle- and lower-class audience. Shifting to ballet as a profession was a very big step. Gene came to the conclusion that he did not want to do ballet exclusively for the rest of his life. He felt a strong urge to develop his popular dancing to a higher level. He also wanted to explore modern dance because of the work of Martha Graham, another Pittsburgh native who was making an impression nationally at the time. And he readily admitted that earning a good living was important as well. Gene still felt obliged to help his family weather what was left of the Depression.[3]

DANCE STUDIOS

Gene's campaign to make the studios more profitable paid off, but it took several years of hard work. The Kellys took advantage of every opportunity to increase enrollment. The release of *42nd Street* in 1933 represented something of a watershed in the production of movie musicals and also created a lot of interest in Pittsburgh. The movie inspired a new dance uniform for the studio, with girls wearing a blouse with a large collar and long sleeves. Bows were added to their tap shoes, and they wore shorts made of velvet "with three little pearl buttons on each side." Admiring mothers of the girl students embroidered a giant "K" on the blouse for the Kelly Studio. Gene refused to force his boy students to wear tights or short pants even when he taught them ballet steps and poses. The boys were allowed to wear street clothes for their classes. They of course dressed in appropriate costumes for the shows the studio staged for parents and the public. The school also used metal taps on the shoes of both girls and boys, with James Kelly ordering them "a gross at a time" according to Fred. When Shirley Temple started appearing in feature-length films from 1934 on, it created great interest in dancing. "Every time Shirley Temple made a movie," Fred recalled, "our studio enrollment doubled. We had one hundred girls in our studio who all looked exactly like Shirley Temple! . . . We couldn't stop it. So we went with it."[4]

Gene gave up the chance for a ballet career but he never regretted the decision. Instead he intensified his work at both studios, continued to stage the annual shows for Beth Shalom, and accepted jobs anywhere in Pittsburgh that involved choreographing, creating, or managing entertainment. Essentially he continued the extracurricular activities he had started in college with no other end in sight than to continue helping his family and making a living.

Gene taught in his dance studios for seven years. To keep in shape he danced energetically with the kids as he taught them. By 1935 there were 350 students combined in the Johnstown and Pittsburgh schools. There was less competition in Johnstown, so the classes there tended to be larger than at Squirrel Hill. The family decided to move the Johnstown school to its third location at Franklin and Vine Streets where they had the entire second floor to work in. The space also had dressing rooms and an office for James. The two studios were taking in $8,000 to $10,000 per year by the late 1930s. The family emphasized that Gene was the youngest member of the Chicago National Association of Dance Masters, as well as the American Society of Dancing Teachers, to promote their Squirrel Hill location.[5]

The high interest in dancing that prevailed in Johnstown brought many young boys and girls in touch with Gene. Ironically, he met his future second wife this way. Jeanne Coyne was twelve years old when her mother took her to the Gene Kelly Studio of the Dance at Franklin and Vine in 1935. She remembered entering a huge ballroom for her initial lesson. The first thing Gene said to her was, "You have good legs for a dancer. You'll have a lot of fun here." Coyne soon developed a crush on the twenty-three-year-old dance instructor that eventually blossomed into love.[6]

Al Checco of East Liberty always remembered what he learned at the Gene Kelly Studio of the Dance in Squirrel Hill. He was impressed by the number Gene and Fred did on roller skates "going up and down steps." He also recalled, "I had to follow that act . . . singing 'Brother Can You Spare a Dime'!"

Gene taught him how to take a bow. "There was an ovation and I wanted to run out [on the stage], but he said, 'Hold it, kid. Let 'em want you more.'"[7]

Gene masterminded a big show mounted by the students of both dance studios every year. "Gene Kelly Studio Presents Its Annual Revue of the Dance," read the program for the 1938 show, which blended the Johnstown and Pittsburgh talent. It was directed by Gene, Fred, and Louise Kelly and consisted of two acts. The first contained twenty-two numbers, one of which involved twenty dancers, while the second had thirty-four, with Gene and Fred doing a dance near the end. Racelle Lazar, a star pupil of the Squirrel Hill location, performed in five numbers. Marjorie Spector, also a student at Squirrel Hill, was in two dances. Jeanne Coyne from Johnstown was one of several students who performed in "Presenting the Holidays Throughout the Year." She also appeared in "Prince Charming and the Sleeping Beauty" with another girl and in "Valse Viennois."[8] Coyne not only found her future husband but also developed her talent for a career in dancing as she continued to study at the Gene Kelly Studio of the Dance.

JEWISH COMMUNITY

Racelle Lazar, a Jewish student of Gene's, represents an interesting angle on Kelly's life. The Squirrel Hill studio was right in the middle of an increasingly Jewish section of Pittsburgh, and the family made lasting contacts with many Jewish families who sent their children to study there. Moreover, Beth Shalom was only two blocks south of the school's location on Forbes Avenue. In addition to teaching many Jewish children at his studio, Gene continued managing Beth Shalom's yearly Kirmesses. A few years later, he exercised his irreverent sense of humor by telling an interviewer that he had worked for the synagogue for seven years and "If I'd remained another season they were gonna Bar Mitzvah me! Imagine, an Irish Hebe!"[9]

Ruth Portnoy was ten years old when she became one of the thousands of students who enjoyed Gene's work for Beth Shalom. She recalled that Fred always acted as Gene's assistant and Harriet, Jay, and Louise sewed or at least supervised the making of the costumes. Gene and Fred also did their "breathtaking routines on skates" at the Kirmesses. "My memories of Gene Kelly as my teacher are crystal clear," Portnoy wrote in 1996. "He loved to dance, he loved to see his pupils dance, he loved life." Portnoy "knew total joy" when Gene taught her and her sister an Irish jig duet for the recital.[10]

As Portnoy indicated there was a special relationship between the Jewish community of Squirrel Hill and Gene, the Kelly family, and the Gene Kelly Studio of the Dance. They all were good for each other. Gene agreed to participate in several events for the community. He staged a children's dance for the Ladies' Hospital Aid Society in December 1933, performed at a Men's Club event in January 1934, and entertained at a supper club for members of Beth Shalom in February 1935. Gene also took part in the Purim Dance Masquerade for Century Court in March 1936.[11]

The family placed ads for the Gene Kelly Studio of the Dance in local newspapers such as the *Jewish Criterion* and the *American Jewish Outlook*. Robert Lazar, Racelle's brother, formed his own band and developed a lifelong friendship with Gene and Fred. The connections Gene crafted with the Jewish community of Squirrel Hill lasted beyond his departure from Pittsburgh. He telegraphed his congratulations to Bobby Lazar for his Bar Mitzvah in 1938, adding "probably be married next thing I hear." Ruth Portnoy wrote to Gene several times during his film career. She not only wanted to congratulate him but also to let him know "what he'd meant in my life." She was delighted that he responded each time with personal letters. Portnoy believed, "it summed up the nature of the man . . . the goodness and grace of the man who was my teacher."[12]

These personal and business connections with the Jewish community reinforced Gene's distaste of ethnic prejudice and created an enduring sense of community across religious and ethnic boundaries. Gloria Elbling Gottlieb, who had been a student in the Kirmess productions, recalled this connection in a 1990 oral history interview sponsored by the National Council of Jewish Women. "He was very friendly, very personable," she said. "The whole family, I would say, were very friendly with the Jewish community." The times seemed to foster this kind of connectedness. "We were all living through a Depression and living in this particular community we each depended on each other."[13]

CAP AND GOWN

Gene also became involved, as an alumnus, in the Cap and Gown Club shows. It was "the pinnacle of success in Pittsburgh at the time, for anybody connected with the dance," to be part of these shows, he recalled. A year after graduation, Kelly served as chorus manager of the 1934 production of *Hello*

Again. The next year, he was promoted to dance director of *In the Soup*. He held two-hour rehearsals every Monday and Wednesday evening at the Y hut on campus. A reporter named Ben Baskin was impressed by his professional manner. "Okay, fellows, it's 8 o'clock . . . what say we get started?" he yelled to the forty performers while standing on a chair. "Girls line up in the front, fellows in the back." Of course, the "girls" were really male members of the club assigned to the female roles. "Okay, are you fellows in the back line finished making wisecracks about the girls up front? . . . If you are, we'll get started." Gene tried to get the dancers to reach a faster pace, what he called "jazz tempo." And he made them practice high leg kicks. "Hey, you in the yellow suspenders, keep your knees stiff and point your toes," he shouted.[14]

G. Norman Reis made an amateur film of *In the Soup* during its 1935 run at the Nixon Theatre. The choreography and the inclusion of a blackface number were similar to previous productions. Nevertheless, Gene managed to impart a faster and more energetic tempo. He developed an amusing number involving two Southern gentlemen who wanted to dance in a slow, dignified manner but the two girls with them preferred a wild dance. The routine started with the slow dance, but progressively the wild dance took over as the two gentlemen caved in. Gene was a success in his first effort as dance director in a Cap and Gown show. After the premiere, the "girls" in the show lifted him onto their shoulders, took him through the stage door into the street, and carried him around the block in celebration. As part of the program, Fred Kelly, now a student at Pitt, danced in a tuxedo—with great enthusiasm but not much body control. He did his trademark roller-skate dance dressed as a bellhop. At one point, he spun rapidly around with outstretched arms.[15] The move, which we call the Airplane Propeller, became one of Gene's trademarks in his film dancing to come. The same move was performed by Nick Long Jr. in "I've Got a Feelin' You're Foolin'" a few months later in *Broadway Melody of 1936*, released on September 20, 1935. The Airplane Propeller obviously was used by a number of popular dancers of the era.

For the 1936 production of *Out for the Count*, Kelly was promoted to associate director. Reis took some backstage home movies showing Gene dressed in a suit and sporting a huge smile for the camera. Sadly, the show once again had a blackface number. Although it was traditional for Cap and Gown to get a director from New York, the 1937 production of *Trailer Ho!* appointed Gene as the director of the entire show. Reis once again shot backstage footage showing Gene completely at ease as director. The film of the production shows that the dance tempo was fast and energetic, although the steps were quite simple. Unfortunately, even this production had a blackface number. And Fred once more danced in his tuxedo and on roller skates as in his previous outings with the club. But there were new elements as well. Several dancers did the Airplane Propeller this time. Gene even had a number involving a row of performers dressed as cowboys doing another step that would become a trademark in his dance films. They balanced themselves with one hand on the floor behind them and kicked their legs out toward the audience.[16] We call this Gene's Prone Kick.

Gene was once again the director for the entire show of *Pickets, Please!* in 1938, his last Cap and Gown production. He was also the choreographer, while two senior students wrote the play. It premiered at the Nixon Theatre on April 4 and ran for one week.[17] *Pickets, Please!* ended a long association with college theatrics for Gene. He literally worked his way up from specialty dancer to director and choreographer of the most prestigious amateur show in town, participating annually from 1931 to 1938. In the process, he deepened his experience at managing and staging large productions and imparted something of his own style of dancing to them. The Kelly approach to mass entertainment is evident in his work for Cap and Gown.

PREPARING FOR NEW YORK

Gene also branched out as a show doctor in Pittsburgh. He lent his energy and talent to any production that needed advice, including shows on the vaudeville circuit, in nightclubs, and visiting productions that came through town. This gave him greater exposure in Pittsburgh and, more importantly, outside town as well. Late one year, Broadway choreographer Robert Alton came to Pittsburgh to stage a Christmas show for the Stanley Warner Theatres circuit. The show took place at the Stanley Theatre on Seventh Street in downtown. Gene took half of his students to participate in the show and Alton was impressed by their skill. He urged Gene to come to New York "to be his assistant or perform in a show," according to Kelly. But Alton was thinking only of dancing. Gene very much wanted to be a choreographer, so he did not go to New York just then.[18]

Hollywood beckoned in a small way. During the summer of 1935, after Gene finished his master classes in Chicago for that year, the family visited relatives in California. It was a good chance to take up RKO Studios on an offer made by one of its representatives, a Mr. Willey, who had visited

Pittsburgh earlier that year and told Gene to drop by for a screen test if he ever was in town. The make-up artists spared no paint. "I remember thinking that I looked like a raving fag by the time they put the cameras on me," Gene recalled years later. "I'm sure they just took one look at it and laughed." But he met Fredric March while in California, "which was quite a thrill for me."[19] He would act with March twenty-five years later in *Inherit the Wind*.

Robert Alton provided the spark to get Gene interested in Broadway. Not long after the choreographer's visit to Pittsburgh, Kelly became serious about going to New York. "For a while I thought that all I wanted to do was teach dancing," he later recalled. But a Broadway career as a choreographer now became more attractive. In the summer of 1937 he received an offer to choreograph a number in a Broadway show and accepted it. But upon reporting for his new job Gene was sorely disappointed to find out that the offer had been changed from choreographing the number to simply being one of the dancers in it. This was far from what he wanted or expected, so Gene refused the offer. He spent a couple of days trying to sell himself around town as a choreographer but without luck. Gene thought his years of doctoring shows in Pittsburgh would qualify him at least for consideration, "but nobody in New York seemed to know that fact or care either."[20]

After returning to Pittsburgh, Gene decided he needed more experience in choreography, and he got it in a production at the Pittsburgh Playhouse in April 1938. *Hold Your Hats* was a musical revue by Charles Gaynor who hired Gene as dance director. The revue ran for a month at the Pittsburgh Playhouse and received notices in national entertainment publications. Gene also appeared in six of the sketches and performed a solo called "La Cumparsita" in which he further developed his interest in Spanish dancing.[21] In fact, he was so fascinated with the Spanish style that he used parts of this dance later in *Pal Joey* and in *Anchors Aweigh*.

Gene now felt ready to give New York another shot. He had an added incentive to try the Big Apple once more. He had met his first serious girlfriend, Helene Marlowe, in 1937, but kept the relationship hidden from his family. Helene was a Jewish dancer from New York City and was in Pittsburgh working as a chorine in local shows. She later participated in Pittsburgh's summer stock. Born Helene Staniloff in New York City on September 11, 1916, she was four years younger than Gene. The family lived in a fashionable residential area in the Bronx and Helene's father worked in the garment industry. She was a "tall, dark-haired beauty with an engaging personality" who studied dance and took her brother's first name, Marlowe, as her stage name, recalled

Figure 3.1 The ballet lessons were the basis for this graceful ballet jump in Gene's fantasy Spanish dance. (Still from *Anchors Aweigh*, 1945)

a cousin who grew up with Helene. As mentioned earlier, in 1937 Kelly was appointed the director of the Cap and Gown show, which was to premiere on May 3. He took Ben Baskin and other chorus boys, who were to play the "girls" in the show, to the backstage of the Stanley Theatre on March 15. Here, Helene and another chorine, Ethel Ebert, showed the boys how to dance as girls. A photo of the four was published in the *Pittsburgh Post-Gazette* the next day.[22] Unfortunately, the photo is too dark to be reproduced, but one can see that Helene was indeed tall, dark-haired, attractive, and had a huge smile.

Some previous biographers of Kelly have stated erroneously that Helene and her family were from Pittsburgh and that she went to New York to try her luck. They also wrongly claim that when Kelly went to New York in 1937, he returned without meeting Helene and she was hurt by this. Helene was actually in Pittsburgh in the summer of 1937, giving Gene an incentive to rush back after his disappointment in the big city. This also explains why he did not try to see Alton at the time. But Helene was back in New York in 1938, and there is no doubt that Kelly wanted to try his luck there one more time in part because she lived there.

The final and main consideration, however, was a realization on Gene's part that Pittsburgh had already offered him all it could in the way of a career in entertainment. "I . . . wouldn't make any more money at 50 than at 25," he admitted later, "it was a dead end." Five years later, while developing his film career in Hollywood, Gene told a reporter that he considered himself to have been an adolescent until he reached the age of twenty-four in 1936. "By his gauge," wrote the reporter, "you reach maturity when you start directing your own life instead of letting outside forces direct it for you. Then he struck out the way he wanted to go." Gene made arrangements for Fred and Louise to do all the teaching at the Pittsburgh and Johnstown studios. Then, with $200 in his pocket and a one-way ticket to New York, he left Pittsburgh for good on August 5, 1938.[23] But the town that had shaped his youth would have a lasting effect on his life.

CHAPTER 4

Starting on Broadway, 1938–1940

Gene Kelly was twenty-six when he committed himself to making a career on Broadway. "I knew I could work," he told high school arts students at Sacramento in 1982, "because I could dance well enough—in fact, I was a little cocky about it." He also knew that "the basic training in Pittsburgh" had prepared him to be competitive in New York.[1] And Kelly was determined to do well. The one-way ticket he bought himself was symbolic—he had to succeed this time or else.

Gene arrived in New York on Friday, August 5, 1938, and checked into the 44th Street Hotel. The next day, he received his first job offer but turned it down. It was for a featured solo dance in *Sing Out the News*, but the producers offered him $35 a week, the same pay as members of the chorus. Gene refused to be exploited this way; he insisted on starting his Broadway career on his terms (if he could get them) and walked out of the theater.[2] *Sing Out the News*, a musical revue, opened at the Music Box Theatre on September 24, 1938, and ran for 105 performances—but without Gene Kelly.

LEAVE IT TO ME (1938)

On Monday, August 8, Gene met Robert Alton, and his prospects brightened considerably. Alton called his agent and manager and introduced him to Gene. "This is Johnny Darrow. He's going to look after you. Do as he tells you. He's a good guy." Thus Kelly had his first agent. But Darrow's first suggestion was that Gene change his name to Frank Black. Not surprisingly, Kelly refused. Darrow also messed up Gene's second job offer, this one from the famed Shubert brothers. They offered him $150 a week, which was a good rate for an unknown performer. But Darrow insisted on $300 in a misguided effort to help Gene. The Shuberts refused. Kelly took the disappointment well and never blamed Darrow for the mistake. Once again Alton came to the rescue. He gave Gene a part in *Leave It to Me*, the show Alton was choreographing, at $75 a week.[3]

This was not Gene's real ambition. He had always wanted to choreograph or direct on Broadway but did not have the reputation or experience to do that yet.[4] He now became a dancer and actor to break in and gain an income.

Leave It to Me was a Cole Porter show that tried out in New Haven and Boston beginning October 13, 1938, and opened in New York on November 9. Gene was cast as the secretary to Alonzo P. Goodhue, the "woefully confused" US ambassador to the Soviet Union, played by Victor Moore. Gene was happy to be in a Cole Porter show but recognized that his part was minor. He delivered a telegram to Goodhue at one point without a word spoken. He played a second role where he participated in a show-stopping number by Mary Martin, who also made her Broadway debut in *Leave It to Me*. Martin sang and danced to "My Heart Belongs to Daddy." She played a young woman on the loose, stranded at a railroad station in Russia. Gene was one of five young men who constituted the chorus for her number, "bundled up" as Russians (*not* Eskimos) in freezing Siberia. "The boys would pick me up, sling me around, pass me from hand to hand," Martin recalled. She hit the right note of seductiveness and innocence in her performance. The number became the hit of the show and started her long career on Broadway. "I liked him from the first day," Martin wrote about Kelly. "He was so talented, had so much drive. I've never known anybody who worked so hard perfecting his art. . . . From the beginning I knew he was going to be somebody great." Years later, whenever Martin and Kelly met, they had fun talking about their first Broadway show together.[5]

Now that he had a job, Gene moved out of the 44th Street Hotel and into a small apartment on 55th Street, between 5th and 6th Avenues, sharing it with a dancer from the show. He also reconnected with Helene Marlowe, spending time with her between rehearsals and performances.[6]

A Russian singer who was working with the production noticed the potential in Gene's singing voice. He offered to give him vocal lessons for "practically nothing." It meant taking the subway to Astoria twice a week. The singer gave Gene scales to sing and, more importantly, breathing lessons. Almost immediately his voice sounded better because he was singing from his diaphragm instead of his throat. But Gene's new residence was not a fit place for a performer to rehearse. The apartments were small and the walls were paper-thin. He tried to practice at the theater but was embarrassed when the cleaning ladies stared at him. So he rented a shabby rehearsal hall for fifty

Figure 4.1 Kelly with Mary Martin and four other chorus boys, dressed as Russians in freezing Siberia, in *Leave It to Me* (1938). (Still from *Anatomy of a Dancer*, 2002)

cents per hour, paid a pianist another fifty cents per hour, and continued to practice his singing after the show opened.[7]

Alton gave Gene the opportunity to create a dance routine in *Leave It to Me*. It was not a featured solo but a background divertissement during a period of lengthy dialogue necessary for story development that tended to slow the pace. Gene did not know how to choreograph the number because it was unrelated to the plot. So Alton made up a motive for the dance. He told Gene to think of a girl on a date with a man she does not love, sitting in a crowded room, and watching a man dancing his own loneliness. The two are attracted to each other in a wordless way. Now Gene had a motive and in less than an hour had worked up a wonderful little number.[8] It was Kelly's first choreography for Broadway.

Cole Porter frequently visited the theater during rehearsals for *Leave It to Me*. He was still in a wheelchair because of a riding accident the year before in Central Park. The horse he had been riding fell on his leg and Porter faced years of agony as he tried to recover. One day Porter saw Gene reading a book off to the side rather than interacting with the other performers. He became curious and asked Alton who that young man was. Alton introduced him to Kelly, and Porter asked Gene about the book he was reading. The two then got into a conversation about Aldous Huxley's novel *Point Counter Point*, published ten years before. Porter realized that Gene was college-educated, asked him about his future plans, and promised to help him if he could. Gene and Porter often continued their conversations during the run of the show. "He was very charming and very polite," Gene recalled.[9]

Porter also invited Gene to parties at his apartment. The young man was impressed by the high life in New York but felt uncomfortable with it as well. He especially disliked the way Broadway backers treated the young men in their shows as "second-class citizens." They treated the girls in the chorus much better than the boys.[10] It brought up the resentment that Gene had always felt toward those who failed to treat everyone equally well.

Leave It to Me played at the Imperial Theatre and ran for 291 performances. It received generally favorable reviews, but naturally no one mentioned Gene's limited role in the show. He stayed with the production only three months.

ONE FOR THE MONEY

Kelly's contract did not specify a commitment to the run of the show and Darrow found a better role for him in another production, *One for the Money*, at a substantial raise to $115 a week. It opened at the Booth Theatre on February 4, 1939, with Alton as the choreographer once again. It was a revue aimed at a wealthy audience and had no stars. The cast consisted of six costars who rotated in and out of several roles, supported by the chorus. Gene was often costumed in a tuxedo and white gloves as he handled seven different roles. William Archibald, who became his friend, also had seven roles, while Keenan Wynn performed nine roles. Gene moved once again, leaving his 55th Street address and sharing an apartment with Archibald in Greenwich Village, a haven for artists. *One for the Money* offered Gene a wider range than he had in *Leave It to Me*.[11] He sang and danced, gaining much-needed experience as a Broadway hoofer in 132 performances.

For Gene, *One for the Money* was an important experience because of its director, John Murray Anderson. "I learned more about staging a show from Murray than anyone else in the business," he said. "His timing was superb. . . . He'd watch a song, then make one simple suggestion that would turn a good number into a hit." Anderson had a habit of creating nicknames for everyone. Alton became "Fleming" to him, but he could not find an appropriate nickname for Gene so he just called him Kelly. Gene was delighted when

Anderson complimented him for his work in *One for the Money*. It was the biggest boost to his self-esteem yet in his life. Gene later talked of graduating from the school of John Murray Anderson and identified him as his primary mentor on Broadway. He forever remembered Anderson's brilliant use of colored lights on stage to create moods and tried to duplicate that technique in his later movie career.[12]

One for the Money was fun to be in and it had some unexpected moments. One day Keenan Wynn caught the flu and Hugh Martin replaced him. A young writer from Alabama just beginning his career, Martin was an understudy for Wynn and did well during the first act. But the teeter-totter number that started Act 2 was a different story. Seven couples on teeter-totters started with the guys in the air. After eight bars they went down and the girls were up for the next eight bars. But Martin, who was short and skinny, was forty pounds lighter than his partner Maxine Barrat, who was slim but tall. Without wanting to, he arose immediately after going down, well before the second eight bars had been played. He could not go back down, even with huffing and puffing, and hung in the air by himself, completely out of sync with his colleagues. Everyone in the audience laughed uncontrollably, and even the musicians in the pit had to stop playing because they were overcome with laughter. The stage manager finally brought down the curtain and the show was stopped for five minutes to allow everyone to compose themselves. Gene loved it. During the five-minute break he "tried to keep me from going to pieces," Martin recalled. "'Hugh!' he cried, giving me that famous Kelly grin and a bear hug to go with it, 'Hugh, you were a smash! They ought to keep it in the show!'"[13]

Kelly and Martin became good friends. Hugh thought Gene's singing voice was small but pleasant. He wanted to coach him but knew that Gene could not afford to pay him, so the two worked out an exchange. Martin would coach Kelly on his singing and Kelly would coach Martin on his dancing, even though Martin admitted he was a klutz. Despite Gene's firm belief that *anyone* can dance if they just try (which he put to good practice at his dance studios), they got to the point where he gave up, saying, "Hugh, you don't look good even when you get it right." Hugh appreciated Gene's honesty and never took another dancing lesson.[14]

The producers took *One for the Money* from New York for a six-week run at the Selwyn Theatre in Chicago during the early summer of 1939. Gene, Archibald, and another performer named Robert Smith rented a suite at the Ambassador East Hotel. They met John Barrymore, who was in a play at the Harris Theatre next door to the Selwyn, but found him so drunk most of the time that they did not interact with him. Chicago offered Gene an opportunity to expand. Many performers had replaced the original cast, and Alton had gone on to another show. As a result, Anderson relied on Kelly to coach the newcomers. Gene's long experience in Pittsburgh came into play; he did not alter Alton's choreography but adapted it to the abilities of the replacements, many of whom had little dancing experience. Anderson was very pleased with the results.[15]

SUMMER OF 1939

One for the Money's six-week Chicago run ended in June 1939. Gene and Bill Archibald decided to take a summer vacation. They drove to Orr's Island, located off the coast of Maine ten miles south of Brunswick. They rented a rundown cottage and for six weeks did little more than relax, eat inexpensive, fresh seafood, and try to write. Bill's ambition was to be a writer, which served as inspiration to Gene. But the experience of writing on Orr's Island proved to be a disappointment. Kelly managed to rough out half a three-act play about a man who went to New York City and got into trouble, "and then I got stuck. It was a pretty frustrating business." He abandoned that project and started a stage comedy, mimicking the style of Samuel N. Behrman. Gene managed to get two acts on paper and again gave up. "It just wouldn't come to me," he said years later. "And I realized, that summer, that writing was definitely out. I had to move about, run into the wind, swim—anything, in fact, that kept me active and burned up my energy. Writing was too sedentary for me. And far too lonely an existence." The six weeks at Orr's Island ended not only Kelly's hope of being a writer but also his six-month friendship with Bill Archibald. They argued about many things in Maine and went their separate ways upon returning to New York. Gene visited the Kelly home in Pittsburgh in early August when the dance schools were in session. Although it was a short visit, he was happy to see that both studios were doing well with a total enrollment of 500 students. All the family was well, too.[16]

Soon after returning to Greenwich Village, Kelly met Betty Comden and Adolph Green, who would play a major role in his film career. The two writers had their hearts set on performing and had created a group called The Revuers with Judy Holliday and others in 1938. Their first performance, a series of skits on current events, took place at the Village Vanguard in 1939. When

Gene heard they were planning to perform at the famous Westport Country Playhouse in Connecticut in a couple of weeks, he offered to emcee their show and perform at the end.[17] At this point, Comden and Green had no real idea of Kelly's talents, but they knew of his dance experience and found him likeable. So they agreed to let him join their group for the show.

The Westport Country Playhouse was founded by Lawrence Langner in 1931. After a long association with the Theatre Guild, Langner became frustrated with their decisions "by committee" and wanted to create a summer theater where he and his wife Armina could make all the decisions. The Playhouse became a "tryout house" for "plays that might later go to Broadway as Theatre Guild productions." It became the setting for "premieres of plays by Bernard Shaw, Noël Coward, and William Inge," as well as a "magnet for actors" including Ethel Barrymore, Helen Hayes, and Tyrone Power.[18]

There were occasional guest productions at the Playhouse and this is how The Revuers became part of the Westport program in August 1939 with a show called *Magazine Page*. Gene emceed with sophistication and humor, and in his performance at the end, he demonstrated in an amusing way how different kinds of dancers might deal with tap dancing. To close his performance he employed a routine that became one of his trademarks for years to come. He sprang sideways across the stage, bouncing on his hands, with his legs stretched out behind him.[19] We call it Kelly's Crab Bounce.

Magazine Page was very well received, and Gene quickly made many friends at Westport, even celebrating his twenty-seventh birthday there on August 23. This kind of revue had been an important part of his experience as an entertainer in Pittsburgh, and he was superb in it. Richard Somerset-Ward, who wrote a history of the Westport Country Playhouse, commented on *Magazine Page*: "There was a lot of talent on stage. . . . But Gene Kelly stole the show." Kelly also got rave reviews in the local press, and Comden and Green were immensely impressed by him. Comden found him "attractive, . . . adorable, . . . and very funny." Green saw him as a handsome, charming young man who did not even seem to be a dancer until he got on the stage, and then "it was a different story. He was full of grace and vitality, and what I remember most of all, was the effect he had on an audience. They just loved him. . . . There was this magic—this 'star quality' he exuded. His dancing was very athletic and he had the wonderful ability to make the most complicated things look ridiculously simple." Green recalled a "street-boy earthiness" that combined with a "terrific outgoing quality." His future was not in question as far as Green was concerned: "You just knew he was going places."[20]

Kelly, Comden, and Green had connected in an enduring way, but the time for their true collaboration was still in the future. Comden and Green had to get the acting bug out of their system and find their niche with writing *On the Town,* a pathbreaking stage musical in 1944. Kelly still had much work to do before he was ready for a starring role either on Broadway or in the movies. But all three were well on their way.

FALL OF 1939

After this invigorating experience, Gene and his father took a month-long road trip to Mexico in September 1939. They drove south from Pittsburgh by way of the Great Smoky Mountains of Tennessee, and then through New Orleans and Laredo, Texas. In Mexico, they stopped at many towns and had a good trip overall. The only downside for Gene was being appalled at all the gold ornaments and opulence in Catholic churches, which contrasted with the grinding poverty of most villages.[21]

As a result Kelly continued to be ambivalent about his religion. Still, he admitted in an interview in 1980 that he would spend much time drinking with friends in New York only to break away from the party at 4:30 A.M. to attend early morning mass at St. Malachy's "with all the other drunken Irishmen. I was that dyed-in-the-wool Catholic."[22]

On returning to New York after the Mexico trip, Gene moved out of Greenwich Village because he had no immediate job prospects. He rented a tiny, one-bedroom apartment with a bath and kitchenette at the Woodward Hotel, at 55th and Broadway. He had to live on Social Security at $15 a week while looking for his next job. Kelly frequented a diner called Beck's and ate breakfast at Chock full o'Nuts, where he could buy a doughnut, grapefruit juice, and a cup of coffee for only 15 cents. "It was a good breakfast," he insisted.[23]

While he waited for his next work opportunity, Gene wanted to keep up with his dancing. There was an old rehearsal hall close by that he could rent cheaply. It had a piano, but he needed someone to play for him. Kelly met an unemployed pianist named Richard Dwenger and invited him to move in with him. But instead of sharing the rent, he would play the piano for Gene. Dwenger, an aspiring playwright from Ridgewood, New Jersey, agreed, and they put up two army cots in the bedroom. The arrangement worked out well and the two soon became close friends.[24]

Kelly also acted on the advice of Katherine Cornell, who he had met during the Chicago run of *One for the Money*. She had suggested he visit a diction coach she knew on 57th Street in New York. "I've never had a good speaking voice, but . . . my flat Pittsburgh accent must have sounded really terrible." The diction coach taught him to deal with words such as "water" (which he pronounced as "wadder") and "orange" (which he pronounced as "ooringe"). She eliminated some of that Pittsburgh accent. In addition to keeping up with his dancing and polishing his diction, Gene often visited the Museum of Modern Art to browse its collection of books and films about dancing, continually expanding his knowledge of dance.[25]

THE TIME OF YOUR LIFE (1939)

Gene's persistence at improving himself in all these ways was soon rewarded. An opportunity developed for a role in William Saroyan's *The Time of Your Life*. It was the second Broadway play by this Californian and would be one of the best known of his productions. Saroyan was having the time of his own life, enjoying an explosively popular ride. In fact, his biographer calls 1939 his "miracle year." Saroyan wrote his second play quickly in May and it opened in New Haven, Connecticut, early in October 1939. It is set in a San Francisco bar and features a succession of "gutter" people—outcasts from society who develop their own twisted ideology. Joe the bartender, a kind of alter ego of Saroyan's, is the ringmaster for his circus of depraved humanity.[26]

One of these misfits is Harry the Hoofer. "He is a dumb fellow," Saroyan wrote of this character, "but he has ideas. A philosophy in fact. His philosophy is simple and beautiful. The world is sorrowful. The world needs laughter. Harry is funny. The world needs Harry." Saroyan conceived of him as a study in contrasts. While "dumb," his dance is actually supposed to be energetic and forceful. Yet no one in the bar is interested, and they continue doing their own thing as Harry tries hard to make his philosophy work.[27]

Harry was a difficult character to create and Martin Ritt, who opened the production of *The Time of Your Life* in that role, was having trouble making it work. It was not just Ritt; there were many problems with the New Haven tryout. Eight actors, including Ritt, were replaced. Saroyan decided to take over the direction of the play even though he had no experience to justify it. Charles Walters was a frontrunner as Ritt's replacement. Born in New York City a year before Gene, Walters was at this time far ahead of Kelly as a desirable dancer. But he turned the role down because it paid only $175 a week.

Darrow, who was also Walters's agent, told Gene of the opportunity. But Theatre Guild's Lawrence Langner, who had appreciated Gene's sophistication and humor at his Westport Playhouse, was reluctant to audition him because he seemed wrong for the role of a social misfit like Harry. Gene talked him into an audition, but Langner and Eddie Dowling found him too clean-cut for the role. Learning from that miscue, Gene went deliberately unshaven and sloppily dressed for a second audition, this time with Saroyan. Ray Middleton was being seriously considered for the role, but Saroyan thought he was not shouting loud enough. When Gene overheard this, he yelled from the back of the theater, "I can shout!" Saroyan liked his gumption and asked him to shout his monologue from the stage. It worked. Gene not only could yell but also looked the part, and his dancing was terrific.[28]

Kelly watched the play at New Haven the day after this audition to get an idea of how to approach the character of Harry. It was not an easy job. According to Kelly, Saroyan told him, "you've got to get up and dance and move the people. And I said, but you've written the part so the fellow can't dance. He doesn't know anything. He said, that's right. I said, how can I do both things? And he said, I don't know. Work it out." Even though that sounds like a hopeless scenario, Gene managed to get into the character and decided the dance had to appear spontaneous and natural. If he could hook the audience immediately with native charm, the character's inherent contradictions could be reconciled. Within a week he performed the role in Boston.[29] Kelly learned a good deal about fitting dance to a character that would benefit his later career.

Saroyan appreciated Gene's talent and his contributions to the production. "Gene Kelly helped me get the play in its true dimension of theatre," he commented. Audiences suddenly began to like the play. While the production was strengthened by the addition of William Bendix and Celeste Holm, Saroyan noted that Kelly "was a very significant part of that about face" in the fortunes of the play. He especially liked Kelly's ballet leaps in Act Two and his "tap-dancing, moving in and out of the action," which he saw as a "kind of new Greek chorus comment on what was going on." Saroyan recognized that Gene was "a great man of the theatre."[30]

Kelly's performance in Boston started October 14, 1939, and he opened the production at the Booth Theatre on Broadway on October 25. The bugs had been largely worked out by then and the opening was a success. "I knew if I didn't make it that night I might as well pack up and go home," Gene said. For the first time he received personal recognition for his stage work by the

Figure 4.2 Kelly with Julie Haydon and others in *The Time of Your Life* (1939). (Library of Congress)

public and in the New York press. An outlier, Richards Watts Jr., who totally misread the play as showing love for the human race, merely referred to the "dancing comic" without mentioning Gene's name. But First Lady Eleanor Roosevelt was so impressed by Kelly's performance that she gave him full credit in her syndicated newspaper column "My Day," writing, "Gene Kelly does some exceptionally good dancing." Kelly received wide coverage of his most important role on Broadway thus far in Pittsburgh as well.[31] The play ended its Broadway run on April 6, 1940, after 185 performances. Kelly and Saroyan became good friends through this collaboration.

The Time of Your Life opened when Richard Pleasant and Lucia Chase were in the process of forming Ballet Theatre to highlight artistic dancing. Pleasant was interested in getting Gene to choreograph for their new group. He had seen *The Time of Your Life* and was greatly impressed. Pleasant viewed Gene's contribution to that play's success as essential. But Kelly was much too involved in the Broadway production to take on anything else. Pleasant finally signed Anton Dolin as choreographer but still asked Kelly to keep in touch so he could work with their group in the future.[32]

Kelly never found time to contribute to Ballet Theatre's success. In 1957 its name was changed to American Ballet Theatre, and today it is the flagship ballet company in the United States. Gene had turned down an opportunity to perform for the Ballet Russe de Monte Carlo in 1933 and now turned down work as a choreographer for what would become an American ballet institution.

With his focus on the popular music world, Kelly was keenly aware of Harry the Hoofer's importance to his development as a stage performer. "I became a dancer who did his own choreography in a play that won the Pulitzer and the Drama Critics' Prize and created a lot of attention." He appreciated that he had been picked for what was essentially a dramatic role but still did not think of himself as a full-fledged actor.[33] But he was selling himself short.

HOLLYWOOD'S INTEREST

The Time of Your Life prompted the first serious interest by the movie industry in Gene Kelly. Actually, a talent scout for Metro-Goldwyn-Mayer (M-G-M) had known of him even before he came to New York. Fred Finklehoffe had sent a telegram to M-G-M announcing: "Have young genius in believe it of all places, Pittsburgh. Please come." But no one had paid attention to this signal, even after Finklehoffe urged the studio more than once. Only after the Broadway premiere of Saroyan's play did the film company become serious about considering Gene.[34]

Producer Arthur Freed came to New York specifically to see Kelly in *The Time of Your Life*. He was impressed and met Gene backstage to discuss a movie career with him. Born in Charleston, South Carolina, of Jewish parents, the forty-five-year-old Freed had a successful career as a song lyricist during the early days of talkies. He parlayed that beginning into a job as a rising producer at M-G-M, mostly through his work on *The Wizard of Oz*, released on August 25, 1939, and *Babes in Arms*, released only a few weeks before, on October 13, 1939.[35] It would be several years before anyone could talk about the "Freed Unit" within M-G-M and the successful film musicals it would create, but Freed was certainly an up-and-coming power within the studio.

Freed and Kelly had a good chat backstage, which Gene later called a "soft sell." Freed wanted him to come to Hollywood, but Kelly demurred, saying he had to learn how to act before he could risk a movie career. "And he said that was fine and that maybe we'd talk again."[36] Thus ended Gene's introduction to the man who would later play an important role in his career.

Kelly was right; he had never worked on his acting ability during the long years of tutelage in Pittsburgh, and his roles thus far offered him few opportunities to improve. In addition, Freed caught Gene when the young performer had little time or thought for film work. He was too busy building his résumé on Broadway. There was a bit of stage snobbery in his attitude as well. He had "no idea or even any dream of dancing for motion pictures. At that time, I foolishly didn't think it held enough challenge or enough promise."[37]

CHOREOGRAPHING A SHOW AND MEETING BETSY

Meanwhile, his prospects in New York continued to grow. An opportunity to choreograph came Gene's way in January 1940, while he was acting in *The Time of Your Life*. John Murray Anderson had directed *Billy Rose's Aquacade* at the 1939 World's Fair in New York and directed other productions at the Diamond Horseshoe, Rose's nightclub in the basement of the Paramount Hotel on Times Square. He was the director for the new show as well. Rose wanted Robert Alton to choreograph it, but Alton was unavailable. Anderson recommended Gene, who he said, "would be as good if not better than Alton." Rose talked with Kelly on the phone and asked how he would choreograph the show. Gene talked for an hour and Rose was pleased. But he offered only $100 a week. A verbal battle ensued, until Rose finally consented to raise the offer from $100 to $135 a week.[38]

The stint at the Diamond Horseshoe not only gave Gene an opportunity to choreograph popular entertainment at a club considerably above the "cloops" of Pittsburgh, but it also introduced him to his future wife. The International Casino Club closed down just before Rose began rehearsals for his new production. So, Rose invited all the dancing girls from the casino to audition for him. This brought sixteen-year-old Betsy Blair to the Diamond Horseshoe. Born Elizabeth Boger, she had grown up in Cliffside, New Jersey, just across the river from New York City, and had attended dancing school, performed in amateur shows, and graduated early from high school. Her father was an insurance broker who worked in New York and her mother was a public-school teacher.[39]

"I always dreamed of a dancing career," Blair recalled, but that would take some doing. Her father wanted her to be a secretary, but the precocious girl managed to win a scholarship at Sarah Lawrence College in Yonkers. During the interview, the college admissions staff found her immature and suggested she take a year of junior college first. But Betsy was set on dancing and happened to see an ad for dancers by the International Casino Club. Her mother understood her ambition, helped prepare her for the audition, and Betsy was hired. By now even her father was willing to support her decision to be an entertainer and drove her to work and back home every evening. Betsy danced in the chorus at the Casino for three months before the owners "disappeared with the money" and the place shut down.[40]

This closing and Rose's invitation to the Casino girls brought Betsy into Gene's life. She came the day before the audition and saw Kelly as he was moving chairs and tables around. She assumed he was a busboy, and Gene did not disabuse her of that notion. He told her to come back the next day and asked if she could dance well. Betsy boldly told him, with some disdain, that she was a terrific dancer. She was chagrined the next day to see that 600 girls had come to audition and that the "busboy" was the choreographer. Gene saw something in her spirit that he liked and fought for her in the crowded field. Rose needed only a dozen dancers and one understudy. If not for Gene's persuasion, she would not have been hired. Betsy later admitted that she was "besotted" with him from that moment on.[41]

As unlikely as it seems, there actually was a future for this immature sixteen-year-old upstart and the twenty-seven-year-old mature man of many talents, although Gene's interest in Betsy blossomed more slowly than her infatuation for him. By early 1940, Kelly had developed a deep friendship with Dick Dwenger and had persuaded Rose to hire him as rehearsal pianist. Dick initiated contact with Betsy, chatting with her during the lunch break and inviting her to eat with himself and Gene. He was a year older than Kelly and the two treated Betsy like a kid sister, but she was grateful to share their company. By the last week of rehearsals they took her to their favorite haunt, Louis Bergen's Theater Bar and Restaurant on 45th Street between Broadway and 8th Avenue. The three were forming a tight-knit trio, with the two men intent on exposing Betsy to the culture of New York. "Gene was extremely ambitious, artistic, learning everything like a demon," Betsy later said. "We went to museums, dance recitals, concerts, everything, all the time. Because I ended up not going to college, Gene is the one who gave me a sort of college education."[42]

It took Betsy a long time to make sense out of what she was feeling in those first months of her life with Gene. Even though she never figured out why he took such an interest in her, there can be no doubt that her intelligence, eagerness to learn, and enjoyment of life appealed to him. At eleven years his junior, she was something like the bright female students to whom he had taught dancing in Pittsburgh and Johnstown. As far as he was concerned, it would take a while for romance to enter into the relationship.

Meanwhile, Kelly continued to see Helene Marlowe. The *Miami News* ran a photo of the pair on March 29, 1940. "Helene Marlowe, the show girl, and Gene Kelly of *The Time of Your Life*, holding hands," read the caption.[43] We were unable to locate the photo, but the description shows that the two were still dating at that time.

From Betsy's perspective though, she was in love. No wonder that she broke down on the opening night of the new season at Diamond Horseshoe when she saw Gene with another woman. While dancing on stage, Blair saw him come in with Dick Dwenger and "a beautiful brunette" she had never seen before. They stood in the back watching the show, and it seemed obvious to her that Gene and the woman were close. Betsy was heartbroken and cried as she danced. Nevertheless, she had dinner at Louis Bergen's with Gene and Dick between shows and did the midnight show as well.[44] Betsy claims she never asked Gene about the woman, but it was obviously Helene Marlowe.

Little is known of the relationship between Kelly and Marlowe, how serious it became, or whether they ever planned to marry. Hirschhorn writes that Helene very much wanted to marry Gene but he hesitated, and her Jewish parents fiercely opposed the union, unable to accept an Irish Catholic in the family. The Bridesons claim that the two were engaged from 1937 to 1942.[45] The latter assertion is definitely incorrect. Gene and Betsy were married in 1941, and their daughter was born in 1942. And even as early as 1939, Gene took a six-week vacation with Bill Archibald and a month-long vacation with his father, which hardly suggests someone engaged to be married. In 1940, he saw less of Helene as he hung out with Dick Dwenger and their protégé Betsy Blair.

Much later, Betsy believed she had been in desperate need of being loved during those early days of her infatuation for Gene. For some time she had grown emotionally distant from her father because of his cheating on her mother. As Gene was older and more mature than her, he seemed an ideal object for her affection. "Our needs meshed perfectly," she wrote in her memoirs. "My need to be swept away by a man, to be held securely and adored by a man, and his need to find the girl who would be pliable and receptive to his idea of a couple, who wouldn't question his unspoken authority."[46]

Kelly was serious about schooling Betsy in a variety of topics, and that included introducing her to left-wing politics. He knew Lloyd Gough, an actor and member of the Communist Party. Born as Michael Gough in New York, he was five years older than Gene. Gough was one of several actors on the East Coast who mixed their careers with active political lives. This was a new departure for Kelly. In the diverse and exciting atmosphere of New York City, Gene's tendency to question his conservative father and his traditional Catholic religion flowered. He never became a Marxist, as Betsy soon learned, but he was conversant with its theories and could argue with Gough over a drink at Louis Bergen's about its validity. He was what Betsy called a "strong sympathizer" with some of the goals of the Marxist state but remained highly critical of its lack of democracy and individual freedom. Both Kelly and Dwenger read Arthur Koestler and George Orwell, who were severely critical of Soviet authoritarianism. Gene and Dick "were good left-wing people who believed in all the right things—trade unions, anti-racism."[47]

Gene and Dick wanted to expose Betsy to these ideas, and she was fascinated by the heated discussions at Louis Bergen's. Now and then Gene thought Gough pressed his case too hard on her. "Leave her alone. She's just a kid," he told Gough. Betsy insisted, "No, no! I want to learn." This was the beginning of Blair's own political life, which took her farther along the road toward left-wing politics than it did Kelly, who never went beyond spirited discussions with Marxists. Gough asked Betsy to attend a Marxist study group held at his apartment. He and a man named Paul cotaught the class, which met two days a week for two hours in the evening. Five other students besides Betsy were in attendance. She remembered they used a very boring textbook, but wrote: "The cultural side of the meetings was great." While Betsy "very diligently" attended every class, Gene never participated in the study group.[48]

Gene's commitment to labor unions and racial justice was real and enduring, but he never committed to socialism or Marxism. They were interesting and provocative concepts to him but, in his view, not workable or necessary for American society. How far Betsy developed a genuine commitment to socialism or Marxism is open to question, although she took both more seriously than did Gene.

SUMMER OF 1940

All through spring Kelly was playing Harry in *The Time of Your Life*, but as summer approached, he lined up his first summer stock production in 1940. This was a revue called *Two Weeks with Pay* at the Ridgeway Theatre in White

Plains, New York, in late June. The play was based on a 1921 silent comedy with the same title starring Bebe Daniels and was about a working girl's vacation. It was being tried out at Ridgeway with hopes of getting to Broadway. Gene was hired to develop the choreography. While he was working on this production, Westport Country Playhouse "put out an emergency call" for Kelly. Johnny Haggott, codirector of the Playhouse, was substituting for John Ford as director of Lynn Riggs's *Green Grow the Lilacs*, which the Theatre Guild had produced on Broadway in 1931. They were doing it as a musical now, and "choreography was needed in a hurry."[49] From his getting to know Gene in the summer of 1939 when he had appeared in *Magazine Page*, Haggott knew Kelly was perfect for the job.

Haggott located Kelly at Ridgeway and brought him over just in time to work on staging several square dances and folk dances because the music written by Bethell Long consisted of "lively old cowboy songs." Gene developed "some pretty good choreography" according to Somerset-Ward, historian of the Playhouse, and the show played July 15–20. Elaine Anderson Scott, the assistant stage manager, recalled fifty years later that the opening night "was a smashing evening." Terry Helburn of the Theatre Guild saw the potential in the show and contacted Richard Rodgers, who came from his nearby home in Fairfield, saw it, and agreed with Helburn. It was transformed into *Oklahoma!* with music by Rodgers, lyrics by Oscar Hammerstein II, and choreography by Agnes de Mille.[50] The show premiered on Broadway in 1943 and became an icon of stage musicals.

Haggott then asked Kelly to choreograph another summer production at Westport, *The Emperor Jones*, which was to play August 5–10. Gene had another summer commitment to appear in *The Royal Roost*, written by Dick Dwenger, at the Community Playhouse in Stamford, Connecticut, July 29 to August 3. But he agreed to choreograph the Westport show without compromising his commitment to his friend's play. The tryout for *The Royal Roost* was fine but it did not go further. "The play has a good idea," Kelly told a newspaper reporter, "but is better movie than play material."[51]

The Emperor Jones, written by Eugene O'Neill, starred Paul Robeson, who had played the role before in a 1923 version when it was still called *The Silver Bullet*. He had also acted in the 1933 movie and was very familiar with the role. It was a story about a brutal "Pullman porter who sets himself up as a Caribbean dictator."[52]

Gene was excited to choreograph for the all-male troupe from Harlem that appeared in *The Emperor Jones*. "I really was working with all men and I could give them the strongest movements, and they were all big, tough bruisers. They all had muscles. They all could jump and leap and kick. It was wild. It was jungle stuff." His choreography worked well for the subject and the actors. "I remember I felt that that was the first time professionally I had done a real, superior job" he recalled in 1975.[53]

There is no evidence that Robeson and Kelly met at Westport as some previous biographers claim. The Westport Country Playhouse is briefly mentioned in Robeson's biography, but Kelly is not referred to in that context. And Kelly never mentioned meeting Robeson at Westport in his many interviews over the years. Robeson had a singing engagement in Philadelphia in early August 1940.[54] Given his tight schedule as well as his familiarity with the role of Emperor Jones, Robeson arrived in Westport just for the performance, August 5–10. And given Kelly's commitment to *The Royal Roost*, playing July 29–August 3, he coached the Harlem troupe before the performance of *The Emperor Jones* and left for Stamford prior to Robeson's arrival.

Hugh Martin recalls that, "just before he took New York by storm in *Pal Joey*," Kelly had a meal with him at Childs Restaurant on Broadway and 46th Street. It was late summer 1940, and Gene told him, "I've made a decision about my career, Hugh. I've accepted the fact that I'm never gonna make it as a performer. I have hopes for myself as a choreographer or maybe, a director, but as for Gene Kelly, performer—never gonna happen."[55] It was an unusual moment in his life, which normally was filled with brash optimism. It also highlights Kelly's conception of himself as primarily a creator and manager of entertainment rather than a performer.

SIGNING ON FOR *PAL JOEY*

But his rise as a performer was just about to take off. Richard Rodgers and Lorenz Hart were planning a stage musical based on two stories written by John O'Hara in what came to be known as the Pal Joey series. The short stories were published in *The New Yorker* beginning in October 1938. O'Hara was born in Pottsville, Pennsylvania, in 1905. He had achieved early success with two novels but was now best known for his short stories published in *The New Yorker*. "Bow Wow" and "A Bit of a Shock" became the basis for Rodgers and Hart's plan for *Pal Joey*. They were nearing the end of their collaboration on twenty-six Broadway musicals in more than twenty years and were taken with O'Hara's portrayal of Joey Evans, a likeable cad and nightclub performer who takes advantage of the women in his life and has no sense of responsibility for his actions.[56]

Robert Alton was hired to do the choreography for *Pal Joey*, but O'Hara, Rodgers, and Hart had difficulty choosing the right leading man for this tricky role. Charles Walters was a leading contender to play Joey Evans, but O'Hara was uncertain that he could pull off the characterization of a likeable heel. Rodgers had seen Kelly in *The Time of Your Life* and thought he was a good prospect. He called Johnny Darrow, who arranged an audition.[57]

Gene arranged singing lessons because the audition was only for his singing; Rodgers had already seen him act. But Gene almost wrecked the audition. He naively decided to sing a ballad written by Rodgers, unaware that this would appear to be kowtowing to the composer. It was a difficult song as well, and Gene barely got through it. Although Hirschhorn identifies the song as "I Didn't Know What Time It Was," Gene indicated later that it was "Blue Moon." "I was *terrible!*," he admitted. Rodgers took the audition in stride; he did not protest or insult Kelly but calmly asked him to sing something else. Falling back on his Pittsburgh days, Gene dug a song out of his mental archives—"It's the Irish in Me," a snappy ditty that reflected pride in his Irish heritage. It "had a lot of pep and dash to it, and . . . I knew how to put [it] across," Gene said. The song worked. O'Hara, sitting in the back of the theater, jumped up and shouted, "That's it. Take him." But Rodgers and Hart still hesitated. They wanted to explore all possible talent. After several weeks, however, they decided on Gene at $350 a week, his highest salary yet on Broadway.[58]

About this time, the Theatre Guild planned a second, short Broadway run of *The Time of Your Life* in the fall, to be followed by a tour. Gene, of course, was now focused on *Pal Joey* and declined the job. When a suitable replacement could not be found to play Harry the Hoofer, Gene recommended his brother Fred. He argued that Fred looked like him, he was a good dancer, and Gene would coach him. The producers brought Fred to New York for an audition and hired him. Gene showed him the routine and recalled later with brotherly pride that Fred picked up the steps easily.[59] After this, Gene took some time off to see the tryouts for Saroyan's "Sweeney in the Trees" at Cape May, New Jersey. He predicted it would be better than *The Time of Your Life*. Saroyan asked Kelly to be in "one of the three new plays" he had written and "to stage the dances for a revue" that would have music by Kurt Weill.[60] But Gene did not commit to anything. His whole focus was now on *Pal Joey*.

From Cape May, Gene drove to visit his family in Pittsburgh over Labor

Day weekend in early September 1940. By now his success in *The Time of Your Life* had garnered increased attention in his hometown. Harold Cohen interviewed him for his column in the *Pittsburgh Post-Gazette*. Cohen was impressed when Kelly told him that M-G-M had been ready to offer him a long-term contract, but he had insisted on holding out for a deal involving just one film so he could have the freedom to return to Broadway. Gene thought this was a real possibility if *Pal Joey* was successful enough to give him the clout to negotiate a movie career on his terms.[61]

When he returned to New York, his brother Fred rode back with him, geared up for the second Broadway run of *The Time of Your Life*. Fred was well received when the show began on September 23, 1940. In particular, critic Richard Watts Jr. paid more attention to Fred than he had to Gene in that role. Watts thought the revival was at least as good as, and in some ways better, than the original. Fred was "splendid in the part," according to Watts. After the second Broadway run ended on October 19, 1940, the production hit the road.[62] Until then, Fred had been content with the dance studios at home and small performances here and there. Now, by getting a role on Broadway for his brother, Gene had given Fred a chance at a larger career outside Pittsburgh.

As for his own career, Gene now was fully absorbed in preparing for his toughest job to date. His success in *Pal Joey* would not only help him make it big on Broadway, but it would help him get the type of deal he wanted from Hollywood.

CHAPTER 5

Triumph on Broadway, 1940–1941

The role of Joey Evans held the potential to become Gene's breakthrough in New York, but only if he mastered the daunting task of creating a complex character—a man with no morals who is nevertheless appealing. Kelly's dancing, singing, and acting would be viewed more critically than at any previous stage of his life. If he could pull this off, it would open a hundred doors to the future. If he failed, it could shatter his apparently unbreakable self-confidence.

PAL JOEY (1940)

Returning to New York after the Labor Day weekend in Pittsburgh, Kelly immersed himself in preparations for *Pal Joey*. He worked closely with dance director Robert Alton, who once again came into focus as Gene's mentor. Born in Vermont forty-three years before, Alton had "revolutionized American show dance" in the words of film historian Larry Billman. Working on Broadway by 1919, Alton broke up the single line chorus that had been traditional on stage and organized it into small groups. Gene explained in 1958 that this innovation allowed greater flexibility in choreography.[1] Alton richly earned his reputation in New York as a choreographer who could quickly invent fresh steps, manage large groups of dancers, and bring a sense of excitement to the musical.

Gene understood how important Alton was to the success of *Pal Joey*. "Things happened dance-wise in that show that perhaps wouldn't have happened with another choreographer," he mused. Alton encouraged him to work out his own steps but always maintained the right to approve everything before it went into the show. "He would chuckle when I would try things that nobody else was doing," Kelly said. "He'd say 'My God! Where did you pick that up?' And I'd say, 'Oh, I just made it up.' And he'd say, 'Now isn't that silly.

That's great.' And he'd incorporate it in the dance."[2] Kelly always remained grateful to Alton for encouraging him to find his own style. He created a mélange of many dance styles including tap, Spanish, and ballet. But in terms of choreography, expressing the essence of the character in dance movement was the rule he meticulously followed.[3]

Creating Joey Evans was not easy. Gene had to work on the characterization for a long time. The basic problem was that Joey was not a traditional hero but he had to be liked by the audience or *Pal Joey* would bomb on opening night. Joey is a fourth-rate performer with big dreams but not enough brains or heart. Although he has a girlfriend (Linda), he starts courting a married socialite (Vera) to get money for his own nightclub on the South Side of Chicago. He also has affairs with other women he meets. And yet, he is gullible and soon blackmailed out of his club. The show ends with a lonely Joey realizing he has only himself to blame for his misfortunes.[4]

A good illustration of Kelly's inventiveness occurred when he developed a dance to accompany a song by Vera and Linda about Joey. Called "Take Him," it illustrates how fed up both women are with their problem lover. Gene was supposed to dance on the side of the stage and knew that a typical tap dance, knees bent, would not work for this lyrical song. He developed a dance that would be focused on the melody rather than the rhythm and the percussion. This turned tap on its head but it worked beautifully, creating "a strutty kind of dance . . . a tap done in tango rhythm," in Gene's words. He wanted to achieve "that Spanish arrogant look."[5]

Gene also consulted with director George Abbott. They agreed he had to dance well to impress the audience, and to connect positively with the audience as a character. Gene and Alton worked together, combining "unusual and energetic steps that might be done in a kind of a cheap act, but would be exciting at the same time." This would wow the audience but not be considered high art. Gene could use his ballet training for the dream ballet inserted into the show. Dream ballets were extended dance numbers that explored a character's emotions or fantasies. It was becoming very popular to do this on Broadway in the late 1930s. Joey would imagine he could dance well in this piece; it gave Gene the opportunity to do "a pas de deux with a nice little ballet dancer" hired to support him in this number. Kelly recognized that Joey Evans had a lot of similarities with Harry the Hoofer; both characters were limited in their intelligence and morals, yet both had to dance well, a paradox that Gene dealt with magnificently.[6]

Figure 5.1 Kelly as Joey Evans with Shirley Paige in the dream ballet of *Pal Joey* (1940), in an advertisement for the show. It is the only instance we have come across where Kelly signed his first name as “Eugene.” (New York Public Library)

Kelly and Abbott agreed that the key to making the character work was energy. “If a young man came into a nightclub and he was going to make passes at all the chorus girls and take them to bed one by one, . . . he would have to have a lot of energy and that would have to be conveyed to the audience.” So he worked in a lot of fast tap dancing, some leaps, and some “good old-fashioned acrobatic tricks.” In short, Kelly could draw on all the steps he had created or adapted for his many performances as a young man in Pittsburgh. And he had more than enough energy to pull it all off. As critic Jack Holland later noted, Gene played Joey “with a twinkle in his eyes—and with his irrepressible smile.” Kelly remarked that it worked well. “I never was hissed nor had rotten tomatoes thrown at me!” Much more than with Harry the Hoofer, Gene learned how to act in *Pal Joey*. “I became an actor, or an actor-dancer, if you will.”[7]

Pal Joey was previewed for a select audience in New York and was well received. Then it opened in Philadelphia for its three-week tryout and some problems surfaced, including a nervous Gene Kelly. A song had to be dropped, and some revising of the book was in order. Notices, however, were good. Robert Sensenderfer called Kelly “the most ingratiating young actor that has stepped into musical comedy in several years.” He noted that Gene “was running down a bit toward the close” of the Philadelphia premiere because his was a long, tough role. “But he had already made himself with his audience.” Sensenderfer correctly pinned Kelly’s vocal capability by writing that he did not have “a good singing voice but he knows how to make the most of what

Figure 5.2 Kelly as Joey Evans with a chorus girl in *Pal Joey* (1940) depicting Joey's energetic wooing of women. (New York Public Library)

he has." The key to his performance, however, was his energy, as Abbott and Gene had known. "His enthusiasm is contagious," wrote Sensenderfer.[8]

The short run in Philadelphia worked wonders. When the show premiered at the Ethel Barrymore Theatre on December 25, 1940, it was ready for New York audiences. Gene opened the show by singing about Chicago, solo and unaccompanied by the orchestra, for thirty seconds. Then the orchestra came in, the complex characterization and the dances with their fresh choreography started, and the New York audience was taken by storm. Mother Harriet and sister Louise were there to see him. Betsy Blair could not attend the show because she was in the chorus of *Panama Hattie*, but she joined Gene for the party at Lorenz Hart's apartment that night.[9]

Critics loved the show and they singled out Kelly as the chief reason for it. Richard Watts Jr. called it "a hard-boiled delight. It is a bitter, satirical and yet strangely realistic account of the flora and fauna of the night clubs, done with such real and scornful relish that it achieves genuine power." Watts thought Gene had "guilefully played" Joey, combining "a certain amount of straightforward personal charm with the realism of his portrait." As a result, Joey became "at once heel and hero." Without Kelly's success at creating this role, in Watts's view, the show would not have worked.[10]

Burns Mantle also liked Kelly's performance, and was grateful that his dance style ranged widely across the spectrum. Walter Terry agreed: "His performing is directed right at the audience with the hail-pals spirit of the old vaudeville days, but his tapping is nicely mated with the ballet touch of the contemporary style. There are leaps and spins and intricate rhythms which Mr. Kelly puts across in engaging fashion."[11]

Three reviewers thought the show was uneven, although their opinions about pacing were contradictory. One reviewer thought it started slowly but then picked up steam in Act Two. The other two thought the opposite—that the high energy and inventiveness slacked off in the latter scenes, and one of the reviewers blamed Abbott for this.[12]

Brooks Atkinson admired much about the production, including the dream ballet and Kelly's dancing. But he could not accept the character of Joey Evans. "Can you draw sweet water from a foul well?" he asked his readers. Atkinson admitted that Gene portrayed Joey with success and was "a brilliant tap dancer." He offered Gene a left-handed compliment by writing, "If Joey must be acted, Mr. Kelly can do it."[13] There is no doubt that without Gene the show would not have succeeded. As Sidney Whipple put it, Kelly "is made for the part of Pal Joey. He brings out the amusing worthlessness of the young man, his cocky self-confidence, his magnificent pretentions. . . . and he is extremely attractive. Mr. Kelly dances amazingly."[14]

Indeed, *Pal Joey* was more than a personal triumph for Gene. It represented something of a watershed in the musical theater, "a complete departure from the goody-goody, make-believe world of most musical comedies," according to historian Roy Hemming. "There had never been a musical like *Pal Joey*," Gerald Mast concurred, "bitter, cynical, seamy, sordid, with no romantic resolution, no change of heart, no happy ending."[15] Such attributes made it a sensation for the avant-garde New York audience and for most critics, but it understandably restricted its popularity.

Writing for *Theatre Arts* in 1946, Hermine Rich Isaacs summed up Gene's triumph in *Pal Joey* by discussing his limitations as well as his strengths. "Although his acting had not been schooled, he already had the tools well in hand: a dancer's body, a good enough voice to do what he needed, and a combination of economy and sincerity in his playing that reached straight across the footlights. As for his dancing, its inventive patterns [and] its lusty vitality schooled with precision were like an electric charge through the fabric of the show."[16]

Gene naturally became a bit proprietary in the stage characterization of

Joey Evans. Atkinson's comment that one cannot "draw sweet water from a foul well" bothered him for months afterward. According to Helen Dzhermolinska, who interviewed him in April 1941, Kelly objected to Atkinson's take on Joey. If such a character had been included in a drama instead of a musical comedy, he could be taken as serious social commentary, but the expectations for stage musicals were different. "In defense of Joey and his story," Gene told Dzhermolinska, "I will say that as long as there are sewers, you can't help breeding rats."[17] Gene went on to explain how he viewed the character. "Joey isn't a bad guy. He's not immoral. He's just amoral. He's only trying to get along the best way he knows how. Anybody that's ever worked in the racket understands what makes Joey tick." Kelly knew that someone living a comfortable middle-class life in a suburb would be shocked by Joey. "He belongs to another world, another race of people."[18]

During the run of this exciting show Kelly developed a routine as he prepared for each performance. In fact, he changed his habits to be better prepared for its demands. He had worked so hard in rehearsals that his weight dropped from 163 to 147 pounds. Alarmed, Kelly consulted a doctor, who gave him vitamin B-1 supplements, and his weight increased a bit. The other reason for his exhaustion was that he accompanied O'Hara and Hart when they hopped from one club to another until 4 A.M. But when the show opened, Gene became more disciplined. For dinner he ate "plain spinach with a little piece of lamb." For thirty minutes before the curtain rose, he vigorously warmed up. After each night's performance he ate a steak, drank one beer (all the liquor he consumed that day), and was normally asleep by 1:30 A.M.[19]

A member of the audience sneaked a camera into one of the performances of *Pal Joey* and exposed a few feet of film depicting Gene dancing in the major numbers.[20] It was only the second time Kelly's dancing was filmed, and a huge difference can be seen compared to the Cap and Gown productions. After five summers of ballet training and his experience in *The Time of Your Life*, it is obvious Gene had learned a great deal about body control and dance technique. He had also developed a wider conception of dance styles—everything that worked to make him a top-notch performer. His choreography, in consultation with Alton, is spirited and exciting, his energy level is high. Whereas his electric smile was the only real attraction in Cap and Gown, there is genuine brilliance in all aspects of his dancing as Joey Evans. Kelly had finally come into his own, and at age twenty-eight, he was just beginning the major part of his career.

There were a few mishaps. Gene fell down during a solo number one night

Figure 5.3 Vivienne Segal (as Vera Simpson) and Kelly (as Joey Evans) had a wonderful time performing together in *Pal Joey* (1940). (New York Public Library)

and "the audience laughed." Recalling this to a group of high school arts students in 1982, Kelly mused that "it's OK for singers to forget lyrics—but if a dancer falls down, he's a bum." On the night of January 16 he was not well enough to perform and his understudy, Davy Jones, took over. A bug must have been circulating among the cast because Leila Ernst, who played Joey's girlfriend Linda, also was too ill to go on. Two days later, Vivienne Segal, who played Vera, was coming down with something. Mostly though, all went smoothly. Gene thoroughly enjoyed working with his costar Segal and all the other members of the cast. "Vivienne sang—& I danced, & we had fun every night—She was great," Gene wrote on the cover of the song sheet for "Bewitched (Bothered and Bewildered)" in his personal collection.[21]

Two members of the cast who filled minor roles in *Pal Joey* went on to much more visible careers in show business. Stanley Donen, a teenager from South Carolina, played the part of Albert Doane, a waiter. He did not get to know Gene during the run of the show but later recalled how impressed he was by Kelly's ability, focus, and drive. Not long after, Kelly noticed Donen and became an important sponsor, mentor, and friend, providing the ambitious young Southerner with many opportunities to craft a career for himself.[22]

Van Johnson had a bigger head start on Donen, having performed obscurely in many shows by the time of *Pal Joey* where he filled the role of

Victor, another waiter. He also did not get to know Gene personally during the run of the show but always remembered him. One night during the rehearsal period, after working hard from nine in the morning until midnight, he was on his way out of the theater when he heard someone tap dancing on the back part of the stage. Johnson went back and saw Kelly "stripped to his shorts and under a single light bulb," intensely focused on getting the steps right. He watched for ten minutes as Kelly worked, and years later he recalled, "It was a tricky number. Time and again he leaped in the air and, it appeared, almost floated through space."[23]

The success of *Pal Joey* gave Johnny Darrow the idea to introduce Kelly to wealthy nightclub audiences in New York. He arranged for Gene to do a cameo performance at the Rainbow Room, located on the sixty-fifth floor of 30 Rockefeller Plaza and geared for the richest New York clientele. It was a long way from the "cloops" in Pittsburgh, and Gene did not do well in that venue. Jack Cole, born in New Jersey and a year older than Gene, was the regular star of the Rainbow Room. Darrow was also his agent, and Cole agreed to bring Kelly in for a tryout. Cole had performed thus far in four Broadway productions. He thought Gene simply did not have what it took to succeed in a nightclub for the rich. "He was a nice-looking man," Cole recalled years later, "but not a beauty—and he didn't have the kind of false, idiot social bit that people like Charles Walters had—which was essential to Rainbow Room audiences." Making it worse, the orchestra leader introduced Kelly as "George Murphy" and then played the accompanying music incorrectly, making it difficult for Gene to dance to it.[24] The experience was a disaster and Kelly never tried to do something like this again.

The Rainbow Room fiasco was a minor slip in a season of success. *Pal Joey* garnered Gene far more publicity than he had ever enjoyed. In addition to several major newspaper interviews, dance critics continued to write about the show for months after its opening. Robert Van Gelder did an extensive interview for the *New York Times* in which Kelly expressed the concern of his friends that he might be typecast as a heel. "Well, if that is to be, let it," he told Van Gelder. He loved the fact that not only was his role good, but "the whole show is gutsy." The songs had a bite to them. Gene admitted that he had limitations as a singer. "My feet are all right but they tell me that when I sing all I need do is make certain that the audience can understand the lyrics. There is no use my trying to let my voice out because there is not enough of it to show."[25]

Helen Dzhermolinska interviewed Kelly for an article in *American Dancer* during the spring of 1941. She noticed that his dressing room at the Ethel Barrymore Theatre had congratulatory telegrams from Cole Porter, Victor Moore, Lorenz Hart, and Gene's brother Fred. Dzhermolinska was a serious dance commentator, and Gene readily spoke of things important to him. "He believes, and with justice, that the virile male dancer is the most commanding figure on the ballet stage, but virile he must be," she wrote. Dzhermolinska was impressed with Kelly's control, his "coordination between feet, arms, ears and chin." He was a tap dancer "who doesn't flail his arms about like a windmill gone berserk." No one seemed to match Gene in combining ballet and tap, mixed with an "animal nervousness" to create Joey Evans. "I don't believe in conformity to any school of dancing," he told Dzhermolinska. "I create what the drama and the music demand of me. While I am 100% for ballet technique, I use only what I can adapt to my own use. I never let technique get in the way of the mood or the continuity."[26]

While Kelly appreciated a more elevated discussion of dance with Dzhermolinska, he could not resist the temptation to reveal his down-to-earth side. He told her of his love for teaching children. "I was behind the eight ball myself as a child in dancing class so I know what kids really like and want." He also joked about being "the best polka dancer in any part of the world and I don't care who knows it." Regarding *Pal Joey*, Gene confessed he felt like a kid again "who has just been handed a carnival on a platter and doesn't quite know why, or what to do about it."[27]

Commentator John Martin pinpointed a key innovation that Kelly used—the ballet technique to solve the problem of the torso when tap dancing. Others had solved the problem without employing ballet. Fred Astaire and Bill Robinson avoided ballet like the plague but found "natural means" to make use of the upper body. Martin noted that Paul Draper and George Tapps also blended ballet with tap, but Draper had gone too far in using ballet until it overwhelmed his tap dancing. Martin thought Gene did well in "the oppositions and balances of the various parts of the body though in his arms he has a trifle more of the academic port de bras than is good for him." Nevertheless, Martin concluded that Kelly "has a natural lightness and excellent elevation, and could without doubt become a good ballet dancer if he put his mind to it."[28]

While Gene performed in *Pal Joey*, Betsy Blair's career slowly progressed as well. Kelly and his friends had advised her to get out of the nightclub circuit and into musical comedy. After Betsy was turned down for *Louisiana*

Purchase, Robert Alton gave her a job in the chorus of *Panama Hattie*, which he was choreographing. Gene also introduced Betsy to William Saroyan, who gave her an important part in *The Beautiful People*. It was a straight dramatic role and the pay was $100 a week, the most she had ever made.[29] It opened at the Lyceum Theatre on April 21, 1941, but ran for only 120 performances, making a loss of $12,000.

BEST FOOT FORWARD (1941)

Gene's work in *Pal Joey* was going strong when he was given the opportunity to choreograph an entire Broadway show, *Best Foot Forward*. It was the kind of job he had been pining for ever since he came to New York. Hugh Martin and Ralph Blane wrote the songs and music for the show, but rehearsals were not going well. The choreographer simply was not in tune with the spirit of the story, set in a high school; the show needed fresh dance steps and more energy. Martin convinced Richard Rodgers, a silent partner in the venture, who talked director George Abbott into buying out the choreographer's contract.[30]

Martin writes in his memoirs that he prayed at St. Thomas's Cathedral at 5th Avenue and 53rd Street for guidance. He was inspired to ask Gene to take over the job of choreographing *Best Foot Forward*. Martin thought it would be a stretch to ask Kelly to do this at the height of his success. Nevertheless, he asked Kelly during an intermission of a matinee performance of *Pal Joey*, and Gene was stunned. Hugh was not aware of the extent to which Kelly had created his own dance steps and felt he was going out on a limb in offering him this job based only on his inspiration. "I don't even know whether you do that or not," he asked. "Do you?" Gene could not contain his excitement. "Yes!," he exclaimed. "I want it more than anything. Much more than performing." Martin said he felt strongly that Gene might "have that touch" that was needed to save *Best Foot Forward*. Kelly asked him how he knew it, and Martin did not tell him he was inspired after much praying. He simply said he didn't know how, but he just knew. Kelly responded, "Hmm. Clairvoyant yet. Well, kid, I've got news for you. I do have that touch. And I've been hankering for a long time to prove it."[31]

Pal Joey would have a four-week hiatus that summer and Gene offered to work on the choreography of *Best Foot Forward* during that break. Rodgers was pleased with the arrangement, but Abbott hesitated. He was not sure

Kelly had the ability to handle the job and he also wanted the choreographer to start right away. If it was to be Gene, Abbott was concerned about Kelly's working on two Broadway shows simultaneously. He went to talk with Gene after an evening performance of *Pal Joey*. "He insists that he is a choreographer at heart," Abbott told Rodgers and Martin the next day. "Before he came here, he and his brother, Fred, ran a dance studio for kids in Pittsburgh. To make a long story short, I made a deal with him, and he starts work next Monday."[32]

Martin vividly remembered the start of rehearsals that Monday. "There was electricity in the air," he wrote. The actors were in awe of Kelly because of *Pal Joey* and eager to see what he would do with the show. The effect was immediate. Gene began turning the production around. Even Martin's weakest song, "Don't Sell the Night Short," came to life with Kelly's fresh dance steps and vigor. "Being so aware of the power of choreography, I felt my morale zooming into outer space as I watched Gene Kelly turning my mediocre song into a snappy opening number." Martin also noticed the effect Gene had on the dancers. "Their eyes were bright, their limbs seemed supercharged, and there was more than a little laughter." Gene had borrowed from John Murray Anderson and Robert Alton the tendency to assign nicknames to his dancers, and it helped to create a familiar bond between himself and his "gypsies."[33]

After five weeks of rehearsal *Best Foot Forward* held its out-of-town premiere in New Haven, Connecticut. In front of the entire cast, Abbott gave full credit to Martin for having the idea to hire Gene. *Best Foot Forward* was a make-or-break project for Martin; it was his first big show and it succeeded with Kelly's involvement. "I am convinced that without his contribution, the show would have failed, and I would have had no career whatsoever," Martin wrote years later.[34]

Kelly brought Jeanne Coyne to New York at this time. She had initially met him as a student in Johnstown when she was twelve years old. Jeanne had kept in touch, seeing him briefly when he returned to town and writing letters. He always replied cheerfully to those missives. "More than anything else, those letters made me keep up with my dancing," Jeanne later wrote. Now Gene wrote and told her to round up some of his former students and bring them to New York to audition for a place in *Best Foot Forward*. It was ideal because the cast needed young dancers, and he knew the capabilities of his former pupils. Gene met the group at the train station and took them to see *Pal Joey* that night. He also introduced them to Betsy Blair. Coyne, now eighteen, could tell that Betsy was "something special in his life."[35]

Figure 5.4 Choreographing and training dancers for *Best Foot Forward* (1941). (Still from *Anatomy of a Dancer*, 2002)

In the end, Coyne did not get a job with *Best Foot Forward*, but Kelly helped her to get into the chorus of *Pal Joey*. He also arranged for her to stay at the same hotel that Betsy lived in. Helen Dzhermolinska saw that Jeanne was not just another chorus girl to Gene. "There is a dancer who comes from his school in Pittsburgh, and he beams on her like something he has just hatched personally out of the egg."[36] Coyne later replaced Blair as "dancing girl" in *Panama Hattie*, where she rubbed shoulders with future greats such as Lucille Bremer, June Allyson, and Vera-Ellen. She stayed in New York several years after Kelly left for Hollywood, dancing in *Something for the Boys*, *Mexican Hayride*, and in *Are You With It*; in the last one, she played a snake charmer's daughter and danced in the ensemble as a replacement.

Stanley Donen had been nothing but a chorus boy in *Pal Joey* without getting to know Gene. Because Abbott was slated to direct *Best Foot Forward*, he asked Donen to come to that production as well in a similarly marginal role. Donen's biographer writes that Donen was the only one Kelly knew (at least by sight) in the chorus of *Best Foot Forward*, and so he asked Stanley to be his assistant.[37] It was the beginning of a mutually beneficial relationship between the two.

The show opened for a two-week run in Philadelphia before its Broadway premiere on October 1, 1941. It ran for 326 performances, a sterling success with the audiences even though the critics were not always generous in their praise. Richard Watts was not enthusiastic about the show but praised Gene's choreography for having "the proper freshness and enthusiasm" demanded of the plot and characters. Brooks Atkinson liked the show a lot and even praised Kelly for producing "some droll and whirling dances."[38]

THE HOLLYWOOD DEAL

When Kelly achieved the highest plateau in his stage career through *Pal Joey*, Hollywood became more interested in him. Judy Garland saw *Pal Joey*, met Gene backstage after the performance, and became an instant and lifelong friend. Her own film career had just skyrocketed along with the rising career of producer Arthur Freed through *The Wizard of Oz* and *Babes in Arms*. Garland's personal traumas were only a few years in the future—for now she was the darling of M-G-M Studios. She invited Kelly to dinner with a large party that consisted of her mother, three press agents, her personal agent, and an adviser. The group went to the Copacabana and danced until 3 A.M. Then Judy asked her mother's permission to walk with Gene through Central Park. During the course of a two-hour walk, Judy expressed her desire to someday make a movie with Gene.[39]

Joseph Pasternak, a producer of musicals for M-G-M, also saw *Pal Joey* and thought Kelly was "superb." But he did not make a move to approach him for film work. It was Fred Finklehoffe, M-G-M's talent scout, who once again alerted Freed to the possibility of signing Gene after he saw *Pal Joey*. Freed had already tried and failed, so he urged studio executive Louis B. Mayer to have a go at Kelly. Mayer went to New York, saw the show, and the next day called Darrow to arrange for an interview with Gene at M-G-M's New York office. Kelly met with Mayer and was interested in pursuing an opportunity with the studio. But he wanted to finish the run of *Pal Joey* first and then do a screen test in California because he had heard that the screen tests M-G-M made in New York were terrible. Mayer told him there was no need for a screen test at all.[40]

But soon after that meeting Kelly received a call from M-G-M's New York office to come in for a screen test. Gene assumed at first that it was a mistake. But Hirschhorn has written that the New York office produced a memo from Mayer asking for the test. Kelly was furious and wrote an intemperate letter to Mayer calling him a liar and saying he would prefer to dance in saloons rather than work for him. Sadly, Gene never forgot the incident and never forgave Mayer for it. Hugh Fordin has tried to explain the incident as arising from a misunderstanding on the part of Al Altman in the New York office. Freed had asked Altman to send him publicity photographs of Kelly because he was considering him for the part of Willie in *Strike Up the Band*.[41] But that request had been made in mid-December 1939, soon after Freed had seen Gene in *The Time of Your Life*. How this request could have confused Altman with Mayer's offer early in 1941 is a mystery Fordin does not explain.

Unfortunately, M-G-M destroyed the bulk of its memos in the 1970s as part of their major housecleaning, so there is nothing in the archives on this issue. It seems unlikely that Mayer would assure Kelly he did not need a screen test and immediately dictate a memo asking for one. If Mayer changed his mind on the issue, he would have informed Gene. One possibility is that Mayer's staff, unaware of Mayer's promise to Kelly, sent the memo for a test as a routine procedure before sending a contract. The memo may have indicated that it was "from Mayer" also as a routine procedure.

Another possibility is that someone in Mayer's office was aware of the promise but sent the "routine" memo anyway. For example, Eddie Mannix, the studio manager, often interfered in the work of colleagues when it came to recruiting and using talent.[42] Either he or someone with the same attitude may have been responsible.

Gene could have discovered what happened and straightened it out with a phone call or a professional letter to Mayer. Instead he acted in anger and cut off any possibility of going to M-G-M for the time being. Part of the reason Kelly behaved this way was that he always had a problem controlling his anger and tended to act hastily when provoked, as he admitted in later years.

The other reason is that at this stage he was ambivalent about a film career. Helen Dzhermolinska nailed it correctly when she pointed out that "the instinct of self-preservation keeps him from taking the plunge. He looks at Hollywood with a question in his eyes. Broadway is his stomping ground." According to Dzhermolinska, Gene thought "that any creative work in the dance must necessarily be done on the stage, not in the movies."[43] So he was not concerned that the M-G-M offer fell through. A short while later,

Paramount Studios courted Kelly for a film tentatively called *Burlesque*. Even though it was a musical, Gene did not like the project and declined Paramount's offer.[44] He was quite content at that point to remain on Broadway.

It took a maverick producer like David Selznick to get through to Kelly. Born in Pittsburgh ten years before Gene, his father had been an early motion picture promoter and his brother was a talent scout in Hollywood. Selznick worked for M-G-M as assistant story editor and for Paramount as assistant general manager before marrying Mayer's daughter Irene in 1930. He then worked for RKO before joining M-G-M in 1933 as the head of a production unit. Only two years later, he left the studio to become an independent film producer. Selznick International Pictures had its greatest financial success with *Gone with the Wind*, which was distributed by M-G-M in 1939.[45]

Unlike M-G-M's purging of its office records, Selznick's papers are well preserved and provide rich details of what happened. Selznick found out about Kelly through Katherine "Kay" Brown, perhaps the most aggressive talent scout in the film industry. Based in New York, she had worked for Selznick International since the company was founded and had been the one to alert David to Margaret Mitchell's novel. Kay had also been instrumental in recruiting Ingrid Bergman and Alfred Hitchcock to work with Selznick. She was convinced that Gene was a hot prospect after seeing him in January 1941 in *Pal Joey*. Calling him "a magnificent hoofer," she sent a telegram to Dan O'Shea, Selznick's chief subordinate in California. Aware of M-G-M's interest in Kelly, she ruthlessly added that she was determined "to take away from Metro every person in whom we and they are interested. I am not at all concerned on what basis I take them."[46]

Despite Al Altman telling Kay that M-G-M had "first refusal" on Gene with a verbal agreement stemming from Arthur Freed's initial offer to him, she urged Darrow to send Kelly to see her at her office, which he did in mid-February 1941. After meeting Gene, she wrote to Selznick and O'Shea: "I think he would be a very valuable property. Kelly is small like George Raft and slick in the same way, and my guess is that he can be photographed very well. He is an unpretentious sort of person with his feet on the ground. He would like to do movies but he doesn't want to sign a term contract until he knows what his first picture will be."[47] And yet Selznick did not act, most likely because he had no interest in musicals and was not sure of Gene's potential as a straight actor.

A few months went by, and it was almost inevitable that Hollywood would make another try at luring Kelly to California. John Martin predicted it in a

New York Times piece that ran on June 8, 1941. He thought no other Broadway personality had Gene's "natural ability" and that he had not yet reached his full potential. Not since Fred Astaire had gone from a long career on the musical comedy stage to Hollywood had such an exciting dancer and "so promising a talent" been ready for film work. In addition, "He is personable and probably photogenic." Martin thought the only sad thing was that "one who can act as well as Kelly will gradually be weaned away from dancing."[48]

Indeed, soon after this, M-G-M made a contract offer to Gene in late June. For $1,000 a week, Kelly could star in *As Thousands Cheer* (as the project was tentatively called then) with a start date of October 1 and then go back to Broadway to direct and star in Saroyan's "Sweeney in the Trees." After that M-G-M would have yearly options starting at $750 a week for seven years, with a $250 increase each year. Gene could also work on one film per year for Twentieth Century-Fox during his time at M-G-M. Darrow approved the generous terms by July 1, but Kelly wanted to clarify a couple of points first. The contract did not mention a screen test, but he wanted assurance on this. He was actually ready to do a screen test now, even in New York. He said if a test was needed, he would rather do it soon, because if it failed, he wanted to start planning the production of "Sweeney in the Trees." The second question he had was whether the start date of October 1 was for rehearsals or production of *As Thousands Cheer*.[49] He had not yet received an answer when he heard from Selznick.

After hearing about M-G-M's firm offer to Gene, Selznick now wanted to grab Kelly for himself. He, Kay Brown, and Dan O'Shea were all matched in aggressiveness and lack of scruples. O'Shea had talked to Darrow, who told him that Gene was about to close on M-G-M's offer. O'Shea advised Selznick that if he offered Kelly $1,000 per week and no screen test, they could get him. Brown urged Selznick to do this and he agreed. She offered to have lunch with Kelly and Darrow to make the offer, but Selznick decided to fly over and join them. Selznick also approved the idea of naming a film project if it would entice Gene's interest. Hitchcock, as a contract producer for Selznick, had mentioned *Saboteur* as his next project. The Selznick team rightly judged that this would appeal to Kelly, and decided to mention it in their discussion to tempt him. And as another way to outdo M-G-M, Selznick planned to see Betsy Blair in *The Beautiful People*. That was a powerful indication of how serious Gene and Betsy's relationship had become by then and how widely everyone knew of it. Selznick heard that Betsy was very good in the play and mused, "Who knows but that she is a better bet than Kelly."[50] Selznick's memo clearly shows that he still harbored doubts about Gene's potential and was doing all this mainly to grab someone M-G-M wanted.

Selznick and Brown had lunch with Kelly on July 15 in New York. Selznick put on the charm and Gene saw him as an honest and straight-talking guy. "Your father-in-law is a son-of-a-bitch because he lied to me," Kelly told him. Selznick already knew of the controversy over the screen test. He laughed and asked, "Do you want to sign a contract with me?" The two hit it off very well, and Gene was especially keen on doing a Hitchcock picture. He decided to sign with Selznick, apparently without much consideration of the details. The truth is that Selznick was not sure he wanted to make the Hitchcock movie and had mentioned it simply as an enticement. In fact, Brown cautioned O'Shea in a memo after the lunch that Kelly was counting "one hundred percent" on the Hitchcock picture but "it was impossible" and should not be made an issue in the contract.[51] The name of the Hitchcock project was never mentioned to Gene.

After the lunch, Selznick wrote to his father-in-law to tell him he was signing Kelly, expressed a good deal of frustration at how M-G-M had treated his company in the past, and then suggested Mayer find out "who was the culprit who told you that Kelly had been offered a deal, when all he had been offered was an option and a test."[52] This is a clear indication that Selznick suspected that Mayer was not the originator of the request for a screen test from Gene and that someone in the office was changing the terms. Selznick must have expressed the letter overnight because it created an instant reaction in California.

Mayer was upset that his son-in-law would steal a prospect from M-G-M. He realized that he could not compel Kelly to accept his offer but was anxious to convince him to seriously consider M-G-M. He tried to call Selznick but could not reach him. At this point, Mayer asked Leland Hayward to intervene. Hayward had been enlisted by Darrow to represent Gene in California because Darrow had not yet established himself as an agent in Hollywood. Hayward was, in effect, the subagent for Kelly and was in the middle of a thriving career, representing everyone from Astaire to Garland.[53]

Hayward tried to call Kelly but could not reach him. So, on July 16, the very next day after Gene's lunch with Selznick, he wrote a long letter reminding Kelly that he and Mayer had worked a deal as early as July 1 and reiterated the generous terms. He cautioned Gene not to ignore all his interactions with M-G-M and suddenly switch to Selznick. "You are starting out your career in pictures at best with a bad odor to the negotiations. Metro is a very important company—the most important. They have great assets and will be in business a long, long time." Hayward was hinting at how unstable Selznick International was, and he was right. By this time, Selznick was mainly a peddler of people and projects rather than a moviemaker. Hayward also pointed out that Kelly was throwing over M-G-M, which had invested a lot of time and effort on him to take up another offer after only a brief lunch meeting. "This is not an entirely honest thing to do and I don't like to see you do anything that you can be severely criticized for."[54]

Hayward sent a copy of his letter to Gene for Selznick to read and added, "there is no question there was a commitment made to Metro by myself and accepted by Gene Kelly." When Selznick read Hayward's letter, he immediately wrote his father-in-law that he did not like the implication that Gene should accept M-G-M's offer because the studio was big and important. He added, "I will also be very much surprised if Mr. Kelly doesn't offer to beat up Mr. Hayward for calling him dishonest."[55]

Gene wrote to Hayward arguing that he did not have a deal with M-G-M and resented the implication that he had acted unethically. He felt he had the right to choose the person who would "guide his future career."[56] Ironically, Kelly made a poor choice in that aspect, as he soon found out.

M-G-M and Selznick International Pictures squared off on Gene Kelly. The former insisted that they had offered him a detailed, long-term contract while the latter argued that it was only for a test and an option. When Hayward called Dan O'Shea and told him everyone had a moral obligation to honor previous M-G-M negotiations with Kelly, O'Shea told him it was not his concern.[57]

Selznick won his battle with M-G-M over signing Kelly through a combination of factors. The crossed wires at M-G-M over the screen test were the key; this opened the door for someone like Selznick who could relate well to Gene in face-to-face negotiations. Added to the mix was an artful misrepresentation of M-G-M's offer by the Selznick group. The offer *did* contain options that the studio could exercise if they chose to do so after Kelly's initial film proved successful, or they could have dropped or traded him elsewhere if they chose. All this was standard practice in Hollywood, and Selznick's contract contained the same clauses. But the Selznick team acted as if M-G-M's contract was not a real commitment.

Gene did not closely compare the actual merits of the two contracts. His aversion to Mayer based on his erroneous assumption that Mayer had lied to him, and his instant liking of Selznick, seem to have been the basis for his choice. As a result, Kelly lost an opportunity to go directly from Broadway to M-G-M, a studio with a *long* record of making musicals. Instead he signed with a studio that had *never* made musicals and showed little interest in them.

The Selznick contract guaranteed him five weeks at $1,100 per week. After this, Gene would have to stay in California for retakes at $550 a week. Selznick agreed to reimburse his transportation costs to California and his return to New York for the Saroyan play after the initial film was completed. The Hitchcock project was mentioned, but Selznick reserved the option of changing it to a different film before October 1. Selznick retained options just as M-G-M had but with a wider salary range than M-G-M had offered, from $1,000 to $2,250 per week. Like M-G-M, Selznick also reserved the right to assign Kelly's contract to a major studio.[58]

The deal was not completely sewn up until Gene signed the contract. Selznick had urged O'Shea and Brown to draw it up "with lightning speed to avoid the possibility of shenanigans with Leland and of boosted prices from Metro before we get him signed." In fact, the contract was written so fast that someone used the standard form that contained a clause about wardrobe for female stars. A few days later O'Shea had to send the clause applicable to male wardrobe as a substitute. The contract was expressed to Kelly to reach by 6 P.M. on Friday, July 18. For unexplained reasons the contract still had not been delivered by July 21, causing great anxiety at the Selznick office. Selznick was so nervous he even told his crew that they could offer to loan Kelly out to M-G-M for *As Thousands Cheer* if needed to secure him. "Kelly possibly most important young player on New York stage today," Selznick wrote to his publicity contact as he told her to break the news to the media the moment Kelly signed, or sooner. After Gene inked his name on the contract, everyone at Selznick International Pictures could breathe normally. Selznick wrote a brief note telling Kelly "how much I look forward to working with you."[59]

There were now a few fences to be mended. By now Hayward wanted to keep Kelly as a client and was entirely on his side, telling the actor that the Metro offer was at best "a test deal." Hayward also assured Mayer that Gene was not at fault in the controversy and argued that it was at worst a misunderstanding. For his part, Selznick wrote a conciliatory note to Mayer, addressing it as "Dear Dad" and promising he would explain everything privately to him.[60] How he spun the tale to Mayer no one knows. By now Selznick was denying that he even knew of M-G-M's offer to Kelly, even though there is a trail of memos showing that both Darrow and Hayward had specifically told Brown, O'Shea, and even Selznick of M-G-M's offer, including its details.

Gene would not report to work at Selznick International Pictures for a couple of months. In the meanwhile, Selznick began to worry because he really did not have anything in mind for him. Selznick's staff was concerned about another issue—that Kelly may be subject to the draft that had been passed into law earlier as a way to prepare the United States for possible entry into World War II. Someone checked into the details and found that the upper age limit was currently twenty-eight.[61] Gene was a few days short of twenty-nine and so barely missed it.

Hitchcock wanted to start production on October 1, but Selznick was already having second thoughts about the project and its high preproduction costs. By September 10 he was seriously considering Kelly for a different project, *The Keys of the Kingdom*. Written by Joseph Mankiewicz, the script excited Selznick more than any script he had seen in the last few years. Afraid Kelly would lose interest in his studio, Selznick urged Brown and O'Shea not to tell Gene that he planned to sell the Hitchcock project to another studio. He even talked about making a screen test of Kelly in New York. Brown reminded her boss that Gene would not be happy if told he had to do a test in that city. "We are in desperate need of a good test of Kelly," Selznick responded, "especially since actually we have no film of him at all." Brown agreed to broach the issue gently with Darrow.[62] While we do not know the details of that conversation, we do know that Gene did *not* make a screen test in New York.

Selznick and his staff were still not honest with Kelly regarding the Hitchcock film. Instead of telling him that the project had been sold, they told him it was postponed. As they began to consider him for *The Keys of the Kingdom*, Brown wondered which role would be right for Gene. The plot concerned a Catholic priest from Scotland who is sent to a mission in China. It also involved an "atheist doctor." No one had any idea how Kelly would do in these or any other roles; he was an unknown quality when it came to acting a straight dramatic role in a movie. Basing her judgment *only* on Joey Evans, Brown was uncertain if he could fill any role that required "Passion and Romance."[63]

The Selznick group had gone to great lengths to acquire Kelly but now had no good ideas for what to do with him. The basic problem was that Selznick was not interested in film musicals. While he recognized the potential in Gene as an actor, that potential was only a glimmering possibility. Kelly could only be said, at this stage of his budding career, to be a fledgling actor of unknown depth. Selznick would scratch his head for some time trying to decide how to explore that unknown.

Gene was disappointed at the "postponement" of the Hitchcock film but excited by a project that Kay Brown mentioned as a substitute, an unidentified story about a sailor and a girl. Ben Hecht also was keen on involving Kelly in his newest film project, but Selznick warned his staff not to mention it to Gene because "it might confuse him." Hayward, who now was working completely for Kelly's benefit, told Selznick that if he could not find a good film project he ought to let Gene stay in New York a while and act in *Hotel Splendide*, a play with producers who were keen to have Kelly in it. Even though Selznick had nothing ready for Gene, he refused, saying that he worked his film projects on a tight budget and could not afford to let Kelly loiter in New York.[64]

Ironically, Selznick also was interested in signing Betsy Blair. "Believe it or not her face and personality have stayed with me amazingly, more so than any other girl I saw in New York other than [Dorothy] McGuire." He even thought she might be "a unique Lillian Gish kind of personality." He urged Kay Brown to have Betsy do a reading but thought a screen test probably was not needed, given that Twentieth Century-Fox had done one with her. Selznick specifically thought of her for *Claudia*, a story of a young bride who has a lot of growing up to do.[65] Eventually he sold the rights to Twentieth Century-Fox, which used McGuire, who had created the role to great acclaim on Broadway. The 1943 film's success led to *Claudia and David* (1946).

PREPARING FOR HOLLYWOOD

Gene and Betsy's relationship had come a long way from their initial meeting when she mistook him for a busboy at Billy Rose's Diamond Horseshoe. At first it was based on friendship as she became part of the life Kelly and Dwenger lived in New York. Gradually Gene saw less of Helene Marlowe, his first serious girlfriend, and more of Betsy.

Helene went on to live a happy life, marrying Floyd B. Hall, a photographer, at the onset of World War II. She worked as an assistant art director on live television at CBS after the war and also designed clothes. She and Floyd had a long marriage and one son. They lived for many years in Darien, Connecticut, where Helene died on August 26, 2015, only two weeks short of her ninety-ninth birthday.[66]

Betsy remembered that for a long time Gene kept their relationship platonic. In fact, she began to wonder why he did not get more physical in their "pure" relationship. "I was doing everything in my power for it to be a bit less pure," she admitted years later, "but until Gene considered it was 'serious' enough, he didn't touch me. His *not* making love to me was his way of showing me that he *did* love me."[67]

By May or June 1941, however, they became lovers. When preparing for his move to California, Kelly popped the question. "He sort of said, 'I can't leave you at the mercy of New York, and I want you to be the mother of my children.'" Betsy, of course, was ecstatic. Gene insisted they have a Catholic ceremony. According to Blair, he only half-jokingly told her, "Of course it has to be in church—do you want to kill my mother?" Gene had to ask Betsy's father for permission as she was not yet eighteen. Approval was gladly given, and the two sets of parents became part of the wedding plans.[68]

With his upcoming marriage, preparing for Hollywood, and working on *Best Foot Forward*, it is understandable that Kelly did not want to be in *Pal Joey* in its second Broadway run starting September 1, 1941. But Abbott talked him into continuing to play Joey Evans in the first two weeks to let his replacement George Tapps ease into the role. For those two exhausting weeks, Kelly worked on rehearsals for *Best Foot Forward* in the mornings and acted in *Pal Joey* in the evenings. Tapps, who had been in a couple of Broadway productions before this, could not carry the show like Gene. A year older than Kelly, Tapps was a good dancer but did not have the star quality or the acting ability to succeed in this complicated role.[69] *Pal Joey* closed on November 29, 1941. Gene's creation of the role made the show a hit, and his exit lowered the curtain on it.

A week after finishing his portrayal of Joey Evans, Gene and Betsy got married in Philadelphia while *Best Foot Forward* was still on tryout. "A Wedding Between Rehearsals" is how the Philadelphia *Evening Bulletin* put it on September 22, 1941. Both families were present for the ceremony that day, but Betsy admitted later that she had to put on a show for the priest and Harriet, promising to convert to Catholicism and to raise their kids in the church. "It was all done with Gene's collusion. He told me we had to perform this farce" for his mother's sake. Gene and Betsy enjoyed a wedding breakfast at the Bellevue-Stratford Hotel and then he rushed back to the Forrest Theater to put "finishing touches on new numbers" in *Best Foot Forward*.[70]

When the Selznick people heard about the wedding Kay Brown advised Selznick to give them a wedding gift on their arrival in Hollywood. Gene had planned to leave with Betsy on October 2 for their road trip to California. He wanted to take a leisurely trip to recuperate from his weight loss while doing two shows simultaneously, but he could get there by November 1. This was fine with Kay. They could take as long a car trip as they liked because Selznick was going to reimburse only the equivalent of a first-class train fare. But now, two dancers were replaced in *Best Foot Forward* and Abbott asked Kelly to stay back to rehearse the new people. Not having anything urgent for him, Kay postponed his start date from November 1 to December 1, 1941.[71]

As soon as his work on *Best Foot Forward* ended, Gene and Betsy set out on a nearly two-month honeymoon trip. Gene purchased "a little Ford convertible roadster" and the two said goodbye to Dick Dwenger, who had been instrumental in getting them together and was a dear friend to both. From New York they motored down through North Carolina and Tennessee to New Orleans, where they spent a few days before catching a boat to Vera Cruz. Driving in Mexico, they once ran out of gas in the middle of the night. Gene made sure Betsy was safely locked in the car and went to find someone who could help.[72]

Sometime later he came back riding on a donkey cart with a man and a little girl, about seven or eight. Stopping at the car, Gene alighted and held out his hand to the girl with a grand sort of gesture. She was equal to the moment. Sporting long braids and with "enormous black eyes," the girl came out of the cart "with a natural elegance equal to Gene's" and took his hand. "He twirled her around, set her down on the ground, skipped around her, and bowed. She didn't giggle like an American child; she watched him with a grave little smile and curtsied back." Her father filled the gas tank and refused payment. It was one of those delightful moments in life that stick in the memory, and Betsy was certain Gene recalled it when he choreographed his dance with Sharon McManus in *Anchors Aweigh* four years later.[73]

In Mexico, the couple visited Mayan temples and villages. In Mexico City, they went to museums, cathedrals, bars, and dance halls. They then drove through Texas, New Mexico, and Arizona to San Francisco, where they met William Saroyan. Through their week in the city, Saroyan tried to involve them in his new play, "Sweeney in the Trees." Gene had already seen tryouts of it at the Cape May Playhouse in New Jersey and had been keen on directing and acting in it, but the play never came off. Saroyan's biographer called this and another of his plays, *Love's Old Sweet Song*, "unredeemable disasters." The latter was coproduced by the Theatre Guild and lost more than $31,000 on Broadway in 1940. The Sweeney play never made it to Broadway. But those days of discussing the play in San Francisco bred a pair of private nicknames—Gene called Betsy "Sweeney" and Betsy called him "Geney."[74]

From San Francisco they drove down to Los Angeles and arrived in Hollywood on December 7, 1941, just as news of the bombing of Pearl Harbor reached the West Coast.[75] America plunged into World War II at the same time that Kelly took on Hollywood.

Taking on Hollywood, 1941–1944

Gene came to California with a contract that allowed him to make one movie and then return to Broadway, but the path of his life was not that simple. In fact, within a few months of his arrival, he became fascinated with the process of presenting dance on the two-dimensional format of a movie screen and decided to stay in Hollywood to work out this problem. He had been so thoroughly absorbed in stage performance all his life that the technical challenges of this new medium had never entered his mind. Now he took on Hollywood and never looked back.

Kelly's decision to stay in California took some time to jell. First he and Betsy found a place to live, renting a one-bedroom house in Laurel Canyon, at 8415 Lookout Mountain Drive, set among wooded hills. The Kellys had to negotiate ninety-nine stepping-stones to climb up to the house.[1]

KELLY AND SELZNICK

Before Gene could make his first movie he had to navigate the uncertain waters of David Selznick's mind. Described by film historian Aljean Harmetz as "obsessive, indecisive, recklessly extravagant, [and] undisciplined," Selznick was also unpredictable. With a tremendous energy level boosted by Benzedrine, he constantly jumped from one line of thought and action to another.[2] Selznick International Pictures had released only eleven movies from its inception in 1935 to 1940. None of them were musicals. When Gene came on the payroll, the company was floundering artistically and economically, headed by a compulsive man who had a great deal of trouble making up his mind about what to do next.

"Gene Kelly presents a problem," Daniel O'Shea wrote to Selznick even before Gene arrived in Hollywood. "So far I haven't had any success in lining up a picture for him." The Hitchcock film had never been a real option. Selznick had already sold it to Universal and independent producer Frank Lloyd in late fall 1941. It was released in April 1942 as *Saboteur*. There was a possibility that theatrical producer Jed Harris would be interested in Gene for a film project, but Harris insisted on a screen test. Kelly was also considered for the title role in a projected film about the life of Rudolph Valentino and for the lead in an adaptation of the novel *G String Murders*, which they planned to sell to Columbia.[3] None of these possibilities materialized.

Selznick finally settled on using Kelly in *The Keys of the Kingdom*, the story of a Catholic priest's experience as a missionary in China. He talked to Gene about it on December 18, 1941. Though he was willing to play the priest, Gene was more eager to play the role of Willie Tulloch, the atheist doctor. Both roles required a Scottish accent, and Selznick asked that a dialogue coach begin working with Gene while he lined up screen tests of Kelly for each character. He wanted to use the best cinematographer and director for the tests because they were "so important to Kelly's whole future."[4]

But these tests were still not made in mid-January 1942, when Kay Brown urged Selznick to purchase the rights to Katharine Brush's novel *But Always You*. Brown thought it would be a good vehicle for Kelly "if we intend doing anything with him." Instead, Selznick thought that if Gene was not suitable for *The Keys of the Kingdom*, he should be loaned to another studio. For a good price he was willing to give Columbia the original Joey for its own *Pal Joey*.[5]

Meanwhile, the office circulated biographical information on Kelly for publicity purposes that emphasized his strong work ethic growing up in Pittsburgh. It also listed Gene as five feet, nine inches tall, 155 pounds, with black hair and brown eyes. Even while they kept him in the public eye, Gene "went off salary" at Selznick International Pictures on January 3, 1942, which was "the end of his five-week guarantee." The studio had until March 19 to pick up its option on him, and that option would not begin until May 6, 1942.[6] Thus far Gene had received $5,500 for five weeks of doing nothing but taking dialogue training.

With very little to occupy his time, Gene had the chance to roam about Hollywood a bit. He visited Paramount Studios and met Fred Astaire for the first time. Astaire was then involved in filming *Holiday Inn*.[7] The film, costarring Bing Crosby, was released later that year.

While waiting for the dialogue coaching to be done, Selznick thought a test of Kelly as "a modern character" should be made just in case his accent did not turn out right. In a screen test made on February 6, 1942, Kelly performed a scene from a Warner Brothers movie released nearly two years before called *Saturday's Children.*[8] Selznick was not planning to remake this movie; the object simply was to get Kelly on film in some way, and the role of an inventor with few prospects seemed right for Gene.

Finally, in mid-February, Kelly did the screen test for *The Keys of the Kingdom*. It was delayed by six weeks of work with a dialogue coach in Pasadena. Even after that intensive training, Kelly's Scots accent was terrible. He and Selznick laughed when viewing the test.[9] Gregory Peck ended up playing the priest and Thomas Mitchell the atheist doctor.

"You, you are a great actor," Kelly remembered Selznick told him during this period of his career in Hollywood. "This nonsense about your doing musicals, that's fine. You can do them for a hobby." Gene insisted that dancing was the key to his future but he failed to see that Selznick could not help him. "We became great friends," Kelly recalled in numerous interviews, and "had a lot of fun and several good drinking bouts every month."[10] The two men hit it off so well on a personal level that both were blinded to the fact that Selznick International was not the studio for Gene.

Selznick was frustrated at his inability to find a good role for Kelly. He was angry when Leland Hayward urged him to let Gene go to M-G-M, telling the erratic producer "how much better off he would be and how he'd be working." Obviously, Hayward was right. Mayer's studio was interested in putting Kelly into a musical produced by Arthur Freed, *For Me and My Gal*, opposite Judy Garland. But M-G-M wanted to secure Kelly's entire contract rather than take him on loan. There was not much hope he could be loaned to Columbia to make *Pal Joey*. Columbia wanted to change the storyline a good deal and was undecided on the lead. Gene had not acted in any movie at this point, so Columbia's hesitancy in using him was understandable. With no good options left, Selznick was willing to let Gene work for M-G-M if Mayer's studio purchased half his contract, with a proviso that Selznick International Pictures could use him for one film per year.[11]

M-G-M agreed to Selznick's proposal to share Kelly's contract. Gene started working there on February 19, 1942, even while the details of his contract were being worked out between the two studios. His salary would be $775 per week from Loew's (M-G-M's parent company), but Selznick also paid him $1,550 per week. This was for a full year, until February 18, 1943. The option date for continuing his contract was set as January 19, 1943, and the option salary would be $1,000 a week from Loew's and $2,000 from Selznick. Selznick also at this time reimbursed Kelly for his travel from New York to California but for a one-way train fare and not a round-trip as per the original contract because there was no question now of his going back to do a play on Broadway.[12] It seems incredible that Selznick would pay such a huge ongoing salary for an actor not even working for him. But this was the price he had to pay to allow Gene to start his movie career at another studio and still retain rights to part of his contract.

Gene's only real disappointment during his short time at Selznick International Pictures was in the dashed hope to start his movie career in a Hitchcock film. He assumed it was for *Strangers on a Train*, but that picture was released by Warner Brothers many years later, in 1951. The only possibility could have been *Saboteur*. But years later, when Gene asked Hitchcock about it, the director frankly told him he had never discussed Kelly with anyone for any of his movies.[13] The entire discussion of the Hitchcock project with Kelly had taken place simply to entice him to go with Selznick and had never been a reality.

It was around this time, in mid-February 1942, that Betsy found out she was pregnant. Her doctor pointed out that climbing ninety-nine stone steps would be dangerous, especially when wet. The couple rented a house owned by Yip and Edie Harburg at 506 North Alta Drive in Beverly Hills. M-G-M, now actively in charge of Kelly, found the house for them, moved their belongings, and arranged for Betsy to interview three housekeepers. Built in 1929, the two-story, 3,000-square-foot house was huge compared to the chalet-like home on Lookout Mountain Drive, and far bigger than the young couple needed. Betsy furnished it with some antiques including nineteenth-century "English-style" chairs and tables. She also obtained her first driver's license, prompting Gene to purchase a new car, a Pontiac convertible.[14]

FOR ME AND MY GAL (1942)

Fred Finklehoffe played an important role in securing a role and thereby a contract for Kelly with M-G-M. Freed had asked him to do some rewrites on the screenplay of *For Me and My Gal*. Finklehoffe told Freed that Kelly would be perfect for the role of Harry Palmer, vouching for him based on knowing him briefly in Pittsburgh and after seeing him on Broadway.[15] Gene was now eager to work, even for Mayer, because M-G-M had a going prospect that he could step immediately into and play opposite someone he knew and liked a great deal.

Rehearsals for *For Me and My Gal* started February 19, the day Kelly began to work for M-G-M.[16] It was an ideal vehicle for his first film. He created Harry Palmer, an ambitious hoofer whose ultimate goal was to play the Palace and who initially did not mind taking advantage of Jo Hayden (played by Garland) to get there. Of course, as love developed between them, Harry changed and eventually was redeemed. Thus Gene had an opportunity to duplicate some of the same characteristics that made Joey Evans so unusually attractive for sophisticated Broadway audiences. But he also could make Harry a good guy in the end for mass audiences in middle America.

Judy Garland was in an interesting phase of her life and career. Only a year older than Betsy, Judy had been born in the entertainment world, sung before audiences since childhood, and worked at M-G-M since age thirteen. She had just married bandleader David Rose the year before, and at the time was happy in the union. But her personal problems had already begun—pill-popping for energy, an overbearing stage mother, and the pressures of being a moneymaker for a powerful studio. At this point Garland was able to cope well enough so as not to delay production of *For Me and My Gal* too much. Nevertheless, the assistant director's report shows that rehearsals, tests, and recordings were cancelled for three days in February, six days in March, and eight days in April due to Judy's illness.[17]

On the days she showed up for work, Garland was bright and energetic. Delighted to be working with Gene, she played a large role in helping him adjust to the intricacies of filming. Kelly remembered that he "watched her to find out what I had to do. She pitched her voice and gestures very low, because she knew—which I didn't—that the soundtrack and the camera pick up everything." The two had great chemistry on the big screen. Gene always recalled that certain scenes in which he and Judy just talked were among the best acting he had ever done. "Kelly and Garland convey a sense of pleasure in working together and a mutual respect that is unmistakable," wrote film historian Jeanine Basinger.[18] This is particularly evident in their first number together, performed to the title song of the film in a deserted diner late at night. They dance charmingly together, and before the dance they sing a duet at the piano. This was Gene's first song on film. His voice is much higher here than in his other films to come, but it blends beautifully with Judy's.

Gene's entry into the picture ruffled the feathers of his other costar, George Murphy. Ten years older than Kelly, Murphy gained experience on Broadway before moving to California in 1934 and had a modestly successful film career. He had been considered for the lead before Kelly was brought in as Harry Palmer. Murphy was deeply disappointed. "Once again I was relegated

Figure 6.1 Kelly, with Judy Garland, singing his very first song in a film. (Still from *For Me and My Gal*, 1942)

to the part of the *shnook* who never gets the girl," he wrote in his autobiography. Murphy carried on, smothering his resentment in order to finish the film, but never forgot how bringing in Kelly spoiled what he thought was his best chance at a first-rate film portrayal.[19]

Kelly learned a great deal not only from Garland but also from director Busby Berkeley. "I had to teach him the tricks of using his eyes to give expression and animation to his facial projections," Berkeley said of Kelly. In addition, Gene carefully watched Berkeley to learn about basic camera work.[20]

Gene and Judy rehearsed their title number on the first day of work, February 19, and continued every day until February 25. George Murphy started rehearsals on March 16. A number of photo and sound tests took place, with Kelly and Garland prerecording their songs beginning March 21. Filming began April 3.[21] The first routine Gene performed in his first film was the tramp number—Harry Palmer's clown act for vaudeville. It came straight from his Pittsburgh experience. The assistant director noted in his report that technicians rigged up a "nose lighting gag on Gene Kelly" on April 4.[22] Kelly had always liked clowns, but for this number the wardrobe department went a bit overboard with his make-up and costume.

Gene's facial expressions and overacting in the tramp number fit the role

Figure 6.2 Eagerly learning about dance direction from Busby Berkeley during the filming of *For Me and My Gal* (1942). (Still from *Anatomy of a Dancer*, 2002)

Figure 6.3 Dressed as a clown in his very first dance in a film. (Still from *For Me and My Gal*, 1942)

of Harry Palmer, a vaudevillian so hungry for applause that it hurt. He used all three athletic stunts from his repertoire since his days in Pittsburgh—the Airplane Propeller, the Prone Kick, and the Crab Bounce. It is obvious that dance director, Bobby Connolly, allowed Kelly to choreograph his own material even in his very first film.

There was a cut in the number to show the audience and people watching from the wings. Gene had no idea this was being done, as it was his first dance in his first film. He never allowed this to happen again, understanding the importance of keeping the dancer in the frame throughout the number.

Gene and Judy did a spirited routine to "Ballin' the Jack" that was filmed in one day, May 23. It was a complicated dance done at fast tempo, and Garland, who was not a trained dancer, had to pick up everything in rehearsals. Kelly always praised Garland for her ability to learn fast. "She could hear a tune once and walk away knowing every step," he recalled many years later. "We called her Old Tin Ear."[23] Gene worked the Airplane Propeller into "Ballin' the Jack," but this was one step Judy simply could not do. Her attempts at it are halfhearted at best, demonstrating her limitations as a dancer. Eight years later, the two made a joke about this in *Summer Stock* (see chapter 11).

The only problem with *For Me and My Gal* was that, as originally written, Harry Palmer was not a hero. In order to avoid being drafted into World War I on the eve of playing at the Palace, he deliberately broke his hand by smashing a heavy trunk lid on it. As written, he was only trying to postpone being drafted for a couple of weeks so he could play at the Palace and marry Jo as planned. After that he wanted to fight in the war. But he ended up crippling his hand, so he could never join the army. No one (including Jo) could accept that he did intend to join the army in two weeks. Everyone saw him as a heel. It broke up his relationship with Jo, whose brother had just been killed in France. Still, the scriptwriters managed to reconcile the two lovers by the end of the movie.

Filming ended May 23, 1942. After editing, *For Me and My Gal* was shown to a preview audience, which clearly registered a major complaint. A whopping 85 percent thought George Murphy's character should have got the girl. They saw Harry as a draft dodger, missing the subtleties of his intentions. They also did not seem to mind that Murphy's character cheats a French cab driver and thinks it is funny. Ironically, Murphy had warned Freed that showing the lead as something of a draft dodger only a few months after Pearl Harbor was a mistake, and he took some degree of satisfaction in seeing his prediction come true.[24]

But Mayer's decision to reshoot the ending of the film, which of course was the right thing to do, aggravated Murphy further. Kelly's character was transformed into a military hero, and Murphy's character was written out of the last number in the movie. Murphy still steamed over this development when he wrote his memoirs decades later. Parts of the new ending were filmed on June 26 and the rest on July 27 and 29, 1942.[25]

Harry winds up in France as an entertainer and finds himself near the front lines during a developing crisis. He takes the initiative to wipe out a German machine-gun nest to save American ambulances carrying wounded to the aid station. He and Jo are reunited at an event to entertain soldiers in an emotional and uplifting ending. It made sense to end the film with the couple singing just two lines from the title song in a low-key, emotional way while hugging each other, instead of a trio jauntily singing an entire number called "For Me and My Gal."

After five and a half months of hard work on his first picture, Gene had to wait several more months for its release. It premiered in New York City on October 21, 1942, but Kelly did not see it then. Bosley Crowther of the *New York Times* found Gene's performance a bit strained: "He has been forced to act brassy like Pal Joey during the early part of the film, and then turn about and play a modest imitation of Sergeant York at the end. The transition is both written and played badly. Mr. Kelly gets embarrassingly balled up."[26]

A month later Gene saw the finished version of *For Me and my Gal,* "magnified 20 times" as he put it, at a theater in Riverside, California. It was a revelation to him. "I was amazed," he told an interviewer much later. "This was a picture about things I had done in nightclubs from my old days working with my brother. I knew it well, I knew it was sleaziness and cheap clubs. I was a walking encyclopedia on this. But it wasn't translating well." When dwelling on this over the next few weeks Gene came to realize how ignorant he had been about dealing with the camera as a medium for dance. The process of filming movement was not as simple as he had imagined. The same movements performed on stage simply did not work on film.[27] Nobody had brought this up during rehearsal or filming, and Gene concluded that there was a general lack of awareness or interest in the problem. Gene soon decided he had to stay in Hollywood and meet this intriguing artistic challenge head-on.

Kelly certainly was guilty of overacting in some scenes, especially those that emphasized the brassiness of Harry Palmer, but other people also overact at times in this film. It has an over-the-top emotionalism that can carry you along one moment and seems overdone the next.

While John Updike has argued that Judy carried the movie, others firmly believed that Gene stole the show. "Kelly is amazingly fresh," wrote Pauline Kael, "his grin could melt stone." Jeanine Basinger thought that "the role of Harry Palmer was tailor-made for Kelly." All agreed that Murphy would have been wrongly cast as the hero of this film. "I can remember sitting up and taking notice the moment he [Kelly] began to dance," wrote John K. Newnham four years after its release. "His acting was a trifle brash, maybe, but it was obvious that he was a newcomer worthy of attention."[28]

For Me and My Gal was a stunning financial and critical success. It cost nearly $803,000 but grossed $4,371,000 during its initial release.[29] Selznick could not have offered Gene a vehicle remotely like this, so well suited to his talents. Not only would Harry Palmer be the closest to Joey Evans of his many future film roles that mimicked the Broadway character, but from the very beginning of his movie career Gene was involved in supporting the war effort. Released less than a year after Pearl Harbor, *For Me and My Gal* was more relevant to the audience as a World War II movie than as a World War I film. Despite Crowther's complaint about the bizarre plot twist, it worked for most viewers.

"I found myself a star in Hollywood," Gene recalled. "It seemed very quick." The title number was released as a single by Decca Records and reached number two on the *Billboard* chart.[30] Any doubts about Kelly's vocal abilities should have been quelled by success like this, but Gene continued to be very modest about his singing.

On March 22, 1943, Kelly and Garland performed a half-hour radio version of *For Me and My Gal*, sponsored by Screen Guild Theatre. This is one of thirty radio programs we listened to that Gene participated in from 1943 to 1959 (see appendix for full list). Dick Powell substituted for George Murphy, who had the measles. The show focused on the highlights of the film. Both Gene and Judy read their lines *exactly* as in the movie and were very much on cue. Only the last scene was changed, with more lines added to compensate for the lack of visuals, but it missed the impact of the film's less verbose but emotionally satisfying ending. Another thirteen-minute radio program to promote the film included only the songs, which Garland, Kelly, and Murphy sang live on radio, and Garland introduced Kelly as "from the New York stage" to tie in to his *Pal Joey* fame.

Gene changed his mind about California. "I didn't like Hollywood at all at first," he confided to interviewer Dale Pollock in 1984. "I never thought I'd be in the movies for long." But his first film created a deep interest in pictures.

Kelly remained devoted to the theater, but he could not resist dealing "with all the intricacies of translating dance to film. There were so many inventive things to do with it that I was determined to stay in movies."[31]

The urge to go back to New York and choreograph shows surfaced now and then, but M-G-M would not hear of it. The studio recognized Kelly's potential after his first outing. William Saroyan tried hard to pull Kelly back to the theater. During the filming of *For Me and My Gal,* Saroyan talked to Gene about his new script for the stage, *Get Away Old Man*. He wanted Kelly to play the main character, a screenwriter who challenges "the old man." Saroyan did not tell Gene why he wrote the play. M-G-M had bought Saroyan's novel *The Human Comedy* for a hefty $50,000 and also allowed him to work on the screenplay and to coproduce the picture. They refused to let him direct it, however, based on his terrible direction of a one-reel film done as a test. As his "revenge," Saroyan wrote *Get Away Old Man*, in which, as Saroyan's biographer writes, the "egomaniac Jewish studio head was clearly Mayer." The play opened in November 1943 to scathing reviews—"vicious caricature," "bile and buffoonery do not blend well"—and it closed in one week, a complete failure. Fortunately for Kelly, he did not get involved in this abysmal venture even though Saroyan tried to tempt him by suggesting that Betsy could play the female lead. It is possible that Gene read the script and was turned off by the vicious tone. In any case, he simply claimed he was too busy, and Saroyan finally accepted Kelly at his word, saying, "naturally the studio will very much want to keep you busy . . . which isn't such a bad thing for you at that."[32]

PILOT NO. 5 (1943)

In fact, M-G-M put Kelly in a dramatic role next in *Pilot No. 5*. Gene was pleased because it gave him a chance to show his acting ability.[33]

The film was a potboiler that mixed commentary on political corruption with early war sacrifice in the Pacific conflict. Set during the Japanese conquest of the Dutch East Indies, five pilots are available to fly one plane for a possibly suicidal attack on the enemy fleet, and a Dutch officer has to decide which one to select. Franchot Tone starred as a lawyer corrupted by politics but eager to atone for his past. Gene played his friend, Vito Alessandro, who had flirted with corruption as well. Vito is angry, callous, and opportunistic but becomes better by the end of the film, somewhat in the nature of Harry Palmer. Kelly's character loves Tone's fiancée (played by Marsha Hunt) but sacrifices his feelings to help the two reconnect after a long separation and get married. Van Johnson played one of the other pilots. Only Kelly and Tone portrayed multi-dimensional characters in this one-dimensional plot, filmed immediately after Gene's work in *For Me and My Gal.* George Sidney directed his first film with *Pilot No. 5*. He would direct Kelly in three more movies in the near future—*Thousands Cheer* (1943), *Anchors Aweigh* (1945), and *The Three Musketeers* (1948).

Betsy recalled that Gene was very excited during the filming. He remembered what Berkeley had done in his previous picture and watched carefully as Sidney lined up the camera to catch mood, emotion, and atmosphere. He also began to think about how to do this while filming dances and was convinced it had to be done in full figure with no cuts.[34] For all its banal effects and forgettable drama, *Pilot No. 5* played an important role in the development of Kelly's views on filmmaking. He was learning how to direct for the camera and how to master the technology of cinema.

Gene still had not mastered the finer points of acting for the camera. Years later he admitted a continual problem of overacting in this movie. He felt that he was fine in long shots but could not master the close-ups. "On Broadway I was a damned good actor. I could hit that fourth balcony without any trouble at all. But I needed to *see* three thousand pairs of eyes to do it. On the screen it was a different story altogether."[35] He clearly missed the contact with an audience, which was a central aspect of his stage performances ever since his Pittsburgh days. It would take some time for Gene to learn to perform before a camera.

Pilot No. 5 was released on June 24, 1943, nearly a year after it finished filming. It was a cheap movie churned out to fill the slots in the studio's string of movie theaters where one picture after another was shown. In fact, movie viewership soared during the war years, and simplistic films like this were mainstream viewing. Nevertheless, Dore Schary, who later succeeded Mayer as head of M-G-M, wrote in his autobiography that the picture received "excellent reviews." Author Tony Thomas wrote that Kelly's performance surprised and impressed those who considered him mainly a dancer. One viewer who liked Gene's acting enormously was David Selznick. He "was very pleased with and proud of you," Selznick wrote in a congratulatory note. "I think you would be an acting sensation if only they could forget that you know how to hoof." Gene was very happy with the letter, saying it "was better than a week's salary." Calling Selznick "the tycoon with a heart," he assured him that he and Betsy "love you dearly."[36]

DU BARRY WAS A LADY (1943)

Kelly was assigned next to create the role of Alec Howe/Black Arrow in *Du Barry Was a Lady*. The film was based on a popular stage musical of the same name by Cole Porter. It ran for 408 performances from December 6, 1939, to December 12, 1940, with Hugh Martin doing the choral arrangements and Ethel Merman and Bert Lahr starring.

Du Barry Was a Lady was at best a fluffy bit of entertainment rather typical of Porter's work. Gene was less than enthusiastic about the prospect. He asked Freed, "Why are you doing this?" before starting production. Freed told him the studio owned the rights, wanted to recoup something on its investment, and assigned it to him, so he had no choice.[37] Gene did his best, but the vehicle offered him no opportunities to experiment or innovate. Pitched as a comedic vehicle for Red Skelton and Lucille Ball, Kelly was just along for the ride.

While Gene could not work on the problems of conveying dance on film in this project, he certainly could do the best job possible of executing the little dancing assigned to him. But he ran afoul of Seymour Felix, who had been a dance director in Hollywood since 1933. Twenty years older than Kelly, Felix had an old-fashioned attitude toward dancing on the screen that Gene could not accept. Kelly called Johnny Darrow in New York to see if Robert Alton could be secured to replace Felix, but Gene's mentor was busy working on two Broadway shows. So Gene asked Darrow for Charles Walters instead. Darrow not only was Walters's agent and best friend but also shared a house with him at the time. Walters had been in only one movie so far, concentrating on stage performance and choreography for most of his career. Gene had a habit of calling him "Charlie," which Walters did not like, but there was plenty of mutual respect between the two and Walters agreed to replace Felix.[38]

This move not only pleased Kelly but started a long film career for Walters. The new dance director studied the script to understand the context and characterizations. He developed an insightful idea about how Gene could transition from singing a love song to Lucille Ball's character, May Daly, in a dressing room to a spirited stage performance, both set to Porter's "Do I Love You." He wanted Gene to start the dance immediately after leaving the dressing room, building up to the point where he jumps triumphantly onto the nightclub stage with something to dance about—May's admitting her love for Alec. When Walters told Freed of his idea, the producer was impressed. He thought it sounded like a director rather than a choreographer.[39] Gene's singing of "Do I Love You" was his first solo song in a movie. He sang very well—in tone, pitch, and emotion.

Gene's only real dance in the movie was to "Do I Love You." Ironically, after being instrumental in bringing Walters on board as dance director, Kelly was allowed by Freed to choreograph and shoot his own number because Walters was busy choreographing and shooting the other numbers.[40]

Keeping in mind Walter's suggestion to start the number as he comes out of May's dressing room, Kelly had Alec run out of the room filled with excitement that May loves him. The next bit involved the breaking of a racial taboo that was little noticed. Alec encounters May's African American maid, Niagara (played by Louise Beavers), and does a spirited little dance with her—a one-way dance, admittedly, for Niagara is so stunned at his behavior that she does not respond at first. But he touches her arms and dances with her and her face lights up with a smile. In these few moments, Kelly created a little instance of racial equality rarely seen in films of that era. It presaged his dance with the Nicholas Brothers to come in *The Pirate* (1948).

For his remaining choreography, Alec waves jauntily to Niagara, runs to the auditorium, jumps over a chair and onto the stage, and performs his dance with spirit. Gene starts his main number with balletic steps (as in *Pal Joey*), then dances with a chorus of twenty girls, ending the routine with the Crab Bounce. But this time he bounces under a semicircular line of the chorus girls, each girl jumping over him as he approaches them in a fascinating display of coordination and daring. What could have happened if someone mistimed her jump is painful to contemplate. Also, in the middle of the dance, Gene jumps over two of the girls in one leap, demonstrating his talent for athletic stunts on the dance floor.

While filming "Do I Love You" Gene became a father. Betsy's doctor had arranged for a bed at Good Samaritan Hospital with a plan to induce labor because hospital beds were hard to come by during the war. Her mother Frederica Boger had taken leave from teaching in New Jersey to be with her. The plan was to induce labor on October 16, 1942, but Gene had to be on the set that day to film his big number. A newspaper reporter who was present noticed how nervously Gene worked with the chorus girls. "There I was, dancing for the cameras, and there she was, having a baby," Kelly recalled. "I was so nervous I kept missing cues and delaying production. It wasn't until ten o'clock that night that I wound up the routine and headed for the hospital." Betsy was a little short of nineteen when daughter Kerry was born that day. Three days later, one of Selznick's staff members found out about

Figure 6.4 Singing his first solo in a film. (Still from *Du Barry Was a Lady*, 1943)

Figure 6.5 Most unusual for the time, Kelly is dancing with and touching African American performer Louise Beaver. (Still from *Du Barry Was a Lady*, 1943)

the birth and sent flowers to "Betsy, Gene, and Kerry" with a card from the Selznicks.[41]

Betsy admitted that instead of growing up as a result of motherhood she continued to be a little girl pampered by her husband. "I spent my adolescence as a married woman and was completely happy." With hindsight, Blair remembered feeling like "the eldest daughter in a motherless house." At the time, however, she had no thought of resentment or rebellion about her life with Kelly. "I was delighted to be taken care of, spoiled, adored."[42]

To make life easier for Betsy, Gene created charge accounts everywhere—the grocery store, the drugstore, the bookstore, the gas station, department stores, and dry cleaners. He created a joint checking account so Betsy could spend $100 a week freely. In New York, Betsy was used to saving half her $35 weekly salary in a bank. Now, "I quickly developed the knack of never thinking about money at all," wrote this well-to-do woman who claimed to be a communist.[43]

Filming of *Du Barry Was a Lady* wrapped up fairly quickly after Kerry's birth. Gene participated in the closing number, set to Porter's song "Friendship." There was movement but no real dancing in this number staged by Walters. "I just did my own individual shtick which will not shake immortality to its timbers," Gene later said of not only this number but the entire picture. The film was released on August 13, 1943, to roaring box-office success. Costing a little over $1,239,000, it grossed $3,496,000. Financial success failed to create any sense of artistic fulfillment for Kelly. He later called *Du Barry Was a Lady* an "atrocious" film.[44]

Du Barry is by no stretch of the imagination a good movie, but it does have some entertaining elements. Skelton and Ball were old pros by this time, and their scenes together work well. The storyline is strong and makes sense, but Freed inserted many irrelevant numbers and performances by people who were not characters in the movie. This is what takes away from the integrity of the film and colored Gene's evaluation of it. *Du Barry* is far from the integrated musical that Kelly achieved consistently in his career.

Kelly sang "Do I Love You" effectively, and his dance to the same song was spectacular. In terms of his character, Alec Howe is not like Joey Evans or Harry Palmer. He is a good-hearted and loving person with no need of redemption. Even as the Black Arrow (Alec's character in Red Skelton's dream of living in the age of France's King Louis XV), Gene is effective. He sings a rabble-rousing song to incite the peasants to revolt against the king, only to be stopped by the French army and slated for beheading. He performed all his scenes well. Yet, Kelly was capable of doing far more than this potboiler offered him in terms of both acting and dancing.

THOUSANDS CHEER (1943)

Gene was put into *Thousands Cheer* immediately after finishing *Du Barry Was a Lady*. He had been tentatively slated to do a film version of the stage musical *As Thousands Cheer* even before coming to Hollywood, and the studio finally was ready for it. Irving Berlin had written the music and Moss Hart the book for this musical revue, which played on Broadway from September 30, 1933, to September 8, 1934. The original screenplay was only about a soldier, a girl, and her army father, estranged from his wife. But producer Joseph Pasternak enlisted many M-G-M entertainers to do skits as part of a huge show that the main characters put on at an army camp. Kelly engaged scriptwriter Isobel Lennart in numerous conversations about the screenplay. She recalled that he had many good ideas and was interested in making the whole film better rather than embellishing his own part in it.[45]

Pasternak helped Gene with his role in the film. Born and raised in Transylvania, Pasternak had worked from the ground up in Hollywood to become a producer at M-G-M. He gave Kelly sage advice: "You want to steal the movie? All you have to do is one dance that is new and original. Everyone else is doing their usual 'shtik'—you be different." So Gene developed the famous Mop Dance, staged while his character was assigned extra duty cleaning up the post exchange. "I used where I was and I used the props that were there," he recalled. It was the first time in his career that he experimented with a concept termed "bricolage"—incorporating props into a dance routine. Fred Astaire had already used bricolage in his numbers, so the Mop Dance was an innovation only in Kelly's personal career. But film scholar Jane Feuer later observed that whereas Astaire seemed to use props because no real partner could match his grace, Kelly used bricolage to display "good old American inventiveness."[46]

Kelly used both a mop and a broom, the former made up to resemble a woman. He developed a choreography that mixed ballroom dancing, tap dancing, and athletic stunts. Gene kicked a drum and two buckets, jumped on furniture, danced on the bar, drew soda from fountains, and wiggled empty glasses with spoons in them to make noises that were incorporated into the music of the number. Kelly danced briefly while sitting down, something he would do for "Moses Supposes" in *Singin' in the Rain*. In contrast, while lying on his back on a tabletop, he powerfully jumped up without using his arms to lift himself. He used this remarkable step later as well; we call it his Prone Jump. He also employed another of his favorite steps—the Airplane Propeller.

There is no doubt that the Mop Dance stole the movie from the many other entertainers who, as Pasternak aptly put it, did their old shtick. It is not true, as some previous biographers have stated, that this was the first time Kelly choreographed his own routine. He had been doing that ever since his first number in his first movie, as shown by the incorporation of his characteristic stunts and steps into all his numbers to date (as well as from Gene's many interviews over the years). Although working in films that had a dance director, Kelly was allowed from the start to be his own choreographer.

Unlike the joyful Mop Dance, the character he played (Eddie Marsh) was grumpy and angry, even with the girl he loved, played by Kathryn Grayson. Eddie had been brought up by the Flying Corbinos, a family of aerialists, and had a good deal of difficulty adjusting to army life. Once again, Gene had to portray an outlier in society. His regimental colonel asked the Corbinos to remind Eddie how important teamwork was just before they perform at the army show. Once again, his bad-boy character was redeemed in the end.

Despite his athletic dancing, Kelly was reluctant to do dangerous stunts for fear of hurting himself and ruining his dance career. A stunt double was hired for Gene's performance on the high wire "because the guy did a double somersault without a net (laughter), and I can't do that!"[47]

Overall there is little of redeeming value in *Thousands Cheer* except for Kelly's performance. The plot is weak and there is little character development. The film is somewhat redeemed by the huge camp show that takes up nearly half the movie. But some of the comedy routines are awful and many musical numbers are not very good. Only the Spanish dance by Maxine Barrat and Don Loper is a standout, but it is overshadowed by dross.

Yet the film became very popular soon after premiering on September 13, 1943. Reviewers recognized the banality but singled out Kelly as the highlight. Latter-day commentators always mentioned Kelly's Mop Dance as the high point of the film. John Russell Taylor and Arthur Jackson noted "the bouncy ebullience, the broad humour (always a nudge in the audience's ribs), [and] the slightly over-emphatic masculinity" that would come to characterize so many of Gene's film performances. But as Jeanine Basinger wrote, the Mop Dance hardly fits the character of Eddie Marsh. It "comes out of nowhere" much as the many M-G-M performers come out of nowhere for the camp

Figure 6.6 In an outstandingly acrobatic routine, Kelly starts with gentle ballroom dance steps with a mop, posed to look like a girl. (Still from *Thousands Cheer*, 1943)

show.[48] In *For Me and My Gal* and *Du Barry Was a Lady*, Gene's dances made sense within the context of his character development and the plot. But lack of continuity in character and plot were common failings of Pasternak's films compared to those that Freed produced.

LIFE AT HOME

The steady pace of Kelly's work for M-G-M during the shared contract period allowed him enough time for a social life. With their move to the huge North Alta house in Beverly Hills, Gene and Betsy actually had room to invite people over, and they held "a kind of open house every Saturday night." At 5:30 P.M., guests streamed in to play ping-pong or a particularly competitive game of charades, with Gene captaining one team and Betsy another. After that there was impromptu entertainment by the guests; sometimes Gene would dance, but mostly everyone sang songs around the piano until one or two in the morning.[49]

The Kellys developed their own social life in Hollywood. They were rarely invited to the upper-crust parties. "We were the working stiffs," according to Gene. But Kelly was glad to be excluded. He was uncomfortable with superficial interactions. "I'm sure a lot of people considered me anti-social, which I wasn't. It's just that my social life took place in my home." As Betsy accurately put it, her husband "had no pretensions, no 'society' aspirations."[50]

Writers for the fan magazines recognized that Gene was different from typical Hollywood stars. "Kelly's a quiet-mannered guy, who thinks more than he talks and smiles more with his eyes than his mouth. He is sensitive, gentle, well-bred, well-read." Surrounded by pine paneling on the walls and nineteenth-century English-style chairs and table, Gene was correctly presented as a serious-minded man who could "talk intelligently on any subject." To further promote his regular-guy image, the studio sent a photographer to take pictures depicting their home life. Gene played with Kerry while Betsy borrowed an apron from their housekeeper Mamie and pretended to cook.[51]

All the stories about the Kellys were positive, but one reporter went against the trend. When Kerry was only six months old, gossip host Jimmy Fidler announced on his radio program that Kelly had moved into a hotel, leaving his wife and daughter. Actually the couple had gone to a friend's house to help with a new baby. Gene initially laughed at this miscue by Fidler, but when friends and family members began calling, he became angry. He considered filing a lawsuit against Fidler but was persuaded not to do so. M-G-M, however, barred Fidler from the studio from that point on.[52]

By the middle of 1943, Kelly was beginning to be recognized on the street, and Gene Kelly fan clubs were popping up across the country. The studio kept in close touch with these clubs, sending out portfolios of publicity photographs when the clubs had at least ten members. Several of Kelly's publicity photographs are preserved in the New York Public Library. These photos supposedly were autographed by Gene, but Betsy revealed in her memoirs that he signed one that was then copied by a studio employee on the photos sent out. This was common practice at the studio for all its stars.[53]

SELZNICK GIVES UP KELLY TO M-G-M

When Selznick shared Gene's contract with M-G-M back in mid-February 1942, he retained an option to use his new star in one film during the year. Only a month later, Selznick complained to O'Shea that his father-in-law's studio had "out-traded and out-smarted us" by keeping Kelly too busy. In April 1942, he suggested to Mayer that Kelly could be the new Dr. Kildare in a continuing series of films after Lew Ayres dropped out. He urged Mayer to make a test of Kelly for the role.[54] Gene was busy with *For Me and My Gal* at the time.

Just eight months later in October 1942, Selznick became worried that his option on Kelly would run out before he found a suitable role for him. He waited for the reviews of *For Me and My Gal* in order to gauge the critical reaction; he was greatly encouraged when those reviews praised Kelly's performance. During the war Hollywood was making more movies about servicemen than ever. Selznick reconsidered Gene for the project Kay Brown had mentioned to Kelly earlier called "Sailor and a Girl" opposite Jennifer Jones, Dorothy McGuire, K. T. Stevens, or Joan Tetzel. He also liked the idea of placing him as the star in "The Life of Gershwin."[55]

None of Selznick's ideas worked out. He seemed unclear as to the terms for sharing Kelly with M-G-M and wondered if Selznick International could force Gene "out of a picture to which he has been assigned." O'Shea told him it was not possible and also that they had to give M-G-M notice of their intent to use Kelly in a film thirty days before the starting date of the production. But Selznick was not thinking of placing Gene in a production of his own because he essentially was out of the moviemaking business for the time being. In fact, Selznick was trying to sell Kelly's services to other studios at a profit. He initially offered Gene to Twentieth Century-Fox for $40,000, but after seeing how "absolutely wonderful" and "irreplaceable" Kelly was in *For Me and My Gal* Selznick thought a better price would be $75,000 or even $100,000.[56]

Because M-G-M was assigning Kelly to project after project, Selznick finally tried to sell his interest in the actor's contract to that studio for $100,000. Eddie Mannix—now convinced of Gene's worth in front of the camera—played hardball with Selznick. He insisted on adhering strictly to the contract terms concerning how and when Selznick could use Kelly, while taking his time to consider the offer to purchase the rest of Kelly's contract. Bennie Thau at M-G-M warned Selznick that Kelly was reclassified as 1-A by the local draft board, and therefore would be eligible for service very soon. Selznick thought that M-G-M knew this all along and had withheld the information from him. It was part of that studio's "machinations," he concluded, "even more macheavillian [*sic*] than I figured out." To Selznick, it all amounted to efforts by his father-in-law's company to prevent Selznick International from using Kelly at all. But when he called Gene, Kelly told him his classification actually was 3-A, which meant a deferment from service because he was a father.[57]

"I think we should put a note on our calendars not to get pushed around further on Gene Kelly," Selznick told O'Shea on December 19, 1942. When Mannix offered $75,000 for the rest of Gene's contract, Selznick was in no mood to agree. He wanted O'Shea to take the lead in tough negotiations with M-G-M. Selznick "had such unpleasantness at Metro on the Kelly situation originally" that he did not want to be involved in talks personally, especially with Mayer. He laid out possible terms—sell Gene's contract for a suitable amount of cash or receive as compensation another actor, director, or movie project from M-G-M.[58]

To help O'Shea's negotiations, Selznick wrote a strong letter to Mannix on January 27, 1943: "We made what in my opinion is the worst deal we have ever made on a personality when we gave you Kelly exclusively with the exception of one picture yearly, in order to secure for him a part in a picture which turned out much better than it had promised." Selznick was referring to *For Me and My Gal*, in which Gene created a dicey character for a war movie. Harry Palmer "was calculated to ruin a new personality just as much as to make him." But Gene pulled it off brilliantly, and M-G-M took advantage of the success. "You have already used Kelly in many more pictures than you contemplated and have received benefits from him far beyond those which you anticipated, whereas we have yet to receive our first dividend."[59] Selznick was tired of this outcome, which he saw as the result of M-G-M's tactics.

Mannix was willing to talk. Even as he advised Selznick that Gene was slated for several projects, including "Marriage Is a Private Affair" and "Army Chaplain," he agreed to a lunch meeting so "the Kelly matter can be thrashed out." They came to an understanding that was finalized by February 13, 1943, whereby M-G-M would buy out the rest of Gene's contract for $85,000. Gene became an exclusive employee of M-G-M for the next dozen years. A year later, Selznick told O'Shea that he should remind the studios that had not been interested in Kelly as a loan-out "of their lack of foresight and faith in our judgment."[60]

Selznick's fortunes declined soon after he let Gene go. He dissolved Selznick International Pictures in 1943 and replaced it with Vanguard Films the next year, producing a total of eight films over the next four years. But his financial troubles continued. By 1945 he was $9.5 million in debt.[61]

Despite the fact that Selznick was never able to use Gene in one of his productions, or even loan him out to another studio except M-G-M, the maverick producer played an important role in Kelly's early film career. It was Selznick, not M-G-M, who convinced Gene to try Hollywood. Selznick's deep sense of competition with M-G-M worked to Kelly's benefit. In the end,

Gene found his true home in Hollywood at M-G-M. While he did nothing for Selznick other than make two screen tests, he played a major role in no less than four films with M-G-M within just one year.

THE CROSS OF LORRAINE (1943)

By the time M-G-M bought out the rest of his contract, Gene was involved in his fifth project for the studio. *The Cross of Lorraine* was a significant departure for his career. This movie follows the trials of five French prisoners incarcerated by the Germans when France fell in the spring of 1940. Kelly portrayed Victor, the only character in the movie with more than one dimension, offering Gene an opportunity to act with a range of emotions and attitudes. His character is the most angry and defiant of the group and is therefore subject to cruel torture and beatings by the Germans that temporarily break his spirit. Gene goes from a strong, violent man to a shattered one, displaying his tortured and mutilated face in close-ups. A prison break leads several members of the group into the French countryside, but they are caught in a village whose residents are being rounded up as laborers by the German army. Victor snaps out of his passivity and depression after witnessing the cruelties of these soldiers. He leads the villagers in a savage revolt, killing the Germans and streaming into the countryside to join the French Resistance.

The Cross of Lorraine belongs to a class of war movies in which emotion overrides everything. Characters and incidents are blown up bigger than life. While the Germans treated conquered peoples with horrible brutality, the truth is that the 1.8 million French military prisoners taken into custody during the spring of 1940 were mostly treated humanely. The majority were released to work as agricultural and industrial laborers, and 73,000 escaped. But reality was less important than the overwhelming need to arouse the American spirit to fight evil—and Kelly played his part in this with gusto. His tendency to overact worked well in a picture in which director Tay Garnett encouraged overacting by everyone.

Released on November 12, 1943, the film garnered good reviews with praise for Kelly's performance, and made a small profit for M-G-M. "I thought I did quite well in the first half," Gene said, "but missed towards the end." Kelly was not satisfied with his close-ups; they "just weren't registering what I wanted them to." Yet he recalled having fun during the filming. He did not have to "wear any make-up" or "bother about shaving," and "it was great pleasure to be able to get dirty without having the wardrobe department jump down your throat."[62]

COVER GIRL (1944)

Having used Kelly in five films in a little more than one year, and securing his full contract from Selznick, M-G-M now loaned him to Columbia for a musical called *Cover Girl.* The impetus for this loan started when Columbia bid for the rights to *Best Foot Forward*, which Freed was keen on producing. M-G-M worked out a deal to pay Columbia $25,000 *not* to bid for the rights to *Best Foot Forward* (so M-G-M could buy them) and the loan of Kelly for one film.[63]

The loan-out to Columbia was a turning point in Gene's career. He had done some good work in those first five projects but had no opportunity to experiment with creating the kind of dances that were uniquely suited to a movie camera. He barely had time to begin developing a distinctive dance style of any kind other than to mainly replicate in his first three musicals what he had been doing for years. If he wanted to make a distinctive mark in film, Kelly needed leeway to experiment, an opportunity to influence more than just his own dances, and a supportive studio administration to provide the money necessary to realize his dreams.

Ironically, he found all that at Columbia, which was one of the smaller top-rated studios in Hollywood. It was not noted for making dance films, and a tough executive tightly controlled the studio. Harry Cohn was a New Yorker who had worked his way up from being a song plugger to controlling a major studio. Cohn developed a bruising managerial style, regularly insulting and challenging employees to see how they reacted. If they fought back, he respected them. If they continued to argue passionately for their needs when he routinely said no the first time, he assumed they knew what they were doing and approved. Cohn kept a tight rein on his limited assets and could be overbearing one minute, supportive the next.[64]

Kelly came to understand and appreciate Cohn. "There was a toughness and an honesty about Cohn which I liked," he recalled. "I may have recognized something of myself in him—especially in my tough early Pittsburgh days. . . . I think I understood him better than most people." Gene knew that Cohn was the chief and had to be convinced of everything before the innovations he wanted to create in *Cover Girl* could be attempted. While he crafted these innovations at Columbia, he had to fight tooth and nail for every opportunity. And Gene had to put up with insults as well. One day Cohn called him into his office to complain that Gene was stealing scenes from his costar, Rita Hayworth. Kelly exploded with anger. He had been trying to do just the opposite—crafting dances that would enhance her native ability—and he threatened to punch Cohn in the face. His boss quickly gave in: "Of course you're making Rita look good. I just wanted to see what you'd say."[65]

Hayworth was a wonderful partner for Gene. He had studied with her uncle, Angel Cansino, who had told him about Rita when they socialized in Chicago. Trained in Spanish dancing, Hayworth had enough familiarity with ballet to handle almost any type of dance style. She excelled in ballroom movements, and Gene regretted that they could not work a ballroom dance into the movie. They do dance briefly in that style to "Long Ago and Far Away" and Kelly admired her ability to move fluidly. "She can bend and sway and follow like a part of you," he wrote of her.[66]

Kelly also worked for the first time with Phil Silvers on *Cover Girl*. They became instant friends and supported each other on the screen beautifully. A year older than Gene, Phil had been performing ever since he was a child but appeared in his first picture only in 1942. *Cover Girl* was his big break, and Silvers claimed that Kelly talked Cohn into signing him for the movie, taking him away from Twentieth Century-Fox. Gene insisted that Phil join him and Rita in at least one major number even though Silvers had never danced.[67]

Gene, Rita, and Phil formed a powerful onscreen trio that underpinned the plot and emotions of *Cover Girl*. They were strongly supported by Saul Chaplin, a musician who had worked for Cohn for many years. Chaplin's experience was typical of the industry. His job was to write songs for particular moments in a film and no one told him why it made sense within the plot flow or character development; they were just inserted for entertainment purposes. But Gene was different. He told Saul all about the plot, the characters as he saw them, the set, and the need for a particular mood in a particular place. Chaplin at first was overwhelmed, but Kelly made it simple for him: "Look—make Phil as funny as you can and don't worry about me. I'll take care of myself." Saul was very impressed and excited. "I had never met such an unselfish actor," he wrote of Gene. They ended up working together for many years. Chaplin recalled that Kelly's "attitude never changed. He was always concerned with the entire project and was indeed capable of taking care of himself."[68]

Saul recalled coming to work in the morning and hearing gales of laughter from Gene, Rita, and Phil in the rehearsal hall. The trio clicked off screen as well as they did on camera. Gene and Phil constantly teased Rita, and she enjoyed every minute of it, creating the right kind of atmosphere for moviemaking.[69]

Kelly's ability to shape the filming of *Cover Girl* extended far beyond merely making its female star happy. For the first time in his film career, Gene tried to influence every aspect of the project. He wanted *Cover Girl* to be as light as possible but director Charles Vidor had an opposing view. Chaplin characterized Vidor as "humorless." He had also never directed a musical before. He and Kelly often argued on the set, even engaging in a fistfight one day over their different visions for the picture.[70]

Neither man fully won their struggle for control. *Cover Girl* has a strange mixture of light and dark—a melding of sad, bittersweet, and hopeful moods that mark it as unique among film musicals. Its exuberant numbers appear as desperate efforts to push back the doubts and anxieties that lie at the heart of the plot. Gloom and hope seem to contend for control of the movie.

But *Cover Girl* starts with a bit of wry humor. Gene did not like "The Show Must Go On," an ensemble number by the showgirls in his character's nightclub, which had been filmed before he signed on. Cohn refused to drop it, so Kelly filmed scenes of his character watching the number from the wings, shaking his head, and wincing.[71] It was a clever way to make use of the number.

Gene worked hard to create his character, Danny McGuire, a nightclub owner in love with his star performer Rusty Parker (played by Hayworth). He tackled a love ballad, "Long Ago and Far Away," written for the film by composer Jerome Kern and lyricist Ira Gershwin. Kelly was self-conscious of his limited singing ability, especially when it came to lyrical ballads, but by concentrating on the emotion he delivered the song with great success. Kelly had to record it the old-fashioned way—still used at Columbia—singing while wearing headphones in a booth a hundred feet from the orchestra. He came out of the booth ready to apologize to Kern for his limitations, but the composer liked it very much. Gene went on to make three more takes but Kern insisted on using the first one. The song ran for twenty weeks on radio's *Your Hit Parade* after *Cover Girl*'s release and was nominated for an Academy Award for Best Song.[72]

It is interesting that Kelly segued into the song by first humming the tune as he did later for "Singin' in the Rain." Even as early as this movie, Gene was reluctant to insert songs and dances into the film in an artificial way and worked to make the transitions natural and believable.

On May 4, 1944, Kelly was a guest on NBC's "Kraft Music Hall," a thirty-minute show hosted by Bing Crosby. Crosby and Kelly sang a comedy song together and plugged *Cover Girl*. But unfortunately, instead of Gene singing "Long Ago and Far Away," Bing sang it, and it fell far short of the emotional impact of Gene's rendering.

"Make Way for Tomorrow" became the major dance number performed by the trio. Gene had to argue with Cohn to break down the walls between two soundstages to create a long street scene. He wanted room for a traveling number expressive of their characters' friendship and hope for the future. Kern and Gershwin had written the song for the Allied war effort, but it fit the trio perfectly. Gene's innovation with the set broke many film-dance conventions. It destroyed the sense of a proscenium arch and opened up the dance space enormously. And Gene's choreography brought the trio along by incorporating many street features as props, representing his second foray into bricolage. He had the three of them bouncing along, jumping up and down steps, and using trash cans as well as a passing milkman as divertissements in the dance flow. It was a brilliant piece of film staging and "became a very big factor in a lot of later dancing that I did," Kelly said. In his view, "movement and space" were the keys to the number.[73]

Phil Silvers had never danced before, and the studio was reluctant to let him. But Gene insisted, saying, "Phil will dance because I'm going to show him how, and make steps to fit him." He choreographed the number to accommodate Phil's limited dancing skills, coached and encouraged him to learn, and assigned Stanley Donen to drill him in the lessons. Donen had moved to California and secured a small role in the chorus of Freed's *Best Foot Forward* (1943). He then helped with dance rehearsals for M-G-M musicals but refused when told to fill in as an extra, believing it was beneath his dignity. M-G-M fired him and Gene brought him over to Columbia to help with *Cover Girl*, saving Donen's Hollywood career. Silvers "worked on the edge of embarrassment and anger; dancing does require a special physical skill and Gene forced me to keep up with him and Rita." It was tough, but Silvers persisted. "I couldn't fake it. In the end I had a great feeling of accomplishment: I felt I could do anything."[74]

Betsy Blair thought that Gene had Dick Dwenger in mind in creating "Make Way for Tomorrow." They had not seen Dwenger since leaving New York for California, but both always remembered him with love. Dwenger

Figure 6.7 Kelly with Rita Hayworth, Phil Silvers, and an unnamed specialty dancer as the milkman in the joyful number "Make Way for Tomorrow." (Still from *Cover Girl*, 1944)

also had played the key role in getting Betsy and Gene together as a couple. "All the warmth and fun and friendship we had is there in those scenes," Blair wrote. Tragically Dwenger died only a few months after the number was filmed and before *Cover Girl* was released. Married to a Broadway dancer named Flower Hujer in June 1942, Dwenger soon after joined the Navy Reserve. He was serving as a yeoman first class on the destroyer *USS Buck* when a German U-boat torpedoed it off the coast of Italy near Salerno on October 9, 1943. Dwenger was among ninety-seven crewmen lost. Initially listed as missing in action, his body was never found, and in October 1944 he was reclassified as killed in action.[75]

Gene never gave any indication that "Make Way for Tomorrow" was connected to his closest male friend. Even though it made Betsy feel good to think that Dwenger was the inspiration for this number, it does not seem to be the case. Had it been a tribute to Dwenger, Kelly would have mentioned it in his interviews over the years. More importantly, the number comes straight out of the storyline where three characters who are very good friends have great fun together. It also accurately reflects the fun and joy the three actors shared behind the scenes. The number naturally emerges from and reflects the story as well as the backstage reality.

Late in life when Kelly donated song sheets to Boston University, he scribbled his last public thought on "Make Way for Tomorrow": "What a pleasure to work on this number with Rita & Phil! We should have payed [*sic*] Harry Cohn for letting us do it!"[76]

This unusual number spiked audience attention in *Cover Girl*. It marked an important new path for Kelly's aesthetics, the first real effort to create a dance for film, the beginning of an inspired new kind of choreography, and the true beginning of a multitalented force to be reckoned with in cinema.

Kelly took the escalation of his achievement in *Cover Girl* to a new level when he created "Alter Ego," the most innovative dance number yet filmed in Hollywood. Cohn had told Kelly that he wanted a solo number for him in *Cover Girl*, so "I just dreamed it up," Gene said about "Alter Ego." "I sat down one day and said 'What can I do that I can't do on the stage?" and came up with the idea of dancing in tandem with himself. Kelly developed every aspect of the number, focusing it on the "emotional struggle" of Danny McGuire as he contemplates whether he should let Rusty Parker take a chance on a bigger career, risking the real possibility that he will lose her love as well. He conceived it as a "pure cine dance" on a deserted street at night—a fight between two opposing aspects of Danny's feelings for Rusty. How to sneak it into the film without rupturing the continuity was a problem, but Kelly solved it by introducing the theme slowly, starting with Danny noticing his reflection in the glass windows of shops along the street. It escalates into a confrontation—a fight within himself—expressed physically in a competitive dance between the character's two selves.[77] Kelly worked a fast Airplane Propeller into the dance, with both his images doing it simultaneously and exactly alike. All the steps are thoughtfully choreographed to show the intensity of emotion and the internal struggle, which capture the parameters of a dream ballet.

In filming the number, Kelly relied on Donen's help. According to Betsy, Gene "considered Stanley bright and talented, and recognized that he would need him" to guide the cameramen for "Alter Ego" as Gene himself would be dancing.[78]

Strangely, Donen's biographer Stephen Silverman claims that Stanley thought up the concept for "Alter Ego," but that is not true. Donen often claimed credit for Gene's ideas and work, and did so even in this case in some interviews. But Donen himself admitted in an interview with Ronald Davis

Figure 6.8 In "Alter Ego," innovative for its time, Kelly dances in "double" to show the conflict he feels about the Hayworth character. (Still from *Cover Girl*, 1944)

that it was Gene's idea, and that his own (Donen's) interest in technical aspects enabled him to help Kelly in the number. Moreover, Saul Chaplin, who was involved in creating the music for the number, has written that it was "Gene's concept from start to finish."[79]

Selling the dual-self concept to Cohn was not easy. Kelly cleared it with producer Arthur Schwartz and brought in an orchestrator for the music who Chaplin had recommended. Informed that no one had panned or dollied a camera in double exposure before, Gene gave it a lot of thought. "I just sat and thought all that out in an armchair, battling with myself like a writer." He came to believe it was possible and worked out a budget for nine days of filming. The concept was presented to Cohn, who reluctantly approved, while insisting that it be filmed after all other work on the picture had ended.[80]

Kelly choreographed the dance for both parts of himself in "Alter Ego," taught it to two assistants, Donen and Alex Romero, and let them dance the two parts, "so he could see what it would look like when it was filmed." Described by Chaplin as "a sweet, gentle man," Romero became one of Kelly's favorite dance assistants. Born in 1913 after his family moved to Texas (his given name was Alexander Bernard Quiroga), his father had been a Mexican general and politician. Romero taught himself how to tap dance as a teenager and performed ever since. He also developed into a good choreographer. Once Kelly was convinced the dance would work, he replaced Romero, who had other commitments, and danced with Donen. During the chase section of the number, Gene tried to get as close to Donen without catching him, but Donen was much slower than Kelly. "The air was constantly filled with 'Stanley, move your fat ass!'" recalled Chaplin. When sliding down a telephone pole, Gene was so quick that he practically sat on Donen's head by the time the two neared the floor.[81]

Because the number had to be filmed with a fixed-head camera, there was no wriggle room for Bernie Guffey, the cinematographer. Donen counted out the timings, keeping Guffey on track, as Kelly insisted on endless rehearsals so that dancer and crew were in synchronization. Because of this thorough preparation, the actual filming went pretty smoothly. Vidor was not interested and let the team of Kelly and Donen handle all the filming. The number had to be filmed twice to show Gene dancing in tandem with himself. Chalk and tape were used to mark where the camera should be for both sessions and to mark Kelly's steps for the first filming. The second filming was done with black velour draping the background so that only Gene would be photographed, and he had no marks on the floor to dance to. Thus Kelly had to sense where to step, but he accomplished it with great precision, according to Donen. It was "tortuous work," Gene recalled.[82]

For the climax of "Alter Ego," Kelly had to stand ten feet from a plate-glass window and throw a garbage can through it. Not only was this a dangerous stunt, with the possibility of glass shards flying in his direction, but there was a war on, and plate glass was not easy to come by. They could get no more than three plates. On the first try the can bounced off, merely cracking the glass. On the second try it shattered the plate, but not at the exact spot where the alter ego would appear on film. Splinters flew past Kelly, who protected himself with his hands. Fortunately for everyone, the third effort worked beautifully.[83]

After a month of preparation, ten days of filming, and an expense of $100,000, Gene had planned, choreographed, directed, and danced his five minutes of "Alter Ego." It was an impressive aesthetic and technical achievement, unmatched in film musicals to date. Much later he still said that it was "the most difficult thing I've ever done." But he gained immense satisfaction with the completion of this complex number that the best cameramen of the day said could not be done. Chaplin recalled that "Gene shot the number himself," meaning that Kelly lined up the camera angles and gave overall directions to the cameramen. Chaplin wrote further that "no one else could have shot it as well as Gene" because "he knew exactly what he wanted it to look like."[84]

What had started as a four-week loan-out for *Cover Girl* evolved into a four-month project. Gene started rehearsals in early April 1943 and began filming in May. "Alter Ego," the last segment to be filmed, was finished by early August. Months of postproduction followed. But when the picture was previewed at the Crown Theatre in Pasadena, the audience laughed at "Alter Ego," leading Cohn to insist it be cut from the release print. This remarkable number was saved when the manager of the theater told Cohn he had just shown *Flesh and Fantasy* before *Cover Girl* and that the other film included a sequence in which Edward G. Robinson talked to his own reflection in a store window. The coincidence was too much for the audience. Another preview was arranged and the audience loved the number.[85]

With its release on April 6, 1944, *Cover Girl* greatly impressed reviewers and drew a large popular audience. Critics highlighted Gene's dancing, singing, and acting, and also noted that Rita Hayworth danced far better than she had in earlier films. Many thought the two actors made a perfect onscreen couple. One Hayworth biographer wrote that Gene's dancing is remarkable and "the numbers choreographed by Kelly stand out in sharp contrast to the rest of the film." Later commentators continued to be impressed by Gene's performance, seeing it as a "giant-step forward" in his career. *Cover Girl* itself is viewed as a "major turning point" in "the history of the Hollywood musical."[86]

Because Kelly exerted so much influence on every aspect of *Cover Girl*, it became a more fully integrated piece than was typical of previous dance movies where the songs and numbers were pasted onto a thin plotline with little character development. Kelly made sure that the songs and dances made sense within the context of both plot and character, and he taught Chaplin how to write music with the whole project in mind. Because of Gene, *Cover Girl* marked the beginning (along with M-G-M's *Meet Me in St. Louis*, released the same year) of the Golden Age of Hollywood musicals. Kelly was undoubtedly the driving force behind the finished product, marking the movie as the start of his auteur status in film history.

Cover Girl also was the start of the Kelly-Donen collaboration, the first time that a choreographer (who was also the dancer) had full control not only of performance but also of cinematography (through his assistant helping the cameraman with timing the shots). It was a revelation and a revolution for Kelly. "Alter Ego" "really turned things around for me," he later said. "That's when I began to see that you could make dances for cinema that weren't just photographed stage dancing. That was my big insight into Hollywood." He was now hooked on filmmaking in California and gave up all thought of returning to New York.[87]

Unfortunately, Kelly would never have the opportunity to work for Columbia or with Hayworth again. He became the pawn in a struggle between Harry Cohn and Louis B. Mayer. After Gene's brilliant success with *Cover Girl*, M-G-M refused to loan Kelly out again even though Cohn very much wanted him for other films. In particular, Gene would have been perfect for the part of Daniel Miller in *Down to Earth*, once again paired with Rita. Cohn, who had purchased the rights to *Pal Joey* earlier, now wanted Gene to re-create his role on film, but that was never to be.[88] Frank Sinatra eventually played Joey Evans opposite Rita in Columbia's version of that stage classic; it was released in 1957 and fell very far short of doing justice to the original.

Kelly always wondered how different his career might have been if he had worked under a long-term contract for Columbia. Cohn gave him the freedom to do whatever he wanted but only after a tough battle over every penny spent. Gene also knew that if *Cover Girl* had not been successful, Cohn "would have kicked me in the derriére. That was . . . the reason I could never have been under long-term contract to him. He would have exhausted me long before I could have exhausted him." But Gene noted that M-G-M, because of *Cover Girl's* success, gave him much more latitude to craft films as he wished.[89]

In *Cover Girl*, Gene reverted to his early role as teacher and started a related role as mentor. He taught Saul Chaplin how to envision his music to fit with every other aspect of the film. He brought out Rita Hayworth's best dancing on the screen and jumpstarted a higher level in Phil Silvers's movie career. Kelly saved Donen's career by taking him on as an assistant at Columbia after he was fired by M-G-M. He also gave Donen his first job helping with camera work and pointed him toward his forté.

With his work on *Cover Girl*, Kelly offered a lesson to Hollywood on breaking the conventions surrounding dance musicals. "Alter Ego" is a major cine-dance that broke completely new ground. "Make Way for Tomorrow" is another cine-dance that greatly expanded the dance space and incorporated bricolage in interesting ways. Both numbers registered enormously with critics and viewers. Gene flowered as a multitalented entertainer, handling choreography, dancing, singing, acting, and shooting dance numbers with great success. Kelly had taken on Hollywood in 1942 and was winning two years later.

CHAPTER 7

Dancing Sailor, 1944–1946

When Gene returned to M-G-M in September 1943, the studio could not know what he had done in *Cover Girl* until the film was released seven months later. As a result, it tried to do the same thing with him that Selznick had futilely attempted—placing him in an ethnic role in a film set in China. This time it was *Dragon Seed*, an adaptation of a Pearl Buck novel about a family caught up in the Sino-Japanese War of the late 1930s. Gene was to portray Lao Er Tan and Katharine Hepburn was to play his Chinese wife. While Kelly was eager to work with Hepburn, the oriental makeup produced a terrible screen test. Kelly later joked that he looked like an Irish oriental. M-G-M traded him to Universal for one picture in exchange for Turhan Bey.[1] Hepburn and Bey performed in *Dragon Seed*, which was released in August 1944 and pretty quickly forgotten.

CHRISTMAS HOLIDAY (1944)

Universal wanted Kelly for a dramatic role in *Christmas Holiday*. Gene welcomed the chance to alternate between drama and musicals, afraid of being typed only as a hoofer. Astaire never deviated from his dance-film roles early in his career, but Kelly felt it was important to become a well-rounded performer.[2] In this film, he portrayed a disturbed character imprisoned for murder, who breaks out of jail and tries to kill his wife, played by Deanna Durbin. It was the first dramatic acting for Durbin.

To his credit, Gene did a fine job of playing a part very different from his onscreen roles. His character, Robert Manette, is the son of an old New Orleans family that has gone to seed. Overwhelmed by a dominating mother and addicted to gambling, he ends up murdering a bookie. The mother rejects her daughter-in-law, blaming her as the cause of her son's downfall. The young wife winds up singing in a disreputable nightclub. When Manette breaks out of prison, he is so angry to know she works at this place that he tries to kill her, but he is shot and killed by the police instead.

Christmas Holiday is a potboiler melodrama, but Kelly did a skillful job of portraying Manette. His is the only multidimensional character in the sordid plot. Gene had to go from a well-meaning but weak character to portray a man who has lost everything, becoming crazy and vicious by the end of the film. Kelly is chilling in the tense climax of the picture. Playing Manette allowed him to show acting skills not seen before, nor in his later film roles. *Christmas Holiday*, released on July 31, 1944, was not a major achievement for Universal, but it gave Kelly an opportunity to stretch himself.

HOME LIFE

Busy as he was with work, there was always time for letting off steam over the weekends. The Saturday night parties became bigger and more intense as Gene invited nearly every new colleague to join in. During and after *Cover Girl*, Saul Chaplin and his wife became regulars at the parties. Many games were played, but none of them with the brutal intensity of charades. Everyone broke up into two teams, one captained by Gene and the other by Betsy, and both captains played to win. Chaplin was astonished by the sudden change in atmosphere when charades started, seeing "the savage competitiveness of Betsy and Gene." For Chaplin, "it was scary watching our easygoing hosts turn into veritable storm troopers right before our eyes." Gene laced his coaching with a good deal of "verbal abuse." After charades, the atmosphere returned to normal with impromptu songs until late in the night.[3]

Chaplin introduced actor Farley Granger to the Kelly open house. Gene and Betsy were "generous and gregarious hosts," recalled Granger, and noted that the entertaining was the highlight of the Saturday gatherings. But Granger found the extreme competitiveness of charades (and later, of the volleyball games) "off-putting." He thought most guests simply put up with it in exchange for the good times they had during the rest of their visit.[4]

Gene never lost the intensely competitive attitude he developed as a boy fighting on Pittsburgh streets and later on high-school sports teams. And yet, he was not at all competitive in his work. He strove for perfection but was generous to colleagues, helping them do their best, so that the whole project shone. It was only in playing games that this serious flaw in his makeup emerged. It seemed deeply embedded in him that in games you win or you lose—without an appreciation for simply enjoying the experience.

When Hugh Martin and his collaborator Ralph Blane moved to California in April 1942 to work for M-G-M, Gene extended a standing invitation to attend the open house every week, and Martin hugely enjoyed the get-togethers. He was struck by the Kellys, getting to know Betsy for the first time. The two "were probably the most romantic couple in Hollywood," he thought. "They were newlyweds, almost honeymooners." Martin was impressed by Betsy's "sharp, rebellious, non-conformist brain" and thought this must have been the chief attraction Gene saw in her. Kelly himself "was as strong intellectually as he was physically, and it must have intrigued him to meet his match in someone so young."[5]

"I, too, found Betsy stimulating," Martin later wrote, "and I became closer to her than I was to Gene." He tagged along when she invited him to attend classes on dialectical materialism. "I didn't know what it was then, and I still don't." Martin went along simply to enjoy the "innocent fun" the two had while Gene was at work. Martin had an opportunity to read Blair's memoirs decades later and was surprised that they revealed a more complicated person than he had known. "I realized I hadn't understood Betsy any better than I had dialectical materialism."[6]

Given his continued rise to prominence in Hollywood, publicity about Kelly soared. Maxine Garrison interviewed Gene in October 1944. Kelly talked of his wish to direct a movie, of his interest in the technical side of filming, and of his desire to round out his skills in moviemaking. Gene was "anything but the scatterbrained, high-flying matinee idol of yesterday," Garrison commented.[7]

THE PITTSBURGH CONNECTION

Writing for the *Pittsburgh Press*, Garrison finished her piece with Kelly's praise for his hometown. "Pittsburgh's a swell town. I was born there, and I love the town and I love the people. And it isn't so doggone dirty as people make out, either."[8] Now and then Gene and his family went to Pittsburgh to visit his parents. They were seen eating with family members at Kahn's restaurant on February 22, 1943, during a one-week stay on their way back to California from New York.[9] Kahn's was located on Murray Avenue, near Kelly's dance studio.

Gene kept in touch with Robert Lazar, the brother of his star student Racelle in Pittsburgh. Lazar had found some success with his own band and he kept abreast of Gene's career. Thanking Lazar "for your swell letter," Kelly expressed his appreciation for "your constant boosting" and asked Bobby to give "my love to all your folks as I am the worst writer in the whole world." He was looking forward to the time when Lazar had his "first big Coast-to-Coast Broadcast."[10]

POLITICAL ACTIVISM

Kelly became active in political causes for the first time in his life during this phase of his Hollywood career. He told Maxine Garrison that it was important for him to get involved in the causes he believed in. "If it's going to keep people away from the box office because I'm openly interested in the future of my country, then I don't care if my kisser never gets on the screen again!"[11]

Moviegoers may not have cared very much whether Gene had a political life or not, but the Federal Bureau of Investigation (FBI) certainly was interested. The FBI began compiling a secret file on Kelly as early as July 1942, after he had been in California only six months. That file was declassified in January 2004 and offers the most detailed information on Kelly's political activism to be found. It is impossible to understand this phase of his life without obtaining a copy of the file through the auspices of the Freedom of Information Act, as we did.

The FBI maintained top-secret files on hundreds of Hollywood personalities. Writer and director Herbert Biberman circulated a proposal for a full-page ad urging the Allies to mount an invasion of France and open a Second Front against Hitler to help the Soviet Union, which was engaged in a life-and-death struggle against the Germans on the Eastern Front. The proposal met with a mixed reception among the film community, but Kelly was one of half a dozen who agreed to sign their name to the ad. Ultimately, the ad never was placed, but the FBI kept a record of everyone willing to support it.[12]

Kelly also sponsored the creation of the Artist's Front to Win the War in October 1942, which FBI officials noted. They listed it as "a Communist front organization" because it included Paul Robeson and Canada Lee, who they considered communists. The Joint Anti-Fascist Refugee Committee included Laslo Benedek, a Hungarian-born writer and director "known to associate with various Communists," according to the bureau. Benedek's address book was examined by an FBI informant, and it showed that Gene contributed $10 monthly to the refugee committee and that his phone number (CR-5-1720) was also in the book. When the Musicians' Congress staged a symposium on "Culture and Democracy" at the Women's Club of Hollywood on May 24, 1944, informants told the FBI that Kelly had agreed to give a talk on "The Role of the Actor" and that communists controlled the Musicians' Congress. So the FBI filed this in Kelly's dossier.[13]

Gene increased the tempo of his political involvement in 1944. When the Hollywood Democratic Committee (HDC) was created in July of that year, he was elected vice chairman. An informant assured the FBI that Kelly was "considered an ardent follower of the Communist Party line," and the House Un-American Activities Committee labeled the HDC as "a Communist front organization." When the Young Voters for Roosevelt Committee was founded, Gene became a member and supporter. Canada Lee was also involved in it, and thus that committee was tainted in the eyes of the FBI. The National Council for American Soviet Friendship held a rally at Madison Square Garden on November 16, 1944, to celebrate eleven years of diplomatic relations between the United States and the Soviet Union. Kelly was one of seven Hollywood actors who sent telegrams of support. Because the council was "engaged in activities that propagate the Soviet cause in the United States," this became another item in the file.[14]

An informant also told the FBI that Gene had been approached by William Young of the Bay City Club, believed to be a front of the Communist Party, to solicit financial aid to set up a "new Communist book store to be opened in Santa Monica." The informant said that Young spoke of Kelly "as a very favorable person."[15]

Betsy was more active in political causes than was Gene. "Life seemed great," she later told interviewers of this time period, and "I was always on the very left side." With time on her hands and a reliable housekeeper who took care of not only 506 North Alta but also Kerry, Betsy threw herself into a number of causes. She addressed envelopes, called people to solicit donations, and became involved in agitation over the Sleepy Lagoon case. Sparked by the murder of a young Hispanic man who was found dying near a reservoir called Sleepy Lagoon, authorities in Los Angeles County rounded up seventeen members of local Hispanic gangs and placed them on trial. Fear of a crime wave perpetrated by gangs drove the jury, despite flimsy evidence, to convict nine defendants of murder and the rest to lesser charges. Area citizens created the Sleepy Lagoon Defense Committee to help the accused. By tapping the phone of Mrs. Charles Glenn, believed to be the head of the Communist Party in Los Angeles County, the FBI knew that Betsy hosted a meeting of the Defense Committee at her house on November 5, 1943. Gene Kelly was among several prominent Hollywood actors who contributed funds to help the accused Hispanics. The FBI and Jack Tenney, the most prominent communist hunter in the California state legislature, were convinced that communists dominated the Defense Committee. They thought the party was trying to gain members from oppressed ethnic minorities.[16]

Both Gene and Betsy threw themselves into the politically charged atmosphere of Hollywood, joining many organizations to which Gene could devote relatively little time. He mostly lent his name and occasional presence at meetings to publicize the groups. Neither could know that the FBI was keeping tabs on their activities or that these groups were tainted with communism in the minds of investigators in both Washington, DC, and in Sacramento.

Gene was equally generous with his name and appearance for other causes. He received a citation for contributions to the Motion Picture Relief Fund in 1943.[17] Keen to support the war effort, he performed in several radio programs to help the Armed Forces. The FBI did not record such contributions even when it illustrated his patriotism.

In the spring of 1944, the Hollywood Victory Committee asked Kelly to organize a tour of military installations across the country to offer entertainment to hospital patients. He put together a group of performers, crafting a kind of Broadway revue, and also performed in the show. The group did three weeks of "one-nighters" across the East, South, and Midwest. It was a grueling pace. Gene got very tired after five days and ran on "nervous energy" after that, catching sleep in the passenger cars while traveling from one hospital to another.[18]

True to his connection with the Jewish community of Squirrel Hill, Kelly supported the creation of a Jewish homeland after World War II. In 1944, he played the lead in a radio program called "Going Home" on *Palestine Speaks!* sponsored by the Zionist Organization of America. In the story, he is David Rothman, one of 800 Jewish refugees escaping the Nazis from Romania on a ship. After eleven weeks on board and stopping at five ports on the Black Sea only to be refused admission, the captain is ready to return to Romania. Rothman, whose parents and siblings have already been killed, argues with the captain, telling him all 800 refugees would be killed if they went back. He urges the captain to take them to Palestine, where they would be welcome. The captain and crew abandon the vessel, leaving behind a note that this is

Figure 7.1 Outside Kennedy General Hospital in Memphis where Kelly went to entertain servicemen in 1944. The hospital, built in 1943, specialized in surgery and neuropsychiatry but treated all war casualties; it closed in 1967. (Albert J. Flogge Performing Arts Collection, Series 1, Box 4, Folder 11, Special Collections and Archives, Kent State University)

the chance for the refugees to save themselves. Rothman takes over and appoints other men in charge of the engine room and navigation. As they take the ship toward Palestine, water starts coming in rapidly through a ruptured seam. Some passengers want to go to the nearest shore to escape drowning, but Rothman is determined to make it to Tel Aviv. When in sight of land, the sinking ship hits a rock and starts to break up. People watching from the shore rush into the bay and form a human chain to rescue the exhausted but grateful passengers.

"Going Home" was Kelly's most fervent effort to support the creation of a Jewish homeland, and it tied in with his larger support for cooperation to create a better world. In 1944, Gene played an American sailor in "Shilling for Luck" on radio. His character interacts with a British sailor on a voyage from New York to England. The latter gives him a shilling "for luck" and talks of his grandson. The ship is torpedoed and sinks. Kelly's character is the sole survivor and he attributes this to the lucky coin. On being rescued and taken to England, he gives the shilling to the man's grandson, who meets the love

Figure 7.2 Outside Kennedy General Hospital, hugging Mary Elizabeth (née Snyder) Keller, a hospital recreation worker from the American Red Cross who also was a Kelly fan. (Albert J. Flogge Performing Arts Collection, Series 1, Box 4, Folder 11, Special Collections and Archives, Kent State University)

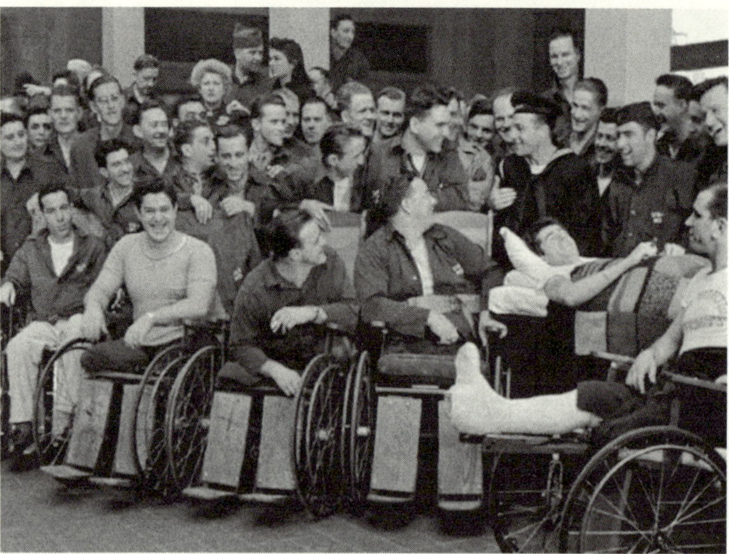

Figure 7.3 Chatting with and entertaining wounded servicemen outside a hospital in 1945. (Still from *Anatomy of a Dancer*, 2002)

of his life (played by Shirley Temple) through the shilling. The coin is passed on and on, bringing luck to all its temporary owners. The story ends with a British Colonel (played by Ronald Colman) whose life is saved by the shilling during a dangerous mission on D-Day.

ZIEGFELD FOLLIES (1946)

As soon as Gene returned from his exhausting tour of military hospitals in the spring of 1944, he went to work on a major project celebrating the twentieth anniversary of M-G-M's founding. Arthur Freed produced *Ziegfeld Follies*, essentially a giant revue.[19] A total of forty people contributed to the writing of the film, with seven directors working on individual segments. To showcase the many stars the studio had under contract, twenty-one principals were rounded up for the major parts and 122 others constituted the supporting cast.

Freed initially wanted to pair Gene with Lana Turner in "Everywhere I Roam," a sketch described as a dance pantomime about a sailor and a pinup girl. Instead, he paired Gene with Fred Astaire. By this time all commentators recognized that Kelly alone was in Astaire's league, and everyone tended to assume there was intense rivalry between the two stars. Nothing could be further from the truth, but Freed planned "The Babbitt and the Bromide" to parody the supposed rivalry.[20] Gene had met Fred soon after his arrival in Hollywood but had little if any contact with him before the start of rehearsals for *Ziegfeld Follies*. The two thoroughly respected each other's accomplishments, and neither saw the other as competition because their dance styles were so different.

"The Babbitt and the Bromide" was a comedy sketch by George and Ira Gershwin written for Fred and his sister Adele in the 1927 stage musical *Funny Face*. Gene was not entirely happy with this number, wanting to do something more up to date. But Freed insisted because he had seen Fred and Adele perform the number years before in another stage musical called *The Band Wagon*. Kelly said later, "I wish we could have tried to dance against each other in our own style instead of trying to amalgamate our things. Nevertheless, it was fun."[21]

Vincente Minnelli directed this segment of *Ziegfeld Follies*. Minnelli was born into an entertainment family and had a strong reputation for set design and decor on Broadway. Freed talked him into coming to M-G-M, where he found his forté as a director. Starting with *Cabin in the Sky*, he reached his stride with *Meet Me in St. Louis*.[22] Minnelli was a key player in M-G-M's success at revamping the film musical with top-quality songs and dances and, more importantly, interweaving them into a substantial plotline with strong characterizations. There was no opportunity to do anything like that in *Ziegfeld Follies*, but Gene and Minnelli were destined to collaborate on future projects that would allow both men to spread their creative wings.

Rehearsals began in mid-April 1944 with stagehands literally locking the doors to the set as Astaire and Kelly tried to work out their choreography. Because they had not previously worked or socialized with each other, both men were unusually careful not to offend each other. "The rehearsals were maddening," Minnelli admitted. "Astaire would demonstrate an idea for a step and ask Kelly what he thought of it. Kelly would say, 'fine, great, swell.' They tried to convince each other and be so polite." Gene admitted he usually gave in and tried to conform to Fred's style, knowing that Astaire had other serious and difficult dances to perform in the film.[23]

If he had been able to choose his own music, Kelly would have preferred "Pass That Peace Pipe," a number written by Roger Edens, Hugh Martin, and Ralph Blane. Kelly thought it had good rhythm, was upbeat in tone, and brand-new. But Astaire preferred "The Babbitt and the Bromide" and Kelly deferred. "Pass That Peace Pipe" was introduced in *Good News* (1947) and was nominated for an Academy Award. Bing Crosby later sang it to great acclaim.[24] It would have been better if Kelly and Astaire could have introduced it in *Ziegfeld Follies* rather than using a twenty-year-old song about the banality of people.

It took six days to rehearse the number and one day to record the song. Filming began on May 20 and was done over four days. One sequence, filmed on the third day, was shot twenty-one times. The number, which lasted 7 minutes, 13 seconds, cost nearly $79,000.[25] It became an instant classic because it matched the two greatest film dancers in history, overwhelming the rest of this long, cumbersome picture.

Dance historian John Mueller has carefully analyzed the number to document the extent to which the two stars, who had seriously differing dance styles, melded their steps. He describes the first of three segments, the initial meeting of the Babbitt and the Bromide on a park bench, to be "a thorough amalgam of the styles of both dancers." Mueller identified "two specific trademarks." One is a hop to the side by one dancer, immediately followed by the other. Kelly had done this with himself in "Alter Ego" in *Cover Girl*. The first segment also has "one of the sprawling, sliding back kicks" that Astaire liked to do.[26]

The second segment, depicting the two men ten years later with both sporting mustaches, is more focused on Kelly's style. Mueller identifies a "loping, casual soft-shoe, with the arms swinging freely" that Kelly often did. There is "a leg-over-leg jump" that both men did, but Kelly liked to repeat it several times while Astaire normally did it only once. It is done only once here to suit Astaire.[27]

Mueller concludes that the third segment, depicting the Babbitt and the Bromide in heaven, is mostly oriented to Astaire's style. It contains "satiric waltz choreography" that "looks better on the fluid Astaire than on the chunky Kelly," even though both men splendidly perform everything. Kelly liked to do several "heel-clicking leaps," and they are included. Also, in their pirouettes, Kelly turned left and Astaire turned right, "their preferred directions." The finale of the third segment, however, is "pure Astaire," according to Mueller. It includes "swivel-hipped tapping," "precise hesitations," and a "traveling pattern," all of which are "Astaire signature steps." "Kelly keeps up gamely but is pretty well outclassed in this last sequence," Mueller concludes. Kelly realized it as well. "I hated the third section," he is quoted as saying, "I thought I looked like a klotz[*sic*]!" That was a reaction that no one else, even Mueller, would support. Jack Martin Smith, a set designer at M-G-M, recalled how much fun it was for the crew to stand on the sidelines and watch these two masters at work.[28]

Overall, Mueller feels that "The Babbitt and the Bromide" was geared for Astaire's preferences. He explains that in terms of dance style, Kelly "often takes standard steps from the tap, character, or ballet vocabulary and incorporates them wholesale into the dances." Mueller also notes that "The Babbitt and the Bromide" is a cynical commentary on banality, and in fact the entire film has a dark, cynical, almost bitter tone, strange characteristics indeed for a celebratory pageant.[29]

Ziegfeld Follies was not released for a long while after Gene and Fred finished filming their number in May 1944. The movie was nearly three hours long when previewed on November 1, 1944, and had to be trimmed, re-edited, and one new comedy segment added. Gene and Fred's number, however, was not touched during this long period of revising. The second preview on March 12, 1945, resulted in more re-filming. Costing more than $3 million, *Ziegfeld Follies* finally was released on April 8, 1946, grossing more than $5 million. Critics singled out "The Babbitt and the Bromide" as the highlight of

Figure 7.4 With Fred Astaire in "The Babbit and the Bromide." (Still from *Ziegfeld Follies*, 1946)

this cinematic revue. Using phrases such as "sheer delight" and a "dance for the archives," they urged viewers to put up with the "spectacular boredom" of the rest of *Ziegfeld Follies* "just to watch Astaire and Kelly together."[30]

Over the years, this number has been subject to a considerable amount of analysis given its historic nature as the only pairing of these two greats while they were in their prime. Freed wanted the two to make fun of the idea of competition between them, and they do so through dialogue and their dance routine, knocking each other's hats off or kicking the other in the seat or the nose. Joseph Epstein found moments such as these to be darkly indicative of how ugly a real, heated competition between these two greats might have been. If dance contest it is, then some commentators thought Gene won while others gave the palm to Fred. And yet, the message that there was no rivalry between the two came across clearly. Peter Levinson noted that Kelly and Astaire "had an obvious chemistry," while Stanley Green and Burt Goldblatt wrote that their dance was "full of gaiety and mutual admiration." Most serious commentators found the tone of "The Babbitt and the Bromide" beneath the dignity of either dancer's abilities (matching Kelly's own concern about the choice of the song) but have been content to bask in the pleasure of seeing the two together on the dance floor.[31]

Kelly voiced his dissatisfaction with the song for this number to Minnelli sometime after it was filmed. The director mentioned it to Astaire, who retorted, "What does Gene mean by unchallenging? Didn't we beat hell out of the floor together?" As late as 1954 Kelly told Hedda Hopper that "we should have done a much better number together."[32]

But Kelly did not hold this against Astaire. Both men had nothing but positive things to say about the other for the rest of their lives. About their dance together, Gene said in 1973: "That was as pleasant as it could ever get. . . . We did our best to make each other comfortable." Astaire had earlier supported this sentiment in his memoirs, published in 1959. In fact, their collaboration on "The Babbitt and the Bromide" was the beginning of a lifelong friendship between the two. "We got to know each other and like each other very much," Gene said. "We've been fast and firm friends ever since."[33]

ANCHORS AWEIGH (1945)

With *Cover Girl* garnering critical acclaim and huge box-office returns, M-G-M finally directed Kelly into another dance musical in 1944. In fact, the studio had decided to pair him with Judy Garland again for *Anchors Aweigh* as early as October 1942, soon after *For Me and My Gal.*[34]

But many factors delayed and altered initial plans until two years later Kathryn Grayson replaced Garland as the female lead. Joe Pasternak produced, George Sidney directed, and Isabel Lennart wrote the screenplay. So far, Gene had worked with all of these people before, but new faces included Frank Sinatra as his film buddy.

The movie has a thin plot but it works for the most part. Because Gene's character, Joe Brady, saved the life of Frank's character, Clarence Doolittle, while both were on naval duty, Joe "owes" him something according to Clarence. But he is willing to relieve Joe of his responsibility if he will get Clarence a date. On shore leave, Joe and Clarence meet a boy played by Dean Stockwell and through him meet his Aunt Susie, played by Grayson. Joe immediately tries to get Susie interested in Clarence and persists even after realizing his own attraction for her. But Susie reciprocates Joe's feelings and Clarence later prefers another woman, a waitress, so it all works out. Some roadblocks as well as humor are provided as Joe and Clarence try to meet José Iturbi to interest him in giving Susie an audition.

The length of the movie in conjunction with its simplistic plot offered Kelly many opportunities to craft striking dance numbers along the way. Pasternak gave him free rein in this regard. He admired Kelly's work ethic and found that none of his requests were unreasonable. In fact, Pasternak appreciated the fact that Gene worked to lessen costs whenever possible.[35] Moreover, *Anchors Aweigh* was the venue for Kelly to dance as a sailor for the first of many times in his career.

It was Pasternak's idea to pair Gene with Frank Sinatra at a time when the latter's film career was stymied. Few singers have the kind of explosive early success that Sinatra enjoyed. Born in Hoboken, New Jersey, three years after Gene of Italian and Sicilian parents, he sang for several well-known bands and on the radio, building up a vibrant following among young girls until he reached superstar status. His film career, however, left a lot to be desired. He appeared in five movies before *Anchors Aweigh*, struggling with an acting role in only one of them, while simply singing in the others.[36]

Gene had to deal with a costar who had never danced before and who had little real acting experience. Once again, his love of teaching came to the rescue. "We decided that we were going to get Frank to move," he later stated. Sinatra was willing to try because he was desperate to make it in Hollywood. "I've never had anybody work that hard because he had never done a dance step in his life." Sinatra found the whole experience grueling; he had never been pushed liked this before and often felt depressed over his lack of success in cinema. Kelly buoyed his spirits, gave him hope, and kept him rehearsing long hours every day for eight weeks. Gene sought and drew out Frank's untapped ability to move his feet. At the end of this boot camp in film dancing, Gene said, "Francis, you've worked your way up from lousy to adequate—I'm ready to dance on camera with you."[37]

When rehearsals were over and the filming proceeded smoothly, Sinatra realized how important *Anchors Aweigh* had been for him personally and professionally. He knew Gene had been the key. "Apart from being a great artist, he's a born teacher," Sinatra later said. "I felt really comfortable working for him and enjoyed his company, in spite of his insane insistence on hard work."[38] Not only had Gene rejuvenated Frank's film career, the two developed a lifelong friendship.

Kelly's tutelage paid off. In their first on-screen number together, "I Begged Her," the two perform a short but spirited dance that ends with jumping from one army cot to another for a grand finish. Casey Charness found that Kelly utilized several tricks to help Sinatra along. The two perform simple steps, but the number is filmed at a fast tempo to make them appear more difficult. Even the cot-jumping was "filmed with a fast dolly back" so that the camera

Figure 7.5 Showing off his "lucky dancing shoes." The photo was taken during the filming of *Anchors Aweigh* (1945). On the back of the photo is written: "Gene always starts the first dance number in each of his pictures wearing the shoes." (New York Public Library)

movement enhanced the dance. Kelly's growing knowledge of camerawork allowed him to achieve such outcomes. "The facile steps and deceptive double-timing are part of the dance to enable Sinatra to look good," Charness concludes. And yet, "Sinatra can be seen constantly checking the floor to see if his feet are in the right place."[39]

While filming *Anchors Aweigh* Kelly came to realize that whereas most people got better with each additional take, Sinatra always was at his best on the first take. So it was worth the extra rehearsing with him because filming was then streamlined. "Frank & I in the Dormitory—we had a ball together on this #," Kelly wrote on his song sheet of "I Begged Her."[40] Gene's efforts to make Frank look good in *Anchors Aweigh* expressed two common themes in his career—his generosity to colleagues and his fierce commitment to making the project work.

Isobel Lennart recalled how much Kelly bugged her with suggestions about character development. He urged her to decrease his own role in favor of Sinatra's character, Clarence. Lennart had experienced Kelly's feedback earlier on *Thousands Cheer* and learned to appreciate it. After seeing *Cover Girl* she encouraged his input even more, realizing that unlike most actors who tried to embellish their own roles, he was truly interested in improving the project.[41]

Kelly mentored an aspiring young actress named Sharon McManus for another memorable number in *Anchors Aweigh.* On a set depicting Olvera Street, the heart of old, Hispanic Los Angeles, Joe Brady impetuously dances with a young Hispanic girl. It was staged in memory of the impromptu dance he did with the little girl on the honeymoon trip through Mexico. At least three themes in Kelly's career came together in this number. He had been interested in Spanish dancing ever since taking classes with Angel Cansino in Chicago. His love of working with children was expressed well in this delightful number. Kelly also developed a good deal of bricolage, including candles, pots, an open flame, and a water fountain as props. He designed the choreography for the characters—steps that a child and a grown man can do together.

Kelly held a casting call and chose McManus because of her big eyes, her overall look, and her attitude. But her blond hair had to be dyed black, and she needed makeup to look brown-skinned. McManus performed magnificently after much agonized coaching by Stanley Donen, who disliked her, and she vigorously reciprocated the feeling. But Gene enjoyed working with her and she adored him.[42] Kelly's work with children in his youth helped him create bonds with kids easily.

Once again, Kelly used his understanding of camera movement for improving the number. Charness notes a "pullback to extreme long shot" without a cut in the third shot of the number.[43] It is an example of adapting the camera to complement and enhance the sense of movement on a two-dimensional screen.

Even more impressive is Kelly's fantasy Spanish dance later in the picture, a dream ballet wherein Joe Brady tries to express his feelings for Aunt Susie by conjuring up a scene from Hispanic California. He used a segment from his Spanish dance in *Pal Joey*, literally borrowing the first eight bars of music and steps from it. Even before *Pal Joey*, Kelly had used this routine in a Spanish dance in *Hold Your Hats* at the Pittsburgh Playhouse in 1938.[44] Viewers of *Anchors Aweigh* have no idea that they are seeing something Kelly developed in his pre-Broadway days, then used to great acclaim in New York, and again in Hollywood.

Danced to "La Cumparsita," the Fandango number, also called the fantasy Spanish dance of *Anchors Aweigh*, blended ballet elements with flamenco and tap. It seems like an odd combination of dance styles, to be sure, but Gene pulls it off. "It is Kelly's style alone," Charness concludes.[45] The number

Figure 7.6 Dancing with Sharon McManus (made up as a Hispanic girl) on a set depicting Olvera Street, the heart of old, Hispanic Los Angeles. (Still from *Anchors Aweigh*, 1945)

Figure 7.7 Dancing to "La Cumparsita" (in a costume similar to that of the *Pal Joey* dream ballet) in the fantasy Spanish dance. (Still from *Anchors Aweigh*, 1945)

performed by a "bandit chief" to impress a "princess" includes two fast Airplane Propellers and some Revolving Jetés (twirling and leaping while dancing in a circle) that Kelly repeated later in two dances in *The Pirate*.

The number is climaxed by Kelly's athleticism. Using specifically designed scenery, he runs up the wall of a hacienda and onto an artificial tree, then across a wall to the other side, but he still cannot reach the princess. So he runs back and up steep steps to a strategically placed curtain and, holding it, swings across nearly fifty feet of space to the other side. He then runs down a roof and slides down a pole to finally reach and embrace Kathryn Grayson, who is holding the deep red rose he threw to her earlier. And he does all this in perfect synchronization to the music. The number is expressive of Kelly's developing film aesthetics—melding differing dance styles seamlessly, presenting movement in striking, controlled fashion, mixing in athleticism, and building to a grand flourish at the end. Most of the elements of his success on screen are encapsulated in this fantasy Spanish dance of *Anchors Aweigh*.

But there is an additional element in this movie that has never been discussed before. *Anchors Aweigh* is the first time that Kelly introduced Spanish elements into his films, and it was done only a year after the Sleepy Lagoon controversy. There was no inherent reason within the storyline of *Anchors Aweigh* for any scenes to be set on Olvera Street and no necessity to create a Spanish fantasy as compared to any other kind of fantasy. Kelly most likely inserted these positive, romantic images of Hispanic heritage to educate America, reduce ethnic fear and prejudice, and encourage mainstream citizens to respect diversity. The Pittsburgh boy who had been shocked by ethnic prejudice at Penn State University learned about the insidious nature of all kinds of bigotry after moving to California, and he tried to do something about it.

Kelly also inserted another number into *Anchors Aweigh* that came to be a landmark in his career. It explored the technical aspects of creating a distinctive kind of dance for the camera that could not be done on stage. Stanley Donen had continued at Columbia for a while after *Cover Girl* until he was fired from that studio as well. Kelly once again rescued Donen's career by talking M-G-M into hiring him one more time. It was Donen who had the idea of having Kelly dance with a cartoon partner, and Gene developed the choreography. The result is called "The King Who Couldn't Dance" or "The Worry Song."[46]

The number was not easy to develop. Combining animation with live action went back at least to 1917 with Max Fleischer's *Out of the Inkwell* cartoon series. But it had not been done since the 1920s and was essentially a new concept as far as viewers and critics were concerned. Studio manager Eddie Mannix was not convinced it was feasible and suggested Kelly consult Walt Disney, the leading pioneer in animation. Disney had released *Salutos Amigos* in February 1943, which mixed separate sequences of live action interspersed with animated sequences. He also was currently working on *The Three Caballeros*, which included a similar mix of live and drawn images. Disney showed Kelly and Donen his plans for the latter, but Kelly knew it was not what he wanted. The Kelly-Donen plan was to use interactions in dialogue and dancing between a cartoon character (possibly Mickey Mouse) and a live actor throughout. In that sense "The Worry Song" was a true innovation in film history, bringing the concept to full fruition. Disney refused to let Gene use Mickey Mouse as his dance partner, but he was willing to talk to Mannix and help convince him the number was feasible.[47]

Ironically, the M-G-M cartoon department was fully capable of handling this assignment, but going to Disney first enlisted a potent ally. Mannix was convinced by Disney's endorsement, and thus Jerry the Mouse became famous for dancing with Gene Kelly. Jerry had appeared initially with his partner Tom the Cat in "Puss Gets the Boot" (1940), by William Hanna and Joseph Barbera. M-G-M's animation department was only three years old at that time, but already it vied with Warner Brothers as the only real competition to Disney in the field of animation. The *Tom and Jerry* series lasted fifteen years and won seven Academy Awards. Kenneth L. Muse, who had worked on the first Tom and Jerry cartoon, drew Jerry for "The Worry Song." Ironically, he had also drawn Mickey Mouse for Disney. Seven other animators also worked on the Kelly number.[48]

Isabel Lennart finished drafting an outline for "The Worry Song" on August 10, 1944, including Donald Duck as the dancing partner for Gene.[49] But, as discussed, Kelly preferred Mickey Mouse and settled for Jerry. Gene needed a likeable character, and actually, little Jerry is far more appealing than Mickey Mouse. Other than changing the cartoon figure, Lennart's story outline was closely followed.

"The Worry Song" is the main event in a story Joe Brady tells a group of school children. It is in essence a dream ballet that the children imagine as Joe narrates it. The story begins with Kelly, dressed in a different sailor suit, cavorting in an artificial woodland. He incorporates the athletic Prone Jump from the Mop Dance in *Thousands Cheer*, but this time he jumps up from lying on the grass instead of a tabletop. He then interacts with animated forest animals. The same idea was later used by Disney in *Mary Poppins* in the "Jolly

Holiday" number. The animals tell Joe that the king has outlawed dancing, so he goes to the castle and discovers that Jerry (the king) cannot dance and felt compelled to outlaw it. "The Worry Song" teaches Jerry (and all kids) that *anyone* can dance if they have the right attitude.

In choreographing "The Worry Song," Gene tried "to be as childlike as an adult could be and yet have as much energy and playfulness in this . . . pas de deux with a mouse." Ballet elements are prominent, as *New York Times* dance critic Anna Kisselgoff reminds us. Gene "executes turns à la seconde with Jerry . . . perched on his extended leg." She also contrasts Kelly's "skill and considerable taste" in this dance with the "inept contortions through which Walt Disney put Donald Duck in . . . *The Three Caballeros*." But Gene thoughtfully explained that this was because Disney was not a dancer. In fact, Kelly created the choreography based on the type of movements that would be believable for a cartoon mouse. Based on this, he playfully wrote in a booklet about the dance, "I *didn't* teach the mouse how to dance. *He* taught me. The whole routine was his invention."[50]

Kelly wanted this number to be an object lesson to kids that having a positive, happy attitude toward life is important if you want to enjoy learning new things. The camera moves very little, and the appealing steps incorporate the Prone Kick of his Pittsburgh days as well as Side Heel-Clicks and a move we call the Midair Twist, which he used often in films from this point on. In this move, he runs forward, jumps high, twists around in the air, and lands gracefully.

Filming "The Worry Song" was difficult. The set was draped with blue, and the cameraman kept Kelly on one side of a crosshair in the viewfinder, leaving room for Jerry on the other side. Kelly had worked out the counts for the entire dance, and Donen counted for the camera operator, telling him exactly when to pan. After that, Hanna and Barbera's team of animators spent months drawing Jerry into the picture, matching his movements to Gene's as closely as possible. Only after the number was finished did everyone realize a mistake had been made. Gene cast a shadow but Jerry did not. To correct the problem, animators had to make 20,000 drawings of Jerry's shadow.[51]

Three months later, "The Worry Song" was finished. It cost $100,000, took up eight minutes of *Anchors Aweigh*, and stole the show. M-G-M capitalized on it by inserting animated sequences in several subsequent films. For example, Tom and Jerry swam in an underwater ballet with Esther Williams in *Dangerous When Wet* (1953). When Kelly happened to be in London at the

Figure 7.8 Dancing with Jerry the Mouse in "The Worry Song" (aka "The King Who Couldn't Dance"), an innovative number for the time, mixing live action with animation. (Still from *Anchors Aweigh*, 1945)

same time that Disney was in town, the two had a drink. "Please don't do any more cartoons," Disney half-jokingly pleaded with him.[52]

Soon after *Anchors Aweigh* premiered on July 19, 1945, reviewers agreed that it was Kelly's picture even though Sinatra and Grayson got top billing. They recognized his achievement not only as an actor and dancer but as a choreographer. Writing for the Los Angeles *Daily News*, Wanda Hale thought Kelly was the only male musical comedy dancer in the business who had sex appeal. Gene clipped this review and preserved it in his papers, writing "and I never knew!!" as a playful note in the margin. In Alton Cook's view, *Anchors Aweigh* was the "absolute climax to the brilliant start he has made" in the movies.[53]

"The Worry Song" was hailed as "a triumph of both cinematic technique and dance integration." Sometimes, when asked who his favorite dancing partner was, Gene only half-kiddingly said Jerry the Mouse. Columbia Records talked him into recording "The Worry Song," which sold "zillions of copies," as Gene once said. As mentioned earlier, he wrote a short booklet to go with the record, which was packaged "in a little album box." For decades to come he received fan mail from grownups who fondly remembered listening to it over and over as children.[54]

Kelly participated in several radio programs over time to promote *Anchors Aweigh.* On October 17, 1945, he was a guest on *Songs by Sinatra.* The crowd went wild when Gene, already a lieutenant in the Navy, came on. Sinatra joked that it was bad enough that Kelly stole the movie from him and now he was stealing his radio show. The two friends sang songs and acted scenes from *Anchors Aweigh* and also discussed the plot. They tap danced together to the audience's delight and ended the show with a plea for racial and religious tolerance. On December 4, 1946, Kelly appeared on the *Ford Show* with Dinah Shore. They plugged *Anchors Aweigh* with a lot of silliness about "Petey" the mouse, who supposedly "played" Jerry in the dance with Gene in the film. On December 29, 1947, more than two years after the film's release, Sinatra, Grayson, and Kelly performed a thirty-minute version of the film on *Lux Radio Theater.*

Because Gene inserted Spanish music and dance into *Anchors Aweigh* and because of the Mexican restaurant and the set of Olvera Street, M-G-M recorded a separate release print of *Anchors Aweigh* with the dialogue spoken in Spanish. The studio also created a Spanish language trailer and supported a fifteen-minute radio program summarizing the story in Spanish for broadcast on radio. All of this ethnic marketing took place in the summer and fall of 1946, more than a year after the initial, English-language release of the picture.[55]

For the first time in his film career Kelly danced as a sailor on screen. It was a new wave in art and entertainment. Fred Astaire had done so in *Follow the Fleet*, released in 1936, and dancing sailors had appeared on stage in *Les Matelots* (1925) by Ballet Russe de Monte Carlo as well as in *Fancy Free* by Jerome Robbins, which premiered in April 1944. To commentators the sailor image stood for freedom, and the way in which Gene and Robbins portrayed him denoted the friendly, boy-next-door type.[56] Given the wartime setting of *Fancy Free* and *Anchors Aweigh*, the sailor image also represented patriotism and support for the collective effort to defeat Germany and Japan.

For Gene, perhaps the most important aspect of dancing as a sailor was the uniform. He loved the sailor suit because it was designed to hug the body in key areas, becoming a good substitute for leotards. The uniform neatly outlined the body, highlighting the line of his figure for dancing.[57] He could not have worn a leotard in *Anchors Aweigh*, but a close-fitting white or blue sailor suit, with a cap and tie, perfectly blended the image of Joe Brady and Kelly's dance aesthetics at the same time.

Moreover, crafting a story about sailors on leave enhanced the plot. Not only did the public look up to a sailor as a "cultural hero," but his "carefree attitude" while on leave made him the "ideal musical hero."[58] For all of Kelly's dancing sailors, the story is never set on board a ship but always on shore so the character can interact with civilians as well as with his comrades. We never see the sailor while he is on duty, but instead trying to have as much fun and excitement as he can in the real world. As a result, the dancing sailor we see in *Anchors Aweigh, On the Town*, and *Invitation to the Dance* is an unreal character in an important way—a domesticated warrior who rarely mentions combat or sea duty.

THE NAVY

Ironically, Kelly went immediately from portraying a fictional sailor in cinema to becoming a real one in wartime. Like all young men of a designated age, Gene registered for the draft soon after the Selective Service Act was passed in September 1940, but the call-up for actual service was limited and bypassed him. By the time Pearl Harbor catapulted America into World War II, he was married and thus deferred for that reason when the call-ups increased. Ten months later he became a father, which added another element to his deferment status. But as the war lengthened and the needs of a worldwide military deployment increased, deferments were altered and Gene's classification changed.[59]

By mid-October 1944, about a month before his work on "The Worry Song" was finished, Kelly was reclassified as 1-A, ready for immediate service. His local draft board scheduled him for induction in about four weeks, just enough time to finish the number. "I was ready to go," Gene told a reporter, "but I also wanted to get that dance on film. By literally working night and day we managed."[60] Kelly finished his part of the number on Sunday, November 12, and the next day reported for his physical exam by military doctors. The physicians were impressed by his condition, and he told them that making dance films was like a "professional boot camp. Contrary to popular impression, dancing is plenty tough work."[61]

During the filming of "The Worry Song" Kelly nursed an injury to his hand. In the earlier filming of the fantasy Spanish number, a wire in the stem of the artificial rose used as a prop had punctured his hand and created a mild case of blood poisoning that included "shivers and a fever." Gene had to soak his hand at night and wear a bandage around it while rehearsing. He took off the bandage only when filming. The infection was still not gone when he reported for his physical exam. Gene did not understand why everyone chuckled when they saw the bandage. Then he realized they had seen *For Me and My Gal* and remembered how Harry Palmer had tried to postpone being drafted by smashing his hand with a trunk lid.[62]

A week earlier, on November 6, 1944, Kelly participated in a radio broadcast called "The Night Before the Election," sponsored by the Democratic National Committee to help Roosevelt retain the presidency. It was hosted by Humphrey Bogart, and several other actors participated. Judy Garland sang campaign songs. Actors and ordinary people made brief comments, everyone stressing the continuation of social programs under the New Deal and the need for an experienced man like FDR in the White House who would work with other nations for world peace. Several said that Thomas Dewey was controlled by isolationists and conservatives of the Republican Party, and as governor of New York he had passed legislation making it impossible for thousands of servicemen from the state to vote.

A ninety-four-year-old man talked of shaking Abraham Lincoln's hand in Galesburg, Illinois, in 1858, and said he would vote for FDR. A veteran said he had been in the Navy during World War I and was part of the Bonus March of 1932 where he saw two of his friends killed when President Hoover called in the army to roust peaceful demonstrators from the Washington Mall. Everyone agreed the country needed to keep FDR in office and continue his policies domestically and internationally and not retreat to the days of Hoover. FDR himself spoke from his home in Hyde Park, New York, in a typical Fireside Chat, warning against a return to isolationism and urging the need for America to engage the world and work with other nations. Kelly was one of many actors who came on just to say who they were and a brief phrase. "Gene Kelly, army-bound, but not before I vote for Roosevelt," he said. Happily, FDR won reelection very easily with 432 electoral votes to Dewey's ninety-nine.

On November 20, 1944, Kelly was inducted into the Armed Forces and chose to serve in the Navy. "I'm used to the uniform," he quipped to an interviewer. Thirteen weeks of boot camp at San Diego followed, from late November 1944 to late February 1945. It was anything but pleasant for Kelly. He was several years older than everyone else and was shocked at the regimentation and indoctrination of the military system, which was so different from the life he had crafted in Hollywood. When he finished, Kelly was assigned to make movies for the Navy. This initially upset him because he wanted to fight in the war effort, but he soon realized that applying his special skills to a needed task was the best way to make a contribution.[63]

MAKING FILMS FOR THE NAVY

Right after boot camp, Kelly started working at the Naval Photographic Center at Anacostia, near Washington, DC. His first assignment was to star in a film on combat fatigue. In preparation for the role, he spent two weeks at a rehabilitation hospital near Philadelphia, pretending to be a patient. He was allowed to go out at night, and after some people spotted him, reports spread that he was a genuine patient at the institution.[64]

Lieutenant Hugh McMullin wrote and directed the film. It was made with lightning speed in March and April 1945.[65] Kelly starred as a sailor affected by the stress of war in the thirty-five-minute film. All the characters are fictional but true to life. The film used real sailors for the most part; only Gene, Jocelyn Brando, Marlon's older sister, and Lauren Gilbert were professionals among the onscreen appearances.

Gene played Bob Lucas, a fireman in the hold of the battleship *Montana*, who had to stay down in the cramped space to tend valves and gauges. He was frustrated because he wanted to be outside and participate in the fighting. Then a torpedo attack blew him out of the vessel and into the ocean. Lucas was glad to be out, but after seeing the bodies of his crewmembers around him in the water, he felt guilty to be alive. All of these conflicting feelings led to his nervous breakdown. It is the only time that Kelly's character cried on screen, revealing yet another untapped part of his acting ability.

Betsy was impressed by *Combat Fatigue Irritability*, calling it "simple, compassionate, and hopeful." Both she and Gene saw it as a promising sign that he could act in a "serious drama" on screen.[66] His roles in *Pilot No. 5*, *Christmas Holiday*, and *The Cross of Lorraine* had already demonstrated his acting ability, but those films were made in Hollywood and had some unreal aspects. They lacked the element of subtlety, and even honesty, that *Combat Fatigue Irritability* offered him.

Figure 7.9 Acting as sailor Bob Lucas experiencing battle tension in the engine room of his vessel. (Still from *Combat Fatigue Irritability*, 1945)

Soon after finishing the film, Kelly was commissioned as lieutenant, junior grade, on April 26, 1945. He had earned a reserve officer's training certificate at the University of Pittsburgh, which was important in obtaining the commission.[67]

Right after receiving his commission Kelly took a film crew to New York City to interview crewmembers of the *USS Franklin* (CV-13) as his second assignment. An *Essex*-class aircraft carrier, *Franklin* had been hit by a Japanese bomber fifty miles from the coast of Honshu, Japan, on March 19, 1945. The huge ship nearly sank and more than 800 crewmen died, but the survivors refused to abandon the vessel and managed to save it. After emergency repairs in the Pacific, *Franklin* steamed under its own power through the Panama Canal and reached the Brooklyn Navy Yard on April 28.[68]

Previous biographers and film writers mistakenly claim that this was Kelly's fifth or sixth film for the Navy, with Hirschhorn claiming that it was made after the war. Actually, when the ship docked on April 28, 1945, the crewmembers were ready to go home or to other assignments and let workers fully repair the damaged vessel. To interview and film them before they left, Kelly and his team had to get there immediately. Had this been Kelly's fifth or sixth film, or made after the war ended, the ship's crew would have dispersed

Figure 7.10 Lucas experiencing a nervous breakdown. (Still from *Combat Fatigue Irritability*, 1945)

Figure 7.11 Lieutenant (junior grade) in the United States Navy. (http://weheartvintage.co/2013/05/11/gene-kelly-in-uniform/)

months before and Kelly could not have interviewed and filmed them at the Brooklyn Navy Yard as he did.

Gene and his colleagues worked for one week on *Franklin* after it docked, filming footage of its survivors. After that they interviewed relatives of crewmen who lived in New York and also shot film throughout the city. Julius Epstein, who had written the screenplay for *Casablanca* (1942) with his brother Phil, was now serving as a naval officer. He and Kelly wrote a scenario for a film about the *Franklin* crew. Kelly found that it was possible to "steal" shots of the city without having to get permission or use a line of policemen to hold back gawking spectators. Wearing his officer's uniform, he simply knocked on doors of buildings that had windows opening out on the scenes he wanted to film and asked residents if they would let him in. They always agreed, and it was easy to set up the camera in their living room, point it out a window, and get what he needed. If he was filming extras on the street, he stationed a man there to signal him when the coast was clear of unwanted passersby. The man simply waved a white handkerchief and Gene told the camera operator to start filming. He was also able to film at Grant's Tomb and the Brooklyn Navy Yard without being bothered.[69]

This improvised filming made a big impression on Kelly. He was convinced that even a feature-length dance picture could be done in similar ways, although it would be four years before he had a chance to try it in *On the Town*, shot in part at the same Brooklyn Navy Yard that repaired *Franklin*.

Gene's film about the crew of *Franklin* was never completed. He was recalled to his station in Washington, DC.[70] The Navy issued an official documentary film, *The Saga of the Franklin*, in 1945. Twenty-four minutes long, it consists entirely of color footage of the carrier before, during, and after the horrific experience of March 19, covering its last deployment and the trip to New York City. But none of Kelly's footage is included.

What probably happened is that initially Navy officials thought it would be a good idea to interview crewmembers and include that in the film along with city footage. So they assigned Kelly to the task. Meanwhile, others were working on the documentary about the ship's misfortunes. When this part was completed, the Navy officials realized that the dramatic documentary could stand alone. They rightly decided not to dilute its impact by including crewmember interviews or city scenes.

When Kelly returned to Washington, he was assigned to edit footage that Navy cameramen had accumulated and stored at the Naval Photographic Center in Anacostia. Most of it was of operations in the Pacific, and some consisted of captured Japanese film. The Navy assumed that anyone associated with movies would have the knowhow, but Gene had no idea how to edit film. Fortunately a man already working at Anacostia, who had known Kelly before the war, taught him the basics and he "learned a lot of things." It was the first time he worked with a Moviola machine, a device that stopped the film frame-by-frame for examination and cutting.[71] This experience introduced Kelly to the art of film editing, and he took every opportunity to learn it. Later, he was able to collaborate with editors on his dance films as a result of digging through and editing thousands of feet of disparate and repetitive images of Navy planes and ships.

Kelly then embarked on his third Navy film project, a documentary about a new foam designed to smother gasoline fires on board warships. By April 1945, the Japanese had deployed Baka bombs, which were specially designed planes with a large bomb load in front and three rockets in the tail. It was manned and designed to deliberately crash onto an American ship as a suicide bomber. The new foam was developed to quickly extinguish fuel fires that resulted from such attacks. The Navy assembled twenty-four airplanes, spilled fuel over them, and detonated a fire through explosions. Gene directed thirteen cameras to film the conflagration from several angles while firefighters used the foam to put it out. Fleet Admiral Ernest J. King saw the film, was convinced the foam was effective, and ordered it deployed in the Pacific.[72]

For his fourth assignment, Kelly documented a newly built cruiser named *Fall River* (CA-131), which had an advanced type of radar. Gene and his crew boarded the heavy cruiser at Philadelphia for its initial voyage to Cuba after the vessel was commissioned on July 1, 1945. He had no idea how to proceed, not being at all familiar with the ship, but was delighted to learn that Captain David Stolz Crawford had been an acquaintance of his from the University of Pittsburgh and was ready to help. Kelly and his crew filmed everything they needed on the way to Cuba and then flew back to Washington.[73]

Kelly's fifth assignment involved deployment to the Pacific to film the Navy's part in the planned invasion of Japan, scheduled for November 1945. Gene and eleven crewmembers left San Francisco in early August. "I was scared to death," he admitted years later. Then the first atomic bomb was dropped on Hiroshima on August 6; Kelly and crew were detained at Honolulu pending developments. Gene described the next few days as "a sort of drunken nightmare to me, as I was waiting to see what was going to happen next." The second bomb was dropped on Nagasaki on August 9. After that it was only a few days before the Japanese government agreed to a cease-fire on August 14. Kelly and crew returned to San Francisco and then to Washington, his fifth assignment cancelled by the ending of World War II.[74]

With the war over, Kelly's sixth Navy assignment was to commemorate a little-known aspect of the Pacific conflict—the use of American submarines to eviscerate Japanese seaborne supply lines. Either Kelly or one of his superior officers decided it would be helpful for him and his crew to actually ride in a submarine to taste the experience. For Gene it proved to be more difficult than anticipated. He felt a bit claustrophobic but soon overcame that feeling and began to understand what existing deep underwater could be like. In the end, he crafted a film using stock footage of submarines.[75] But based on experiencing a ride in a submarine, he was able to write the narrative and narrated the film himself. It is thirty-seven minutes long, in black and white, and was released as *Submarine Warfare.*

Kelly's seventh and final assignment for the Navy was the easiest. He took charge of the Navy's part in a joint publicity effort called *Army-Navy Screen Magazine.* It was a semiweekly film compilation of news mixed with entertainment in the form of cartoons and variety shows, each episode about twenty minutes long, and designed for viewing by military personnel. *Army-Navy Screen Magazine* had been in production since June 1943. With the war over, it was in its final stages and ended in 1946.[76] Perhaps the best part of this assignment was that Gene could move to his beloved New York City.

LIFE IN THE NAVY

During his brief but hectic service in the Navy, Gene was able to be pretty close to his family. When he finished his basic training at San Diego and was assigned to the Naval Photographic Center at Anacostia in February 1945, Betsy gave up the rented house on North Alta Drive and took Kerry to Georgetown, where she rented a house. Kelly was able to live there with them, commuting to the center. Their housekeeper Mamie got a job in a munitions factory in California and would never work for the Kellys again. When Gene was deployed to the Pacific early in August 1945, they gave up the Georgetown house. Betsy and Kerry traveled by train to Los Angeles to see Gene off and then returned to the East Coast to stay at Betsy's parents' home in Cliffside, New Jersey. When Kelly was assigned to edit *Army-Navy Screen*

Magazine after completing his submarine film in fall 1945, the couple rented Apartment 12-D at 128 Central Park South in Manhattan.[77]

Kelly's few months of residence in the Washington metro area during 1945 exposed him more deeply to racial prejudice than he had ever known. Washington had always been a southern city, and in this era it began to segregate blacks from whites on the tennis courts and in public parks. Sixty-five organizations banded together to fight this move, and Gene was upset by it as well. Georgetown had historically been mostly black but it was being invaded, so to speak, by well-to-do whites who were pushing for the segregationist ban. Betsy had inadvertently become a part of this whitening of Georgetown when she rented a house there. While living in the area, Gene had enjoyed playing tennis in mixed-race doubles. "For weeks he and young Negroes and whites played tennis, became good friends," wrote a reporter for *Ebony* magazine. When the segregationist ban went into effect, Kelly said "he would play anyway, 'and if any police care to stop me, I would be most anxious to know on what grounds.'" Kelly was transferred to New York City for work on *Army-Navy Screen Magazine* before the segregation controversy in Georgetown came to a head.[78]

While Gene and Betsy lived in New York, Kerry continued to stay at her grandparents' home. The parents saw their daughter only once a week. It was an unusual decision, for Gene normally was a devoted father. "I guess Betsy and I fancied ourselves as Zelda and Scott Fitzgerald and just wanted to have a good time," he admitted years later. "A child would have been in the way."[79] The lure of New York and the opportunity to re-create their early months together in that city overpowered the parental sense for a time.

Service in the Navy did not prevent Kelly from continuing to perform public service in his spare time. On January 30, 1945, in the middle of boot-camp training, he participated with other actors such as Myrna Loy, Danny Kaye, and Margaret O'Brien in celebrating Franklin D. Roosevelt's sixty-third birthday. Although the president did not attend the ceremony in Washington, DC, it was intended as a promotion for his "pet personal project," the National Foundation for Infantile Paralysis.[80]

Also in January 1945, the FBI resumed tracking Kelly's activities. "A highly confidential and delicate source" in New York City assured the bureau that Kelly's name and phone number were in the papers of Julia Dorn Wood, who was believed "to be a close contact of reported Soviet espionage agents." A few months later, in July 1945, the FBI noted that both Gene and Betsy were listed as charter members of the Los Angeles branch of the National Citizens' Political Action Committee. The national organization was believed to be infiltrated by communists, and it later changed its name to Progressive Citizens of America.[81]

Ironically, around the same time, on July 10, 1945, Lieutenant (junior grade) Gene Kelly and Lieutenant Robert Taylor emceed the inaugural *Navy Hour* radio program. The broadcast, aired from George Washington University, praised the Navy and supported its recruiting efforts. A few months later, on November 18, 1945, Kelly was honored on the *Radio Hall of Fame*. On a forty-eight-hour pass from the Navy for the show, Kelly was asked how he would spend his time in New York. He joked that he would visit the Museum of Natural History and Grant's Tomb, presaging the opening of *On the Town* to come and amusing the live audience. Popular singer Martha Tilton offered to drive him around but he refused, saying that Navy men did not accept rides from strange women, which further tickled the audience. Then he and Tilton played the "Pet Shop" scene from *Pal Joey*. Gene also talked of seeing vaudeville shows at the Davis Theatre in Pittsburgh every Saturday afternoon as a child, did some tap dancing to piano music, and sang a jingoistic song about the Navy winning the Pacific War.

The FBI files do not mention either of these radio programs or Gene's role in supporting the Navy. Instead they note that a "technical surveillance" of the office used by Elaine Mendelsohn Rose, the field representative of the Los Angeles County branch of American Youth for Democracy (AYD) and a suspected member of the Communist Party, revealed that Rose had called Kelly at the suggestion of John Garfield. The latter was high on the FBI's list of suspected communists in Hollywood. Rose asked Kelly to help in a program called "Sweethearts of Servicemen," sponsored by AYD. The bureau was convinced that the Communist Party controlled AYD for its own purposes.[82]

Whether Gene actually did anything for the "Sweethearts of Servicemen" program is not known, but he did participate in an event that apparently was sponsored by AYD. It took place on December 12, 1945, at the Hotel Roosevelt in New York City to honor returning veterans. Called "Welcome Home, Joe," the ceremony also honored Jane Froman, a singer and actress who had been horribly injured in a plane crash near Lisbon, Portugal, on February 22, 1943. Traveling with a USO contingent to entertain the troops, she was among fifteen survivors among the thirty-nine people on board. But her left leg and right arm were nearly severed. After a year of painful recuperation, Froman resumed performing in a wheelchair and a heavy leg brace while entertaining troops in Europe. Kelly presented an award of appreciation for her "courage and inspiration to wounded soldiers" at the Hotel Roosevelt ceremony.[83] It is strange that the FBI would note Kelly's participation in honoring a courageous singer who battled against terrible physical infirmities. But the bureau was simply in a mode of filing everything for the record if there was any hint that the sponsoring agency was on its suspect list.

The FBI did not record the fact that Gene appeared on a *Victory Bond* radio show with Bing Crosby on December 6, 1945, or that he received a citation from the US Treasury Department for help in selling war bonds. Neither did they note that Kelly accompanied Myrna Loy in visiting wounded servicemen to cheer them up or that he appeared in two back-to-back *Treasury Salute* radio programs on January 25, 1946, to highlight the physical and emotional trauma that soldiers endured after the war. But because the Independent Citizens' Committee of the Arts, Sciences, and Professions (ICCASP) was suspect, the bureau did record that Gene donated $100 to help fund a meeting designed to organize physicians in New York City for the committee. It also noted that Kelly presided over a meeting hosted by the Veterans Council of ICCASP held at Madison Square Garden on May 16, 1946.[84]

Meanwhile, Kelly's fame continued to grow. When *Anchors Aweigh* was released on July 19, 1945, it built on what he had achieved in *Cover Girl.* The Newspaper Guild of New York City gave him its Page One Award at a ball held at Madison Square Garden on December 6, 1945. The committee consisted of newspaper critics including John Martin of the *New York Times.* The award was "for outstanding performance in the field of dance for 1945," with particular reference to his "inventive utilization of the motion picture camera in widening the scope of the dance on the screen in *Cover Girl* & *Anchors Aweigh.*"[85]

A month later, in January 1946, a news release informed the country that Kelly had been nominated for an Academy Award as best actor for *Anchors Aweigh.* Gene recalled that he was on a cruiser in the Pacific at the time (although he never explained why) when he received word to see the captain. "I was scared," he told a high school audience in 1982. But the captain told him, "it just came over the wires—you've been nominated for an Academy Award!" The news surprised him because he had not expected it. But the Navy was very proud that one of its own had been honored. Secretary of the Navy James V. Forrestal congratulated Kelly in a letter dated January 28, 1946.

"As a very infrequent goer-to-the-movies, I can add my own testimony that it was a well merited choice. You made 'Anchors Aweigh' into intelligent and imaginative entertainment."[86]

Kelly, however, did not win the Oscar. Competing with Bing Crosby, Cornel Wilde, and Gregory Peck (ironically for his role in *The Keys of the Kingdom*), he lost to Ray Milland for *The Lost Weekend. Anchors Aweigh* had been nominated for best picture as well but was edged out by *The Lost Weekend.*

Soon after missing out on his Oscar, Kelly was interviewed by Hermine Rich Isaacs. She could not help but notice the "unmistakable tang of Pittsburgh" in his voice and emphasized his everyman qualities. Gene "still drives an unobtrusive car and when he chooses his eating place in New York it is likely to be a joint aptly nicknamed 'ptomaine palace.'"[87]

Even before his discharge from the Navy, movie agents were in touch with him about projects. Leah Jayne Salisbury tried to interest Kelly in a story called "Arthur Was Not an Ordinary Acrobat," written by one of her clients, but he passed this on to M-G-M. The studio "own[s] me but lock, stock, and barrel. If they show any encouraging signs, please let me know."[88]

Gene was discharged from active duty on May 13, 1946 (which the FBI carefully noted), but he continued to serve in the Navy Reserve at his rank of lieutenant, junior grade, for the next eight years. He received the World War II Victory Medal and the American Area Campaign Medal. By this time Johnny Darrow and Leland Hayward were no longer Kelly's agents. He was represented by Roy Myers of MCA, and when Gene called him about work, Myers reported that M-G-M had no projects for him yet.[89]

So Gene and Betsy continued to live in New York after his release from active service, taking an extended vacation before going back to California. Gene felt he had put on weight while in the Navy and wanted to get back in shape before resuming his film career. For three weeks he worked out at Charles Weidman's studio. Kelly often ate at Toots Shor's, downing a steak with spinach and broccoli every night, but he asked Toots not to allow any fan to buy him liquor. After three weeks M-G-M told Gene to take more time, and he continued working out at Weidman's studio for another three weeks.[90]

When Kelly returned to California in early July 1946, there was an addition to his professional life—a personal secretary. Gene had met Lois McClelland, a WAVE (Women Accepted for Volunteer Emergency Service) soon after boot camp. She was a script clerk on *Combat Fatigue Irritability*. Later they met again at the Naval Photographic Center at Anacostia. Lois came from what she described as "an upstate New York Republican family" and had never known a movie star before meeting Kelly. "He was so human, so natural, so absolutely lacking in affectations," she wrote. McClelland did secretarial work for Kelly and proved to be so helpful that he wanted her to continue working for him after they were discharged. Betsy liked her from the start. "Tall and strong, with a great figure and a wide smile, Lois is gently spoken, loving, and loyal. She was also a very good secretary" and quickly became a friend to the entire family.[91]

While Gene continued to work out at Weidman's and to enjoy the brief extension to his stay in New York, Lois accompanied Betsy and Kerry to California in late June 1946 so they could look for a house before Gene arrived. In her memoirs, Blair mistakenly reports that this took place in August 1945 and does not mention the long stay she and Gene enjoyed in New York through mid-1946. Johnny Darrow, who now was a real estate agent in California, found a house for the Kellys that Betsy thought was perfect. Located at 725 North Rodeo Drive in Beverly Hills, it needed renovation but was available at $42,500. Betsy liked it so much she talked Gene into letting her buy it before he came to California.[92] It would be the family's home for the rest of Gene's life.

Kelly's brief Navy experience was vitally important to his development as a filmmaker. Working for only about a year, he went through a crash course in the basics—learning how to edit film, acting in ways he rarely had a chance to in Hollywood, and making films for a specific and important purpose quickly and with limited resources. Working with *Franklin* crewmembers gave him his first exposure to location filming. The reinforcement of Kelly as the all-around filmmaker—the auteur—took place while he was in uniform working for Uncle Sam.

CHAPTER 8

Restarting His Career, 1946–1948

When the Kellys moved back to California in July 1946, Gene faced the daunting task of picking up his career where he had left it before his Navy service. For a time there appeared to be no good project for him. Meanwhile, the family settled into the new home at 725 North Rodeo Drive. The house was nearly thirty years old. It was, as Gene told a reporter, "a converted farm house, . . . a remodeled Belgian Provincial" with a white exterior and red trim. Until M-G-M called him for work, Kelly puttered about remodeling the place. He made tables and chairs and even dismantled some walls. The five-bedroom, three-bath house was big enough—it just needed remodeling to suit the family's needs.[1]

LIVING IN A BIG WAY (1947)

The studio put Kelly into one of his least satisfying films, *Living in a Big Way*, for his first project after the war. The primary purpose of this picture was to launch Marie McDonald as the studio's newest star. Gregory LaCava, the director, had the original idea for a story about returning veterans and housing shortages, but nothing was written yet. He and screenwriters, Charles Lederer and Harry Kurnitz, flew to New York to talk with Gene about the project even before he moved back to California. But Kelly was not impressed by the ideas.[2] They made the picture anyway.

Gene plays Leo Gogarty, who marries Margo Morgan nine days after meeting her and just before going to war in 1942. They seem to be carried away by the moment rather than being in love. When he returns, her family has become wealthy through lucrative war contracts, and she wants to divorce him. The plot revolves around Leo's effort to help his army buddies solve a housing shortage and trying to decide whether he should fight for Margo. Neither of them seems to truly care for the other. In fact, Margo admits she married him only because he looked good in a uniform. Most of the characters are one-dimensional and not very likeable. *Living in a Big Way* ranks as one of the least enjoyable of Kelly's movies, and it failed to jump-start McDonald's career.

When the movie was finished, the studio thought it needed something more, so Kelly was asked to add three dances to "pep it up," as he later put it.[3] Two of the three dances are good, but one is terrible.

The first number is typical of Kelly's romantic film dances. It is similar to the graceful number he does with Leslie Caron on the banks of the Seine in *An American in Paris* and to dances in many other Kelly films with other co-stars. Here, it is set to "It Had to Be You," and surprisingly McDonald dances well and matches Kelly in grace. The number is inserted right after the two were dancing in a nondescript way in a crowded ballroom and come out on the terrace for a kiss and to say goodbye, so it works well with the plot.

The second dance is set in the garden of Margo's palatial home supposedly to win her back, and the song starts with "Fido and Me." The plot placement works, but the sequence is contrived and unappealing. The dog does a few tricks while Kelly prances about and Margo smiles as she watches from her bedroom window. Yet, one does not sense any love between the two, and Kelly's overacting and exaggerated facial expressions are a turnoff. The second segment, where he interacts with the statue of a woman, is even worse. There is so much silliness and hammy posing that even the brief sections of ballroom steps, Spanish dance, and jitterbug are all difficult to watch. The finale combines tap and modern dance but it is nothing new for Kelly; tagged on to the end of a farcical number, it does not redeem it. When the dance is over, Leo looks up and Margo's window is vacant. That is the only honest moment of the number—it is truly unwatchable and a great waste of Kelly's talents. It is difficult to understand why he planned such a grating number here rather than dancing his love seriously to win her back. Perhaps it was to match the cavalier attitude that the characters seem to have about each other. And yet, a love dance would have redeemed Leo at least and compensated for the sorry plot.

The third number, though, is unique and memorable. Kelly developed a routine using an unfinished apartment building as a prop, and incorporated a number of children into the number. The dance combines varied steps with many acrobatic stunts to showcase Kelly's athletic ability. Only the placement of the dance is questionable. It is inserted right after Margo dumps Leo a second time, so the exuberance of the number is out of place.

Putting aside the scene's poor placement, the dance itself has much to offer.

Building on his appealing dance with Sharon McManus in *Anchors Aweigh*, Kelly jumped full-scale into the world of children, their games, and their enthusiasm in this number. He choreographed Leo playing street games with boys and girls and then leaping onto the unfinished building. The structure becomes his jungle gym as Gene incorporates several dance traditions in his spirited romp between studs and across rafters. Finally, he swings on a tall ladder from one part of the structure to another, with the bottom end of the ladder fixed to the floor of the studio. Kelly did his own stunts in the number, just as he performed a similar swing high over the set in the fantasy Spanish dance of *Anchors Aweigh*. Descending, Leo once again interacts with the kids before collapsing in mock exhaustion. The dance exemplifies Kelly's love of interacting with children and his willingness to give a great deal to entertain them.

Referring to his jumping around on the high rafters, Kelly said, "Any gymnast can tell you that's an easy trick to do." Viewers are awed only because it was done at a considerable height above the floor. He appropriately chose to wear work clothes for this number on the unfinished building. Kelly found that a tee shirt, jeans, and "a Navy working cap—the kind they still wear on aircraft carriers" worked well. "I tried Marine caps, but they weren't as effective."[4]

Art director Preston Ames, who did not work on *Living in a Big Way*, nevertheless was greatly impressed by the Building Dance and Kelly's nerve in tackling the complicated routine that took him into and out of so many spaces on the set. Ames also noted that it was "very rough on the cameraman" to film the number. Cinematographer Harold Rosson was rushed due to the tight schedule for framing and shooting this complicated routine. Charness believes "the camerawork is awkward and unsatisfying" as a result. Stanley Donen worked with Gene on this and the Fido/statue routine and received credit with Kelly for creating and directing the dance sequences.[5]

Living in a Big Way premiered in Los Angeles on June 10, 1947, and in New York on October 9, but lost money. Critics generally panned the movie except to praise Kelly's numbers. Virginia Wright thought the dances grew out of the story and were "as much a part of the action as the dialogue." In an interview with Philip Scheurer, Kelly emphasized that engaging in children's games was a way to "bring dancing closer to everybody and take away the 'highbrow' curse" often associated with dance. One can imagine Gene's pleasure when Martha Graham, who he called "my idol, and my goddess," told him that she liked the dance with the children and she "was happy to see popular stuff," as

Figure 8.1 Playing games with children as a prelude to a dance. (Still from *Living in a Big Way*, 1947)

Figure 8.2 Dancing on the rafters of an unfinished building, while the children he just played games with gaze up at him. (Still from *Living in a Big Way*, 1947)

Kelly put it. Graham "just tickled me pink when she said that." But strangely, she also praised the number with Fido and the statue.[6] It is not clear why Graham, a pioneer of modern dance, liked this number with its hammy overacting, uninventive choreography, and unappealing characterization.

Unfortunately, *Living in a Big Way* was an inauspicious start to Kelly's postwar career despite Graham's praise. Kelly was capable of far better choreography and performance than the Fido/statue dance.

THE KELLY TEAM

Gene's home life at this time, however, was comfortable and cozy. Lois McClelland lived with the Kellys for two and a half years before getting her own apartment. She became a trusted personal manager. One day Gene said to her, "Loie, . . . see that we save some money. I don't care how you do it—but do it, hmmmm?" So Lois put both Gene and Betsy on a strict budget and managed their money for some time.[7]

Jeanne Coyne—his former dance student, soon-to-be dance assistant, and future wife—came to California while *Living in a Big Way* was in production. The Kellys put her up in their house too, sharing a room with McClelland. Gene arranged a job for her at M-G-M and also introduced Coyne to Donen. Kelly was putting together a personal team, with Donen assisting him on the filming of dance sequences, Coyne serving as his dance assistant, and McClelland handling his fan mail, daily schedule, and bank account. Donen and Coyne were paid by the studio, but McClelland was paid by Kelly.[8] Carol Haney joined the team as another dance assistant a year later.

About a year and a half after Coyne joined Kelly's team, she and Donen decided to marry. Jeanne did not tell her mentor about it until the very day of the wedding, April 12, 1948. When she broke the news at ten in the morning, Gene took charge of the event. He told Lois to arrange for flowers and champagne, and he gave the bride away at the ceremony, which took place at two that afternoon in Santa Monica.[9]

GIVING UP DREAMS OF BROADWAY

Despite his desire to stay in Hollywood and continue to work in films, the lure of New York tugged at Kelly in the postwar years. He and Betsy were

Figure 8.3 The Kelly Team (in 1951): *from left*: Jeanne Coyne, Stanley Donen, Gene Kelly, and Lois McClelland, with Carol Haney sitting on the floor with her back to the camera. (Photographer Maurice Terrell, Library of Congress)

subscribers to the Ballet Society but could not attend the opening on November 20, 1946. George Balanchine suggested that Kelly give his and Betsy's season tickets to someone else, and Gene readily agreed. He replied that he would give the tickets to students who could not afford to be members. "When I'm in town I'll sneak in somehow," he joked.[10]

Kelly recalled later that in those days the urge to do a play on Broadway came back now and then. Of course, it was not possible given his M-G-M contract. But every time he finished a film, the Kellys would go to New York to at least *see* a play on Broadway.[11]

William Saroyan persisted in trying to get Gene to do more projects with him. He reminded Kelly that "Sweeney in the Trees" was still an option either on the stage or on screen if he was interested. Another possibility was a new play called "Jim Dandy, Fat Man in a Famine," an update of *The Time of Your Life* with a surrealistic tone and setting but again filled with "civilization's wreckage and assorted castaways." The play had a strange mixture of cynicism and hope, with a great deal of Christian symbolism unusual for Saroyan.

He wanted Gene to play a character in this production, which never made it to Broadway because the Theatre Guild rejected it. So did Gene. A third suggestion Saroyan made was John Millington Synge's *The Playboy of the Western World*, an "Irish Irish" play that was "a natural for you."[12]

Saroyan also tried to lure Kelly into a film version of *The Time of Your Life*. Produced by William Cagney, it would include his brother James and sister Jeanne in major roles. Producer Cagney very much wanted Kelly to re-create his role as Harry the Hoofer, but M-G-M refused to loan him. Gene suggested his brother Fred, who was still living in New York at that time. "The Cagneys would be crazy not to use him," he told Saroyan. The playwright was deeply disappointed, considering Gene as the ultimate Harry, but he supported Fred as the next best option. In the end William Cagney offered the part to Paul Draper. When released in September 1948, the film was widely criticized and lost money.[13]

Despite Saroyan's attempts to collaborate, it was fortunate that Gene never did because most of the playwright's work failed to register with the public after his initial success during the late 1930s. M-G-M wisely refused to loan Kelly, placing his career high on its priority list as a successor to Astaire, who had gone into retirement by this time. Some commentators thought that Gene's visibility and success thus far fell short of Astaire's but he had the potential to work up to and exceed it. John Martin wrote that Kelly could be "the most important figure on the Hollywood dance scene at the moment. Not only has he a lively imagination as a dancer and a creator of dances, but he is also keenly aware of the camera's unique possibilities, which most dancers are not."[14]

These were heady words for a performer just back from military service and having dished out the disappointing *Living in a Big Way*. Hometown folks too continued to be proud of their favorite son. The Johnstown Junior Chamber of Commerce issued a certificate of appreciation to Gene "in recognition of success in your chosen field of endeavor. It is a symbol of the high esteem in which you are held by your friends and former associates of this city."[15]

THE PIRATE (1948)

Soon Gene was placed in a film project worthy of his talents, an adaptation of the stage play *The Pirate*. Originally a comedy by the German playwright

Ludwig Fulda, it had been revised by Samuel N. Behrman into a vehicle for Alfred Lunt and Lynn Fontanne in the 1940s with a few songs interspersed. Lunt and Fontanne had great success with the production, so M-G-M purchased the rights and invested a good deal of time and money in working up an appropriate screenplay.[16]

Much to Kelly's fortune, Freed assigned Vincente Minnelli to direct the film. Gene had not been able to interact with the director very much while filming "The Babbitt and the Bromide," but on *The Pirate* the two forged an exciting collaboration. Kelly often pinpointed Minnelli's *Meet Me in St. Louis* as his favorite musical, admired the director's use of color, and appreciated his willingness to explore innovative staging and cinematography. "We complemented and supplemented each other quite well," Kelly said of his colleague. Gene thought Minnelli stayed largely on the surface, spending hours minutely composing a scene, while he himself paid attention "to the guts" of the scene—the characters, the movement, how it fit into the plot. Preston Ames thought that Minnelli could be frustrating to most people, but not so for Kelly. If the director took too long to arrange the extras, Gene only had to say, "Come on, we are an hour behind; let the girl cross her legs the other way." Minnelli caved in and the scene was filmed. "So we were a good team, and we enjoyed each other," Gene concluded.[17]

Minnelli reciprocated these feelings. Like Gene, he enjoyed discussing every aspect of a picture before the cameras started to roll and found that they usually thought alike concerning camera angles, continuity, and other aspects of the filming process. But Minnelli was famous for being unable to express what he wanted actors to do and recalled that sometimes even Kelly found it difficult to understand him. "I'd tell him to make a scene more jaunty. Gene would look quizzically at me. He was, of course, the definition of the word, jaunty."[18]

The pair had their greatest fun developing Gene's character, a traveling actor named Serafin who impersonates a famous pirate to win the heart of Judy Garland's Manuela. But his plan backfires and he is arrested and nearly executed before Manuela's fiancée, the mayor of her town, is exposed as the real pirate. Kelly and Minnelli thought Serafin should be a parody of John Barrymore and Douglas Fairbanks Sr., played with a lot of bravado and cockiness.[19] This sort of acting held a special place in Gene's heart because of the many Fairbanks movies he had seen as a child in Pittsburgh, and he threw himself into the characterization with gusto.

Kelly also valued the opportunity to work with Garland again. He had gone to the set of *Meet Me in St. Louis* to watch and applaud her work under the hand of Minnelli, who had not yet become her husband at the time. Now Garland and Minnelli were married, but their union was beginning to show signs of fracture. Garland's personal problems with drug abuse and her recurring feelings of inadequacy also increased during the production of *The Pirate*. Kelly worked around the problems created by Garland's frequent absences, eternally grateful for her early support of his career.[20]

The Pirate was blessed with an almost perfect team, and Kelly worked beautifully with all of them. Robert Alton had been lured to California well before this time and was an experienced film choreographer, especially adept at large ensembles. He and Kelly divided up the work, with Alton handling everything but Kelly's own dances. Cole Porter was hired to write the songs for *The Pirate* and produced a handful of classics. Kelly was responsible for one of them. When everyone thought a lighthearted number was called for in a particular spot of the film, he visited Porter in Brentwood and explained what he needed. Porter, of course, remembered Gene from *Leave It to Me* and graciously wrote exactly what he was asked in the form of "Be a Clown." Kelly said, "It surpassed anything I could have imagined. It was brilliant. Each verse was more stunning than the last."[21] He and Minnelli used it twice in the picture.

In the first use of "Be a Clown" Gene danced with the Nicholas Brothers, the same team that he and his brother Fred had replaced in Cab Calloway's show at Altoona in 1931. The three of them wore identical clown costumes and performed a lively, acrobatic routine. Kelly included his Midair Twist and Crab Bounce. He also incorporated his Prone Kick but with a modification—rapidly switching the hand each dancer rested on, to make the step even more impressive. Gene also used acrobatic steps the brothers had performed before, creating an unforgettable number.

Short, wiry, and brilliant flash dancers, the Nicholas Brothers had performed in several Hollywood movies but usually in discrete segments so their numbers could be deleted from release prints sent to the segregated South. Gene refused to kowtow to this marketing strategy and insisted they dance with him as an integral part of the plot. It was the first time that a white performer danced with African American dancers in a major studio production. Gene was forging ahead with his attack on racial prejudice; both Minnelli and Freed supported him in it. Fayard Nicholas remembered that Kelly, when reminded of the Southern market, replied "I don't give a damn! It'll play the same all over the world, so why do we have to just think about the South?"[22]

Figure 8.4 Kelly and the Nicholas Brothers, Fayard and Harold, leap high and touch their toes in the acrobatic "Be a Clown" number. (Still from *The Pirate*, 1948)

In the second rendition of "Be a Clown," Gene and Judy, also dressed as clowns, were clearly performing on a different stage and to a different audience to show that Manuela had now joined Serafin's act and that the two of them were a couple. Their chemistry and sense of enjoyment in doing this number created an upbeat ending for the movie.

Kelly expanded on his previous work to create elaborate, colorful dances that fit tightly into the plot and characterizations of *The Pirate*, making it one of the most thoroughly integrated dance musicals ever made. The "Niña" number, taking place relatively early in the film, was set as an impromptu dance through the streets of Port Sebastian on a mythical Caribbean island so Serafin could promote his upcoming show that evening. It is a traveling dance during which Serafin flirts with local girls as he climbs up and over the buildings and segues into an energetic dance with the girls on a pavilion. It ends with Gene performing Revolving Jetés and then running up steep steps to point dramatically to the promotional poster for the show.

The number demanded a big set and complicated details to give Kelly maximum range for athletic stunts mixed in with vigorous choreography. Set

Figure 8.5 In the final shot of the "Be a Clown" reprise, which is also the ending of the film, Gene and Judy come across as themselves rather than as Serafin and Manuela, which actually adds to audience delight. (Still from *The Pirate*, 1948)

designer Jack Martin Smith created a pavilion with poles set on ball bearings, so Gene and the chorus dancers could spin around. "He got whatever he wanted" from Freed in the way of props for this number, Smith recalled. The set designer enjoyed working with Gene on the intricate details. He designed it "so that Gene could run up and down it like a cat."[23]

The most elaborate and complicated number, the "Pirate Ballet," marked a new level of achievement for Kelly. As discussed earlier, Gene had created three film ballets so far, "Alter Ego" in *Cover Girl* as well as "The Worry Song" and the fantasy Spanish dance in *Anchors Aweigh*. All three were standouts, but this number went even further.

The "Pirate Ballet" is Manuela's fantasy about the pirate who has always fascinated her, and thus it delves into psychological implications. As she watches Serafin dancing around a mule, he changes in her imagination to the blood-thirsty pirate. Vincente and Gene pushed barriers in this number in every way, symbolically as well as physically. Dressed in a tight-fitting pair of shorts for the first and only time on screen, Kelly chillingly created a ruthless pirate who not only terrorizes women and steals gold, but kills his own men

Figure 8.6 It is clearly Kelly, and not a stuntman, going up the rope to the crow's nest to throw a lighted torch down. This is the only time Kelly wore shorts in a film. The number is the "Pirate Ballet." (Still from *The Pirate*, 1948)

when they try to steal his booty. "Niña" was a tour de force, but the "Pirate Ballet" surpasses it in bravado. Kelly grabs a rope to ride up to the crow's nest of a tall mast and then tosses down flaming torches to the deck. After that he rides down again; both trips were filmed fully to clearly show Gene doing his own dangerous stunts.

He ends the ballet with a stunning spear dance to express the unbridled demonic energy of the pirate. "He whips the weapon into a horizontal position behind him," as Douglas McVay has so aptly described it, "sends it back to a vertical line, snaps it in two and continues a whirling dance with one half of it."[24] The dance ends with Revolving Jetés as the pirate transforms back to Serafin dancing around the mule while Manuela slowly emerges from her fantasy.

As an authentic film presentation of a demented outlaw, the "Pirate Ballet" is unsurpassed. It is a unique Kelly product that stretches many conventions to the breaking point and was a pyrotechnical achievement. "We pretty near burned down the studio putting it on," commented Jack Martin Smith, "but it was a hell of a number" with "savage, beautiful, piercing music."[25]

Kelly insisted on doing his own stunts in *The Pirate*. Not only did he climb all over buildings in "Niña" and ride up and down the mast in the "Pirate Ballet," but he also fought four guards in an athletic tour de force at the start of the ballet. And unlike the stage play, where Lunt (as Serafin) had faked the tightrope scene, Kelly actually walked across a tightrope to enter Manuela's bedroom. A wire was attached to Kelly's back and mattresses were placed on the floor of the set, out of camera view, in case he fell.[26]

The Pirate was the most exciting, enjoyable, and fulfilling film that Kelly had made yet in his career; he was certain it would be a smash hit. Filming ended on December 20, 1947, and the picture was released on June 11, 1948. Initially it did well at the box office and received overwhelmingly positive reviews, but repeat viewings (always the key to box-office success) dropped and the movie fell out of public view. It failed to recoup its costs in the initial release but over time made a profit for M-G-M.[27]

Kelly was deeply disappointed by the reception of *The Pirate*. His expectations were so high that the limited public response impressed him more than the many positive comments by critics. "Vincente and I honestly believed we were being so dazzlingly brilliant and clever that everybody would fall at our feet and swoon clean away in delight and ecstasy—as they kissed each of our toes in appreciation for this wondrous new musical we'd given them. Well, we were wrong. About five and a half people seemed to get the gist of what we set out to do." Kelly partly blamed himself, saying he could not pull off the parody of Barrymore and Fairbanks properly.[28] But he was taking unnecessary blame for the lack of widespread appeal.

Initial reaction to *The Pirate* by critics was clearly positive; the audience was the real problem. Most viewers did not get the tongue-in-cheek quality of the production. Arthur Freed correctly predicted that viewers would get it twenty years later. By the 1970s a resurgence of interest in *The Pirate* sprang up, and it became a cult icon for some people while receiving accolades as a landmark musical from writers in the mainstream as well. Gay viewers came to embrace it for many reasons, and film historians often called it the perfectly integrated dance picture.[29]

The Pirate is an important landmark in Kelly's film career. He flourished as a multitalented artist in it. As with most of his previous films, Gene choreographed his own dances, but this time he did not film them. Neither did he need Donen to help on this project. Minnelli was not only a congenial collaborator but also a superb director of dance numbers, so Kelly had no need of a technical assistant to guide the cameraman for his dances. Those numbers are hallmarks of his choreographic abilities and his keen sense of performance. Serafin is charmingly portrayed as an egotistical but good-natured artist, and when Kelly danced there was magic. Gene really came into his own as a major film star with *The Pirate*, building on prior achievements in *Cover Girl* and *Anchors Aweigh*.

Kelly also learned from watching Minnelli. He had become even more interested in directing due to his filming experiences in the Navy, and now he picked up lessons from a master. Minnelli used the boom to increase camera movement vertically as well as horizontally. His camera fluidly follows Gene during his romp over the buildings of Port Sebastian in "Niña."[30] In contrast, when George Sidney's camera captures Kelly's similar romp over the structure of the hacienda in the fantasy Spanish dance of *Anchors Aweigh*, it is stationary and on the floor of the set. When he became a director in his own right, Kelly would use boom shots and keep the camera moving whenever possible.

HOME LIFE

The Kellys lived a comfortable, upper middle-class lifestyle on Rodeo Drive. They had a maid named Bertha who lived in the back of the house with her husband, a post office worker. Gene continued to putter around with making furniture and enjoyed the bliss of domesticity. "Children are close to the Kelly heart," commented Dorothy O'Leary for *Silver Screen*. "He remembers with unabashed Irish sentimentality the happiness of his own childhood." Gene was careful about Kerry's education, preferring she attend a public school rather than be "'contaminated by some of those kids with turned-up noses' in private schools."[31]

Gene told a reporter in 1953 that Kerry wanted a pool, and Betsy was keen on it too, but swimming gave him sinus trouble and the ocean was not too far. So they built a volleyball court instead because Kelly needed something for vigorous exercise to keep in shape. In her memoirs fifty years later Betsy misremembered it, writing that Gene wanted a swimming pool but she refused as it was too "Hollywood." As for his daily routine, Gene went to bed at 10 P.M. if he had to report to the studio in the morning. When he could stay at home, Kelly was up until 2 or 3 A.M. working out dance routines in his mind or on his feet in the den, and slept until noon the next day.[32]

The famous Kelly parties restarted almost as soon as the family moved

Figure 8.7 Gene and daughter Kerry skating on their driveway at 725 N. Rodeo Drive in 1951. (Photographer Maurice Terrell, Library of Congress)

back to California in 1946. The Saturday ritual began with dinner for about a dozen people, followed by games for additional guests until twenty to twenty-five people regularly came to blow off steam, relax, and enjoy the company of interesting and entertaining people. Ping-pong continued to be a feature of these gatherings, as well as charades, songs, and piano-playing.[33]

Singer Lena Horne and her husband, musical arranger Lennie Hayton, were regulars at the Kelly house parties. Horne always was aware that her

Figure 8.8 Betsy, Kerry, and Gene skating on their driveway, with their house in the background in 1951. (Photographer Maurice Terrell, Library of Congress)

color separated her from white Hollywood and resented the assumption that she was to "sing for my supper" at posh gatherings. She gravitated toward "the Gene Kelly group, the Easterners who had been transported out West and who did their best to transpose their old style of life as well." Horne did not necessarily like everyone else who attended these Kelly parties, but "they were decent and interesting" people.[34]

Gene also started a new tradition of volleyball games. The new volleyball

Figure 8.9 Dancing with wife Betsy Blair at one of their open-house parties on Saturday nights in 1951. Lena Horne is singing near the piano (behind Gene), and Lois McClelland (Gene's secretary) is sitting on the sofa with her back to the camera. (Photographer Maurice Terrell, Library of Congress)

court became the venue of intense competition between scratch teams every Sunday at noon. One pair of teams played and then showered in the upstairs bathrooms while the next group took the second shift on court. After volleyball, a potluck buffet was assembled because Sunday was Bertha's day off. This was followed by watching movies projected on a large screen in the living room.[35]

Gene let his innate competitiveness flow without restraint on the volleyball court. "It was his backyard, and his volley-ball, and he wanted to be king," choreographer and dancer Bob Fosse recalled years later. "I'd never seen anyone so fierce about a so-called friendly game in my life . . . He had a competitive streak in him which was quite frightening." But just when it became unbearable, Gene often flashed "that smile at you and all was well." Some guests could not stand it. Composer Andre Previn eventually came less often to the Kelly parties because he could no longer put up with Gene's "desperate need always to prove he was the best."[36]

Broadway playwright and screenwriter Arthur Laurents was a regular at the Kelly parties even though he disliked Gene immensely. Laurents, a promiscuous gay man, admitted to sleeping around since age fourteen, going, in his own words, "from house to house like the Avon lady." He came to the Kelly parties to pursue actor Farley Granger, who was dating another man at the time. Granger was a regular, so Laurents became a regular as well. He enjoyed playing charades and quietly counted up many personal reasons to hate Gene while accepting his hospitality. Noël Coward once joined the Kelly group and became the center of attention. Betsy recalled the evening with pleasure. Not only did Coward play the piano and sing, but others also entertained, with Comden and Green performing, Judy singing, and Gene dancing. But the way Laurents described that evening was only that Kelly tried to outdo Coward by trying to dance on the living room rug with little effect. Laurents especially was contemptuous of what he called the "secretary-fans" at Kelly's parties, apparently referring to the close inner circle of McClelland, Coyne, and Donen. "They were all battling hard to please the lord and master." Laurents even criticized the house as furnished "with an absence of taste: uncertain colors and islands of plaid." He hated the "slapdash pot-luck meals" and Betsy's interjection of politics into the conversation.[37]

Despite Laurents's obvious disdain for Kelly, which tainted much of his recounting, there is no reason to doubt at least the outline of his version of a controversial incident in Gene's life. On Sunday, October 12, 1947, Kelly broke his right ankle. Exactly how that happened has been obscured by a number of different stories, but Laurents was present and saw it happen. On that day Gene divided the volleyball players into an A team of skilled players like himself, Donen, and Richard Conte, and a B team of what Laurents called "duffers like Farley and me and Betsy." The teams were to alternate on the court. Gene's A team (split into two opposing groups) had its first game and then rested on the lawn while the B team (also split into two opposing groups) tried to finish their game. But they could not, because no one played well and so no one scored. They could feel the tension building as the A team became eager to have the court again. It was too much for them, and the B team "began to laugh like bad kids. The harder we tried to stop, the less we succeeded"—and the longer the game continued. According to Laurents, players on the B team knew Gene was getting angry and dared not look at him.[38]

Then the ball flew away and hit Gene on the head. Kelly lost his Irish temper, sprang up from the lawn, and yelled at the B team for taking so long. They offered to quit, but Gene took it as an accusation that he was being unreasonable. Angrier, he stomped toward the house, opened the kitchen door, and stepped partway in. Kelly turned for a final outburst at the group and

Figure 8.10 Kelly and guests playing in the family's volleyball court behind the house in 1951. (Photographer Maurice Terrell, Library of Congress)

stomped his right foot down very hard. He happened to step directly on the doorsill and fractured his ankle.[39]

Worried about what the studio would think, Gene spun a story about how the accident happened. He told studio executives he broke the ankle while rehearsing at home. That story was repeated in the *Los Angeles Times* a couple of days later, specifying that he was dancing on a hardwood floor. Other reports circulated that it happened as he played touch football or softball.

Even in 1974, when confiding to an interviewer that it occurred while playing volleyball in his backyard, Kelly could not bring himself to admit exactly how the accident took place. He did acknowledge that he had been "an idiot" to have let it happen.[40]

It is interesting that with two teams of guests present and witness to the injury, no one except Laurents revealed how it happened. Only Laurents, who despised Kelly, broadcast what happened in his memoirs and also in an interview for *Anatomy of a Dancer*. Everyone else kept silent to protect Gene, showing how well-liked he was, even among people who disliked his extreme competitiveness in games.

EASTER PARADE (1948)

The ankle break, a serious injury for a power dancer like Kelly, took place at a critical point in his next movie assignment, *Easter Parade*. Before the accident, Freed wanted to reunite the team of Minnelli, Kelly, and Garland, but it did not work out that way. Returning from her recuperative stay at the Austin Riggs Foundation, and at the suggestion of her therapist, Garland insisted that she not work with her husband any longer. Their marriage was essentially over anyway, so Freed dropped Minnelli from the project and brought in Charles Walters, who got along very well with Garland.[41]

Robert Alton worked with Gene on the dance numbers, and Kelly played a large role in selecting Irving Berlin songs for the movie. On the cover of "Play a Simple Melody," Gene wrote "Irving wanted me to do this in Easter Parade—finally nixed it." He nearly approved "Ragtime Violin" but decided at the last minute against it. "Say It with Music" also was "an early candidate for 'Easter Parade,'" according to Kelly. "I Want to Go Back to Michigan" also "almost made it into" the picture. Berlin wrote new songs specifically for Gene, such as "Drum Crazy" and "Steppin' Out with My Baby," that made it into the film.[42]

The Kellys left for their first vacation in Europe in late August and returned to Hollywood by mid-September 1947. Frances Goodrich and Albert Hackett worked on the screenplay of *Easter Parade*, completing it on September 17. Gene had already started rehearsals two days before that date. He worked on "Drum Crazy" and "A Couple of Swells," the latter with Garland. As the two continued to rehearse, a mini-drama unfolded over the screenplay. Walters read it and reacted very negatively, calling it "terrible" because Gene's character (Don Hewes) was too harsh and mean toward Judy's character (Hannah Brown). He told Kelly and Garland "it stinks and the audience is going to hate you both." The two agreed that Walters should work with writer Sidney Sheldon on revisions because Goodrich and Hackett were now on vacation in Europe. In fact Gene and Judy raised the idea with Freed and helped persuade him to allow it. Sheldon worked on it from October 20 to November 14, 1947. Everyone was happy with it, but our careful comparison of the original with Sheldon's work reveals that the revisions are not drastic—in fact much of the harshness of Hewes was retained by Sheldon.[43] He merely toned down the character rather than making major revisions.

Rehearsals went along well until Kelly broke his ankle on Sunday, October 12. Doctors told him he had to wait at least six weeks before he could do any dancing on it. M-G-M chief Louis B. Mayer naturally was upset. The studio had already invested from $100,000 to $200,000 in the project, and a good deal of work had already been done on crafting the songs for Kelly. When the news broke in the *Los Angeles Times* on Tuesday, October 14, Fred Astaire called Gene to commiserate with him. Astaire had gone into retirement two years before, having reached a point of exhaustion in making dance musicals. He had kept in touch with Kelly and sent him congratulatory telegrams on the release of each new movie.[44]

According to Astaire, one hour after he hung up the phone M-G-M executive Louis Sidney called and asked him to replace Kelly on *Easter Parade*.[45] Gene has always taken credit for suggesting that Astaire replace him but never specified exactly when he did so. It is most likely that Astaire's friendly call planted the seed of this idea in Kelly's mind and he told the studio to get Astaire to replace him. Given the fact that the studio acted immediately on it, Kelly's idea was readily accepted.

"I was taken by surprise and told them I'd have to think it over," Astaire recalled. Actually, just the day before, he had listened to a recording of "Jack the Bellboy" by Lionel Hampton and got the itch to dance again in the movies. So the idea of jumping into *Easter Parade* was inviting. Astaire went to Culver City to talk with Sidney in person. He did not want to barge in on Kelly's project, so he once again telephoned Gene. The two had a frank discussion, with Gene reassuring Fred that he would consider it a favor because he was feeling bad about causing so much dislocation in the schedule. Then Astaire questioned Kelly about the nature of the dances. Gene assured him "they were adaptable to my [Astaire's] style." Finally, Fred wanted assurance that

Gene was not able to come back quickly to his work. When Kelly convinced him that was impossible, Astaire accepted M-G-M's offer.[46]

The news that Astaire was coming out of retirement broke on October 16. Gene told a reporter that he regretted losing *Easter Parade* but was very happy that Fred was working again. In fact, Kelly had told another reporter earlier, in April 1947, how much he wished Astaire would come back so the two could do a full movie together.[47] Thus far their professional paths had only intersected in "The Babbitt and the Bromide" of *Ziegfeld Follies* and now tangentially in *Easter Parade*.

Kelly's and Astaire's styles were quite different, and there has always been some discussion about how the latter adapted to the concepts already worked out for the former. Astaire contended that a lot of revision was needed before he felt comfortable with "Drum Crazy" and "A Couple of Swells." Those were the only two numbers Kelly had a chance to impress his style on during rehearsals. He and Garland had just begun to work on "I Love a Piano" before the accident. Fred also pointed out that with the Sidney Sheldon revision the characters were a bit different. In fact, Astaire asked Sheldon to further revise at least one scene of his revised screenplay to soften Don Hewes even more.[48]

Years later Kelly contended that most of his conception of "Drum Crazy" and "A Couple of Swells" was retained by Astaire. Fred merely had to "adjust the steps. But he kept pretty much the same kind of ideas, like the drum dance I had all finished. But he changed the steps so they'd look like his style. I don't think he kept all the camera moves."[49]

It demands a fine eye to detect whether these two numbers in *Easter Parade* reflect Kelly or Astaire. "If you look very closely," commented the film's director, Charles Walters, "you'll see that the numbers don't really fit Fred." Walters was speaking only of "Drum Crazy," because he thought "A Couple of Swells" was in Astaire's style. Dance historian John Mueller believes that neither of these numbers "seem out of keeping with Astaire's style," but he found "A Couple of Swells" to be a mix. It has "the galumphing" quality that Mueller interprets as a Kelly attribute along with "meticulous attention to mime and sly, throwaway humor" that he connects with Astaire.[50]

The original conception of "Drum Crazy" by Goodrich and Hackett was a joyous romp by Don Hewes who intensely enjoyed banging away on drums, "much to the delight of the kiddies" as the screenwriters put it.[51] They did not envision Don in competition with a surly kid for a stuffed toy. Moreover, it is unlikely that Kelly would have framed that number as a contest between himself and a child, and one must assume this was Astaire's idea or at least a concept with which he felt comfortable.

"Drum Crazy" was in fact the only film dance with a child that Astaire ever did, in contrast to Kelly's many film dances with children.[52] And in that one dance, Astaire competes with the kid and tricks him. In contrast, Gene always framed his dances with children as fun, cooperative, and bonding experiences between adults and children.

Easter Parade began filming on November 25, 1947, and finished the following February. When the picture was released on July 8, 1948, it took the country by storm, making a huge profit for M-G-M and rejuvenating Astaire's film career. Gerald Clarke, Garland's biographer, always critical of Kelly, wrote that, "The more sophisticated Astaire was a far better match for Berlin's succulent melodies." But Walters also thought that Astaire "was so much righter [*sic*]" for the role.[53]

In contrast, dance historian Mueller wrote that *Easter Parade* "might be considered less an Astaire film than a Gene Kelly film starring Fred Astaire." Then in a seeming contradiction, Mueller said that the end product "betrays no evidence of its origins and seems ideally suited to Astaire."[54] The truth is that Astaire had a hand in shaping the character of Don Hewes, had full control over most of the dances in the film, and compromised with Kelly's work on the numbers Gene had worked on before his accident. And yet, Kelly's mark is noticeable to those in the know. So, Mueller's first assessment seems to be from a historian's perspective and his second from the viewpoint of a movie audience, and considered in this way, both views make sense.

Kelly always regretted missing out on *Easter Parade* but recognized he had no one to blame but himself. He especially missed performing "A Couple of Swells," tailor-made for him and Garland, reminiscent of their "Be a Clown" in *The Pirate*, and inspired by its success. Garland was good at mime and comic skits and used this routine in her well-received stage show in the 1950s. Kelly admitted to "a twinge of regret" every time he saw the number in *Easter Parade*.[55]

CHAPTER 9

Red Scare—First Wave, 1946–1949

Kelly broke his ankle at a critical time in the history of postwar Hollywood. The House Un-American Activities Committee mounted a full-scale assault on the film industry in the fall of 1947. It subpoenaed nineteen people in the movie business to testify on suspicion that they were aligned with communist causes and organizations. Gene was not one of the nineteen, but he became heavily engaged in efforts by concerned members of the film community to counteract this attack, which they argued violated freedom of speech and many other liberties. Gene became a warrior for values he deeply believed in while stumping about on a crutch only days after the ankle break.

"I was always in the so-called left wing of Hollywood," Kelly commented years later about his political views. As he saw it, that meant "anyone who voted for Roosevelt." Kelly correctly saw that conservatives viewed politics as bluntly divided into two camps. They made no differentiation between the Democrats and the extreme left wing (communists and socialists) while placing themselves in the "American" wing. He accepted being labeled as a liberal because of this lumping together of divergent political views. But Gene also recognized that his solid New Deal principles actually put him in a group he called "the in betweeners," occupying an uncomfortable position between political extremes. On the right were conservatives "who hated Roosevelt" and on the left were communists and socialists whose philosophies Kelly rejected.[1]

Historians, however, take the differences between the extreme political left (the Communist Party and the Socialist Party) and the Democrats (liberals and moderates) seriously. Nevertheless, they conclude that both groups reduced in numbers from the 1930s to the 1940s. Kelly was one of the more prominent members of the liberal group during the war and the postwar years. George Murphy, his disgruntled costar in *For Me and My Gal*, was one of the more vocal conservatives. Murphy wrote of an imagined "all-out Communist effort to capture the movies" in his memoirs.[2]

Kelly's politics stemmed less from political ideology and more from a basic desire to see everyone treated fairly despite their skin color, ethnicity, or social and economic distinctions. He consistently supported and voted for Democratic candidates and liked the spirit of the New Deal programs. Giving a fellow an even break was the basis of his civic ideals. Gene never embraced socialism or communism, and Betsy's understanding of those political philosophies is questionable. Kelly was naturally frustrated to be lumped together with the far left by narrow-minded conservatives who readily branded anything outside their own political views as un-American.

Kelly first became politically aware in New York, but his political activism started in Hollywood and deepened during his naval service. As discussed in chapter 7, the local authorities began to racially segregate public facilities as whites invaded Georgetown. Gene enjoyed playing mixed doubles with African American friends and threatened to violate the local ordinances. "At the time I never felt like a protagonist or a champion of anything or anyone," he told *Ebony* magazine a short time later. "Being told who my friends might or might not be, I strongly believe, usurps the idea of democracy. If we're going to beat this thing I think that a good place to start would be the athletic fields and playgrounds of the nation."[3] As mentioned earlier, Kelly was transferred to New York City before anything came of this brewing problem.

Gene was active in many political events while in the Navy. He joined other actors, including Paul Robeson, in speaking on "The Artist as a Citizen" on the evening of January 6, 1946, at Henry Miller's Theatre in New York. The event was sponsored by the Theatre Division of the Independent Citizens' Committee of the Arts, Sciences, and Professions (ICCASP).[4]

The New York branch of ICCASP sponsored a rally called "One World or None" at the Hotel St. George in Brooklyn on May 4, 1946. Kelly mixed a good deal of self-deprecating humor with his political message. On rising to speak he pretended to start a dance then stopped himself. "I fooled you. No footwork tonight. This is serious business." The purpose of the rally was to encourage the United States and the Soviet Union to cooperate. "I don't want another war," Gene told the large gathering. "This one-world idea must be A.B.C. logic if it can even get through the skulls of hoofers and actors." Kelly defended Frank Sinatra for speaking out against prejudice and argued that "the people who really count will respect you when you fight for what you believe in and when the thing you believe in is right and just." He then went on to joke about playing a Brooklyn-type character so often on the stage and on the screen that he "might as well call this my home and figure that I'm a commuter to Hollywood."[5] Gene also spoke at a Veterans Peace Conference held at Madison Square Garden later in May 1946. Sponsored by the Veterans Council of ICCASP, it pushed for national action to deal with employment and housing problems facing returning servicemen as well as protested against racial and religious discrimination.[6]

Kelly's secret FBI file illuminates his political activities after his service in the Navy. It shows that he further deepened his political activism after returning to California from New York in the summer of 1946, initiating a year and a half of very intense involvement in public affairs. Gene supported the veterans of the Abraham Lincoln Brigade, consisting of volunteers who fought for the leftist republican government of Spain against Francisco Franco's military forces; the latter received help from Hitler and Mussolini. When the veterans group held a national convention in New York City on September 22, 1946, Kelly sent a congratulatory telegram that was published in the *Daily Worker*, the official newspaper of the Communist Party of America. "Please allow me to join in paying tribute to the men who fought Fascism before it was popular to do so," he wrote.[7]

Gene became involved in mediating a labor dispute in Hollywood. A messy and sometimes violent confrontation ensued between rival labor unions representing electricians, stagehands, and other behind-the-scenes workers in the movie industry. Roy Brewer headed the Hollywood office of the International Alliance of Theatrical Stage Employees (IATSE). A New Deal Democrat like Kelly, Brewer positioned himself as an enemy of communism. Battling against IATSE was Herbert Sorrell's Conference of Studio Unions (CSU), an organization widely believed to be genuinely influenced by communists. Brewer played up that angle in his publicity war against CSU, while Sorrell accused IATSE of widespread corruption. The two organizations (IATSE with 17,000 members, and CSU with 10,000 members) had been at loggerheads throughout 1945 and 1946 over jurisdictional disputes. CSU called a series of strikes in September 1946 that turned violent the following month.[8]

The Screen Actors' Guild (SAG) supported Brewer and IATSE, and because Gene had become involved in SAG by this time, he took an active part in the labor controversy. SAG formed a committee to write a forceful statement condemning CSU and appointed Gene to it, along with George Murphy and others. SAG also encouraged its members to break CSU picket lines. Gene agreed with this philosophically but found it difficult to put into practice. Reporter Adela Rogers St. Johns interviewed him after he recognized a Navy comrade who was walking in a picket line he just broke. Gene immediately called the man's wife and asked her to tell him "it was the toughest thing I ever

Figure 9.1 Kelly speaking fervently at a labor rally. (Still from *Anatomy of a Dancer*, 2002)

had to do." Kelly also wanted her to tell him "we're doing it *for* him. . . . We have got to make everybody see jurisdictional strikes are wrong."[9] He strongly believed that differences should be arbitrated.

SAG tried to calm the troubled waters. Eleven members, including Kelly, traveled to Chicago to appeal to a convention of the American Federation of Labor (AFL) for help in mediating the trouble. The answer was yes, so Gene tried to talk Brewer and Sorrell into going back to Chicago with him to consult with AFL representatives. Brewer and Sorrell refused to do that, but both agreed to a telephone conference with AFL representatives, which failed to settle the labor troubles with any finality.[10]

Kelly lent his name to another troubling issue that failed to be resolved. When Paul Robeson spearheaded a drive to pressure Congress for federal antilynching laws in September 1946, Gene was one of many sponsors who allowed him to use his name publicly. The FBI believed that communists may have been behind Robeson's effort in order to create more racial tension in the country. That year witnessed more lynchings since 1942, and yet all the pressure that Robeson could bring to bear did not work—Congress failed to pass legislation.[11]

The FBI received an anonymous and undated letter written on M-G-M letterhead on November 22, 1946. The writer stated that Kelly was a "proven Communist." But the agents noted that, "No facts substantiating this allegation were given."[12] Apparently someone at M-G-M had a grudge against Gene and lied to get him into trouble. But with no evidence provided, the attempt failed.

Kelly continued to be very busy with political work early in 1947. He participated in a benefit at the Los Angeles Philharmonic Auditorium on February 6 to raise $6,000 for striking workers in Hollywood. Gene was one of many actors who appeared in a short-subject film produced by David Selznick to promote American Brotherhood Week. The National Conference of Christians and Jews sponsored the Brotherhood Week movement, which was endorsed by Harry Truman. Selznick's film was screened during February 16–23 and included Lionel Barrymore, Gregory Peck, Dick Powell, and June Allyson in addition to Kelly. Gene also sent "first anniversary" greetings to the People's Songs of California, a branch of the organization founded by Pete Seeger a couple of years before. The California branch was headed by Mario Casetta, who the bureau believed was a member of the Communist Party, and so the FBI noted that Kelly sent greetings for the occasion.[13]

Gene tried to help the Joint Anti-Fascist Refugee Committee when it sponsored a meeting at the Los Angeles Biltmore Hotel on February 21. O. John Rogge, a former special assistant to the United States Attorney General, was slated to give the main speech but could not get to Los Angeles in time. Kelly agreed to read Rogge's speech, but he became ill just before the event so Betsy gave the talk. The FBI noted all of this.[14]

When Dorothy O'Leary interviewed Kelly in the spring of 1947 and asked him about his political activity, he was not shy in responding. "I'm a Democrat and I made speeches for the Democrats in the Fall campaign," he told her. "I don't know why I shouldn't say so. We're still guaranteed freedom of speech. A good thing, too. Imagine an Irishman named Kelly not wanting to make a speech about something or other!" But Kelly spoke more seriously to an interviewer from *Movieland* two months later. "I don't think being an actor exempts you from being a citizen," he bluntly stated. Gene took his civic responsibilities as seriously as his responsibilities toward his daughter and his wife. "This country is my country, and I intend to keep my mind and my eyes open, and my voice loud, to help make it run smoothly, efficiently, and democratically."[15]

By the fall of 1947 the House Un-American Activities Committee (HUAC) began pushing at Hollywood. Historians have conjectured that conservative disgust with pro-Soviet movies produced by the industry during World

War II, when the Russians were our allies against Hitler, rankled for years. Created initially to investigate the American Nazi movement in the late 1930s, HUAC turned its critical gaze on American communists after the war.[16] While the pro-Soviet movies of the war years may have been a factor, there is also no doubt that unscrupulous politicians saw attention-getting potential in slamming the movie community.

Calling for "a cleansing of the film industry," HUAC subpoenaed forty-one men in September 1947. Nineteen of them were labeled as "unfriendly" witnesses, suspected of ties to communists. Thirteen writers, four directors, one producer, and actor Larry Parks constituted the Hollywood Nineteen. The other Hollywood people subpoenaed were "friendly" witnesses, expected to provide evidence against the nineteen. The friendly witnesses included Roy Brewer, Ronald Reagan, Louis B. Mayer, Adolphe Menjou, and Walt Disney.[17]

The subpoenas created an immediate backlash from the left wing of politically divided Hollywood. The Progressive Citizens of America (PCA) protested HUAC's move with vehemence. Created by the merging of two other organizations late in 1946, PCA had several communists in its ranks. Many moderates and liberals in Hollywood refused to join it for that reason. Within the PCA, a cleavage between radical leftists and liberals developed by the summer of 1947, with Kelly becoming a major spokesman for the liberal group. PCA held the "Conference on the Subject of Thought Control in the United States" at the Beverly Hills Hotel on July 9–13, 1947. The organization was therefore ready to strike back as soon as HUAC began to target Hollywood two months later.[18]

Apparently Kelly was not involved in the well-publicized conference on thought control, but he became energized by PCA's action to defend the Hollywood Nineteen. The FBI noted that Gene hosted an executive meeting of PCA at his house on October 6, 1947, to plan its campaign. Gene also allowed himself to be listed as national chairman of the Young Progressive Citizens' Committee of PCA, with chapters created at various universities and colleges.[19]

But the most prominent Hollywood reaction to HUAC was mounted not by PCA but by a new group formed early in October 1947 by directors John Huston, William Wilder, and Philip Dunne called the Committee for the First Amendment (CFA). Huston strongly asserted that no one in the CFA was a communist. The group's primary objective was "to defend the principles indorsed in the Bill of Rights," as Huston put it. CFA grew quickly to 500 members, including Gene, and was endorsed by several US senators.[20]

CFA and PCA worked independently of each other in those hectic days as concerned citizens scrambled to prepare for the October 20 start of the Hollywood Nineteen hearings. Gene was deeply involved in the efforts of both organizations. PCA hosted a massive rally at the Shrine Auditorium in Los Angeles on October 15, 1947, to drum up public support for the Nineteen. Gene was the master of ceremonies. Taking place only three days after he broke his ankle, Kelly managed to take the stage with a heavy cast on his lower right leg to direct the event. Two FBI agents, Leslie Warren and Emmett McGaughey, attended the rally and reported on what Gene said while introducing Larry Parks. "Can it be that they feel he is afraid or can be intimidated because he is on the threshold of his career?" Gene asked the crowd. "If so, I believe they are in for a surprise, and you will agree with me after listening to Larry Parks."[21]

"We thought that the mood in Hollywood was absolutely great," remembered Betsy Blair of those heady days just before the hearings started. In fact there was a large groundswell of reaction against the politicians in Washington, and Betsy can be forgiven for assuming "that Hollywood was with us, and that we would triumph. We didn't believe that America could go so wrong."[22]

But Gene and Betsy underestimated the countervailing forces in Hollywood. Not only were many movie people deeply conservative, but the studios, always with a mind on money, were understandably scared of the controversy surrounding the Nineteen. As noted earlier, Mayer himself was a friendly witness for HUAC. Louis Sidney, Mayer's assistant, who played a role in getting Fred Astaire to replace Gene in *Easter Parade*, visited Kelly at his house and "begged him" not to participate in a planned trip to Washington, DC, hosted by CFA to witness the hearings.[23]

That famous trip to Washington became the most visible expression of Hollywood's reaction to HUAC. Organized by CFA, which chartered an airplane and recruited twenty-nine well-known actors to go along, it was designed to offer moral support for the Nineteen. In addition to Kelly, the flight included Humphrey Bogart, Lauren Bacall, Ira Gershwin, Danny Kaye, John Garfield, and Paul Henreid. It was timed so the group would arrive in Washington after the friendly witnesses had spoken and when the Nineteen were scheduled to begin their appearance. Despite Sidney's plea, Gene was determined to go on the trip. The chartered flight left Los Angeles on October 26, stopped in Kansas City, and arrived at Pittsburgh on Sunday, October 27, on the way to Washington.[24]

In his hometown Gene garnered a lot of attention, and Kaspar Monahan interviewed him for the *Pittsburgh Press*. Kelly said he was afraid that this was only the beginning of an effort to politically censor movies, but he also talked about his career and his ankle. The cast was due to be removed in December, and he anticipated that he would rely more on his left leg in dancing as a result of the injury.[25]

The CFA group went to Washington with high hopes but they were surprised by what happened there. Only eleven of the nineteen witnesses appeared before HUAC. They refused to cooperate and in some cases were rather bellicose in their comments. The CFA liberals had expected more cooperation, more dignity, along with a firm refusal to go beyond a certain line in testimony and commentary. Committee chairman J. Parnell Thomas abruptly called off the hearings on the afternoon of October 30 before the other eight unfriendly witnesses were heard. Expecting something like a "movieland" climax where right triumphed and everyone cheered for the underdog, the CFA people were confused when the reality of hardball politics came into play. Thomas had heard enough and wanted to move on to the next step—consideration of criminal charges against some of the Nineteen for their refusal to cooperate with the committee.[26]

Soon after this, a disturbing rally took place at Independence Square in Philadelphia, sponsored by PCA on behalf of the accused, where twelve of the Nineteen appeared. The crowd of 1,200 people was openly hostile to the group. "Shut up, you Communists," yelled members of the audience. "Go back to Russia, you bums."[27]

While in Washington, the CFA group presented a signed petition to the clerk of the House of Representatives. Kelly's signature was on the petition, which asked the House to address violations of civil liberties by HUAC. Gene also participated in two radio programs funded by CFA called "Hollywood Fights Back." They were broadcast on October 26 and November 2, 1947, and included a stunning list of thirty famous movie stars who spoke for a few minutes each on the need to protect free speech.[28]

The first "Hollywood Fights Back" program aired on the ABC radio network on October 26, the very day that twelve of the actors who participated in it started their flight to Washington. Those twelve, including Kelly, prerecorded their contribution. At a cost of $8,000, the half-hour program included prominent entertainment figures and four Democratic senators.[29] We listened to a recording of the program, and it was an impressive political statement. Gene spoke early and belittled conservative fears that the movie industry was being taken over by communists. He asked listeners, "Did you happen to see *The Best Years of Our Lives*, the picture that won seven Academy Awards? Did you like it? Were you subverted by it? Did it make you Un-American? Did you come out of the movie with the desire to overthrow the government?"

The second broadcast on November 2, 1947, was aired live. The hearings had just been abruptly cancelled, and Kelly spoke from New York City.[30] We also listened to a recording of this program. Kelly referred in his remarks to a "violent physical attack" a few days earlier by protestors opposing the peaceful Independence Square rally in Philadelphia. He mentioned that they even struck an eighty-one-year-old man. Gregory Peck also talked of the mob breaking up that rally. Richard Rogers and Leonard Bernstein were among those who spoke.

Both "Hollywood Fights Back" shows were put together with a canny mix of idealism and common sense. The actors knew how to appeal to the values of middle-class America. But their primary point—that everyone deserved the right to think what they wanted to and that Hollywood was not trying to subvert the American way—went only so far in the face of the Red Scare. Emotion tended to overwhelm logic, especially when unscrupulous politicians used that emotion for partisan gain. The two broadcasts are the most visible expression of values held by the embattled liberals of Hollywood during this era.

But did the broadcasts do any good? For a couple of weeks following the abrupt ending of the HUAC hearings there was reason to hope. One could say the opposing forces had achieved something of a stalemate in the contest. But then HUAC took legal action against ten of the original Nineteen, initiating a new level of confrontation. HUAC cited the ten, now referred to as the "Hollywood Ten," for contempt in November, and a grand jury returned indictments against them the next month. Hollywood liberals folded. Their idealism had been soiled by the action of those who had testified in October and who had been "shrill and defiant in their demeanor," as Marsha Hunt put it. And then the studios stopped being quietly worried and began to place open and unrelenting pressure on their actors to avoid politics. Those who refused faced a blacklist that now began to develop in Hollywood. All HUAC did was to threaten studio profits and it gained a big ally in the fight to attack suspected communists in Hollywood. Only the hard-core leftists in the film industry refused to kowtow and they suffered greatly for it.[31]

Even the Screen Actors' Guild joined the bandwagon. Ronald Reagan won election to its presidency against Gene Kelly and George Murphy on

November 17, 1947. Gene instead was elected one of three vice presidents. Reagan built a coalition of conservatives and moderates by arguing that SAG should work to keep the studios open during ongoing labor strikes resulting from the clash between Brewer's IATSE and Sorrell's CSU. The only way to do that was to continue crossing picket lines, a controversial tactic that created many enemies among both unions.[32] After his election, Reagan pushed through a resolution requiring that anyone seeking office in SAG had to sign an affidavit "stipulating that he was not a member" of the Communist Party. Kelly did not protest or oppose this resolution.[33]

Gene also joined with Edward Arnold to push through a resolution curtailing an initiative to pressure the studios into allowing more African Americans to have roles in movies. Gregory Peck had spearheaded this initiative back in September 1946, but little had come of it and the Anti-Discrimination Committee charged with the task had been dissolved in March 1947. The committee was later rehabilitated and achieved some success before disbanding once again. When a resolution was moved to resurrect the committee in November 1947, Kelly and Arnold proposed a counteraction that the resolution not be considered. They cited statistics indicating that more African Americans had worked in Hollywood during the past year and also stated that they did not want to antagonize the studios any more over this issue given the developing atmosphere in Hollywood over communism. The countermotion was carried and the committee was not resurrected.[34] This was the only time in his life when Kelly backed off from a fight concerning racial equality, and there can be little doubt that the devastating impact of the Thomas hearings and the criminal charges against the Hollywood Ten were the reasons for it.

Marsha Hunt, one of Kelly's costars in *Pilot No. 5*, served on the SAG board of directors. She later thought of herself as politically naive in the fall of 1947, but Hunt had participated in one of the "Hollywood Fights Back" programs and was not afraid to speak up in board meetings. One day Kelly gave her helpful advice. "Marsha, save your fire for when it matters. You are beginning to be heard. You're perfectly right about what you say; I agree with you. But don't waste your fire. Save it for a big issue, and then come on with your big guns. I know this board." Hunt came to realize he was right. The SAG board of directors, in her view, were mostly "extremely conservative. There were a few of us who were more liberal."[35]

As Kelly bluntly explained to Hunt, his political strategy was simple—choose the most important battles, back off when necessary, and rebound when possible. Indeed, in the wake of the "Hollywood Fights Back" failure, the liberals backed off under pressure from the studios to end political activism. Most Hollywood liberals tried to disassociate themselves from the far left and from the Hollywood Ten. They continued to uphold the principle of free speech, but that was a thin reed in a storm of conservative anger at anything that smacked of left-wing politics. Humphrey Bogart exemplified the dramatic change by publicly recanting when pressed to do so by Warner Brothers. He wrote an article for *Photoplay*, published in March 1948, titled "I'm No Communist" in which he stated that the trip to Washington had been a mistake.[36]

Bogart's stunning recantation did a great deal to quiet liberal activism. It "was such a body blow to all the rest of us on that plane," recalled Marsha Hunt, "because Bogie had been in the forefront. We were aghast at his turnaround." We do not know how Gene felt about Bogart's new position, but Betsy was not surprised by it after having met Bogart informally and observing his "macho" posturing.[37]

Not only Bogart's recantation but the entire trip to Washington was "a sobering experience," according to Hunt. Seeing firsthand how the congressmen of HUAC conducted themselves, and reading a lot of "devastatingly critical" newspaper commentary on the actors for mounting this protest, both angered and saddened the politically naive entertainment people. CFA changed its name to the Committee of One Thousand soon after the trip but "was moribund" by 1948.[38] Studio pressure to stop actors from being involved in politics was the final factor in the collapse of organized liberal activity in Hollywood.

Kelly never recanted or apologized for his role in the liberal movement, but "he came back disheartened by the tragedy that was happening," recalled Blair. When the Actors Division of the PCA sponsored a full-page ad in support of Larry Parks, published in *Hollywood Reporter* on November 3, 1947, Betsy was among those who signed the ad but Gene did not.[39]

A few months after the crisis of October 1947, Kelly once again openly supported liberal causes. He organized a party at his house to raise money for the National Association for the Advancement of Colored People. Paul Robeson sang "Ol' Man River" and spoke movingly to the group; they raised "a lot of money," according to Blair. Kelly also hosted a reception at his house in March 1948 for Anna Louise Strong, who had been invited by the American Russian Institute of Los Angeles to speak on "World Peace and the Russians."[40]

The 1948 presidential election was one of the most hotly contested in American history, with isolationist Republican Thomas Dewey seeming to have the lead on incumbent Democrat Harry Truman. A third candidate,

Henry Wallace, ran on an avowedly socialist platform. Norman Mailer, who had just written *The Naked and the Dead*, came to Hollywood for two weeks to campaign for Wallace. Even though Kelly strongly supported Truman, he raised money for Wallace because Betsy liked his candidacy. FBI informant "T-24" reported that Gene invited about twenty friends to his house and asked them to contribute $100 each to Mailer for Wallace. Gene and Betsy took an instant liking to Mailer and later visited him and his wife Beatrice in Brooklyn Heights. "They were very kind and courteous to us," Kelly recalled.[41]

Truman won with 303 electoral votes to Dewey's 189 and 49.6 percent of the popular vote compared to Dewey's 45.1 percent. Kelly attended Truman's inauguration along with other supporters from Hollywood.

Farley Granger recalled that Mailer also attended a gathering at Kelly's house to support the Hollywood Ten. "Everyone in Hollywood who was not an extreme conservative was there," Granger wrote. Mailer gave a passionate speech and then asked the guests to sign a friend-of-the-court petition to be presented as part of an appeal to the Supreme Court against the conviction of the Hollywood Ten. Granger and Shelly Winters wrote checks for $100 each, but later Mailer returned the checks. Only Granger and Winters had signed the petition and others had given cash so as not to create a paper record of what they had done. Mailer tore up the petition because he did not want Granger and Winters to get into trouble, either.[42]

In February 1948, nearly four years after Kelly performed in *Palestine Speaks!* to support the creation of a Jewish homeland, he and Gregory Peck acted in a dinner drama sponsored by the Los Angeles chapter of Hadassah to raise money for medical care in Palestine, the area where efforts were under way to create separate Jewish and Arab enclaves. Hadassah, the Women's Zionist Organization of America, had been working since 1913 to support medical care for all races and religions in Palestine. The Los Angeles chapter was trying to raise $90,000.[43] Only three months later, the state of Israel was established.

Throughout all this, the FBI kept track of Kelly's activities. Informant "T-32" told the bureau about a meeting of the Hollywood Motion Picture Film Council, created to improve the movie industry's image following the crisis of 1947. Dore Schary of M-G-M was its chair. The meeting took place on January 25, 1949, and Schary defended Kelly when the subject of Frank Fay came up. Fay, a stage and film actor who had long since gone to seed, was one of the most thoroughly disliked figures in the business because of his white supremacist, anti-Semitic views. Even when not spouting ultraconservative

Figure 9.2 President Harry Truman with Hollywood supporters at his inauguration in January 1949. Kelly is sharing a pleasantry with Jane Powell; twelve-year-old Margaret O'Brien is on the left side. (Truman Library)

rhetoric, he was an abrasive, unpleasant personality. Fay had identified Kelly and Sinatra as communists or at least fellow travelers at a public meeting held in Boston. Schary called Fay "a drunken bum, a crack-pot" and asked the Hollywood Motion Picture Film Council to vote a resolution of support for Kelly and Sinatra. Other members of the council were reluctant to do that, and nothing came of Schary's motion.[44]

On May 20, 1949, FBI director J. Edgar Hoover told his Los Angeles office to see if there was any real evidence that Kelly had been affiliated with the Communist Party or any organizations that could be considered a front for the party. But he cautioned: "It is not requested that you conduct an open security investigation concerning this individual in view of his prominence in public life." The Office of Military Intelligence had indicated that Kelly was a member of the Navy Reserve, so Hoover intended to forward the results of this investigation to the Navy as well. Agent Marcus Bright issued a twenty-five-page report on July 27, 1949, listing all the pertinent information his Los Angeles office had gathered on Kelly. Bright concluded that "Subject [Kelly] has several times denied being pro-Communist and no reliable evidence of actual Communist Party membership is known." Yet, Bright also pointed out that Kelly "has consistently supported causes either knowingly or unknowingly which were backed and often inspired by Communist Party elements." After digesting the contents of Bright's report, Hoover forwarded a copy to the director of Naval Intelligence on September 2, 1949, noting that it was confidential.[45]

Kelly had become one of many Hollywood liberals classified by historians as graylisted. That is an intermediate category below the blacklisted people (the Hollywood Nineteen, the Hollywood Ten, and others) who were known to be members of the Communist Party or so closely working with it as to be lumped into the same category. The graylistees generally did not have much trouble making a living in Hollywood even though unsubstantiated rumors, fears, and worries centered on them among enemies and friends alike. As long as the people who counted in their careers (studio executives, friends, and supporters) continued to believe in them, they had a good chance of weathering the political storm that still had not spent itself in Hollywood.

One of Kelly's supporters was gossip columnist Hedda Hopper. Born twenty-seven years before Kelly in Hollidaysburg, Pennsylvania, ninety miles east of Pittsburgh, Hopper's family later moved to Altoona. She had a modest career on stage and in films before becoming a columnist for the *Los Angeles Times* in 1938, aggressively battling Louella Parsons for juicy bits about famous actors. Eventually 35 million people read her syndicated column. Ironically, Hopper was an archconservative, a driving force in creating Hollywood's infamous blacklist. But she liked Kelly. It is obvious in their several interviews that Gene did his best to ingratiate himself with her as far as he could without compromising his political views.

Their discussions usually centered on his personal life, but now and then Hopper passed judgment on his politics as well. "Tho sometimes he is identified with radical groups, I learned, thru talking with him, that his philosophy is based strictly on Americanism," she concluded in a column published on October 9, 1949.[46]

Another prominent figure was not a Kelly supporter. Jack B. Tenney, born in St. Louis in 1898, had moved to California with his family as a child. A lawyer, he also wrote successful songs, including "Mexicali Rose," but politics was his forté. Elected to the California State Assembly in 1936, he headed the California Committee on Un-American Activities (the "Tenney Committee") from 1941 to 1949. Tenney pursued allegations of communist influence in Los Angeles with fervor, especially targeting the Sleepy Lagoon Defense Committee and actor Edward G. Robinson.[47] He often named Kelly in his reports, but only as one of dozens of other targets.

Tenney's strategy was to argue that the fellow traveler was the enemy. The communist threat had to "be measured in terms of their ability to direct or influence other organizations and groups who have many times the membership that the Communist Party claims," he asserted in his 1947 book *Red Fascism*. This, he believed, was the real "Communist menace to America." So Tenney reported on any organization he felt was influenced by the party, including many that Gene was involved in, and thereby smeared his name in an off-handed way. "I do fear for the liberal and progressive who has been hoodwinked and duped into joining hands with the Communists," he wrote.[48]

"I don't know what Mr. Tenney's talking about," Gene told a reporter for the Los Angeles *Daily News* in an article published on June 9, 1949. "I am not a Communist, never was, and have no sympathy with Communist activities. The only line I know how to follow is the American line." Gene was commenting on Tenney's latest report, published in June 1949, which drew a lot of criticism from various people. Tenney had written his committee's reports for 1943, 1945, 1947, and most of 1948, but he hired Edward Gibbons, editor of the anticommunist newspaper *Alert*, to write the 1949 report. The *Los Angeles Times* also blasted the report by printing statements of many actors, including Kelly, denying the accusations contained in it. Widespread disgust with Tenney built up, and he was dumped as head of the committee in 1949.[49] He had never uncovered original evidence of his own, merely repeating what he found in public documents, and no one called to testify before his committee was ever indicted.

Gene and other Hollywood figures had an opportunity to more fully defend themselves when Edward L. Barrett wrote a book about the Tenney Committee and invited them to contribute letters. Kelly wrote one of the few long letters he ever composed to explain and defend his political views. Gene admitted to emceeing the Shrine Auditorium rally of October 15, 1947, but it was *not* to support the Hollywood Ten, as Tenney incorrectly stated. The rally was held to protest HUAC's characterization of the Hollywood Nineteen as unfriendly witnesses and "smearing them publicly before they had a hearing."[50] Also, as this was *before* the hearings and *before* anyone was charged, there was no "Hollywood Ten" at this time. Tenney twisted facts to make it appear as if everyone involved in the rally was trying to help known communists.

Kelly was also angry at Tenney's note that he was one of several sponsors of the Actors' Laboratory Theatre, another suspect organization. "We bought a group of tickets and got seats to see the best theatre presentations then existing in Los Angeles. Imagine having the finger of suspicion pointing at you because you go to the theatre!" He pointed out that returning veterans sponsored by the GI Bill studied at the Actors' Laboratory Theatre after the war. "Does this implicate General Omar Bradley?" Kelly denied that the Committee for the First Amendment or the Hollywood Democratic Committee had any connections to communism. He also pointed out that, contrary to what Tenney reported, he never spoke at a symposium sponsored by the Musicians' Congress.[51] Tenney's mode of operation was typical of the prominent communist hunters of the era, blending a mix of inaccurate information with baseless assumptions and cynical twists of logic and fact to embellish what little they knew. Gene thought that if someone should compile a complete list of everyone mentioned by Tenney in his many reports as having links with communism it would be so long as to "be ludicrous."[52]

Betsy was largely on the sidelines during the Hollywood Nineteen phase of the Red Scare, but she was energized by the controversy. In fact, Blair tried to join the Communist Party either in 1947 or 1948. By this time Lloyd Gough had moved from New York to Hollywood for a modestly successful film career, and he was given the task of explaining to Betsy why the party did not think it was a good idea for her to join. Blair recalled that she and Gough drove out into the Hollywood Hills for their private conversation. "I was married to a very important man who wasn't a member of the Party and I could be just as useful outside," was how she remembered Gough's explanation. It was for the best, as far as Gene was concerned. "You'll be the worst Communist in the world," he told her. Both Gene and Betsy disliked regimentation and thought control, and the Communist Party was the most regimented and dogmatic political group in the world. The party clearly saw Kelly as a fellow traveler even though Gene did not consider himself as such. Blair's membership would complicate that delicate scenario.[53]

In later years, Blair would come to realize that Gene had been more discriminating about negotiating the dangerous political waters of Hollywood during this era of the Red Scare. He certainly "was wiser than I was" when it came to signing petitions, Betsy told an interviewer. She recalled that, unlike her, he would actually read the petition and decide whether to put his name to it.[54]

On December 2, 1947, FBI informant "T-23" told a bureau agent of a conversation that he or she had with Kelly. Gene expressed worry about what HUAC might continue to do in the wake of the Hollywood Nineteen crisis. "Kelly appeared to be concerned over what effect it might have on his own career," in the words of the FBI agent.[55] Such concern was natural. Gene was absorbing the shock and disappointment of the HUAC hearings and the collapse of liberal efforts to combat the wave of developing hysteria that contributed to the indictment of the Hollywood Ten only a few days after he shared this worry with the informant, who must have been a close "friend."

As it turned out, Kelly's career was not in jeopardy. His name never made it onto a blacklist—those people were the ones whose careers and lives were at least temporarily ruined. As a graylistee, Kelly continued to work in Hollywood, and he even continued his political activity.

Gene also helped those unfortunate enough to be blacklisted. He gave money to their families and tried to find jobs for them. "Gene's politics never really changed," Betsy asserted. Writer Ring Lardner Jr., one of the Hollywood Ten, later told interviewer Patrick McGilligan that Kelly was one of those liberals "who were against the Party and skeptical of the Soviet Union, but who continued a staunch defense of our rights." Lardner included Marsha Hunt, John Huston, Groucho Marx, Danny Kaye, and Frank Sinatra in that list. Kelly joined Katherine Hepburn and several others who wrote letters of support for Lardner, which obviously did no good. Lardner served one year in the federal prison at Danbury, Connecticut. Kelly's letter is among the Lardner records classified as "specially protected documents and are not available to researchers."[56] It was in 1965 that Lardner finally obtained screen credit for the work he had been doing surreptitiously for years.

Many years later, Gene now and then made a public comment about these tumultuous times in Hollywood. He continued to assert his dislike of blacklisting. "I thought that even members of the Communist Party should be allowed the right to work," he told Franciscan priest Jack Wintz in a 1980 interview. "I still think so, . . . especially in the creative arts." Given that the Communist Party was a legal organization in America, obviously its members should have had the right to work. But M-G-M even shied away from movies that had strong political or social content, as did most large studios, for fear of losing the audience.[57] So it is understandable how easily HUAC could push the movie industry around.

During those difficult days of 1947, Mayer reportedly told someone that Kelly "couldn't possibly be a commie because," as Gene recalled it, "I was a Catholic who loved his mother."[58] It is very easy to believe a story like this, considering Mayer's schmaltzy patriotism and his maudlin worship of motherhood.

Kelly dated his political awakening to his time on Broadway when he soaked in New York intellectualism. It was such a different atmosphere compared to Pittsburgh, a conservative Republican city before Roosevelt's New

Deal coalition began to take shape in 1933. When he went to Hollywood, Kelly found the movie capital to be a "company town" with a strong tendency toward conservative Republicanism as well, especially among the powerbrokers in the studios. Catholics also tended to be strongly conservative in politics, as exemplified by his own father. In fact, Pittsburgh's Catholics divided over New Deal agencies, with a vibrant left-wing movement among them fighting tooth and nail to support Roosevelt's policies in the Smoky City. Pittsburgh also became a major center of controversy over the issue of communist infiltration of American life after the war. Left-wing Catholics had to battle the charge that they were fellow travelers while simultaneously fighting to maintain New Deal initiatives against a conservative backlash that tried to roll back Roosevelt's legacy. Because of his support for progressive causes ever since he came to Hollywood, Kelly was never considered "a very good Catholic," in his own words.[59] If Gene had continued to live in Pittsburgh, he most likely would have aligned himself with his fellow left-wing Catholics who fought for the goals important to him.

On May 18, 1949, the New York *Daily Compass* listed the names of 128 prominent artists and educators who had been identified by the American Legion as "unsuitable or in-appropriate for Legion sponsorship." The *Compass*, a leftist newspaper, meant to highlight the absurdity of such a list. Kelly's name was among the 128.[60] It was an ironic case of a veteran being blacklisted by the oldest organization of veterans in the country.

"The people who criticize me for taking an active interest in the government of my own city, state and country are cockeyed," Kelly told reporter Jack Howard in November 1949. "Men of note in other professions use their influence for or against legislation. Why shouldn't actors?"[61] Gene wanted entertainers to have equal opportunity with all other citizens to voice their political views.

Betsy called her husband "a good left wing Democrat all his life," but Lois McClelland spelled this out in more detail and without linking him to party affiliation. "Gene is actually a citizen of the world," she wrote in a fan-magazine article published early in 1950. "He takes his rights and privileges as an American seriously, and exercises them. He belongs to forward-looking political groups, not just in name, but in body and spirit. He's amazingly well-informed, and believes in the rights of the individual to express himself, be he factory worker, congressman, or movie actor."[62] We can assume that Lois showed this statement to her boss before sending it to the editor; Kelly must have loved it because it accurately described his political beliefs.

CHAPTER 10

Surging to the Top, 1948–1949

Kelly weathered a crisis related to his political beliefs during the fall of 1947 as the trauma associated with the Hollywood Nineteen and the Hollywood Ten played itself out. But his ankle healed rapidly, and his film career soared in the wake of the first Red Scare in Hollywood. On December 29, Kelly appeared on *Lux Radio Theater* with Frank Sinatra and Kathryn Grayson to promote *Anchors Aweigh* (as mentioned in chapter 7), and the live audience asked him at the end of the program if his ankle had recovered. In response he danced energetically—as heard by his rapid taps—to wild applause. The cast had come off in December and, after a few months of further healing, M-G-M offered him a role he personally loved very much. Ever since a boy growing up in Pittsburgh, Gene had been enthralled by Douglas Fairbanks Sr., and the swashbuckling roles that made him famous on the silent screen.

THE THREE MUSKETEERS (1948)

The studio was set on remaking *The Three Musketeers*, and Kelly was overjoyed to play D'Artagnan, the rough newcomer to the trio of Athos, Porthos, and Aramis. "I had the image of Douglas Fairbanks Sr., still fresh in my mind when I made it," Kelly told an interviewer. "I never escaped the influence of Fairbanks." He knew he did not have the "brio" to pull off the athletic stunts as did Fairbanks, but he had the physical ability to do any of them in his own style.[1]

As soon as his ankle was healed, Kelly trained for two months. Fencing expert Jean Heremans of Belgium was hired to coach him in swordplay. Gene found an important similarity between fencing and ballet; in both one had to keep the feet pointed out so as to move quickly side to side "and to use your body to the full." More difficult for him was to deflect an opponent's thrust and then resume his stance as quickly as possible. "That was a skill I had to acquire through sheer hard work and practice."[2]

Kelly was determined to make the fight sequences different from those of other action pictures of the day. He wanted to link the fighting with dancing and to make sure the audience saw that he was doing the stunts rather than relying on a double. For all these reasons he insisted that D'Artagnan take on the three musketeers in a "get-acquainted" fight filmed in a wide-open space outdoors to give him plenty of room to choreograph the action. Kelly was nicked in the face and bruised more than once while filming his fight scenes, but he persisted.[3]

Two men, Russell Saunders and David Sharpe, worked as stunt doubles for Kelly when he had to ride a horse. Gene was most reluctant to ride, viewing a horse as "the dumbest animal in the world" and unpredictable. "He can be standing still and a fly will go by, and he'll go 'Bl-eh-le-eh,' and you'll be on your derriere and the horse may be on his, too, on top of you." When he had to be on horseback in a close-up, he would talk the wrangler into selecting a mount to suit him. In *The Three Musketeers* one scene shows the heroes riding furiously along a beach, but stunt men were in the saddle.[4]

Kelly told an interviewer how he accidentally broke Lana Turner's elbow while filming a scene. Turner played the evil Lady de Winter, who kills D'Artagnan's love interest, played by June Allyson. In a heated scene in which he tries to wrench information from her, D'Artagnan was to push Turner, but Gene was doing it gently, afraid he would hurt her. Turner was irritated and insisted he push her really hard, so he finally did, with the result that she broke her elbow.[5]

When it was released on October 20, 1948, *The Three Musketeers* proved to be a huge moneymaker for M-G-M and one of Kelly's personal favorites.[6] But this color film, two hours long, has a convoluted, hardly believable plot and comes across as a potboiler rather than a work of film art. Watching Gene do his many acrobatic stunts, especially in the sword fights, is interesting, but he counterbalances that with some of the worst overacting he ever committed to film. Comparing his work with that of Douglas Fairbanks Sr. in the 1921 silent version of *The Three Musketeers* confirms what Kelly himself admitted—Fairbanks does his stunts with less athleticism than Kelly but with a great deal more flair.

Film historian Jeanine Basinger praises Kelly's stunts as "magnificently choreographed" with "stunning jumps from [a] balcony." But she is highly critical of his overacting. "He wriggles his rear tauntingly at rival duelists, kicks the floor like an infant denied food when he first spots Allyson, and generally runs around like the village idiot."[7] Nevertheless, *The Three Musketeers*

Figure 10.1 Dressing as D'Artagnan in *The Three Musketeers* (1948) for a shooting on location, with his dressing trailer in the background. The signature seems to have been made by a studio employee, a common practice in the Golden Age. (New York Public Library)

remained close to Kelly's heart for decades to come. By 1958, Gene admitted that he had gone overboard in some scenes. "I did a lot of bad things in it," he said in an interview. "Some of it was pretty awful, but some of it was pretty good." Planning and executing the fight scenes was "rollicking good fun." Even in 1975 he called it his favorite nonmusical picture, saying, "I enjoyed it so much because, again, it's that little boy thing."[8]

The movie was plugged on two radio programs in January 1949. The first was the *Sealtest Variety Theater* with Dorothy Lamour and Dennis Day on January 13. Kelly and Lamour performed a comedy sketch about a husband and wife traveling by train to Reno for a divorce but reconciling when someone says they look like newlyweds. The second was the *Maxwell House Coffee Time* with George Burns and Gracie Allen on January 27. In a comedy sketch, Gracie talked Gene into "playing" George, proposing to her and kissing her, and has her friend record this on film to give George as a birthday present. Someone sees them kiss and tells George, and hilarity ensues with all the misunderstandings that follow. Both programs also plugged Kelly's performance in *Words and Music*, which had just been released in late December.

"SLAUGHTER ON TENTH AVENUE" (1948)

Words and Music is a massive film biography of American songwriting partners Richard Rodgers and Lorenz Hart, written by Fred Finklehoffe and produced by Arthur Freed.[9] It includes nearly two dozen songs and dances taken from the voluminous stage work of Rodgers and Hart.

Kelly was assigned to choreograph and perform in the dance number "Slaughter on Tenth Avenue" in *Words and Music*. The number, originally choreographed by George Balanchine, had been a ballet in the Rodgers and Hart stage musical *On Your Toes*, which had a successful run on Broadway from April 11, 1936, to January 23, 1937.

The plot of *On Your Toes* is unbelievable and too complicated to fully explain here. "Slaughter on Tenth Avenue" was its climax. The hero, Phil Dolan (played by Ray Bolger) has written the music of a stage show. An evil Russian impresario, who claims to have written it instead, sets up Phil for murder by two Russian hitmen. Phil's dancing partner (played by Tamara Geva) is killed by mistake by a hitman aiming at Dolan. Phil holds on to her body to shield himself while he continues to dance. The key then to "Slaughter on Tenth Avenue" in the Broadway production is a desperate dance for life by Dolan until the police come and arrest the hitmen.

When Warner Brothers made a film version of *On Your Toes* in 1939, Balanchine once again choreographed "Slaughter on Tenth Avenue" but made changes to fit the revised story. This time Phil (played by Eddie Albert) and Vera (played by Vera Zorina) are in a stage performance in which the plot calls for Vera to shield Phil from a bullet and die. Instead of holding her body to protect himself, Phil is supposed to dance in grief and then shoot himself. The hitmen are in the audience, know the plot (of the stage performance), and plan to shoot Phil exactly when he "shoots" himself on stage. Phil learns of this and keeps dancing nervously to avoid getting to that part. This segment is far too drawn-out and is wearying to watch. Moreover, Albert was not a trained dancer, and most of the time the camera focuses only on the dancer's feet—obviously someone else's—which takes away from the integrity of the dance. Not surprisingly, Kelly wanted to get away from both the stage and the movie versions. He planned to do something quite different, new, and exciting with the old, threadbare idea.

The first thing Gene did was to select the right dancing partner, and he found her in Vera-Ellen. Born in a German American community in a suburb of Cincinnati, Ellen had been "driven and manic" about dancing ever since her high-school years. Her biographer writes that Ellen's mother had taught her to be finicky about food, and she suffered all her life from what most likely was anorexia nervosa. Ellen almost landed the part that made Mary Martin famous in *Leave It to Me*, but the producer thought she did not have enough sex appeal. She went on to roles in *Panama Hattie* and the Rodgers and Hart shows *By Jupiter* and *The Connecticut Yankee*. Ellen's career was built largely on being a small, cute woman who could be tossed about by her husband and two other men in a moderately successful stage show. The act was part dance and part gymnastics. It was good enough for Samuel Goldwyn to costar her with Danny Kaye in *Wonder Man* (1945) and *The Kid from Brooklyn* (1946).[10]

But a limited shtick like hers could take Vera-Ellen only so far in Hollywood, and she was ready to return to stage work when Gene tapped her for his version of "Slaughter on Tenth Avenue." Kelly saw the potential in Ellen and wanted to develop it. "Vera could do practically anything," Gene said. He particularly wanted his version of "Slaughter" to be sexy, or "voluptuous," as Kelly put it. This was pushing Vera's envelope the most because she excelled at perky, bright, and cute rather than sexy.[11]

Ellen embraced the opportunity with enthusiasm, and it changed her career. Before this role, "I had just danced in a thoughtless, easy-going way," she admitted. But M-G-M voice and acting coach Marie Bryant "made me 'think' my dancing and Gene made me take it seriously." Marie coached her to get away from her usual Shirley Temple persona for the mature role Gene wanted her to play. And Gene made her aware of her dancing potential.[12]

In developing "Slaughter on Tenth Avenue," Kelly was well aware of Balanchine's versions. He had seen Ray Bolger perform it on the New York stage and liked aspects of the number. It had a comic element that had made Gene laugh. But it was a dark comic touch for a man to use a dead woman's body to shield himself from a bullet. Also, Balanchine's incorporation of American jazz dance was done to satirize Russian ballet. In contrast, Kelly always melded different dance styles to create joyful numbers rather than to mock any tradition. Gene wanted to do the number as a tragic ballet or grand opera in which both he and the girl dance ecstatically until they are shot down by a jealous thug in a seedy bar. He also shortened the ballet from eleven to under eight minutes, making it more compact and with greater dramatic flow.[13]

Unlike the previous stagings, Gene starts the dance in his bedroom above the bar, then down to the street where he meets the girl, and the two perform their mutual attraction in a brilliant, energetic dance in the street and then in the bar. The thug appears and tried to pull the girl away, but she is not interested. For the climax, as the thug aims to shoot the man, Gene kept the part from the *On Your Toes* film about the girl shielding the man to take the bullet. But he also envisioned the rage of the man, his trying to avenge his lover's death, and getting shot by the thug. Wounded, he carries his lover's body up the steps, then falls and dies next to her for a Romeo-and-Juliet touch.

In developing the choreography, Kelly relied heavily on Alex Romero, who had just been hired by M-G-M after leaving Jack Cole's dancing group. Gene asked Alex, whom he had known since *Cover Girl*, to suggest moves in Cole's style for his dance on top of the bar. Romero did so and Kelly worked out the finer points. For the rest of the number, the two men began by experimenting with lifts. Ellen was good at this as well, and both men became engrossed in different lifting moves, critiquing them to see if it would look good on the screen. In the process, Ellen developed black and blue marks all over, but as Kelly recalled, she did not mind because it was fascinating to her as well. Eventually Kelly and Romero realized they were developing nothing but highlights for the number and were losing their focus on the plotline, so they threw out most of those balletic lifts. Kelly later told an interviewer that having a complete dancer like Romero to help him was very important. Romero's biographer writes, "The collaboration with Kelly on 'Slaughter on Tenth Avenue' was pivotal in Alex's career." Stanley Donen was little more than a hoofer and had long since given up even that limited experience at dancing. With Romero to help him, Kelly did not need Donen's assistance.[14] Kelly and Romero worked out a tightly wrought dance that brilliantly told a dramatic story in less than eight minutes. Kelly and Ellen's lively and spectacular dancing makes it even more poignant when they both are shot down.

Kelly used the "free style," or what he often called "American style," in "Slaughter on Tenth Avenue." He described it as "a mélange of ballet, modern and general masculine movements" suitable for "the American male and the American medium."[15]

Robert Alton, musical director of *Words and Music*, gave Kelly free rein to choreograph "Slaughter on Tenth Avenue" but contributed greatly to an innovative staging of it. Alton had the idea to create the building on a turntable to allow the camera fluid movement in getting Gene's character from his bedroom onto the street and into the seedy bar. Set designer Jack Martin Smith took Alton's idea and made it into reality.[16] It goes against an aspect of cine-dance in that it replicated a stage show's design for the camera but produced a fascinating departure from typical camera staging that is still a delight to watch.

Figure 10.2 Gene Kelly and Vera-Ellen in the electrifying "Slaughter on Tenth Avenue" number. (Still from *Words and Music*, 1948)

Kelly pushed the envelope when he insisted on an extreme close-up of Vera-Ellen at the moment her character died. The rule at M-G-M was to use nothing less than a 40-millimeter lens for its female stars. If it was a close-up, cinematographers were supposed to use a 50-, 75-, or 100-millimeter lens. But to get the shot he wanted, Kelly arranged for placing the camera in a pit near the spot where Ellen was supposed to be and used a 28-millimeter lens. "The executives raised a little hell about it," he recalled years later.[17] Indeed, the shot distorted her image a bit but created a striking departure from the norm and used the camera to good effect.

What Kelly conceived for "Slaughter on Tenth Avenue" was in so many ways dramatically different. The number was rehearsed for six weeks, and Vera-Ellen became so engrossed in rehearsing that her feet often bled or blistered at the end of the day. But she never complained, delighted to be working on something challenging. *Words and Music* began filming on April 4, 1948, and finished production by July 14. When the film was released on December 31, 1948, it was an instant success, grossing $4,552,000 for a cost of $2,800,000. Reviewers pinpointed "Slaughter on Tenth Avenue" as the best component of this biopic. "Gene Kelly and Vera-Ellen are electrifying," effused Lew Sheaffer in the *Brooklyn Eagle*. John K. Newnham put up with many dull moments in the film until "Slaughter on Tenth Avenue" burst on the screen with "so much vitality." It was "a brilliant ballet, . . . superbly staged and perfectly executed." Newnham went on to say that "Slaughter" confirmed his long-held belief that Kelly was "the best of the screen's male dancers." He concluded that whereas Astaire was "very much of a specialist, Kelly is a ballet dancer of the first order, and his control of movement in the *Slaughter on Tenth Avenue* ballet is a sheer joy to behold."[18]

The number has been highlighted by dance and film historians as a milestone in the successful employment of modern dance styles in popular cinema. Roy Hemming has written that Kelly "revolutionized movie dance" in this number by proving that "movie audiences would accept this style of dance enthusiastically." Jeanine Basinger has appreciated the dance for its "stylized rendering of an underworld milieu" and its "sense of urban tension and underlying violence."[19]

Not everyone praised Kelly's version of "Slaughter on Tenth Avenue." Ray Bolger disliked that Kelly altered the "comic ballet" to a "serious ballet" by changing the context. A couple of commentators found it either pretentious or predictable. But most critics and audiences loved what Kelly had done, and Vera-Ellen was forever grateful to Gene for the experience. It rejuvenated her film career and made her a major star with a seven-year contract from M-G-M. She even received marriage proposals in the mail because of her sexy performance. It was not just Vera whose performance was sexy. As Basinger writes about the number, "Kelly's masculine strength exemplified by his strongly muscled body was never put to better use."[20]

Kelly's tutelage also brought out deeper emotion in Ellen's dancing. "Slaughter" remained her favorite role for the rest of her life. Gene's influence as a teacher cannot be better exemplified than in the transformation of Vera-Ellen from a doll figure in the pictures to a serious dancer in the cinema.

TAKE ME OUT TO THE BALL GAME (1949)

Kelly's next project was one he developed on his own in the form of *Take Me Out to the Ball Game*. Producer Joe Pasternak had an idea of pairing him with Sinatra again as two entertainers who purchase a wreck of an aircraft carrier from the Navy and convert it into a floating nightclub. Gene liked the idea of teaming with Sinatra again but hated the Navy aspect. The concept was first pitched to him while he was still serving in the Navy and living in New York City. To dodge this project, Kelly came up with a story inspired by the team of Schacht and Altrock, two players turned coaches who entertained baseball audiences with comedy routines on the playing field.[21]

Al Schacht, known as "The Clown Prince of Baseball," was a pitcher for the Washington Senators and became third-base coach from 1924 to 1934. Nicholas Altrock, also a pitcher-turned-coach for the Senators, paired with Al for twelve years of field antics. The two also performed on the vaudeville circuit during the winter months. Gene's love of baseball and his boyhood dream of becoming a shortstop for the Pittsburgh Pirates must have contributed to the inspiration for the plot.

Kelly called in Donen to help him develop the idea during a train journey from New York to Washington, DC, to be discharged from active service in the Navy in May 1946. The two worked on the story, stretching Kelly's initial ten-page scenario to fifteen pages. This scenario was not good enough for M-G-M to base a decision on, so Kelly verbally pitched the idea to his agent Roy Myers in mid-July 1946 after returning to Los Angeles. Myers asked him to write a better proposal about "the general background, environment, and situation ideas" of the concept. Gene wrote a letter to Myers on July 27 further explaining his ideas before committing them to an extended proposal. He wanted to present Sinatra similarly to how he had been presented in *Anchors Aweigh*. He would still be a "nice, modest guy," but instead of a sailor he would be "a helluva 2nd baseman." Kelly knew that the gangster angle of his plot was "old hat" but he thought "this kind of stock characterization" worked well in musical comedy. He wrote that these guys should be just menacing enough so the audience could hiss at them but not be worried about their heroes. He predicted lots of laughs built around the climax as the baseball players beat up the gangsters and Kelly finds out that Sinatra had deliberately knocked him out with a weighted ball and runs after him.[22]

In short, Kelly gave a lot of thought to developing the storyline and the characters. Apparently Donen only helped build the initial scenario while they were on the train; there is no evidence he contributed anything to the further development of it after Gene got back to California. Even so, Kelly listed Donen as a partner in the story development, and Donen's name appears as coauthor on the final synopsis of *Take Me Out to the Ball Game* dated September 27, 1946. Freed liked the project and pushed M-G-M to buy it for $25,000, which Kelly split evenly with Donen.[23]

Gene saw the two main characters (shortstop and second baseman) as more interested in vaudeville than baseball. This would explain the many dances he envisioned. He wanted real baseball manager Leo Durocher to play the first baseman so the three could be a trio—O'Brien, Ryan, and Shaughnessy. Kelly planned to suffuse the storyline with nostalgia by placing it in the period 1905–1915 and using many Irish songs of the era such as "McNamara's Band" and "Dear Old Donegal." He wrote, "I've worked out an Irish jig that Sinatra and Durocher will be able to dance" and humorously added, "which will carry on the myth of Frankie's terpsichorean ability." He also thought Sinatra could sing a ballad. Gene wanted Jimmy Durante to play the role of a trainer. He had seen Durante's routine filmed for the *Army-Navy Screen Magazine*, thought it hilarious, and picked out a spot in the film for it. He also envisioned a "baseball ballet—very masculine, very exciting" and knew exactly where it should go. Kelly suggested Kathryn Grayson as the female lead and based his conception of Sinatra's character knocking out his character on a real incident between Schacht and Altrock that ruined their friendship.[24]

This is how *Take Me Out to the Ball Game* started, but it wound up significantly different. Freed had George Wells do a treatment based on Kelly's synopsis of the project on August 12, 1946, and a script by October 10. But Harry Tugend and Harry Crane worked on rewrites in the spring and summer of 1948 to produce the final screenplay.[25] Durocher was replaced by Jules Munshin (as a Jewish character) and Durante by Richard Lane, and both did well in their roles. Only one Irish song and dance found its way into the final production.

Kelly deserves credit for initiating a film project that was very profitable for M-G-M and has a good many entertaining songs and dances, but he was incapable of bringing it out in the way he initially conceived it. Gene always had difficulty writing an extended piece, whether it was a screenplay, a stage play, or even a personal letter. Other men produced the script that the final product was based on. Moreover, most films are group projects—in working out the details over time, many things inevitably change.

Busby Berkeley was the director for the film. He had suffered a nervous breakdown and labored under alcoholism in recent years, and Freed wanted to give him a chance at a comeback. Gene's involvement in the rehearsal and production phases of *Take Me Out to the Ball Game* was more intense than usual because it was his project from the start. He became impatient with Berkeley, who seemed stuck in the past and who admitted he was tired. Both Kelly and Donen "used to make fun of" Berkeley behind his back, according to Betty Garrett, who played Sinatra's love interest in the picture. Donen later admitted they "made jokes about" Berkeley's famous musicals of the 1930s and early 1940s, which were centered on huge choruses of female dancers in geometrically designed numbers. During the filming of the climactic baseball-game sequence, when Berkeley loudly called for his cinematographer to frame the shot so the entire field could be within view, yelling "Back! Back! Farther Back!," Kelly said under his breath, "Yeah, back to 1930." Kelly and Sinatra were also extremely rude to Berkeley in front of the crew, laughing at his direction during rehearsals of the first number, when Busby was panning left and right and swooping in and out on the crane, while Romero performed the dance. Gene ended up directing the number with him and Frank on stage as vaudevillians.[26]

On May 26, 1948, two years after hatching the project, Kelly began rehearsals for the dances in the film. Gene directed all of them except "It's Fate" with Sinatra and Garrett, which Donen directed. As Garrett recalled, Kelly insisted on thoroughly rehearsing all the numbers so they were "up to 'opening-night' perfection."[27]

Kelly had Kathryn Grayson in mind for the female lead, but Freed wanted Judy Garland. Judy's continuing drug problems and absenteeism on other films, however, led to this idea being dropped. Freed then thought of June Allyson, but she was pregnant and declined. Esther Williams, who had been very successful in a string of movies in which she swims, was next. "When the studio began methodically going down their list of possible replacements, there I was," Williams wrote, admitting she was less adept at acting and dancing than swimming but that she tried hard nonetheless.[28]

Unfortunately, Kelly and Donen mercilessly badgered Williams as soon as she joined the project. Ironically, Kelly had stated in an article published in 1944 that he thought Williams was the most beautiful woman in film partly for her looks but mostly for her athletic ability and grace. But now he and Donen began making juvenile jokes about her, knocking the sides of their heads as if waterlogged and pretending they could not hear. Williams noted that she became "instant friends" with Sinatra, but she developed a justified disdain for Kelly and Donen due to the immature way they treated her.[29]

Apparently it was acceptable in Hollywood in the 1940s and 1950s to mock Williams. In *Silk Stockings* (1957), Janis Paige plays an actress who became a success with a string of movies in which she swims, clearly suggesting Esther Williams. The character is portrayed as rather stupid and is constantly trying to knock water out of her ears. This does not excuse Kelly and Donen's behavior but simply points out that making fun of Esther Williams was not uncommon in that era.

Esther admitted she was not a good dancer, but Gene "was nothing less than a tyrant behind the camera—at least with me." She could plainly see his "mounting aggravation" with her. And yet, with other costars who were less adept Kelly was patient and understanding. It is possible that Williams truly had more trouble learning dance steps compared with Sinatra or even Phil Silvers for *Cover Girl*, and Kelly apparently could not tolerate that. This tied to an aspect of his social life at home. Andre Previn remarked that "Gene and Betsy had an unforgivably conceited intolerance of untalented people." If a guest "wasn't particularly good" at playing charades, "they showed their displeasure."[30]

The plan for *Take Me Out to the Ball Game* had changed so much that when Williams came on board she was trapped in a full-blown dance musical. Kathryn Grayson was not a dancer either and had not danced in *Anchors Aweigh*. Initially, Kelly had planned to keep the female lead out of the dances here as well, especially with all the Irish numbers mentioned in his synopsis. But when screenwriters revised the script, only one Irish song was kept. So Gene planned two other dances with Sinatra and a third with Sinatra and Munshin. He and Donen also envisioned the number "Strictly U.S.A." as an innovative crowd dance. Garland was still being considered at this time, so that would have worked easily. But when Freed brought in Williams instead, Kelly and Donen did not want to give up their big ensemble number and they could not keep Williams out of it. So they were forced to work with her until she was passable.

"I wasn't used to a back seat," Williams frankly wrote in her memoirs, and perhaps that is another reason Kelly and Donen ragged her so much. Yet another explanation for Gene's inexcusable behavior is that Esther was noticeably taller than him. Given his lifelong sensitivity to his perceived shortness, Williams tried hard to bend when doing scenes with him, but "Kelly just looked at me as if I was hopeless." While filming a scene in which they sit on a loveseat, Kelly turned to Donen and said "You know something? This sonafabitch even *sits* tall!" It is shocking that he could be so rude, but Williams stood up to him on this occasion and lectured him about this remark. She also said, "For this scene, . . . try tucking a foot under your ass."[31]

To ease the bad blood, Berkeley developed a dream ballet sequence in which Esther would be swimming in a rushing river as Gene reached out to her, losing his grasp and trying to regain it, as a symbolic way of expressing his character's attraction to the lady ballclub owner. Both Freed and Williams liked the idea very much and storyboards were made, but Kelly bluntly refused to do it. When Esther tried to discuss it with him, "his tone was patronizing and arrogant." She zinged him by suggesting it was because he could not swim. "He gave me a death-ray look and said, 'I know how to swim, smartass.'"[32]

A possible reason for Kelly's adamant refusal of the dream ballet is that no one could match Esther's grace in the water and he did not want to be upstaged. When he helped dancing partners do their best, it improved the project, and yet they could never supersede him because he was such a great dancer. Another reason may be that swimming gave him sinus trouble, which is why he had opted for a volleyball court rather than a swimming pool in his backyard. He may have not wanted to admit this for fear of appearing sickly. A third reason may be that he could not have worn his hairpiece under water. The assistant director's report specifically mentions Sinatra's and Munshin's hairpieces, and it is generally known that Kelly and Astaire used these as well.

Berkeley already was going to seed as a director by this late stage in his career, but the water ballet had invigorated his zeal for this film. When Kelly refused to do it, Berkeley lost a lot of interest in *Take Me Out to the Ball Game*. Kelly devised a tepid number based on the song "Baby Doll" as a substitute for the water ballet. It was poorly conceived and executed. Alex Romero recalled that Williams wore a huge skirt to hide her "squat" dancing aimed at lessening her height to suit Gene. When Freed saw the number in rehearsals, he immediately nixed it.[33] Included in the DVD release as a deleted number, the steps Williams does as a "doll" are awkward and ungainly, and Kelly's steps as a mechanized toy soldier are not appealing, either. It is clear that the number richly deserved to be dropped.

Kelly and Donen directed the second half of the film when Berkeley lost interest. Williams wrote that they continued their snide remarks, causing her "pure misery." She thought they were comparing her to Garland and bemoaning her lack of talent. Soon after, Williams was slated to star in *Pagan Love Song* with Donen as director, and she absolutely refused to do the project until he was replaced by Robert Alton.[34]

In "O'Brien to Ryan to Goldberg," Kelly, Sinatra, and Munshin sing about their characters as an "unholy trio," based on the famous double-play team of Joe Tinker, Johnny Evers, and Frank Chance of the Chicago Cubs from 1902 to 1912. One could call the Kelly-Donen team an "unholy duo" at least as far as Williams was concerned. Whether it was because Williams was a success based mainly on her swimming talent, or because she had difficulty learning dance steps, or because she was taller than Kelly, there is no excuse for the callous and juvenile way Kelly and Donen treated their colleague.

It is worth noting that in referring to the making of the movie, Betty Garrett said, "Oh that was absolutely a ball."[35] The rest of the cast had a wonderful time and seemed unaware of the treatment dished out to Williams. Garrett was well aware of the jokes about Berkeley, so Williams may have exaggerated a little, or possibly Kelly and Donen made these remarks only when the others were not around. Or the cast may have been aware of all this but ignored it. Interestingly, in the finished product, Williams acts well, dances passably in "Strictly U.S.A.," and performs pretty well in the reprise at the end—better than Garrett. She even gets to swim and sing in a pool as the three ballplayers admire her beauty and grace from an upstairs window. And in "Strictly U.S.A.," Williams sings very well, as do Munshin, Kelly, and Sinatra, of course. Only Garrett is noticeably off-key. Yet she was never harassed by Kelly and Donen.

Production of *Take Me Out to the Ball Game* started on July 28, 1948. While filming the baseball sequences on August 18 and 27, Kelly and an extra were accidently hit on the head with a baseball. Kelly decided simply to rest a bit to recover, but the extra was given a medical checkup to ensure she was okay. The assistant director's report also reveals that Kelly was requesting extra takes and discussing scenes with Berkeley prior to shooting, showing his gradual taking over of direction.[36]

For his solo number, Gene selected "The Hat Me Dear Old Father Wore," a jaunty Irish song by Jean Schwartz and William Jerome that he prerecorded on September 23. After rehearsing and laying out the sets, Kelly began to film it on September 27. He exposed forty-one takes during the course of the day, taking only nine minutes to rest in midafternoon. On September 28, with nine takes filmed between 11:02 and 11:55 A.M., Kelly finished production on what would become one of his most impressive dance numbers in cinema.[37]

"The Hat Me Dear Old Father Wore" exemplifies the kind of Irishness that was so important to Kelly's public persona, an image he cultivated throughout his career. He had always admired George M. Cohan and modeled this performance on him. "Cohan set the style for the American song-and-dance man," Kelly stated, "a tough, cheeky, Irish style, . . . a jaw-jutting, up-on-the-toes cockiness—which is a good quality for a male dancer to have." The number consists of three sections, starting with a tour de force of muscular dancing, segueing to a reflective, almost dreamy section, and ending with another propulsive section that celebrates the Irish style Kelly so loved to project. He performs the number "with the jaunty ease of a professional leprechaun," as an observer has written, but "The Hat Me Dear Old Father Wore"

Figure 10.3 Kelly's Irish dance—the only Irish number to be retained out of several in his original plan for the film. (Still from *Take Me Out to the Ball Game*, 1949)

is more than that. Commentators write "it is a number rich in variation of mood, dance style, lighting, and setting, splendidly photographed," and Kelly, "not weighed down by a partner," does strong, assured, and joyful dancing, "making it the high point of the film."[38]

"Strictly U.S.A." was written for *Take Me out to the Ball Game* by Roger Edens, Freed's assistant, and inserted late as a big production number. It takes place at a landing during a clambake and offered Kelly and Donen an opportunity to work with a large crowd of extras. As Casey Charness puts it, they packed a "tight mass of people in a confined space" and always had at least some of them moving at all times. The camera moves a lot as well. The effect is to incorporate the extras into the dance number not only as spectators but as participants, supporting the movement as well as the décor.[39]

Kelly and Donen demonstrated a real departure from the way Minnelli used crowds as background for dance numbers in his films. While Minnelli used people as elements in a meticulously planned décor, standing largely as statues to frame and decorate the scene, Kelly and Donen choreographed the crowd in an ever mobile background. While Kelly did not have the spectators move in "The Hat Me Dear Old Father Wore," most of them have broad smiles, laugh, and applaud vigorously as they watch him dance. In that way, they become part of the event. In numbers that Minnelli staged in his films, the extras do not even smile for fear of breaking their image as statues. The Kelly-Donen strategy is much more vibrant, engaging, and effective.

Gene became ill during the latter stages of filming *Take Me Out to the Ball Game*, a not uncommon occurrence for him in the strenuous period of production. He missed a couple of days of work, forcing the company to do other needed tasks around him. *Take Me Out to the Ball Game* finished production on November 4, 1948. Preview audiences overwhelmingly cited Kelly's dances as the highlight of the film. "I never tire of watching Kelly dance," was one comment that observers overheard during the first day of release. Opening on April 1, 1949, the movie was extremely profitable, grossing $4,344,000 in its initial release for a cost of $1,726,000.[40]

Take Me Out to the Ball Game takes some of Kelly's stock-in-trade to a new level in his musicals. Developing a brassy character, performing spirited athletic dances, and indulging in hammy acting are characteristics starting with *For Me and My Gal*. But here his Eddie O'Brien is more pushy and insensitive than in previous musicals, and he barely changes over the course of the picture. Only in "The Hat Me Dear Old Father Wore" does Eddie's brassiness play well within the context of a Cohan-style dance performance. In "Yes, Indeedy" Kelly and Sinatra turn in one of the least attractive numbers either committed to film. They hammed it up, overacting shamelessly to lyrics by Betty Comden and Adolph Green that were mostly funny but often tasteless. The dance to the title song, which starts the film, also has some comic moments but works well. It is nicely performed by Kelly and Sinatra, incorporating a Prone Kick and Side Heel-Clicks. Sinatra seems to have come a long way since *Anchors Aweigh* in terms of his dancing.

Many years later Kelly admitted that much of the movie was "overplayed and overblown and very corn pone," but the public ate it up anyway. "Buzz [Berkeley] always let us overplay, he always liked to let us ham it up, and it was very easy for me to do that!"[41]

Reviewers liked the picture but did not take it seriously. They recognized that it had a flimsy plot with shallow characters, but it was put together with a lot of entertainment value. Because the concept was initiated by Kelly, and because he ended up directing much of it, as well as choreographing and starring in it, Kate Cameron of the New York *Daily News* aptly termed it "a thoroughly Kelly project."[42] There is a youthful vigor in *Take Me Out to the Ball Game* that is still exciting to experience, and it set up a similar tone for his next project, which followed soon after.

Figure 10.4 Kelly and Sinatra as vaudevillians (who alternate as baseball players) performing the Side Heel-Click, a Kelly favorite. (Still from *Take Me Out to the Ball Game*, 1949)

ON THE TOWN (1949)

On the Town was the first of a trio of film musicals that represented the pinnacle of Kelly's career. It was based on the stage musical *On the Town*, which had its origins in a short modern ballet called *Fancy Free*, with music by Leonard Bernstein and choreography by Jerome Robbins, about three sailors on leave in New York City. Comden and Green were inspired by this piece to expand the concept into a full-blown musical comedy with Bernstein and Robbins. The stage version of *On the Town* opened on Broadway on December 28, 1944, only six months after *Fancy Free* had opened. Comden and Green not only wrote the book and lyrics but also played roles in the production, with Comden as Claire the anthropologist and Green as Ozzie, one of the three sailors, and they positioned their own roles as the most prominent.[43]

The stage version of *On the Town* took critics and patrons by storm with its fresh vitality, its joyful spirit mixed with bittersweet moments as the three sailors meet their girls but have to part at the end of their brief shore leave. Scene designer Oliver Smith put it well when he recalled that the heart of the musical was "the enormous love each of us felt for New York City. It was a valentine to New York." In his mind, this was the "unifying theme" of the production. Kelly saw the show while he was still in the Navy and loved it. He especially was taken by the "melting pot" aspect of the Comden and Green concept, depicting different races and ethnicities in a realistic way. Sono Osato, born in the United States of a Japanese father and an Irish–French Canadian mother, played the important role of Ivy Smith, and an African American woman danced with a white man. Gene thought it would be possible to film it on the streets of New York City and called Freed about it. He found that M-G-M had already purchased the rights even before the Comden and Green production premiered. In later years Kelly claimed he talked the studio into buying the rights, but that was not the case.[44]

Gene did have to fight for two years to convince M-G-M to actually make the movie because, after seeing the stage version, Mayer was turned off by the melting-pot aspect. It did not fit his view of "pure" Americanism, but the studio was stuck with it. After a great deal of prodding, Freed finally got the green light to start work on the picture in 1948.[45] Comden and Green were slated to write the screenplay; Kelly would star and also direct, in association with Donen. It would be the first full picture the two would codirect.

Converting the stage version, which appealed to the sophisticated audience of New York, into a general-release film to appeal to the average American in the Midwest demanded substantial changes. Freed thought Bernstein's music was too "avant garde," and he did not like the "campy manner" of the stage performance. Bernstein was not interested in the project, so Freed obtained a "free hand" to change as he saw fit, and much was done.[46]

Comden and Green made the sailor Gabey the focus of the film to give Kelly his due as the star, and Vera-Ellen was brought in as Ivy, his love interest. Sinatra, Munshin, and Garrett, who had made a good team in *Take Me Out to the Ball Game*, were also included, with Garrett as Sinatra's girl and Ann Miller cast as Munshin's. The melting-pot aspect was kept through shows the group visits around New York.

Kelly admired Robbins's staging of the Broadway show but departed drastically from it. Most of the bittersweet element was eliminated, and a lighthearted tone infused the movie. The film would have a dream ballet as did the Broadway production, but of very different setting and tone. Robbins had a huge chorus to represent New York, but Kelly based his screen choreography on the six principal characters and avoided big production numbers involving a lot of people. Instead, he relied on shots of the city and the atmosphere of New York "to provide the background and the chorus." Kelly knew that three sailors on leave is a potent source of almost any kind of dancing, acting, or storytelling. In fact, three men dancing (whether in or out of uniform) had been a common theme in stage entertainment back to the previous century.[47] Actually the three sailors did not dance by themselves in the film, but the title song with all six principals on a soundstage and the backlot set of a New York street is one of the exuberant highlights of the picture.

Kelly talked Freed into bringing Saul Chaplin over from Columbia to work on the project, and Chaplin did most of the musical arrangements. It led to his residency at M-G-M for the rest of his career. Chaplin kept most of Bernstein's instrumental music as the basis of the ballet. Only four songs from the Broadway production were retained, and seven new ones were added. Comden and Green wrote lyrics for the new songs, and Roger Edens wrote the music. In "New York, New York," which was retained, they had to change the lyrics from "a helluva town" to "a wonderful town." Some of the dropped songs were beautiful ballads, but Kelly thought they would slow the pace of the film too much. Freed agreed and decided to drop the songs.[48] Freed and Kelly were right because the ballads are so slow (as heard on the DVD of *Musicals Great Musicals*) that they would not have fit the film's fast pace and energy.

Rehearsals began on February 21, 1949, and proceeded smoothly. Within four weeks the cast was ready after having a lot of fun preparing for production. Kelly worked briskly, developing choreography that enhanced Garrett's limited experience with dancing. He insisted she practice in front of a mirror to make sure her arms and her upper body worked in coordination with the rest to create a holistic image of grace and coordination. Gene made no effort to change Ann Miller's dance style. Ever since an early age, the Texas-born Miller had been uninterested in anything to do with ballet technique but found her groove in rapid-fire tapping to peppy music. She was very good at this limited range and had no desire to explore anything else, so Gene choreographed for her accordingly.[49] Miller was able to dance along with the rest of the ensemble in the limited steps Gene worked out for everyone, but her solo piece in "Prehistoric Man" was pure Ann Miller.

To introduce Ivy Smith, Kelly created the unique "Miss Turnstiles" number, the first ever to showcase the character of the female lead in a dance. He used short pieces of film strung together to demonstrate Ivy's versatility, ranging from a devotee of art to just being a "regular gal." Gene worked out a system of hard cutting to quickly transition from one segment to another. He also worked with set designer Jack Martin Smith to eliminate the line in the visual image where floor met wall to create an effect similar to an illustration in a magazine or a "curved cyclorama," as he put it.[50] The most vigorous segment mixes athletics with dance—a favorite theme of Kelly's. Several male dancers pose as "jocks" that Ivy supposedly punches. They all are excellent gymnasts, and their flying around as she "punches" and "kicks" them is amazing to watch. All of these elements along with Vera-Ellen's perky performance make this a striking number.

Kelly fought for permission to film at least part of the movie on the streets of New York City. M-G-M was reluctant, expecting many difficulties and expenses. They imagined "fifty policemen surrounding the area." But Kelly explained how he had shot scenes after the *Franklin* had reached the city in 1945 and argued that it could be done expeditiously. Eventually Mayer allowed him only five days of production in the city. The Navy gave permission for filming in the Brooklyn Navy Yard and for using real sailors in the shots because Kelly "was one of their boys."[51]

In preparation for the location shooting, M-G-M sent a second unit headed by Hungarian-born director Andrew Marton to New York on March 21, 1949. The purpose was to check out the locations and methods of filming that Kelly wanted to use a couple of months later. For several days Marton had a great deal of difficulty with overcast skies, rain, and generally unfavorable conditions for filming. He experimented with placing a camera in the back of a station wagon to expose footage of street scenes on the go. Haze and smoke proved to be a problem at the Brooklyn Navy Yard, but the crew watched as a ship came slowly to dock because they knew that Kelly wanted a similar shot of a vessel leaving the dock. Marton could not get permission to film on top of the Empire State Building and had to shoot from the top of the Rockefeller Building instead.[52] But this footage was not used.

By the time Kelly and the other principals were ready to go to New York, the season had moderated and there were more possibilities for filming. Gene left California on May 4 and arrived early the next morning with Munshin on the same flight. His crew reached town later that day, and the other principal actors arrived on May 7 and 8. On May 9, they began an odyssey that would become almost legendary in film history. Kelly rehearsed real sailors on a destroyer tied up at the dock at the Brooklyn Navy Yard and shot all the opening scenes. Rain prevented the crew from filming the next day. On May 11, they rehearsed and filmed the ending of the movie. This was the only working day for the three women because they were only in the ending scenes for location shots. Finally, having waited a long time for the destroyer to leave the dock and sail away, Kelly and Donen decided to scrap their plans for this parting shot. Instead, they set up a camera on a dolly and rigged a hand car, moving it alongside the ship with "the girls on the car to simulate the ship leaving the dock."[53] But this ending shot was not used. In the actual last scene, the ship stays put and a new batch of sailors runs ashore excitedly, with three of them singing "New York, New York" for an upbeat ending.

On May 12 the crew filmed on top of the observation deck of the RCA Building, 30 Rockefeller Plaza, the camera panning 360 degrees to capture the three sailors excitedly looking at the expansive view of New York. This was the same building that housed the Rainbow Room, where Kelly had bombed in his test performance before a snobby nightclub audience eight years earlier. Over the next few days, the crew rapidly filmed many scenes on various streets of New York, capturing well-known location shots to create the atmosphere of New York. Kelly, Sinatra, and Munshin rode in a taxi, hiding Sinatra on the floor to avoid crowds of his fans, and Kelly and Munshin often hid too, to make it look like an empty cab. Kelly placed the camera in the back of a station wagon as Marton had done to get many of his shots. But now the photographers had to lie on their stomachs to avoid being seen. The taxi followed, and the actors had to jump out and sing "New York, New York" in different locations and jump back in to avoid being mobbed. "We did it with stopwatch timing," Kelly said. They hired a dozen extras for some scenes, but bystanders are seen as well. On May 17 they filmed at the fountain of Rockefeller Plaza and went back to the Brooklyn Navy Yard the next day for more crane shots. Due to a technical problem they had to reshoot the long shot of the final scene on May 18 using doubles for all six principals. Fortunately the close-up shots in the ending were fine. Everyone but Kelly had left New York by then, and there was no sense in putting Gene in the long shot if the other five had stand-ins. The company returned to California on May 22.[54]

The footage shot in New York made up the introduction as well as the ending to *On the Town*. The introduction in particular became the highlight of the movie, remembered for decades to come as a breakthrough in film musicals. Kelly used hard cutting to go quickly from one short piece of film to another, imparting the sense of excitement expressed by the three sailors during their first visit to New York. "That really made the picture, that opening," commented Betty Comden.[55] Incidentally, the introduction includes a clip of the three sailors riding horses in Central Park where Gene looks very confident, grinning as he gallops along, despite his aversion to horseback riding.

After returning to the studio, Kelly threw himself into "A Day in New York," conducting rehearsals for this dream ballet until the company was ready to start shooting on June 28. Kelly and Ellen were the only principals participating in this ballet because Sinatra, Munshin, Garrett, and Miller were not up to the kind of dancing he envisioned. Gene asked Alex Romero to be one of the four specialty dancers, and brought in Carol Haney, on Romero's suggestion. Haney was a Massachusetts native who had worked as one of Jack Cole's dancers. M-G-M immediately offered her a long-term contract, and she joined Jeanne Coyne as Kelly's dance assistant. Alex Romero also suggested Lee Scott for the ballet as well as for "Miss Turnstiles." Marie Groscup, a Broadway dancer, made up the last of the four specialty dancers in the ballet; it was not Jeanne Coyne, as many writers have mistakenly claimed.[56] In addition to many invigorating steps, the three men performed Gene's Midair Twist, and Kelly also did his Side Heel-Clicks and Revolving Jetés when he danced by himself. The three women did vibrant dancing as well, the kind Kelly had Vera-Ellen perform earlier in *Words and Music*.

A ballet called "The Dream Coney Island" had been inserted into the stage version of *On the Town*. Sono Osato danced in it as Ivey Smith, but Ray Harrison substituted for John Battles, who played Gabey, apparently for the same reason that Sinatra and others did not take part in Kelly's dream ballet. In other words, there was a precedent for the use of professional dancers as substitutes for principal actors. The same thing had been done in the ballet of the stage version of *Oklahoma!*, which Kelly thought worked well. But what worked for the Broadway audience did not always work for the film audience. Later, when *Oklahoma!* was made into a screen musical, many viewers were confused by the substitution. Gene hoped that his own substitution in *On the Town* would work, but eventually came to believe that it did not. Even so, most commentators thought the transition from recognized star to talented dancer was smooth and believable in the film version of *On the Town*. Casey Charness writes that the ballet "effectively substitutes two real dancers for Sinatra and Munshin, paving the way for later similar ventures."[57]

"A Day in New York" is in fact the most effective film ballet Kelly ever created. It has a strong emotional impact in portraying the suffering that Gabey feels at losing Ivy so suddenly, taking him through sections in which he feels the exhilaration of finding her and the acute pain of losing her.

Charness points out that the ballet is staged theatrically rather than as a cine-dance, but he calls it "the very center of the picture."[58] He is right. It perfectly captures the heart of the story. Kelly never danced emotional highs

Figure 10.5 Kelly and Vera-Ellen perform an exuberant dance as part of Gene's dream ballet "A Day in New York." (Still from *On the Town*, 1949)

and lows better in his career, aided by his inspired choreography, which is a mix of modern and athletic styles.

Nestled within the dream ballet is a segment pairing Ivy and Gabey at the barre, but even here the moves are modern and deliberately sensual. Kelly was captivated by the application of color to this sequence, believing it was "rather dull" when he saw it in black and white rushes. Once the Technicolor people finished bathing the sequence in rich colors, especially red, everything jelled. "It heightened the fact that these two people were yearning for each other," he recalled. But Gene's choreography also highlighted that yearning. He developed some of the most sensual moves of his career as the two slide together over and around the barre assembly to Bernstein's bittersweet music. "Yet I never laid a glove on her. There was nothing the censors could say."[59]

Kelly finished filming "A Day in New York" on July 2 but encountered difficulties on the last day. He had practiced sliding across the floor on his knees the day before to get it just right. After he left for the evening, workers heavily waxed the floor to be helpful—but did so without orders. When Kelly filmed the emotional ending, including the sliding, on July 2 he slid much farther than intended and almost fell off the stage. A grip had to stop his fall. Gene ripped his pants and his knees began to bleed. They had to sand the floor to

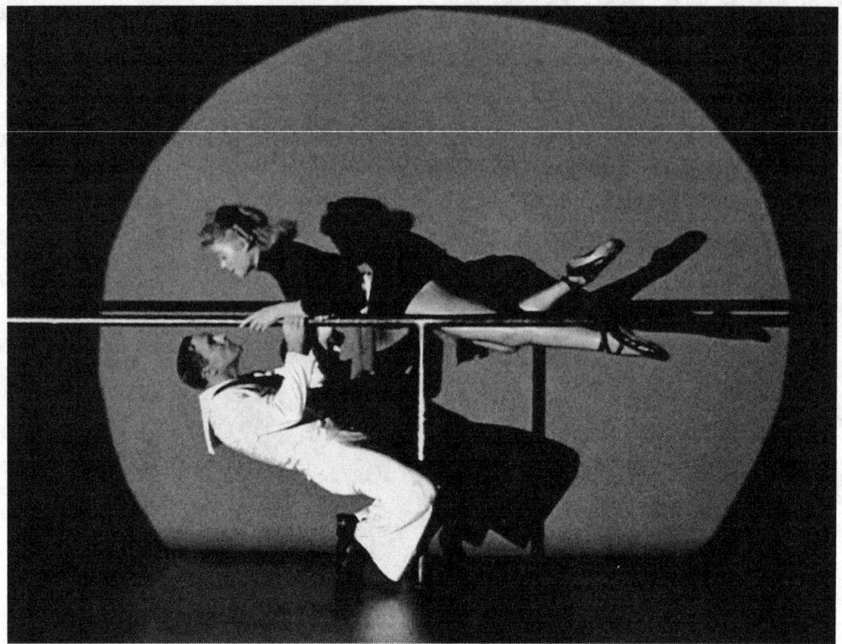

Figure 10.6 Kelly and Vera-Ellen in the sensuous dance at the ballet barre, nestled in the dream ballet "A Day in New York." (Still from *On the Town*, 1949)

make it less smooth. Technicians fitted him with knee pads, and he continued to film the ending. He had to express his shock and sadness in losing Ivy and then slide to her photograph, all in one shot. He did all this perfectly on take eleven, but a grip forgot to close the stage curtain to end the scene. Kelly wound up filming a total of twenty-six takes to get the final scene of the ballet to his satisfaction. He had "sore knees for a while."[60]

After two months of postproduction, a preview took place on September 9, 1949, at Pacific Palisades, followed by a second preview on November 22 in New York City. Preview audiences raved about the film, and *On the Town* was released December 30, 1949. Freed loved the movie from the moment he saw the first version of the edited dances, calling them "the greatest and most inspiring works I have seen since I have been making moving pictures." Both Freed and Kelly were flooded with letters praising the film for going beyond typical musicals. The picture bowled over audiences on its release, grossing $4,440,000 for a production cost of $2,111,000. Critics loved the dream ballet for its energetic dancing and its emotional impact in contrast to many latter-day commentators who coldly and excessively criticized it. Reviewers united in praise, calling it the best postwar film musical yet produced and lavishing attention on the location shots at the beginning of the picture. Film historian Thomas Schatz writes that *On the Town* was the "first all-out dance musical" and was the most effective "in blending story and music, song and dance into a seamless, integrated whole."[61]

One reviewer, Otis Guernsey, was aware that Kelly shared directing credit with Donen but he suspected Gene "was the guiding spirit in both performance and staging." He was right. And despite the fact that most commentators gave the bulk of the credit to Kelly for his directorial debut in this film, Kelly was always careful to give Donen credit for his contribution to this and every picture they collaborated on.[62]

In contrast to Kelly's generous and gracious attitude toward Donen, the younger man exhibited a crass, grasping, and selfish attitude toward his mentor. Donen admitted that at age twenty-four he felt as if he had "arrived" on the set of *On the Town* and was "kind of snotty about it." In later years he consistently tried to take all the credit for this and other films he made with Kelly. Unfortunately, Donen biographer Stephen Silverman took an even harsher stance, consistently blasting Kelly and excessively praising Donen's work, elevating his subject to a position of importance that is not in the least supported by the evidence. For example, Alex Romero recalled that Donen "never once, never once came into the rehearsal hall . . . never once," in referring to both *Take Me Out to the Ball Game* and *On the Town*.[63]

In addition, the assistant director's report demonstrates how importantly Kelly influenced every aspect of production in comparison to Donen. Taking part of a single day as an example, we learn that the two split on April 2 with Kelly's unit on Stage 25 preparing to film scenes inside the museum. Donen was assigned to film "Miss Turnstiles," which Kelly had choreographed, at the same time. But Stanley could not even start without Gene's approval. Kelly rehearsed Garrett in her dance steps and "outlined setup to camera crew." At that point, word came that Donen's unit was "ready to shoot." Kelly left to consult with Donen and gave him the green light to film. He then returned to the museum set, rehearsed the principals (including himself), and shot three takes in three minutes. Again Kelly went back to Donen's unit to check how they were doing. He returned to shoot thirteen more takes on the museum set. He then rehearsed Miller and Munshin for their duet and filmed four takes of this.[64] There can be no doubt that Kelly was the senior partner in this collaboration and that he had to approve everything Donen did—even in directing.

Kelly always retained a soft spot in his heart for *On the Town*, calling it his favorite. He believed that other works he did, such as *An American in Paris* and *Singin' in the Rain*, were better films, but shooting in New York and using quick editing were innovations of which he was forever proud. Director François Truffaut later told Kelly that the picture, especially its quick editing, had an important influence on the new wave of filmmaking in France. Gene also achieved the goal of integrating music and dance with the plotline and character development more than in any previous film. Commentators praise the flow, the integration, the vitality, and the uniqueness of *On the Town* as a milestone in Kelly's career as well as in the evolution of the dance musical.[65]

Zenith, 1949–1952

By 1949, the thirty-seven-year-old Kelly reached the zenith of his film career. Of the sixteen movies (including eleven musicals) that he had performed in so far, *Cover Girl* and *Anchors Aweigh* had been huge successes and *The Pirate* would be viewed as a masterpiece in years to come. He had already made the classic film *On the Town*, and soon would throw himself into the very successful *An American in Paris* and *Singin' in the Rain*. Kelly and the Golden Age of the film musical reached a satisfying plateau in their mutual development with all of these pictures. There is a noticeable maturity in Kelly's performance, especially in *On the Town* and *Singin' in the Rain*—less hammy acting and more serious dancing to express the inner character.

BLACK HAND **(1950)**

But, true to Kelly's complicated career, he was eager to do straight, dramatic roles to continue developing his acting skills, and M-G-M obliged by placing him in *Black Hand*. He created the role of Johnny Columbo, originally meant for Robert Taylor, a young Italian American in 1908, whose father had been murdered in 1900 by a mob known as the Black Hand. Johnny vows revenge and works with a police detective in an ultimately successful effort to break the mob.

Black Hand is a tightly wound, well-crafted crime drama that carries the viewer along despite the oversimplified, melodramatic nature of the plot, writing, and character development. Johnny wins in the end by the skin of his teeth in true movieland style. With a wig of black, curly hair and some makeup, Gene was made to look the part, and he spoke several lines of Italian in a plausible way. He performed very well, normally commanding the scenes when on screen, although his role did not allow much room for nuance or multidimensional development.

Filmed in only twenty days, *Black Hand* was released on March 12, 1950. The film was moderately praised by critics, but Kelly's performance was called "eminently forceful." The movie was quite popular with audiences and made a hefty profit for the studio. In one scene Kelly thought he saw the trained dancer as he moved about. "I just look at that and I see myself being ballet boy all over again," he commented years later. Soon after making it, Gene and his family took off on a European holiday.[1]

"JUST PLAIN KELLY"

Not long after returning, Hedda Hopper interviewed Kelly at his home. He spoke of his desire to do more straight acting roles like that of Johnny Columbo, assuming that he could not dance forever. Gene also was interested in making a picture about a clown but could not find the right story for it. Kelly yearned for more opportunities to direct movies, but his studio wanted to maximize the profit from his dancing roles, creating a constant tug-of-war between them. From observing little Kerry's reactions to his pictures, Gene became interested in making a series of films for kids between the ages of four and ten that could be used in schools. He realized that other than cartoons there were virtually no films aimed at this age group, and he believed in the power of the medium to educate as well as entertain.[2]

SUMMER STOCK (1950)

Kelly accepted his next role, playing the aspiring Broadway producer and actor Joe Ross in *Summer Stock*, mainly as a way to pay back Judy Garland for the support she had given him early in his Hollywood career. The plot and characters of this Joe Pasternak production did not appeal to Gene, and for good reason. It is a patched-up job imitating the old saw of putting on a show in a barn, hoping for the big break. Garland was at a low ebb in her career, increasingly haunted by her private ghosts—a serious weight problem dogging her persona and a frenzied addiction to sleeping pills and pep pills. The result was frequent absenteeism on the set. Her problems became everyone's problems—director Charles Walters claimed he got an ulcer because of the repeated delays she caused, which stretched the production schedule out for months beyond the original plan.[3]

Kelly saw that his most important job was to support Garland, and he went out of his way to help her. "I'll do anything for this girl," he told Pasternak. "If I have to come here and sit and wait for a year, I'd do it for her. That's the way I feel about her." Pasternak was forever grateful to Gene for this, calling him "a saint." Phil Silvers also had a role in the picture and tried whenever possible to raise Garland's spirits. Saul Chaplin, who also worked on the picture, was impressed by Gene's loyalty, which "was really put to the test. His patience and indulgence were amazing." Walters also observed their interactions, calling Gene "marvelous." He would "placate her and hold her hand and [ask], 'Anything I can do today?'" Walters says he was able to film Gene's natural "gentility" toward Judy in the number "You Wonderful You."[4]

As filming progressed sporadically, Gene noticed an awful odor emanating from Judy's mouth when they did close-up scenes. He decided to tell Dore Schary about it, worried that she was indulging in something much worse than pills. As Schary recalled it, Kelly described the odor as something like formaldehyde. Schary consulted a doctor who told him it probably was paraldehyde, a drug in use to help alcoholics out of delirium tremens. Schary had to see for himself. Asking Garland in for an informal talk, he sat near her and "got Kelly's message—strong and overpowering." Schary told Gene what he had found later that day, but apparently neither did anything about it. Schary recalled that "trouper and loyal friend to Judy that Gene is and was," he just put up with the odor and the delays.[5]

Despite her many problems, Judy tried to push herself when it came to Gene's choreography. "She was determined she wanted to dance a little better in that picture," Kelly recalled. "I guess it was for old time's sake . . . and maybe she felt it was our last picture together." Garland asked Kelly to develop harder dance steps, and he did so in a sequence depicting the characters rehearsing for the big show. Although fifteen pounds overweight, Garland "danced up a tiny whirlwind." Kelly admitted that Garland "was a good dancer, but not a fine one." She excelled at learning something well and gave "it an authenticity and authority that made her look a far better dancer than she was technically."[6] In the "Portland Fancy" number the two inserted a private joke. Gene performs various complex steps and Judy quickly imitates him and dances well. But when he does the Airplane Propeller, she simply gives up and they both laugh. This was a tie-in to her not being able to dance this move in *For Me and My Gal.*

Perhaps the strain imposed on everyone by Garland's problems led to some testiness on Kelly's part. Nick Castle was the dance director for *Summer*

Stock, although Gene collaborated with him on some numbers while developing his own routines on others. Born in 1910, Castle had experience dating back to the 1930s but tended to be "hot-headed," according to historian Larry Billman. Assistant director Al Jennings remembered that Kelly and Castle nearly came to blows one day over some choreographic argument. He felt compelled to step between the two—"You two little boys!" he yelled. "I really let them have it."[7]

Kelly also rubbed Carleton Carpenter the wrong way. The six-foot, three-inch actor had a supporting role in the picture, and apparently Gene did not like to be filmed too near him, once again sensitive about his perceived short height. Carpenter recalled that Kelly would ask him, though "always with a smile," if that was where he was going to stand in the next scene. If he said yes, Kelly would talk with Walters, and Carpenter was instructed to stand farther away.[8]

Despite the problems and the hackneyed plot, Kelly turned in a stellar performance in *Summer Stock*. At least three numbers are notable in one way or another for his film career. "Dig for Your Dinner," written by Saul Chaplin, features an impressive power dance by Kelly with a very enthusiastic ensemble backing him up. Joe Ross and his adoring young troupe arrive at a farm where Garland's Jane Falbury is barely managing to survive, and they use her barn as a rehearsal hall. But Jane insists that the troupe do their share of farm chores as well, so Kelly and Silvers lead the way with this cleverly written patter song about working for your keep. Kelly dances in a low, crouched athlete's stance, rapidly tapping out his steps. He winds up with an elaborate performance of the Airplane Propeller, rapidly changing directions while spinning around. Making this number even more memorable is the tightly coordinated support of the troupe members who crowd around Kelly, interact with him, and egg him on. Kelly liked to actively incorporate the chorus into dance routines, and "Dig for Your Dinner" is a tour de force of his achievement in that concept.

Kelly's performance in the unusual "Heavenly Music" highlighted his delight with clowning around on stage and screen. In this case, it is a spoof of hillbilly stereotypes, written by Chaplin originally for Kelly and Garland, but Silvers replaced Judy. They prerecorded the song on March 6, 1950, and filmed the sequence the next week.[9] With costumes, wigs, and makeup to highlight the characters they play, both Kelly and Silvers are very believable as unwashed, illiterate hillbillies. They also have huge rubber feet, and both actors play the possibilities here to the hilt. Their chorus is a large and raucous

Figure 11.1 Clowning around with Phil Silvers in "Heavenly Music." (Still from *Summer Stock*, 1950)

group of dogs. The number obviously was meant to replicate the spirit of "Be a Clown" from *The Pirate*, but Silvers carried the comic element off just as well as Garland.

Kelly's Squeaky Board and Newspaper dance became another highlight of his career. Left alone in the barn late one night, coming to grips with his developing love for Jane, Joe idly notices how a floorboard squeaks when stepped on. He then notices the noise made when tearing a newspaper laying on another part of the floor. Kelly developed a routine in collaboration with Castle that mixed these two aural elements with vigorous tapping. The result was a unique number in his life's work.

But arriving at the finished product was complicated. One afternoon when the company was dismissed due to Garland's absence, Kelly visited Castle at his house, where Nick demonstrated to him the sound produced by tearing a newspaper. Gene loved it. This led to a complicated search for just the right kind of newspaper to produce the right kind of sound. They collected many old newspapers that Gene danced on to split them until, as he recalled, he almost got a hernia. They finally settled on the *Los Angeles Times* of 1932 and 1935, and bought all the copies the property guys could find. But Kelly wanted another sound to pair it with, and that produced another lengthy search. He and Castle walked the streets of Culver City and Los Angeles for ten days "scraping our feet" on gutters, grates, and sidewalks, kicking windows, and sliding on grass. Then one day Gene noticed the floorboards of the barn set and wondered why he had not thought of them before. "It seems simple now," he later admitted, "I was just too dumb to think of it ahead of time."[10]

It was harder to develop this number than any other in his career, according to Kelly. He often said it was his personal favorite as well. "It was torture to put on—but I got great joy out of it." As film critic Jane Feuer has put it, Kelly developed many "environmental conceptions" in his dance career, meaning numbers that grew out of the staged environment. Of them all, the Squeaky Board and Newspaper routine "gives the greatest impression of spontaneity." Spontaneous it appears, but as Kelly told an interviewer, "the boards didn't really squeak, we dubbed all that in."[11]

Production of *Summer Stock* finally came to an end by the late spring of 1950 after six months of patient exhaustion. On its release on August 31, film critic Bosley Crowther admired Kelly's "beautifully disciplined style" in the Squeaky Board and Newspaper number, and the film went on to do fairly well with other critics and the viewing public. It was the last time Gene ever worked with Judy. But the two were tied forever by mutual admiration and devotion. She "is the greatest all-round performer living," Kelly wrote in a *National Women's Weekly* article that appeared in the summer of 1952. "I have always been left in complete awe at the amazing amount of talent which is tied up in this one person." But there was a bittersweet tone to his love for Judy. "I won't discuss her," he told Hedda Hopper in 1954, "it's too sad a story."[12]

IT'S A BIG COUNTRY (1951)

After *Summer Stock*, Kelly was placed in a film cowritten by Dore Schary called *It's a Big Country: An American Anthology*. Consisting of eight separate stories to illustrate the breadth of ethnicities in American society and designed to promote tolerance and understanding, its aims were consonant with Kelly's philosophy and political leanings. But the stories tend to be overly simplistic and the characters often unpalatable.

Kelly's "Rosika, the Rose" was not as bad as some episodes but still not praiseworthy. Janet Leigh was Rosika Szabo, the daughter of a Hungarian father, played by S. Z. Sakall, who hates Greeks simply because he claims

Figure 11.2 As Icarus, getting to know Rosika (Janet Leigh). (Still from *It's a Big Country*, 1951)

that all Hungarians hate Greeks. Gene was Icarus Xenophon, a young Greek, who falls in love with her and has to deal with her father's prejudice. Comic elements are deliberately factored into the plot, and Sharon McManus played one of Rosika's sisters. The episode is difficult to believe, greatly undercutting its message of tolerance and understanding even though the father reluctantly caves in at the end to approve the love match. Although Kelly acted well, the story was weak and the dialogue was poor. It took a while for all eight segments to be filmed, so the release was delayed to November 1951. Not surprisingly, the movie was a huge failure at the box office.

AN AMERICAN IN PARIS (1951)

Gene went from one of his most forgettable roles to a film most fans consider a classic. Arthur Freed originated *An American in Paris* with a desire to highlight the work of George Gershwin. He worked out the right to do so over a game of pool with George's brother Ira. Freed selected Vincente Minnelli to direct, Saul Chaplin to work on the music, and Alan Jay Lerner to write the script. Freed and Minnelli wanted a ballet in the film, which led to choosing Kelly over Astaire. Gathering everyone into a conference room, Freed told them, "Now, here's the idea: It's an American and he lives in Paris." The team took it from there.[13]

Spurred by the example of *On the Town*, Freed wanted to film 40 percent of the movie in Paris. But the cost and logistical difficulties were daunting. Also, the city government was reluctant to grant Freed's request to film in Paris. Most importantly, Kelly and Minnelli looked at location stills and realized how difficult it would be to shoot a ballet on Parisian streets. A second unit shot 10,000 feet in Paris for the "opening montage," but only 500 feet wound up in the release print. Everything else was done in the studio.[14]

In a letter to his fan club Kelly explained that failing to film on location made little difference because the studio allowed its team maximum latitude to create sets that would duplicate the aura of Paris. M-G-M's legendary largesse was still in vogue by 1950. Freed especially encouraged his unit to shoot more rather than less during production so he could have choices about what went into the release print. Moreover, art director Preston Ames had lived for five years in Paris and technical adviser Alan A. Antik had been born and raised there.[15]

Kelly and Chaplin spent a good deal of time in Ira Gershwin's house going through George Gershwin's voluminous output of songs. George had long since passed away, in 1937 at age thirty-eight. They wanted songs typical of his work that could be fitted into the story, working closely with Lerner to identify key moments in the developing plot and figuring out which songs would support those moments. Chaplin assembled a list of strong possibilities. Decades later, Kelly wrote cryptic notes on the Gershwin song sheets in his private collection as he recalled the process of selection. "Somebody Loves Me" was "a probable for Amer. In Paris—Rehearsed but Never used." The same occurred for "Soon" and "Tip-Toes." Although "Mine" was Ira's "big favorite," the team decided not to use it. In the end sixty-two musical segments were filled by twenty-five pieces of Gershwin music. The size of George Gershwin's musical legacy made the selection process the most difficult Kelly could remember, and then trying to work the chosen ones into a developing plot added more time and tedium to the preproduction phase.[16]

An American in Paris reunited Kelly and Minnelli, once again, in a mutually enjoyable and productive partnership. Costar Leslie Caron recalled that Minnelli and Kelly liked and respected each other. If their ideas differed, Minnelli found methods to quietly circumvent opposition and get his way.[17]

Finding Leslie Caron was not easy. Initially Cyd Charisse was considered, but Freed decided he wanted a real French girl for the role of Lise Bouvier opposite Kelly's Jerry Mulligan. Gene agreed. "There shouldn't be anything 'phony French' about her," he told Schary. Kelly had seen Leslie Caron, a young French ballerina, two years before in Roland Petit's ballet *La Rencontre* in Paris. Caron played the role of the Sphinx to great acclaim in that production, and Gene went backstage to meet her only to find she had gone home. He now thought she would be perfect for Lise. Freed later claimed that he asked Kelly to test Caron for the part. Gene maintained that he thought of Caron on his own and was asked by Freed to go to France and test another ballerina, Odile Versois. Leslie also recalled that when they met in the spring of 1950 Kelly told her he only had authorization to test Versois but he wanted to test her as well.[18] There is no doubt Kelly deserves the credit for discovering Caron.

Born in 1931 of a French father and an American mother, Leslie suffered serious malnutrition during the grim days of the German occupation during World War II. But she was a gifted dancer who drew the attention of Roland Petit. In 1948, she became an overnight sensation as the Sphinx at age sixteen, which is when Kelly saw her. "I was made to dance," Caron has stated. "My limbs just live it."[19]

When Freed and Minnelli saw the screen tests of both Versois and Caron, they agreed with Kelly that Leslie was perfect for the role. Everyone was impressed by her dancing skills and her fresh quality. Two or three weeks after the screen test in Paris, M-G-M called to offer Caron a seven-year contract. Three days later she was off to California with her mother as chaperone. Everyone failed to understand that her complete lack of experience in filmmaking would be a problem. Caron herself says she was not really interested in making movies but agreed just to please her mother. It was up to Gene to handle, mold, and encourage the teenager before she could carry the weighty role offered her.[20]

Rehearsals started on June 5, 1950, and Gene had to become more than a colleague for Caron. Her mother, worried about spending too much money, checked out of the Beverly Wiltshire and into a seedy, ill-reputed hotel in Culver City. When Gene found out he was shocked and made them move immediately to a hotel closer to the studio. He continued to watch out for Leslie. When she came to work late one morning he was surprised to learn that she had no alarm clock. "You don't? Well, let me tell you something, the war is over, kid. You can buy one now in any drugstore." It was "a new concept" to Caron, who had been accustomed to persistent shortages of everything in postwar France. Suffering from anemia, Caron often grew tired long before the end of her eight-hour day and Kelly had to coax her to continue. Just before filming was scheduled to begin, Leslie decided she would look better with short, straight hair and cut it one night. The next morning this created a minor crisis because all decisions about her hair had already been made. She was grilled by a committee of exasperated executives who thought a wig would not work for her. They sent her home and had to postpone filming her parts for three weeks to let her hair grow back. "They fire girls for less than that, you know!" Gene told her.[21]

The problems continued after filming started on August 1, 1950. Caron had just turned nineteen, and her mother returned to Paris. Kelly felt even more responsible for Leslie now. When she developed mononucleosis, Kelly arranged for her to take every other day off and the studio doctor gave her injections of vitamin B12 and B complex. Caron writes that she was very inhibited at the time, unable to express herself in words, and her English was less than perfect. She sweated through intimate scenes with the much older Kelly, mainly because she had not experienced any romantic relationship in her life so far and feared looking ridiculous.[22]

But Kelly did whatever was necessary to help her. "He guided me in front of the camera with a good deal of humor," Caron wrote. As he did with many colleagues, Gene developed a nickname for her—"Lester de Pester"—which is at once an expression of affection and frustration. Caron admits she wanted to hide from the camera and Kelly would say, "Lester, if you want your mother to see you in the film, you had better turn this way when you speak!"[23]

To prepare Caron for his choreography, Gene had the staff assemble excerpts of his major dance numbers from several of his movies. Caron was "really impressed," calling it "forty-five minutes of remarkable skill, precision, and invention performed with cocky charm and apparent facility." She had never really understood the career of the man who had taken her under his wing and blurted, "What tremendous fun you must have had!" In response, Gene gave her a five-minute lecture on how hard it was to achieve perfection on the screen. "That was lesson number one," Caron admitted.[24]

After all was done, the two achieved a warm, mutual admiration for each other and a lasting friendship. Kelly predicted a marvelous future for her in the movies the year after *An American in Paris* was released. Caron forever admired Gene's informality and his help in dealing with colleagues. As a mentor he gave approval "in measured tones." But "his disapproval was sharp, straight-forward, and didn't allow for any excuses. His rebukes were feared by one and all in the studio." She admitted she "could lose my confidence in front of him." Caron found Kelly to be very quick in assessing the strengths of his colleagues and "knew how to make the most of them." He was "a born leader, and liked to take command." As a dance partner Kelly was "strong, skillful, and with a perfect sense of rhythm." She also came to his weekend parties on a regular basis, surprised by the simplicity of his home and the informality of his gatherings. She recalled that as Betsy sang enthusiastically but completely off-key, Gene "did the Irish thing—drink whiskey and talk."[25] Kelly invested the most intense and comprehensive mentoring for Caron that he ever did for a colleague. He literally made her into a movie star. Only the mentoring he did for Stanley Donen approached this level, but the difference was that Caron remained forever grateful and honored him for it.

Another costar, however, could not be molded by Gene. Oscar Levant, a fellow Pittsburgher, clashed with Kelly behind the scenes. A gifted pianist with a long list of personality problems and addictions, he had his own ideas about how to play one of Gershwin's few waltzes, "By Strauss." He added a Viennese after-beat, with hesitations and accents. Kelly thought that would not work for the dance he wanted to do with an elderly lady and knew it was not part of the original music. But Levant refused to give in at first. "What started as a normal discussion soon turned into a shouting match," remembered Chaplin, "with Gene threatening to hit Oscar, who threatened to sue Gene if he did." Levant walked out of the studio but came back the next day as if nothing had happened, and they got along fine after that.[26]

Dance assistants Carol Haney and Jeanne Coyne were invaluable to Kelly during preproduction of *An American in Paris*. Haney especially was good at training dancers. Kelly trusted her keen eye for precision when it came to choral dancing, and she drilled everyone until they got it right. Haney also suggested choreographic movements to Kelly, who used them if he thought they would work. Coyne had a wonderful eye for how costumes aided or hindered dance movement. Kelly had the idea to light up the stairway steps used in George Guetary's "Stairway to Paradise," and Haney flipped the switches to light up each one as Guetary climbed them during his song.[27]

The first major sequence filmed was the introduction of Jerry Mulligan, waking up in his artist's garret. "I'd like to do something which makes me look like I'm a pretty smart guy," Kelly said, and developed a Buster Keaton routine of maximizing space by turning his bedroom into all other rooms of his residence. It had to be carefully coordinated with the set designers and then choreographed in fluid movements. Minnelli suggested that Gene think of it as moving underwater—no matter how much you try you cannot move too fast, but it gives the appearance of energy in a small space. This worked very well, but for the "Tra-la-la" number in Levant's apartment, Minnelli told Kelly to "clown it up" and to be "giddy and almost drunklike" because he is in love.[28] As a result, the number, though fine in terms of dancing expertise, is unappealing, especially with all the hammy acting by Kelly and Levant. It is a huge contrast to the universally loved title number from *Singin' in the Rain* where Kelly demonstrated how best to dance as a man in love.

By pairing with an elderly lady in "By Strauss," Kelly expressed his long-held view that everyone could and should dance. Minnelli thought that with anyone else this might look "cloying" but recognized that Gene was one of the rare performers who could get away with it. He thought the dance added "a lovely touch." Indeed, while some commentators thought it schmaltzy, others praised "Kelly's easy charm" and his "flair for comic pantomime" in the number. Levant, possibly stung by his argument with Kelly, could not bring himself to approve. "As talented as he is, Gene is not averse to a good dose of corn now and then," he commented in his memoirs.[29] What Levant may have been referring to is the segment leading up to the dance, where he, Gene, and even Guetary grossly overact in a supposedly comic routine. It is similar to the silly and crude overacting in the "Yes, Indeedy" number in *Take Me Out to the Ball Game* discussed in chapter 10. Fortunately, the positive things Kelly contributed far outweighed such segments.

Feeling compelled to include "I Got Rhythm"—the most famous of Gershwin's songs—Kelly had to think hard about how to present it with a unique twist. He decided to use it as a way to teach French kids some English words. The result was a beautiful expression of Kelly's Pied Piper ability to interact with children. Many of the kids were from French families living in Southern California, which added a touch of authenticity to the number. Minnelli stated that he let Kelly direct this number because it was Gene's idea and he had worked out the movement so closely. It shows in the finished product—the kids are a vocal, mobile chorus for Kelly's singing and dancing rather than decoration for the number, as was Minnelli's tendency. Even Levant liked it.[30] Of course, one does not feel it is Jerry Mulligan in this number but Gene Kelly. But it makes no difference to the audience. In no other number can one see Kelly's gift for working with young people so vividly displayed, producing electricity that is unique in film between actor and children.

The romantic number between Kelly and Caron is charmingly performed

Figure 11.3 Happy interaction with kids in "I Got Rhythm." (Still from *An American in Paris*, 1951)

with similar moves as in Kelly's other romantic dances on film. In a prerelease radio promotion on September 24, 1951, this part of the picture was highlighted in "Movie Time USA," which aired on CBS to celebrate the fiftieth anniversary of the film industry in Hollywood. Kelly gave the background of the story, then he and Caron read their dialogue near the Seine, and Gene sang "Our Love Is Here to Stay." The segment ended with Caron suddenly having to leave and the two making plans to meet the next day, as in the movie.

The sequence to introduce Caron to *An American in Paris* viewers was filmed after everything else except the ballet. Kelly copied the similar "Miss Turnstiles" number from *On the Town*. But unlike Vera-Ellen, who was proficient in many dance styles, Caron knew only ballet. So Kelly decided to showcase her in different costumes and performing difficult ballet moves in adagio (very slowly) to emphasize her body control. Minnelli decided to cue each section of this montage with different colors and décor, but he let Kelly direct the number. A woman from the Breen Office, which oversaw compliance with industry codes, came to watch rehearsals. Caron remembered that the woman was taken with Kelly, who in turn charmed and distracted her so that all she asked for was to reshoot one segment in a slightly different way and Caron "moderated my relationship with the chair." Kelly later admitted that he always tried to outwit the censors in some way to achieve the look he envisioned.[31]

Everyone wanted a big ballet in *An American in Paris*. Chaplin recalled that the very first meeting to discuss music for the film included a consensus that they must have a ballet. There was some resistance to the idea outside the team, but Schary fought hard for its approval. Even well-wishers such as Irving Berlin thought it risky, while Betty Comden and Adolph Green found it unnecessary, but the team was fiercely committed to the project. Initially it was planned for the middle of the picture, but Freed insisted it would be better at the end. Serious planning did not begin until the rest of the film was nearly shot.[32]

While Nina Foch, who played Jerry's patron, was recovering from chicken pox that she caught from one of the kids in "I Got Rhythm," Minnelli and Kelly worked up a six-page scenario for the ballet by September 6, 1950. Kelly wanted the extended number to tell an actual story as in the emotional ballet of *On the Town*, but Minnelli vetoed the idea and wanted everything to be jumbled in Jerry's mind in "a kind of delirium." Unusually for him, Kelly caved in. They decided that the ballet would represent a painter's thinking about Paris and what the city means to him and illustrate it with famous French paintings as well as images of Paris. The work of Raoul Dufy, Pierre-Auguste Renoir, Édouard Manet, Maurice Utrillo, Henri Rousseau, Vincent Van Gogh, and Henri de Toulouse-Lautrec, plus the Place de la Concorde, figured into the planning. Jerry's falling in love with Lise and losing her would be woven into all this. It was the most elaborate of Kelly's film ballets and a labor of love for Minnelli. It involved dozens of dancers and extended through seventeen minutes of screen time. Hundreds of costumes were used, along with several major sets of intricate props and décor. Irene Sharaff was responsible for 300 costume designs, and the art directors handled the sets and paintings.[33]

Transitioning into the ballet was tricky. Kelly and Minnelli decided to use a drawing of the Place de la Concorde, a rose, and color (versus black and white) as the key motifs to go into and out of the fantasy. Minnelli had the idea to stage a Beaux-Arts ball before the ballet with people in black-and-white costumes to accentuate the explosion of color to follow in the fantasy. Interestingly, set decorator Keogh Gleason criticized the masquerade ball. "There was just no sense or rhythm or design to it. It was just a mass of black-and-white moving things." Editor Adrienne Fazan concurred, complaining that she had to sift through a mountain of film to try to make some sense of it. For the ballet itself, thirty painters worked for six weeks to reproduce dozens of paintings as backdrops. Chaplin worked up the music for the ballet from Gershwin's tone poem that lent its name to the movie. In awe of Gershwin's talent, Chaplin felt a bit queasy about changing segments of the music to match sequences in the ballet. Kelly, however, thought that the music was critical and the paintings had to be "subjected to the music" in order to create a thoroughly integrated ballet.[34]

Minnelli left to direct *Father's Little Dividend* on October 6, finished it by November 1, and returned in time to begin filming the ballet on December 6. While he was gone, Kelly worked hard on choreography and rehearsals. He had acceded to the idea that "the décor and the color" were more important than the choreography in this piece; even so he developed vibrant, arresting steps that matched the elaborate set decoration and costumes in every scene. He inserted some ballet movement for Caron and himself in several segments. He used tap in a section showing American servicemen, where he danced with four male dancers (including Alex Romero) with Cohan-type cockiness. In the same segment, Caron and a large group of female dancers used ballet movement, modified to match the men's dance steps. The result is typical Kelly choreography, a mélange of styles crafted for the characters, the moment, and the emotion.[35]

The most memorable choreography in the ballet centers on Toulouse-Lautrec's painting *Chocolat Dancing in the Irish and American Bar*, featuring an African American jockey. Kelly had always been intrigued by this man and conducted research but could not determine the type of dance he did in Paris. He devised his own choreography, inspired by the jazzy music of Gershwin and the pose of Chocolat in the painting. He even inserted the modified, more vigorous Prone Kick that he performed with the Nicholas Brothers in *The Pirate*. The result was, as one film critic put it, a "perfect coincidence between the frame of cinema and the frame of painting."[36]

Preston Ames designed the Place de la Concorde set. The actual Place de la Concorde contained the Obelisk of Luxor in the center and two fountains designed by Jacques Ignace Hittorff, when the eighteen-acre public square was created in the 1750s near the Seine. Kelly told Ames the obelisk would get in the way of his choreography and that there was no need for two fountains. So the obelisk was dropped and sculptor-modeler Henry Greutert created a model of one fountain, which was used to build a three-fourth scale fountain for the set. Minnelli wanted water to squirt out of the fountain, but that was impossible with people running about. So they designed plastic tubes with dry ice to simulate flowing water. Kelly used the fountain to work out the

Figure 11.4 Dressed as Chocolat for the ballet in *An American in Paris* (1951), Kelly checks on the camera setup with Minnelli. (Still from *Anatomy of a Dancer*, 2002)

choreography in and around the set of the Place de la Concorde. It was the key set of the ballet because Jerry starts in it and returns there to end his interior journey through Paris as he finds love and loses it.[37]

After a month of filming, the ballet was finished by January 2, 1951. All that was left was the ecstatic reunion of Jerry and Lise on the steps, which was filmed on one flight of stairs used for *Kismet* (1944) and reproduced as three flights by studio processing. This was finished by January 8. Kelly now had a seventeen-minute ballet that cost $450,000. Irene Sharaff recalled that everyone involved in the number had a stronger than normal sense of excitement about it. People not involved in its production regularly came to the studio to watch them work. There was a general feeling that it was something unusual.[38]

The reaction to the ballet proved them right. Most critics who loved the picture cited the ballet for its stunning visual impact. Released on November 11, 1951, the film garnered more than $8 million in revenue for a cost of less than $3 million. It won Academy Awards in seven categories, including Best Picture of 1951. In addition, Kelly won an honorary award for "his extreme versatility as an actor, singer, director, and dancer but specifically for his brilliant achievement in the art of choreography on film." Gene was unable to accept the award personally because he was filming in Europe when the awards were given on March 20, 1952.[39]

But does a sweep at the Oscars indicate a great movie? Film historian Donald Knox writes with reference to *An American in Paris* that "Academy Awards do not necessarily indicate excellence." Moreover, Howard Strickling, in the publicity department at M-G-M, revealed that after the film was nominated the studio made sure every Academy member saw *An American in Paris*, even setting up special screenings, which might explain the unusual number of awards the film received. Freed admitted that, despite good reviews, critics did not like the weak story. Bosley Crowther said, "Mr. Kelly's the one who pulls the faint thread of Alan Jay Lerner's peach-fuzz script into some pattern of coherence." British director and film critic Lindsay Anderson wrote that the script was "constructed with confusion and lamely written." And yet Lerner received an Oscar for the story.[40] In fact, it was only Kelly's special Oscar that was not explicitly tied to the picture. That award recognized all his film work to date including directing, choreography, acting, dancing, and singing.

The French theme of *An American in Paris* was a key element in the film's success with audiences. The Kelly-Minnelli vehicle started a trend that has been termed "Frenchness" films, including the Freed-Minnelli picture *Gigi* (1958) starring Caron and *Irma La Douce* (1963). While the French took to these films enthusiastically, they are thoroughly American views of France, its people, and its culture. As author Tony Thomas has put it, *An American in Paris* is "a pleasant fantasy barely related to reality, . . . a purely American idealization of things French."[41]

The visual appeal of the ballet was the other key to the film's appeal. Kelly and Freed showed the picture to Raoul Dufy in the summer of 1952 in Paris. The elderly painter loved the movie and asked to see the ballet again. But not everyone felt the same way about the ballet. Several critics thought it overblown. Anderson agreed that the extended number generated excitement as a spectacle but rightly pointed out that its brilliant color and decoration had subverted the purpose of the piece within the flow of plot and characterization. He saw *An American in Paris* as a struggle between Kelly's "naturalistic, dramatic musical" (as in *On the Town*) and Minnelli's "pure confection, with style and design to match." Anderson liked *On the Town* better, both its ballet and the picture as a whole.[42]

Our own assessment of the two films exactly coincides with Anderson's rather than with the majority of critics. Unlike *An American in Paris*, *On the*

Town has an appealing story and likeable characters, and its ballet effectively touches heartstrings. We also find that the number that introduces Caron is far less appealing than the "Miss Turnstiles" number with energetic dancing by Vera-Ellen and the male gymnasts.

Anderson's critique also mentions that not only the idea behind the ballet but also the montage introducing Caron were taken from *On the Town*. He concludes, as we do, that both fell far short in execution.[43]

Another major problem in our opinion is the characters of the two leads. Lise misses Henri's special performance, even though he took care of her during the war and she is engaged to marry him, for a rendezvous with a man she hardly knows. As for Jerry, he is abominably rude to Milo, who is his patron. He is also unnecessarily rude to a female college student from America who stops by to discuss his paintings.

Similarly, Stephen Harvey calls Lise "thoughtless" for missing the premiere of fiancé Henri's number to dance with Jerry and says Jerry is "outright callous" to Milo. He points out that Milo and Henri have more depth and sensitivity. This is true. In fact, Freed dropped scenes that portrayed these two supporting characters even more sympathetically so as not to overemphasize Jerry and Lise as selfish.[44]

Harvey also wrote that Jerry's paintings, executed by Gene Grant, do not express the advanced style of art in the 1920s much less that of 1950.[45] We agree with this criticism. Moreover, Jerry's paintings look very much at odds with the paintings of the artists who supposedly inspire him.

Over the years, more and more people have become critical of the film's weak story and unappealing main characters. *An American in Paris* is included in the "Ten Most Overrated Films of All Time," where the plot is criticized as "creaky and nonsensical," the film for its lack of wit, and "unlike *Singin' in the Rain*, it is a forgettable experience."[46] It is also included in the "20 Most Overrated Movies of All Time," a 2006 poll by *Premiere* magazine, where Kelly's character is described as "predatory" and "leering." Indeed, this description fits with his behavior in the nightclub scene where he inveigles an acquaintance with Lise. Ironically, this is where Caron's lack of acting experience is painfully evident. She looks like a schoolgirl who has no idea why she is in the scene or what she is supposed to do. Her lack of expression in the nightclub scene makes it difficult to believe that Jerry would fall so hard for her, especially when Milo, an attractive and supportive woman of his own age, is interested in him.

Caron later said that the problem with her acting arose because Minnelli was incapable of expressing what he wanted from actors. This was just one of the many problems of this splashy but weak movie. As Nina Foch so aptly put it, "You can't take *An American in Paris* seriously."[47] But none of these obvious flaws seem to matter to mass audiences. *An American in Paris* often ranks second only to *Singin' in the Rain* as the general public's favorite Kelly movie.

DONEN AND COYNE

Before embarking on *Singin' in the Rain*, Gene agreed to a cameo role in the first film that Stanley Donen directed on his own, *Love Is Better Than Ever* (1952), starring Elizabeth Taylor and Larry Parks. Gene appeared briefly as himself as a way to help his protégé in the project. The film, however, lost money.

Donen's marriage to Jeanne Coyne reached rock bottom at this time. It had never been a strong union. Coyne was eager for a real home life with children and dinners at home, but Donen could not offer these things to her. He made $500 a week yet claimed he could not afford children. Coyne testified that they had dinner at home only three times in three years and that he ignored her when they were in public. The Bridesons write that the failure of the marriage was due to "Donen's immaturity and callousness, characteristics also evident in his behavior with colleagues at M-G-M." Coyne asked for a separation around Christmastime in 1949. The relationship simply worsened after that, with her losing fifteen pounds due to stress and nervous exhaustion by the time Donen consented to the divorce on April 21, 1950. The pair finally obtained a divorce on May 18, 1951, with Coyne reclaiming her maiden name and waiving alimony.[48]

SINGIN' IN THE RAIN (1952)

Kelly moved on to his next major project almost immediately. *Singin' in the Rain*, widely viewed as the pinnacle of his career, was also a catalogue picture, like the Gershwin project, but featured the songs of lyricist Arthur Freed and composer Nacio Herb Brown. The pair had used their output in many movies before, starting with the groundbreaking *Broadway Melody* (1929), but *Singin' in the Rain* capped Freed's obsession with using his own songs in his movies. Comden and Green worked on an original script for a year before production began, writing one of their finest pieces. Kelly loved the project and agreed to create the role of Don Lockwood, a silent screen star who struggled with the transition to sound pictures. He was also slated to direct, with Donen as codirector. The screenwriters were old friends with both directors, and there was quick and easy communication between all of them. Comden and Green admired the visual creativity and pacing in *On the Town* and knew it would be re-created in this project.[49]

Donald O'Connor was brought in as Kelly's costar, creating the role of Cosmo Brown. A gifted dancer and comedian, O'Connor's breezy style and technical perfection made him one of the hottest film dancers of the era. But his talents had never been honed to a fine point because of the less than perfect film projects in which studios like Paramount, Universal, and Twentieth Century-Fox placed him. Kelly and O'Connor liked each other right away and danced together better than any other male partner Gene ever encountered. Thirteen years younger than Kelly, O'Connor occupied the same age group as Betsy Blair, Jeanne Coyne, Stanley Donen, and many other protégés and students that Gene influenced, mentored, or taught. O'Connor learned something about total body control during rehearsals, having been a hoofer, comic, and stunt dancer his whole career.[50]

The other major costar was Debbie Reynolds, a nineteen-year-old newcomer who had turned in only small acting appearances in a handful of pictures. Whether Kelly wanted her for the role of Kathy Selden, Don's love interest, or had her pushed onto him by Mayer, who saw star potential in her, is a matter of debate. What is certain is that Kelly faced a daunting task in teaching her to dance so she could hold her own with two masters. Reynolds worked hard to catch up, complaining at times about Kelly the taskmaster, but she brought her dancing up in time to contribute greatly to the success of *Singin' in the Rain* and remained forever grateful to Kelly.[51] As with Vera-Ellen and Caron, Gene made Reynolds's long career as a star possible.

Jean Hagen was chosen to play Lina. Kelly thought she was perfect for the role—pretty enough to be believable as a movie star but, more importantly, very funny. "We were damn lucky" to have her for the role, he said. Cyd Charisse was picked for the ballet when Donald O'Connor had to leave for other commitments and Freed did not want Carol Haney, who Gene first recommended. Charisse had been trained as a ballet dancer before coming to Hollywood and had appeared in a few films with ballet themes. But Kelly saw the potential in Charisse and had to rethink the entire ballet so he could showcase her talent. Under his guidance, Cyd learned how to dance steamy and sexy, wowing the audience with a vamp performance and creating a watershed in her career that made her a major star.[52] The Kelly touch was never better employed than in seeing and developing the dance potential in underutilized performers like Charisse.

Since Freed's songs mostly came from the days of early sound pictures, Comden and Green decided to place *Singin' in the Rain* in that era. This led to a good deal of research into the movie industry of twenty-five years before, with Kelly and others studying photographs, interviewing people at the studio who had been active in those days, and finding old equipment in studio storehouses.[53]

Much time was spent deciding which Freed-Brown songs would be used. As he did for his other song sheets donated to Boston University, Kelly wrote short notes on the songs used in *Singin' in the Rain*. "Loved dancing to this," he commented about "Broadway Rhythm," the main theme of the ballet. For "Fit as a Fiddle," he wrote "O'Connor & Kelly—A couple of hams! Came off well." And for "Singin' in the Rain," the title song and ultimate film dance of Kelly's entire career, he wrote "What can I say?"[54]

Nineteen-year-old Rita Moreno got a big break when Kelly cast her in a supporting role in *Singin'*. "It was refreshing," Moreno recalled, because Kelly chose her not for an ethnic role but for the brassy Zelda Zanders. She remembered working hard to perfect "the intricate steps laid out by Gene Kelly," but those scenes along with others she was in were dropped from the release print. Moreno also stood up to Kelly one day when he told her that, to be consistent with the styles of the era, she would have to cut her hair. The young Puerto Rican refused, giving Gene a mini lecture on why that was not done in her culture. "It is a point of feminine pride!" She recalled, "He caught his breath. I don't think young actresses countered his requests very often. Then he said in that mellifluous voice of his, 'Okay, you'll wear a wig.'"[55]

Intense rehearsals ended when production began on June 18, 1951. In "Beautiful Girl" and the montage that preceded it, Busby Berkeley's famous kaleidoscopic patterns were used partly as homage to the past, but mainly to poke gentle fun at it. Kelly and Donen wanted an extremely high angle shot to end "Beautiful Girl," looking straight down at singer-dancer Jimmy Thompson surrounded by girls, all looking up. For this they needed two cameramen because the chassis had to move forward as the crane lifted the camera thirty-five feet above the studio floor in order to keep everything in balance. Frank Phillips worked the gearhead while another camera operator handled the chassis, both men looking through the same viewfinder. It was an unusual, difficult procedure, but they managed to capture it perfectly on the third try. Yet Phillips was frustrated that this "monster of a shot" was less impressive visually than it should have been considering the trouble involved in shooting it.[56]

Classic numbers in *Singin' in the Rain* that would live forever included "Fit as a Fiddle," depicting Don and Cosmo's lean years as vaudeville performers, and "You Were Meant for Me," a love song between Don and Kathy performed on an empty soundstage. "Make 'Em Laugh" gave O'Connor an opportunity to do his unique combination of dance, comedy, and athletic stunts all wrapped up into one number. It is certainly the highlight of his film career. "Good Morning" joined Kelly, O'Connor, and Reynolds in their only number as a threesome with utterly delightful choreography and performance. Rarely has a trio danced so well and so joyfully on the screen. "Moses Supposes," pairing Kelly and O'Connor in a stunning display of coordinated, vigorous tapping, often ranks as one of the very best dances of Hollywood's Golden Age.[57]

The title number was never meant to be a classic for all time, but it became one under Kelly's choreography, direction, and performance. Gene found the task of creating a number to "Singin' in the Rain" quite easy as the lyrics that drive the action are straightforward. He realized that it had "to be *played* more than it's danced." To have the room to play it out fully, Kelly thought it best to place the number on a street. With the help of art director Randall Duell and Jeanne Coyne, he picked a side street of the New York set in M-G-M's backlot. Deciding the number should take place at night, Kelly had the technical crew rig black canvas so it could be filmed during the daytime as M-G-M preferred. The crew set up pipes to bring in the "rain" on cue and even chipped out one puddle in the sidewalk and a large gutter pool exactly where Kelly wanted them. A special covering had to be made for parts of the camera equipment, and operator Frank Phillips, who was often soaked, had to wear gloves to stop getting electric shocks when touching the equipment. Director of photography Harold Rosson had to backlight the rain so it would show better on film and "front light" Kelly's dancing. Kelly always commiserated that the dance was much harder on the cameramen than it was on him.[58]

"Singin' in the Rain" was filmed on July 18, 1951, and part of the next day. Kelly had a fever of 103 degrees due to a sinus infection in the days before filming. He probably got it rehearsing in the cold water, just as he often did after swimming. He had not fully recovered but decided to do the number anyway. Kelly also rode the boom to check out high camera angles and approved

Figure 11.5 Dancing up a storm with Donald O'Connor in "Moses Supposes." (Still from *Singin' in the Rain*, 1952)

all the camera movement before filming. The highlight of this classic dance number has Kelly swinging his open umbrella as he twirls around while dancing in a wide circle, filmed by a crane shot. "It is a case of motion within motion," Casey Charness writes, "the finest single example of the application of camera knowhow to a dance movement." The number also tracks dance movement toward the left of the screen to impart a kinetically effective image of dance action on a flat screen.[59]

Kelly found the aesthetics of "Singin' in the Rain" relatively easy to accomplish. He wanted to impart a sense of childlike joy that was implicit in the lyrics of the song. In this case the number was strategically placed right after his love for Kathy reaches its peak, so Don had something important to dance about despite the downpour. He added bricolage, using iron grates, water puddles, downspouts, and his umbrella as props—all of it to enhance the joy he felt as Don. Technically he worried about slipping on the wet pavement and had to deal with the fact that his wool suit kept shrinking constantly, not to mention that he was still feverish. Watching him film the number left Rita Moreno in awe. She could see he was ill and how hard the cold water hit him, and yet he was a trouper—his magnetic smile never faded. "Gene Kelly

Figure 11.6 Singing "The sun's in my heart" from the title number. (Still from *Singin' in the Rain*, 1952)

remains in my mind a classy performer in a classic film, showing the ultimate in classic determination. I was inspired—for life."[60]

As with *An American in Paris*, the ballet of *Singin' in the Rain* was the last segment to be shot. Quite different in tone and décor, it tells the story of an aspiring hoofer who comes to Broadway and makes good, developing a romantic crush on an unattainable woman kept by a mobster. Although the story is only loosely tied to the rest of the film, the ballet is a well-crafted, extended number with some of Kelly's most accomplished choreography and dancing. The best thing about the ballet is Gene's singing and dancing to "Broadway Melody" and "Broadway Rhythm," the two most popular songs in the Freed-Brown catalog, which had been used many times before in films. Gene performs Revolving Jetés in the early segment and rapidly repeats the Airplane Propeller several times here as well as in the finale. He sings both songs well, and his throaty, enthusiastic rendition of "Gotta Dance!" is emblematic of his entire life. He dances with more verve than usual in the finale of the ballet, which sums up his life and career.

Two behind-the-scenes photographs shared with us by cinematographer Roy Wagner nicely illustrate how Kelly managed to coordinate the tasks of directing and performing. In one photo, Kelly, in a tuxedo, is standing on a ladder looking through the viewfinder and consulting with three cameramen, two of them crouching on a platform that is eye-level with him. In the other photo, Kelly, in the same tuxedo but now with hat and cane in hand, is in front of the camera setup he just approved. Based on his clothes and his stance, he is clearly singing "Broadway Melody" for the finale of the ballet as the cameramen film him. Donen is not in either photo.[61]

Charisse played an important role as the vamp in the ballet and remained forever grateful to Kelly for this important break in her career. Her introduction, dressed in a tight-fitting green dress, wowed audiences even while offending censors in some foreign countries. Her other major part in the ballet—dressed in white and manipulating a long white veil in a dreamy dance with Kelly on a virtually bare stage—also offended censors and was very challenging in technical execution as well as artistic expression. Kelly felt the thirteen-minute ballet needed to be trimmed for the release print, but he could not figure out how to do that without cutting Charisse's screen time, which he refused to do because she needed every minute of it to establish herself as a major film dancer. "I have Gene to thank for bringing Cyd to life," Freed wrote after seeing the rushes of her next project, *The Band Wagon*.[62]

Singin' in the Rain was premiered on the East Coast in March 1952 and on the West Coast in April. It received overwhelmingly enthusiastic reviews and widespread audience approval. At a cost of $2,540,800 it grossed $7,665,000, giving Kelly unprecedented clout at M-G-M. The film's early profile was dampened slightly in terms of audience numbers because it came out when public adulation for *An American in Paris* was at its height, but it quickly outpaced its predecessor, and its appeal grew with time. *Singin' in the Rain* has regularly been named the best musical of all time and placed among the top ten best films ever made. For its melding of artistic merit and viewer appeal, *Singin' in the Rain* is the pinnacle of Kelly's lifelong effort to excel in both areas simultaneously.[63]

During 1948 to 1952, Gene reached the zenith of his career, producing major dance musicals that would live forever. No one—not even Fred Astaire—had risen so sharply to such heights. Even though Astaire's dancing tended to appeal a bit more to some critics and viewers, Kelly's movies tended to be more successful than those of his older colleague. Most of them were far better integrated, told weightier stories, and achieved a blending of talents better than the films that merely tended to showcase Astaire's great talent while leaving everything else behind. A huge part of Hollywood's accomplishment in the Golden Age of the musical was built by Kelly's drive, artistic vision, and skill as a choreographer, dancer, director, and mentor of young talent.

CHAPTER 12

Turning Point, 1951–1953

By the end of 1951, immediately after finishing work on *Singin' in the Rain*, Kelly embarked on a risky venture that was dear to his heart. He had for years wanted to make a film that highlighted serious dancing and the artists who performed it. A devoted ballet lover, he had long been frustrated that the general public had so few opportunities to see ballet. M-G-M, like all other studios, sought properties for mass distribution and it was understandably reluctant to sanction this scheme. Even Freed could not bring himself to approve it—that is, until Kelly had reached the peak of his value to the studio with an impressive string of financial and artistic successes.

In October 1951, a month before the release of *An American in Paris*, columnist Edwin Schallert identified Kelly as a quintuple threat in the movie business—dramatic actor, song and dance man, choreographer, director, and writer (the last for *Take Me Out to the Ball Game*). Interestingly, Schallert added "writer" as a category but still came up with only five categories, as did Kelly's special Oscar, because he lumped dancer and singer into "song and dance man." Pointing out that literally no one else qualified "in all those spheres," Schallert rightly concluded that "Kelly is today unique in pictures." Gene modestly credited the studio for giving him unusual latitude to work in all these areas. He also told Schallert that he needed a rest, having "cut short a European trip to prepare for 'Singin' in the Rain.'"[1]

With Kelly's heightened clout, M-G-M was now willing to give him even more leeway. Other considerations also led them to negotiate an unusual deal with their multitalented star. In December 1951, the US Congress passed a law allowing an American citizen to work outside the country up to seventeen months out of eighteen without paying US income tax. It was aimed primarily at oil industry men who were beginning to develop the rich oil resources of the Middle East, as well as at individuals working for the US Defense Department. Lew Wasserman, Kelly's agent since 1946, had the idea of encouraging his clients to take advantage of the tax break. He not only alerted Kelly to the opportunity but also rounded up twenty-four other M-G-M actors who were willing to make movies overseas for the studio. Gene's contract was due to expire at the same time, giving him even more leverage in negotiating the terms of his employment.[2]

For M-G-M, this was good business. The company had a movie studio in England, at Borehamwood, Elstree, just north of London, since 1937. Variously known as M-G-M Elstree or M-G-M British Studios, it had turned out products mostly for people in England and was largely staffed by British employees. The parish of Elstree hosted seven film studios, making up the largest concentration of moviemakers outside Hollywood. M-G-M agreed to let Kelly make his ballet movie there so it could use up funds frozen by the British government—that is, money that could be spent only in Britain.[3]

Kelly was ecstatic. He considered London, which was close to Elstree, to be the dance mecca of the world. Moreover, European dancers would be more likely to go to England than to the United States. He made arrangements to fly the rushes to Culver City, where Freed could handle editing and pass final judgment on the scenes.[4]

Kelly would have to handle everything else associated with his project in England. The arrangement meant he would be the writer, director, casting master, and uncredited coproducer. He would have to oversee virtually everything associated with making a feature-length movie without the support of the well-developed resources of the M-G-M studio at Culver City. He would be working with an array of staff and crew he had never met, at a studio he had never visited, to produce a film with a risky premise—the assumption that average film viewers wanted to see the highest level of art dancing. Only an artist of Kelly's temperament, drive, and work ethic would have taken on something like this, especially when years of innovative work had brought him to the pinnacle of success in producing films that appealed to average as well as elite audiences.

Personal financial considerations played a role in this decision. Kelly's new contract, signed in December 1951, paid him $2,500 a week. That was in stark contrast to the average income of $75 per week in the country that year. Yet he was not satisfied. In an interview with Tom Dancy, Kelly noted that his films had grossed $75 million for M-G-M, that he received lucrative offers of up to $10,000 a week from producers of stage shows in Las Vegas, and that he should have received a higher salary from the studio because he worked in so many areas of film production. Moreover, Kelly admitted he had saved only a small amount of his salary thus far due to extensive traveling with his family.

In her memoirs, the would-be communist Betsy Blair wrote that "it was a fine joke on the IRS" to take advantage of the tax break. She mentioned in an interview that Gene had no interest or time to dabble in the stock market or seek other investment opportunities.[5] He counted on salary increases or income-tax breaks to improve his financial situation. In short, money matters intermingled with the desire to make an experimental film about ballet dancers served as the motivation for Kelly's extended stay overseas.

Gene flew to Europe in late February 1952, followed by Betsy, Kerry, McClelland, Coyne, and Haney by sea in March. They met Gene in Paris. Coyne was in bad shape physically and emotionally after her traumatic marriage to Donen, and Kelly convinced the studio he needed her in Europe. It was a rehabilitative experience for her.[6]

THE DEVIL MAKES THREE (1952)

To meet the studio's terms, Kelly had agreed to star in two films produced in Europe in addition to making his ballet movie. The first was *The Devil Makes Three*, a potboiler about Nazi remnants who try to make a return to power in Germany soon after the end of World War II. Directed by Andrew Marton, who had shot the second-unit footage in New York for *On the Town*, Kelly had the undemanding role of US Army Air Force Captain Jeff Eliot opposite newcomer Pier Angeli who was twenty years his junior. Kelly was frustrated with the poor plot but had no opportunity to improve it. Before filming began he developed appendicitis and had to undergo surgery. He recovered at the Hotel Lancaster in Paris and then at Klosters near Zurich.[7]

Filming of *The Devil Makes Three* took place in Germany and Austria, with Gene only half-interested due to the unbelievable aspects of the plot (smuggling gold by making car fenders out of the precious metal, for example). Despite his frustration, Kelly turned in a good performance. He was effective in expressing a wide range of emotions from gentleness to anger in dealing with Pier Angeli's character, who is being manipulated against her will by the Nazis. He also acted believably in fighting or tricking all the tough guys surrounding him during the buildup to the climax.

The ending of the plot involves a chase of the Nazi leader that takes everyone to the wreckage of the Berghof near the city of Berchtesgaden in Bavaria. The Berghof was Hitler's personal residence, one of several constructed for the Nazi dictator across Germany. It had a huge plate-glass window overlooking the mountain scenery that appears in many photographs dating to the 1930s. When Marton filmed the climactic scene of *The Devil Makes Three* in the ruined shell of the Berghof, highlighting the huge window without its plate glass, he produced a striking visual image that resonated with a dark and horrific page in European history. The Berghof was completely destroyed a few months later by the new German government to prevent it from becoming a mecca for Nazi sympathizers.

While Kelly was filming *The Devil Makes Three*, Freed called him on March 29, 1952, to tell him that *An American in Paris* had won big at the Academy Awards. Gene's own special honorary award, for all his film work to date, was the biggest and best news from America. Johnny Green, conductor of the M-G-M orchestra, was not the first to nominate Kelly for this award and assured Gene that it received "unanimous approval" by the board. "We knew that he was terribly, terribly pleased," Lois McClelland told an interviewer, "because he underplayed it so."[8]

Kelly finished work on *The Devil Makes Three* early in April 1952 and vacationed with his entourage at Klosters. Released on September 19, 1952, the film lost money at the box office. It was "practically unnoticed," as Blair put it, noting that this was "the first time this had happened to Gene." After Klosters, the group moved to London. Betsy secured a job as dialogue coach for director Anatole Litvak in Paris, and Kerry attended the Royal Ballet School in England. Freed, Lela Simone, and Johnny Green came to visit on May 7. Freed and Gene made a brief trip to Scotland to scout possible filming locations for *Brigadoon*. Green and Freed flew back to Culver City on June 1, but Simone remained behind to help Kelly with his ballet film.[9] Haney, Coyne, and McClelland were also set to support Kelly's work.

INVITATION TO THE DANCE (1956)

By midsummer 1952, Kelly threw himself into his heart project, which now was called *Invitation to the Dance*. He claimed to have been interested in this idea ever since he arrived in Hollywood—to have ninety minutes of serious dancing with no plot. But when M-G-M finally approved the project, Gene frankly admitted that "I started getting cold feet. I began to think what would happen if it really flopped." That sudden lack of confidence led to serious alterations in the plan. He now envisioned several separate stories that would be expressed solely through dance movement, with no dialogue. Although he had not planned who would be in the film, studio publicity as early as November 1951 identified Leslie Caron as a star in the ballet movie while emphasizing it would be crafted with "an unorthodox and experimental approach." Later, M-G-M insisted that Kelly himself star in the film as a way to hedge their bets at the box office.[10] This led to further alterations in Gene's plans.

During the summer of 1952, Kelly rented a small house in a village near Chartres in France. This was done not only because he loved the country, but he could not work for more than 186 days per year in England to avoid paying tax to the British government. Most of the work involved in preparing *Invitation to the Dance* took place here near Chartres. Gene traveled to Elstree for a conference on July 10, 1952, to introduce the plan of the movie to studio staff. It would consist of four stories—"Circus" (set in 1830), "Ring Around the Rosy," "The Popular Song Ballet," and "The Children's Ballet" (the last to consist of live action and animation). Kelly planned to start with the first and work his way through the lineup by December in a complicated and tightly woven schedule of rehearsal and filming. He recognized that the animation may need to be done in Culver City.[11] Gene now had to recruit players, develop set and costume design, and handle many other details at the same time. Agreeing to do two other movies while in Europe had greatly constricted the time available for *Invitation to the Dance*. He was in for the most intense period of work in his career.

"Circus" was the first to be developed and filmed. To write the music, Kelly enlisted Jacques Ibert, who almost literally composed the score on the rehearsal stage to catch the nuances of Kelly's developing choreography. "Circus" demanded more unique costumes than any other part of his film project, and Kelly pored over all designs before approving them. Gene experienced a moment of despair when he and Lela Simone watched *Les Enfants du Paradis*, a 1945 film by director Marcel Carné in which Jean-Louis Barrault portrayed a clown in exactly the way Kelly had envisioned playing his own clown in "Circus." "What do we do now?" he asked Simone.[12] But Kelly continued with his plan because Barrault's portrayal was not unique. He had borrowed heavily from a stock character in European popular culture called Pierrot. Kelly drew his inspiration from the same character, dressed in a white, flowing costume—who on the surface was a silly clown, but inside, a frustrated lover.

In "Circus," Kelly came close to realizing his initial dream for the picture. He recruited Moroccan acrobats for an athletic segment in which he participated. He also signed Igor Youskevitch and Claire Sombert, two professional ballet dancers who had never performed for the camera, to star in the story while he played the clown who dies tragically in trying to prove his love for Sombert's character. Gene moved back to London in time for the start of filming and was his usual taskmaster. He insisted that Youskevitch do difficult double-turns exactly on the mark for the stationary camera, and the dancer found it very difficult to land so precisely. Youskevitch hurt his knee after landing on the concrete floor, and had to rest before completing the shot. Gene agreed to move the camera after that to make it easier for him. For the clown's walk on the high-wire (that results in his death) and for Yousevitch's high-wire walk, Gene hired the Fellers, German professionals, to double for both him and Youskevitch. But for the close-up of himself on the wire, Kelly first mastered walking on a wire two feet above the floor and shot the scene. Later he practiced more and refilmed his walk on a wire five feet above the floor, which according to Simone "made the shot much more exciting."[13]

The death scene proved to be almost too much for the two neophyte film stars. Youskevitch and Sombert found the mood of the moment so strange they began to giggle during filming. Kelly knew it was because of their inexperience and was patient. He told them to be quiet and instructed the camera operator to keep rolling the film because it would be too difficult to get back into the mood if he stopped. "I wish I had that film," Gene later mused. "That would be very funny."[14]

Keeping tabs on progress from his Culver City office, Freed worried about delays in the schedule. Ben Goetz, manager of the Elstree studio, reported that Kelly was overworked with various duties in addition to performing, directing, and supervising. He had also introduced several new ideas after the start of rehearsal that had not been part of the original plan. Work on "Circus" extended for more than double the time initially allotted as a result. Simone reassured Freed, who remained in the United States, that Kelly was working very hard all day and evening. Unlike his usual perfectionist self, Gene was highly conscious of cost overruns and seeking to get the job done in "the most practical and economical way."[15]

A large part of the problem lay in the fact that the Elstree studio had never made this kind of film before. Its departments often were baffled by Kelly's wants, and the equipment was not the most modern. The wardrobe and makeup departments were not up to speed, so Gene had to supervise many "petty details." The camera crew was not familiar with moving the boom to musical counts. The pace was slower than at Culver City with mandated afternoon tea breaks. The playback machine burned out just when it was needed the most, and a small fire broke out in a corner of the set building during filming one day.[16]

"Circus" has a good deal of ballet dancing and is the closest to anything Kelly did to honor his great respect for the art form. In a section involving a troupe of dancers and jugglers, Kelly himself dances chorus types of ballet steps. More muscular and earthy than the other dancers, Kelly nevertheless creates a creditable performance in this dance style. But Gene also incorporated several of his favorite moves, doing the Midair Twist, the Prone Kick, and Side Heel-Clicks with the other dancers and the Crab Bounce by himself. Perhaps he did this to ensure that the film would be popular with mass audiences.

As he made progress through "Circus," Kelly hit his stride when it came to the rhythm and speed of his work. "His shooting is fast," wrote visiting journalist Stephen Watts, who found Kelly's working style "wearingly intensive, pleasantly informal and highly efficient." Kelly was frank with Watts. "I'm going out on a limb with this one," he told the journalist. "But I firmly believe people are going to like it." Famed war photographer Robert Capa dropped by the studio during production of "Circus" to take a number of photographs showing Gene behind and in front of the camera, often in the clown costume of his dance with the troupe.[17]

In "Ring Around the Rosy," Kelly largely reverted back to his normal mix of tap and modern dance style with only two brief ballet sequences. Claude Bessy, who was in one of these, had never performed for a camera, but she remembered decades later that Kelly eased her into it. "There was no problem working with Gene Kelly," she told the authors in an email interview. "He knew exactly what he wanted. He really explained to me the character and the situation."[18]

Based on Arthur Schnitzler's 1897 play *Reigen*, the story involves a bracelet passed around from one person to another in a tale of adultery and misplaced affections. In addition to Tommy Rall's performance as a "sharpie," this segment's highlight is a modern dance between Kelly and Tamara Tamanouva, the latter portraying a prostitute. Tamanouva, a classical dancer, was performing in a dance style alien to her experience. Yet she did it well, and there is an electrifying chemistry between her and Kelly. Also, Gene's leaping from the ground unaided onto the post of a stairway railing is astoundingly athletic. Kelly experimented technically with the ending of "Ring Around the

Figure 12.1 Kelly rehearsing ballet leaps with the troupe in 1952 for "Circus" from *Invitation to the Dance* (1956). Unfortunately, this sequence is not in the film. But the photo gives a clear indication of Kelly's ballet skills. (Photographer Robert Capa, Library of Congress)

Figure 12.2 Kelly, in costume, directing dancers during rehearsals in 1952 for "Circus" from *Invitation to the Dance* (1956). (Photographer Robert Capa, Library of Congress)

Figure 12.3 Dancing with Tamara Tamanouva in "Ring Around the Rosy." (Still from *Invitation to the Dance*, 1956)

Rosy," shooting scenes of a cocktail party at three different speeds with key parts of the set collapsing around the extras. Simone found this "a very weird and amazing shot."[19]

For the popular song segment, eventually titled "Sing Me a Song," Gene's initial idea to use Judy Garland and Frank Sinatra perform the songs fell through. He used English performers, none of whom would have been recognized by an American audience. He himself played a supporting role in the segment, which was fully filmed but later dropped from the release print.[20]

That left only the children's animated segment, but time was running out due to the tight production schedule mixed with unavoidable delays. On October 26, 1952, Kelly submitted a revised production schedule to Simone, which astonished her. It was far too ambitious to be practical. Right after that, as was typical of his career, the intense work involved in the production phase of his films led to illness. The company had a break of several days as Kelly recuperated at home, while Haney, Coyne, and Simone caught up with a variety of chores left undone in the hectic pace thus far. "Only through his tremendous will-power did he somehow manage to get back on his feet again" by October 30. The revised schedule was discarded and Kelly faced the fact that he could not finish *Invitation to the Dance* before leaving Europe. He became ill on November 17 as well, causing more delays in his schedule.[21]

Exhausted, Kelly vacationed with his family and his assistants over Christmas at Klosters. He even invited Simone, who told Freed, "I found him well but terribly depressed." According to Simone, Gene was aware that he had not achieved all he wanted in the work thus far on his pet project. Maybe his state of mind led to an accident on the slopes, when Kelly fell and a ski pole punctured his upper thigh. This led to three weeks of enforced idleness before he could go to work again.[22]

While resting during the early weeks of 1953, Kelly absorbed Freed's appraisal of *Invitation to the Dance*. The producer loved "Circus" but was disappointed by "Ring Around the Rosy." "Sing Me a Song" was not acceptable. It needed to be done with "great stars" as planned. As for the animated segment, Freed urged Gene to wait and make it in Culver City. Freed even urged him to get "a real rest," work on *Brigadoon*, and then tackle the animated segment. The two then talked by phone, and Freed suggested Kelly increase his presence in the movie, for example, in the Popular Songs segment. Gene wrote back saying he already was in two songs and it would be best just to drop this segment. He mentioned he had abandoned the idea of filming the animated story in Malta (where military hangers could provide a huge soundstage) and agreed to wait till he returned to Culver City. Regarding "Ring Around the Rosy," Kelly felt that English composer Malcolm Arnold's score was too heavy-handed and "all the humor is gone."[23]

***THE CREST OF THE WAVE* (1954)**

After the Klosters vacation, the Kellys moved to London and rented actor Robert Donat's house. Gene now fulfilled his other film commitment for M-G-M by creating the role of Lieutenant Bradville in *The Crest of the Wave*. Written, produced, and directed by brothers John and Roy Boulting, it was filmed at the Elstree studio after plans to shoot it on location in Scotland were cancelled. Kelly portrayed a US Navy lieutenant detailed to supervise torpedo experiments by a team of British personnel after World War II. Based on the successful London play *Seagulls over Sorrento*, the movie stressed British-American cooperation, a subject Kelly liked, and the movie did very well in London under the original title. But when released in the United States on December 6, 1954, it did no better with American audiences than had *The Devil Makes Three*. "It just was a bomb," Gene laughingly recalled years later.[24]

EUROPE

As we have seen, Kelly was having serious doubts about his heart project as well. Ironically *Invitation to the Dance* was receiving more prerelease interest on the part of the media than any other of his movies. Interviews and articles were appearing in major publications such as the *New York Times*, the *New York Herald Tribune*, and *Look* magazine. Kelly's multitalented career and his driving work ethic were highlighted in this publicity, along with his relatively lavish lifestyle while in Europe. Author A. H. Franks invited Kelly to write an essay about the film for a book he produced titled *The Girls' Book of Ballet*, published in 1953. In it Gene promoted his pet project as an exercise in varied dance styles so it would appeal to ballet lovers as well as the general public. He also wrote that it was suitable for audiences around the world because there was no dialogue to create language difficulties.[25] Never before and never since did a Gene Kelly movie get so much exposure even before it was finished.

After finishing *Crest of the Wave*, Kelly spent the rest of his time in England as a vacation. By now the flood of Hollywood people who had taken advantage of the tax break became a matter of public interest. Unions were complaining that people for whom the tax break was not intended were reaping the benefits, and because Kelly led the way in this he became a target of investigative reporting. Journalist Joe Hyams estimated Gene would garner $370,000 in tax-free income from his European stay. M-G-M's official line was that "it is just coincidence that his schedule calls for him to be in Europe eighteen months." When asked about it, Kelly told Hyams, "I can't see where income tax enters into it." He said his studio told him to make films in Europe and he obeyed. Both M-G-M and Kelly were telling white lies. It was important to both the studio and Kelly that he not appear as a tax evader. There is no question, however, that Kelly's trip to Europe was directly motivated by the tax break, as discussed earlier. Kelly himself admitted this frankly in later years. In fact, the studio was very careful even about his avoiding British tax. A staff member reminded M-G-M studio manager Eddie Mannix on November 24, 1952, that Kelly had already been working in England for 141 days as of November 18. According to the staff member's calculations, he could stay no more than forty-one additional days to avoid British income tax.[26]

The Kelly entourage enjoyed the remainder of their stay in Europe. Gene and Kerry took a ten-day boat trip up the Thames River, staying at inns along the way. Betsy joined them at night and traveled back to London for the day.

They watched the procession at the coronation of Queen Elizabeth II on June 2, 1953. On their way to the London office of MCA on a rainy day, a loudspeaker played "Singin' in the Rain," and the crowd packing the street took up the song, providing Kelly and his family a warm welcome as they crossed the street. Kelly had taken on some of his father's Irish-bred distrust of the English, but this moment changed all that. He fell in love with the English people.[27]

By early August the Kellys had to return home. Gene told a reporter, "You can't beat the United States, and that goes for life in Pittsburgh as well as Hollywood." Carman Pantages, wife of an M-G-M producer, had rented his house while the family was away and needed it a bit longer. So Kelly rented Gene Tierney's house at 9646 Heather Road in Beverly Hills with plans to move back to his own home on November 1. Ironically, stung by public criticism concerning Hollywood's elite taking advantage of the tax break, Congress had repealed it the previous May. The normal tax regulation allowed Kelly to keep the first $35,000 he earned overseas tax-free, but he was taxed on the rest.[28]

Swallowing his disappointment at losing the tax break, Gene was excited by the fact that Marc Houlihan, a graduate student at the University of California, Los Angeles, was writing a Master's thesis about dancing in commercial films. Gene gave Houlihan an interview on September 5, 1953, and stated that "Alter Ego" was without doubt his favorite number (at this point in his life) because "it is pure dance for the cinema." Kelly was now so far away from his Broadway experience and deeply into experimenting with dance for the camera that he admitted he probably could never go back to a stage show. "When I dance, I try to tell a complete story, . . . some idea I want to convey, and it must have a complete meaning."[29]

"SINBAD THE SAILOR" (1953)

At the time he gave this interview Kelly was deeply involved in the third and final segment to be included in *Invitation to the Dance*, "Sinbad the Sailor." It was a completely different concept than the original children's ballet except that it too would mix live action with animation. Gene would play "Joe Sinbad from Pittsburgh, Pa." according to his scenario notes dated August 12, 1953, which included the outline of the segment as well as aspects of the dances.[30] The first part was filmed entirely as live action as Sinbad the Sailor

Figure 12.4 Sinbad bonding with the boy genie (David Kasday) in "Sinbad the Sailor." (Still from *Invitation to the Dance*, 1956)

wanders through a Middle East city and purchases a lamp from which a genie (played by eleven-year-old David Kasday) appears. The two get to know each other and perform a sailor dance, showing not only young Kasday's dancing skills but also Kelly's talent for working with children.

After this comes the animated part where Sinbad and the boy genie enter the pages of a magical book and start their adventures. The same idea was later used by Disney in *Mary Poppins* (1964) where Mary, Bert, and the children jump into chalk art on the sidewalk and cavort around in an animated version of the drawing.

Sinbad first dances with a dragonlike serpent tamed by the genie's flute-playing. Then he is captured by two palace guards and has to dance with them to keep from being killed. This is an extended dance similar to the one with Jerry the Mouse in *Anchors Aweigh*, except that Sinbad has an animated guard on either side imitating him perfectly. The three perform only one of Kelly's favorite steps, the Airplane Propeller, but also perform other steps, including the Charleston, as Sinbad tries to flee his captors. Aimed at children, it is a humorous segment filled with energetic dancing.

Kelly and Kasday had to be filmed against a blue or white backdrop, and then animators drew in other characters and the background. For

Figure 12.5 Doing Side Heel-Clicks during a charming sailor dance with David Kasday in "Sinbad the Sailor." (Still from *Invitation to the Dance*, 1956)

Figure 12.6 Dancing with two animated guards to distract them from trying to kill him in "Sinbad the Sailor." (Still from *Invitation to the Dance*, 1956)

cinematographer Joseph Ruttenberg it was a tedious, exacting process to film the actors with a steady camera so the animators could match their drawings frame-by-frame to Kelly's movements.[31]

As planned by Gene, the Sinbad segment also included an extended love dance with an animated princess. Kelly worked closely with the artists until they drew just the kind of woman he envisioned. He showed them a painting by Pierre-Auguste Renoir and said, "This is the type I want with an American figure." Gene filmed some of his movements in slow motion and others while swinging twenty-two feet above the studio floor. Props covered with blue or white cloth had to be used so he could move up or down ramps to simulate the kind of effect he wanted to create in his dancing.[32]

Filming began on October 3, 1953. In an email interview with the authors, Kasday said he worked comfortably with Kelly. His French-born mother had put him into ballet lessons at age six, and he had participated in several television and film projects. Gene had already used him in three instances. He had appeared in "I Got Rhythm" and the ballet of *An American in Paris* and also at the start of *Singin' in the Rain*. Kelly had planned to use Kasday for the original conception of the animated children's ballet to be filmed in Europe, but as we have seen, the plans for that idea fell through. Kasday told the authors that Gene treated him like an adult while filming "Sinbad," which he very much appreciated. Kelly walked him through everything he had to do, and nothing Kasday did was cut from the film. He remembered that Haney worked closely with Kelly as a partner in the dance rehearsals, and Coyne took notes and did a number of other chores connected with the production.[33]

Joe Barbera and William Hanna created the animation with their team of artists. It was a tedious, months-long process of matching thousands of drawings to Kelly's steps. Haney imitated the movements of the dragon that Gene danced with, but the animators used her movements only "as a general reference" here rather than literally. Haney also danced the part of the princess for the ballroom part of the love dance Kelly choreographed, which was followed more closely by the animators.[34]

For the rest of the love dance, Gene and the princess were shown in animated drawings of hills, streams, and gardens. Kelly danced joyously to express his falling in love. He included graceful leaps and performed ballet steps that a principal ballet dancer would do. This is the only evidence on film that Gene was fully capable of performing ballet as opposed to merely adopting the form to support other dance styles. Unrestrained by another person's movements as he danced alone against a plain backdrop, Kelly was free to

Figure 12.7 Rehearsing with Carol Haney in 1953 for the ballroom part of the dance with the animated princess (so animators could copy her movements) in "Sinbad the Sailor." (Still from *That's Dancing!*, 1985)

Figure 12.8 A very effective love dance with the animated princess in "Sinbad the Sailor." (Still from *Invitation to the Dance*, 1956)

imagine a partner moving fluidly with him, and his facial expressions and body movements convey deep emotion. The animators drew the princess to copy Kelly's movements and expressions as much as possible. Set to the music of Nicolai Rimsky-Korsakov's symphonic suite "Scheherazade," the number with the animated princess is one of the most effective love dances of Gene's career.

Kelly directed "Sinbad" with his usual attention to detail, often riding the boom to check out camera angles. Filming ended after ten days of shooting. "Sinbad" cost $947,659, of which $323,025 went into the cost of the animated segment. But *Invitation* underwent an unusually long period of postproduction that lasted two and a half years. In part this resulted from the need to coordinate work between Culver City and Elstree, with Freed and other M-G-M people telling the staff in England what needed to be done and then waiting for the result. Malcolm Arnold's musical score of "Ring" was dropped and Andre Previn was assigned the difficult task of writing a new score for an already filmed story. Freed arbitrarily made several cuts in "Sinbad" that distressed Kelly, but the latter gave in to most. He did insist on reinstating two cuts, one at the end and especially the one at the start because that cut "eliminates whatever charm the beginning of the dance had." Freed replied that Schary could not see any difference with the cuts, but he did not want any more delays arguing back and forth, so the two cuts were reinstated.[35]

Kelly told a reporter that the Breen Office objected to Tamanouva's sensuous dance with him in "Ring," but a search of the office archives tells a different story. The staff member who screened *Invitation* reported "no adultery, no illicit sex, no seduction." He must have slept during "Ring" because the entire segment, one-third of the movie, is built on all three things. Every other censor organization besides the Breen Office also overlooked "Ring," giving the picture a pass for adults as well as young people.[36]

Then M-G-M engaged in a long struggle with how to market *Invitation* because it was so different from its normal product. As early as June 1952, even before filming started, Freed announced that it would not be generally released like other films but targeted for art theaters and marketed as a theatrical show. The studio's marketing staff used derogatory phrases in their notes such as "long-hair promotion" and "load it with snob appeal," also mentioning that Freed wanted them to "sell it like a Cadillac." But Kelly rebelled against that approach. He wanted it released generally to reach the widest possible audience. To accommodate Kelly's wishes, Howard Hertz in the marketing department wrote, "What we have to sell is 'class.' Who to sell it to is 'everyone.'"[37] Whether that was a viable strategy is open to question, but the tension between targeting an elite audience and generally distributing the film prolonged the release for months and never was resolved to Kelly's satisfaction.

It cannot be said that M-G-M ignored *Invitation* or sabotaged its promotion. But the delay in promoting it extended the film's release into the years when musicals were in an obvious decline and studios had become more frugal. Hertz developed an elaborate marketing plan that involved heavy personal involvement by Kelly in promoting the picture through touring several major cities and giving interviews. But this was never done, probably because M-G-M balked at the expense. Studio personnel struggled a great deal with the trailer, viewing it as the key to achieving the difficult task of marketing a product that mixed high art with popular entertainment to both an elite audience and general viewership. They thought of getting Edward R. Murrow to narrate a script for the trailer, and to have Ed Sullivan interview Kelly on his popular television show about the making of the film. Neither approach was taken, without explanation. An idea of inserting scenes from *An American in Paris* and *Singin' in the Rain* to bank on the success of these recent films was dropped as irrelevant. It was suggested that Kelly could do the narration for the trailer himself. But he refused, thinking it inappropriate to promote his own creation. He did approve the first part of the trailer, which showed scenes from the film.[38]

M-G-M also negotiated with William Saroyan to write a foreword to the movie and Saroyan was happy to do so. But the studio did not use it because Saroyan began to argue about the terms of his financial consideration and made an absolute pest of himself.[39]

Despite the marketing problems, *Invitation* remained Kelly's dream project. "It made his eyes sparkle" to talk about it to journalist Marjorie Trumbull after giving a lecture at the San Francisco Museum of Art in October 1954. But he became frustrated by the long delay in releasing the film. "Is it going to be shown at any festival?" he wrote to Freed in August 1955 while in France. "Is it going to be shown [at all]??" But Gene was only half right when he later concluded that M-G-M "didn't know what to do with it."[40] Kelly misread Freed, who he thought had agreed with him that the movie should be both an artistic and a commercial success. Instead, Freed had always thought of positioning it as an art film because he did not believe it would work commercially.

But Kelly disagreed. "You shouldn't underestimate the intelligence of the movie audience," he told an interviewer. "The public today likes challenging entertainment," he told another interviewer, "and the man who makes pictures has the responsibility of catering to the highest level in the public's sense of appreciation. . . . I've learned never to sell the public short." Gene was encouraged by the reception to the ballet of *An American in Paris* to think that *Invitation* could also be widely applauded.[41]

There are many reasons why that analogy is false. The ballet in *An American in Paris* was nestled within a Hollywood dance musical with a proven formula for popular success. Gene was the main dancer in the ballet, which made it even more appealing to the public. He used many of his personal dance styles throughout the ballet that were already popular with mass audiences. *Invitation* did not meet any of these criteria. But Kelly did not seem to recognize these marked differences between the two products.

This is one of those instances when Kelly's sense of aesthetics intertwined with his political ideals. It was the New Deal Democrat—the believer in the best aspirations of the common man—who was speaking when he asserted that everyone had the ability to appreciate good dancing no matter how artistic it might appear to be. Freed and everyone else at M-G-M doubted that Kelly was right, yet they could not bring themselves to openly oppose him. This was the real source of tension in the marketing and release of *Invitation.*

When it was finally brought out for widespread release, the film tended to support Freed's view that it would appeal mostly to the elite. A splashy world premiere took place at Zurich, Switzerland, on April 9, 1956. It was warmly received by critics and—spiked by Kelly's personal appearance—by the audience. *Invitation* premiered in the United States on May 22 as a benefit event to raise money for Ballet Theatre in New York, and a special screening was enthusiastically appreciated by the Dance Alliance. The movie won first prize at the Sixth International Berlin Film Festival, receiving the Golden Bear statue, and the Tenth International Edinburgh Film Festival gave it a Diploma of Merit.[42]

At a total cost of more than $1,400,000, *Invitation* grossed just over $600,000. Two-thirds of that gross, more than $400,000, came from foreign distribution.[43] Indeed, there would be no prizes or frenzied reception at home for the film. It was shown at art theaters as well as conventional venues, and did well with the smaller, elite audience but received little attention from mainstream moviegoers.

Some reviewers, such as Rose Pelswick, offered praise for *Invitation*, calling it delightful, brilliantly created, and excellently danced. But other reviewers were highly critical. Those who saw it as an art film thought it did not go far enough. Aubrey Haines was deeply disappointed with Kelly's choreography and the relatively little amount of serious dancing, despite the promising idea. Those who viewed it as a popular film also thought it missed its mark. Hazel Flynn criticized Kelly for getting out of his zone of strength as a performer and choreographer and venturing into elitist art that she thought was of limited appeal.[44] Kelly wound up failing to find enough supporters in either camp to carry the picture through its trial before the public.

Bosley Crowther, who often was critical of Kelly's most accomplished work, penned not one but two reviews of *Invitation to the Dance*. He liked marginal elements of the film such as the décor, color, and musical scores. He thought that "Circus" had "a nice, formal ballet" but that "Ring" was "rather banal." He found "Sinbad" to be "technically clever" but not as irresistible as the animated dance in *Anchors Aweigh*. The entire movie "throws a heap of hoofing of a rather gaudy sort into one show." Crowther admired Kelly's ambition and guts in his "departure from the ordinary song-and-dance film" but was convinced he had failed. The picture was "a brave experiment," but Kelly should have been "more fertile with ideas and less inclined to overdo." Crowther pinpointed a key flaw in the film—the lack of a unifying theme other than stories told through the medium of dance. He also mentioned the lack of a common dance style or theme of movement and pegged *Invitation* as "a variety entertainment that features dance."[45] Actually, the film *does* feature ballet in all three segments, but because it also includes a wide range of dance styles it fails to highlight ballet as originally envisioned by Gene.

Kelly retained a deep resentment toward M-G-M for what he saw as its limited marketing plan for the movie. He wanted the studio to pursue the international market more vigorously and place it in small-town American theaters rather than art venues. Frustrated, he recruited a group of investors, raised a million dollars, and tried to purchase the film from M-G-M, but the studio refused. He blamed the advent of television for much of its failure with the public. Indeed, the small screen was beginning to broadcast a variety of dance styles directly into American homes by 1956. Kelly continued to be touchy when interviewers brought up the failure of *Invitation*. "You go ahead or try to go ahead, and if you have a flop it's no big deal." He referred to his idealistic desire to elevate the artistic taste of the masses as "part of my Excalibur ideology." As time went by, Kelly realized more deeply that, artistically speaking, *Invitation* had not turned out as he had hoped. It "wasn't a great picture, but it had some very good things," he said in 1988. Blair put it well when she wrote that *Invitation* "was perhaps too ambitious, and the ambition was misdirected."[46]

Kelly reached the zenith of his popular film career with *Singin' in the Rain* and then abruptly took a dramatic new turn by going to Europe. He missed the joy of basking in the overwhelming public reception of *An American in Paris* and *Singin' in the Rain*, missed accepting his honorary Oscar, and was isolated 6,000 miles from Hollywood while making three movies, none of which achieved the critical or public acclaim that he had grown accustomed to thus far in his career. The only reason Kelly chose to go to Europe at this time was the tax break, and ironically in the end he could not garner the benefit of that break. Moreover, his excitement about going to Europe to make his cherished dance film ended in personal and artistic disappointment. Although Kelly continued to make a handful of major dance musicals, none of them achieved the success of those he made before 1952. His career had changed dramatically, but it had by no means ended.

CHAPTER 13

Red Scare—Second Wave, 1950–1954

Kelly's European trip coincided with a renewal of the Red Scare in Hollywood. In addition to Kelly, fellow liberals such as Gregory Peck and John Huston, as well as archconservatives such as Ward Bond and Gary Cooper, were going overseas to take advantage of the tax break. While money was the prime motivation for all of them, some observers assumed the liberals wanted to escape red-baiting as well.[1]

But this was not true for Kelly. John Cogley, a journalist who exposed the details of blacklisting in a two-volume report in 1956, wrongly claimed without any supporting evidence that Gene Kelly had been "so harassed that he went to Europe." English authors especially like the idea that Kelly was a political refugee from America because he spent much of the time in England during his European stay. Film critic Peter Wollen stated that "Kelly was driven into exile by McCarthyism," and that he was "forced to leave the US for Europe." Both Cogley and Wollen based their assertions simply on coincidence; Kelly happened to leave when the second wave was taking shape. But these are pure speculations with no evidence to back them. In fact, as discussed in chapter 12, the evidence shows that Gene left entirely because of the tax break and to work on his dream project. Kelly himself consistently said so later in life.[2]

Moreover, during the second wave Kelly was not targeted by the House Un-American Activities Committee (HUAC), nor was he questioned by the FBI. He had survived his great public exposure in the first wave and had little to worry about in the resurgence of conservative witch-hunting. Kelly's name appeared on some lists, but there is no evidence he was aware of this. Ironically, he received far more attention for taking advantage of the tax break than for being an ally of communists during this time.

The second wave of the Red Scare started officially in 1951, but earlier events that led to it need to be reviewed to fully understand this unhappy period. As mentioned in earlier chapters, Kelly's FBI file offers invaluable evidence that he was an object of concern but in a secret rather than a public way, and only within the bureau. The information in that file allows us to present a comprehensive picture of why Gene was not affected by the second wave.

During the first wave of the Red Scare, Kelly's name had popped up in secret information provided by Louis J. Budenz to the FBI. Budenz was the most famous turncoat of the Red Scare, having been a member of the Communist Party from 1935 until renouncing his membership ten years later. In the interim, Budenz had been managing editor of the party's newspaper, the *Daily Worker*. After switching sides, he provided thousands of hours of testimony to the FBI. Budenz stated in 1947 that Kelly was mentioned favorably by the Communist Party, but he did not know if the actor was a member. Then, in 1950, he changed his story to say that three party officials had told him in the early 1940s that Kelly was a member. The FBI did nothing with that information at the time.[3] Kelly, of course, had no idea of Budenz's claim.

In November 1949, two years after the liberals' devastating failure to stem the tide of red-baiting, Gene told reporter Jack Howard, "I'm a middle-of-the road liberal, and I get pasted all the time. The Communists hate me and the Republicans hate me." He admitted it would be easy to keep his mouth shut about politics, but "then some guy in Alabama gets lynched or some kid gets his eyes blacked because he's Jewish." In such cases he had to speak up even if it drew more attention to his political views.[4] Kelly could not keep quiet in the face of continuing affronts to civil and humanitarian values.

In the early 1950s, communist hunters turned their attention to liberals, but it did not affect Gene or his career. Betsy, however, became a target of this inquisition. In June 1950, the right-wing journal *Counterattack* published a book called *Red Channels: The Report of Communist Influence in Radio and Television*. It named 151 people in the entertainment industry—including Betsy Blair. Soon after, Blair spoke at the groundbreaking of a new building for the Actor's Lab in Los Angeles, an organization suspected of links with communists. A reporter then informed Blair that she would be replaced in *Kind Lady* even though preproduction had gone very far on that project. Blair fought to keep her role, even meeting with Louis B. Mayer, who spent most of the meeting telling her how good America was and how grateful she should be for it. In the end, he agreed to keep her in the film.[5]

Gene had talked earlier with Mayer to help Betsy. In addition, after filming for the day, he went back to Mayer's office, where the studio head and Betsy were meeting. Mayer told him, "Well, Gene, it's just as you said. She's a fine girl and as American as you and me." But the truth was, as Blair later realized, that Mayer wanted to avoid any taint on Gene's public image. The only way he could do so was to keep Blair in *Kind Lady*. But after that she became persona non grata at M-G-M, not working for the next four years.[6]

According to information in Kelly's FBI file, Betsy participated in a meeting to protest *Red Channels* at the new Globe Theater in Los Angeles on November 10, 1950. She criticized a proposal that actors take a loyalty oath before they could be allowed to perform in films. Informant "T-9," identified as an M-G-M employee who was "personally acquainted" with both Kelly and Blair, told the FBI that Gene had assured Dore Schary that Betsy "entertained no Communist sympathies whatever." But after the meeting of November 10, according to the informant, M-G-M wanted to drop Blair from *Kind Lady*. T-9 further noted that Kelly told Schary that Blair was willing to sign a loyalty oath, which she did in order to retain her role in the film.[7] However, there is no evidence in Blair's memoirs or interviews, or in Kelly's many interviews, to support any of T-9's testimony.

Meanwhile, Budenz had started to make a living out of being a turncoat, writing books, giving lectures, and securing teaching appointments based on his notoriety. One such effort to make money was the compilation of a list of 400 people he called "concealed communists" in 1950. The list was designed to promote a book titled *Men without Faces: The Communist Conspiracy in the USA*. Budenz included Kelly in this list, along with many other Hollywood liberals. HUAC called Budenz to testify in March 1951. Because Budenz was scheduled to talk publicly about the list, the FBI asked him to write memos on each individual he named and to specify where he obtained his information. At the same time, the bureau scrambled to compile information on each person named on the list so it could cross-check Budenz's information. When Robert Lichtman, a lawyer turned historian, later obtained this list through the Freedom of Information Act, he found that all but about fifty of the names had been redacted, showing that the FBI realized the lack of evidence supporting Budenz's allegations. Lichtman noted that "the listees in any case were unlikely to be aware that he had named them."[8] This further corroborates the fact that Kelly knew nothing about Budenz's claim and it therefore did not influence his going to Europe.

Behind the scenes, however, Blair's troubles and Budenz's claims rejuvenated the bureau's interest in Kelly. FBI director J. Edgar Hoover told his agents in November 1950 to reopen Kelly's case and "determine whether or not his present activities warrant making him the subject of a Security Index Card," which allowed for the detention of people deemed a security risk to the nation in case of war or national emergency. In other words, the writ of habeas corpus was legally denied anyone listed on the Security Index. But only two months later, in January 1951, Marcus Bright noted that seven informants who had been in the party, or were closely associated with it, agreed that Kelly had never, to their knowledge, been a member. They acknowledged that he had formerly been willing to support causes supported by the party, and that Blair was "a little closer" to the party's goals, but there was no evidence to back up Budenz's claim.[9]

The second wave of the Red Scare started with a bang on March 8, 1951, when HUAC mounted its second investigation of Hollywood. It called forty-five unfriendly witnesses for the purpose of getting middle-of-the-road liberals to name people who were considered dangerous left-wingers. There was no organized resistance because of the dismal failure of the Hollywood Fights Back effort in 1947 and because the studios wanted to disassociate themselves from political controversy at any cost. HUAC was backed by pressure from many Hollywood conservatives and quite a few organizations, including the American Legion. In 1951, thirty witnesses named about 300 people during the HUAC hearings, but Kelly was not among those who were named.[10]

Also in 1951, J. B. Matthews spurred renewed interest in Hollywood's liberal community. A former socialist turned commie hunter, Matthews published a widely read article titled "Did the Movies Really Clean House?" in *American Legion Magazine* in December 1951. He not only reviewed the people and organizations that were suspect in the first Red Scare wave of 1947, but he also contended that most of the liberals suspected of communist alliances were still making movies. Matthews listed a total of fifty-one films being produced that year made by these suspect liberals. The list included three by Kelly.[11] The FBI did not take the list seriously.

In the same year, two informants gave information about Kelly. Informant "T-4," a former member of the Communist Party, told US Army security officers in June 1951 that Betsy and Gene had attended Lloyd Gough's classes in New York during the late 1930s, which was not true in Gene's case. This person did say it was not clear whether Gene had been recruited. The Army sent a copy of this testimony to the FBI. Informant "T-3," a woman in the Cultural Section of the Los Angeles County Communist Party, reported in November 1951 that Kelly had never been in the Communist Party. In fact, she noted that the party considered him "somewhat of a problem" because he was "more anti-Party than pro" and tended, especially after the war, to disapprove of whatever little Betsy was doing when she appeared at public functions of interest to the party.[12]

Weighing all the evidence, the FBI did not think it worthwhile to pursue Kelly. There was "no admissible evidence" that he had ever held party membership. And he had not been named thus far by any friendly witness in the HUAC testimony. Because of this and because he was not working in an industry considered vital to national security, the FBI decided that no interview with Kelly was needed and there was no need to create a Security Index Card for him. Hoover made the final decision on Kelly's file, noting on January 4, 1952, that it would not be productive to pursue his case any further.[13]

But only one month later, when Kelly was filming *The Devil Makes Three* in Germany, new "evidence" popped up to add to his file. Dr. C. Russell Anderson of Beverly Hills came to the Los Angeles FBI office to unburden his conscience about startling information given to him by a patient. Max Nathan Benoff, a New York born freelance comedy writer, came to see Anderson about a skin rash in 1945. Benoff grew to trust the doctor and admitted his problem was probably caused by stress. In addition to writing for Fanny Brice's popular radio program *Baby Snooks*, he was a member of the Communist Party and subject to a great deal of work in the evenings and on weekends for the cause. Benoff mistakenly believed that Gene was a member of the party and told Anderson this, saying he "greatly admires" Kelly. Anderson did not think much of the information in 1945, but when the second wave of the Red Scare began in 1951, Benoff told his doctor that he had quit the party. Anderson suggested his patient talk to the FBI, but Benoff was reluctant because he did not want to name people. The doctor therefore decided to tell what he knew to the bureau on February 28, 1952.[14]

Bureau agents at first took Anderson's information seriously. If Benoff was right, the bureau could actually place Kelly within the ranks of the party. Of course, officials never found confirmation of Kelly's membership because he had never even considered joining the party. It was just another red herring. Nevertheless, Anderson's decision to see the FBI betrayed Benoff's secrecy and he was called to testify before HUAC on March 24, 1953. Benoff did a masterful job of shuffling around, pretending to be a naive writer who had only flirted with party membership for three or four months in 1944, mostly to meet people who could advance his career. He claimed he dropped membership because the meetings were too dull. The fact that his testimony conflicted with what he had told Anderson is obvious—but it worked. HUAC treated him as a friendly witness even though he named no one.[15]

At this time in March 1953 Gene was still in Europe with no idea that he had been placed on any lists. He was aware of the HUAC hearings but he had not been named, so there was nothing for him to be concerned about.

But this was also the time period in which the studios began a general "clearance" process. "Clearance," as it was called in Hollywood, was an effort to repair the damage caused by both waves of the Red Scare. It was an internal process within the studio system (and the unions that supported the industry) to clear the names of graylistees so they could work without suspicion of collaboration with left-wingers. In effect, clearance was a public relations campaign to restore public confidence in the stars and the movie industry. The studios approached the American Legion in early 1952 and arranged a cooperative relationship whereby the Legion provided files on up to 300 Hollywood individuals who were suspect. Many of those individuals wrote letters to the Legion, at the urging of their studios, to clear themselves. Each major studio assigned a staff member to handle it quietly. But Roy Brewer, powerful president of the International Alliance of Theatrical Stage Employees, became a major figure in the process. He worked closely with many individuals who had been targeted by the Red Scare and urged them to publicly renounce their past associations or to join a pro-American organization that would provide them the stamp of approval, after which he would lobby studios to find jobs for them.[16] Kelly, of course, had not lost his job and had not been openly targeted. When push came to shove, M-G-M did not suggest that he clear himself.

Nevertheless, Cogley alleged that Kelly cleared himself after returning to Hollywood in the fall of 1953 by giving a speech at a meeting of the American Federation of Labor (AFL) Film Council. In this speech Kelly praised Roy Brewer for his work with the Hollywood labor movement. He also praised Irving Brown, the AFL representative in Paris, and his efforts in Europe to persuade French labor to align with American labor in its opposition to communism.[17] However, Cogley was making an assumption that the speech was part of a clearance process. It was not. Kelly's speech was aimed at redeeming himself in the eyes of unions that had previously criticized him for trying to take advantage of the tax break in 1952.

Given his strong support for labor unions, Kelly had been troubled ever since they had criticized him regarding the tax break. While he was still in Europe he worked to restore his image with labor unions. The AFL had

Figure 13.1 With daughter Kerry on a trip to Paris from England. (Library of Congress)

mounted a publicity campaign in Europe to counter Soviet propaganda. It was overseen by Irving Brown, the AFL representative in Paris. Along with other Hollywood liberals like John Huston and Humphrey Bogart, Kelly agreed to participate in a public rally. He also made radio broadcasts criticizing Soviet anti-Semitism. Brown was grateful for Kelly's participation and suggested that Gene talk against communism at a conference for French actors and writers influenced by fellow-traveler programs of the communists. So Kelly gave a talk about "the fight against the Commies in Hollywood," in the words of journalist Victor Riesel.[18]

It is understandable that observers may have seen this as an attempt to clear himself during the Red Scare, but the fact is Gene was solely concerned with patching up his relationship with labor unions and the AFL. He was not targeted in the second wave, and M-G-M never asked him to do anything to clear himself.

After settling back in Hollywood after his Europe adventure, and immersed in "Sinbad" and *Brigadoon*, Kelly was surprised when early in 1954 the Navy informed him that it intended to conduct a review of his loyalty. Because Gene had served in the Navy Reserve since his discharge in 1946, the Office of Naval Intelligence had asked the FBI for all its current information on Kelly in 1948. Hoover complied by sending a report in September 1949. Nothing was done then because there was nothing of concern. In the wake of Budenz's sensational list of 400 concealed communists, however, the Navy decided to prepare a loyalty review for Kelly in late 1952, as they did for hundreds of others under the auspices of the Service Loyalty Program. It took a while for the Loyalty Review Board of the Bureau of Naval Personnel to get around to Kelly's case. Budenz wrote a statement about Gene to be used as an exhibit in that hearing. Dated March 20, 1953, the statement claimed that three men—the editor of *The Communist*, the supervisor of cultural activities of the Communist Party, and a member of the party politburo—agreed that Kelly was a "concealed Communist." When Kelly was informed of the pending review in early 1954, he was understandably angry that the Navy would suspect him. Gene immediately wrote back that he wished to resign from the Navy Reserve. The Navy refused to accept the resignation, arguing—for Kelly's sake—that resigning while a loyalty review was pending would make him ineligible for veterans' benefits.[19]

Kelly did not attend his review proceeding, which took place in the spring of 1954, but he wrote one of the few long letters of his life, which was submitted as part of the paperwork for the board to examine. Dated March 27, it contains much of the same commentary that Kelly made in the relatively rare interviews in which he discussed his political views. The Great Depression had conditioned him as a young man to embrace Roosevelt's New Deal in spirit as well as in practice. He was dedicated to social reform so that no generation would ever have to endure that awful trial again. "In my own family and among all my relatives I saw them all victims of want and fear in the midst of plenty," Kelly wrote. The spirit of the New Deal "symbolized the best hope politically for this country."[20]

Kelly bemoaned the fact that conservatives lumped the social reformist with the communist. He pointed out that the former wants social reform within democracy, in contrast to the latter, who wants to overthrow democracy. He noted that, while serving as vice president of the Screen Actors

Guild, "I was one of several actors who in 1946 broke the Communist-dominated unions who were trying to gain control of the labor side of the motion picture industry." The next year, he participated in Hollywood Fights Back because he opposed the work of HUAC and went to Washington to voice that opposition. "My mind was immediately changed on this by the attitude of the ten men cited for contempt." After that, he "refused to participate in any more activities in their behalf." Kelly also pointed out that he supported President Harry Truman in the 1948 election, just as he had worked for Roosevelt in 1944.[21]

It was an effective letter. His loyalty review proceeded smoothly and concluded that "there is not, upon full review of the record, substantial reason to doubt the loyalty of the respondent." Nevertheless, Gene persisted in his wish to resign from the Reserve. He was still offended that the Navy would question his loyalty. The secretary of the Navy accepted Kelly's resignation from the Reserve force "under honorable conditions" on August 13, 1954. Gene's long letter to the loyalty review board was sent to the FBI for inclusion in Kelly's file.[22] Many years later, that letter was released to researcher Sue Cadman when she requested Kelly's FBI file under the Freedom of Information Act, and she posted excerpts of it on her website dedicated to Gene. But inexplicably it was not included when we obtained the same file, even though our request was routed to the Navy as well as to the FBI.

Kelly weathered the second wave better than did Betsy Blair. After four and a half years of inactivity because of her placement on the blacklist, Blair landed a plum role in the film *Marty* because of her friendship with the writer Paddy Chayefsky. Nonetheless, United Artists, which released the film, had raised the issue of her being blacklisted with the producers. Even though this project had nothing to do with M-G-M, Gene talked to Schary about it, saying, "You know her. You've played charades with her. You know she's not going to overthrow the country." Going out on a limb to help Betsy, he threatened to drop out of filming *It's Always Fair Weather* if something was not done. Schary called the American Legion "in front of Gene and said he would vouch for me," Blair recalled. The Legion cleared her based on Schary's call.[23]

Even though *Marty* was released to widespread acclaim in 1955, and Blair was nominated for an Academy Award and won Best Actress at the Cannes Film Festival, she never was offered another role in Hollywood. Betsy appeared in several European films but gave up her American career until many years later. She felt very bitter about her experience during the Red Scare. Upon obtaining a copy of her FBI file in 1998, she found out that it covered nineteen years of her life. What upset her more than anything was the evidence that informants—some of whom she was convinced were personal acquaintances who had attended the Kelly open-house gatherings—had been spreading misinformation about her. Rather than "friends," she referred to these people as "rats."[24] There is no indication that Gene ever viewed his FBI file.

It has been estimated that 250 Hollywood figures (including Betsy Blair) were blacklisted during the second wave of the Red Scare. An additional one hundred were graylisted. As historian David Caute writes on this era, "Those graylisted were normally the victims of rumors or remote guilt-by-association." The lingering effects of the Red Scare finally dissipated by about 1959. When the State Department filed a report with the FBI on Kelly's application for renewal of his passport in 1960, the bureau reported back that his file had been closed.[25]

Kelly never let the Red Scare affect his political views. "He believed in unions," Blair proudly wrote of Gene, in "freedom of thought, social justice, and racial equality. He never wavered from his democratic principles. And he acted on his beliefs." Blacklisted director Jules Dassin recalled that at the Cannes Film Festival he involuntarily ducked when he saw Gene, not wanting the star to be embarrassed by being seen with an outcast such as himself. Kelly saw this, quickly caught up with him, and said, "What the hell are you doing? Are you avoiding me?" Then Gene deliberately took Dassin's arm and walked with him into the Palais. "He was the only one I knew willing at that time to be photographed with me."[26]

"People like myself were used by the Communists at times," Kelly admitted in 1958. "I'm amazed to have found out later that I participated in things with Communists who misrepresented themselves to me." But he thought it never "caused any harm to our country." As time went by, Kelly became angrier about that terrible period of Hollywood history. He spoke "with some bitterness" of it at a film festival devoted to his movies held in England in the early 1970s. By that time Hollywood was changing dramatically in terms of its politics. During Kelly's heyday, it was deeply divided between conservatives and liberals. "You'd go into someone's living room and talk about voting for Roosevelt for president, and two people who were Republicans would get up and leave." But by his later years the political allegiances in Hollywood shifted toward the liberal side of the political spectrum. "Thank God, that kind of stuff is long gone," Kelly said of Hollywood conservatism in 1984.[27]

CHAPTER 14

Sunset of the Golden Age, 1953–1955

The arc of Kelly's career was deflected not only by his trip to Europe and his participation in three films (that failed to register with the public and critics), but also by fundamental changes in the film industry that led to a marked decline in the making of dance musicals. Federal antitrust action forced Hollywood studios to gradually divorce themselves from controlling the distribution of their own films. Eventually, there would be no preset venue for showing any movie the studios produced, which had been the key to the success of the studio system that had prevailed for decades. In addition, television was drawing viewers away from movie theaters.

The decline of the Golden Age is most evident through statistics. From 1948 to 1952, according to one estimate, the film industry lost close to 75 percent of its audience and 50 percent of its revenue. By the mid-1950s, studios were more cost-conscious. Technicians were laid off and producers began to shift from expensive Technicolor to cheaper and poorer quality Eastman color. Expensive dance films were the first to suffer as the industry entered the sunset era of the musical.[1] It took a while for the effect of all these trends to manifest themselves. Meanwhile, members of the Freed Unit at M-G-M continued their work with an assumption that it could go on forever.

BRIGADOON (1954)

Gene's next project was a film version of *Brigadoon*, and it proved to be one of the more frustrating efforts of his career. It was based on the stage musical by the team of Alan Jay Lerner and Frederick Loewe that ran on Broadway, from March 1947 to July 1948, for 581 performances. Arthur Freed and director Vincente Minnelli wanted to film much of it on location in Scotland. Freed and Kelly had scouted sites in June 1953, but later the producer cancelled plans for location shooting because of the difficult weather in Scotland. They then scouted sites in Southern California and found a mountainous locale near Big Sur that they thought would work. But budget cuts were mandated, leading to the final decision to film everything at the Culver City studio.[2]

Kelly and Minnelli were deeply disappointed. Both had been excited about using the new broad-screen Cinemascope technology during location shooting. They thought they would do what Western films had already been doing—filming the great expanse of the outdoors—but incorporate it into a dance musical. Years later Kelly recalled that filming on location as well as the widescreen format had been seen as remedies for the decline of the film musical. Television "was kicking the life out of the motion picture industry" and "the bottom was dropping out of the musical comedy business." Location shooting and Cinemascope were, in other words, seen as possible answers to stop the decline of the Golden Age. He and Minnelli "were very disappointed that we couldn't be the first to shoot a musical in Europe." Seeing the clans come marching over real Scottish hills would have been a sensation, he believed.[3]

Instead, Kelly and Minnelli were constricted to the confines of a soundstage. Both men were unusually disappointed and it shows, at least in Kelly's performance. "We never felt that it was *our* picture," he admitted while asserting that everyone did the best they could. With hindsight, Kelly believed that the shift from location filming to the soundstage should have led them to reorient the film from a dance movie to a largely singing picture.[4] But that was not done.

Was it really so important to film *Brigadoon* outdoors? Many thought not. Cinematographer Alfred Gilks, who had worked on *An American in Paris*, argued that shooting in the studio offered everyone far more control over the elements that could affect the quality of filming. If everything worked well during location shooting it could have produced something boldly new, but according to experts like Gilks, the odds were not in favor of success.[5] It also has to be pointed out that the Golden Age of the film musical had been almost entirely achieved by studio filming—it was a system that worked brilliantly for many years. Up to that point, the only excursion into the real world in dance film production had been Kelly's New York shooting for *On the Town*. But that location film constituted only a few minutes of the picture and did not involve any dancing at all. It could not be taken as proof that an entire dance movie could be made on location.

To compensate for the lost opportunity to film outdoors, Minnelli and the decorators went out of their way to make a huge set that attempted to capture the reality of Scotland. It was a staggering 75 feet tall, 250 feet long, and 150 feet wide and covered nearly 38,000 square feet of floor space.[6] They achieved a unique product that dazzles the eye but merely emphasized the fact that the film was made in a studio. It was too stagey. The set—complete with distinctive breeds of animals to be found in eighteenth-century Scotland—has the same effect on the eye as the brilliantly decorated set of the ballet in *An American in Paris*. It diverts attention from the dancing, music, and plot. Ironically that plot (about a mythical Scottish village that appears every hundred years for a short time) is tailor-made for a dreamy, mystical, and ephemeral setting. They could have minimized the setting with a misty, foggy space that would have created the right atmosphere and drastically reduced costs.

It was not just the overpowering set that was a problem. The plot had many defects. Kelly played the role of Tommy Albright who, with his cynical friend played by Van Johnson, stumbles upon the mythical village during a hunting trip in Scotland. He falls in love with the character played by Cyd Charisse, but he and his friend find it as hard to understand the rules of the village's existence as does the audience. The village would apparently disappear forever if someone leaves, but it is unaffected when the two strangers arrive. A wedding takes place, but an admirer of the bride creates havoc, resulting in the whole clan chasing him over hill and dale to prevent his leaving the village or else it would be lost forever. Like many of Lerner's plots, the story is paper-thin at best and the characters are not well developed.

Filming began December 9, 1953, and continued until the following March. Under the best of circumstances it would have been difficult to make *Brigadoon* work on the screen, but the process of filming was more difficult than usual. Kelly had to alter his choreography to the wide screen, calling it an "abomination" for a dance film because so much space is not used. He said it only worked well for group dances. Minnelli also thoroughly disliked Cinemascope because he could not use close-ups. And yet Freed filmed *Brigadoon* not only in Cinemascope but in widescreen and used stereophonic sound that altered natural tones. The company also used two color processes, Kodak and Ansco, requiring two cameras on the same boom and making camera movement difficult.[7] The picture became a test case of desperate innovations to arrest the decline of the film musical.

Possibly the worst part of *Brigadoon* was that Kelly did not appear as his normal buoyant self. Despite his later assertions that everyone did the best they could, his lack of enthusiasm compared to his performances in other films is obvious. Minnelli dealt with his disappointment better than Kelly, urging him to find a spark of inspiration to liven his performance. Minnelli also admitted that he "didn't know if the slender thread of a story would go over."[8]

It is true that the story lacks appeal. But Kelly's energy might have saved it. Even his choreography is unimaginative for the first time. In his dances with Charisse, he plays the typical male ballet dancer, mostly supporting Cyd in her poses. For his own dance to "It's Almost Like Being in Love," his choreography is nothing like his usual standout style, blowing the opportunity to inaugurate this classic song on screen in a memorable way. His singing too is not up to his usual mark—his voice sounds weak either because his heart was not in the project or because Frederick Loewe's composition was set too high for his vocal range. The stereophonic sound may have worsened the effect.

When *Brigadoon* was previewed on June 4, 1954, it received surprisingly positive responses from the audience. But more people thought Charisse and Johnson had better performances than Kelly, which was highly unusual because typically Gene had the highest ratings in his films. When released on September 8, 1954, it made $3.3 million for a cost of $2.3 million.[9] But the profit was not enough to offset the cost of advertising and marketing now that the studio no longer owned the distribution outlets.

Unlike the preview audience, reviewers were less than enthusiastic. *Dance News* thought Agnes de Mille's choreography for the stage version had been much better than Kelly's choreography for the movie, and noted that Gene "shows signs of tiredness" especially in his dancing. His steps tended "to be cliché ridden and obvious." Everyone seemed disappointed that there was no sword dance in the movie as there had been on stage. Bosley Crowther called the film slick and mechanical, Kelly's performance "thin and metallic as a nail," and Charisse "solemn and posey." He noted the lack of warmth and whimsy. Even Harold Cohen of Pittsburgh agreed with Crowther. "There is no joyousness at all in Mr. Kelly's numbers. . . . they are desperately stylized and painfully purposeful. Only their feet are in them, never their hearts." Over the years *Brigadoon* has drawn similarly negative comments from film critics and historians.[10]

Perhaps to compensate, Kelly and Charisse did a radio program called "Salute to Brigadoon" as part two of *Best of All* on NBC on September 27, 1954, less than a month after the film's release. Gene briefly shared the plot and talked about how he had wanted to star in the movie even before its stage

Figure 14.1 Dancing with Cyd Charisse in the balletic "Heather on the Hill," filmed in Cinemascope. (Still from *Brigadoon*, 1954)

run after hearing the songs at the invitation of Lerner and Loewe. He mentioned touring Scotland with Freed, standing on "Brigadoon"—the old stone bridge over the Doon River, and being "thrilled by the beauty and rare color of all of Scotland." He and Cyd then talked about the huge film set and how beautiful it was, in a vigorous plug for the movie. Kelly mentioned that Van Johnson, a friend since his stage days, came to Hollywood only weeks after he did, that the two wondered if they had made a mistake, and that later they reminisced about old times on Broadway. Gene sang parts of "Heather on the Hill," "Almost Like Being in Love," and "Go Home with Bonnie Jean." The program ended with Kelly thanking Freed, Minnelli, and everyone associated with *Brigadoon*.

DEEP IN MY HEART (1954)

Kelly soon rejuvenated himself with his next project, which reunited him with his brother Fred in a short but spirited number in the Sigmund Romberg biopic *Deep in My Heart*. Roger Edens, who produced the picture, had the idea of uniting Gene with Fred to portray the O'Brien Brothers in "I Love to Go Swimmin' with Women." It brought back the old Pittsburgh days when Gene and Fred struggled to help the family through the Depression by performing in "cloops." It was the first and only time they danced together since Gene left Pittsburgh in 1938, and both brothers had a lot of fun.[11]

Fred Kelly had crafted an entertainment career for himself that was entirely separate from his famous brother. He married just before being drafted

Figure 14.2 Re-creating their "cloop" dancing, with his brother Fred, in "I Love to Go Swimmin' with Women." (Still from *Deep in My Heart*, 1954)

into the Army early in World War II. Because he had been a premedical student for a time at the University of Pittsburgh, the army initially slated him to go into the Medical Corps but soon shifted him into entertainment duties. He directed and played in musical shows at Camp Stewart, Georgia, that were much like the Cap and Gown programs. His talents became widely known and in 1942 Fred participated in a major Broadway show, Irving Berlin's *This is the Army*, which involved 300 soldiers. He appeared in and choreographed the film version of the show for Warner Brothers the next year. After that Fred went to England, where Dwight Eisenhower recommended him to teach ballroom dance to Princess Elizabeth and Princess Margaret. After the war, Fred worked in New York on the stage and especially in the television industry, where he directed many shows. He is credited with introducing the mambo to America in 1948.[12]

The brothers worked for one week on the number for *Deep in My Heart*, framing it as a vaudeville performance dressed up in M-G-M Technicolor. Fred had taken ballet lessons while performing in New York early in his career but obviously had not incorporated them into his performance.[13] The number offers a wonderful opportunity to study Gene's dancing style in comparison with his younger brother.

Gene developed nothing new in the way of dance steps for the number, throwing in all his usual tap routines, including the Midair Twist and Airplane Propeller. Fred and Gene do everything together, and it is fascinating to see how alike and how different they are at the same time. Technically Fred does well in all the steps except the Midair Twist, which they repeat several times; his upper body is horizontal, parallel to the floor, seemingly less in control. Gene has much better control, holding his upper body straight in the same move, which looks more athletic yet graceful. At the end of the number, Gene smiles with confidence while Fred laughs in an amateurish way; he seems relieved that the number is over and is eager for applause. The only explanation for why Fred did not have a career in films is that he lacked Gene's star quality.

UNREALIZED PROJECTS

As early as January 1951 and extending throughout the time period of *Brigadoon* and *Deep in My Heart*, Freed wanted to make a film based on Mark Twain's *Huckleberry Finn*. Lerner wrote a screenplay, with Kelly and Danny Kaye in mind to play the Duke and the Dauphin and Minnelli as the director. Minnelli began to rehearse on August 28, 1951, and Gene took a break from filming *Singin' in the Rain* to work with him from September 11 to 14. By October Freed decided to postpone work on *Huckleberry Finn* because Kelly was going to Europe and Kaye was committed to star in *Hans Christian Andersen* for Samuel Goldwyn. Kelly was eager to do the picture. He told Edwin Schallert in October that the team wanted to present it "the way Mark Twain would have adapted his story for a musical picture." He claimed they were conducting "extensive research in order to obtain the proper viewpoint."[14]

We will never know what that meant because *Huckleberry Finn* was not made. Kelly's trip to Europe took the momentum out of the project. Lerner was keen to restart work in late 1953 when Kelly was still absorbed with "Sinbad the Sailor" and began to film *Brigadoon*. Lerner kept asking Freed about the shooting schedule and said the project was "absolutely marvelous for Gene." But Freed put it on the back burner indefinitely. It is unclear why—he had a script, several songs were written, and a nearly full slate of actors had been named. Speculation ran rampant. Lela Simone later claimed that Kelly did not wish to work with Kaye. Peter Wollen has argued that Yip Harburg (who wrote the lyrics) and Donald Ogden Stewart (who wrote the original screenplay) were targeted by the Red Scare and therefore Freed was reluctant to go on with the project. But in 1959, Freed announced he was going ahead with the movie.[15] By that time the Golden Age was almost over and the film never materialized. As for the speculations, Simone's claim is ridiculous. Kelly and Kaye were warm friends and shared strong liberal convictions. When Kelly later appeared on Kaye's television show, their performance together was magical. Wollen's conjecture also does not ring true because Freed had replaced Stewart's script with Lerner's. Freed never explained why he put the project on hold for so long. *Huckleberry Finn* could have been a great dance musical, but fate ordained otherwise.

In December 1953, Freed placed high priority on a film based on Cole Porter's music and wanted Kelly to star in it, but it also never happened. Neither did "St. Louis Woman" for which he was slated. At the same time, Kelly had an idea for a project he wanted to do with playwright Thornton Wilder, "which I think can be the most exciting thing ever done in the theatre." But he never explained on paper what the idea was, except to say it was "not a musical comedy."[16] This idea also never turned into a full-blown project.

But Gene still wanted to work on a theater project at this time. He visited William Saroyan in Malibu in the fall of 1954 to discuss a "dance-play" or "Ballet-Opera-Play" called "Life's Dance." Saroyan saw it as an innovative form melding classic dance with contemporary movement, which greatly interested Kelly. Gene thought they could create a company to produce it "so that we can really keep the money we get out of this." Later, Saroyan sent him an outline and Kelly wrote back, "I've never been this excited about anything since I first became a part of show business." At the same time, he found parts of the outline "too melodramatic." Saroyan, eager to get Gene on board, responded that they could drop the first outline if needed.[17]

Several months later, in April 1955, Kelly and Saroyan met again, and Gene was even more deeply excited by the prospects. Based on their discussions, Kelly typed out a scenario that was less than a page of text. It starts with a masquerade ball held by the elite. "The cast, primarily being dancers, should be dressed in costumes that bespeak movement and have a litheness about them." Into this setting comes a stranger who is a product of the tough streets. But he impresses everyone because he is so different. His cynicism and bitterness are changed quickly after meeting the heroine, who also is part of the elite but seems out of place in it. Within a remarkably short space of time she redeems him, but he is shot tragically as the lovers start to leave the ball.[18]

It sounds as if Gene saw this as a real ballet, with plot and characterization compressed into poetic form and expressed primarily through dance. It was up to Saroyan to write the full script. Kelly asked Saroyan to consider whether their hero should be a repairman, the victim of mistaken identity, or a fugitive. He suggested that the heroine be engaged or married to create more obstacles. He wanted everyone to talk about their philosophies of life and what they would do differently if there was reincarnation. He suggested a wide range of philosophies that would lead to more varied dance action. Gene was ready to begin working out choreography but he needed more substance concerning characters and plot development. He was even wondering if the masks at the ball should be full-face or half-face and thought this too would be directed by the plot details.[19] Kelly had many ideas and suggestions but was incapable of developing them into a usable script.

But Saroyan seems to have found it even more difficult to develop a coherent plot. He tried for several weeks and came up with alternate scenarios for the hero to be either innocent or guilty and always lost steam. "I guess I just can't work when I know before I start what I am supposed to be doing. I have better luck when the life of the thing itself chooses its own nature as it grows." Saroyan sent Kelly his latest scenario for the hero as an escaped convict that reads like a potboiler of a plot more suited for the *Suspense* radio show that Gene enjoyed listening to in the late 1940s than serious drama. He included a note saying, "I'm sorry if it's all useless. If you want to drop the whole project . . . that will be ok with me."[20] Apparently, that is what Kelly decided to do.

IT'S ALWAYS FAIR WEATHER (1955)

With no theater project in the offing, Kelly came up with the idea for his next M-G-M film, *It's Always Fair Weather*, based on Alexander Dumas's *Twenty Years After* about the Three Musketeers meeting after two decades. He applied it to the three characters of *On the Town* meeting ten years later and planned to bring back Frank Sinatra and Jules Munshin. Betty Comden and Adolph Green agreed to write the screenplay, although they later claimed to have thought up the idea in the first place.[21] Whoever had the brainstorm, *It's Always Fair Weather* was in many ways a throwback to the height of the Golden Age and was a way to remind viewers how good those musicals could be.

But it did not quite turn out that way. The team encountered many difficulties and changed the nature of the project during its development. Sinatra's demands were too difficult for the studio to stomach and he was ruled out, and Munshin was not available. So they recruited veteran hoofer Dan Dailey and choreographer Michael Kidd to be part of the trio. Although Kidd had never danced or acted on screen, he was a dancer as was Dailey. As a result, the team decided to include more dancing than originally planned. They also changed the characters—no longer would it be the trio of sailors in postwar America but three army veterans who had served together in Europe. The idea was to show how the three grew apart after ten years, highlighted by a day in New York as they try to rekindle their old camaraderie. Kelly admitted it was "an experiment by treating a serious subject within the context of a musical comedy."[22]

Indeed, in contrast to the lighthearted themes of dance musicals, there is a dark atmosphere to *It's Always Fair Weather*. In part that comes from the use of dull tones associated with the cheaper Eastman color process and in part from the script and the music, but also because much of the time the three men are soured on each other and have their own problems to work out.

As with *Brigadoon*, this picture would be filmed in Cinemascope. Kelly once again shared the direction with Stanley Donen, and the two worked out different ways to use the wide screen to their benefit.[23] One measure they employed was the use of triptych sequences. One such sequence showed what the trio did in the ten intervening years before they met again. Another depicted them sitting together at lunch after ten years, with each one musing to himself to the song "I Shouldn't Have Come" as he realizes that he does not like his comrades anymore. A third showed the three dancing separately in different venues but doing the same steps to "Once Upon a Time" as they show sadness that their friendship has ended. It is an imaginative format that works very well in all three cases.

Other measures were taken to allow dancers to use the wide space more effectively. The three men fill the screen as they dance side-by-side in the "Binge" and the "Ash Can" numbers. The three dancers also move swiftly toward the camera, using space effectively and energetically. In Kelly's "Roller Skate" dance, he skates fast and effortlessly along sidewalks, filling the entire screen very quickly as pedestrians watch with appreciation. In Charisse's and Dolores Gray's solo dances, male performers dance around them to fill the wide screen. Finally, Kelly did not hesitate to use close-ups. He employed them to convey intimate conversations and situations very effectively in marked contrast to the cumbersome widescreen with tiny figures in most of *Brigadoon*.

Rehearsals began on Kelly's birthday in 1954 and filming started October 13. Unfortunately, friction developed between Kelly and Donen. For the first time in their collaboration, Kelly and Donen could not see eye to eye. Kelly could not, or would not, say later exactly why this happened, but he never made a big deal of it. In contrast, Donen was extremely negative in his comments, calling their codirecting on the film a nightmare. But Donen later confessed the real reason for their disagreement: he had progressed by this time as a solo director and was not happy sharing credit anymore. He said he would have quit halfway through production but felt obliged to continue.[24]

The assistant director's report indicates that the directors cooperated well enough to get the job done. Each one handled a bit of everything associated with directing a picture without a clear and consistent division of labor. They did some filming on location for a few combat scenes, lighting off numerous explosions at Bronson Canyon in Griffith Park, Los Angeles. When Donen was ill, Kelly handled all directing duties for the day and vice versa. They often agreed on whether a scene was good enough or if more takes were needed. Also, Dan Dailey said he encountered no problems, the directors let him work out his own solo, and he enjoyed rehearsing the trio's dances together.[25] So, it is obvious the Kelly-Donen disagreements were not universal, no matter what Donen claimed with his usual hyperbole. Also, the directors clearly worked together to improvise clever ways to use the widescreen format.

Their major disagreement centered on Michael Kidd, who struggled with his acting role. Donen had recently formed a friendship with Kidd while working on *Seven Brides for Seven Brothers* (1954), in which Kidd created impressive choreography. He tried to get more lines for Kidd's character even though Kidd comes across as the neophyte actor he was, at least during the early part of the film. Even Kidd's dancing is not up to that delivered by Dailey and Kelly. He does well when the three perform the same step together, but in his brief solo routines in the "Binge" and "Ash Can" dances his movements are jerky and lacking in grace. But Donen was determined that Kidd have a solo dance number. Gene agreed at first as a courtesy to Kidd. Ironically, the assistant director's report indicates that Donen, who directed this number, had great difficulty with it. Donen dropped lines from it off the cuff, was repeatedly dissatisfied with the dance action, and acceded to Kidd's desire to do four more takes of a scene that he already was satisfied with, only to be dissatisfied with the new takes. Kelly rightly dropped the number. He also dropped a number that he and Cyd Charisse filmed, just as he did with his own numbers in other films. Unfortunately, Donen and Kidd mercilessly criticized Kelly for axing Kidd's solo. Even Andrew Previn, who wrote ten minutes of music for the number, criticized Kelly for dropping it, and suggested that Kelly was jealous of someone else's number with children.[26]

It is impossible that anyone, least of all Kelly, could be jealous of the number. Kidd had created a bizarre routine called "Jack and the Space Giants." His character, a cook at a diner, tells a story to children about cooking for space giants. One look at the deleted number on the DVD edition of *It's Always Fair Weather* shows that Kidd's movements are extremely graceless and jerky, the story impossible to accept, and the handful of kids involved merely stand around as if they have no idea why they are there. All in all, "Jack and the Space Giants" would have hung around the neck of *It's Always Fair Weather* like a leaden weight. Gene was right to drop this fiasco. He always tried to do what was best for the project, and in this case, he actually helped Kidd by not showing such an unflattering performance of his to the public.

Ironically, while Kelly and Donen agreed to keep Dailey's solo in the film, it too should have been dropped—but for different reasons. Dailey choreographed and performed it well based on the lyrics and the plot, but it was Comden and Green who had introduced an unnecessarily negative element here. It was fine to show Dailey's character regretting that he went into advertising instead of becoming a serious artist. But for him to physically and verbally abuse his colleagues in a drunken state shows him in a very bad light. One cannot excuse his behavior by saying he was drunk because it is one's true essence that emerges when drink or medication removes inhibitions. In view of this, it is less convincing for Ted (Kelly's character) to say he respects his friends and wants to win their respect. Such a line would have worked if Dailey's number had been an introspective musing.

Despite the friction and the negativity of the film, the team produced a major dance musical with several interesting numbers. The "Ash Can" dance was one of the more difficult of Kelly's career because each member of the trio locks a foot under the handle of an ash can lid, which he then uses to tap dance. "You get a lot of good [sound] effects from them," Kelly said. He developed this concept in true bricolage fashion, by walking the street and looking for props in everyday life.[27] Kelly also developed a stunning number for Charisse in "Baby You Knock Me Out," in which she dances in a recreation of Stillman's Gym in New York to highlight Kelly's longtime association of dance with athletics.

It is unclear who choreographed Dolores Gray's humorous "Thanks a Lot, but No Thanks," with several accomplished male dancers doing acrobatic tricks. It is not in Kelly's style, and Donen was not a choreographer. The number is very similar to Judy Garland's "Get Happy" number from *Summer Stock*, which was choreographed by Charles Walters. It is possible that, just as the directors let Dailey and Kidd plan their own numbers, they asked some of the male dancers who had performed in "Get Happy" to come up with a similar routine for Gray. Indeed, some of the faces are the same in both numbers. No matter who created it, the choreography is memorable.

The highlight of *It's Always Fair Weather* is Kelly's "I Like Myself," danced on roller skates along M-G-M's outdoor New York set. Even Donen told an interviewer, "I thought Gene did it very well. [It] is probably one of his best numbers." Whether on ice skates or roller skates, Kelly had been a whiz since childhood. Later, Gene and his brother Fred had done a routine on skates in Pittsburgh where they went up and down steps. One day Comden and Green saw him skate on the tennis court of the house they were renting while working on the film and urged him to create a number incorporating skating into the dance movement. Kelly purchased the skates from Pioneer Hardware on Beverly Drive and did not alter them in any way or lock them to his shoes. As documentary film producer Robert Trachtenberg explains, "so when he tapped in them he had no help."[28]

Actors had appeared on skates to musical accompaniment before in the movies, including Charlie Chaplin in *Modern Times* (1936), Fred Astaire and Ginger Rogers in *Shall We Dance* (1937), and Donald O'Connor in *I Love Melvin* (1953). Chaplin of course did not dance or tap on skates, but simply skated fast and spun around with confidence. The others also mainly skated, O'Connor with more confidence than Astaire and Rogers. The three did some dancing moves but very little tapping—nothing like the sustained and difficult tapping Gene did on skates.

Astaire's biographer Peter Levinson writes that Fred resisted this number and had to be convinced to do it. Moreover, it took thirty-four hours of rehearsal and 150 takes. Historian Roy Hemming concludes that "neither Astaire nor Rogers look at ease or completely comfortable in this number."[29]

In contrast, given his skill and experience in dancing on skates, Gene made "I Like Myself" into a hallmark of his athletic dancing style and his bravura sense of presentation. Moreover, the dance represents the redemption of Kelly's character, and the obvious joy and love he exudes as he skate-dances makes this number very appealing. It truly is the last great Kelly dance to appear in a Golden Age musical.

The preview on June 25 received very strong approval, with Gene once again getting far higher ratings than the other performers as was typical except for *Brigadoon*. In terms of dancing, the "Roller Skate" number had the highest ratings, and the audience almost unanimously said they loved the

Figure 14.3 Ending the roller-skate dance "I Like Myself" to enthusiastic applause from the public. (Still from *It's Always Fair Weather*, 1955)

film. When released on September 1, 1955, *It's Always Fair Weather* received strongly positive reviews from critics who often cited "I Like Myself" and the satirical view of early television as the highlights. These two aspects along with the "Ash Can" dance also tend to draw the most attention from film scholars. The movie came to be seen as the last in a long string of Hollywood musicals celebrating the serviceman as hero, although doing so with a strangely dark tone. The criticism also focused on the poor color and Previn's uninspired musical score.[30]

Most of the principals involved in making the movie were pleased with it but had some regrets. Comden and Green believed they did not set out to write such a dark-toned movie. And they were furious at M-G-M for marketing it in a very limited way—in drive-ins instead of theaters. As a result of the limited distribution, the picture barely made $2.5 million on initial release for a $2 million cost. Previn was not satisfied with his score. Kelly bemoaned that the visual aspect of the film was so dark and remarked that even the prints deteriorated because of the cheap Eastman color process, which produced less durable dyes than Technicolor. And yet, Kelly and the writers recognized that the film itself was good, even with the dark tones in story, music, and print. At wide variance with them was Donen, who believed the film had nothing new to offer and was a failure. He also differed from them in saying "it's not cynical or downbeat—it's all sugar-coated if anything."[31] Actually, despite the cynical tone that suffuses most of the picture, the ending is somewhat positive as the trio rejuvenate the camaraderie they once shared. Even with its limitations, *It's Always Fair Weather* has survived as one of the more enjoyable products of the Freed Unit.

New Directions, 1956–1960

In the mid-1950s, Kelly's career and personal life took dramatic new turns, forcing him to adjust to changes in both areas. With the decline of the Golden Age, there was no possibility of making one dance film after another as he had been doing since 1942. His marriage to Betsy Blair, seemingly rock-solid for so long, developed fissures that led to divorce. Gene became a single father and an independent producer, director, and actor at the same time. He also initiated a long career on television, finding the new medium a welcome home for his talents.

The Freed Unit at M-G-M began to fall apart soon after the release of *It's Always Fair Weather*. Freed himself became an independent producer with *Silk Stockings* (1957), released through M-G-M, and Roger Edens went to Paramount with many unit members to work on *Funny Face* (1957). Kelly had little to gain by finishing the remaining two years of his seven-year contract, signed with M-G-M in 1950, and wanted out of it. The studio was willing if Kelly did two more films over the next five years, in addition to giving M-G-M first refusal on the distribution of his first independently produced movie. That deal was acceptable, and the old contract was cancelled in January 1956.[1]

THE HAPPY ROAD (1957)

Gene wasted no time in his new role as an independent producer. His first project was *The Happy Road*, "a nice, small-budget picture in Europe," as he called it. He produced, directed, and starred in this film about busy single parents losing touch with their kids. Kelly's character and the one played by Barbara Laage are thrown together because their children, away at a boarding school, take off across France to find their parents. It is a chase movie that self-consciously promoted international cooperation, something that Gene was happy to support. The filming was stressful due to poor weather and the triple responsibilities Kelly bore, but he thought it "a sweet little picture."[22]

Critics liked *The Happy Road*. Even Bosley Crowther praised Kelly for "functioning most effectively" in all three roles (producer, director, and star), called his acting "outstanding," and cited him as "a propagandist for brotherly love." *The Happy Road* opened June 20, 1957, and soon after was shown as a fundraising effort for a French hospital. The film was a "modest success" and received several honors—the Hollywood Foreign Press Association Award for "the picture contributing most to international understanding," *Parent's Magazine*'s Gold Medal, and a certificate from the Southern California Motion Picture Council for "outstanding merit." The British Film Academy cited it for the film best illustrating the principles of the United Nations Charter.[3]

CHANGES IN FAMILY

Gene's father passed away during the filming of *The Happy Road*. Kelly made a week-long trip from France to Pittsburgh to attend the funeral and console his grieving mother. James Kelly was eighty when he passed away on July 11, 1956, and he was buried at the Calvary Cemetery in Pittsburgh.[4]

Gene was also going through a divorce while filming the movie. Four years earlier, during the summer of 1952, Blair began to have affairs in Paris while Kelly was working on *Invitation to the Dance* in England. She continued a series of overlapping affairs after returning to California. In 1956, Betsy fell in love with a Frenchman in Paris while Gene was working on *The Happy Road*. She broke the news to her husband, admitting all the previous affairs as well. He said he had known and was waiting for her to get over her wild period. But Blair wanted to craft a different life without him. "The time had come to grow up," she wrote in her memoirs.[5] Apparently her view of being "grown up" was to have a string of affairs for four years while Gene supported her financially and in other ways.

Kelly hoped to work things out, but Blair was set on starting a new life. Kerry, who was fourteen when her parents told her of the impending divorce, was deeply shocked. Gene asked if it would help if Jeannie (Jeanne Coyne) came over, and Kerry eagerly agreed. She had always considered her a second mother. Coyne flew to Paris from California to help Kerry at this difficult time.[66]

On returning to California, Gene and Betsy decided to live separately in their home until the divorce. But when it came to the financial settlement,

Blair became bitter. Even though she had cheated on Gene for several years while he remained faithful to her, and although she was the one who wanted the divorce, she hoped to use California's community property law to get half of his assets as the former wives of other actors did. Gene did not want to split the assets evenly. He explained that in the other cases it was the men who wanted out of the marriage and dividing the assets equally was a way to get their wives to agree to a divorce. But Betsy refused to acknowledge the difference in the situations and insisted on half the assets. Gene's lawyer then told Betsy's lawyer that Gene could accuse Betsy of adultery to bypass the community property division. He also mentioned her having given $10,000 to the Red Chinese. Betsy was furious at the last suggestion because she had invested the money for a film in China, which was hardly the same thing. She could have denied that charge but not the charge of adultery. So she agreed to receive $180,000 over ten years. Even though this was pretty generous (nearly three-fourths of the $250,000 that a 50-50 split would have given her), she carped about it in her memoirs, claiming that it was less than the interest she could have earned on the money she would have received through community property division.[7]

The divorce was granted on April 3, 1957, in Las Vegas. They received joint custody of Kerry, and Kelly paid Blair $100 a month for child support. He agreed to let Blair cite "mental cruelty" as the grounds for divorce.[8] In the absence of "no-fault" divorces, this was viewed as the most convenient category. Still, Betsy does not acknowledge in her memoirs Gene's generosity in agreeing to these grounds even though she was the one causing him pain by leaving. Nor does she seem to recall that he had gone out on a limb to allow her to keep her prized role in *Marty* despite knowing at the time that she was cheating on him. Also, she does not mention that while she received child support, Gene funded Kerry's education in Switzerland as well as her other expenses as Kerry continued to live with him when school was out.

After Betsy left, Jeannie moved into the guest quarters to support both Gene and Kerry. She had been in love with Kelly for many years without anyone knowing it. As Coyne was not the type to break up a marriage, she kept her feelings hidden and even married Donen to try to get on with her life. As we have seen, that marriage was a disaster. Later, according to Cyd Charisse, Coyne had a brief romance with Dan Dailey while the two worked on *Meet Me in Las Vegas* (1956). But now Coyne had a chance to get close to Kelly. She became a surrogate mother to Kerry as her relationship with Gene deepened. Betsy admitted that Jeannie was more mature than she had been when she fell in love with Gene and that Jeannie did not feel threatened by Kelly's importance as had Betsy.[9]

LES GIRLS (1957)

Kelly's next project was a curious throwback to his early film career. In *Les Girls* he was merely a player. Kelly did not produce the film, he did not direct it, and he was not the official choreographer. Jack Cole was assigned choreographic responsibility because, as he claimed, M-G-M was exasperated that Kelly went overboard in creating *Invitation to the Dance*. Of course, Kelly choreographed dances in *It's Always Fair Weather* after *Invitation to the Dance*, so that reasoning is faulty. Gene explained that this was one of the two films to play out his contract with M-G-M, and he did not want to add choreography to his roles of star and dancer. Cole's style differed markedly from Kelly's. It tended toward a vigorous modernist attitude and more intently blended international dance traditions. "It opens up a new vocabulary of movement, different ways to approach the problem, rather than a balletic way," according to Cole. Jeanne Coyne, dance assistant on the film, had worked for him earlier, and Cole considered her "a very nice girl and a very good dancer." Coyne was concerned when Cole tried to work out steps for Kelly during rehearsals for *Les Girls*. She told him Gene was too advanced in his career to learn new tricks.[10]

But Kelly was more flexible than Coyne imagined and tried to do what Cole developed. In a number with Taina Elg that involved the two pulling at opposite ends of strings running through a hole in a raised stage, Cole planned modernist moves that barely resemble dance steps. Ironically, Cole became ill partway through rehearsals and had to leave the project, with Gene taking over the choreography for the film. But rather than changing the plan for this number, he tried to do it as Cole had envisioned. Kelly had already choreographed a number with Kay Kendall to the song "You're Just Too, Too!" That dance is heavily laced with bricolage and has only a few simple steps because Kendall was not a dancer. Gene did not get official credit, not even shared credit, for choreography, but it was not a big deal to him. He pointed out that he did not get credit for creating dances in *For Me and My Gal*, *Du Barry*, or *Cover Girl* either, nor did he and Astaire get credit in *Ziegfeld Follies*. That was the studio system and he accepted it.[11]

Kelly also choreographed the biggest number of the film, "Why Am I So

Figure 15.1 Dancing with Mitzi Gaynor in "Why Am I So Gone About that Girl?" (Still from *Les Girls*, 1957)

Gone About that Girl?" with Mitzi Gaynor. The number is a parody of Marlon Brando's motorcycle movie *The Wild One* (1953) with Kelly dressed in black, dancing romantically with Gaynor, but leaving her callously at the end to go off with the pack. Except for the sad end, the number could be the highlight of the film. Jeanine Basinger says it "is a nearly perfect piece of film choreography," and Clive Hirschhorn calls it "a delightful moment" and "the best thing in the film." Historian Tony Thomas writes that Gaynor won the starring role in *South Pacific* based on this performance.[12] The dance is pure Kelly with a mix of ballet, modern, tap, and athletic jumps. Both Kelly and Gaynor perform it beautifully. It has some similarities with Kelly's dance with Tamara Tamanouva in "Ring Around the Rosy" from *Invitation to the Dance*. In both numbers, he upsets the girl, but then lifts her all curled up and placates her. They make up and dance energetically together, but he walks away from the girl at the end.

Les Girls is not a bad movie, but it failed to make much of an impression during the decline of the Golden Age. Based on a stage musical by Cole Porter, it has a convoluted plot about Barry Nichols (Kelly) and the three women in his entertainment troupe. Barry starts out as a manipulator but is redeemed by the love of one of those members and does the right thing to help the other two out of their difficulties. The picture has an uneven quality that entertains one minute and frustrates the next.

Gene later admitted he did *Les Girls* "without much heart" because he was contractually obligated to the studio. And yet his acting is very good in it. With the film's release on October 3, 1957, Bosley Crowther wrote that Kelly was "more winning" here than in *An American in Paris*. Other commentators, however, have criticized different aspects of the movie, such as the story or Cole Porter's score.[13]

"THE LIFE YOU SAVE" (1957)

While working on *Les Girls,* Kelly stretched himself as an actor by appearing as a one-armed handyman in "The Life You Save," an episode of the *Schlitz Playhouse* television program aired by CBS on March 1, 1957, with a rerun on September 6.[14] This was Gene's plunge into television. Many other Hollywood personalities were also exploring television with greater or lesser success.

The episode was based on a short story by Flannery O'Connor, well known for her gritty stories about working-class Southerners. Published in 1955 as "The Life You Save May Be Your Own," O'Connor depicted Tom Shiftlet as an unredeemed soul who agrees to marry a deaf-mute girl but then abandons her on their honeymoon trip to continue living the wandering life. In the adaptation for *Schlitz Playhouse*, his name was changed to Triplett, and his character is far better than in the original. The girl is played by Janice Rule and her mother by Agnes Moorehead.

The interesting thing about "The Life You Save" is how well Kelly pulled off the difficult role of a one-armed itinerant handyman, which was at such variance to anything he had done. He duplicates a Deep South accent with surprising effectiveness. Within a few minutes of this short drama we forget we are watching Gene Kelly and buy into the character of Tom Triplett. He does a very good job of acting greatly against type. In musicals Gene often played a mixed-up man who finally redeemed himself. Here, he seems mostly okay throughout, helpful and decent, but suddenly—on seeing an opportunity for what he thinks will be freedom—he takes it. But Triplett encounters a boy running away and cleverly gets him to go back home. Then he sees a billboard that advocates careful driving because "The Life You Save May Be Your Own." He makes the connection between the boy he just saved, the billboard, and his own life. Triplett then goes back to the girl, leading to a happy ending, unlike the story on which the episode was based.

"The Life You Save" demonstrates beyond doubt that Gene and television were made for each other. Kelly had genuine ability as an actor in dramatic roles, and his large screen persona could comfortably fit on the small, intimate screen viewed in people's living rooms.

Figure 15.2 Kelly does an excellent job playing a one-armed handyman in "The Life You Save" (1957) on the television series *Schlitz Playhouse*. His costars Janice Rule and Agnes Moorehead are on the porch in the background. (General Still Photograph Collection, 1957–1958, Box 2, Binder 5, Image 51, Special Collections Research Center, Syracuse University)

Kelly's second foray onto the small screen related to his love of sports. He agreed to host "Salute to Baseball," which aired in color on the night of April 13, 1957. Comedian Ed Garner and eighteen major league players, including Mickey Mantle, appeared on this half-hour variety special that aired on the NBC network.[15]

MARJORIE MORNINGSTAR (1958)

Gene's next project was a film by Warner Brothers. He undertook a dramatic role by portraying Noel Airman in a screen adaptation of the Herman Wouk novel *Marjorie Morningstar*.[16] The book had been published in 1955 to great interest. The star of the picture, and Kelly's love interest, was Natalie Wood. She was twenty-six years his junior, but an age difference was written into the plot. Airman is a man of talent who has never been able to make it on Broadway. Kelly imbued the role with a good deal of bittersweet remorse. It required of him more nuance and feeling than he was used to portraying in his dance film career, and Kelly pulled it off effectively. Unlike many of his previous characters, Airman is not redeemed by love and becomes a tragic figure, incapable of personal growth and knowing he is his own worst enemy.

Gene was given a great deal of latitude in developing Airman's character and enjoyed the challenge. "I thought it was the most interesting thing to do," he said in an interview. But the initial screenplay, which would have produced an overly long film, had to be trimmed drastically. Kelly felt that this process shortchanged his role. "It became most difficult really to make this a well-rounded characterization." In the end he was not fully satisfied but concluded that "it was a good try."[17]

Kelly was being too hard on himself. The film was released on April 24, 1958, and the end product is more than just a good try. Gene very affectingly sings "A Precious Love" to set the bittersweet tone of the picture. He also pushes himself in a dramatic moment that represents all the frustration, anger, and bitterness of his character when he berates a group of well-meaning backers for his show who simply do not understand him. In an unusual display of his acting ability, Kelly forcefully expressed all these emotions only to whine like a child as soon as the backers walk out on him. Never in any other screen depiction, except perhaps in *Combat Fatigue Irritability*, did Kelly turn in such an emotional performance.

After the filming of *Marjorie Morningstar* and before its release, Kelly suffered a serious injury while skiing at Klosters in December 1957. "I had the cartilage ripped off my knee," he said, and had to limp painfully for a quarter of a mile to seek medical assistance. A local doctor wanted to operate but Kelly refused, believing it would worsen the damage. Even so, he could not dance for a couple of years and greatly toned down his steps after that hiatus. Klosters, with its 275 miles of skiing slopes, had drawn a wide variety of actors, writers, and elite socialites throughout the 1950s and early 1960s. But now it lost much of its attraction for Kelly.[18]

THE TUNNEL OF LOVE (1958)

Soon after the Klosters accident, Kelly embarked on an assignment to direct *The Tunnel of Love*, the last commitment in his revised contract with M-G-M. It was a film version of a Theatre Guild stage comedy just ending its Broadway run, which in turn was based on a novel by Peter DeVries. For the first time Gene would direct a film but not act in it.

Even so, it seemed to some that he could not help but act. Journalist Joe

Hyams was amazed to see Kelly infuse his direction of actors by demonstrating how he wanted them to move. "Bouncing in and out of character like a rubber ball, Kelly acted every part in the movie." Richard Widmark, who starred in the production, was also impressed. "Movie actors often complain they miss the audience. But not with Gene around. He's not only an actor, producer and director. He's a whole audience, too."[19]

The picture was released on November 7, 1958. Kelly's success as a director was limited by the improbable and convoluted plot of *The Tunnel of Love*. Widmark and Doris Day played a childless couple wishing to have a baby. An attractive adoption caseworker tricks Widmark into believing he had a one-night stand with her and takes money from him to have the baby, which she will then give him and his wife to adopt. Day realizes later that the woman was hiding her own pregnancy, jumps to the conclusion that Widmark is the illegitimate father, and is ready to leave him and the adopted baby. In the end, the other woman confesses that there was no affair, she is married and just needed money, and the baby she gave them to adopt is not hers. She returns the money she took from Widmark, saying her husband is doing well now. Widmark and Day reconcile, and Day suddenly becomes pregnant.

Bosley Crowther aptly observed that "it boils down at the finish to a wholesome and virtuous little tale." He thought "one could not expect much more with a plot containing "one minor gag that wears awfully thin before the finish." And yet he believed that Kelly guided everyone to the point that "they have played it competently."[20]

With *The Tunnel of Love,* Kelly had now directed two nondance films toward a solid accomplishment. The first, *The Happy Road*, won many awards. *The Tunnel of Love* has an interesting introduction involving aerial photography of the couple driving along a parkway to their home (foreshadowing the exciting train sequence that would later open *Hello, Dolly!* under Kelly's direction). His camera placements and angles, as well as his pacing, are very well done. They keep audience attention on the story and characters rather than on the director and are consistent with Kelly's longtime focus on doing the best thing for the project rather than hogging the limelight.

LOOKING FOR NEW PROJECTS

After finishing *The Tunnel of Love* Kelly was no longer tied to M-G-M. He became a completely free agent. Gene had already begun crafting new directions in his career with his triple role in *The Happy Road*, his foray into television, and his dramatic role in *Marjorie Morningstar* with another studio. Part of that crafting was the never-ending search for new projects. Several that he seriously considered never developed.

Gene bought the rights to a short novel by Félicien Marceau called *The Diamonds of Mlle. Antoinette*; he intended to star in, produce, and direct a film based on it. Kelly was to portray a jewel smuggler who transformed Gina Lollobrigida from "a drab girl into a glamorous Parisienne beauty." Gina liked the project and signed up for it. The movie was slated for filming in France during the spring of 1958, but for some reason, the project never got off the ground.[21]

Kelly purchased the rights to David Lord's *The Fancy Dancer* with the intention of producing a film and starring in it. The story revolved around a Latin American dancer who witnesses a miracle that changes his life. This project also failed to gel. Gene was excited about directing, choreographing, and starring in a movie project called "A Gentleman's Gentleman." It was to be a musical comedy set in London. The story was about a romance between an English butler, who worked for an American millionaire, and a maid. The maid would be played by Moira Shearer, and the songs would be written by Sammy Cahn and Jimmy Van Heusen. "It's certainly going to be fun to be dancing again," Kelly told a reporter. But like the other projects, this one never materialized. It was to be produced by Arthur Rank in England, but he lost interest. As always, Gene also tried to put together something for the stage. He considered working with ballet choreographer George Balanchine to create a new production of *The Nutcracker*, but neither he nor Balanchine could devise a significantly new way to present this old classic.[22]

FLOWER DRUM SONG (1958)

Nevertheless, Kelly was able to return to the stage through the aid of Richard Rodgers and Oscar Hammerstein, who needed a director for their new production *Flower Drum Song*. Based on a novel by Chin Yang Lee about generational tension within an Asian American family over marriage traditions, it was hot off the press and receiving rave reviews when Rodgers and Hammerstein decided to transform it into a stage musical. They initially wanted Yul Brynner to direct, but he was tied to a contract with Twentieth Century-Fox. They next turned to Gene, who flew to London in early 1958 to meet Hammerstein. "I was very favorably impressed," the lyricist cabled his partner.[23] Carol Haney was to choreograph. A few years earlier she had left Kelly's circle to perform with great acclaim in the stage musical *Pajama Game*, which ran on Broadway from 1954 to 1956, and in the movie version that was released in 1957.

Gene was venturing into unknown waters but was excited about the project. It had been seventeen years since he had done anything on Broadway, and he had never directed a stage musical. His first job was to scour the country for Asian American talent able to handle Haney's choreography, which ran the gamut from modern to ballet. Auditions held in New York, Philadelphia, Boston, and Los Angeles netted fourteen little-known actors. "What most of them lack in show business experience they more than make up for in willingness, charm, and inherent talent," Kelly said.[24]

With Kerry attending school in Europe, Kelly, Coyne, and McClelland moved to New York by late August 1958, taking up residence in Milton Berle's apartment while Berle's family stayed at the Kelly residence at 725 North Rodeo Drive. Rehearsals began September 1. Kelly rehearsed the cast for six weeks and then tried out the show in Boston where some fine-tuning was required. Although Gene talked with Carol Haney about the choreography early on, he left her alone to work out the numbers. She put a lot of dancing into the show. At one point Rodgers had to remind her and Gene that songs were the key to a successful Rodgers and Hammerstein show. True to her tutelage under Kelly, Haney pulled movements from virtually every dance style imaginable, including some traditional Chinese movements, and concentrated on working up the dances from the mood of the songs.[25]

Rodgers worried about Kelly's direction, complaining that he concentrated too much on technicalities and less on shaping the actors' performances. "He flounders so," Rodgers wrote in a letter. Stage manager Jamie Hammerstein echoed that criticism, viewing Kelly's direction as uncertain. In part the problems stemmed from the lack of experience among the cast and what some people identified as the inherent shyness of Asians, limitations that Rodgers and Jamie Hammerstein thought Kelly could not overcome through his direction. But one wonders if Rodgers really understood what was going on. The composer had a habit of criticizing everyone during the rehearsal and tryout stages of every production and he often fell asleep during rehearsals. In his memoirs, Rodgers wrote, "we did the unexpected" in choosing Kelly. But he added, "We were confident he could do a beautiful job. He did."[26] Indeed,

Figure 15.3 Directing Pat Suzuki (as Linda Low) in the Broadway show *Flower Drum Song* (1958). Kelly often acted out exactly what he had in mind, making it very easy for actors to follow his direction. (New York Public Library)

archival photos show Kelly working closely with the actors, just as he did when directing films.

The show opened at the St. James Theatre in Manhattan on December 1, 1958, and ran until May 7, 1960, for a total of 600 performances. Critics liked it but did not love it, which for Rodgers and Hammerstein amounted to something of a failure. But for Gene, it has to be counted as a success. "Gene

Kelly . . . has organized a warm, radiant, fluid performance," wrote Brooks Atkinson, while Walter Kerr called the show "placid, unruffled, cheerfully confident." Audiences loved the show for these qualities even if reviewers were not overly impressed. Advance bookings totaled $1.5 million, and Kelly received a percentage of the gross.[27]

Kelly was satisfied with his first and only Broadway production as a director. He had no illusions about the material. "I knew that as long as I crammed the show brim-full of every joke and gimmick in the book, I could get it to work." He had nothing to do with the film version that was released in 1961. When Chin Yang Lee sent him the script for his next project two years later, Gene said he was unable to go back to Broadway. Instead, he offered to see if there was any interest in making a film version of it, but that did not happen.[28]

With little possibility of making major dance films anymore, Kelly was at a pivotal point in his career. Could he have gone on to do more Broadway shows? When asked to share his thoughts, Kelly admitted that Broadway had changed since his early experience in New York. Shows were beginning to deal with more serious plots and incorporated better music and dance than was common seventeen years before. He recalled *Pal Joey* as uniquely advanced in those ways and thought it had helped to start these trends. But the "thoroughly commercial" nature of Broadway disturbed Gene. In fact, it was "the most commercial thing I have ever been connected with." Its goal was "nothing higher than pleasing the public." The only thing to counteract this attitude was the inspiration of talented artists.[29]

Ironically, Kelly had spent the previous seventeen years in a film industry that was no less commercial. The difference was that he had been cocooned within the Freed Unit at M-G-M, surrounded by creative people of all kinds, and did not have to deal with financial matters as he had to now as a free agent. This is why he did not bemoan the commercialism of Hollywood.

"DANCING: A MAN'S GAME" (1958)

The growing medium of television offered Kelly a plum assignment, one in which he could explore an issue that had bothered him since childhood. Robert Saudek, who had known Kelly while growing up in Pittsburgh, recruited him to put together an episode for the popular *Omnibus* television show he produced. Gene wanted to deal with gender prejudice concerning dance and signed the contract in June 1958.[30] Immediately, he began working on "Dancing: A Man's Game," with the intention of proving to America that dancing was allied to sports and should not be considered a sissy endeavor.

Kelly initially wrote notes concerning what he wanted to do on a large manila envelope in which Saudek had sent information to him. Those notes were later typed up by Lois McClelland, and Gene continued to sketch out his ideas by handwriting further notes on sheets of paper. The first draft of the script for the show, dated December 11, 1958, also had marginal notes written by Kelly as he further explored how to present his views. The second draft is dated five days later but has fewer notes as Kelly veered toward a deadline. "My 2 loves" he wrote, crossing out "hobbies" to substitute "loves," "are dancing and sports. I love to watch them & I love to participate in them. I know that the foundation of my dancing style is a 50-50 mixture of ballet and athletic training, & where one leaves off & the other begins I am never quite sure." He credited his experience as a counselor at a boy's camp for helping him see that dancing was not effeminate. "Athletes there didn't think it was sissy—[they] recognized bodily prowess."[31]

Kelly was dismayed that dancing had been dominated by women for many decades and men's opportunities to be taken seriously as dancers had suffered as a result. He was determined to prove that athletics and dance were intimately related, and did so by recruiting a couple of dozen well-known athletes from several sports to demonstrate their technique and compare the body movements to typical dance steps. Kelly also wanted the hour-long program to be an introduction to dance history in America, in which he would narrate and demonstrate dance heritage with the help of musicians and dancers. It was an ambitious and deeply personal program that only television could offer him.[32]

On December 19, 1958, two days before the live performance of "Dancing: A Man's Game," Edward R. Murrow interviewed Kelly on his *Person to Person* program, broadcast live on CBS television. Gene appeared alone in Milton Berle's Park Avenue apartment, showing America a few things he brought from California to decorate the place, including a montage of photographs of Fred Astaire and himself while working on "The Babbitt and the Bromide." "Fred is always with me," he joked of the montage. When Murrow asked him if he was good at business, Kelly replied: "Can I use the word lousy? I'm pretty much bored with business dealings. I don't sneer at money, I like to get paid well but sitting in on a business deal or trying to wrangle something I find I'm not good at." Gene agreed that Americans were getting too soft and urged anyone who wanted success in show business to "work hard, learn your craft, and like your job."[33] The twenty-minute program came off very well, showing Kelly at ease with the small screen and ready to share selected aspects of his personal life with millions of viewers.

He also plugged his upcoming show, said he had been training for his own dancing in it for the previous two weeks, and asserted his basic premise that athletics were the foundation of masculine dancing. He showed Murrow's television audience the mass of papers laying on the dining table that represented the working out of his packed hourlong presentation and admitted that television was a demanding medium. As codirector of the show as well as narrator and performer, he would have to deal with the fact that television cameramen often used "at least 5–6 cameras, and one can't get in the way of the other."[34]

Parts of "Dancing: A Man's Game" were taped on December 19–20. Then everyone did a full run-through of the live-action parts on Sunday, December 21, at 11 A.M. After lunch, another dress rehearsal took place at 2:45. Kelly had a half-hour break before the live broadcast began at 5 P.M. from NBC's Studio 2 in Brooklyn. Alistair Cooke, the regular host of *Omnibus*, began the program and soon introduced Kelly to take over. Cooke called the program a "well-disciplined orgy of nothing but dancing."[35]

"Dancing: A Man's Game" impresses as a unique attempt to enlighten America about an important misconception and to educate the country about its own dance history. In the program, Gene blended themes personally important to him and enjoyed his widest exposure as a teacher. The first section involved many professional athletes in a complicated sequence of moves that still fascinates today, and the message is made abundantly clear that dancing involves the same kind of physical activity that underlays athletics.

Planning the unusual program involved coordinating the appearance of twenty athletes, five to ten dancers, and half a dozen musicians, and Kelly intermingled with all of them on the show. One of the highlights is a tap routine done to "Broadway Melody" with boxer Sugar Ray Robinson. It did more to prove Kelly's point than any other moment because Robinson holds his own with ease in this demanding dance.

Gene hits a rather coarse note when he argues too strenuously that male dancing is different from female dancing. That point is appropriate for some types of dance, but Kelly pandered to male chauvinism by stating that "we men are always ready to admit that women can do a few things better than men. They can bear children, and they can sing soprano. On the other hand, they'd look a bit ridiculous growing a beard or playing football." He

Figure 15.4 With boxing champ Sugar Ray Robinson, both hoofing expertly. (Still from "Dancing: A Man's Game" on NBC's *Omnibus*, 1958)

differentiated between feminine grace and masculine grace both on the athletic field and on the dance floor. Kelly argued that men should not mistake "beauty of movement with effeminacy of movement. I believe that that is a prime reason for making the American man afraid of the words 'grace' and 'beauty.'"[36] If Kelly pushed this point a bit too far, it grew out of decades of frustration he felt at unfair cultural labels that could be countered only by vigorous assertions. No other television program went to such lengths as Kelly did in dealing with this issue.

For the rest of his *Omnibus* program Gene became a teacher of dance history. He went through a good deal of it, now and then demonstrating a step as illustration. He started by praising Russian ballet for being innovative in the early 1900s and sweeping away old concepts. But for the rest of the show, he stressed the development of a distinctively American dance style built on popular music, tap, and jazz. Nevertheless, he urged the American dancer to begin by studying ballet to develop an appreciation of "line and form," then go on to study modern dance. He explained his own training when telling America, "We know we need the line of the classic ballet, we know we need its training for precision and control. . . . We use the modern dance for strength and emotional expression. These, mixed with the movement of sport gives us what we might call *an American style*."[37]

In some ways this teaching part of "Dancing: A Man's Game" is less effective than the first part. Kelly tried to pack too much information into it, not allowing himself time to explain his points more deeply or allowing his audience—for most of whom all this was completely new—enough time for it to sink in. At times the pace of this live broadcast wore on him; he was a bit out of breath in places and running a bit behind now and then, which forced him to rush through a sentence. But the live performance also highlighted his personal charisma—it is a delight to watch and listen even as he breaks his train of thought and quickly regroups. His sincerity and love for the topic shine through, producing a unique viewing experience.

"Dancing: A Man's Game" received overwhelmingly rave reviews from critics. They were struck by the mix of entertainment and learning as well as by the demonstration of Kelly's previously unknown talent for teaching. Bob Hull called it "an extraordinary march through terpsichore history," and J. Water Thompson found it "a stunning production, expertly directed and executed." Although not his debut on television, "Dancing: A Man's Game" seemed to many Kelly's coming-of-age on the small screen. It was "as entertaining and illuminating as bright conversation," according to Ann Barzel in *Dance Magazine*. One viewer, however, criticized Kelly for paying more attention to popular dance than to ballet. Another viewer, Irma Duncan, the adopted daughter of Isadora Duncan, was irritated that Kelly did not mention her mother.[38]

Kelly received a special award from *Dance Magazine* and a nomination for best choreography from the National Academy of Television Arts and Sciences for this program. The show has worn very well over the decades, garnering from observers the same kind of adulation written by reviewers right after its airing. Kelly remained delighted with it the rest of his life, especially appreciating the fact that Saudek allowed him to write and say exactly what he wanted to. He was more proud of this show than anything else he did on television and received letters about it for decades after. People who were young when they saw it in 1958 wrote to him later to say it had influenced their thinking.[39]

Ironically, only two months after this television triumph, Kelly nearly lost his life in a freak airplane crisis. After a trip to Switzerland with Coyne and Kerry, he flew to London to see if "A Gentleman's Gentleman" could be salvaged. Kerry returned to school in Switzerland, and Coyne flew back to California. Kelly had no luck with the project, and while flying back to the States the Boeing 707 he was in almost crashed. The pilot had put the plane on automatic to mingle with the many celebrities among the 114 passengers, and something went wrong. The plane went into a deep dive and was barely brought out of danger at the last minute. It landed at Gander, Newfoundland, and another plane took the passengers to New York. Kelly recalled that the pressure of the 30,000-foot rapid descent "pinned me to my seat," and before the plane was righted he came to the conclusion that he would die at any moment.[40]

THE GENE KELLY PONTIAC SPECIAL (1959)

After Kelly survived this near tragedy he soon began to prepare for his next television project. The success of "Dancing: A Man's Game" led to a variety show (sponsored by a major automobile manufacturer) called *The Gene Kelly Pontiac Special*. He began working on it in February 1959 and planned a number of innovative ways to entertain television audiences. Kelly commissioned America's most famous poet, Carl Sandburg, to write a new poem to which he would dance. He recruited three ballerinas (Claude Bessy from the Paris Opera, Gerd Andersson from the Royal Swedish Ballet, and Judith Dornys from the Berlin Opera) to do a jazz ballet called "Coffee House" to music by Henry Mancini.[41]

Perhaps the most striking innovation was the debut of Liza Minnelli at age thirteen. The daughter of Judy Garland and Vincente Minnelli had not shown interest in a show business career, but she could sing well. Gene attended a party at Ira and Lee Gershwin's house where Roger Edens persuaded Liza to sing a song. Kelly was struck by her ability and wanted her to perform on his broadcast special. After gaining her parents' permission, he worked up a charming duet singing "For Me and My Gal." Although Liza did well in the rehearsals, when it came time to tape the number Kelly suddenly worried that she might falter in front of the large, live audience. He feared her mother would "scold the hell out of her" and yell at him too. Luckily, Liza "kept cool as a cucumber, and it was I who was nervous as a cat. I remember quivering like a leaf."[42]

The special aired on CBS on the night of April 24, 1959, and was an overall success. Kelly's number with Liza was one of the highlights. It was the first small step for Liza in what would develop into a spectacular career in show business. Kelly was amazed that she did such a good job. He recalled that only two years earlier, Liza, then eleven, had played in his backyard and he had gone out a few times to show her some dance steps. "But I didn't see that she had any greater flair for it than most kids do." Even after the show Liza did not tell anyone she wanted a career in show business.[43] Another highlight was Kelly's soft-shoe with six-year old Cherylene Lee, who had performed at age five in *Flower Drum Song*. The Sandburg piece, "A Poem to Dance To," is not much to write about, and Kelly had to stretch his imagination to come up with dance steps to illustrate it.

In an email interview with the authors, Claude Bessy, one of the three ballerinas, was enthusiastic about the show, calling it "a very interesting and enriching experience."[44] Unfortunately the talents of the three are underutilized. They do some ballet steps while Gene taps to music from *Les Girls*, but their big number, "Coffee House," is a jazz ballet and contains nothing that showcases their balletic talents. It has the flavor of "Slaughter on Tenth Avenue" from *Words and Music* but is performed in a comic way. Kelly interjected a good deal of commentary throughout the show, including the idea that ballet should not be stuffy and therefore the ballerinas would mostly be doing popular dance, much in the way that *Invitation to the Dance* had included some ballet but mostly popular dance.

Gene also gave a mini-lecture on basic popular dance steps with himself in split screen, reminiscent of "Alter Ego" from *Cover Girl*, which is very effective. Both images of him sing to "Any [Dance] You Can Do I Can Do Better," adapted from *Annie Get Your Gun*, to add a competitive but humorous note. In this number, Kelly demonstrates the Airplane Propeller, the Midair Twist, and other steps such as the Maxie Ford. In fact much of the Pontiac special is suffused with segments of Gene's famous dance duets of his film career that he performs with the three ballerinas in turn. The program ends with a scaled-down reprise of "Singin' in the Rain" replete with rain on the soundstage soaking him as he exits with a splash—both figuratively and literally.

GENE KELLY AND THE COLD WAR

Throughout 1959 Kelly became an increasingly vocal critic of Russian dancing. The coming to power of Soviet premier Nikita Khrushchev earlier in the decade had ratcheted up the Cold War with overheated comparisons between the two countries. "American dancers are the best in the world," Kelly told a reporter in February 1959, basking in the wake of critical applause for "Dancing: A Man's Game." In contrast, he said, "Russian dancing today is static, conservative, almost reactionary, while ours has advanced." Comments by Khrushchev probably prompted this assertion from Gene. The Soviet premier added fuel to the fire when he visited the United States during the last half of September 1959. He had lunch with hundreds of Hollywood personalities on September 19, and in his comments following the meal he criticized America for not providing government funding for ballet and opera. He praised Russian ballet as the best in the world and said this was largely because it was funded by the Soviet government.[45]

This prompted Kelly to write a letter to *Esquire* magazine in which he ignored Khrushchev's sound suggestion about government funding for the arts and focused on the comparison between American and Russian dancers. He argued that American popular dance was sweeping the world with its distinctive energy and vitality. He had discussed this idea the year before in an oral history interview for Columbia University, arguing that an American dancer moved in such distinctive ways that one could identify his nationality even without credits or titles. "He's as indigenous as the coke or the hot dog," Gene said. "He just moves around and you know he's American."[46]

Kelly followed up his letter to *Esquire* with an interview for the *Indianapolis Star* in which he continued to criticize Russian dance. "It's very old hat," he said of their ballet. "I don't think Khrushchev knows as much about dancing as some of us think." He characterized Soviet culture as "very reactionary in the arts. I admire their skill but I don't like the fact that they still concentrate on the classics." Pushing the New York City Ballet as the best in the world, Gene noted that "our classical ballerinas can do musical comedy and get more scope." One could enjoy watching Russian ballet in the same way that one enjoys "looking at a picture book," but there was no growth in it.[47]

This commentary on Cold War tensions started Kelly's reputation as a public authority on dance. It was a role he enjoyed, starting slowly at first and then accelerating during the 1960s and 1970s until he was widely acknowledged as the unofficial Ambassador of Dance in America by the 1980s.

"THE GENE KELLY SHOW" (1959)

The first Pontiac special went over so well that Kelly agreed to do a second one, called "The Gene Kelly Show," to be aired as part of the new *Pontiac Star*

Parade series on NBC. Kelly not only put the show together with his own choreography but served as the executive producer. Unlike the first special, this was filmed in color. He tried to create a more smoothly flowing program than the first with less awkward segues from one unrelated number to the next. The cast spent five weeks rehearsing and two weeks in preproduction before taping the one-hour show over three days. Kelly commented on the rushed schedules in television, noting that movie production allowed far more time to rehearse and film.[48]

When it was aired on the night of November 21, 1959, "The Gene Kelly Show" far outshone his first Pontiac special, becoming one of the best programs Gene produced for television. Much of that effect came from using Donald O'Connor in the show, making full use of his friend's enormous talent and displaying the close camaraderie between the two performers. It was the second time Kelly and O'Connor worked together, and one wishes it had not been the last. They obviously loved working together, and Kelly was never teamed with a better male dancing partner. The other guest star, Carol Lawrence, who had created the character of Maria in *West Side Story* on Broadway in 1957, was a good fit for Kelly and O'Connor.

The start of the show, "Has Anybody Here Seen Kelly?," is a rousing Irish romp that brings the program to the audience with verve and skillful tapping by Kelly, backed by a chorus of male dancers. This is followed by Kelly and Lawrence singing and dancing to "Shall We Dance?," an energetic yet romantic number. The highlight of the program is a charming duet by Kelly and O'Connor in which they joke, sing, and dance, sitting on chairs for part of the number as they tap their feet to musical excerpts from their most famous film dances. The segment ends with them dancing vigorously, using the chairs as they did in "Moses Supposes" to the audience's delight.

With "The Gene Kelly Show" Gene consolidated his hold on television, completing the first phase of a long association with the small screen. He brought to it a previously unseen talent for character acting in "The Life You Save," a high-profile role as educator in "Dancing: A Man's Game," and an easy grace while presenting variety entertainment in the two Pontiac broadcasts. One of the best things about television is that it offered the viewer a personal glimpse of Kelly. In "Dancing: A Man's Game" and "The Gene Kelly Show" one can see Kelly between numbers, sometimes out of breath or laughing at O'Connor's antics. We never see such moments in his films. It simply endears him to the audience rather than taking away any illusions. Kelly found his medium, and the audience gets a good idea of what it might have been like to see him perform live.

INHERIT THE WIND (1960)

Even as he was preparing "The Gene Kelly Show," Gene geared up for a supporting role in *Inherit the Wind.* It was a Stanley Kramer adaptation of the stage play by Jerome Lawrence and Robert E. Lee that ran on Broadway from 1955 to 1957 for 806 performances. Kelly portrayed cynical journalist E. K. Hornbeck, based on the 1920s social critic H. L. Mencken, a role created by Tony Randall on stage. Lawrence and Lee freely adapted their script from the actual trial of John T. Scopes for violating a state law prohibiting the teaching of Charles Darwin's theory of biological evolution in the small town of Dayton, Tennessee, in 1925.

Kelly liked the social message of *Inherit the Wind*, which was to attack intolerance and thought control, but the main reason he agreed to play Hornbeck was to work with the film's stars, Spencer Tracy and Fredric March. He had met March on his first visit to Hollywood in 1935 and admired his accomplishments, but Gene was more curious to see how Tracy worked. He kept a keen eye on both of these "giants of the American motion picture," as he called them. March and Kelly seemed to share a common tendency to act for a live audience, displaying emotion so even those in the back rows could see it. But Tracy played for the camera. During filming it seemed as if little was happening, but when Kelly saw the rushes it all came "pouring out of his face." Tracy was "the embodiment of the art that conceals art." Kelly could learn from March but he found it impossible to do so from Tracy. "All I learned from Spence was that no matter what I did, I'd never be as good as he was."[49]

The film was released in July 1960 with a premiere in Dayton, Tennessee. Kelly did well in his limited role as Hornbeck, and *Inherit the Wind* has good qualities. But its overall tone is much too harsh and unhistorical if one compares it to the reality of the Scopes trial.

Critics generally liked the film. Bosley Crowther correctly noted that the main focus of the picture was the titanic struggle between the characters portrayed by Tracy and March with everyone else in relatively minor, supporting roles. One of the other supporting characters was Bertram Cate, Lawrence and Lee's version of John T. Scopes, effectively portrayed by Dick

York. Crowther thought Kelly portrayed Hornbeck "briskly and glibly," but Gene had a different reaction. "I wanted to hide under the seat when I saw that film! I walked like a damn ballet dancer, turn-out and all!"[50]

By the time *Inherit the Wind* was released, it had been eight years since Kelly's supreme achievement in *Singin' in the Rain*. Yet his career was very far from over; it had merely taken several new directions into directing, producing, serious acting, and television.

New Life, 1960–1969

During the 1960s, Kelly continued the new directions in his personal life and his career that had taken place in the second half of the 1950s. His marriage to Jeanne Coyne in 1960 greatly changed his home life, and he once again became a father. Gene returned briefly to stage work, devoted a good deal of time to television, and engaged in the never-ending search for new projects. He acted or danced a small role in a feature film now and then and also developed his career as a director to its highest degree. Kelly enjoyed the first retrospective on his movie legacy in the early 1960s as his film-dance career began to be viewed as history. At the same time, he continued to be viewed as a cultural commentator and the unofficial Ambassador of Dance in America. His interest in politics revived with the ascent of the Democratic Party to power once more after nearly a decade of Republican domination. In every way, the 1960s demonstrated that Kelly adjusted well to the end of the Golden Age of the Hollywood musical, to his divorce from Betsy Blair, and to changing times in politics and the entertainment industry.

Another continuing theme of Kelly's life was his love of Europe. He spent an increasing amount of time there during the 1960s. Gene came up with an idea for a television series called "At Your Service," as part of *General Electric Theater*, about a man, played by Van Johnson, who ran a tourist assistance office in Paris for American visitors. To a degree Kelly planned this to have an excuse to be in Paris and to be closer to Kerry, who at seventeen was still at school in Switzerland. He spent six weeks in Paris to make the pilot in March 1960.[1] The pilot, with background music from *An American in Paris*, was nothing much, typical television fare, and the series never materialized. However, CBS recycled the half-hour show as a television movie called *American in Paris* in 1964.

PAS DE DIEUX (1960)

But soon Kelly had another good reason to stay in Paris. Claude Bessy had encouraged him to develop a production for the Paris Opera Ballet, of which she was lead dancer, when she was filming *The Gene Kelly Pontiac Special* in 1959. He accepted the invitation and worked on it throughout the spring of 1960. Gene called the ballet *Pas de Dieux*, a pun on "pas de deux," meaning a dance for a couple. But literally, the title "Pas de Dieux" could mean "Dance of the Gods" or also "Not Gods," and both terms fit the plot he created about dancing Greek gods with human failings. It was set to George Gershwin's *Concerto in F* and represented a dramatic departure for the Paris Opera Ballet in terms of dance styles. Clive Barnes, who saw the rehearsals, thought Kelly's scenario was similar to *La Belle Hélène* developed by choreographer John Cranko for the Paris Opera Ballet in 1955 in which Bessy had also performed. Barnes knew that Kelly had seen Cranko's work, which Barnes called a "Grecian folly," and liked it.[22]

Whether Kelly was influenced by Cranko's ballet is not clear, but as the first American to choreograph anything for the Paris Opera Ballet, Gene certainly developed a thoroughly American style for *Pas de Dieux*. He spent two weeks teaching the ballet troupe how to perform in a jazzy way. Kelly admitted his French was not so good, but it improved greatly because few of the dancers could speak English. Three of the troupe dropped out because they did not like the kind of dancing Kelly was offering them. Gene thought that, compared to American dancers who could pick up steps easily, French dancers had trouble in this regard and they lacked "crispness even in the things they did best." He had to repeat lessons over and over. The strain told on Kelly. Barnes thought he was "somewhat less than jaunty," while Gene admitted that "training a whole group of classical dancers to dance in an American idiom was pretty tough."[3]

Kelly developed a scenario that revolved around the theme of marital infidelity. Zeus is married to Aphrodite (played by Claude Bessy), who cannot keep her eyes off other males (gods or mortals). She first makes out with Eros, and then the two go to Earth to find mortal paramours. Zeus, who sees all this, comes down to Earth, sends Eros back and tricks Aphrodite by disguising himself as a mortal man. When she is attracted to him, he grabs her and administers a sound spanking, followed by their reconciliation. Each amorous adventure was expressed through jazzy modern dance, including the reconciliation. Kelly also spiced everything up with flashy props—such as chariots descending from heaven and floating beds—as well as inventive choreography.[4]

This first jazz production by the Paris Opera Ballet premiered on July 6, 1960, to thunderous applause. Gene took Grace Kelly to the premiere. Although the main performers were okay, he was not satisfied with the performance of the ensemble. "I felt like weeping," Gene told an interviewer years later. But it made no difference. The audience loved the production for "its newness," as he accurately put it. The performance received a fifteen-minute ovation, and Kelly was made a knight of the Legion of Honor at a reception following the show. Clive Barnes thought *Pas de Dieux* was "a quite terrible ballet but Kelly's guts, humor, panache, and risk-taking still made it an occasion." In her email interview with the authors, Bessy thought the ballet, which she had encouraged Kelly to undertake, was a huge success.[5]

The State Department took notice of *Pas de Dieux* and considered sponsoring a road trip of the show to other countries to promote goodwill for America. That thought never was put into action, but Gene's creation had a life. It remained in the repertoire of the Paris Opera Ballet for nearly ten years, and Bessy mounted it again in 1975 for her farewell performance as lead dancer. She felt it was unfortunate that previous biographers of Kelly did not give the ballet the attention it deserved. Kelly also was irritated that his *Pas de Dieux* was not included in a list of ballets staged by the Paris Opera that appeared in Agnes de Mille's book *To a Young Dancer*, published in 1962. "It has since proven to be their most popular ballet," Kelly wrote of his creation, "and the only one done in what we might loosely call an 'American' style."[6]

LET'S MAKE LOVE (1960)

From trying to crack open traditional European ballet, Kelly went to a cameo role in a forgettable movie called *Let's Make Love*. Yves Montand plays a man who pretends to be an actor to get close to Marilyn Monroe's character. Neither the plot nor the characters are believable, and the whole is marred by the most blatant kowtowing to the lowest common denominator among audience members. The only good part of the picture consists of cameo appearances by Milton Berle, Bing Crosby, and Gene Kelly. Montand wants lessons in comedy and contacts Berle, who performs his usual funny shtick in a futile effort to teach him comedy, then suggests he learn to sing instead. Crosby, in a shorter cameo, finds out that Montand cannot sing either and suggests he learn to dance. Gene's role is the shortest of the three cameos. He is astonished at how badly Montand moves and gives him a mini-lecture on the importance of dancing with his entire body, ending with a slow dance to show him how to partner a woman. Montand's business manager, played by Wilfrid Hyde White, happens to see them and moves away embarrassed, as if there is something romantic between them. Gene's expression suggests he is wondering if the guy thinks he is a sissy because he is a dancer. Although much too short, Kelly's cameo brings in several themes of his dance career to make it more than just an amusing moment in his film work.

NEW HOME LIFE

On August 3, 1960, a month after the premiere of *Pas de Dieux* and a month before the release of *Let's Make Love*, Kelly visited Hedda Hopper at her office for one of their interviews. They spoke of many things relating to his personal life including the woman he recently took to dinner at Dinah Shore's house. Kelly told her it was Jeanne Coyne but did not elaborate. "She was a beautiful girl," Hopper commented. Three days later, on August 6, Kelly and Coyne went to the county courthouse in Tonopah, Nevada, to be married. Lois McClelland and producer George Englund were their witnesses. The couple thought they had tricked the media by their secrecy, but after flying back to Los Angeles they were greeted by a mob of reporters.[7]

Their married life together was vastly different than Kelly's previous marriage to Blair. Kelly was nearly forty-eight and had already achieved many of his career dreams. Coyne, at thirty-seven, was a mature woman whose focus was her family and a comfortable domestic life. She had been happy to work as Gene's assistant for many years mainly to be close to him and to help him. But now she was content simply to be his wife and gave up her work. Gone were the intense, competitive parties of the old days. Instead, the Kellys rarely entertained. They were very happy living a private life of their own. Tim was born March 3, 1962, followed by Bridget on June 10, 1964.[8]

GIGOT (1962)

Jackie Gleason provided Gene with yet another excuse to spend several months in Paris. The "Great One" wrote the scenario for and planned to star

Figure 16.1 Gene and Jeannie, delighted to be Mr. and Mrs. Kelly. (Still from *Anatomy of a Dancer*, 2002)

in *Gigot*, a film about a deaf-mute living in Paris. It was a Gleason product from start to finish—he even wrote the musical score. Gleason considered a number of directors before settling on Kelly. It was the second time that Gene directed a film without starring in it, and he had no control over any other part of the development or production of *Gigot*. Gleason's expensive tastes and ego-driven decisions led to building enormous sets with a production cost of $5 million, more than double what a typical film musical of the Golden Age demanded and far more than a nonmusical. It was an astoundingly high cost for a straight dramatic film with comedic overtones.[9]

Kelly worked well with Gleason and the mostly French cast, directing them in their native language during the four-month production phase in the summer of 1961. Gleason and the young Diane Gardner were the only Americans in the cast. Reporter Eugene Archer observed Kelly at work and noted that a dancer was the best director for a comedian because timing was so important to both arts. Once when Gleason forgot some small business before the camera, he threw off the complex tracking plan and Kelly had to ask for a retake. He did so "with some trepidation" because of Gleason's well-known temper and the fact that he so dominated the plot of the film. "Jackie has to draw a thin line between pathos and burlesque," Kelly told Archer, "without a word of dialogue. No matter how closely we try to work out every move, we still have to improvise—and that means throwing a lot of footage away." But the Great One obviously bowed to Kelly's viewpoints—Archer saw a hand-lettered sign hanging on his dressing room door that read "'GENE KELLY IS RIGHT.'"[10]

Kelly was not involved in the editing of *Gigot*, and Gleason did not own the rights to the final cut. The production company, Seven Arts, did the editing without consulting either one. When the movie premiered in September 1962, both Kelly and Gleason were unhappy with the result. "It was not the picture I directed," Kelly said. "It was good but not great, as it could have been."[11] Viewing *Gigot* today it is difficult to know what Gleason and Kelly did not like about the edited version because no one has seen the version they had approved. The film works as it is—Gleason puts in a good performance and Kelly's direction is quite effective.

Gleason's biographer William Henry offered gentle criticism of Gene's direction: "Kelly's genial, nice-guy humor had almost no point of connection to Gleason's plot with its rituals of cruelty and submission." He also criticized the narrative as "fragmentary rather than cumulative" and the ending as offering "no promise of happiness." Critic Bosley Crowther thought that Gleason's schmaltzy and scene-hogging presence on the screen was the major problem.[12] We disagree with these criticisms. The movie works well even if it might have been better without further editing by Seven Arts.

In the draft of an article Kelly wrote for Crowther, he said the production company "had made some forty-odd cuts and changes" to his version. "To say they've altered the look and 'feel' of the movie is putting it mildly." But he urged everyone to see *Gigot* "to watch the phenomenal Gleason at work. He's a joy!" Nevertheless, based on the high-handed way they handled this picture, Kelly managed to get out of his agreement to do two more films for Seven Arts.[13]

GOING MY WAY (1962–1963)

For his next project, Gene accepted a job that brought him much closer to home in more ways than one. He took on the role of a Catholic priest named Father Chuck O'Malley in the television series *Going My Way*, based on the popular Bing Crosby film of the same name released in 1944. Joseph E.

Figure 16.2 Gene as Father Chuck O'Malley with Leo G. Carroll (as Father Fitzgibbon) and Nydia Westman (as the housekeeper). (Still from the television series, *Going My Way*, 1962–1963)

Connelly, who coproduced the long-running *Leave It to Beaver* series (1957–1963), produced this series, which premiered on ABC on October 3, 1962. Leo G. Carroll portrayed O'Malley's superior, Father Fitzgibbon. Gene played the star role differently than had Crosby, making him "more of a fighter."[14] Dick York joined the show as the head of a boy's club in St. Dominic's Parish.

The role allowed Kelly to stay at home more often and do something quite different from his previous work. The first episode was the only time he danced. He performed an Irish jig with Father Fitzgibbon, very similar to his brief, joyful dance with the coaches in *Take Me Out to the Ball Game* before his Irish solo. He also sang a ballad and did well even in the high notes. Lauren Gilbert, who played Dr. Nash with Gene in *Combat Fatigue Irritability* seventeen years earlier, filled the role of Dr. Warnaker. In the same episode, Kelly inserted a private joke saluting his uncle, both brothers-in-law, and older brother when Father O'Malley said to the crowd at a party, "You all know Gus Curran, Mike Radvansky, Bill Bailey, Jim Kelly—the choir." In a later episode, Gene inserted a similar inside joke, saluting his parents and siblings when Father O'Malley read pledge cards for donations to St. Dominic's by reciting the names of Harriet, James, Eugene, Louise, and Frederick.

Kelly created an athletic priest in Chuck O'Malley, throwing a boy on the mat during judo practice and playing ball with the neighborhood kids. He showed his athletic prowess even in catching fly balls while walking by as the kids are playing. He portrayed an activist priest who becomes a positive part of the working-class Manhattan community the parish serves.

Kelly was frustrated when the network, in deference to the church, cancelled a planned episode in which a girl who is thinking about abortion seeks O'Malley's help.[15] Nevertheless, many episodes hit serious themes in effective ways while inserting a good deal of gentle humor, warmth, and solid moral values. The series did a fine job of showing what it was like to live in a Catholic environment during the 1960s.

Gene's mother was happy her son was portraying a priest on television. By this time she had given up the Kensington Street house and had moved to Kenmawr Apartments on Shady Avenue in East Liberty. Harriet watched *Going My Way* religiously. When he called her early in December she "chided him slightly for what she regarded as mumbling certain of his lines," according to reporter Fred Remington. "I guess he got kind of mad," Harriet admitted.[16]

Dick York greatly admired Kelly, having seen him on the screen while growing up in rough Chicago neighborhoods. He was taken by the fact that Kelly portrayed characters who were tough and vulnerable at the same time and appreciated Gene's ability to move the audience either joyfully or sorrowfully. The two developed an easy working relationship. When York brought his wife, Joey, to the set Kelly kidded her by saying, "'My God, Dick, she isn't ugly at all," which made them all laugh. York had badly injured his back while filming *They Came to Cordura* (1959). Twenty-five episodes into *Going My Way* he experienced a difficult period with back pain and restricted movement. Without consulting him, Kelly persuaded Connelly to install ramps on the sets and create places where York could ease into a comfortable position while waiting for his call. York always remembered Kelly fondly, and called him: "A cool man. A kind man. A perfectionist. A tireless worker."[17]

Going My Way did relatively well with the audience but not well enough when placed in competition with *The Beverly Hillbillies* (1962–1971). After one season it was cancelled, with the last new episode airing on April 24, 1963, and reruns taking it to September 11 of that year. Although a bit frustrated at the limitations placed on the development of his character, Kelly retained fond memories of the show. "I liked it very much," he told an interviewer in 1971.[18]

Soon after *Going My Way*, Kelly joined his friend Danny Kaye for a delightful performance on *The Danny Kaye Show*. He appeared on the fifth episode of the first season, which aired October 23, 1963. Watching the two interact reveals what a delight *Huckleberry Finn* could have been. They sing several songs from Kelly's Broadway and film career and do a soft-shoe routine, all the time lacing their performance with comments and personal asides that make the show very appealing.

THE FIRST RETROSPECTIVE (1962)

The early 1960s introduced the beginning of retrospective looks at what the public considered Kelly's most important work of the past. In 1962, the Museum of Modern Art hosted complete showings of nine films and excerpts of two others from September 2 to October 6. The complete films ranged from *For Me and My Gal* to *Les Girls* and the excerpts were "Slaughter on Tenth Avenue" and "The Babbitt and the Bromide." In the catalogue to accompany this retrospective, Richard Griffith penned one of the earliest evaluations of Kelly's film legacy. Griffith wrote in very complimentary terms, stating that Kelly "has made the dance come alive to millions of people who previously eyed it with suspicion." But when analyzing Kelly's objective in melding dance into the plot and characterization of a film, Griffith was less than successful at making his points. Gene appreciated the attention but years later criticized Griffith for not interviewing him. Kelly found some of Griffith's points to be contradictory and others "I frankly don't understand." At the time, however, Kelly attended at least some of these showings and composed an article for Bosley Crowther in which he wrote that the enthusiasm shown by the audience "was a source of great joy to me. . . . It made all those sweaty hours behind and in front of the camera very worthwhile."[19]

Retrospectives are curious things. They are tacit acknowledgements that an artist's best days are past, but at the same time they can rejuvenate current interest in his legacy. Ironically, Kelly was continuing to build his legacy even as this retrospective immortalized him as an icon of film history.

SEARCHING FOR PROJECTS

Gene continued his quest for major projects throughout the early 1960s. *Le Jazz Hot* was to be filmed in Paris and London, and *The Bohemians* was to be filmed in New York, both projects to take place in 1960 or 1961. Kelly was to direct and star in the former, and star and do the choreography in the latter.

Neither project materialized. Two years later, in 1963, Kelly agreed to a three-film deal with Warner Brothers. He would produce one film, costar in another, and direct the third, with Frank Sinatra to star in all three. But this fell through when Sinatra delayed coming to California from New York for so long that Kelly became exasperated and dropped out of all three projects. The two had a frank discussion about this and remained friends, but it is an example of Kelly's strong sense of professionalism that he refused to put up with such a lackadaisical attitude about work. Universal arranged for Kelly to direct *Beau Geste* and then a film version of the stage comedy *Send Me No Flowers*, but he backed out of both projects due to conflicts concerning control and hiring actors. Gene developed the idea for a musical about a pilot in World War I with George and Ira Gershwin songs, but that too never got off the ground. In one of the more outlandish possibilities, the producers of *Hair* tried to talk Kelly into directing a film version of the innovative stage musical. He was not impressed that "they had no script, and you can't ad lib a movie musical. . . . You need discipline and coordinated teamwork." Obviously, he refused.[20]

Gene also considered going back to the stage if he found worthy projects. Jerome Lawrence and Robert E. Lee finished a script for a stage musical with Sinatra and Kelly in mind. Set in 1938 and titled "The New Yorkers," the draft notes do not look too interesting, and it is not surprising that the show was not made. Kelly briefly worked with playwright Samson Raphaelson, evaluating "Here We Are, Alone Together," but the play was never produced. He politely demurred when Samuel and Bella Spewack tried to talk him into appearing in their remake of *Leave It to Me* in 1967. In the same year, the New York City Ballet wanted Kelly to choreograph a production of "Slaughter on Tenth Avenue" for the stage. Unfortunately, Gene had to decline that request as well because he was heavily involved in three major television and film projects.[21]

ENCOURAGING YOUNG TALENT

Kelly also began to emerge as a national cheerleader for the performing arts in America during the 1960s. He expressed optimism that Hollywood was entering a golden age of film production despite the demise of the old studio system. He was no longer so optimistic about Broadway but saw regional theaters as "mushrooming" both in quantity and quality. "There is a real cultural boom," he gushed in 1965. "It could rival the Renaissance in Italy." But in

"Some Notes for Young Dancers," published in *Dance Magazine*, Kelly warned aspiring artists that dance had to be adapted to the cinema by growing it out of plot and character development. Otherwise it was just a stage dance in a film.[22] He was trying to teach the younger generation what he had practiced since the early 1940s in terms of fully integrating dance into film musicals.

When Kelly was invited to write the introduction to John Springer's pictorial history of film musicals, published in 1966, he pointed out that Hollywood excelled in this area. The movie musical was "one of the few peculiarly American art forms" he wrote, "and, at its best, it certainly is art." He drew international attention as an expert on the future of the film musical. The editor of the French journal *Cinema 64* corresponded with him about "la nouvelle vogue," which was inspired by Kelly's *On the Town* to emphasize quick cutting and location shooting. In a 1965 article for *Sound Stage*, Gene effectively traced the history and development of the film musical from the 1930s to the 1960s and expressed excitement that good ones were still being made now and then. He pushed for more filming of musicals on location and regretted that he could not do this with *Brigadoon*. Nevertheless, he noted that it was very expensive to make a film musical, and an audience had to be willing to pay for it before production companies were willing to risk the venture. He realized this kept many aspiring young dancers from trying their hand at cinema, in contrast to the days of the studio system.[23]

Gene did what he could to encourage young dancers. He was disappointed that no one was documenting the leading dancers of the day to serve as learning tools for beginners. "My own generation has done very poorly at this," he admitted while he encouraged the creation of "a dance film library." Agnes de Mille, whose book *To a Young Dancer* Kelly admired as a teaching tool, completely agreed with Gene. Noting that there were up to 5 million dance students in America during the 1960s, she scolded the country for offering them little in the way of making a living by their art. Having criticized Soviet premier Nikita Khrushchev after he said the same thing in 1959, Kelly did not openly second de Mille's concern. But he tried to help by allowing the American Ballet Theatre to use his name in fundraising drives.[24]

POLITICAL ACTIVISM

After nearly a decade of Republican domination in Washington, Kelly again became active in political efforts during the early 1960s. He joined a group called SANE (Stop All Nuclear Explosions), which pushed for limitations on nuclear testing worldwide. He joined nearly ninety Hollywood personalities to support Democratic candidates in the 1960 general election as the political tide in Hollywood shifted toward that party. He agreed to speak at a rally held on the night of April 13, 1962, to protest the bombing of homes belonging to two ministers who criticized right-wing extremists for calling anyone who supported the United Nations a communist. Many Hollywood liberals shied away from this rally fearing retribution, but Kelly boldly participated.[25]

Hollywood was bowled over by John F. Kennedy, the charismatic Democratic president elected in 1960, and Kelly gave himself up to the Kennedy aura. He was an emcee at the Democratic Gala to raise funds for the party in January 1963, attended by the president. Gene asked each performer to sing something Irish, but no one did until Kennedy himself stood up and volunteered to sing "The Wearing of the Green" with Kelly. At a special party for seventy-five guests at Lyndon Johnson's vice presidential home following the fundraiser, Kelly danced as Carol Burnett sang "Singin' in the Rain." Gene also developed a friendship with Kennedy's younger brother Robert, who served as attorney general. Gene was among the guests at a party fundraiser in New York in December 1965 where Robert was the guest of honor. At a rally for Robert in Los Angeles during the run-up to the 1968 election, Bobby was late so Gene entertained the crowd by waltzing and fox-trotting with a volunteer to thunderous cheers.[26]

"I've always been a Democrat," Kelly told Tony Thomas. He was proud to have been included in White House invitations by Franklin Roosevelt and Harry Truman but was especially thrilled "to become a good friend of John F. and Robert Kennedy. I had good times with them and I believed in what they were trying to do." He did not consistently support all Democrats, involving himself only in the fortunes of "those in the Democratic party about whom I have felt strongly."[27]

INTERNATIONAL AMBASSADOR OF DANCE

Kelly's many new roles in the early 1960s—including his international stature, his developing profile as a cultural commentator, and his connections to the administration—combined to offer him a unique opportunity. The State Department wanted him to tour internationally as a cultural ambassador for America. He would take along a forty-five-minute film consisting of excerpts of his best cinema dances along with a projectionist and show them in central African nations over a three-week span early in 1964. Most of those nations were newly independent, former French colonies that were being courted by the Soviet Union. Once again, Cold War angles came to play a role in Kelly's work. He was not expected to perform—just to show his film, lecture, and interact with the people.[28]

Gene left Washington, DC, on January 3, 1964, to begin his journey. The first stop was Dakar, Senegal, where he spoke in French to secondary-school and university students, and showed 16-milimeter prints of excerpts from *Anchors Aweigh*, *Words and Music*, *An American in Paris*, and *Singin' in the Rain*. He went on to the Ivory Coast, Upper Volta, Niger, Congo-Brazzaville (Republic of the Congo), and Congo-Kinshasa (Democratic Republic of the Congo). Kelly found that many of the young Africans knew him far better for *The Three Musketeers* than for his dance films. The audiences at his talks varied widely from a handful of people to several thousand. He spoke to educated, sophisticated people in some cities and to poor, rural people in other areas. Wherever he went, though, Kelly was energized by common interest in the dance. "Africans love the universal language of dancing and they responded so well to the film clips." He thoroughly enjoyed mingling with people, trading dance steps, and talking about dance movement. It was not easy traveling through the rural areas, especially due to anxiety about catching an illness through a mosquito bite, but the three weeks were worth the risk, in his view.[29]

In Ghana, an English-speaking country, the government strongly leaned toward the Soviet Union. Mark B. Lewis, an employee of the US Information Agency in Accra, the capital, had been a moving force behind Kelly's visit. To prepare the way, he first showed Gene Kelly movies in local theaters. They were such a huge hit that 3,000 people greeted Gene at the airport when he arrived, and many more lined the streets to watch him pass by. A theater happened to be showing *Singin' in the Rain* and the car stopped to let Gene introduce himself to the owner, who "nearly fainted" when he realized the star himself was in town.[30]

The next day a woman cosmonaut from the Soviet Union arrived in Accra and received full coverage in the news media with only a small photograph of Kelly tucked away in a corner of one newspaper page. There was a caption but no story about his visit to Accra. To compensate for this official neglect, theater owners who had prints of his movies placed huge ads to say that Kelly was in town and would appear at some of the theaters showing his films.

Thousands of eager spectators thronged the theaters and the streets hoping to catch a glimpse of the actor and Gene made the most of it. He went to as many theaters as possible, "parted the curtains and appeared on stage under spotlight. There was such happy pandemonium and tumultuous cheering" that Kelly could not speak until the delighted audience had quieted down. He also lectured at the university and other venues and was genuinely interested in African culture. He often asked people at his talks to show him typical dance steps. "Oh boy, I wish I could do that!" Lewis recalled him saying, as he tried a few steps. There was no doubt in Lewis' mind that Kelly's five-day visit to Accra had a noticeable effect, as anti-American rhetoric by the government decreased. Even the newspapers came to publish lengthy stories about his visit. "I am convinced that Gene Kelly was one of the most effective representatives of the United States abroad in my 25 years as a USIA foreign service officer," Lewis wrote more than thirty years later. He credited this to Kelly's "friendly, unpretentious nature, his openness and cheerful manner." Lewis was also impressed that Gene's "approachability off-stage matched his professionalism."[31]

WHAT A WAY TO GO! (1964)

From the heights of his African tour to the reality of making a living in post–Golden Age Hollywood, Kelly agreed to a role in *What a Way to Go!*, a black comedy with a screenplay by Betty Comden and Adolph Green. Gene had taken an option on the property three years earlier when it was called *The Richest Girl in the World* but sold it to Arthur Jacobs, who now produced it.[32]

What a Way to Go! premiered in May 1964. Shirley MacLaine as Louisa Foster marries a series of men, all of whom die and leave her a great deal of money. Kelly played Pinky Benson, husband number four. When they meet he is dancing and singing in a clown suit at an Italian restaurant, thoroughly ignored by everyone except Louisa. They marry and live on an old houseboat. A dream ballet on the deck of a ship signifies their happiness. But Louisa then encourages Pinky to drop the clown suit in his act. He does so, and now suddenly everyone notices and applauds him. In fact, he becomes the hottest act in show business. It goes to his head, and he is killed by a stampede of adoring but maniacal fans.

Kelly choreographed his dances and the ballet with MacLaine, although he received no credit for it. The pair worked out for a month to get into shape

Figure 16.3 Entertaining an indifferent audience as Pinky Benson the clown. (Still from *What a Way to Go!*, 1964)

even though their dance together was not very demanding.[33] In his own numbers, Kelly used many familiar steps, including the Midair Twist. Comden and Green incorporated several sly references to *Singin' in the Rain*, including the premiere at the beginning of that film. Gene went along with this, playing "Don Lockwood" in his final scenes, smiling and blowing kisses to the fans before the crowd stampedes over him. He carried off his performance with a pleasant, tongue-in-cheek air appropriate to the screenplay.

MISSED OPPORTUNITY

Gene missed an opportunity to become involved in an iconic film of the era when he turned down an offer to direct *The Sound of Music*. Ernest Lehman wrote a screenplay adaptation of the Rodgers and Hammerstein stage musical, which was doing very well on Broadway. When Lehman visited Gene at his North Rodeo Drive home, Kelly made it abundantly clear that he was not interested in the project. The reason was that the stage version was widely panned as too saccharine and many artists were reluctant to take part in it. Even Julie Andrews hesitated until she was convinced that the film version would be drained of much of the unnecessary sugar. While critics wrote very harshly of the stage musical, in which Mary Martin starred, audiences loved it so much that this last Rodgers and Hammerstein collaboration ran for 1,443 performances and garnered six Tony Awards. Robert Wise directed the picture, much of which was filmed in Europe, and it became an instant success in the United States and internationally. Eventually *The Sound of Music* earned $286 million, becoming the fifth-highest grossing film in history.[34]

Whether the film would have turned out the same if Kelly had directed it is not easy to say. The fact is he shared many people's concern about turning the stage version into a film musical. It turned out all of them were wrong. Still, Gene very soon thereafter appeared as a guest on *The Julie Andrews Show*. The taped episode was aired on November 28, 1965, on NBC. They performed a medley of songs from *Singin' in the Rain* with umbrellas and a curtain that sparkled to roughly simulate rain drops. Gene also danced an Irish jig, a sailor number, and some of his favorite moves, including the Crab Bounce.

Critic Jack Gould thought Kelly "has never been seen to better advantage on TV."[35] This, of course, is not true. Gene's television appearances by himself, with Donald O'Connor, and even with Danny Kaye are far better. Nevertheless, it is an interesting show, partly for the irony that Andrews was about to experience a tremendous high in her career because of the movie that Kelly refused to direct.

GENE KELLY IN NEW YORK, NEW YORK (1966)

Kelly's next television production was *Gene Kelly in New York, New York*, a one-hour variety show reminiscent of the film musical of the Golden Age but set in a modern urban environment. With director Charles Dubin, Kelly taped for two days in the studio and an additional five days on location in October 1965. The most difficult part was an all-night filming at the Museum of Modern Art's Sculpture Garden for a five-minute sequence in the special. Many things went wrong. Water had to be hauled in for the fountains from outside the state because of a water shortage in New York. Plywood that was needed to cover the marble floor of the garden (for camera movement) got stuck in traffic, so Masonite boards found in the museum were deployed. The generator used to power the lights ran out of gas and caused more delays. The dancers huddled in winter coats while all this was taking place until the cameras were ready to roll, finally finishing this exhausting process just before dawn. A reporter thought Kelly's sense of perfectionism was another cause for the drawn-out process. He reshot many scenes, examining each shot on tape before deciding whether to keep or redo.[36]

The special is a tribute to New York that mimics the spirit of *On the Town*, replete with an introduction that takes Kelly to many well-known buildings, parks, and landmarks in the city. Gene ice-skates at the Rockefeller Center and roller-skates with children in Central Park. Woody Allen provides some comedy, and British entertainer Tommy Steele tries his hand at tap dancing. The sequence filmed at the Museum of Modern Art is the highlight of the show. Despite the many difficulties, it comes off well, with Kelly dancing in sequence with several women and in varied moods and tempos.

When it aired on February 14, 1966, on CBS, *Gene Kelly in New York, New York* was not well received by Jack Gould, who had delighted in Kelly's pairing with Julie Andrews the year before. He found it "a tepid facsimile of an old-fashioned film musical." Eulogizing a city had worked well in 1949's *On the Town*, but it seemed old hat by the time of the gritty 1960s. Gould found a "clinical tone" and wished Kelly had not danced all the main numbers. Gower Champion appeared as a guest, but Gould felt his talent was wasted in simplistic choreography. Only Steele seemed to present a fresh face, and Gould was sorry that he did not do more on the program. All told, *Gene Kelly in New York, New York* probably was too much nostalgia, too much trying to remind the audience of past glories, and not enough keeping up with the times.[37]

JACK AND THE BEANSTALK (1967)

From that limited success Kelly went into a project that meant something more to him. He once again tried to fashion entertainment for children that could also appeal to adults by asking Joseph Barbera if they could do an animated special for television. Barbera was interested and suggested the story of Jack and the Beanstalk. Gene created a role for himself as Jeremy Keen, an unusual peddler who not only provides the magic beans for Jack but also accompanies him up the beanstalk to best the giant. Eight-year-old Bobby Riha played Jack.[38]

As producer and director, Gene carefully went over an early script and marked it up. When Jeremy was to cook an Irish stew for the giant, Kelly crossed it out, wrote "No like!" in the margin, and it was cut. He nixed many other elements such as the "talking" cow, a song called "I Sure Hate Love" that Jack was supposed to sing, and character names such as "Goosey Lucy." He introduced Jack's mother and an entertaining dance with two "Woggle Birds" into the story. Kelly added a bittersweet ending to the part with the animated Princess Serena. She goes home alone on the goose while her newly found love, Jeremy, has to return to "reality." But Jeremy's meeting Jack's mother, also called Serena, makes it a happy ending. The many differences between the early script and the finished product demonstrate how much Kelly was involved in preproduction. Three four-by-six index cards filled with Kelly's handwriting also demonstrate how minutely he planned Riha's dance with a corps of animated mice in the "Upper Lip" song. This is one of the few extant sets of notes produced by Kelly that show how he worked out choreography.[39]

Kelly and Riha performed three dances together. The first was set outdoors to "Half-Past April" on their acquaintance. The second was in the giant's colorful garden after they climb the beanstalk. The third was on the giant's table jumping and dancing on a giant-sized knife and fork as bricolage. Riha danced well for an eight year old. His singing was dubbed by thirty-nine-year-old Dick Beals, whose voice sounds perfect for young Bobby.

Riha recalled the experience in a phone interview with the authors. Two to three months of rehearsal took place at an Episcopal church in Los Angeles followed by another two to three months of filming on two soundstages in the studio. Kelly knew "exactly what he wanted" both in the rehearsals and the production phase and guided Bobby's dancing minutely with tips such as "take bigger steps here." When Riha could not, after many tries, get the timing right for yelling, "A giant is coming!," Gene had an animated mouse do it. Riha remembered that the wooden floor was marked to block out the action and a large trampoline was used for jumps. Bright blue painted foam served as the background so animators could add "scenery" later. The "knife" was a rectangular box on cables. The fifty-foot fiberglass beanstalk, a well-behaved cow, and harnesses to take the costars twenty-five feet into the air also made an impression on the young actor. He recalled that Kelly nearly fell at one point when they were in the air. Riha said he grabbed at Kelly and wondered if Gene was afraid of heights.[40] Obviously that was not the case as seen in Kelly's many aerial stunts in various movies. But in their second dance in the giant's garden, Gene does wobble dangerously in an aerial scene. The harness seems to have been mainly at the waist rather than the shoulders, or it may have come loose, causing him to tip forward precariously and nearly fall.

In planning the Woggle Birds sequence Kelly once again made detailed notes concerning action and dance steps. He wrote phrases such as "maybe fanny stuff, crouched & bouncing," "turn into tango," "bird squats to other side," "woggly walk," and "peckin' walk 1½ bar, into fanny twist 1 bar." For the end, where he escapes from the Woggle Birds, he wrote, "gallop, hand over eyes, I peek on 3rd bar—they pass me on the 4th & 5th bar." Riha recalled

Figure 16.4 Gene's first of several dances with Bobby Riha (as Jack). (Still from the television special, *Jack and the Beanstalk*, 1967)

Figure 16.5 As Jeremy the peddler, performing a highly entertaining dance with animated Woggle Birds. (Still from *Jack and the Beanstalk*, 1967)

Figure 16.6 Jeremy and the animated Princess Serena in a love-dance to "One Starry Moment." (Still from *Jack and the Beanstalk*, 1967)

watching Kelly film this number and how he danced alone on a huge soundstage. He called Gene "bigger than life."[41]

Alex Romero worked as Kelly's assistant for *Jack and the Beanstalk*. He danced in for Gene, performed as a Woggle Bird during rehearsals, and observed Kelly's performance while filming.[42] In short, he did what Carol Haney and he himself had so often done for Gene in the movies.

Karel Shimoff, who had performed as the Sugar Plum Fairy in the London Festival Ballet's production of *The Nutcracker*, danced the part of Princess Serena in rehearsals. But during filming Kelly danced his part of that sequence alone. It was another love dance with an animated woman, performed to Sammy Cahn's "One Starry Moment." The precision had to be exact in matching the scale of the animated figure with Kelly, or else he would be looking beyond her head instead of into her eyes. Hanna and Barbera did not hit the mark exactly, as one can see from a careful viewing of the finished product. Kelly admitted that mixing live action with animation demanded precision but argued that it did not inhibit creativity or spontaneity.[43]

There are obvious parallels between *Jack and the Beanstalk* and the "Sinbad" segment of *Invitation to the Dance*, but there are differences as well. In both stories a man meets a young boy, a woman, and some threatening characters. Whereas the snake, the dragonlike serpent, and the guards in "Sinbad" are subdued with music, the giant in *Jack* is killed. Gene's only dance with David Kasday in "Sinbad" is extended and more complex than all his dances with Riha and makes good use of the eleven-year-old Kasday's terpsichorean skills. His dance with the animated Woggle Birds is similar to his dance with the animated guards in "Sinbad," although the latter is longer and has more demanding steps. His love dances with the animated princesses in both venues are similar, but again the one in "Sinbad" is more extended and complex. Both stories have happy endings with the trio on their way to becoming a family. Perhaps due to the limited appreciation that *Invitation to the Dance* received, Kelly wanted to re-create the magic of "Sinbad" and he did just that with some modifications in *Jack and the Beanstalk.*

Aired on February 26, 1967, on NBC, *Jack and the Beanstalk* was a sterling success. Touted as the first television special to mix live action and animation, it won an Emmy for Outstanding Children's Program.[44] If Kelly had made "Sinbad" as a children's special for television, it too would likely have won accolades and awards.

THE YOUNG GIRLS OF ROCHEFORT (1967, 1968)

Kelly's optimism about the future of the film musical led him to appear in Jacques Demy's *The Young Girls of Rochefort*. Demy was a rising director and writer who had achieved acclaim for *The Umbrellas of Cherbourg* (1964), a musical that blended elements of operatic convention with popular music. All dialogue was sung, all movement planned for dance effect. He wanted to do the same for *Young Girls*, and Kelly was taken by the concept. "It may be another breakthrough," he told an interviewer in 1966. "Another new style for musicals. How well it will succeed, I don't know yet."[45]

But Demy missed his cue with this one. The film's most prominent impression is one of artificiality. The plot is too thin, the characters undeveloped, the situations unbelievable. The constant singing with sophomoric lyrics is grating. The picture has too much dancing of an undistinguished character, and even Kelly does not appear at his best. He is unusually thin, apparently having lost a good deal of weight and muscle mass. His dancing lacks spark or feeling; it tends to mimic old moves such as the Airplane Propeller but without the verve and muscularity of the past. He spoke his dialogue in French, but his singing along with that of all the principal actors was dubbed. Even the spoken lines that lead into songs were dubbed. The voice used for Gene did not work. It detracted from anything enjoyable that might have been there.

Critical reviews and audience reaction were mixed when the film was released (March 1967 in France and April 1968 in the United States). Surprisingly, some people liked the movie. But it has to rank at the bottom of Kelly's musical projects for the big screen. When he returned to California after production in France, Kelly regretted being away for six weeks while his two young children were growing up quickly. "My kids looked as though they were twenty years older." He decided to be more careful about choosing roles that required long absences from home.[46]

NEIGHBORS

An unusual insight into Kelly's life at this time comes from his neighbors. The Zekaria family moved in next door in the summer of 1967. Ruth Zekaria Levy, who was six years old at the time, told the authors in an email interview that Gene was a quiet, friendly neighbor. He was a loving husband to Jeanne and an affectionate, involved father to his children. Ruth remembered Jeanne Coyne as "very sweet and warm" and Tim and Bridget as unaffected by their father's fame. When Ruth broke her leg at age eight, Kelly saw her being carried to the car for transport to the hospital and rushed out of his house with a pillow to be put under her leg. When she was back home, he visited her and gave her a stuffed toy animal.[47]

Ike Zekaria, Ruth's brother, told the authors in an email interview that, even though Tim and Bridget were older, they invited him to play. Sometimes when he played in his backyard with a friend, a ball would go into the Kelly's backyard ("mostly by accident," he humorously added) and he and his friend would go over to retrieve it. Gene was always reading or working in the living room, but he answered the door and chatted with the boys for a few minutes. Ike said Kelly was "always friendly and welcoming" even though the ball incident happened fairly often.[48]

Ruth also mentioned that Lois McClelland was a very nice lady and very friendly. She sometimes called to request that they keep their dog indoors in the morning so the barking would not wake Mr. Kelly. When the Zekaria children were older and had a Fourth of July party, playing loud music "with amp and mic" by their pool, Kelly walked in through the back gate while all their friends stared at him. He "very sweetly and quietly explained" that he was trying to listen to Vivaldi records and if they could lower their volume, he could enjoy his music.[49] All these refreshing memories shed an interesting light on Kelly as a good and thoughtful neighbor.

A GUIDE FOR THE MARRIED MAN (1967)

After his return from France, Kelly could stay at home for the next major film of his career, directing *A Guide for the Married Man*. Frank Tarloff wrote the screenplay after talking with friends about their extramarital affairs, putting in actual incidents about how they made mistakes and were caught by their wives. The film literally is a guide for successful infidelity. Producer Frank McCarthy at Twentieth Century-Fox wanted Frank Tashlin to direct it, but Tarloff disagreed. "It had to be done with style and class, or otherwise it would be sleazy." Tarloff thought of Kelly; a copy of the screenplay was sent to him while he was still in France, and Gene agreed. "I liked him. He was very easy to work with," Tarloff noted.[50]

By all accounts, Kelly worked well with everyone involved with the project. Tarloff established a good rapport with him from the start, asking Gene when he should bring up a suggestion if he had one. Kelly told him he should do it after he set up a shot, and Tarloff cooperated. If an actor asked him about how to deliver a line, Tarloff referred them to Kelly. McCarthy appreciated Gene's work ethic and his focus on getting the movie filmed on time and under budget. "He had a job of work to do and he did it with a professionalism almost unique in my experience of the industry." McCarthy also admired Kelly's way of dealing with the players. "His touch was so light with actors that he almost danced behind the camera. He allowed each of the guest stars to 'do their thing' yet he managed very subtly, quietly and diplomatically, to make them fit the structure of the story." Kelly had a gift for talking to actors, knowing "how to cater to their whims, while at the same time being firm."[51]

Walter Matthau, the star of *A Guide for the Married Man*, developed a good working relationship that developed into friendship with Kelly. Matthau thought Gene had "a definite flair for comedy and directing comedy." The only troublesome actor was Robert Morse, whose fame had come from creating the role of J. Pierrepont Finch in the 1961 Broadway stage musical *How to Succeed in Business Without Really Trying*. After 1,417 performances, and because he was currently starring in the film version (also in production at this time), Morse wanted to play Ed Stander exactly as he did Finch. That was impossible but Kelly eased Morse away from that idea with gentle coaxing that was "a work of art" in McCarthy's view.[52]

As with most of his projects, Gene took every opportunity to learn something new about his craft. He spent hours listening to sound tracks, observing the editing process, and "trying to absorb as much as he could, as often as he could," in McCarthy's words. He experimented with dialogue that overlapped scenes, with quick editing, and with other techniques that seemed to fit the style and pace of the film's content. "At times he seemed to choreograph the film along the lines of a fast-paced modern dance, often shouting out the rhythms he wanted as if he were a ballet master."[53]

A Guide for the Married Man glamorizes infidelity while also poking fun at it, a direction in storytelling that was possible in the late 1960s with the decade's changing cultural values and social mores. But one does wonder why Kelly found it an appealing storyline with the breakup of his first marriage in mind and given that it did not comport with his personal values. It is possible he took it on simply as a directorial challenge. From a purely technical viewpoint, he did a magnificent job of directing the picture. Camera setups are interesting, the acting is right on cue, and everything is done with a crispness that is refreshing. If one can overlook the fact that many of the characters and situations are painfully mean-spirited and that the plot makes light of marital cheating, which usually poisons and embitters the people involved, then it is possible to enjoy the film.

The film was a big critical and popular success on its release in May 1967. Bosley Crowther highly praised Kelly's "lively direction," done with speed and "freedom from the leer," which made the film "thoroughly disarming and delightful." "Wouldn't Lubitsch love this!" wrote Samson Raphaelson to Kelly after seeing the film. "Right from the beginning of your picture, touch after touch gladdened my heart." Box-office receipts delighted everyone at Twentieth Century-Fox. Kelly was quickly signed up to direct *Tom Swift and His Wizard Airship* with McCarthy as producer. But that project fell by the wayside because Gene was offered *Hello, Dolly!* instead by the same studio.[54]

In *A Guide for the Married Man*, Kelly continued to prove his prowess as a director. He mastered the technical aspects, molded performances from recalcitrant actors, delivered the project under budget, and appealed to a wide popular audience. He pleased everyone with his efficiency, his good-natured interactions, and his commercial success. Also, Gene demonstrated once again his touch for light comedy that deals with a potentially controversial issue.

Directing certainly appeared to be Kelly's most important opportunity by the late 1960s, but a guest appearance on *The Jackie Gleason Show* demonstrated that his dancing days were not over. The poor showing of *The Young Girls of Rochefort* was completely dispelled when Gene danced with the June Taylor Dancers to "Shall We Dance?" The episode was aired on February 22, 1969, and gave Kelly an opportunity to perform good choreography with great vigor and joy. No matter how much he aged, Gene could pull out a great performance when he had the chance.

HELLO, DOLLY! (1969)

Based on the success of *A Guide for the Married Man* and critical praise for Kelly's direction, Richard Zanuck at Twentieth Century-Fox gave him the job of directing *Hello, Dolly!* The project took Kelly's career as a director to new heights. But the story of how it did so is complicated.

The plot of *Hello, Dolly!* began with an English play of 1835 that became the basis for a German play of 1842 and was transported to Broadway in 1938 by Thornton Wilder's *The Merchant of Yonkers*. Wilder revised it fifteen years later as *The Matchmaker*, which ran for nearly 500 performances. It was made into a film by Paramount called *The Matchmaker* in 1958. Later, a stage musical version called *Hello, Dolly!* opened on January 16, 1964, with David Merrick as producer and Carol Channing as Dolly Levi. It played on Broadway until December 27, 1970, with 2,844 performances. Richard Zanuck purchased the film rights for $2.5 million but was contractually obligated to wait until the show closed before releasing his picture.[55] Nevertheless, Twentieth Century-Fox threw everything it could into the project, authorizing a ballooning budget that even producer Ernest Lehman could not control.

Kelly knew he was taking on the most difficult directing job of his career when he agreed to join in Zanuck's wild ride. He worried about making a two-and-a-half-hour movie based on a smash Broadway hit that admittedly had a pretty thin storyline and only one really big song. "Then, my curiosity and the challenge took over," he wrote, "and I accepted the job." Lehman was happy to have Gene on board, seeing his talent and experience as essential for the project. Lehman also hired Michael Kidd to choreograph the many dances so Gene could devote himself entirely to directing.[56]

The old studio system was long gone, so Kelly could not count on a readily available troupe of contract dancers to use in *Hello, Dolly!* "We scoured the

Figure 16.7 Director Gene Kelly, producer Ernest Lehman, Shelah Hackett (Kidd's assistant and future wife), and choreographer Michael Kidd, taking a break during the filming of *Hello, Dolly!* (1969). (Ernest Lehman Collection, Harry Ransom Center, University of Texas, Austin)

English-speaking world for people who could sing and dance and at the same time play comedy," auditioning 1,500 of them and running lots of film and television footage to find more. After a busy preproduction phase, filming began on April 15, 1968, in California and continued until the end of May.[57]

Then the company moved to Garrison, New York, a small community on the eastern bank of the Hudson River fifty-five miles north of New York City. Kelly finally realized his long-cherished dream of filming dances on location. Garrison was remodeled into Yonkers for several sequences, most importantly for a major dance to "Put on Your Sunday Clothes." The lead-in to this dance had already been filmed at the Twentieth Century-Fox studio in California, but the rest of the number would be shot on the streets of Garrison and nearby Cold Spring. During his visit to the area in February, Kelly had picked the exact buildings and streets to be included in filming. Kidd choreographed and Kelly directed forty-two dancers and a hundred extras on June 18 and 19.[58]

The result is a magnificent realization of his dream. Dancers as well as the camera setups move fluidly from indoors to outdoors to take full advantage of the open space. Groups of dancers move from right to left of view in the typical way Kelly liked to film dance movement. Main characters, supporting characters, and extras gather at the platform of Garrison's train station as the principals prepare to go to New York for a day of excitement and romance. Kidd's choreography—always better than his dancing—is superb. Kelly climaxed the number by filming from a helicopter as the train pulls out of Garrison. He also had arranged for helicopter shots to vitalize a long and exciting sequence for the opening credits of *Hello, Dolly!*, depicting the train moving toward Yonkers from New York through the beautiful Hudson River Valley.

If Kelly and Vincente Minnelli could have achieved results like this from location-filming on *Brigadoon*, then perhaps that troubled project could have been redeemed. Kelly had to wait fifteen years for the chance to realize some of what he envisioned by breaking out of the studio to make a dance musical. "Put On Your Sunday Clothes" is confirmation of his vision, representing the real possibilities of creating a new style of musical.

Kelly's ability to keep the cast on target was tested to its utmost on *Hello, Dolly!* Barbra Streisand, who was just on the cusp of an explosive career at a young age, was in many ways miscast as Dolly Levi. She was much younger than the character and had been chosen for her extraordinary singing ability. But as one of her biographers points out, it was more than a mismatch of age. "She didn't have Dolly's maturity, confidence, or warmth." To make matters worse, Streisand had little respect for Kelly, disdaining a tap dancer–turned–director and not at all understanding his achievements or capabilities. She had a need for direction and coddling so deep that probably no director could have satisfied it. Kelly tried to guide her as much as he could, but he had many headaches to attend to, and Streisand had little ability to find her own center of gravity. As Walter Matthau said, she may have been a star, but she was not an actress at that point. Kelly and Streisand maintained a working relationship, but neither was entirely satisfied with the end result of her performance. Nevertheless, Kelly saw the good points in Streisand, praising her intelligence, willingness to learn, and work ethic in an article published on the release of *Hello, Dolly!*[59]

As for the costars, Streisand and Matthau engaged in a legendary feud. Matthau was thoroughly disgusted at Streisand's constant overstepping of her bounds in trying to tell Kelly what to do. He knew what a great director Kelly was from having worked with him previously and resented Barbra's self-importance. The result was a persistent bad mood on the set that often exploded into tense confrontations. The worst of these occurred when Bobby Kennedy died of an assassin's bullet on June 6, 1968. The next day, the news saddened and depressed everyone on the set at Garrison. Matthau exploded at Streisand, and Kelly had to call off work for three hours while he calmed the two of them down. Michael Crawford, an actor in the film, was greatly impressed that Kelly, who was crushed by Bobby's assassination given their personal friendship, was still able to handle the emotional crisis between his stars. Streisand's troubles were not solely directed against Kelly or Matthau. She argued with many people in the production (including Irene Sharaff, over costumes). One biographer writes that her insistence on repeated takes for *Funny Girl* had been enormously costly for the studio, and it was not just for *Hello, Dolly!* that she was so insecure.[60]

Gene's patience with Streisand and with the enormous job of directing this movie had its limits. The massive parade sequence along Pico Boulevard involved 3,000 to 7,000 people, according to different sources. The three-day event taxed Kelly to the limit, but he was able to handle the task for the most part. He had to shout instructions to the huge crowd and lost his voice for several days. Lehman had written into the script that the sequence should end with a wide crane shot with Streisand in the middle of the huge crowd hitting the last note of "Before the Parade Passes By." For some reason Gene wanted to keep the shot long and narrow, not wide, on the end note. When Streisand complained to Lehman, the producer confronted Kelly, who exploded in anger and told Lehman he could direct the shot himself. Lehman was nervous because he had never directed before, but he did it and the wide angle shot worked beautifully. To his credit, Gene admitted he was wrong and that he was glad Lehman redid it.[61]

At other times, Kelly fiercely protected the boundaries of his job as director during filming. When Lehman once made a suggestion to Michael Crawford about how to play a close-up, Kelly told him in no uncertain terms that he had no business directing his players. Kelly felt he had a great deal to share with actors, especially when they delivered songs. He had learned many ways to compensate for not having a powerful singing voice—such as using his arms and body movement as well as emotion to put the number across.[62]

Michael Crawford, an English actor, had been recruited by Kelly for the role of Cornelius Hackl. Crawford had never danced before, had only sung as a teenager on the London stage, and had been focused on acting rather than singing when Gene contacted him. Referring to the character, Gene told Michael, "He's an attractive idiot. Now, my wife . . . well, she thinks you're attractive. And I . . . think you're an idiot." They hit if off from the start. Gene coached him to the point where he sang and danced perfectly for the role. In filming his biggest song, "It Only Takes a Moment," Crawford put "as much honest emotional intensity as I knew how" into it. "I looked up at Gene when I finished and saw he was in tears. He came over and put his arm around me. 'That's my boy!' he said." Crawford was forever grateful that Kelly opened new doors in his career. Gene taught him the value of extensive rehearsal as well as how to deliver a song in a believable way. Crawford's long career was climaxed by creating the starring role of *The Phantom of the Opera* in London in 1986 and bringing it to New York two years later.[63] That stage musical continues to be performed in both cities today. Crawford might not have had as successful a career as a singer if not for Kelly.

Not everyone praised Gene's direction of *Hello, Dolly!*, but their criticism is easily overshadowed by supportive commentary and evidence. Casting director, Hugh Fordin, called him a competent director but thought he could not block out shots from the crane for the parade. Actually, except for the final shot that Lehman redirected, Kelly did a wonderful job filming from the crane. Dance arranger, Marvin Laird, thought Kelly had concentrated too much on camerawork and not enough on coaching the actors. (His criticism is totally based on Streisand's complaints about not getting enough guidance.) Michael Crawford raved about Kelly's efforts in teaching and guiding him and Walter Matthau consistently praised Kelly's direction.[64] This echoes how actors in other films, such as *The Tunnel of Love*, admired Gene's direction in coaching actors. Also, Kelly's expertise in crane work is evident in many of his films, especially *Invitation to the Dance*.

Despite rumors that Kelly and Kidd did not get along, there is ample evidence that they worked well together. The two came to a "broad agreement" about "where a number should take us," but then Kelly let Kidd alone to work it out. At the same time, he wanted to know what Kidd was planning so he could offer "constructive suggestions." The two agreed that they should film as many dances as possible outdoors at Garrison and on the lot at Twentieth Century-Fox. Because of rain delays, Kelly had time to help Kidd rehearse groups of dancers during filming at Garrison. "We didn't have as much collaboration as we would have liked," Gene later said. For example, he could have benefitted from Kidd's help in managing the huge masses needed for the parade sequence, but Kidd was busy preparing for a major dance to be filmed immediately after that sequence.[65]

Production of *Hello, Dolly!* ended in September 1968 with costs ballooning from an initial $10 million to more than $22 million. Kelly received $277,500 in salary. The budget got out of hand mostly due to the elaborate sets and the cost of filming in New York. Release was delayed a year because Merrick continued his Broadway show as long as it was making money. *Hello, Dolly!* finally premiered December 16, 1969, with a great deal of hoopla. Initial public response was high. Advance ticket sales totaled more than $1 million, double that for *The Sound of Music*. But *Hello, Dolly!* did not have the sustaining power of the previous blockbuster, which it sorely needed to offset the huge production cost. After years of television airings, videocassettes, and DVDs, *Hello, Dolly!* finally came close to recouping its cost.[66]

Hello, Dolly! became one of the more controversial movies of its era for many reasons. Its enormous cost—three times that of *The Sound of Music* for far less financial gain—tends to be the main point of criticism. So much money invested in what admittedly is a slender plot is a legitimate point. Critics cite the miscasting of Streisand and her floundering performance, also legitimate criticisms.[67]

But the picture has far more going for it if one looks beyond the legendary cost and Streisand's problems. Clive Hirschhorn calls it "the best film musical of the sixties" and credits Kelly with playing a huge role in achieving that distinction.[68] He is right. After reading for years about how bad *Hello, Dolly!* was, the authors were stunned by its quality on first viewing it. The boldness of the visual imagery is striking, from the initial aerial shots of the train speeding through the picturesque Hudson River Valley to the stunning aerial shot of the wedding on the banks of the same river during the finale. The quaint little chapel for the wedding scene was constructed in California, brought to the campus of the United States Military Academy at West Point, and set up at a location to maximize the scenic beauty of the last shot. There is a sense of grand showmanship throughout the picture that works despite all the plot and character problems.

Zanuck strongly encouraged this larger-than-life aspect of the film, which was why the studio approved such a gigantic budget. Twentieth Century-Fox had invested so much money to obtain the rights to Merrick's play that it "wanted to turn it into a whale of a good show," as Gene put it. But by the late

1960s, Twentieth Century-Fox's musicals were losing money. Spurred on by the astounding success of *The Sound of Music*, Zanuck had authorized *Doctor Doolittle* (1967) with Rex Harrison and *Star!* (1968) with Julie Andrews. Both films flopped at the box office with enormous losses, $11 million for *Doctor Doolittle* and $15 million for *Star!*. Appearing only one or two years before *Hello, Dolly!*, both of those films share equal responsibility with Kelly's movie in closing the curtain on Twentieth Century-Fox's brief moment as the preeminent producer of film musicals in the 1960s. The studio lost $77 million in 1970, with only nine of its thirty-three releases during 1969 and 1970 making a profit.[69]

Yet *Hello, Dolly!* was a huge achievement for Kelly as a director. In it he not only shared his enormous expertise at making film musicals with a new generation of actors such as Michael Crawford, but he was also able to fulfill a long-cherished dream of filming dance sequences on location (and in outdoor settings on the backlot), something not fully possible during the Golden Age of the Hollywood musical. The picture's dance numbers are among the very best ever filmed, even when compared to Golden Age pictures. The fact that the world was changing, values were altering, and youth-driven movies with hard-edged portrayals were becoming the vogue, lends an air of nostalgia to *Hello, Dolly!* that is palpable.

Kelly Resurgent, 1970–1979

After the 1960s, a decade of personal happiness and hectic work, Gene endured the worst phase of his personal life in the early 1970s. His beloved wife, Jeannie, died, leaving him the sole parent for his two young children. Kelly's career continued along the lines already established the previous decade in terms of taking on small acting roles, television projects, and directing. But there was now an added twist—he could accept only those projects that did not take him away from the children too long. At the same time, there was a remarkable upsurge of public interest in Kelly's achievements during the Golden Age of the Hollywood musical. Even as Jeannie dealt with the devastating leukemia that eventually took her life, Gene was becoming the object of much attention as numerous interviewers, oral historians, and biographers viewed him as a cultural icon.

THE CHEYENNE SOCIAL CLUB (1970)

The last feature film Gene directed and coproduced was *The Cheyenne Social Club*, a western starring James Stewart and Henry Fonda. Kelly enjoyed their sense of professionalism after having to deal with Streisand and called it "a lovely picture to do." It was filmed mostly near Santa Fe, New Mexico, with Jeannie and the children in tow. Production was difficult because Stewart's stepson was killed while serving as a Marine in Vietnam. "I knew what he was suffering," Gene recalled, so he filmed around Stewart on the days when the actor found it particularly difficult to concentrate, and Gene sometimes cancelled production for a day to give the star time to reflect. Stewart made it through this difficult period, and the movie was finished on time.[1]

The Cheyenne Social Club, released on June 12, 1970, was at best a modest success. Screenwriter James Lee Barrett was dissatisfied with Kelly, viewing him as "a sweet guy" out of his element as a director of westerns. Barrett even criticized Kelly for coddling Stewart when the actor was stricken with grief.[2] Barrett's criticisms are difficult even to understand much less accept. *The Cheyenne Social Club* is not a typical western. It is a portrayal of the friendship between two men, one of whom has inherited property that turns out to be a house of prostitution. There is more gentle humor than violence, and Kelly handled that gentle humor with skill. Even the gunfight sequence is filmed crisply and with a sense of reality that often is missing in typical westerns. The two actors play their roles with a sardonic edge that works. One gets the impression Kelly had a good sense of what the script called for, and Barrett was unable to explain why he did not like the end product.

In both *Hello, Dolly!* and *The Cheyenne Social Club*, Kelly took full advantage of location shooting, and in the second project he had fun juxtaposing a train with the house to create interesting effects of living near a railroad. Gene deserves a good deal of credit for facilitating the close bond established between the characters portrayed by Fonda and Stewart. These two friends had a long relationship, and Kelly was well aware of it. He facilitated their bonding on screen to allow for the chemistry to come through. By the time of the gunfight the viewer is engaged and excited because by then Gene has well set up the two characters as likeable and their friendship as believable.

Kelly established himself as a good director of big musicals, suburban comedies, and now westerns. His forté was dance films, but he proved his worth as a director of several other genres as well. Kelly was a versatile director who never received the credit he deserved for it because people tended to focus on him as a dancer.

MISCELLANEOUS PROJECTS

Gene's devotion to his family constricted future opportunities to direct. He tended to accept jobs that would keep him near home, and television was the prime opportunity. He therefore agreed to host a comedy-variety series called *The Funny Side*. Premiering on NBC on September 23, 1971, it consisted of skits on a different topic every week and involved five couples to represent the young, the elderly, the rich, the working class, and African Americans. Kelly hosted each episode and participated in some of the sketches and production numbers. The audience seemed to like the episodes better when Gene participated, but the success of the series was limited by stiff competition from the other two networks. The show went off the air on December 7, 1971.[3]

Kelly thought he had an opportunity to work with Liza Minnelli, who had begun developing a career in entertainment, but it proved to be a false call. Cy Feuer was producing a film version of *Cabaret*, a stage musical based on Christopher Isherwood's 1930s stories about gay life in Berlin. Liza was slated to portray Sally Bowles. Feuer wanted Bob Fosse to direct the picture, but his financial backers insisted on a higher profile director, in part because Fosse's latest directorial endeavor, *Sweet Charity* (1969), was a flop. Feuer had to at least pretend to seek a well-known director and approached Billy Wilder, Joseph Mankiewicz, and Kelly to mollify his backers. He considered Gene a friend and felt bad about approaching him because Kelly was genuinely excited about the prospect. "These were only half-hearted interviews," Feuer admitted. "My mind was made up on Fosse before I saw any of them."[4]

Kelly never knew this because Feuer kept his agenda secret. As far as Gene was concerned, he would have liked to direct *Cabaret* but felt he could not because it was to be filmed in Munich and the trip would have taken him away from his family for too long. Kelly recommended Fosse to Feuer, little knowing that Feuer had already decided on him. The producer thought Kelly could have done the picture but it "would have been more . . . frivolous. It wouldn't have Fosse's dark side." That was the key to Feuer's decision. He wanted to develop the mix of music, Nazism, and sexual edginess in the Isherwood stories and the Broadway show based on them. Kelly probably would not have been able to do this to Feuer's satisfaction. Fosse's deep paranoia made filming *Cabaret* a severe trial for everyone, especially Feuer, but the end product was highly successful with the critics, the audience, and the Motion Picture Academy.[5]

The next project that Kelly undertook was a risky venture called *Clownaround*. It was a stage show centered on a large and complicated clown machine from which various actors popped out to perform. Kelly was excited about the project given his lifelong fascination with clowns and the challenge of directing an unusual show. He began auditions for seventy performers in October 1971 with an opening a few months later in Oakland, California. After a few weeks the show closed when the producers ran out of money and also because two dancers fell eighty feet from near the top of this monster prop and were badly injured.[6] *Clownaround* certainly was an experiment but one that failed.

40 CARATS (1973)

Kelly also graced a movie production of *40 Carats* at about this time, lending an otherwise forgettable film an interest that keeps it alive. Based on a Broadway play that ran from December 26, 1969, to November 7, 1970, for a total of 780 performances, it depicted a romance between an older, divorced woman and a young man.

Kelly agreed to portray Billy Boylan, the former husband of the divorcée played by Liv Ullmann. He liked the script and was particularly interested in working with Ullmann. But Jeannie was then ill and he hesitated until his wife insisted he do it. The studio was only twenty minutes away, and Kelly devoted a mere six days of filming to the project. Even so, he did an engaging job of creating the screen version of Billy. At one point Kelly dances with Binnie Barnes, as an older couple might trip it on a dance floor surrounded by young people more comfortable with 1970s dancing. And yet, as Pittsburgh reviewer Dan Lewis wrote, "they appear to be enjoying themselves enormously." Released on June 28, 1973, by Columbia, *40 Carats* was a mild success with the audience. Critic Vincent Canby disliked the movie as a whole but thought Kelly "gives the impression that he might still be as charming as we all remember him in 'Singing in the Rain.'"[7]

LOSING JEANNIE

The early 1970s were the most tragic period of Kelly's personal life. On March 11, 1972, when he was in the Midwest searching for talent to place in *Clownaround*, Jeannie told Lois McClelland of unusual bruises on her skin. Two days later, after Gene had returned to California, she was diagnosed with leukemia. Although doctors warned that she could die in three weeks, Jeannie survived with courage and grace for more than a year. She made many arrangements to help Gene and Lois run the household and take care of Tim and Bridget. Gene's mother passed away during this time on June 1, 1972, at age eighty-six. Kelly had been paying the costs of her residency at the Negley House, a nursing home in Pittsburgh, for ten years. Harriet was buried at Calvary Cemetery where Gene's father had been buried sixteen years before.[8]

Jeannie passed away at the City of Hope Medical Center in Duarte, California, on May 10, 1973, at age fifty. Gene and his small family were devastated and had to cope with their loss. Tim later recalled that his father would psychosomatically suffer illness each year when the anniversary of her death neared. "It was a tremendous sense of loss, of emptiness," Kelly told interviewer John Land in 1980. He was certain that having two small children who needed him was the key to dealing with the loss of his beloved wife. Gene decided that their welfare took precedence over his career. "Daddy has to be there," he said. "I don't want any medals for it. I think you're responsible for anyone you bring into the world." In turn Tim and Bridget helped their father out of depression and hopelessness. Jeannie had prepared them well, and they were strong after she died. "They're my whole life right now. They gave me the will to carry on when I didn't know what to do with my life." In July 1973, the family visited Kerry in London, where she was living with her husband, a Canadian psychologist, and their baby daughter. They also took a trip to the Black Hills of South Dakota in the spring of 1974 as part of their healing and stayed in a cabin.[9]

OL' BLUE EYES IS BACK (1973)

Gene's first work-related activity after losing Jeannie was a guest appearance in *Magnavox Presents Frank Sinatra*, an NBC broadcast on November 18, 1973. It was a comeback for Sinatra after a brief retirement and was so successful that he released an album called *Ol' Blue Eyes Is Back*, which retroactively tended to be viewed as the title of the television special. In fact, Kelly was the only guest star for the hour-long program, but according to scriptwriter Fred Ebb he was not Sinatra's first choice. The singer wanted comedian Redd Foxx. When Ebb felt uncomfortable writing for a comedian and suggested Kelly, Sinatra reluctantly agreed. It is possible he thought Gene was not yet ready for this after his loss. Ebb was surprised to hear Sinatra refer to Kelly as "Shanty," probably a reference to old stereotypes of Shanty Irish on the lowest rung of society, but Gene did not seem to mind. "He was the sweetest man, always humble and gracious," Ebb recalled.[10]

There also was a bit of trouble with a song titled "We Can't Do That Anymore," which Ebb had written for an unrealized stage musical and thought would work well for the pair. Sinatra did not like it. "I don't want to do a number like that with Gene," he told Ebb. It is likely he was afraid Kelly would be offended. They did it anyway because before Sinatra and Ebb could work out this problem, a sound engineer who had no idea of Sinatra's reluctance to

Figure 17.1 Relaxing with children Bridget and Tim in the backyard of their Rodeo Drive home in Hollywood. (Still from *Anatomy of a Dancer*, 2002)

sing it asked Gene if he was ready to record the number. When Kelly eagerly said yes, Sinatra simply went along with it.[11]

Good for the sound engineer, because the number is the highlight of the show. It pokes gentle fun at aging after showing the pair's hit dance numbers from *Anchors Aweigh* and *Take Me Out to the Ball Game*. Then, as they sing about not being able to do that anymore, they proceed to do a little of it anyway. Kelly performs toned-down but still impressive versions of the Airplane Propeller, the Crab Bounce, and the Midair Twist to enthusiastic reception by the live audience. After softly singing a few lines from "For Me and My Gal," Sinatra calls on him to "Sing it!" and, pumped by the excitement and adrenaline, Kelly shouts "I *am* singing it!" The two perform songs from their movies together and laugh about how long ago it all was. Sinatra admits how terrible his movies were before Kelly took him on board. Finally Sinatra sings "Nice and Easy" while sitting down as Kelly dances, sometimes slowly but often breaking into a fast pace that greatly excites the audience. Kelly has to pat down his toupee on both sides of his head after these brief spurts of exuberant dancing. The number ends with the pair walking slowly off stage, with Gene trying to break free a couple of times to dance fast, which the audience enjoys.

It would have been impossible for Sinatra to have had a success like this with Redd Foxx. Kelly and Sinatra obviously enjoyed each other's company, especially when they got into the spirit of old times, and Kelly was mostly responsible for bringing that charm and excitement back to their relationship.

TAKE ME ALONG (1974)

Kelly's next undertaking greatly helped the family to heal from their loss. He agreed to portray Sid Davis in a touring company of *Take Me Along*, a Broadway musical that had run for 448 performances from October 22, 1959, to December 17, 1960. It was a remake of Eugene O'Neill's play *Ah Wilderness!* on Broadway in 1933 in which Gene Lockhart created the character of Sid, a lovable alcoholic whose efforts to woo Lilly continually fail because of his inability to beat his drinking problem. Other characters in the extended family, however, were the main focus of O'Neill's play as they were in the M-G-M movie of the same title, directed by Clarence Brown and released in 1935. A gem of a film, Brown's picture faithfully reproduces the characters, with Wallace Beery offering an endearing portrayal of Sid. M-G-M released a musical version titled *Summer Holiday* in 1948 with Frank Morgan as Sid that utterly failed to reproduce the charm and interest of the 1935 movie. David Merrick's Broadway musical of 1959 featured Jackie Gleason as Sid and changed the characters drastically, making Gleason the center attraction. Not surprisingly, Sid is a bigger-than-life character, brags of his drinking, and clearly wins Lilly in the end, whereas in the original play and movie this aspect is left open.

Merrick's production was a far cry from both O'Neill's play and Brown's movie in spirit as well as detail, and whether one liked it depended on how one felt about Gleason. Kelly agreed to sign on mostly because he was ready, after a year of quiet reflection at home, to do something. Moreover, because it was to be a summer tour of half a dozen cities, he could take the kids along. The company had to recruit local actors in each town for extras, which gave Tim and Bridget an opportunity to "do bit parts or be in the chorus." The kids loved the experience and stayed up till midnight to have dinner with their dad and the cast after the show.[12]

The family flew to Dallas in June 1974 to join the company, and Kelly immediately established a good relationship with his costar Patricia Wilson, who portrayed Lilly Miller. Nearly seventeen years younger than Kelly, Wilson had been singing on stage mostly in touring companies of *Carousel* and *South Pacific*. Her biggest success was in *Fiorella!* on Broadway. Wilson's second marriage, to Art Franklin, was in deep trouble when she took on the role of Lilly. Unable to rejuvenate his own career in public relations, Franklin was jealous of her success. Perhaps that is why Wilson initially assumed the worst of Kelly when he introduced himself, said he knew she was not a dancer, and mentioned something about her height. She could barely control her anger. "Does my height concern you, Mr. Kelly? I'm quite a good method actress. . . . *How tall do you want me to be?*" That brought a laugh from Kelly and the offer of a friendly conversation over a beer. "We'll get along fine, Pat. You'll look great onstage, and that'll make me look good. Call me Gene."[13]

The two became close friends during the summer run of *Take Me Along*. Wilson was impressed by how much Kelly enlivened the cast, bonding with the group and "embracing the role of Sid with Irish charm." He introduced dancing to Sid's character, including tap, soft-shoe, and free style in a number where he meets the townspeople as he steps off a train. In another dance routine set to the title number, he included Side Heel-Clicks and the Crab Bounce even though he was pushing sixty-two years of age. Wilson suggested they do a simple dance when they sing "But Yours," and Kelly worked up something that would not be too challenging for her. Wilson and Kelly sang three songs together including "I Get Embarrassed," after which Sid chases Lilly around the furniture and both end up in a chair. One night she stumbled and both fell into a love seat, Kelly on top of Wilson, and the audience loved it. "Milk it, kid!" he whispered to her, and Wilson "shrieked appropriately," letting her legs fly into the air and showing her bloomers. Both were prepared for the other to improvise. Once, Wilson kicked Kelly in the rear and it was followed by an impromptu look of surprise on Gene's face. For Wilson, trying to deal with an explosive relationship with her husband, the "frisky fun" of "I Get Embarrassed" became a healing experience, and she felt it was the same for Kelly as he continued to deal with his grief.[14]

Opening in Dallas on June 17, *Take Me Along* was an unqualified success mainly because of Kelly. Reporter Aline Wilbur called Gene's dances the highlight of the show. She thought the entire production was faster, tighter, and funnier than the original. Wilson said the reviews were overwhelmingly good, mainly "raves for Gene Kelly." Although Gene had confessed to Wilson that he had qualms about returning to the stage after thirty-three years of movies and television, critics and audiences loved him. At Gene's suggestion, Wilson brought her two daughters along for the tour so they could be part of the group of extras and play with his children. Kelly also brought along Lois McClelland and his cook Bessie for the tour, one day sending Lois to bring Wilson to his room so he could ask her to witness the signing of his new will. When New York producers saw the Dallas show they offered to finance a Broadway run, but Kelly refused because he did not want to disrupt his children's lives with an extended stay from home.[15]

From Dallas the company traveled to St. Louis, where the reception was just as warm. Kelly was in his stride and told a reporter that he would not worry about having enough energy until he was ninety-five. "The minute I hear that orchestra tuning up, I get that old feeling in the tummy" he said, and felt ready to go on stage. Reporter Michele Willens characterized Gene as "a warm, unpretentious man whose eyes carry a non-stop smile." By the time the company reached Dayton, Ohio, Kelly was taking a deeper interest in the orchestra. He personally rehearsed with the musicians, even asking some of the strings to be dropped because he was not satisfied with the harmonies of a certain section. Moving on to Warren, Ohio, Kelly drove his kids forty-five miles northeast to show them Conneaut Lake in Pennsylvania, where he had vacationed as a boy. Many Pittsburghers traveled to Warren to watch their city's favorite son. When the tour ended at Columbus, Ohio, Wilson's hometown, Kelly wanted to make it a special event by upping the enthusiasm of the performance. Wilson recalled that his embrace and kiss at the finale was longer and more fervent than before, which drove the audience wild.[16]

When Wilson and her daughters returned to their California home they found that Art had moved out, ending their troubled marriage. She remained a close friend of Kelly's for many years to come. They often talked on the phone for hours "about books, work, the children, and the sweet mystery of life," but they never developed a romance.[17]

Colleen Lester was another member of the *Take Me Along* production whose life Kelly touched in a memorable way. An apprentice assigned difficult tasks such as keeping the props in order and often bullied by her bosses, Lester was frustrated that she did not have an opportunity to act. Kelly had asked her to stand in the wings where he was supposed to exit because he could not see that spot very well, and in the process he noticed that she seemed unhappy. Lester told him the reasons and expressed a great deal of disgust with certain people in the production. "Don't let them bother you," he told her. "The ones who are the most insecure are the ones who are the meanest.

True talent seems to show itself most often in kindness." Lester was greatly helped by Gene's concern and advice, which made her change her attitude.[18]

Gene's only stage performance after *Pal Joey* was a sweet and affecting experience for everyone he touched, but it would not be repeated after 1974. Kelly slowly began to see other women soon after. By May 1975 he was dating *Los Angeles Times* columnist Joyce Haber enough for reporters to note that there could be a romance developing between the two.[19] But Kelly apparently was not ready for marriage.

REVIVALS AND INTERVIEWS

It is ironic that in the early 1970s, around the time that Kelly had to deal with the illness and loss of his wife, public interest in his career began to soar. He received awards for his contributions to the performing arts from a number of universities and other institutions. Revivals of his best film work picked up, as did a tremendous increase in the number of people who wanted to interview him. These interviewers were mostly interested in his past work, not his current or future projects. They saw Kelly as a part of film history and wanted to record that history from the lips of the man who had made it.

Some of the revivals and interviews took place before Jeannie was diagnosed. A retrospective held in England started the decade in November 1970. Held at Chalk Farm, a suburb of London, it featured several of his Golden Age films and a guest appearance by Kelly, who danced a bit for the audience before settling down for a question-and-answer session. There was also a Gene Kelly Day in London that same month where people gathered to meet him. Only the month before, Kelly saw a long string of interviewers approach his door or write to him asking questions about his work. Kelly admitted to Michael Burrows that it was a tossup between *Pal Joey* and *The Time of Your Life* as to his most satisfying stage work. To Edward Blank, Gene said that his greatest achievement as a director was *Singin' in the Rain*.[20]

Most of the interviews occurred during Jeannie's illness or soon after her death, and Kelly tried hard to comply with requests despite his grief. In 1973, Gene's worst year, film historian Tony Thomas was the first to interview him for a book on Gene's films that he dedicated to Jeannie in 1974. Journalist Clive Hirschhorn, South African–born but working in England, also conducted lengthy interviews with Kelly and many others around this time for the first full-length biography, also published in 1974. In the same year, Gavin

Figure 17.2 Kelly's lifelong ambivalence toward M-G-M chief Louis B. Mayer, and Mayer's reciprocation of this feeling, are nicely reflected in this photograph. (Still from *Anatomy of a Dancer*, 2002)

Millar talked with him for *An Evening with Gene Kelly*, broadcast on BBC Television. In this interview, Kelly continued his petty feud with Louis B. Mayer, complaining that the M-G-M head took little personal interest in the movies he made.[21] Instead, Gene could have been grateful that Mayer funded his movies lavishly and left him alone to do what he wanted with them.

Gene did display a wiser perspective when talking with newspaper reporter Michele Willens in St. Louis when *Take Me Along* hit that city. "Looking back, I wish a lot of things I wanted to do could have been done with less temper," he reflected, "without so much fighting the Establishment. People don't realize that making pictures is a very tough, crude business."[22]

During this period and over the next few years, Kelly gave a series of intense, serious-minded interviews that took him from the typical Hollywood chatter into the realm of oral history. Collectively, these deep interviews today constitute important sources of information on Kelly's life and career. The first of these was a lengthy interview conducted on November 20, 1973, by Jerome Delamater and Paddy Whannel and published in Delamater's book *Dance in the Hollywood Musical* in 1981.[23]

The resurgence of interest in Kelly was then tremendously increased by the release of the M-G-M retrospective film *That's Entertainment!* in 1974 (discussed in the next section). From that point on, public interest continued to climb until there was a virtual renaissance in Gene Kelly's stature as an icon of America's achievement in cinema. This happened quickly and took Kelly to the pinnacle of public adulation.

The second deep interview took place only four days after *That's Entertainment!* came out. Ronald L. Davis, a history professor at Southern Methodist University who was conducting a series of oral history interviews with Hollywood personalities, interviewed Gene on several days in late June 1974. Kelly reflected on how well his Golden Age pictures had held up over the years, expressing some embarrassment that many of them seemed dated. *An American in Paris* was "almost silly in its romanticism, you know, as I look at it today." But he knew that it would have been impossible to achieve what he wanted to do in a project if he thought too much about how future generations would see it.[24]

Possibly the most important oral history was conducted by Marilyn Hunt for the Dance Division of the New York Public Library. She interviewed Kelly at his home March 10–14, 1975, for a total of eight and a half hours, covering his entire career. He said *On the Town* was the best film he ever made and a turning point in making musicals. He told her he greatly admired talented people, and that he liked to be around them and interact with them. Gene admitted he had little interest in reading Donald Knox's *The Magic Factory*, a collection of interviews about the making of *An American in Paris*, which came out two years before. He was among the interviewees, but judging from excerpts he had read, Kelly was most surprised that many people in various departments of M-G-M seemed to be under the impression that they were chiefly responsible for making the picture. He asserted that it was the close collaboration between Vincente Minnelli and himself that was the basis for the film.[25]

THAT'S ENTERTAINMENT! (1974)

These interviews and oral histories, important as they are for the historian, were not significant at the time because some were published obscurely or not published at all. As far as the general public was concerned, Kelly resurfaced with a splash on June 21, 1974, when M-G-M released a retrospective film consisting of clips from its impressive collection of film musicals in *That's Entertainment!*

Musicals had been on the decline since the late 1950s. Arthur Freed had retired in December 1970 and passed away on April 12, 1973. M-G-M stopped producing new films altogether in September 1973.[26] It did not take long for the nostalgia mill to begin cranking out products. The timing was perfect. Most of the movies highlighted in *That's Entertainment!* were already two or three decades old, and there was a ready audience for a compilation such as this.

Written and directed by Jack Haley Jr., *That's Entertainment!* gave a great deal of attention to the song "Singin' in the Rain," showing various versions performed over time and ending with the title scene from the film *Singin' in the Rain.* Introductions to segments were made by various personalities, with Fred Astaire hosting the section on Kelly films. Showing excerpts from the "Worry Song" and the fantasy Spanish dance in *Anchors Aweigh*, the Building Dance from *Living in a Big Way*, and "Be a Clown" and the ballet from *The Pirate*, the segment ended with the full title number performed by Gene from *Singin' in the Rain.* "More than any other star I think Gene Kelly became the symbol of the M-G-M musical of the 1950s," Astaire stated. Gene then hosted the section on Astaire films, and they played "Singin' in the Rain" as he walked in. Frank Sinatra at various times stated that *Singin' in the Rain* was the best musical ever made but admitted that *An American in Paris* was the favorite of many. In fact, *That's Entertainment!* ended with an excerpt from the ballet of the latter film. Produced at a cost of $3.2 million, Haley's picture grossed more than $26 million.

With a record like that, Haley's concept caught everyone's attention. It was released just as *Take Me Along* began its summer run, and Kelly was asked about it during interviews. "The enormous success of 'That's Entertainment' clearly means a lot to Kelly," wrote George Anderson in the *Pittsburgh Post-Gazette* after interviewing him in Warren, Ohio. "It's good that it lets my kids see what their old man used to do for a living," Kelly joked.[27]

THAT'S ENTERTAINMENT, PART II (1976)

The push was on for a follow-up to the successful film, but this time it would be done with self-conscious attention. Astaire and Kelly were recruited as the main presenters, teaming them only for the second time since *Ziegfeld Follies*. Saul Chaplin was hired to take care of the new music to accompany these "performing masters of ceremonies," as Chaplin put it. It was not easy to round them up because Astaire was not very active at this time and Gene had other projects. Chaplin had to talk Kelly into it and Gene talked Fred into it. As part of his job, Chaplin screened more than 250 movies and portions of more than a hundred others, plus about seventy-five shorts and trailers in an effort to help producer Dan Melnick choose clips. The first draft of the film was more than four hours long, which they painstakingly reduced to two hours.[28]

Initially Astaire insisted that he not be asked to dance, even threatening to pull out of the project if it was suggested. No one dared bring it up except Astaire himself. One day while listening to the opening music Chaplin had composed for a segment, Fred wondered if he and Gene should dance a little. Everyone was agreeable, and the pair danced three times in the film. Gene choreographed their routines and assured Fred he would develop easy steps. Astaire trusted Kelly's judgment both as choreographer and as director of their sequences. Even when he wondered if a particular step was good enough, Astaire asked Chaplin's opinion about it rather than tell Kelly. Chaplin relayed Fred's concern to Gene, who changed the step accordingly. These two giants of film dance had so much respect for each other that they were careful to avoid even implied criticism. Even so, they maintained a comfortable friendship for each other that became warmer as they grew older.[29]

"He's a very hard worker, Gene," Astaire said of Kelly. "There was no monkeying around, like 'That's good enough for them.' He was very diligent about being on time and working in between shots. I used to say, 'Direct me! Go ahead and direct me.' He is a damned good director."[30]

Melnick tried to make *That's Entertainment, Part II* something more than the previous effort, with excerpts from seventy-two films that neither Kelly nor Astaire had any hand in choosing. "We don't want the responsibility of saying what's good or bad," Gene stated. Astaire and Kelly films play a large role in the lineup, but many less-known films are included as well. Marge Champion sat next to Astaire during the world premiere on May 9, 1976, and heard Fred mutter under his breath, constantly praising Gene's performances while at the same time criticizing his own.[31]

Astaire and Kelly agreed to promote the film with two personal appearances on *The Tonight Show*, a weeklong tour of Europe, and several newspaper

Figure 17.3 A delightful moment showing the mutual affection and regard between Gene Kelly and Fred Astaire. (Still from *That's Entertainment, Part II*, 1976)

interviews. It opened the Cannes Film Festival that year to uproarious applause from the attendees. Fred and Gene cohosted a full week of *The Mike Douglas Show* on television to promote the film. The company came from Philadelphia to film five hour-long episodes on the M-G-M lot. Astaire was not much moved by the explosion of interest in his movie past. "I'm glad people enjoyed it," he said of *That's Entertainment, Part II*, "but it didn't mean anything to me." For Kelly, however, the picture meant a great deal. Even if it flopped at the box office "it's a compendium of history," he told Robert Lindsey of the *New York Times*.[32] *That's Entertainment, Part II* was certainly no flop. But although it grossed $6.5 million, it was far less remunerative than the first installment.

Comments on this second and last pairing of Astaire and Kelly were mixed. Vincent Canby saw mostly nostalgic value in their pairing and criticized their makeup and false hair. Yet Canby admitted they were "still vital talents." John Updike saw Astaire as looser than Kelly, especially in his arm movements. Greg Garrison, who had directed both men in their respective television specials in the 1960s, thought neither "could hit the curveball any longer" by the time of *That's Entertainment, Part II*.[33] Actually, both men dance with grace and confidence, and Kelly deliberately toned down his performance to match Astaire's concerns about dancing at his age. The film ends appropriately with the two friends shaking hands and smiling at each other.

KELLY AS CULTURAL ICON

The retrospectives sparked new evaluations of Kelly's best work of the past. Joel Siegel wrote a significant reevaluation of *The Pirate* in 1974. Vincent Canby wrote about *Singin' in the Rain* in 1975, calling it "a Hollywood masterpiece," and John Mariani also praised the film in a 1978 article that detailed its making.[34]

The cumulative effects of both *That's Entertainment* films spurred more retrospective showings of Kelly's work. In June 1977, the Regency Theater in New York hosted an eleven-week revival of fifty-two M-G-M pictures, eight of which were Kelly musicals. The list included *Invitation to the Dance*, which Clive Barnes disliked intensely but advised viewers to see anyway because of its historic significance. In December 1977, the American Film Institute showed *Singin' in the Rain*. Gene appeared after the viewing to field questions from an audience of 2,000 people. "Musicals are my real love," Kelly told the group. "I didn't want to make pictures with messages. I just wanted to make people happy and bring joy."[35]

Gene increased his profile among college students after the two *That's Entertainment* pictures as well. His career became the subject of what his publicist claimed was the "first full credit class on an actor and his films ever to be held at a major university," when California State University, Fullerton offered such a course in 1979. The next year Kelly gave a lecture with a question-and-answer session at the University of Southern California.[36]

Gene was increasingly thinking of himself as a factor in film history by the late 1970s, and the reaction to both *That's Entertainment* films confirmed that he had succeeded "in some small way" in bringing joy to audiences. He told interviewer Vernon Scott that he received a thousand letters each week, mostly from young people who seemed to think he was still making movies like those seen in the retrospective pictures. Two teenagers in St. Paul, Minnesota, named David Fantle and Tom Johnson were influenced by these two films to show Kelly's movies at nursing homes to bring joy to the elderly. They began to interview people associated with the Golden Age of the Hollywood musical in 1978, and among the first was Gene. He greeted them when they arrived at his house in June of that year with "a jaunty, confident and athletic stride."[37]

Ironically, even as he basked in retrospectives, increased fan mail, and a string of interviewers, Kelly continued to look for new projects to keep his career alive. He was interested in directing a film version of a Shakespearean drama, but that never materialized. Jeannie's death and his own eye problems caused Gene to say no to directing a musical titled *Moulin Rouge* on Broadway in 1973. The next year, he was happy at the prospect of directing two musical films, "Ondine" and "The Music Chase," with scores by English composer Leslie Bricusse, but neither project came to fruition. Kelly was frustrated that film studios considered musicals too expensive to make. He knew they could be produced at reasonable cost. Gene also disliked the rage for action pictures rather than love stories, and he deplored the increase of nudity in mainstream films. "I don't want to make pictures of this kind," he said. "On the other hand I don't want to make pictures for four-year-olds." Given his need to stay at home, he had to pass on an opportunity to play D'Artagnan again. He also turned down the lead in Cyma Rubin's production of *Doctor Jazz* on Broadway to stay close to his children. It only ran for five performances in March 1975. The Russian government asked him to put together a documentary film about Russian ballerina Anna Pavlova. Kelly estimated it would take him two years to accomplish the project, including extended visits to the Soviet Union, and declined.[38]

Gene continued to serve as a cultural commentator during the 1970s, often assessing the history of dance and film musicals while evaluating the current state of both arts. He thought the democratization of dance had taken place during his lifetime as a result of the impact of cinema and television on American culture. He also noticed a crossover effect between popular dance and classical dance since about 1960 and was happy about it. Ballet was no longer the elitist culture it had been, becoming more popular in his view. But Gene also deplored the deterioration of tap dancing and other forms of popular dance during the previous decade. Popular music was now so loud "it would be impossible to hear the feet." Moreover there were few artists in the 1970s who were trained in a variety of dance styles while having the charisma and acting ability to become well-rounded performers in musicals. He thought John Travolta might be an exception if he kept working at it.[39]

DEALING WITH LIFE

Politically Kelly felt out of sync with the 1970s given the unpopular war in Vietnam and the election of Richard Nixon in 1968 and his reelection four years later. The Watergate scandal soured the country, and Kelly yearned for the days of Roosevelt, Truman, and Kennedy. "I'm going through a period of

Figure 17.4 With President Jimmy Carter in November 1977, Kelly introduces thirteen-year-old daughter Bridget (off-camera) to the president. (Jimmy Carter Presidential Library)

cynicism at the moment," he wrote in 1973 as Watergate absorbed national attention, "which I hope will be short." When Ronald Reagan had tried for another term as Republican governor of California in 1970, Frank Sinatra bolted the Democratic Party to support Reagan. In contrast, Gene supported Democratic opponent, Jesse Unruh, who lost. Nevertheless, when Reagan's son wanted to drop out of college and become a ballet dancer in 1976, Reagan recommended he consult "my good friend Gene Kelly" about it. Kelly encouraged the young man to go to ballet school, and Ronald Prescott Reagan crafted a career for himself in that field.[40] It must have been a relief for Gene when Jimmy Carter was elected in 1976. President Carter invited him to the White House for a visit in November 1977.

With advancing age Kelly had to deal with health problems. He had an operation to remove his prostate in 1975 and a procedure for a minor hernia four years later. Gene was in favor of legalizing marijuana and felt the government had not done enough research on its medicinal benefits. He continued to be active, playing tennis every Sunday early in the decade, but soon there was a noticeable slowdown in his exercise routine. After Jeannie's death, Kelly began to put on weight, a problem he would have for the rest of his life. "It's too much trouble keeping in shape," he told an interviewer in 1979. "I'd rather have a drink and a hearty meal."[41]

Available projects that suited the limitations he placed on work tended to be minor roles in television. He appeared on a special hosted by Steve Lawrence and Eydie Gormé in 1975. Kelly did not want to dance, but Lawrence convinced him to do so. By this time, however, he had reduced his dancing to the most simple and undemanding level until it rather bored him. "You keep in shape for nothing," he admitted. "I go on television, but I just horse around. Everybody thinks I'm dancing, but I'm not; I do a few steps." Kelly also appeared in *America Salutes Richard Rodgers: The Sound of His Music* in 1976, portraying Oscar Hammerstein II as well as sharing the hosting duties with Henry Winkler, who portrayed Lorenz Hart.[42] Such roles were throwaways; Kelly took them to make money because juicier opportunities involved too much time away from the kids.

VIVA KNIEVEL! (1977)

Even when a movie opportunity came along that he was able to accept, it was far from something that matched his talents. One of the least important films he participated in was *Viva Knievel!*, an action picture centered around the popular motorcycle stunt rider Robert Craig Knievel, who promoted himself as Evel Knievel. Kelly initially turned down the part but then reconsidered when his children told him Knievel was a hero to many young people and urged him to accept. Gene did not want to disappoint his kids and said yes. During filming Kelly seemed to enjoy the work. "I don't dance. I don't shave. I don't wear makeup. And I don't get the girl. I'm having so much fun I can hardly wait to go to work in the morning."[43]

Viva Knievel! is not as bad as one would guess, but it ranks very low on the list of Kelly films. The production value has all the feel and look of a television movie instead of a feature film, and it tells a simplistic tale of good and bad. Kelly, as Will Atkins, has the only multifaceted role as a grease-monkey pal of Knievel. Atkins resents his young son because his wife died in childbirth, and he is angry and violent at times. But eventually, he reconciles with his son and helps defeat the bad guys who are trying to use Knievel to smuggle drugs from Mexico. If one looks on this project within the context of television fare, it works well for young viewers with daredevil stunts and thrilling car chases.

Figure 17.5 Kelly's character Will Atkins reuniting with his son Tommy (played by Eric Olson) in an emotional climax. (Still from *Viva Knievel!* 1977)

It gave Gene an opportunity to portray a troubled man with a drinking problem who finds his way out of his tortured life.

After *Viva Knievel!* was released in June 1977, reviewers cited Kelly's performance as the only noteworthy element of the movie. He was "unexpectedly touching in the role of a rummy, embittered old has-been," and his acting "puts [Knievel] to shame."[44]

TELEVISION AND STAGE APPEARANCES

The next year, Kelly starred in another television special, *Gene Kelly: An American in Pasadena,* which aired on CBS on March 13, 1978. It was taped at the Ambassador Auditorium in Pasadena as a benefit for an organization that helped homeless children. This variety show mixed new performances with several guest stars, including Frank Sinatra, and clips from many of Kelly's old film appearances. Several leading ladies from his films—Lucille Ball, Cyd Charisse, Kathryn Grayson, and Janet Leigh—as well as thirteen-year-old daughter Bridget, came on stage to interact and sing with Kelly. Liza Minnelli showed up to reprise their 1959 rendering of "For Me and My Gal," showing a clip from that earlier performance as well. Alex Romero and Danny Daniels joined Kelly for "a precision tap dance routine" that mimicked Kelly's dance with two animated guards in "Sinbad the Sailor" from *Invitation to the Dance*. The hour-long show was heavy with nostalgia for the Golden Age of the Hollywood musical.

The show received positive reviews. John O'Connor noted that Gene was "not quite as agile and athletic" as in the past but he "retains a distinctive dancing manner and can still whip up a class act." The reporter thought Kelly "indisputably talented" but, even more importantly, he was "an irresistible advertisement for nice people."[45]

Also in 1978, Kelly parleyed an offer for a stage show into a family reunion on the East Coast. When Resorts International Hotel Casino asked him to do a week-long show at its Atlantic City hotel, Gene said he would if the company financed "an all-expense-paid family reunion" in addition to his hefty remuneration. They agreed, and Kelly took along his children, Jeanne Coyne's mother, Fred Kelly and his wife, Dorothy, and other family members to Atlantic City. Fred and Dorothy celebrated their thirty-fifth wedding anniversary, and Gene celebrated his sixty-sixth birthday. Kelly reprised his dance with Alex Romero and Danny Daniels from *An American in Pasadena*. For the rest of the stage show Kelly threw together old standbys from his long career, which he believed was what nightclub audiences wanted.[46]

As the 1970s neared an end, Kelly's career decisively entered its nostalgic phase with appearances to celebrate his past. He accepted this inevitable development with grace and gratitude—after all, it was far better than being ignored. His occasional guest appearances on other people's television shows created instant attention merely because he was Gene Kelly. Mary Tyler Moore brought him on for a guest appearance on *The Mary Tyler Moore Hour*, a short-lived (March to June 1979) successor to her very popular *The Mary Tyler Moore Show* (1970–1977). Gene came on as himself in the fifth episode, which aired on April 1, 1979, to wow Mary and her associates by his mere presence.[47]

BACK TO PITTSBURGH

Even before Jeannie's illness and passing, and before the retrospectives, Pittsburgh's natural pride in one of its most illustrious sons lured the dancer back to his hometown roots. Of course, Gene had never forgotten Pittsburgh. Ever since leaving the city in 1938 he returned periodically to visit family members. By the 1960s that included only his mother and his two sisters; his father had passed away, Jim lived in Northern California, and Fred was in New Jersey. The University of Pittsburgh gave him an honorary Doctor of Fine Arts in 1961 for "demonstrating that dance was not only a happy game but a human necessity" and for his "creative exploration" and "vibrant spirit." Kelly had given small yearly donations to the university, but he also knew how to say no when asked to participate in public relations events such as "Alumni Fun."[48]

From 1970 on, however, Kelly began a closer relationship with the university. Virginia Nicklas joined the development and alumni affairs staff in September 1970 and was assigned to serve as the primary contact for Kelly, their most famous alumnus. It was a good choice, because Nicklas had been an avid fan of his ever since she saw *Cover Girl* as a high-school teenager. Of course a good deal of the university's interest in Gene lay in the possibility that he might become a major donor. Nicklas first tried to gauge Kelly's attitude toward the university by contacting people she knew who had met him. She mentioned she was interested in contacting him for "a substantial gift." That led nowhere. Then other staff members tried to obtain public information that could reveal his financial worth. They hired a service to conduct research but only received a Dun & Bradstreet report that essentially told them nothing. Nicklas then wrote to Kelly in February 1971. She told him of her admiration for him and his films and admitted that contacting him was "half business and half fun."[49] This began a long association between Nicklas and Kelly that lasted for nearly the rest of his life.

Gene informed Nicklas that he planned to visit Pittsburgh to attend the Civic Light Opera Dinner and Ball on June 10, 1971. He planned to bring Jeannie and the kids along and visit his and his wife's relatives. Nicklas immediately tried to involve him in campus activities. A busy family schedule prevented Gene from attending a campus production of *The Time of Your Life*, but he participated in the John F. Kennedy Scholarship Award Luncheon hosted by the Irish Room Committee and Gaelic Arts Society. The event raised funds for a Pitt student to study during the summer in Ireland. Three of Gene's Peabody High School teachers and his sister Harriet Radvansky attended. After the lunch, Kelly visited the Irish Room, one of several rooms on the bottom floor of the Cathedral of Learning dedicated to various ethnic groups associated with the steel history of Pittsburgh. Publicity surrounding his visit, however, was muted by the onset of a newspaper workers' strike.[50]

Shortly after meeting Kelly, Nicklas wrote to Paul Pugh that she was assigned to contact Gene "in the hope of interesting him in contributing a sizeable sum to Pitt." She then continued to be in touch with Kelly but more as a "fan," never even hinting at the university's hope. Regarding *The Funny Side* television show, she wrote, "I do think that your talents should be utilized to greater advantage, . . . you have so much more to offer than any of those other people." Later, she complimented Gene's appearance in *40 Carats* but wished the brief dancing sequence with Binnie Barnes had been longer. When she wrote to express her and her colleagues' sympathy at the death of Jeannie, she was touched to receive a handwritten acknowledgement of those condolences from Kelly. Gene probably assumed that the "business" part of Nicklas's contact was to involve him in fundraising activities for the university. He did what he could to help, but her efforts to engage him for personal appearances on campus for fundraising more often received a polite no than an enthusiastic yes.[51]

Kelly's feelings for Pittsburgh remained strong. When he played in *Take Me Along* at Warren, Ohio, in 1974, he told journalist George Anderson, "I love Pittsburgh. It's a whole part of my life, but it just isn't the same for me now that my mother is gone."[52] Nevertheless, Gene joined with Franklin Roberts in urging his high school classmates to plan for a fiftieth reunion in 1979. A committee was formed to work out the details, and Gene was happy to use his name to get more people to attend. "It all sounds like a lot of fun and something I think we all should do while we still have time." He knew where many of his former classmates were living and sent letters to them with "much loving, fond nostalgia and great affection."[53]

When the people at the University of Pittsburgh got wind of the reunion, some of them tried to line up Kelly for their own purposes. The curator of the Curtis Theatre Collection made a pitch for Gene to donate his personal papers to the university, but it was too late. As Kelly politely told her, Boston University had approached him "many years ago," and he had been sending shipments of papers and artifacts to the Howard Gotlieb Archival Research Center at that institution ever since.[54]

Kelly attended his high-school reunion at the Allegheny Club in Three Rivers Stadium on June 15, 1979. He made what Chalmers Roberts called a "sentimental little speech about his high school years" and those classmates who had died during the intervening time. Peabody High School was large enough to have had two graduating classes each year. In Kelly's June 1929 class, 429 students graduated. Of that number, 111 attended the fiftieth reunion and fifty-nine were known to have passed away. "He was the same humorous nice guy we remembered," Chalmers wrote of Kelly.[55]

"I had a wonderful time mixed with happy and sad reminiscences," Gene wrote to a classmate soon after returning to his California home.[56] His attachment to Pittsburgh had now become more public and visible. His life in many ways had come full circle, with a deepening connection to his roots that coexisted with a forward-looking gaze on what was left of his life and career.

Finale, 1980–1996

The decade of the 1980s reflected many of the trajectories in Gene Kelly's life and career that had been developing since the late 1950s. He continued to accept small parts in films and television, tried to develop a stage project, and became an executive producer for a film on dancing. Gene continued to be viewed as an icon of American culture, as an ambassador of dance, and as a subject for a nostalgic interview or a retrospective film festival. Kelly accepted this view of his life and work. He taught America about dancing, encouraged young dancers, and launched an ultimately futile effort to write his memoirs.

XANADU (1980)

The last feature film that Gene acted in was *Xanadu*. It was a well-meaning movie that attempted to bring back some of the charm of the Golden Age of the Hollywood musical, and enrolling Kelly as a costar was important. Gene agreed because he liked much of what the producers were trying to do, and he looked forward to working with Olivia Newton-John. His children were old enough so that he could take on a more extended project, and the thought of playing a character his own age appealed to him. Kelly created the role of an aging entertainer reliving his glory days. The character's name was Danny McGuire, the same as in *Cover Girl*. Initially Gene refused to dance, but after the filming was finished, the producers saw the rough cut and "begged him to film a fantasy dance sequence" with Olivia and he agreed. "I do a little moving, a couple of dance steps, but in all honesty they are just little flashes." It turned out to be the highlight of the film. Choreographer Kenny Ortega worked with Kelly on the steps, as they exchanged ideas with each other. Kelly also roller-skated in the film, although without any dance steps built into the routine. At least one interviewer thought he looked more like forty-five

Figure 18.1 As Danny McGuire (the same name as his character in *Cover Girl*), in a retrospective dream ballet with Olivia Newton-John. (Still from *Xanadu*, 1980)

than sixty-seven, but Kelly easily played an older man comfortable with his memories.[1]

Released on August 8, 1980, *Xanadu* did not do well at the box office or with critics. "It's terrific one minute, lethargic the next," wrote Ed Blank. "What makes the difference is whether Gene Kelly's on camera." Another reviewer thought Kelly was "a powerhouse presence" on screen, reminding the viewer that "something very, very good has survived" in Hollywood. But critical appraisal of the film as a whole tended to be harsh. Gene called *Xanadu* "a terrible picture" but admitted he enjoyed making it. The production process demonstrated to him "how little today's crop of youngsters actually knows about making musicals and that was kind of depressing."[2]

The critics were right that Kelly livened up this movie. The shallow plot, lack of character development, and often inane dialogue are partly offset by his genial performance and by his charming "dream ballet" with Olivia. And although the film did not do well, the soundtrack was a huge hit.

THE MUPPET SHOW (1980)

Less than two weeks after *Xanadu*'s release, Gene made a striking guest appearance on *The Muppet Show*. Aired on August 19, 1980, the half-hour episode was built on the notion that Kelly had no intention to perform but was there merely to watch. His humorous interactions with the Muppets reflected the fun he always had interacting with children. The highlight of the show was Kelly teaching Kermit the Frog how to dance, using the "Worry Song" as the model. His singing "You Wonderful You" to Miss Piggy, and then to Gonzo, was also enjoyable.

Gene sang many of his famous film songs for the Muppets but refused to reprise "Singin' in the Rain." Done as a joke, the Muppets finally cajoled Kelly into singing his most famous number. He even did a tiny dance step on the set they re-created for the number. His appearance on *The Muppet Show* represents the best of what could happen when he appeared on television even at his advanced age of sixty-eight.

ZOETROPE

Soon after his pleasant appearance with the Muppets, Gene was excited by the prospect of reviving something like the old studio system to produce a new wave of film musicals in the fall of 1980. Francis Ford Coppola bought the roller-skate/nightclub set of *Xanadu* and made it into Zoetrope Studios, with stock players and dedicated technical staff and facilities. Coppola hired Kelly, who he called a "creative innovator," to direct a musicals division with responsibility for hiring talent, producing, and directing. *One from the Heart*, a love story and fantasy musical, was to be the first production, with choreography of a few dances by Kelly. Another musical, *Tucker*, would be written by Betty Comden and Adolph Green and directed by Kelly.[3]

There was much to expect from this unusual development, and Gene was wild with excitement. He considered it "the plum job of all time," especially because it would allow him "to teach the one thing I know best of all: the movie musical" to the next generation of filmmakers. But the opportunity soured, and there were many causes. First and foremost, although Coppola appreciated the Golden Age Hollywood musical, he could not give Kelly or anyone else the leeway they needed to make modern versions of those pictures. Mercurial and talented, but also egotistical and overly controlling, Coppola ran roughshod over Gene and everyone else at Zoetrope. He interfered with their work and tried to direct and control everyone on the set from a trailer armed with technology so he could see by remote camera what was happening and shout instructions over loudspeakers. When *One from the Heart*

Figure 18.2 Teaching Kermit the Frog to dance (similar to how he taught Jerry the Mouse in "The Worry Song" in *Anchors Aweigh*). (Still from *The Muppet Show*, 1980)

Figure 18.3 Singing "You Wonderful You!" (which he sang to Judy Garland in *Summer Stock*) to Miss Piggy. (Still from *The Muppet Show*, 1980)

started production in February 1981, Zoetrope was in deep financial distress, and it quickly grew worse. Coppola was wildly careless with money, employing workers on a deferred-pay basis and then being unable to pay them. Gene had hired Kenny Ortega to choreograph while he himself would direct the numbers, but he was greatly dissatisfied with everything. Kelly and Coppola argued vigorously on the set over the quality of dancing by the stars (which was amateurish) and about how to stage numbers. When Coppola told Kelly to conceive, rehearse, and prepare a dance for Nastassja Kinski in only one day, Kelly told him it would take weeks to do it right. The argument that ensued was too much for Gene, who walked out of Zoetrope never to return.[4]

When *One from the Heart* premiered in February 1982, it "flopped instantly" and was a target of severe criticism from reviewers who complained that it had no heart and no mind. When an article published in *American Film* in October 1981 indicated that Gene had done the choreography, Kelly wrote a letter of rebuttal that appeared in the January 1982 issue of the journal. In it he clarified that Coppola had asked his advice and assistance on the set "but in no way does *One From the Heart* represent any of my choreography or direction."[5]

The problems associated with this movie mirrored more general concerns with an effort to replicate the old days of the Hollywood musical. It now cost $10 million to produce a film and another $10 million to promote it, with far less opportunity to recoup the investment for a musical. Ticket sales for musicals had dropped 75 percent by the 1980s compared to the 1940s. The core group of film viewers tended to be young people who had limited tastes in movies, which did not include old-fashioned musicals.[6] Moreover, with videotape technology and cable television, viewers who liked old-fashioned musicals could easily see the originals rather than wait for modern replicas to be made.

In short, Kelly's dream of passing on his dance film legacy to a new generation of moviemakers had little hope of fulfillment in any meaningful way. His legacy would remain firmly tied to the past.

UNREALIZED STAGE PROJECT

Gene was enthusiastic about the prospect of directing "Satchmo," a Broadway musical based on the life of Louis Armstrong. Kelly knew and liked Armstrong and had insisted on including him in the *Hello, Dolly!* title number.

He now felt Armstrong's long and unusual career deserved homage. Gene wanted Ben Vereen to star and held an audition in New York in August 1981 to recruit a twelve- to fifteen-year-old to portray Armstrong as a boy. It was not easy to find someone that young who could sing well, and Kelly was sensitive about the feelings of the boys who showed up to audition. To put them at ease he joked with them, asking if they were married, which always brought a laugh. If someone faltered during the audition, Gene encouraged him. He sang a bit himself to relax the group. Even though his voice was a bit raspy, a fourteen-year-old girl in the audience, who had seen his films and loved them, cried when he sang.[7] All the children were drawn to Kelly—the ultimate teacher and friend of young performers.

"Satchmo," however, floundered on two fronts. "I simply couldn't get anyone to come up with a script that worked," Kelly explained, and with an estimated production "budget of over two million dollars" he could not get funding, either. So Gene had to drop the idea even though he thought "Satchmo's life could make a helluva show."[8]

VIEWS ON RELIGION

Kelly rarely talked about his religious views unless the situation called for it. When a Franciscan priest named Jack Wintz interviewed him in 1980 for a Catholic magazine, Gene spoke very openly about his religious journey through life. As detailed in this book, Kelly was raised in a conservative Catholic family in Pittsburgh and rebelled against that conservatism by flirting with agnosticism and even atheism. Betsy Blair had been raised in a Protestant home and did not take religion of any kind very seriously. As a result, the couple lived without any attention to organized religion. Instead, Gene always had strong moral values as attested by Betsy and others and as seen in his political activism.

When Gene married Jeanne Coyne, she brought Catholicism back to the Kelly household. Organized religion was important to her, and Gene went along with her wishes. The two talked with a Catholic priest who refused to let them be married in church because Coyne had not married Donen in a religious ceremony and both Coyne and Kelly had been divorced. That was why the couple went to Tonopah, Nevada, for a civil marriage. Moreover, the priest told them they could not receive communion. Despite all this, Jeannie and Gene continued to attend Catholic church services and sent Tim and

Bridget to Catholic elementary and high schools. Both children at an early age asked their parents why they were not allowed to take communion. Kelly felt the church was wrong to stick to outdated rules like this and thought such things could be traumatic for children. "We haven't left the Church, in my view; the Church has walked away from us," he told Wintz. "In my own conscience I am at peace with God without needing an intermediary."[9] This is as close as Gene came to spiritual and theological independence from the Catholic Church.

At the same time, he believed that his religious faith had helped him in dealing with the deaths of his parents and Jeannie. In fact, a part of him remained deeply traditional and closely connected with the church of his youth. He continued to go to Mass with his children after Jeannie's passing. But he was unhappy about the changes in Catholic services that took place during the 1960s. These included substituting vernacular languages for Latin, the introduction of guitar accompaniment for singing, and a modernized liturgy. He knew that making the service relevant to younger people was important to the church. "But I'm uncomfortable with it because I was brought up as an altar boy to the echoes of *per omnia saecula saeculorum, Dominus vobiscum* and *et cum spiritu tuo*. That still rings in my ears."[10]

The Jack Wintz interview, published in *St. Anthony Messenger* in 1980, is an interesting expression of views on religion by a high-profile film actor. It thoroughly documents Kelly's spiritual journey and reveals a side of him rarely glimpsed otherwise. Throughout his life, Kelly the free thinker—who rightly trusted his own conscience as a guide rather than relying on religion—coexisted with Kelly the traditional Catholic, who enjoyed the rituals and trappings of the church.

MUSIC INDUSTRY

In 1983, Gene agreed to become the spokesman for RCA videodiscs and players, appearing in numerous ads printed in newspapers around the country. One of them listed all the stores near Pittsburgh where one might purchase these home entertainment devices. Kelly agreed to this because he was convinced that home entertainment was the wave of the future and because he was paid a huge fee. "So now I'm selling," he told journalist Arthur Marx, "just like my father." But Gene recognized that the music industry had gone the way of the film industry. "The young people have taken over." Both were now being created for and marketed to the "very young." He had little interest in continuing to direct within an entertainment culture like that and bemoaned the loss of films meant to be enjoyed by all ages.[11]

THE FIRE

Personal loss once again plagued Gene's life. The house at 725 North Rodeo Drive went up in flames on the night of December 21–22, 1983, caused by a faulty Christmas tree lighting system. Kelly was in the habit of keeping the lights on all night in the bay window as a "gesture to his fans" every Christmas season. This night he was asleep in an upstairs bedroom when the fire started at 1:25 A.M. Tim and Bridget were awake and watching television. Tim went upstairs to awaken Gene, but by the time they began to come down, the stairs were blocked by fire. They had to descend by way of another stairway as Bridget called the fire department and escaped unharmed. Tim was credited with saving Gene's life, both of them suffering minor burns and singeing. The house, valued at $350,000, was completely destroyed with virtually everything in it. Kelly lost his 1951 special Academy Award, his Emmy, his dancing shoes, the notes and manuscript he had assembled for his autobiography, and many other memorabilia.[12]

Gene dealt with this tragedy as he did with all downturns in his life, with courage and grace. He temporarily moved into a small building in the backyard of his neighbors (the Zekarias) so he could oversee the rebuilding of his home. Later he moved into a house originally constructed for Greta Garbo but currently owned by director Jean Negulesco. Kelly had his own house rebuilt exactly as it had been, except a bit larger. When it was finished, the family sent Christmas cards proudly proclaiming "Back In Our House for a Merry Christmas."[13]

Not long after the house was rebuilt, Pat York visited Kelly for a book on how famous people were handling the aging process. Gene quietly reflected on himself, his career, and his life. He said he still was a determined worker at his craft, impatient with any colleague who was "dogging it," but patient with slow learners. He admitted to being "mercurial" in his temperament and thought many of the good things that had happened in his life were the product of luck. But that did not dampen his fierce work ethic. When York asked him for his advice to America, Kelly told her everyone should be prepared to work hard and learn every aspect of whatever they chose to do.[14]

Figure 18.4 The Kelly home at 725 N. Rodeo Drive, rebuilt after the fire of December 1983 in which Gene lost most of his prized possessions, but his life was saved by his son Tim. (Photo by authors)

By this stage of his life Gene had mellowed considerably. He admitted to reporter Patricia Nolan that since the house fire in 1983 he had become less attached to material things and valued friendships more than ever. "I don't like to live in the past, but I do cherish the old friends that I once worked with and the movies that I once did." He and Astaire were "still wonderful friends after all these years."[15]

MORE RETROSPECTIVES AND INTERVIEWS

Retrospective showings of his Golden Age films continued throughout the decade. On May 25, 1980, the British Film Institute hosted an M-G-M retrospective in London that was attended by Kelly. On the previous day, he met with young local dancers who asked him choreographic questions in an informal interview. The Film Forum of New York hosted a showing of *It's Always Fair Weather* in May 1987.[16]

Interviewers also came to his home throughout the 1980s. In 1984, Ron Haver interviewed Kelly for ninety minutes and found in him an "enviable ability to talk intelligently and engrossingly. He has no need of the interviewer's prepared questions." Haver was impressed that Gene did this "between conferences with architects, telephone calls, queries from his secretary, and a dialogue with son Tim about dinner." In 1988, Michael Singer also interviewed Kelly at home on a wide range of topics.[17]

With a few exceptions, the 1980s interviews focused on Kelly's past achievements in cinema and to a lesser extent on the stage. This gave him many opportunities to dwell on his career. He asserted that making dance films was the hardest task and bemoaned the fact that Broadway musicals were failing to incorporate different dance styles into their choreography. He believed that "the more variety in a show, the better it is as a dancing show." He considered *The Time of Your Life* as his big breakthrough rather than *Pal Joey* because it taught him how to use dance in order to create a character. He thought the studio system had been "a form of serfdom" but it offered unusual opportunities to craft top-notch film musicals.[18]

Gene reflected on the role dancing played in his life, calling it "my first love and it's still my number one love." And yet at other times he said the same about choreography and even stated that "performing bores me. . . . The big thrill for me is *creating* something." It is true that "making a moment dance" was what he most enjoyed.[19] Of course this involves choreography more than dancing, but actually the two endeavors went hand-in-hand for him. When Kelly stopped dancing due to the natural process of aging, he stopped choreography as well and focused on directing and lecturing.

Gene admitted to a bit of jealousy when comparing the dancer's decline of physical prowess with the increasing technique and skill of, for example, a violinist. For the dancer, the instrument is the body and it ages rapidly. For the violinist, the instrument never changes but the ability of the player increases with experience. Kelly was becoming incapable of performing challenging physical moves on the dance floor, and it took much of the interest and excitement out of dancing for him. As he told Jack Wintz: "Once you've swum a strong river, you can't get very excited about walking through a puddle."[20]

The continuing interviews offered Gene many opportunities to reflect on his life and work. "I've always tried to reach for perfection in every film I've made, knowing that I could never achieve it." He consistently cited *On the Town* as his favorite because of the breakthrough effect of filming the introduction and ending in New York. The Squeaky Board and Newspaper number in *Summer Stock* was his favorite film dance because of the difficulty of working it out. *Meet Me in St. Louis* (1944) was his favorite musical outside his own work. His favorite film dance, outside his own work, was "Dancing in the Dark," performed by Fred Astaire and Cyd Charisse in *The Band Wagon*

(1953). "It's so beautiful. . . . To me it's the perfect courtship number, and I'm jealous I didn't do it."[21]

"We were giving people magic and joy," Kelly mused about his film dances in 1985. "I figured if I could make people happy by jumping over a couple of couches or dancing in a rainstorm, maybe I was achieving something." And it seemed to work even in the 1980s. He received more fan mail in his sixties than he did in his thirties, mostly from younger viewers who were not even born when his Golden Age pictures were released. Half of them seemed to think that these movies had just been made. It gratified Gene to know that possibly such projects could work even now if there were people to make them.[22] The key to viewer interest was the spark generated by the *That's Entertainment* films and the ready availability of classic musicals on videotape and cable television.

As the wave of nostalgia grew, Kelly became interested in writing his memoirs. "You've got enough for a [book]," he told interviewer and film historian Joseph McBride in 1981, "& I want to do this myself you know." He began writing in October 1983, but his notes and drafts were lost in the fire that completely destroyed his house two months later. After rebuilding, Kelly continued writing, "which takes several hours a day. I stop whenever I run out of steam," he told Pat York. Hugh Fordin, casting director for *Hello, Dolly!*, wrote a history of the M-G-M Freed Unit published in 1975. Gene did not like it. "That book is false on practically every other page," he told Michael Singer in 1988.[23]

EVALUATING NEW DANCE TRENDS

Kelly felt that his extensive reading qualified him as "a walking encyclopedia of dance history. I've been desperately in love with the idea of dance since I was in college." He wrote the foreword to Clive Hirschhorn's *The Hollywood Musical*, published in 1981, and the foreword to David Naylor's *Great American Movie Theaters*, published in 1987. Gene argued in other venues that the film musical exposed more Americans to dance of all kinds than any other medium. Those movies created "America's dance consciousness." But he finally accepted the fact that the Golden Age would never return. "Dance always follows music," he explained, and music changed beginning in the 1950s with Elvis Presley and rock and roll. It became focused on appealing mostly to youth and emphasized people dancing separately rather than couples holding each other. It was impossible to re-create the feel of the 1930s and 1940s with music like this. As a result, there was "not enough soul, not enough feeling and not enough sweetness" in current musicals, in Kelly's view.[24]

"These days, everyone thinks he's a dancer," Gene observed in 1986, referring to performers. He noticed a big reduction in the awareness that one had to train rigorously before reaching a height of achievement in one's dance career. He also disliked current choreographic conventions in popular entertainment, with interchangeable steps for male and female dancers. "It all looks a lot the same," he complained.[25]

Kelly disliked trends in the filming of dance that became evident in popular entertainment during the 1980s, especially music videos. He was shocked that some stars' dancing was dubbed by professional dancers in a way to trick the public. Quick cutting, which he popularized with *On the Town*, was now being used "to hide bad dancing" and to emphasize "the percussive nature of dancing today." He did not like any of these trends, believing they violated every rule of success in creating the Golden Age musicals. In general, there was unnecessary emphasis on special effects, excessive violence, and too much gratuitous sex in the movies for Gene's taste. "I guess I'm an old-fashioned guy," he told a reporter. "I like . . . old values." While Kelly did not dislike rock music, he hated that it was played so loud, and he did find that much of it was "bad music."[26]

Gene saw a few signs of hope in the current culture of music and dance. Mikhail Baryshnikov seemed to fit the model of a musical star of the past. He was widely trained in various dance styles and could act and project personal charm. Baryshnikov was "the best talent that's walked over the hill in many, many years." As for younger performers, Kelly admired Michael Jackson for his singing and dancing and liked John Travolta's dancing. He was also taken with the athleticism and spontaneity of break dancing.[27]

After years of refraining from doing so, Gene advocated government funding for the arts, especially ballet, to give aspiring dancers help in crafting a career. He was convinced that the greatness of America had to be expressed in the arts as well as in finance and industry. But the Republicans were dominant in Washington during the decade and Kelly disagreed with many of Ronald Reagan's policies. He believed in keeping politics and art separate, however, and thus participated in an event at the White House that showcased young dancers in March 1982.[28]

HONORS AND AWARDS

Just as he had in the 1970s, Kelly received honors and awards from a variety of institutions throughout the 1980s for his contributions to the performing arts. In particular, he received a Kennedy Center Honor, only the second film dancer other than Fred Astaire to do so, with a White House reception following the awards ceremony in December 1982.[29]

But the biggest award came when the American Film Institute (AFI) gave Kelly its thirteenth Annual Life Achievement Award. Broadcast on May 7, 1985, it was a gala event and an emotional one for Gene. Many clips from his Golden Age musicals and a long list of family, friends, and colleagues from the past made it a memorable evening. At the end of the ninety-minute broadcast, Kelly gave a short speech as he accepted the award. "It was hard work, but we had fun, we had the *best* of times and I think it was because we all thought we were trying to create some kind of magic and joy. And you know, that's what you do up there, you dance love, and you dance joy, and you dance dreams."

The AFI salute was a beautiful climax to a long career, but as Aljean Harmetz noted, it focused too heavily on Kelly's film dances and short-changed his many other avenues of creative expression. Earlier, Gene too had been bemused and a bit disappointed that the public seemed only to know him as a film dancer, ignoring his many other creative achievements in pictures and on the stage.[30] But at the AFI event, Kelly repeated the old idea that as a boy all he wanted to do was play shortstop for the Pittsburgh Pirates. It was quite possible that at some point in his teenage years that was true, but focusing on this greatly obscures his life and career. The truth is that Gene quickly gave up all interest in making a living through sports and opted early on to make his mark in dancing, choreography, acting, directing, and many other contributions to the entertainment industry.

THAT'S DANCING! (1985)

Kelly basked in his AFI salute as he continued to be active in creating new work. He agreed to become executive producer of a feature film compilation representing the history of dancing, although it took some doing for producer Jack Haley Jr. to convince Gene that he needed him. Trying to replicate the success of *That's Entertainment!*, Haley had accumulated ninety hours of dance footage before he talked Gene into joining the project. Kelly became what he called a "supercharged technical advisor" for *That's Dancing!* The first cut was two hours and forty-five minutes long, and the team reduced it by one hour to make it feasible as a feature-length theater product. As Kelly told an interviewer, "We are trying to get the general public excited about dance."[31]

Released on January 18, 1985, the film was a moderate success. Only reviewer Marcia Pally criticized it as having too much emphasis on Astaire and Kelly work, too little on choreographers, and not much on ethnic diversity. She even criticized the opening sequence, completely mistaking Gene's genuine admiration for the natural dancing done by Africans as a racial put-down.[32] But *That's Dancing!* deserves much more credit than Pally was able to give it. The film is Kelly's deepest, most thoughtful screen exploration of the meaning of dance and its history. It covers more ground than "Dancing: A Man's Game." Kelly wrote and did the voiceover for the introduction, which discusses the primal nature of dance in premodern societies around the world, noting that the beat of the heart is connected to the beat of the feet. He also discussed dancing in silent films of the 1920s before moving into the Golden Age of the Hollywood musical and ended with the modern dance scene of the 1980s. *That's Dancing!* received far less attention than did his *Omnibus* television special, but it has much more to say. Jack Haley Jr. was right that he needed Kelly to give his idea shape and to turn it into a meaningful treatise on dance through history.

Even after *That's Dancing!* Kelly did not want to retire. "I love working too much," he said. He thought retirement tended to take a man "one step closer to poor health and even to death. I can't sit around the house all day and do nothing." So, Gene followed up *That's Dancing!* with small roles in two television miniseries. He portrayed Senator Charles Edwards in six episodes of *North and South*, a potboiler series about the Civil War, late in 1985. Soon after that he portrayed Eric Hovland, a composer and husband of Joan Collins's character, in another potboiler called *Sins* that was set in the modern world. Kelly appeared in only three episodes of this series, which aired early in 1986.[33]

BACK TO HIS ROOTS

Kelly had always felt close to Pittsburgh, but he regretted that since his mother's death in 1972 his visits to his birth city had become less frequent. "I used to come several times a year to visit her," he told reporter Ed Blank in a telephone interview. "If you could—give all my dear friends in Pittsburgh my love and constant affection," he urged Blank. "I still have many friends there. I have a very special feeling for Pittsburgh."[34]

Kelly's attachment to the city deepened in the 1980s. He returned to town for a major event on June 26, 1981, as the guest of honor at the Pink Frolic, a benefit to raise funds for the Pittsburgh Civic Light Opera. At a news conference held at the William Penn Hotel, Kelly was "modest, witty and disarmingly frank," according to reporter Jim Davidson. The audience was eager to know what he thought of Pittsburgh after so many years, and Gene obliged. He recalled growing up during the Great Depression "when 50 cents for a couple hours' work meant a lot." Now, with "Social Security, unemployment insurance and unions," there was far less of a gap between the working class and the elite. Pittsburgh also seemed much cleaner. "I remember when you didn't go out with a white shirt. You'd have to change it in the middle of the day."[35]

During a rally at Mellon Square, just outside the front of the hotel, Anne Greenberg showed up. She had been instrumental in getting Kelly his long-term job with Beth Shalom. Gene danced a bit with her, and Greenberg proudly clutched something called Kelly's autobiography, in which she was mentioned. Exactly what that document was is unclear because Gene did not start drafting his memoirs until 1983; perhaps it was a set of notes. At the rally, Mayor Richard Caliguiri gave Kelly the key to the city and declared it Gene Kelly Day. Gene's visit included a ceremony in which the University of Pittsburgh gave him its Distinguished Alumni Award at a luncheon held at the William Penn Hotel that the family also attended. Virginia Nicklas sent Kelly a scrapbook with photos of his visit and a family portrait, all of which he greatly appreciated.[36]

Pittsburgh had indeed changed a lot since its gritty working-class days. Its population had declined from 670,000 in 1930 to 425,000 by 1980 along with its industrial power. "Aggressive redevelopment" had hit East Liberty during the 1960s with the destruction of 1,500 old houses and the building of 2,000 new apartment and townhouse complexes. Other suburbs were less heavily hit by change, but all of Pittsburgh looked and felt very different compared to the time of Kelly's youth.[37]

Perhaps the most evident change was in the air quality. Pittsburgh was one of the most heavily polluted cities in America when Gene was growing up because of heavy use of coal and a topography that tended to trap smoke.

Figure 18.5 With children Kerry, Tim, and Bridget and brother-in-law Michael Radvansky at the University of Pittsburgh for a special event to honor Kelly in 1981. (Gene Kelly Alumni Files, Archives and Special Collections, University of Pittsburgh)

Beginning in 1941, only three years after he left his hometown, Pittsburgh began to do something about that problem. The city passed a strong Smoke Control Ordinance that year and began to push residents to give up coal and convert to natural gas in 1950. Within ten years there was noticeable improvement in air quality, and the change benefited everyone in town up to the time of Kelly's visit in 1981.[38]

Places dear to Kelly had changed as well. The Gene Kelly Studio of the Dance had been operated by Louise and her husband, Bill Bailey, since Gene left town. They also managed the school in Johnstown, located at the corner of Vine and Franklin, until it closed in 1951. At some point the Pittsburgh location also closed down but reopened as the Kelly School of Dance in Dothan, Alabama, where it is still a dance school. The Nixon Theatre, frequented by the Kelly children and the scene of Cap and Gown performances, closed in 1950 and later was torn down.[39] It was located a block away from Mellon Square and the William Penn Hotel.

Six years after the gala of 1981, Kelly agreed to lend his support to a major fundraising drive launched by the University of Pittsburgh to celebrate its bicentennial. The Campaign for the Third Century aimed to raise $225 million, and Kelly's letter of support, written by Virginia Nicklas and approved by Gene, was sent to 103,000 alumni on November 17, 1986. More than 1,800 people responded to the letter with a total of $150,923 in contributions. Kelly appeared at the kickoff for the campaign on June 22, 1987, and joked with reporters when they asked if his economics degree had helped him. "I can discuss intelligently certain things with the IRS people. That alone is where I have it over all of you."[40]

Gene also was honored during this visit by the placement of a bicentennial medal on the grounds of the campus on June 23. Similar to the Hollywood Walk of Fame, it was a blue star set against a bronze background with wording that honored Pitt's most famous alumnus. In yet another honor, the East Liberty Chamber of Commerce, after a year of wheedling permission from Kelly, declared the block around the East Liberty Presbyterian Church to be Gene Kelly Square. Kelly attended the dedication, but when he started to give a speech it began to rain, which he thought was "fitting." Nicklas noted "there was even a lamppost nearby." Gene was impressed by a steel sculpture titled *Joy of Life* by Italian-born sculptor (and Pitt professor) Virgil Cantini, which stood at one corner of the square. "I felt I had to drop you a line to tell you how much I enjoyed your sculpture," Gene wrote Cantini soon after his return home. Once again Nicklas sent a scrapbook, this time with photographs of the houses where he grew up and of the new Gene Kelly Square, where a banner went up after his speech depicting Kelly as a dancing sailor.[41]

Gene was equally keen to maintain contact with his high-school classmates as he was with deepening his ties to his college and to the city. Emerson Venable kept in touch by sending him copies of yearbooks published during their time together at Peabody High School.[42]

WANING YEARS

"I think it is important to share your life," Kelly told Pat York when she interviewed him. "But, of course, what is more important, and indeed more difficult, is to find the right person." He tried during the 1980s to find someone, dating Sandy Bennett, the former wife of singer Tony Bennett, for several years. In December 1985, while filming a cable television special about the Smithsonian Institution, Kelly met Patricia Ward, a freelance journalist more than forty-six years his junior. Ward admitted that she had never heard of

Gene, never seen any of his movies, and knew nothing of his career. But six months later Kelly asked her to come to California and help him write his memoirs. This proved to be more difficult than expected and took much longer than anticipated, but the two developed a relationship. When Gene was stricken with pneumonia in April 1989, he proposed to Ward in his hospital room at the Cedars-Sinai Medical Center. The wedding took place on July 20, 1990, in Santa Barbara. He was a month short of seventy-eight and she was thirty-one. A newspaper report indicated that Kelly changed his will to leave his $3 million home to her plus $1 million. It was a controversial marriage from the family's perspective.[43]

The couple continued to work on Gene's memoirs, telling an interviewer for *People* magazine in 1992 that Doubleday was slated to publish the book soon. "Abruptly brushing aside personal questions, Kelly wants only to talk dance," wrote the interviewer. The article included a smiling photograph of Gene standing in his dining room.[44] By this time he had lost a good deal of weight.

Kelly continued his close connection with Pittsburgh—"a great and interesting city," as he called it—during the 1990s. The Civic Light Opera created the Gene Kelly Awards to support high school musical theater. Divided into eleven categories and open to nineteen Allegheny County high schools, the awards were given yearly starting in May 1991. "I personally am very proud to have my name attached to this effort," Gene wrote in a note to be read at the first awards ceremony, which he could not attend.[45]

Virginia Nicklas genuinely admired and liked Kelly, filling her shelves with videotapes of his films and maintaining contact with him over the years. But there is no evidence that she ever openly requested a gift for the university, and Kelly may have been unaware that she was charged with such an effort. She admitted in a memo titled "Cultivation of Gene Kelly," dated March 18, 1992, that "efforts to interest Gene Kelly, the most prominent of all Pitt alumni, in financially supporting Pitt have been minimal throughout the past three decades." With the advent of a new chancellor and the fact that Kelly would soon turn eighty, Nicklas suggested several new approaches. But before the university could put her plan into action, she received a proposal from Pat Kelly that sculptor Elizabeth MacQueen execute a life-size statue of Gene in a dance pose and that the university fund it and place it on campus. Nicklas responded that Pitt officials liked the idea and even had a location in mind, but no money. They offered to work with the Kellys to get funding.[46]

In another "Cultivation of Gene Kelly" memo on January 6, 1993, Nicklas reported that she had called the Kelly home the previous day and had a fifteen-minute talk with Pat Kelly. Pat told Virginia that Gene's memoirs were "largely completed as of December 31st and at the publishers. Only 'mopping up' work remains." Pat also reported that she had contacted several organizations in California regarding the MacQueen statue. She wanted to give it to whoever was able to fund it, but she and Gene still hoped Pitt would get it.[47] This phone conversation on January 5, 1993, was the last contact Nicklas had with the Kellys. The statue was never made, and the desired big donation from Gene never materialized.

In May 1993, Kelly agreed to film a brief introduction and ending for *That's Entertainment! III*. The filming of the ending took place on Stage 5 of Sony Studios, which was the old M-G-M soundstage where he had filmed the "Worry Song" with Jerry the Mouse and parts of *Singin' in the Rain*. Gene looked very old by now and had lost much of his vitality. And yet, he conducted himself as "the model of polite professionalism, instantly sensitive to all that was going on behind the camera as well as in front of it."[48] When *That's Entertainment! III* was released on June 16, 1994, it offered his fans Kelly's last appearance on screen.

When the Gap clothing chain ran ads for khaki slacks the same year, the company asked Kelly's permission to include him in the pitch. He agreed, but the ad read "Gene Kelly wore khaki" and the majority of people portrayed in the ad had passed on. Many people wondered if the past tense (and the group he was with) meant he had died, and Gene was flooded with phone calls and letters. He took it all in stride, finding the mix-up amusing, but in truth he was often reminded of his advancing age and the inevitability of death. When Leonard Bernstein passed away, Gene was deeply saddened. He sent a few things written to him by Bernstein to be included in the composer's papers at the Library of Congress, regretting deeply that the rest had been destroyed in the house fire. Earlier Gene had donated more than 200 song sheets that had survived the fire (although several of them had scorch marks) to his own collection of papers at Boston University.[49]

Gene's health had been declining quickly since 1993. Ann Miller recalled that during the filming of his segments for *That's Entertainment! III*. Kelly "could hardly see, he had this bad back." She felt it was "heart-breaking" to see him in this condition. In early May 1994, Gene was hospitalized for cellulitis and suffered a severe stroke on July 22 of that year. The staff at the UCLA Medical Center got the eighty-one-year-old actor in stable condition, and after seven weeks Gene returned home. But Warren Cowan, his longtime

Figure 18.6 As host—in declining health but still in great humor—Kelly talked about Hollywood's golden musicals in his conferred role since the 1960s as the Ambassador of Dance in America. (Still from *That's Entertainment! III*, 1994)

publicity agent, thought Kelly never really recovered from this stroke. He suffered another lesser stroke early in February 1995 and entered Cedars-Sinai Medical Center in Los Angeles under an assumed name to throw off reporters.[50]

According to Betsy Blair, Pat Kelly took increasing control over Gene's life as his health and vigor declined. Pat tried to prevent Bridget from visiting her father in the hospital during recovery from his first stroke on the grounds that it was "embarrassing for him." But Bridget went to see him anyway and saw in his eyes how happy he was that she visited. Pat released Lois McClelland after nearly five decades of employment as Kelly's personal secretary, changed the locks, and hired a new housekeeper. She also changed his doctor, a close friend and neighbor for many years, his business manager, and his lawyer. It became difficult to reach him by phone. Betsy had to insist to Pat that she would come to see him when she was in the area in 1995. Gene was obviously happy to see her. They talked about children, grandchildren, and the old days. Betsy found him "lively and loving." As she was leaving, she kissed him on the cheek and was deeply saddened when he replied, "Good—I don't get any of that." She wrote there was "all the paraphernalia of round-the-clock nursing, but it seemed to me there was no love, no fun, no stimulation." Gene asked her to return the next day and bring Ted Reid, their old friend, with her. But later Pat called and cancelled her visit, saying Gene was not up to it. Betsy believed he was well enough, had been very much enlivened by her visit, and was eager to see her and Ted the next day.[51]

A third stroke proved too much for Gene. He died at 8:15 A.M. on February 2, 1996, and was cremated that morning. The ashes had already been spread before the three children arrived the next day at the appointed time of 6:00 P.M. With no ashes and no marker, the children felt they did not get a chance to say goodbye or to grieve. So they planted a tree in his honor at Will Rogers Memorial Garden on Rodeo Drive only a few hundred yards from the house.[52]

Kelly's passing elicited many obituaries in newspapers and magazines across the country and countless reminiscences by people who had been personally touched by him over the years. For example, Bill Thunhurst, working for the Civic Light Opera in Pittsburgh, recalled auditioning for a part in *On the Town* only to be rejected by Kelly, who told him "no, you're too good-looking." Thunhurst thought "that was the nicest and swiftest brushoff I've ever had." Bob Miller was only ten years younger than Kelly but recalled studying dance under him in Pittsburgh and performing in one of the Beth Shalom Kirmesses. "He took me under his wing—it's like losing an older brother."[53]

Several years before his death, Gene mused on the influence of his childhood, his parents, and his siblings in shaping his life. "We had a great childhood with lots of love," he told Pat York. "A tightly knit family and Irish Catholic on both sides, we never thought of disobeying our parents. . . . It was an old-fashioned bringing up." But his extended family was passing away at the time of his death. His older brother Jim had died a couple of years before and Fred's wife Dorothy nearly a year before. Jay's husband Mike Radvansky also died in 1995 and Louise's husband Bill Bailey the previous May.[54]

The book of memoirs that Gene so wanted to write but could not finish by himself—the project that brought Pat Ward out to California in the first place—has not yet been published after all these years. Whatever he had drafted and his notes for further work went up in smoke during the house fire of December 1983. He apparently restarted the project with Ward's help because by 1992 there were reports that Doubleday was about to publish it. There is no public explanation for why that never happened. "History is a hobby of mine," Gene told an interviewer, and he wanted to set the record straight on his career. ""Everybody tells so many lies. I'm just going to tell the truth." Kelly specifically cited Hugh Fordin's history of the Freed Unit for criticism. "You'd think that when the author was compiling facts, he'd have wanted to consult me. He didn't, and there are several mistakes as a result." He told interviewers David Fantle and Tom Johnson that his autobiography would be published in 1995, but his declining health was the likely reason that did not happen. Then in 2003 there appeared announcements that Pat Ward Kelly's book, based on taped interviews with Gene during the 1990s, would be published by Public Affairs Books the next year. Those plans changed and the book has not yet appeared. Prepublication publicity indicated that the project no longer was Gene's memoirs or biography but was focused on "her [Pat's] life with the screen legend."[55]

Kelly never was able to have his story told in the way he wanted it told during his lifetime. Whether his widow will produce a book that accomplishes this objective remains to be seen. But it is not necessary to wait for Pat Ward Kelly's book. Gene gave literally dozens of major interviews throughout his long life. He wrote several short articles for publication, poured out his life story in several in-depth oral histories, and saw his name mentioned and his career analyzed in dozens of books and articles. There is an astonishing wealth of information about Kelly's life and career that goes far beyond his memories in the 1990s or the taped interviews that he made for his third wife in the waning years of his life. This huge wealth of material is the foundation for our comprehensive study of Kelly's life and career as chronicled in this book.

CHAPTER 19

Renaissance Man

Summing up the career of an entertainer whose talents spread across many categories of creativity is no easy task. Gene Kelly successfully explored more aspects of entertainment than any other star in Hollywood. Yet he tends to be considered by the average fan as mainly a screen dancer. His achievements in choreography, acting, and directing, as well as his work on stage, television, and radio tend to be ignored or only dimly understood. Moreover, the intersections of his personal life and his career have not been thoroughly developed by previous writers. He was a teacher at heart, not only to the students in his dance studio at Pittsburgh and Johnstown but also to most of his colleagues. Kelly was a force to be considered in many areas of entertainment, and his long, involved career is much in need of evaluation.

DANCER

Gene's development as a dancer of power and creativity started on Broadway. In *The Time of Your Life* he created a character through dance for the first time in his career. In *Pal Joey* he took New York by storm with his electric dancing and charmed the audience despite playing a heel. His outstanding talent in dancing is what brought him to Hollywood.

Kelly's film dance career coincided with and defined, along with Fred Astaire, the Golden Age of the Hollywood musical. Reporter Don Alpert wrote in 1964 that "Kelly most likely will be remembered best as a dancer," and he was right. Gene saw ballet training as the foundation of his success in this area. It instilled in him a higher sense of discipline, imparted a greater degree of control over his entire body, and satisfied his intellectual curiosity and interest in dance history and culture. "All the sports in the world can't make you have certain kinds of line and form," he believed, but ballet offered him these important attributes. Nevertheless, he chose to concentrate on popular entertainment to make a living, incorporating many dance styles into a mélange spiked by a good deal of formula to offer mass audiences certain steps and moves that they enjoyed. But Kelly always kept "the classic line," using the total body concept even when he tapped or performed modern dance. His ballet training suffused and underlay nearly all he did as a screen dancer.[1]

Film historian Jerome Delamater has identified at least five major styles in Kelly's film dance career—tap, ballet, modern, ethnic, and athletic. "The simple, down-to-earth part of Kelly's character was manifested" in tap routines and athletic dancing while "the more pensive and soulful part was manifested" in ballet and modern styles. But it was in the assembling of these disparate dance styles into a cohesive whole that formed the basis of Kelly's success. Delamater notes that Gene was not the first or only dancer to mix different styles, but he did so more comprehensively and effectively than anyone else. Kelly was proud of his accomplishment, telling an interviewer that others had to judge whether his mix of styles was good, but no one could take away from him the achievement of having accomplished it through hard work over many years.[2]

How seriously observers took Kelly's expertise in ballet technique varied. Everyone was aware of his interest in classic dance and recognized that it influenced his body control while dancing other styles. Early in Kelly's career, John K. Newnham argued that Gene was "a balletomane, but not a ballet dancer." In contrast, Igor Youskevitch thought Kelly had the potential to become "one of the finest character performers in contemporary ballet" even though he did not have the "proper training." But Youskevitch believed Gene's technique was "not good enough" to place him in the top rank of ballet performers because he did not quite have "the noble bearing of a prince Siegfried in *Swan Lake*."[3]

Gene was influenced by previous trends in ballet to feel strongly that the dancer needed to "subjugate his style to fit the character he is playing." He believed this was easier if the dancer was conversant with a variety of styles. He not only thought it important to link dance performance to character development, but he believed that the dancer had to be able to segue from dialogue into dance and out of it without losing the character.[4] He himself never lost sight of this in his own performances.

Kelly rejected the typical 1930s film dance with its shiny floors and men dancing in tuxedos in favor of jeans, rolled-up shirtsleeves, and loafers. "All my dancing came out of the idea of the common man," he often said, "which is the exact class from which I sprang." Gene saw a tight connection between his early life in Pittsburgh and his art. But he also admitted, "I was influenced very much by my social and political thinking." A side benefit of the way he dressed for dancing was that Kelly could show the line of his body and "not hide it with coats and suits."[5] Of course, his frequently worn sailor suit served both purposes as well—to denote the common man and to show the dancer's body.

Gene was right to bypass classical dance for popular entertainment, the area where his talents led him. As Graham Fuller writes, "It was Kelly's streetwise Everyman figure that did most to liberate the genre from its 'putting on a show' tradition." He also helped to move film dance away from the 1930s ballroom style of Fred Astaire and Ginger Rogers.[6] In the process he popularized dance to a wider audience in America than anyone else.

Commentators have noted that Kelly did not develop a stable partnership with one female dancer as had Astaire, and Gene argued that he never had any interest in being part of an ongoing dance team. It was good for his development to be free to perform with a variety of female and male partners. When he did dance with a female partner, he strongly believed that the attention had to be directed to the girl rather than to him. But whoever he danced with, male or female, "I work doubly hard making the other person look good," so that they would look good together.[7]

Kelly furthered the development of the prop dance or "bricolage" by frequently incorporating items in the set design into his routine and "converting the ordinary into the marvelous," as Gerald Mast put it. Critics were also impressed by Gene's "earthy masculinity," "athlete's grace," and "dynamic style."[8] He inspired the next generation's athletic dancers, such as Tommy Rall, Bob Fosse, and Michael Kidd, who took that theme to its apotheosis, although with little success in using that athleticism to create appealing characters.

And yet, Kelly said he knew what Bill Robinson meant by saying the face was the most important part of a dancer's body. Gene's facial expressions were closely tuned to the feelings he wanted to emote as a dancer. Related to this, he commented that "what goes on in your head is maybe more important than what goes [on] in your calves." But Kelly also thought that arms were very important in dance expression. They differentiated a total body dancer from a hoofer and were "the hardest to use."[9]

Gene was well aware that a dancer reached a physical peak in his twenties and his body wore out quickly after that. Yet he began his film dance career relatively late, at age thirty. That career lasted much longer than he expected, until his last major dance film in 1957 at age forty-five.[10] In some ways, coming to this later in life helped his career, because by then he had the maturity to develop larger goals for his film career—pursue cine-dance, develop film ballet, experiment with technical possibilities—things he probably could not have done as a younger man.

As Fred Kelly said of his brother, Gene was "a natural dancer." Moreover, he had talent as a performer that lifted him above the majority of good dancers. For example, Louis DaPron was "a dancer's dancer," according to Peggy Ryan, but he never performed on screen because, as he put it, "I don't have it from the waist up." Paul Draper excelled in tap and discovered ballet at age twenty-three to revolutionize his individual style. But Draper admitted he lacked the ability to "sell the steps to the audience." In contrast, as film historian Rick Altman writes, "Kelly's talent and style turns the entire world into a realm of gaiety. . . . Watching him dance makes us want to dance, seeing him express his joy makes us joyous in turn."[11] It was a combination of natural dancing ability and charisma that helped Gene to achieve his goal of spreading joy through dancing.

CHOREOGRAPHER

Kelly started devising dance steps at an early age—for the students at his dance schools, Beth Shalom, and Cap and Gown. He then became a "dance doctor" in Pittsburgh, helping other performers improve their routines. On Broadway, Gene's first choreography was for a dance in *Leave It to Me*. He then choreographed his own dances in *The Time of Your Life* and worked closely with Robert Alton to create his numbers in *Pal Joey*, with both shows receiving wide approbation.

Choreography "was my first love," Kelly said in 1958, "and still may be my first love." Although he said the same thing about dancing at other times, creating dance was more enjoyable to Gene than performing the steps. Good choreographers were scarce because it was a "very specialized talent." As Gene put it, "You pull dance out of thin air."[12]

Kelly choreographed virtually every dance number he performed on film and on television, a record unique among major dance figures in either medium. For example, Astaire worked up many of his own numbers but with the aid of choreographer Hermes Pan. In addition, Kelly choreographed many dances performed by his colleagues in most of his films. This unusual achievement came partly from Gene's innate interest in developing dances and partly from his many years of creating routines in Pittsburgh.

But it also came from Kelly's desire to achieve his broader goals in Hollywood—such as using the camera to best advantage and creating cine-dance. He had to control the choreography of his own numbers and those who danced with him if he hoped to achieve those goals. Gene thoroughly enjoyed developing a dance number, calling it his "creative energy and life force." He referred to the perfecting of the dance through weeks of rehearsal as "the sweat, blood, and tears" of the process.[13]

In his many interviews, Kelly explained that each dance had to evolve from elements in the film such as character development and plot advancement. He saw each dance as a short story, having a beginning, a middle part, and an end. The middle was the easiest because this is informed by the choreographer's grasp of various dance styles. Starting the number and ending it were difficult to develop. Most of this work took place in Kelly's head before he ever stood up to work out an arrangement of steps. He kept in mind the need to cut each dance into scenes to make a sequence in which everything flows smoothly. In effect, he created dance steps with film editing in view. He rarely recorded his choreography on paper, at most merely jotting down some basic ideas.[14] We found that his personal papers contain such jottings only for *Jack and the Beanstalk*.

Negative assessments of Kelly's choreography are rare. Only his choreography in *Brigadoon* has been described as listless and uninspiring. As for *Invitation to the Dance*, Clive Barnes thought Gene was out of his element in choreographing "Circus," characterizing him as "a vaudeville choreographer, not a 'serious' choreographer."[15]

But the overwhelming verdict on Kelly is one of accomplishment, praise, and gratitude for his achievement in choreography. Delamater wrote that Kelly not only choreographed far more film musicals than other choreographers but he also used eclectic dance styles as opposed to others who used mainly ballet (Loring), mainly modern dance (Cole), or mainly gymnastics (Kidd and Fosse). Delamater also credited Kelly with a desire to create dances uniquely for the camera, noting that he was adept at developing dance numbers that expanded the constricted space of the viewfinder and took full advantage of a large soundstage and numerous camera angles to portray the number from many angles. Dance historian Beth Genné noted that Kelly did a better job of creating dance to fit the context of the film than did Astaire.

Figure 19.1 Choreographing a dance with the help of Carol Haney and Jeanne Coyne in 1951. (Photographer Maurice Terrell, Library of Congress)

Jeanine Basinger wrote that he "strove to devise a cinematic language of dance . . . which told the audience what the character felt, thought, *was*." As David Atkins put it, Kelly "stretched and redefined the boundaries of film choreography."[16]

ACTOR

Gene was aware that making the transition from dancer-choreographer to actor was a big leap. After the grueling process of learning how to dance at a high level of performance, most dancers found that they had neglected to learn how to act. Kelly argued that a good dancer could act even through dancing, but he knew that was not the same as acting believably in a straight, nondancing role.[17] Nevertheless, although his success on Broadway was tied mainly to his dancing and choreography, Kelly had shown in *Pal Joey* that he was also able to act believably. But acting on stage was not the same as playing for the camera.

On Broadway, Gene had no difficulty projecting his voice and body movements to be heard and seen by patrons in the back rows. That did not work when acting for a camera. Kelly credited Judy Garland and Busby Berkeley for showing him how to act in movies during the filming of *For Me and My Gal.* He watched Judy and noticed she pitched her voice and gestures low. He felt by the end of the filming that he "had picked up quite a lot of know-how, thanks to Berkeley and thanks to her [Judy]." Nevertheless, Gene admitted that during his early years in Hollywood he spent more time on dancing and choreography than learning to tone down his acting for the camera, and as a result he tended to overact. He also hated close-ups because he never got the hang of doing them well.[18] Kelly had difficulty mastering the art of understatement, of distilling emotion into subtle movements and slight facial expressions.

When asked about his acting technique, Gene simply said, "I try to be the person I'm playing. I get there by various and sundry means." And yet, much of his screen success grew out of his forceful personality—a force he could not fully control or manipulate before the camera. He therefore falls into the category of a film star who largely played himself in most roles.[19] Viewers enjoyed his movies because they enjoyed watching him, rarely believing they were seeing Danny McGuire, Serafin, or Don Lockwood.

Kelly certainly was capable of creating a real character to the extent that the viewer forgets it is Gene Kelly they are watching—Tom Triplett in "The Life You Save" on television is the best example. But he rarely was given the kind of character that offered him such a chance. The starring roles he played in his major film musicals were shallow, fluffy characters, and Triplett, in contrast, was a complicated man.

But there is a consistency in his acting that endears Kelly to viewers. He very often played characters who were brash, aggressive, and manipulative to start with, but who learned and matured by the end of the movie. They became more likeable, lovable, and loving with experience, and therefore Kelly had a chance—even with the shallow characters of his major film musicals—to work on more than one dimension. He pulled that off very well.

In the end, Kelly's acting career was mostly carried by his forceful personality, essentially playing himself on the screen. He had that element of stardom that Douglas Newton called "poetic presence" and Robert Trachtenberg called "that X quality." Acting was hard work for him, and sometimes he admitted to not enjoying it. But at other times he proudly pointed to examples of his acting achievement, citing his work in *Christmas Holiday*, *Black Hand*,

Marjorie Morningstar, and *Inherit the Wind* to prove that he was capable of excellent acting on film.[20]

Some commentators have complained that Kelly overacted too much at times. Similarly, Stephen Harvey has noted Gene's "exasperating movie mannerisms," and Rick Altman mentions his "vulgarities." These commentators are obviously referring to the unnecessarily crude segments in some of Kelly's films. Directors such as Busby Berkeley and George Sidney encouraged overacting, but Gene himself enjoyed hamming it up. The gross overacting he indulged in as D'Artagnan in *The Three Musketeers* (1948) is something he admitted late in life.[21] We have discussed similar instances of crass overacting Kelly does—by himself in the "Fido/statue" number from *Living in a Big Way* (1947), with Sinatra in "Yes, Indeedy" from *Take Me Out to the Ball Game* (1949), and with Oscar Levant and George Guetary in "By Strauss" from *An American in Paris* (1951). The silliness in the "Binge" dance from *It's Always Fair Weather* (1955) is different, because it was part of the plot where the men were drunk. The overacting in *The Pirate* (1948) was also part of the plot and of Serafin's character and it was done in an appealing way. Fortunately, there is no hint of crudeness in any of Kelly's films or television performances after 1951. He reached a level of maturity as an actor at age thirty-nine that stayed with him for the rest of his career.

But even before Kelly reached this level of stability, he turned in many fine performances in dramatic roles. As Basinger notes, no other musical star could act as well as Kelly did as a murderer (*Christmas Holiday*), a victim who seeks revenge (*Black Hand*), a French prisoner of the Nazis (*Cross of Lorraine*), and many other impressive character roles on the big screen.[22]

CLOWN

Kelly always had a soft spot for clowns and repeatedly played one in the movies. A reporter for *Nova* magazine wrote in 1972 that he even looked like a clown, "because his eyes are round and black and very bright and his features so humorously mobile that he seems constantly on the point of doing something droll to please you."[23] Gene loved to clown around since boyhood. It was evident in his interactions with students at the dance studios, in his directing Cap and Gown shows, and in his stage, film, and television performances. He always wanted to make people laugh.

Kelly dressed as a clown many times in his film career. His first dance in his

Figure 19.2 As a clown dancing with the troupe to "Broadway Rhythm" in the film's ballet. Future wife Jeanne Coyne is to his right. (Still from *Singin' in the Rain*, 1952)

first film, *For Me and My Gal*, was as a clown (Figure 6.3). He performed two separate numbers as a clown in *The Pirate* (Figures 8.4 and 8.5) and clowned around with Phil Silvers in *Summer Stock* (Figure 11.1). Kelly created the "Circus" segment of *Invitation to the Dance* and played the clown in it (Figures 12.2, 19.3, 19.4). This is one instance where the clown was mainly a sad figure in keeping with the cultural tradition of Pierrot, although he did make the audience laugh at the start of the segment. Kelly played Pinky Benson the clown in *What a Way to Go!* (Figure 16.3). And even in his classic film *Singin' in the Rain*, best remembered for his enchanting dance to the title number, he played a clown in the "Broadway Ballet" (Figure 19.2).

Gene also clowned around in film numbers where he was *not* dressed in a clown's costume. Examples include "Make Way for Tomorrow" in *Cover Girl* (Figure 6.7), the "Fido/statue" number in *Living in a Big Way*, "Yes, Indeedy" in *Take Me Out to the Ball Game*, "Prehistoric Man" and "You Can Count on Me" in *On the Town*, "Tra-la-la," "By Strauss," and "I Got Rhythm" (Figure 11.3) in *An American in Paris*, "Moses Supposes" in *Singin' in the Rain* (Figure 11.5), and "I Love to Go Swimmin' with Women" in *Deep in My Heart* (Figure 14.2). Although a few instances in this set were not so funny due to overacting, most of his clowning performances allowed Kelly to fill people with joy.

SINGER

Fred Kelly recalled that Gene "had a great singing voice" as a boy and was always being asked to sing, "which embarrassed him no end." But when his voice changed, Gene never felt entirely comfortable with it. He recalled that his mother once said, "You'll never get anywhere without voice lessons," but none of the Kelly children were trained in that way. As Saul Chaplin put it, Kelly was "always a little worried" about the quality of his vocal performance, which Chaplin characterized as "a very pleasant Irish voice; it's the most I can say for it." But Chaplin astutely pointed out that this was an impetus for Kelly to figure out how he could put a song across.[24]

Gene focused on the emotion and how to express the point of the lyrics in a believable way. He said composers and lyricists often told him they preferred dancers to sing their songs because singers tended to follow certain rules and stretch words until the lyrics became unintelligible. Kelly zeroed in on "the lyrical interpretation" and sang the words clearly and from the heart. He also knew that "the attitude, [and] the way you use your arms," were very important to convey the song well.[25] Kelly had to learn on the job how to sing effectively. On Broadway, he sang solo, unaccompanied by music, for half a minute before the orchestra came in at the start of *Pal Joey*. The audience loved it all, including his a cappella singing.

For a short while Gene took lessons with a Russian vocal coach in New York but devoted scant attention to voice training after going to Hollywood. Focused on rehearsing the dances, he quickly prepared for the songs only the day before the recording session and, later in life, regretted that he did not spend more time rehearsing his singing. But he also believed that the best preparation for a singer was to learn a musical instrument early in life (as he had done with his violin lessons) to acclimate oneself to read and hear notes correctly.[26] Indeed, he had no problem singing in the correct key.

While many people commented on Kelly's limited ability as a singer, they nevertheless admitted that his voice had a pleasing quality and that he sang effectively. In fact, Kelly made several records, one of them a long-playing album in which he sang popular songs from his hit movies in a variety of styles, tempos, and with some tap dancing sounds mixed in.[27]

Like Astaire, Kelly could not command a strong singing voice. But like his colleague, he became a successful singer nevertheless. Gene utilized sincerity of expression, clarity of pronunciation, and, most importantly, finding the emotional center of the song to express it in a way for everyone to appreciate. Kelly's film songs are loved by his many fans. In particular, his joyous rendering of the title song from *Singin' in the Rain* and the bittersweet "Long Ago and Far Away" from *Cover Girl* are standouts.

DIRECTOR

Although Gene did not direct any shows while on Broadway from 1938 to 1941, he had many years of experience directing shows for his dance students, Beth Shalom, and Cap and Gown. Of course, none of these required camerawork, but it did give him experience in directing actors and dancers.

Kelly became a movie director mostly because of his need to obtain greater control over the process of filming his dances. Once he immersed himself in the task, its challenges intrigued him, and he learned all aspects of the job. Kelly credited Busby Berkeley with showing him how to use the camera for filming dance sequences in *For Me and My Gal*. He learned about boom shots from Vincente Minnelli in filming *The Pirate*. Because he was the star as well in several films, Kelly needed the help of an assistant to guide the cameraman. He brought in Stanley Donen, and they became a cohesive team on several major dance musicals.[28] Later, Kelly worked as the sole director for thirteen film and television projects.

When Kelly came to prominence as a director with *On the Town*, his ideas for on-location shooting and quick cuts were widely admired. His colleagues were certain he would become "one of the top directors in the film colony," according to reporter Morgan Hudgins. There was "a definite style to Kelly's films," wrote Delamater, citing "a conscious attempt to make the camera work unobtrusive" despite "long takes with elaborate tracking and dollying shots." Genné noted that Kelly was the first dancer to become "an important director in his own right." Critic Clive Barnes pointed out that Kelly made "some really beautiful and arresting shots," which were "cinematically a pure joy," and that he has been "underrated" as a director.[29]

Gene directed actors and dancers with clarity and purpose. Astutely comparing the two, he said: "As a director, I would wish that all actors had the discipline of the dancer, and that dancers had the emotional know-how of actors."

But he was also aware that an actor, unlike a dancer, "likes to think it all comes from him." So he was careful in guiding actors to get what he wanted. We have seen earlier how actors in *The Tunnel of Love*, *A Guide for the Married Man*, and *Hello, Dolly!* (except Streisand) praised his supportive direction. But if needed, Kelly also acted out what he envisioned. Photographs in Tony Thomas's book show Gene effectively demonstrating to an extra how to stagger like a drunk in *Gigot*, as well as several other instances where he showed actors the physical nuances of portraying a particular scene.[30] Even in his stage direction, Kelly showed actors how to physically convey something (Figure 15.3).

Of course, Gene easily directed dancers because of his extensive experience in both dancing and choreography. "He knew exactly what he wanted," Claude Bessy told the authors. "He really explained to me the character and the situation, and everything happened without any problem." Fred Astaire worked with dozens of directors during his long career and highly praised Kelly. He called Gene "a damned good director." The same was true for Donald O'Connor, who called Kelly "a great director."[31]

Very few individuals in the entertainment field duplicated Kelly's career in this way. Wendy Toye is an exception. She had danced since age three and even choreographed a children's ballet when she was but a child herself. While she was acting and dancing in a film at age fourteen, the director asked her to take over the camera and film one of the dances. She went on to become one of England's earliest women directors and credited her choreographic work because it made her "sensitive to people. I knew how to place them, how to move them, how to keep things moving on the screen."[32] Toye's techniques and working style as a director are very similar to Kelly's because of their common early experiences.

But Kelly went further than Toye in his grasp of technical aspects. "He's a good technician himself," art director Randall Duell said of Kelly, "and he's knowledgeable in the field of photography."[33] In fact, through his interest and hard work, Gene learned a great deal about filming.

Even in movies codirected with Donen, Kelly was behind the camera, approving the setup before his performance was filmed. We provide an example of this in chapter 11, discussing two photographs tied to the filming of *Singin' in the Rain* where he is behind the camera and then in front of it. Another such example is from the "Circus" segment in *Invitation to the Dance*. Photographs show Kelly dressed as the clown behind the camera approving the setup, then in front of the camera in discussion with the camera operators before they start filming.

Figure 19.3 Directing "Circus" in 1952 from *Invitation to the Dance* (1956), behind the camera with his clown makeup on. (Photographer Robert Capa, Library of Congress)

Kelly preferred to use one camera to better control lighting, movement, and the overall look of a scene, breaking that rule only for the big parade sequence in *Hello, Dolly!* Multiple cameras also wasted a great deal of film, and Gene was always concerned about economy. "Kelly was extremely involved in the camera's movement," said Roy Wagner (who worked on *Hello, Dolly!*) in an email to the authors. Gene admitted there was "a lot of blood, sweat, and tears in making a camera move," but he invested the time and patience to supervise it step by step. In directing dancers, he moved the camera to accommodate the dance, to let it flow naturally rather than keeping it stationary at the most advantageous angle and capturing the movement from one perspective.[34] In short, Kelly refused to let technical constraints restrict the filming of the dance.

Gene never became an editor but he learned everything possible about

Figure 19.4 Fully dressed as the clown—but still directing "Circus" through interaction with the cameraman on the crane (who is not in the photo)—while other dancers are around, one on a teeter-totter, ready to start performing. (Photographer Robert Capa, Library of Congress)

the process while in the Navy, and he later worked closely with cutters, especially on editing his film dances. Kelly soon learned to direct numbers as well as nondance scenes in a way to influence the editing process and achieve the final cinematic effect he sought. "You go up to a certain point and [stop filming], so the editor is forced to go into the angle of the next shot" without taking anything away. It was termed "cutting in the camera," and Gene found that directors as diverse as Minnelli and John Ford practiced it. Roy Wagner told the authors that "one of the techniques Gene perfected" was to start wide and move in, and for the next shot do the opposite. This made editing seamless.[35]

Kelly disliked widescreen technology because it inhibited quick cutting and fast panning, two techniques he particularly liked. He approved the results of Technicolor but thought the process of filming it was cumbersome, as the camera was heavy and difficult to move. One advantage was that the Technicolor people were eager to experiment, and Gene worked with them during postproduction to manipulate the balance of colors. The Technicolor camera was constructed in a way that kept the viewfinder at least eighteen inches from the floor, so Kelly conceived of placing a wooden shelf at the bottom of a crane and putting a mirror on it so the camera could shoot into the mirror and get a lower angle. It was called a "Ubangi."[36] The idea came about because of Gene's thinking like a director as well as a dancer.

"You have to know everybody's job," he once said to an interviewer when asked what makes a good director. "It takes a lot of extra homework." He also acknowledged that a good script was extremely important for good directing but "the director . . . has to discuss with the writer every single word, he has to understand the intent and purpose of each [word]. . . . It takes many hours of discussion and adjustment."[37] In applying himself so thoroughly to all aspects of the job, Kelly became an excellent director, marked by his technical knowledge of camerawork, his attention to writers, and his handling of actors, dancers, and the crew.

TEACHER

Kelly once told Hedda Hopper, "I'm a real teacher at heart" and he meant it. Long before he decided to become a professional dancer, Gene was teaching kids of all ages while he was still a student in high school and college. He retained his love of teaching for the rest of his life. Gene did not see this as a career because the Gene Kelly Studio of the Dance grew to be as large as he could make it, and he did not want to create a chain of studios like Arthur Murray's. He had no interest in teaching social dancing but sought to turn out professional dancers conversant with a wide variety of styles. Kelly saw a tight connection between teaching and choreography because in both areas it was important to show someone how to dance. The only disappointment he felt as a teacher was that most of his students eventually did something else with their lives rather than make dance a career.[38]

Lois Elias was a nine-year-old student of Kelly's during the 1935 Kirmess season at Beth Shalom. At age eighty, she talked with the authors about how important that experience had been for her life. Gene at twenty-three impressed all the students, his charm "enveloping you," and "everybody was just a bit bedazzled by him," according to Elias. She was late one evening for rehearsal, entered the hallway rather noisily, and finally noticed that everyone had stopped rehearsing and was staring at her. Gene beckoned to her, and she was afraid. But he put his hands on her shoulders, leaned down and kissed her on the forehead, and softly said, "Don't be late again." Elias took the lesson to heart, learning how important it was to be on time and thoughtful of others. She recalled that Gene taught the students the importance of body control, showing them how to hold themselves with his back to the class and then turning around to watch them do it until everyone got it right. His method was to teach one step and allow them ample time to learn it well before going on to the next lesson. Elias also recalled that all his lessons were infused with enthusiasm as well as discipline. He had a unique gift as a teacher in making each stage in the learning process fun as well as demanding. She was one of the few Kelly students who went on to dance as an adult. At only five feet tall, Elias performed in specialty roles in off-Broadway stage productions and for many years lived in Paris, where she continued to study dance.[39]

It is true, as Kelly once said, that he never produced a ballet star, but he did teach hundreds of young people a variety of dance styles.[40] More importantly, Gene taught them how to work and live their lives with fun and discipline. Elias would not have been able to enjoy performing her roles throughout her long life without Gene's tutelage.

Kelly touched many people through personal contact and his philosophy of life skills. "I found out that I loved working with children," Gene said in 1975. "They'd laugh at everything I said and they giggled. We enjoyed being with each other. They changed my attitude a lot about dancing." He grew to love teaching, but he also grew to love dancing even more because of the children's influence on him. Out of this association grew a lifelong desire to create entertainment for children. In the fall of 1946, he made three records of fairy tales and one record of nursery songs for Columbia. He also had a long-term wish to make movies for children.[41] Several such plans were not realized. The exceptions were *Jack and the Beanstalk* and "Sinbad" in *Invitation to the Dance.*

But Kelly's love of teaching extended to audiences of all ages. He gave lectures to college students and the general public throughout his career. As early as 1946 he talked about dance and film with students at the University of California, Los Angeles (UCLA). The faculty was interested in having him teach an entire course, but Gene's schedule would not allow it. In 1949, he gave a presentation on the "educational, physical, and historic aspects of dancing" to 950 students and teachers at Pepperdine College. When discussing problems of teaching dance he drew on his own experience at teaching blind, deaf, and physically handicapped students. In a talk at the San Francisco Museum of Art in 1954 about film dancing, Kelly very articulately explained the problems of committing dance to cinema. In a change of topic, Gene spoke to students at UCLA in 1962 about writing rather than dancing. The students were so excited that they would not stop asking questions. "You are undoubtedly one of the most effective speakers ever to appear before an audience predominately composed of young writers," declared the chairman of the committee that had invited him.[42]

Gene increased the number of his lectures in the 1970s and 1980s and spoke at least once to a high school.[43] He was an unusually effective public speaker on issues that moved and excited him, which included virtually anything related to dancing or to creative expression in general. His public speaking career grew out of his larger role as a lifelong teacher.

MENTOR

Kelly continued his role as teacher by mentoring a number of colleagues and costars during his film career. His influence was most importantly felt in what can be termed the "Kelly Team" within the Freed Unit at M-G-M. The first member of that team was Stanley Donen, to be followed by Jeanne Coyne and then Carol Haney. At times, Alex Romero was a member of the team, and Jimmy Thompson was a latecomer who arrived just when the Golden Age was winding down. Kelly's mentoring was vital to the creation of Donen's independent career as a director, and it was equally vital for Haney's independent career as a performer and choreographer. The list of costars and others whose careers were decisively shaped by Kelly's influence and advice include Frank Sinatra, Phil Silvers, Rita Hayworth, Vera-Ellen, Leslie Caron, Cyd Charisse, Debbie Reynolds, and Michael Crawford.

In an article about the women in his dancing life, Kelly offered astute evaluations that well illustrate his judgment of talent and potential in his costars. "The better people you have around you," Kelly said in 1958, "the better work you'll do. It's not only more challenging, but they lift you up." But he also worked hard to help his colleagues reach their potential. With one exception, the team members and costars whose careers were changed by Kelly were overwhelmingly grateful to him and publicly acknowledged his influence.

For example, Vera-Ellen said of Kelly that "dancing with him did the most to advance my career."[44]

But Kelly also touched many lives in quiet ways that were vitally important to them. Luigi Faccuito had begun crafting a career as a dancer until World War II intruded. He survived naval service in the Pacific only to be in a terrible automobile accident after returning to civilian life. Faccuito was in a coma for two months and then faced three years of rehabilitation from paralysis of the left side of his body and face before he could dance again. His face never regained its elasticity, and Faccuito was very self-conscious of his appearance. He was sure it would be noticed when he auditioned for Kelly for *On the Town*. "Okay. Do your thing," Gene told him, and Faccuito nervously performed three or four combinations. Gene astutely said, "You love to dance, don't you, boy?" "I said, 'Yes.' He said, 'You got the job.'" Not only did Faccuito perform in "Miss Turnstiles," but Kelly also gave him a close-up in *Singin' in the Rain*'s "Broadway Ballet" that finally ended Faccuito's self-consciousness about his face. He is the one who opens the peephole in the speakeasy door to check out Gene and his "agent" before letting them in. "I didn't have to worry about my eyes anymore," he said. "Gene Kelly gave me a close-up." Faccuito went on to perform in many dance films and became a dance teacher as well, developing a jazz-based warmup exercise for dancers that became widely popular.[45] His life was dramatically changed not only by Gene's discernment in seeing how important dancing was to him but by his compassion as well.

KELLY AND DONEN

The only student of what Betsy Blair called the "Kelly University" who turned on his mentor was Stanley Donen.[46] His falling-out with Gene became obvious with their collaboration on *It's Always Fair Weather*. After that, Donen developed an openly sour attitude toward Kelly that worsened as he aged. Throughout his long life he claimed more credit than he deserved for the jointly directed movies they created, often laced with criticisms of Kelly. Gene, for his part, studiously refrained from criticizing Stanley, taking the high road in this unfortunate development.

Ironically, even as he claimed undue credit for his work on musicals with Kelly, Donen disparaged musicals in his later career, calling them insubstantial in 1973 and saying that he disliked *Singin' in the Rain* in 1968. Of course at other times he said it was the best movie.[47] Almost everything he said in one interview he refuted in another.

Kelly was clear and consistent about many aspects of his collaboration with Donen. Although he often said they "were a good team," he also clarified that "I was captain. I was the senior." And he was right. Gene went out of his way to help Stanley early in the latter's struggling career and saved him on more than one occasion. At one time Donen honestly said: "I was nothing at the time. A *shlepper*. A real zero." But Kelly saw his potential as an assistant and got jobs for him for several movie projects in Hollywood. At times, Donen was unable to retain his position at various studios and Kelly had to pull strings to get him rehired.[48]

The most important thing Gene did for Stanley was to put him behind the camera (so to speak) as his assistant in filming dances; what Donen actually did was to guide the cameramen as to what Kelly precisely wanted. This was Donen's forté, not choreography or performing. Kelly recognized this, and Donen himself admitted it to his biographer, Joseph Casper. Gene gave him the chance to develop his real talent. And although Kelly appreciated Donen's help in guiding the cameramen filming Gene's dances, he also said, "If I didn't have Stanley, I would have Carol Haney or Jeanne Coyne" as an assistant he could trust.[49] The team of Kelly and Donen certainly was not an even proposition—Kelly was multitalented, much more experienced, and had a far wider vision of what was needed to advance the film musical. It was inevitable that their collaboration would be as senior and junior partner.

And Donen did not complain while it was happening. Instead, he praised Kelly as a "creative genius" and "the most stimulating man to work with." Everyone involved in their joint projects, from costars to technical crews, confirmed that Gene was the senior and Stanley was his assistant. For example, Saul Chaplin has written that "Stanley Donen who had been a chorus boy in New York owes his entire career as director to Gene." Chaplin went on to write that "in every case Gene was the prime mover" of their collaborative work. In fact, it was an act of generosity for Kelly to talk M-G-M into letting Donen direct one number by himself in *Take Me Out to the Ball Game* and to list Donen as codirector of *On the Town*. Gene said he considered Stanley a cocreator rather than just his assistant by that time. Kelly was very willing to give Donen credit for his contributions even though he himself did much more. He also pointed out that the collaboration was advantageous for both men.[50]

Kelly also appreciated Donen's personal friendship and loyalty during the healthy period of their collaboration. Even as late as 1994, he said Donen was like a son to him. During their early association, the younger man spent an enormous amount of time at the Kelly home even though he had an apartment of his own. George Cukor asked the Kellys who was the man always asleep in their living room. As Farley Granger explained it, "Everyone thought he lived there."[51]

So why did Donen turn on Kelly? When he received accolades as a solo director, Donen became focused on his own legacy. He then sought to grab what he could at Kelly's expense from the years of collaboration with the much more famous mentor. He always claimed that Kelly gave him no credit even though Gene consistently praised Donen's contributions in his many interviews. It often happens that people who start out with low self-esteem overcompensate when they achieve some level of public acclaim. They are emboldened to express hidden resentments and to claim much more than they deserve to build themselves further. Perhaps he resented being seen by everyone as Kelly's assistant at the studio when he was treated as a friend at the Kelly house. Whatever the reason, it was tawdry, ungenerous, and unkind of Donen to rail against the man who more than anyone gave him numerous opportunities to blossom as a director.

But as his biographer, Stephen Silverman, writes, this was a man who was proud to claim that he was an atheist all his life and that he was oblivious to World War II, unconcerned about who won. He also had no qualms about faking preview cards and stuffing the response box for *Charade* to falsely portray that audiences wanted more violence just so Universal Studios would leave the violent scenes in the film that it was inclined to eliminate. After *Charade*'s release, reviewers strongly criticized the movie for excessive violence.[52] Kelly's high road in this saga with Donen is obviously related to his far better character.

Donen's constant carping influenced his first biographer, Joseph Casper, and writer Gerald Mast to discuss Kelly-Donen films as if Donen solely directed them.[53] Their poor scholarship is based on failing to conduct adequate research in primary and secondary sources and from being easily guided by an obviously biased source.

The most egregious case of distorting film history is by Silverman, Donen's second biographer. In his book on Donen, published soon after Kelly's passing, he not only repeated Casper's and Mast's errors in saying that Donen directed the codirected films, but he also aggressively sided with Donen on his many false claims despite all the contrary evidence. Worse, he went out of his way to personally attack Kelly throughout his book.[54] Negativity sells—at least among those who thrive on it—as seen in blogs, articles, and commentary by people who seem to enjoy Silverman's book and Donen's caustic remarks and who in turn perpetuate undeserved credit to Donen while maligning Kelly. Sadly this trend continued until Donen's death in 2019.

Fortunately some people have seen through the charade and spoken out against it. Genné has pointed out that several sources refute Silverman's claim that Kelly danced and Donen directed. Indeed, as cited in our 2009 book on *Singin' in the Rain*, everyone present during the codirecting confirmed that Kelly *solely* directed the actors and dancers and that he played the *major* role in the technical directing as well. In an email to the authors, cinematographer Roy Wagner corroborated that all the crew who worked on *Singin' in the Rain*, including cinematographer Hal Rosson and cameraman Frank Phillips, said Kelly, not Donen, designed the shots. Donen then did what Kelly had planned while Kelly performed for the camera.[55]

In addition, as cited throughout this book, the assistant director's reports for all the Kelly-Donen films reveal that Kelly planned the shots, rode the boom, and was deeply involved in every aspect of directing. The reports even mention that Donen often rehearsed players but waited for Kelly's approval before shooting. Kelly's contributions to the collaboration were clearly superior; his mentoring and help to Donen were generous. It is sad indeed that Donen reacted so ungratefully to Kelly, unlike the many other people Gene mentored and helped.

KELLY AND MINNELLI

In contrast to his mentoring association with Donen, Kelly's collaboration with Minnelli was on an equal footing. "Minnelli and I came together as two mature men head on and found this wonderful collaboration" when they worked on *The Pirate*, *An American in Paris*, and *Brigadoon*. Especially for *The Pirate*, Kelly and Minnelli fired each other's imagination and creativity. They worked very closely with each other on developing the character of Serafin, conceptualizing the famous "Pirate Ballet," and filming the project's other spectacular dance numbers. Minnelli consistently praised Kelly's contributions and recalled that working with him was a joy. In turn, Kelly said, "I always felt that Vincente and I brought out the best in each other."[56]

Minnelli loved boom shots and spent hours planning and executing these very difficult camera angles. "Booms are deadly to most directors," stated Walter Strohm, head of production at M-G-M, but Minnelli mastered them better than anyone in the business. Genné writes that Minnelli was an obvious influence on Kelly in using the boom. Gene's previous work had used "a gliding boom," but after his collaboration with Minnelli on *The Pirate* Kelly acquired "a new repertoire of moving boom shots."[57]

KELLY AND ASTAIRE

Ever since Kelly began to receive notice as a fresh new power on the screen, viewers compared him with Fred Astaire. This was natural because, from the beginning, Astaire was the only figure worthy of comparison with him; both of them were the only occupants in the top rank of film dancers. Also, nearly every student of the musical feels compelled to compare the dancing of these two towering figures.[58] We will add our contribution to that overflowing bucket of commentary. But it is also important to compare Astaire and Kelly in many other ways—professional and personal—to more fully understand their relationship as well as their contributions.

Astaire was born of an Austrian father and an American mother in Omaha, Nebraska, in 1899. Just as Harriet Kelly did for her children, Astaire's mother was a driving force in getting the young Fred and his older sister Adele to dance. But Astaire's early life was very different from Kelly's. Brother and sister formed a stage team when Fred was only five, reaching the peak of their success by 1916 and playing in Europe after that. With no stable home life and dropping out of school after fifth grade, young Fred was kept busy performing on the circuits with Adele. Moving back to the United States in 1924, the pair saw their last major triumph on Broadway with *The Band Wagon* in 1931. They broke up the team when Adele married an Irish lord in 1932. Fred married Phyllis Potter in 1933 and kicked off his screen career with *Flying Down to Rio* the same year. The financial success of that film gave Astaire the clout to demand that his dances be filmed full-length with minimal or no cuts, which became the standard method for filming dances. Coupled with a string of commercial successes, Astaire thus lay some of the foundations for dance films to come. Although exposed to ballet as a child, Astaire did not like it. He rejected its regimentation and preferred what he called his "outlaw" style of dancing, a mix of different styles, with mainly tap for solos and "exhibition ballroom" with a partner.[59]

Astaire's dancing style was very different from Kelly's. Astaire focused on lightness and elegance and was a superb partner for a female dancer in a ballroom setting. Kelly focused on strength, dancing a character, and appealing to the common man. Astaire did not like to repeat steps from one film to another, but when he tapped it often looked the same. Kelly also enjoyed innovation and creating new routines, but at the same time he valued formula and repeated popular steps throughout his career.[60]

In 1974, Kelly expressed gratitude that he had developed his own distinctive style before becoming aware of Astaire's. "I didn't get trapped into trying to dance like him, which physically I could never have done." The two were always amazed that people compared them when it was obvious that their styles were so different. Some people understood this. Minnelli thought that Kelly was more intellectual but at the same time more earthy and romantic, whereas Astaire was so light on his feet as to seem almost unreal. Norma McLain Stoop viewed Astaire as essentially a partner—even when he performed solo, his eye and hand action implied that there was someone dancing with him. But Kelly was essentially a solo dancer, performing "his greatest feats alone." Astaire did not have the upper body strength to lift a partner in certain positions. Hermes Pan had to be careful with the choreography when Astaire danced with a tall woman like Cyd Charisse to accommodate his muscular limitations. In contrast, Kelly was so strong in all parts of his body that he could easily maneuver any female partner. With all these differences, comparing the dancing styles of Kelly and Astaire may indeed be "a frivolous pastime." Nevertheless, choreographer Doug Varone spoke for many when he stated that both Kelly and Astaire were his "dance icons."[61]

Both Astaire and Kelly were perfectionists who believed in rehearsing until they got everything right. They also recognized the importance of integrating dances into the film's plot. But film scholars agree that Kelly did a far better job of integrating dances with plot and character in his movies than did Astaire. Kelly's vision of what a dance should be and do within a film was far deeper, more expansive, and more important for the development of cinema dance than Astaire's. He cared about the larger issues, while Astaire focused merely on perfecting his numbers and not worrying too much about the rest of the picture.[62]

Viewers seem divided as to who is the better dancer. Each one has his own following. But even those who enjoy Astaire's screen performances more than they do Kelly's, cannot seem to cite any Fred Astaire movie as the best dance film ever made. In contrast, Kelly's projects are regularly cited for that exalted honor. *Singin' in the Rain* tops the list, but *The Pirate* and *An American in Paris* have also received that accolade. This is because Kelly was far more interested in the picture as a whole than was Astaire and he became a driving force to make it better.

But it was on the personal level that Astaire and Kelly differed even more. "I was a plain, middle-western child," Astaire told oral historian Ronald Davis. He had no more than a fifth-grade education. "I'm never aware, really, of what I do. I just sort of *do* it." That was Fred's stock answer to any question that sought to gain insight into how he became a success. Astaire was deeply interested in clothes, shopping, and horse racing, and took several months off between films to rest.[63] Kelly, who was college-educated and intellectual, poured his thoughts into many interviews. He was not interested in shopping or horse racing and seemed constantly immersed in projects except for his short vacations in Europe.

Fred invested in a national chain of dance studios after his wife Phyllis found out that Arthur Murray was making millions doing so. Astaire did not teach at these studios; it was merely a business investment that ended up losing a lot of money. While filming *The Barkleys of Broadway*, Astaire pressured Ira Gershwin to write a song that could be used to promote his chain. Gershwin refused at first because it had nothing to do with the story but finally gave in when Astaire kept insisting on it.[64] In contrast, Kelly wanted only songs and dances that were integral to the film's plot and never asked for insertions for personal gain. Even with regard to dance studios, Gene had a different perspective. He had been involved as a youth in the two family-run schools during the Great Depression. He thoroughly enjoyed teaching children how to dance, and this had a huge effect on his life and career.

Astaire was relatively insensitive to ethnic and racial prejudice compared to Kelly. Earlier, when it was not uncommon, he performed in blackface for "Bojangles of Harlem" in *Swing Time*. But even in 1943, although concerned that Lena Horne was not allowed to stay at whites-only hotels in Washington, DC, when they were part of a bond drive, Astaire never voiced a protest over it. In the wake of racial violence in the Watts section of Los Angeles in 1965, when writer Budd Schulberg asked him to donate to a program supporting writing workshops for disadvantaged blacks, Astaire bluntly told him, "You've got the wrong guy." Astaire was a conservative Republican mostly because he hated to pay taxes to support social programs.[65] In terms of political and societal responsibility, he and Kelly were very far apart.

Yet the two developed a close friendship that grew out of their shared interest in dancing and their unique position at the top of their field. Starting with their joint effort for "The Babbitt and the Bromide," they instantly became friends. The two got together now and then to chat and to share mutual frustrations associated with their work. Fred's first wife Phyllis died in 1954, but he kept working and his friendship with Gene deepened. During the 1970s Fred became frail and did not like to drive at night. Gene often picked him up to have dinner at a restaurant and get him out of the house now and then. In 1980, Astaire met and married Robyn Smith, a female jockey forty-four years younger than himself. His daughter and sister disapproved of the marriage, believing Robyn was out for his money. Astaire biographer Peter Levinson writes that, late in Fred's life, Robyn changed their phone number and did not inform family and friends, making Fred's daughter Ava desperately worried. She also kept away old friends, isolating him to the time of his death by pneumonia on June 22, 1987.[66]

Ironically, both men said they wanted to make a feature-length film together, but it never happened despite Arthur Freed's support for the idea. Astaire thought it was because their schedules never coincided, but Kelly realized it was a financial decision. He surmised that M-G-M knew it could make more money by keeping their film work separate than by combining their talents. Ironically, Fred's last screen appearance was in a television commercial with Gene for Western Airlines in 1985.[67] It is a shame that these two giants of cinema dance did so little together on the big screen. Their collaboration in *That's Entertainment, Part II* was wonderful but in the final analysis a poor substitute for a film musical they could have done together.

TELEVISION

Kelly turned to television in the late 1950s at roughly the same time as did Astaire. For both, the small screen became a venue for replicating their film dance careers in variety specials that were well received by critics and audiences. It also offered them opportunities for serious acting in straight roles.

"None of us believed that television would ever be *the* first of the mass media," Gene recalled. His view of television mirrored that of many members of the Hollywood community when it began to take hold of America in the early 1950s. They thought it was a good venue for "newsreels and documentaries" but would never replace theaters where feature-length films were shown. When the small screen's allure for most Americans became evident,

Kelly, like many of his colleagues, learned how to work with it. He was able to create dramatic roles like that of Tom Triplett, but dancing was another matter. Gene viewed television as an inappropriate medium for conveying dance movement. He explained that even on a twenty-seven inch screen (considered huge at the time) "the dancer's only as big as your thumb." He thought the viewer would lose a sense of the dancer's personality.[68]

Yet Kelly worked to adjust his presentation to fit that small, constricted screen. Richard Griffith thought he achieved wonders by taking into account the "spatial limitations" of the medium and achieving "a surprising command of its intimacy."[69] "Dancing: a Man's Game" and his two Pontiac specials not only became highlights of his career but were some of the bright spots in television history.

Gene not only succeeded artistically on television but he was well rewarded monetarily. Citing the tremendous exposure to millions of viewers and the "lavish" pay, Kelly asserted in 1975 that "none of us suffered" from this new form of mass entertainment. The variety special became the major way that film dancers transitioned to the small screen. This led to the tendency to revert to the revue format of their old Broadway days. Still, Kelly believed they made these specials with "as much class and distinction as we could."[70] But there were few opportunities to experiment on a grand scale.

Later in life Gene tended to be highly critical of television's impact on American culture. While fourteen-year-old Bridget balanced television viewing with study, many of her friends were glued to the set rather than doing their homework. There was a deadening aspect to the small screen that Gene deplored, telling journalist Robert Lindsey that "television has killed a lot of the good things we had." Lindsey also interviewed Astaire, who complained that good dancing was used only to sell products in commercials. Kelly admitted to Lindsey that the people who created the Golden Age of the Hollywood musical wanted to reach a wide audience too, but the difference was that they also considered "what we did an art form, even though it was popular."[71]

It is difficult to pin down exactly how many television appearances Gene racked up from 1957 to the late 1980s. There were about 160 appearances as himself on various programs, where he made a brief announcement or introduced someone else or was a guest star for a few minutes. One needs only to watch some of Gene's guest appearances on *The Tonight Show* to see how superficial the medium tended to be. The authors viewed the shows originally aired on November 7, 1975, May 4, 1976, and January 24, 1985, at the Paley

Center for Media, located at the Museum of Television and Radio in Los Angeles. Each episode seemed exactly the same. The band played "Singin' in the Rain" to introduce Gene every time, Johnny Carson literally asked the same questions each time, and Gene gave the same answers. It was as if they had never seen each other before.

But there were also about fifty instances of Kelly creating a character on dramatic series or variety specials for television. Some of these, for example "The Life You Save," *Jack and the Beanstalk*, and the Pontiac specials, were outstanding. Others, such as the *Going My Way* series, were also pretty good. In all of these instances, Gene's talents seemed ideally suited for the personal touch of the small screen.

RADIO

Kelly crafted a long career in radio that has rarely been appreciated by his fans or his previous biographers. He started in 1943, soon after reaching Hollywood, and continued to 1959, with more than forty-four radio performances. We were able to listen to thirty of these, and another fourteen or more are listed on Sue Cadman's website (see appendix). This aspect of Gene's career is so obscure because the programs are not as readily available to the public as are his movies, and people today are not so attuned to old radio shows. Kelly obviously enjoyed this part of his work—he performed on many types of radio programs from dramatic shows to comic ones and also as himself. Radio offered him the opportunity to learn how to act with his voice and emotions rather than with his body movements. It was a challenge that he readily mastered.

Many of his radio appearances were aimed at promoting his movies, and M-G-M arranged these. In fact his first radio work was with Judy Garland to promote *For Me and My Gal* and the last such work was with Cyd Charisse for *Brigadoon*. In each case, Gene reprised parts of his role in the picture and sang a song or two as we detail in earlier chapters. Radio programs Kelly did during the war, such as "Going Home" and "Shilling for Luck," are also discussed earlier in the book, as are his performances on variety programs, for the Navy, and as part of his political activism.

Gene also created several dramatic performances on radio. In 1946, he played with John Garfield and Gregory Peck as his brothers opposite Janet Leigh (in her first public appearance) in a Christmas play called "All Through the House." One of Kelly's best dramatic roles on radio was as Bill Hallon in "To Mary With Love" in 1947. It was the story of a married couple and Hallon, their close friend who was in love with the wife, over ten years of their lives.

But Gene also enjoyed stretching himself in certain radio programs. He personally liked the mystery series *Suspense* on CBS and appeared in four episodes. Three of these were from 1943 to 1944. In the episode "Thieves Fall Out," he and Hans Conreid played murderers who, in an interesting twist, are convicted and put to death for each other's crimes. In "The Man Who Couldn't Lose," he also played a murderer who almost gets away but is found out at the last minute. These two episodes aired about the same time he played a murderer in *Christmas Holiday* (1944). In the third program, "Death Went Along for the Ride," he created a character being stalked by mobsters, but the audience is never sure if he is a bad guy himself, only to find out at the end that he is innocent.

In the fourth and most sinister episode, "To Find Help," aired in 1949, Kelly played a mentally unbalanced man who terrorizes the character played by Ethel Barrymore in a stunning portrayal of unpredictable evil. Hired to refurbish her dining room, he goes off-kilter, locks her in a closet, and kills her dog before someone intervenes to rescue her. That Gene had it in him to create a vicious character like this—so unlike his screen persona—is astounding. No studio would have allowed him to do this on screen. His portrayal here was far more terrorizing than in *Christmas Holiday*. He could get away with it because radio programs like *Suspense* reached a more restricted audience and posed no threat to his screen image. Kelly realized that radio offered him opportunities for development as an actor that he could not find elsewhere.

In contrast to these sinister performances, Gene created lighthearted or humorous roles in several popular radio shows. He played a fast-talking screenwriter in Sam and Bella Spewack's comedy "Boy Meets Girl" in 1946, in which he ends up helping a young mother find love and in doing so gets ideas for screenplays. One of the funniest comedy episodes was "Murder at Romanoff's" on *The Jack Benny Show* in 1950, which actually had no killing in the plot but was a spoof of a murder mystery. Kelly appeared as a witness, humorously plugging every movie he had yet made.

Although Gene was not involved in organized religion at the time, he participated in episodes of *Family Theater* in 1948 and 1951. He introduced programs titled "Mother's Halo Was Tight" and "Susie's Prayer Ball" and ended them by speaking of "spiritual values" and the need to pray daily. *Family Theater* was associated with the Family Rosary Crusade, a creation of Father

Patrick Peyton. This Catholic ministries effort ran from 1947 to 1957 with 540 episodes.

Kelly also performed radio roles that were intended to create awareness of social problems. While serving in the Navy, he performed in two episodes of *Treasury Salute* in 1946. In "To Pfc. Marvin M. Leeds," he portrayed an army private who loved to sing. But combat experience in North Africa and Italy left him physically injured and emotionally traumatized, and he lost the joy of singing while sliding into depression. Only his army buddy, who could not carry a tune, was able to bring him out of it. In "What's the Matter with Steve?" Gene played a soldier who did not see combat but yet had emotional troubles. In both episodes, Kelly pursued the same theme he so skillfully explored in *Combat Fatigue Irritability*. In 1959, he made a public service announcement on *You Bet Your Life*, hosted by Groucho Marx, to promote awareness of mental illness, citing that an estimated one in ten Americans suffered from it.

Kelly rounded off his radio career with programs about world issues. He hosted "How Hungry Can You Get" in 1947 to highlight childhood hunger in Europe. In London to work on *Invitation to the Dance* in 1952, he hosted "Jungle in Retreat," organized by the United Nations to highlight international cooperation and to help raise living standards in Southeast Asia.

Radio was a wonderful venue for Gene. It forced him to develop his latent talent for voice characterizations. It allowed him to stretch his creative interests into areas he could not explore on film. And it was obvious he had great fun performing on the air. Radio also gave Kelly the chance to pursue his deeply felt need to serve society during war and in peace.

UNREALIZED DREAM PROJECTS

Radio is a good example of Gene's driving urge to expand his skills in every direction associated with his work. Even during his heyday as a screen dancer there were several projects he yearned to do but was denied the opportunity. Especially after ending his M-G-M contract in 1956, Kelly tried to find and develop worthwhile projects, but they often failed to materialize. We have discussed several such lost opportunities throughout the book. Here we focus on the major unrealized dream projects that Gene looked back on ruefully in his later years.

A movie version of *Pal Joey* was the first one. It was a natural for Kelly, who had created the title role on Broadway. Harry Cohn at Columbia had the rights and was eager to make the film with Kelly soon after *Cover Girl* (1944), but M-G-M refused to cooperate. By the time Columbia geared up to produce the picture in 1957 M-G-M was no longer an obstacle, but Kelly "had lost enthusiasm for it and I thought I was already too old." Frank Sinatra played the title role in a forgettable film version of a stage classic. Ironically, a Broadway revival of *Pal Joey* was staged in January 1952 when Gene had gone to Europe. The revival followed public response to a recording of the play's songs released the previous year. Harold Lang was in the title role and Vivienne Segal re-created her role as the female lead. It ran for 540 performances compared to the 374 performances of the original. The plot was changed to make Segal a widow instead of a married woman, and Joey was reformed at the end. As a result, there were fewer criticisms concerning the amorality of the plot and characters. Some critics thought Lang was a better dancer than Kelly had been eleven years before, but they admitted Kelly acted better, putting Joey Evans over as a sly manipulator better than Lang's one-dimensional portrayal.[72]

If not *Pal Joey*, then maybe Al Jolson. M-G-M signed a deal with Jolson to do a sequel to Columbia's *The Jolson Story* (1946) called *Jolson Sings Again*. The studio and Jolson himself wanted Kelly to play the lead, and Gene was eager to do it.[73] For unexplained reasons, it never happened. Instead, Columbia produced the sequel with Larry Parks once again portraying the legendary singer.

Elia Kazan wanted Kelly to create the role of Biff, the eldest son, in Arthur Miller's *Death of a Salesman* on Broadway. "Gene was thrilled," Betsy recalled, but M-G-M refused to give him leave for the requested six months on the grounds that it was a secondary role and would not help his film career.[74] Arthur Kennedy instead created the part in this classic American play. Interestingly, the production ran from February 1949 to November 1950, so it was not just a matter of six months.

Kelly had a long-term desire to do a film based on the character of Cyrano de Bergerac. It fit neatly into what he had done with *The Three Musketeers* and could have involved a lot of swordplay and stunts. The story appealed to him as well. Kelly conceived of it as either a straight acting role or a musical. But M-G-M was reluctant to present their star player with a larger-than-life nose, afraid it would destroy his commercial value. As he told Hedda Hopper, "Metro thinks that might turn me into a character actor."[75]

A stage musical he wanted to perform in was *Fancy Free*, the 1944 ballet by Jerome Robbins and Leonard Bernstein that was the inspiration for *On the*

Town. "I've always itched to dance that ballet," Kelly said in 1958, "to get in and play one of the sailors." He also was keen to portray Sky Masterson in a film version of the long-running Broadway musical *Guys and Dolls*. "I was born to play Sky the way Gable was born to play Rhett Butler," Gene said. But he lost it due to "a feud between [Louis B.] Mayer and Samuel Goldwyn."[76] Marlon Brando filled the role when it was released in 1955.

"When I look back on my career, there are almost as many disappointments as there are triumphs," Kelly said in the early 1980s, "as many shows that never got off the drawing board as those that did."[77] This was inevitable, especially for an entertainer with many talents, diverse interests, and a driving work ethic who had to depend on the cooperation of others to realize projects. And yet, a man's career is significant not only in the projects he actually finished but also in what he wanted and attempted to do.

LEGACY IN CINEMA

Kelly left a magnificent legacy in the stage work and especially in the films that he actually accomplished. This section examines his legacy in filmmaking. He was unusual—perhaps unequaled—in his thinking about the nature of movies and dancing in American culture. Unlike Astaire, who was only interested in pulling off his dances in the right way, Gene thought a great deal about the link between cinema and American society, about gender and racial issues, cine-dance, film ballet, the genre of dance musicals, and the concept of a film auteur. For Kelly, all these things constituted a holistic approach to his work as an entertainer. He was to a very real degree an educated intellectual. Thinking deeply was part of his everyday life, and he pondered for years on many issues important to his life and to the people he tried to entertain. Kelly left his mark not just on the movies but on American culture.

Gender

Since boyhood Gene was energized by the anger he felt over being taunted as a sissy for taking dance lessons. That emotion drove him to shun dancing for many years until his high-school experience awakened an interest in it. As he gradually developed a desire to make dance his career, he turned the anger into a crusade to prove that dancing was not for sissies.

The best way he could do this was to emphasize the link between sports (which he dearly loved) and dancing. Gene substantiated this link in "Dancing: A Man's Game" as well as in an article and many interviews.[78]

Kelly often argued that there was a masculine form of dance and a feminine form, and it was wrong to interchange them. Astaire, however, seemed to think it was good if women could dance like men. He praised Eleanor Powell for doing so, saying, "No ricky-ticky sissy stuff with Ellie."[79]

Actually, what Gene said is true for ballet and modern dance, but not for all dance styles. In his numbers with Vera-Ellen in "Slaughter on Tenth Avenue" (*Words and Music*) and the *On the Town* ballet, he and Ellen do have different steps and it works well. The same is true for his balletic dances with Cyd Charisse in the "Broadway Ballet" (*Singin' in the Rain*) and "Heather on the Hill" (*Brigadoon*) and in the romantic dances in all his films. What he did not clarify, however, is that in tap dances, the steps are exactly the same for men and women as one can see in "Main Street" (*On the Town*) or "Good Morning" (*Singin' in the Rain*).

Gene was disappointed that there were so few male dance students compared to girls at his studios and he always tried to find promising male dancers to coach and mentor. He was not unique in this concern. Dance scholar Ramsay Burt has noted that since the early nineteenth century dance increasingly became tagged as effeminate because middle-class culture emphasized separate roles for men and women. The latter were the repository of emotion and the former were to be tough and virile. By the early twentieth century these values gave rise to a perceived link between dancing and homosexuality.[80] This notion persisted into Kelly's lifetime and it has not changed much even today.

Ted Shawn, born in 1891, tried hard to change this view. "But, Ted, *men* don't dance" a fraternity brother told him when he said he wanted to dance professionally. Shawn created a successful team with his wife Ruth St. Denis to perform expressive dances to middle-class audiences from 1914 until they broke up in the early 1930s. He then formed Ted Shawn and His Men Dancers, embarking on a quest to teach America that men *could* dance. He disbanded the group in 1940 just as Kelly came to Broadway. Ironically, Shawn also developed a long relationship with one of his chief dancers, Barton Mumaw. Although most scholars praise Shawn for his efforts, they also point out that he tried to interpret male dancing as virile, thus fitting into predominant social stereotypes rather than arguing that those stereotypes were wrong and should be altered.[81] Kelly approached the problem of the male dancer in exactly the same way, by arguing for a link between manliness and manly dancing instead of fighting against stereotypes on principle.

Gene's crusade to prove that dancing was not sissy took his image into areas he had never intended. As film critic Peter Wollen has written, "the presence of the body was all important" to Kelly, "a male body that is acceptably exhibitionist in its athleticism." Gene admitted to an interviewer that he had been aware of his sex appeal to women and "consciously exploited it," in the words of Sheryl Flatow. It apparently worked. Jeanine Basinger has described Kelly as "a master of sexual magnetism." In an often-quoted passage, she mused that "a woman might give her heart and soul to Fred Astaire—but she saved her body for Gene Kelly."[82]

But sexual magnetism apparently goes both ways. Kelly became an object of what gay studies scholars call "queer spectatorial investment." By displaying his body to demonstrate either athleticism or to attract female audiences, Kelly also became an object of gay desire. *The Pirate* and the Chocolat number from *An American in Paris* tend to be cited more often than other Kelly screen images in this way.[83] Ironically, in his persistent effort to prove that male dancing was manly, Kelly drew attention from gay viewers to his dancing.

Kelly's larger attitude toward gays has been questioned by Arthur Laurents who claims in his memoirs that Gene often made jokes about "queers" and flirted with both men and women. But one must realize that Laurents was a severely conflicted person—he wrote viciously of many people in his book, his view of them always filtered through the lens of his own hang-ups and hates.[84] There is no evidence that Gene was prejudiced against homosexuals. The parties at his house were open to people of all persuasions (including the aggressively gay Laurents) and he worked well with homosexual colleagues as he did with everyone.

Unfortunately, Kelly's efforts to make male dancing more acceptable had little effect on America. David Kasday, who danced as a boy with Kelly in "Sinbad the Sailor," told the authors in 2008 that he quit dancing at age 14. "I found it hard to be a normal American male teenager and have my association with dancing, especially ballet. It was hardly considered masculine then and is still subject to scrutiny." Choreographer Twyla Tharp put together *Dance is a Man's Sport, Too* as a television special in 1980, but it garnered less attention than Kelly's "Dancing: A Man's Game." Even today most dancers are female, most choreographers and administrators of dance organizations are male, and it has been estimated that half the male dancers are gay or bisexual. Efforts to counter this situation tend to be the same strategies that Shawn, Kelly, and Tharp used, to highlight sports and the accomplishments of heterosexual dancers, but none of these have worked very well. "The American attitude toward male dancers is certainly not good," Kelly told *Los Angeles Times* correspondent Jack Smith in 1989. "We have tried to break down the barriers but certainly have not yet succeeded as much as we would like." The problem exists in Britain as well as the United States. A man, who signed himself only as "Marc," wrote that while growing up in Scotland during the 1960s, he was mercilessly taunted as a sissy merely for telling his classmates at age nine that he enjoyed watching Gene Kelly movies.[85]

Ethnicity and Race

In addition to gender stereotypes about dance, Kelly was disgusted by ethnic and racial prejudice. Throughout his adult life, he worked to counter bigotry. Gene and his family developed a mutually supportive relationship with the Jewish community of Squirrel Hill, he taught Jewish students in his studio, and he had Jewish friends. His first girlfriend was Jewish, and Donen, a member of the Kelly Team at M-G-M, was Jewish. Kelly participated in radio programs to support the creation of a Jewish state in the Middle East and worked with many Jewish musicians, writers, and actors throughout his long career. For Kelly, talent was everything—he admired anyone who was professional, hardworking, and gifted.

Ever since he saw and copied steps from black dancers in Pittsburgh and danced with Cab Calloway in Altoona, Kelly honored and respected African Americans and their contributions to entertainment. He tried to include them in his dances whenever possible. Recall that his first dance with an African American was in *Du Barry Was a Lady* (Figure 6.5). Gene then recruited the Nicholas Brothers, dancing with them on an equal footing in *The Pirate* (Figure 8.4) and even letting them stand on him in various poses during the number. He also danced with boxer Sugar Ray Robinson in "Dancing: A Man's Game" (Figure 15.4).

Kelly was deeply offended by segregation in Washington, DC, while serving in the Navy, and later he lent his name to efforts by Paul Robeson to fight lynching in the South. Gene hosted a party at his house to raise funds for the National Association for the Advancement of Colored People and tried to produce a Broadway play to honor Louis Armstrong. In 1964, he was a cultural ambassador to Africa, where he interacted warmly with the locals and traded dance steps with them. In his own way, Kelly contributed to a revolution in racial attitudes that slowly took place during his lifetime.

Kelly's work against ethnic and racial prejudice coincided with his political views. He was an unabashed liberal and a New Deal Democrat who battled efforts by conservatives to brand all liberals as communist sympathizers. Prior to the publication of our book, Kelly's political activism was probably the least known and least appreciated aspect of his life—but it was a vibrant and important part of who he was.

Cine-Dance

Even while he fought battles against prejudice, Kelly worked hard on his film career. One of the most important themes of that career was to present dance on the big screen in the most effective ways possible. He had mastered dancing, acting, and singing on Broadway but was unprepared for the challenges found in Hollywood when he arrived late in 1941. Gene "was amazed" that dances which worked beautifully on the stage did not work well on film. Busby Berkeley could not explain why, nor could Judy Garland. Kelly concluded that no one in Hollywood thought much about the whys and hows of making film musicals.[86] Like Fred Astaire, they just did it without analyzing the process.

This question intrigued him and was a major reason he decided to stay in California. The problem lay in the technology of moviemaking. Gene realized that the flat screen presented problems for the dancer. A three-dimensional figure on stage became a two-dimensional image on the screen. Methods of transferring dance from one medium to the other had to be devised. The number had to be shortened and something had to be done to impart a kinetic sense of movement. Techniques were needed to re-create the personal presence of the stage dancer on a strip of celluloid. The result was termed "cine-dance," a dance that was specifically designed to fit the medium of film.[87]

No other entertainer went so far as did Kelly in solving these problems. To impart a greater sense of kinetic force, he found that moving the camera along with the dancer helped. As a director, he liked to have that movement flow toward the left (see "Put on Your Sunday Clothes" in *Hello, Dolly!*). Filming on "streets" on a soundstage or filming outdoors increased the possibilities for this kind of movement, which was one of the reasons that Kelly was so interested in shooting on location.[88]

Gene saw film as the ultimate in reality processing. While the stage was an unreal environment, and therefore audiences more readily accepted the introduction of a song or dance, everything *looks* absolutely real on the big screen. That made it more difficult to introduce dances into the picture because people rarely burst into dance in real life. He had to work on ways to segue naturally from dialogue to song, then to dance, and back again. Most commentators rightly believe that he did this better than Astaire and anyone else.[89]

Kelly expanded the cine-dance concept by utilizing technology as his aid. He danced with himself in "Alter Ego" and in a Pontiac special. He danced with cartoon characters in "The Worry Song" in *Anchors Aweigh*, "Sinbad the Sailor" in *Invitation to the Dance*, and *Jack and the Beanstalk* on television. Obviously neither type of dance could be done on stage.

Many people became interested in the concept of cine-dance by the late 1940s after Kelly began to experiment with it. Filmmaker Maya Deren wrote in 1945 about the concept but did not seem aware of Kelly's work in the area. In contrast, John Newnham lauded Gene's screen dancing in an article published in Britain the next year, adding that Kelly "creates his numbers with the peculiarities of screen technology in mind" and "leaves most of his rivals a long way behind." Jerome Delamater singled out Kelly as someone with a keen awareness of cine-dance and a strong record of creating numbers uniquely for the camera. Critic John Martin praised Kelly's work, writing, "Nobody else in Hollywood has come so near to the pure medium of cinema dance." Gene himself contributed to this public discussion not only with his movies but also with an occasional article and numerous comments in interviews.[90] He was both a creator and a thinker in this discussion. With the demise of the Golden Age of the Hollywood musical, public discussion of cine-dance became a lesson in history. Kelly continued to talk of it for the rest of his life, but no further positive contributions to cine-dance took place in Hollywood as had been the case in the 1940s and 1950s.

Film Ballet

Kelly also was an important force in the development of film ballet, although he did not develop the concept. It originated with the introduction of dance into stage musicals on Broadway that were based on ballet steps, such as "Slaughter on Tenth Avenue" in *On Your Toes* (1936) and an early dream ballet called "Peter's Dream" in *Babes in Arms* (1937), both shows by Rodgers and Hart. The dream ballet expressed the inner emotional conflict of the characters or deepened an aspect of the plot. Agnes de Mille's stage version of *Oklahoma!* (1943) greatly popularized the concept. From that point on the dream ballet flourished on stage. Whereas twelve of twenty-one Broadway musicals had a ballet number in 1944, forty-six Broadway productions from 1945 to 1948 had some kind of ballet, with twenty-one of these dream ballets.[91]

As the concept transferred to film musicals, choreographers did not necessarily use ballet steps but crafted a mélange of styles into a long dance number, which was referred to as a "film ballet." If this number included a dream or represented psychological elements, it was called a "dream ballet." The dream ballet concept did not sweep the film musical as thoroughly as it did stage productions, but there are many good examples of it on celluloid. Either Astaire or Kelly starred in most of them. Astaire performed an early dream ballet in *Carefree* (1938) and then two stellar ones in *Yolanda and the Thief* (1945) and *Ziegfeld Follies* (1946), the latter titled "Limehouse Blues." Gene's first dream ballet was actually on stage in *Pal Joey* (1941), where his character dreams of the club he wants to own someday.[92] He included balletic steps, and the dance was widely praised by critics.

On film, Kelly's "Alter Ego" in *Cover Girl* (1944) is an innovative number with many of the characteristics of a dream ballet. "The Worry Song" in *Anchors Aweigh* (1945) also fits the category. So does the fantasy Spanish dance from the same film, which includes balletic steps. The full-scale dream ballet in *The Pirate* (1948) and the extended "Slaughter on Tenth Avenue" number in *Words and Music* (1948) are excellent examples of film ballet as well.

Kelly was encouraged that "Slaughter on Tenth Avenue," clocking in at something like eight minutes, was one of the longest film ballets yet done on screen and had a huge emotional impact. It was soon followed by a much longer ballet in a British film, *The Red Shoes*, released on October 22, 1948, in the United States. Despite its tragic theme, *The Red Shoes* was a commercial and artistic success. Its ballet—a surrealist exploration of the machinations of an evil magician with leading ballet dancer Moira Shearer as his victim—set a standard that Hollywood would struggle to match.[93]

Gene was challenged by *The Red Shoes* ballet and worked to exceed its level of achievement. In the process, he cranked up his conception of film ballet several notches to produce some of the best examples of it. In *On the Town* (1949), he dove more deeply into the inner emotions of Gabey as he poetically re-created the sailor's search for, finding of, and then losing his true love. Kelly tried to show Gabey "synthesizing mentally everything he had gone through." It was a remarkable expression of plot and emotion through dance movement. Dance historian John Mueller calls this ballet the "most prominent development" of the concept in films.[94]

The overblown ballet in *An American in Paris* (1951), which was created by the joint efforts of Kelly and Minnelli, was an attempt "to reflect what an American studying art in Paris was thinking about," Gene later said. It was meant to be "his completely subjective opinion."[95] As we discuss earlier, Minnelli's emphasis on the paintings plus the reverence everyone felt toward Gershwin's music came to dominate the creation of this ballet until the need to explore Jerry Mulligan's relationship with Lise was overshadowed. The décor and the music overwhelmed the psychological exploration to produce a visually and aurally impressive film ballet, but it could not match the ballets in *The Red Shoes* or *On the Town* in terms of emotional power.

The "Broadway Ballet" of *Singin' in the Rain* (1952) became Kelly's last major film ballet. It was not aimed at exploring psychological aspects but merely told the story of an aspiring entertainer's journey from obscurity to fame, with a bit of unrequited romance thrown in. This long and entertaining film ballet nevertheless succeeded because of its choreography and performance values.

Ironically, Donen, who codirected *On the Town* and *Singin' in the Rain*, thought that the ballet in both pictures was "an interruption to the film's main thrust."[96] He never appreciated the concept of a film ballet.

Astaire also made more film ballets in the 1950s, including "The Girl Hunt Ballet" of *The Band Wagon* (1953) and two dream sequences in *Daddy Long Legs* (1955). Kelly made two more dream ballets in *What a Way to Go* (1964) and *Xanadu* (1980). The demise of the Hollywood musical also saw the demise of the film ballet, but it had been an enduring concept for many years. Wonderful examples can be seen in other films, such as *Carousel* (1956), but Kelly and Astaire overwhelmingly dominated the film ballet during the entire time it held sway in Hollywood.

Musical Genre

For that matter, Fred Astaire and Gene Kelly defined the entire genre of the dance musical during the Golden Age. Any list of important musicals produced in that era includes all their major work and hardly (if ever) that of any other dancer. No one could hope to approach the towering contributions of either man to the film musical genre. The Freed Unit at M-G-M, which both stars were a part of, made that studio the preeminent maker of these movies.

Mueller noted that Astaire appeared in thirty-one film musicals and performed 133 "fully developed dance routines."[97] We catalogued that Kelly appeared in twenty-three film musicals and performed seventy fully developed dances. Kelly appeared in fewer musicals than Astaire because he was thirteen years younger, and started his film career nine years after Fred, but both men stopped performing in musicals at roughly the same time due to the decline of the Golden Age. Gene also had fewer numbers per film because Fred often played a dancer, so his movies tended to have more numbers to fit that role. With a few exceptions, Kelly's characters were not dancers but were simply dancing their love or joy; consequently, the number of dances had to be limited to fit the plot. Another reason why Gene had fewer numbers was that Astaire was focused on his own numbers and not the rest of the film, so the studio tried to give him more dances to utilize his talent. Kelly, in contrast, was concerned with improving the whole project and was also involved in directing and other areas, so it made sense for him to spread his energy across all his contributions.

Gene asserted that the dance musical was the most difficult kind of movie to make, and he knew this firsthand because of his extensive work in nondance films. He could not have achieved what he did without the strong support of Freed (who Kelly always praised), and Freed had the strong support of Mayer (who Kelly always maligned). Gene gave credit to the studio system that accumulated the talent, the capital, and the physical facilities needed to produce one musical after another. This was the economic and administrative foundation of the Golden Age. Kelly cherished the colleagues he worked with at M-G-M, often referring to them as a sort of repertory company. "Everyone was sympatico, one with another. Everyone was pitching in." Their collaboration was driven by a desire to make the dance musical a real form of art as well as mass entertainment.[98]

Sheltered and fostered by the system and the people who managed it, Kelly was largely free to explore the aesthetics of film dance, to experiment with its presentation, and to ponder the result. He enhanced the importance of dance to the musical comedy by inserting a good deal of character dancing into it.

In 1947, Kelly wrote a perceptive article for *Dance Magazine* in which he recognized that as long as dance films were made primarily for commercial reasons there was a limit to the extent that they could progress aesthetically. "Do not look to the motion picture, in its present state, to develop the arts," he warned readers. "But on the brighter side, look to it to popularize them and to raise the level of appreciation."[99]

How far the film musical could go in this regard was an interesting question, and later in his life Kelly had less optimism when pondering it. But regardless of how seriously he had approached film musicals earlier in his career, he admitted during the 1970s that they were "a light hearted and light headed thing to do. You do it to bring entertainment." Rarely could he deal with deep issues, and political commentary of any kind was forbidden. Even so, Gene thought that every dance musical in one way or another commented "on the human condition no matter what you do."[100]

Dance musicals continued to be made now and then after the Golden Age ended in the late 1950s, but the demise of the studio system eliminated the economic and administrative foundations for their creation. Rising costs made the production of these very complex pictures prohibitively high. By the 1970s and 1980s, trends settled in to confirm that the Golden Age was unique in every way. The new generation of directors and producers had not bothered to learn how the older generation made musicals. Instead of filming dancers full-body and with few cuts, they increasingly closed in and cut so often that it devalued the contribution of the dance to the picture.[101] For all of these reasons, we cannot expect another Golden Age of the dance musical.

Kelly as Auteur

Given his many roles in the process of making films—all the way from dancer and choreographer to director—Kelly should be a prime target for those who study the auteur in cinema. But Gene refused to consider himself an auteur, arguing strenuously that dance films were so complex that it was impossible to assign primary authorship to any single person among the many who collaborated in their making. He went further than that, however, and tended to debunk the entire concept of authorship in film—even for nondance movies. He pointed out that most of his pictures were made within the studio system, which was thoroughly controlled from the top down with many layers of oversight, several of them by people not involved in the creation of the picture.[102]

But Kelly did not thoroughly understand the auteur theory of his day and did not study the refinements of that theory after his career ended. Students of the theory have pointed out that many directors identified as auteurs flourished within the studio system and that there is a good deal of flexibility in pondering the nuances of authorship in a medium that obviously relied heavily on many creative people. In short, it was possible to detect signs of authorship in all categories of cinema. As Andrew Sarris, who pioneered in developing the theory of identifying a director as an auteur, expressed it, one must look for "certain recurring characteristics of style which serve as his signature" and examine "the body of a director's work" rather than just one film. The director usually becomes the object of auteur theory, but René Clair, a French director who also worked in Hollywood, thought that writing, cinematography, and editing were the keys to making a film and anyone who controlled those tasks had the best chance of achieving authorship. One could take that theory to an extreme and look for what Satyajit Ray called "the great film, the truly personal film, the film that is shaped and coloured by one man's vision and feeling and sympathies." Ray concluded that such a film was "rare if not altogether extinct."[103] Ironically, Ray the great Indian filmmaker, fits the bill perfectly because he not only produced and directed but wrote the script, did much of the cinematography and editing, and even composed the musical score for many of his films. The only other filmmaker at this level of auteurship is Charlie Chaplin who produced, directed, and financed his silent films, wrote the plot and the music, and starred in them.

In the United States, directors tend to garner all the attention from auteur theorists even though merely as directors they do not even come close to the level of auteurship of Ray and Chaplin. Often cited are Orson Welles, John Ford, and Alfred Hitchcock. The only man associated with musicals to draw attention as auteur is Vincente Minnelli. But Jerome Delamater has noted that the "degree of control which Kelly had over his material" in many of his pictures leads to "manifestations of Kelly as auteur."[104] Indeed, Gene deserves to be included in this very short list of auteurs in the musical genre.

Film historian Gillian Kelly (no relation to Gene) argues for Kelly's status as auteur based on themes of "control, authenticity, and innovations in *mise-en-scène*" that can be detected in several of his major projects, both "on-screen and behind the camera." Gillian Kelly focuses on "attribution of unity" (or consistent themes and styles in several films) to conclude that Gene was able to "impose his . . . creative will on a project." For control, she notes that Kelly's characters often manage and manipulate people and settings, such as Don Lockwood creating the illusions that make up "You Were Meant for Me" in *Singin' in the Rain*, "thus becoming director, technician and performer." She also refers to the character Joe Ross filling every role from writer and choreographer to performer and director in the barn production plot of *Summer Stock*. For authenticity, she sees Gene Kelly's tendency to dance for the common man in an earthy, vigorous style throughout his body of work. For innovations she cites Gene's interest in location filming, combining live action with animation, and experiments in split-screen and widescreen composition.[105]

In addition to these auteur elements, one can note that Kelly as director introduced *On the Town*, *The Tunnel of Love*, and *Hello, Dolly!* not only with shooting on location but with rapid pacing. All three introductions exude energy and joy in using open space. In *On the Town*, the three sailors race downhill or on horses, clearly delighted to be in New York. *The Tunnel of Love* and *Hello, Dolly!* increase that effect of joyous movement with aerial shots of a car or a train moving fast through the countryside. This theme comes from Kelly's boyhood love of running swiftly to enjoy the thrill of air rushing past him. It is something Donen never attempted in his own directorial work and once again demonstrates how Kelly controlled the output of their collaboration. This energetic, joyous movement through open space and quick-cutting were Kelly's ideas, not Donen's.

Gene turned in perhaps the ultimate in examples of the auteur with *Invitation to the Dance*. He wrote the scenarios (there was no dialogue and no script), cast the film, choreographed it, starred in it, directed it, and coproduced it (but without credit for the last category). Of all his films, this one explored the widest range of dance styles, including ballet setups. It incorporated animation and commented on social and moral values. It was a highly personal film expression more thoroughly controlled by one person than any dance musical ever made. The fact that Kelly packed it with so many themes stemming from his life's work as to make it less cohesive than desirable does not detract from the fact that it constitutes a wonderful case study of auteur theory. Despite his protestations to the contrary, Kelly was the true auteur of dance musicals.

Multitalented Entertainer

"When you really look at it," commented documentary filmmaker Robert Trachtenberg about Kelly, "he was starring, singing, dancing, acting, choreographing and directing his own numbers—there is no precedent for this career." Concurring with this assessment, Fred Astaire said about his own role in *Silk Stockings* (1957), "Me? I play Gene Kelly. . . . It's a guy who produces, directs, acts, sings, and dances. . . . Who else could it be but Kelly?"[106]

Gene's multiple talents led to closer collaboration among departments within the studio in making a film musical. During the 1930s in Hollywood, each aspect of a musical production tended to be separate, with little crossover work among the director, choreographer, writer, cinematographer, and editor. But during the Golden Age of the musical (the 1940s and 1950s), there was much closer collaboration between departments, which increased the quality of the dance films in that era.[107] Kelly did a great deal to foster that closer collaboration.

From the time Gene was making *The Cross of Lorraine*, he had a burning desire to branch out from acting and dancing into all the other areas of expertise associated with cinema. Art director Preston Ames recalled that, one day while filming that project, Kelly told him, "I want to dance, and I want to direct, and I want to do . . . this and that and the other thing. He knew exactly what he wanted to do and he was able to sell himself to people like Arthur Freed . . . who had respect for what he had to offer." Many technical people were amazed at Gene's ability to work across departments. "That guy's in everything," commented a cameraman while watching Kelly work. "And the hell of it is, it always turns out right!"[108]

By 1949, with *On the Town*, many critics and reporters came to recognize that Kelly had achieved his career goals. He was "the most versatile man on the Hollywood scene," as Morgan Hudgins put it. "It's doubtful if there is anyone else who can qualify as a headliner in all six fields," Hudgins remarked, adding "writing" to the five established categories of dancing, choreography, acting, singing, and directing. Kirk Honeycutt called Kelly "the rara avis [marvel] of show business" for his multitalented contributions to cinema. Gene admitted to Michael Burrows that he was thrilled by the stimulus of engaging in more than one creative category at a time.[109]

Scholars concur with this assessment. Jerome Delamater writes that Kelly, more than anyone else in the industry, took the movie musical "to something of an apex." He did this through his efforts at integrating different elements and through his multiple talents. Other scholars point to his towering achievements in *On the Town*, *An American in Paris*, and *Singin' in the Rain* and recognize that Kelly spearheaded the development of the Golden Age musical.[110] Equally important successes came with *The Pirate* (although belatedly), and with *Cover Girl* and *Anchors Aweigh*, even if these films no longer get as much attention from commentators as his classic trio of movies.

Although many fans think of Kelly primarily as a fantastic dancer, he was also a talented choreographer, a convincing actor, a singer able to evoke emotion, and a director with vision. Through his multitalented achievements in several categories of filmmaking, Kelly made the dance musical into a coherent product, a work of art and commercial success at the same time. His energy, his precise vision of what he wanted to achieve, and his command of virtually all aspects of filmmaking were the foundations of his stellar career in Hollywood.

Appendix

Theater

Nixon Theatre, Pittsburgh (The Cap and Gown Club, University of Pittsburgh, staged annual performances for a week in April or May)
- Gene Kelly during his student years
  - *What's Up* (1931) [Performer in 2 numbers]
  - *The Silver Domino* (1932) [Performer in 3 numbers]
  - *All to the Point* (1933) [Performer in 2 numbers]
- Gene Kelly as an alumnus
  - *Hello Again* (1934) [Chorus manager]
  - *In the Soup* (1935) [Dance director]
  - *Out for the Count* (1936) [Associate director]
  - *Trailer Ho!* (1937) [Director]
  - *Pickets Please* (1938) [Director]

Pittsburgh Playhouse
- *Hold Your Hats* (April 1938) [Dance director, Performer in 6 numbers]

Imperial Theatre, Broadway
- *Leave It to Me!* (November 9, 1938–July 15, 1939, 291 performances)
  - Performer, 2 roles [Secretary to Mr. Goodhue, Russian dancer]
  - Dance sequence created

Booth Theatre, Broadway
- *One for the Money* (February 4, 1939–May 27, 1939, 132 performances)
  - Performer, 7 roles [Friend, Ensemble, Mr. Gordon, Best Man, Reporter, Singer, Western Union Boy]
  - Dance coach for newcomers in the Chicago run (June 1939)

Westport Country Playhouse, Westport, Connecticut (August 1939)
- *The Magazine Page*
- Performer
- Master of Ceremonies

Booth Theatre, Broadway

The Time of Your Life (October 25, 1939–April 6, 1940, 185 performances)

Harry the Hoofer

Choreographer

Ridgeway Theatre, West Plains, New York (June 1940)

Two Weeks With Pay

Choreographer

Westport Country Playhouse, Westport, Connecticut (July 1940)

Green Grow the Lilacs

Choreographer

Community Playhouse, Stamford, Connecticut (July–August 1940)

The Royal Roost

Performer

Westport Country Playhouse, Westport, Connecticut (August 1940)

The Emperor Jones

Choreographer

Three different theatres on Broadway

Pal Joey (December 25, 1940–August 16, 1941, Ethel Barrymore Theatre; September 1–October 21, 1941, Shubert Theatre; October 21–November 29, 1941, St. James Theatre; 374 performances)

Joey Evans (first run, and part of the second run)

Dance sequences created

Ethel Barrymore Theatre, Broadway

Best Foot Forward (October 1, 1941–July 4, 1942, 326 performances)

Choreographer

St. James Theatre, Broadway

Flower Drum Song (December 1, 1958–May 7, 1960, 600 performances)

Director

Paris Opera House

Pas de Dieux (July 1960)

Director

Choreographer

Oakland Coliseum, Oakland, California

Clownaround (April 1972)

Director

Touring Show, Dallas, Texas / St. Louis, Missouri / Dayton, Warren, and Columbus, Ohio:

Take Me Along (June 18–July 31, 1974)

Sid Davis

[Shows performed in nightclubs, hotels, clubs, etc., are not included here as the focus is on the theater. Shows staged by The Five Kellys, and by Gene for Beth Shalom, YMCA, and involving his own pupils are also not listed here.]

Films

(Dates represent nationwide release or a premiere if a city is indicated.)

For Me and My Gal (October 21, 1942, New York) M-G-M
 Harry Palmer
 Dance sequences created

Pilot No. 5 (June 24, 1943, New York) M-G-M
 Vito Alessandro

Du Barry Was a Lady (August 13, 1943) M-G-M
 Alec Howe / Black Arrow
 Dance sequence created

Thousands Cheer (September 13, 1943, New York) M-G-M
 Private Eddie Marsh
 Dance sequence created

The Cross of Lorraine (November 12, 1943) M-G-M
 Victor LaBiche

Cover Girl (April 6, 1944) Columbia Pictures
 Danny McGuire
 Dance sequences created
 Directed "Alter Ego"

Christmas Holiday (July 31, 1944) Universal Pictures
 Robert Manette

Anchors Aweigh (July 19, 1945, New York) M-G-M
 Joseph Brady
 Dance sequences created

Combat Fatigue Irritability (1945) United States Navy
 Seaman Bob Lucas

Ziegfeld Follies (April 8, 1946) M-G-M
 In "The Babbit and the Bromide"
 Shared dance creation

Living in a Big Way (June 10, 1947, Los Angeles) M-G-M
 Leo Gogarty
 Dance sequences created

The Pirate (June 11, 1948) M-G-M
 Serafin
 Shared choreography and dance direction

The Three Musketeers (October 20, 1948) M-G-M
D'Artagnan
Words and Music (December 31, 1948) M-G-M
In "Slaughter on Tenth Avenue"
Dance sequence created
Take Me Out to the Ball Game (April 1, 1949) M-G-M
Eddie O'Brien
Cowriter of story
Choreographer
Directed dance sequences
On the Town (December 30, 1949) M-G-M
Gabey
Choreographer
Codirector
Black Hand (March 12, 1950) M-G-M
Giovanni "Johnny" Columbo
Summer Stock (August 31, 1950, New York) M-G-M
Joe Ross
Dance sequences created
An American in Paris (November 11, 1951) M-G-M
Jerry Mulligan
Choreographer
It's a Big Country (November 20, 1951) M-G-M
Icarus Xenophon
Love Is Better Than Ever (February 23, 1952) M-G-M
Himself (cameo)
Singin' in the Rain (April 11, 1952) M-G-M
Don Lockwood
Choreographer
Codirector
The Devil Makes Three (September 19, 1952) M-G-M
Captain Jeff Eliot
Crest of the Wave (July 13, 1954, London; December 6, 1954, USA) Boulting Brothers, M-G-M British Studios
Lieutenant "Brad" Bradville (USN)
Brigadoon (September 8, 1954) M-G-M
Tommy Albright
Choreographer
Deep in My Heart (December 24, 1954) M-G-M
O'Brien Brother in "I Love to Go Swimmin' With Women"
Shared dance creation

It's Always Fair Weather (September 2, 1955) M-G-M
Ted Riley
Choreographer
Codirector
Invitation to the Dance (May 15, 1956) M-G-M
Clown in "Circus" / Marine in "Ring Around the Rosy" / Sinbad in "Sinbad the Sailor"
Writer
Choreographer
Director
Coproducer (uncredited)
The Happy Road (June 20, 1957, New York) Kerry Productions
Mike Andrews
Director
Producer
Les Girls (October 3, 1957, New York) Sol C. Siegel Productions, M-G-M
Barry Nichols
Dance sequences created
Marjorie Morningstar (April 24, 1958) Beachwold Productions
Noel Airman
The Tunnel of Love (November 7, 1958, Chicago) Arwin Productions, Fields Productions
Director
Inherit the Wind (July 21, 1960, Dayton, TN) Stanley Kramer Productions
E. K. Hornbeck
Let's Make Love (September 8, 1960) Jerry Wald Productions
Himself (cameo)
Gigot (September 27, 1962, New York) Seven Arts Productions
Director
What a Way to Go! (May 13, 1964, New York) Apjac-Orchard Productions
Pinky Benson
Dance sequences created
The Young Girls of Rochefort (March 8, 1967, France; April 11, 1968, USA) Madeleine Films, Parc Film
Andy Miller
Dance sequence created
A Guide for the Married Man (May 25, 1967) Twentieth Century-Fox
Director
Hello, Dolly! (December 16, 1969) Chenault Productions, Twentieth Century-Fox
Director

The Cheyenne Social Club (June 12, 1970) Eaves Movie Ranch, National General Pictures
Director
Coproducer
40 Carats (June 28, 1973, New York) Columbia Pictures, Frankovich Productions
Billy Boylan
That's Entertainment! (June 21, 1974) M-G-M
Cohost and narrator
That's Entertainment, Part II (May 17, 1976) M-G-M
Cohost and narrator
Performer
Dance sequences created
Director
Viva Knievel! (June 1977) Warner Bros., Sherrill C. Corwin Productions
Will Atkins
Xanadu (August 8, 1980) Universal Pictures
Danny McGuire
Dance sequence created
That's Dancing! (January 18, 1985) M-G-M
Cohost
Executive producer
That's Entertainment! III (May 6, 1994, New York) M-G-M
Cohost and narrator

Television

"The Life You Save" (March 1, 1957, *Schlitz Playhouse*, CBS)
Tom Triplett
"Dancing: A Man's Game" (December 21, 1958, *Omnibus*, NBC)
Writer
Narrator
Performer
Choreographer
The Gene Kelly Pontiac Special (April 24, 1959, NBC)
Star
Choreographer
Executive Producer
"The Gene Kelly Show," (November 21, 1959, *The Pontiac Star Parade,* NBC)
Star
Choreographer
Executive Producer

"At Your Service" (May 22, 1960, *General Electric Theater*, CBS)
Director
Producer
Going My Way (October 3, 1962 to April 24, 1963, ABC)
Father Chuck O'Malley
The Danny Kaye Show (October 23, 1963, CBS)
Guest star
American in Paris (August 3, 1964, CBS) ("At Your Service," 1960)
Director
Producer
The Julie Andrews Show (November 28, 1965, NBC)
Guest Star
Gene Kelly in New York, New York (February 14, 1966, CBS)
Star
Jack and the Beanstalk (February 26, 1967, NBC)
Jeremy Keen, the Peddler
Director
Producer
Children's Letters to God (February 18, 1969, NBC)
Himself
Gene Kelly's Wonderful World of Girls (January 14, 1970, NBC)
Host
The Funny Side (September–December 1971, NBC)
Host
Magnavox Presents Frank Sinatra (November 18, 1973, NBC)
Guest star
The Tonight Show (9 episodes, 1966–1987, NBC)
Guest star
Gene Kelly: An American in Pasadena (March 13, 1978, CBS)
Star
Choreographer
The Muppet Show (February 28, 1981, produced in the United Kingdom and aired in the United States)
Guest star
"Hong Kong Cruise," *The Love Boat* (February 4, 1984, ABC)
Retired spy Charles Dane
North and South (November 3–10, 1985, ABC)
Senator Charles Edwards in six episodes, 1.1–1.6
Sins (February 2–4, 1986, CBS)
Composer Eric Hovland in three episodes, 1.1–1.3

[Television interviews, honors, and awards are not included. Not all guest appearances are included. Biography shows and tributes after Kelly's passing are not included.]

Radio

"For Me and My Gal" (March 22, 1943, ABC) *Screen Guild Theater*
"Thieves Fall Out" (November 16, 1943, CBS) *Suspense*
"Death Went Along for the Ride" (April 27, 1944, CBS) *Suspense*
"The Bing Crosby Show" (May 4, 1944, NBC) *Kraft Music Hall*
"Going Home"[1] (1944) *Palestine Speaks!*
"Shilling for Luck" (1944, Armed Forces Radio)
"The Man Who Couldn't Lose" (September 28, 1944, CBS) *Suspense*
"The Night before the Election" (November 6, 1944) *Democratic National Committee*
"The Navy Hour" (July 10, 1945, NBC)
"Songs by Sinatra" (October 17, 1945, CBS)
"Honoring Lt. (j.g.) Gene Kelly" (November 18, 1945, ABC) *Philco's Radio Hall of Fame*
"Lt. Kelly with Bing Crosby" (December 6, 1945) *Victory Bond Show*
"To Pfc. Marvin M. Leeds" (January 25, 1946, syndicated) *Treasury Salute*
"What's the Matter with Steve?" (January 25, 1946, syndicated) *Treasury Salute*
"Gene Kelly Guest Stars" (April 4, 1946) *The Kate Smith Show*
"Boy Meets Girl" (May 26, 1946, ABC) *Theater Guild on the Air*
"Gene Kelly as Guest Star" (December 4, 1946) *The Ford Show* with Dinah Shore
"All Through the House" (December 24, 1946, CBS) *Cresta Blanca Hollywood Players*
"Hollywood Fights Back, Part 1" (October 26, 1947, ABC)
"Hollywood Fights Back, Part 2" (November 2, 1947, ABC)
"How Hungry can You Get?"[2] (November 20, 1947, CBS)
"Anchors Aweigh" (December 29, 1947, CBS) *Lux Radio Theater*
"To Mary with Love" (December 9, 1947, CBS) *Studio One*
"Mother's Halo Was Tight" (May 6, 1948, Mutual Broadcasting System) *Family Theater*
"To Find Help" (January 6, 1949, CBS) *Suspense*
"Gene Kelly as Guest Star" (January 13, 1949, NBC) *Sealtest Variety Theater*
"George's Birthday" (January 27, 1949) *George Burns and Gracie Allen Show*
"Murder at Romanoff's" (January 8, 1950, CBS) *The Jack Benny Show*
"Susie's Prayer Ball"[2] (April 4, 1951, Mutual Broadcasting System) *Family Theater*
"Movie Time: An American in Paris" (September 24, 1951, CBS) *Lux Radio Theater*

"Jungle in Retreat"[2] (May 20, 1952, United Nations Radio)
"Salute to Brigadoon" (September 27, 1954, NBC) *Best of All*
"You Bet Your Life" (October, 1959, NBC) *Groucho Marx*

Twenty-nine of the above programs were purchased by the authors from Old Time Radio, https://www.otrcat.com. [Most programs identified the network but a few did not.]

1. This program was obtained from Box 11, Zionist Archives LP Collection, YeU.

2. These three programs were listed on Sue Cadman's website (which has fourteen other programs not on our list), https://web.archive.org/web/20171002184846/http://www.freewebs.com/geneius/iheardithontheradio.htm.

Notes

URLs for online sources cited are indicated as "[website]" in the notes and provided in the Websites section of the Bibliography. URLs for film/stage/actor data easily located by readers, such as those for IMDb, IBDb, and Wikipedia, are not included.

Preface

1. Betsy Blair, *The Memory of All That: Love and Politics in New York, Hollywood, and Paris* (New York: Alfred A. Knopf, 2003), 103–104.

2. Andrew Sarris, "Notes on the Auteur Theory in 1962," *Film Culture* 24 (Winter 1962): 7–8.

3. Kelly interview, June 3, 1954, File 1342, Hedda Hopper Collection, AMPAS.

4. Kelly interview, in David Fantle and Tom Johnson, *Reel to Real: 25 Years of Celebrity Interviews from Vaudeville to Movies to TV* (Oregon, WI: Badger Books/Waubesa Press, 2004), 71.

5. Roy H. Wagner, email interview, June 21, 2009.

Chapter 1. Son of Pittsburgh, 1912–1929

1. Sue Cadman, "Gene Kelly" [website]; Hirschhorn, *Gene Kelly*, 8.

2. Stephen A. Otto to Kelly, Sept. 25, 1990, and Kelly to Otto, Feb. 4, 1991, Gene Kelly Correspondence, TU; Hirschhorn, *Gene Kelly*, 7–8.

3. Clipping, Robert Van Gelder, "Mr. Kelly, or Pal Joey," Box 6, Scrapbook 1, Gene Kelly Collection, BU; Hirschhorn, *Gene Kelly*, 5–6.

4. Fred Kelly interview, Rusty E. Frank, ed., *Tap! The Greatest Tap Dance Stars and Their Stories, 1900–1955* (New York: William Morrow, 1990), 171; Hirschhorn, *Gene Kelly*, 8; Blair, *Memory*, 18–19; Pauline Swanson, "Dance!," *Motion Picture* (Dec. 1953): 64.

5. Kelly quoted in Bill Stieg, "Kelly Returns to Help CLO Frolic," *Pittsburgh Post-Gazette*, June 27, 1981; David A. Fryxell, "The Dossier on Pitt's Most Famous Graduate, Eugene E. Kelly, Class of '33," *Pitt Magazine* (Mar. 1987): 18; Clive Hirschhorn, *Gene Kelly: A Biography* (London: W. H. Allen, 1974), 8; Ann Rodgers, "Louise, Last of Five Dancing Kellys, Dies," *Pittsburgh Post-Gazette*, Feb. 24, 2008.

6. James Parton, "Pittsburgh," *Atlantic Monthly* 21, no. 123 (Jan. 1868): 19, 21–22.

7. John Bodnar, Roger Simon, and Michael P. Weber, *Lives of Their Own: Blacks, Italians, and Poles in Pittsburgh, 1900–1960* (Urbana: University of Illinois Press, 1982), 186.

8. Bodnar et al., 186–187.

9. R. L. Duffus, "Is Pittsburgh Civilized?" *Harper's Magazine* (Oct. 1930): 537.

10. Clipping, "Gene Kelly Popular Star in New York," Apr. 23, 1940, in Venable to Kelly, July 25, 1989, Box 1, Folder 10, Emerson Venable Papers, HHC; clipping, Robert Van Gelder, "Mr. Kelly, or Pal Joey," Box 6, Scrapbook 1, Gene Kelly Collection, BU; Fred Kelly interview, in Danny Daniels' History of American Tap, NYPL; Hirschhorn, *Gene Kelly*, 20.

11. Clipping, Hedda Hopper, "The Toast of Paris," Box 3, Folder 11, Gene Kelly Collection, BU; Kelly interview, June 3, 1954, File 1342, Hedda Hopper Collection, AMPAS; Gavin Millar, *An Evening with Gene Kelly* [DVD]; Marilyn Hunt, "Gene Kelly Interview," NYPL, 1; clipping, Ben Gross, "'Dancing Isn't Sissy'—Gene Kelly," Feb. 1, 1959, Box 3, Folder 11, Gene Kelly Collection, BU; Pittsburgh Music History [website]; Kelly interview, Ron Haver, "Kelly," *Film Comment* 20, no. 6 (Dec. 1984): 57.

12. Fred Kelly interview, Frank, ed., *Tap!*, 171.

13. Fred Kelly interview, in Danny Daniels' History of American Tap, NYPL; clipping, Gross, "'Dancing Isn't Sissy'—Gene Kelly," February 1, 1959, Box 3, Folder 11, Gene Kelly Collection, BU.

14. Kelly interview, Haver, "Kelly," 57; Edward R. Murrow, *Person to Person* [DVD].

15. Millar, *An Evening with Gene Kelly* [DVD]; Kelly interview, Haver, "Kelly," 57; Jan Halsey and Tracey Record, "Gene Kelly on Campus," *Dance Teacher Now* 4, no. 6 (Nov.–Dec. 1982): 15; Hirschhorn, *Gene Kelly*, 20.

16. Clipping, "Gene Kelly Popular Star in New York," Apr. 23, 1940, in Venable to Kelly, July 25, 1989, Box 1, Folder 10, Emerson Venable Papers, HHC.

17. Fred Kelly interview, Frank, ed., *Tap*, 172.

18. Clipping, Robert Van Gelder, "Mr. Kelly, or Pal Joey," Box 6, Scrapbook 1, Gene Kelly Collection, BU; Hirschhorn, *Gene Kelly*, 10–11, 15.

19. Kelly on *The Tonight Show*, Nov. 7, 1975; Hirschhorn, *Gene Kelly*, 13.

20. John Land, "Magic Doesn't Age," *Saturday Evening Post*, no. 252 (July–Aug. 1980): 128; Kelly quoted in Hirschhorn, *Gene Kelly*, 14.

21. Hirschhorn, *Gene Kelly*, 14–15.

22. Hirschhorn, 12–13.

23. Hirschhorn, 12.

24. Jack Wintz, "Gene Kelly: Keeping That Singin'-in-the-Rain Spirit," *St. Anthony Messenger* 88, no. 3 (Aug. 1980): 26.

25. Michael Aronson, *Nickelodeon City: Pittsburgh at the Movies, 1905–1929* (Pittsburgh: University of Pittsburgh Press, 2008), 15; Lynne Conner, *Pittsburgh in Stages: Two Hundred Years of Theater* (Pittsburgh: University of Pittsburgh Press, 2007), 95–96; Fred Kelly interview, Frank, ed., *Tap!*, 172.

26. "Reminiscences," [1992], 1, Sanford Baskin Papers, Rauh Jewish Archive, HHC; Kelly interview, Ronald Haver, "Pas de Deux with Saul Chaplin," *American Film* 10, no. 5 (Mar. 1985): 23; Marilyn Hunt, "Gene Kelly Interview," NYPL, 21; Kelly interview, "Dialogue on Film," *American Film* 4, no. 4 (Feb. 1979): 43.

27. Kelly interview, Haver, "Pas de Deux," 23; Kelly interview, "Dialogue on Film," 43.

28. Kelly quoted in Stieg, "Kelly Returns"; Jack Howard, "Gene Kelly," Nov. 21, 1949, Jack Hirshberg Papers, AMPAS; Hirschhorn, *Gene Kelly*, 25.

29. Carrie Rickey, "A Dance Master Dies," *Pittsburgh Post-Gazette*, Feb. 3, 1996; John Franko, "St. Raphael School Alumni" [website]; Kelly interview, Haver, "Kelly," 57; *Babes in Toyland* at St. Raphael [website].

30. Pittsburgh Music History [website].

31. Kelly quoted in Hirschhorn, *Gene Kelly*, 10–11.

32. Bodnar et al., *Lives of Their Own*, 117, 159; Nora Faires, "Immigrants and Industry: Peopling the 'Iron City,'" *City at the Point: Essays on the Social History of Pittsburgh*, Samuel P. Hays, ed. (Pittsburgh: University of Pittsburgh Press, 1989), 17–18.

33. Fred Kelly interview, Frank, ed., *Tap!*, 171.

34. Franko, "St. Raphael School Alumni" [website]; Franklin Toker, *Pittsburgh: An Urban Portrait* (University Park: Pennsylvania State University Press, 1986), 243; Wintz, "Gene Kelly," 26.

35. Chalmers M. Roberts, *First Rough Draft: A Journalist's Journal of Our Times* (New York: Praeger, 1973), 8; Rickey, "A Dance Master Dies."

36. Excerpts, Gene Kelly to Department of Naval Intelligence, [website]; Venable to Peabody Class Reunion Committee, Class of 1929, Feb. 18, 1979, and Venable to Kelly, June 5, [1979], Box 1, Folder 10, Emerson Venable Papers, HHC.

37. Kelly, "Streets," in "Fiftieth Anniversary Reunion, Peabody High School Classes of 1929," June 15, 1979, Box 1, Folder 14, Gene Kelly Alumni Files, UP.

38. Clipping, Robert Van Gelder, "Mr. Kelly, or Pal Joey," Box 6, Scrapbook 1, Gene Kelly Collection, BU; Marilyn Hunt, "Gene Kelly Interview," NYPL, 15–16; Hirschhorn, *Gene Kelly*, 15; Kelly to Venable, July 24, 1989, Box 1, Folder 10, Emerson Venable Papers, HHC.

39. Marilyn Hunt, "Gene Kelly Interview," NYPL, 2.

40. Kelly interview, Haver, "Kelly," 57–58.

41. "Shine on Harvest Moon," Box 27, Gene Kelly Collection, BU.

42. Hirschhorn, *Gene Kelly*, 11.

43. "TV Radio Mirror," *Pittsburgh Press*, Dec. 9, 1962.

44. "Gene Kelly and the Jewish Community" [website]; Hirschhorn, *Gene Kelly*, 23–24.

45. Toker, *Pittsburgh*, 251–252; Bodnar et al., *Lives of Their Own*, 193.

46. Fred Kelly interview, Frank, ed., *Tap!*, 173; Fred Kelly interview, Danny Daniels' History of American Tap, NYPL.

47. Clipping, *The Peabody*, Box 1, Folder 14, Gene Kelly Alumni Files, UP; clipping, "Mrs. Yeamans Selects Cast for Class Play," *The Civitan*, Apr. 12, 1929, in Emerson to Kelly, July 25, 1989, Box 1, Folder 10, Emerson Venable Papers, HHC.

48. "Fiftieth Anniversary Reunion, Peabody High School Classes of 1929," June 16, 1979, in Box 1, Folder 14, Gene Kelly Alumni Files, UP; clipping, "Peabody Questionnaire," *The Peabody*, in Venable to Kelly, Feb. 14, 1992, Box 1, Folder 10, Emerson Venable Papers, HHC.

49. Chalmers M. Roberts, "Class of '29," *Washington Post*, June 25, 1979.

Chapter 2. Dancing through College, 1929–1933

1. Charles L. Clotfelter, "Patterns of Enrollment and Completion," in *Economic Challenges in Higher Education*, ed. Charles L. Clotfelter, Ronald G. Ehrenberg, Malcolm Getz, and John J. Siegfried (Chicago: University of Chicago Press, 1991), 31.

2. Rodgers, "Louise, Last of Five Dancing Kellys"; clipping, "Gene Kelly Popular Star in New York," Apr. 23, 1940, Venable to Kelly, July 25, 1989, Box 1, Folder 10, Emerson Venable Papers, HHC; Fryxell, "Dossier," 18; "Dancing in Rodgers & Hart Show Big Break for Kelly," *Pittsburgh Press*, Dec. 16, 1948.

3. Hirschhorn, *Gene Kelly*, 25–26.

4. Kelly quoted in Hirschhorn, 27.

5. Earl J. Hess and Pratibha A. Dabholkar, *The Cinematic Voyage of* The Pirate: *Kelly, Garland, and Minnelli at Work* (Columbia: University of Missouri Press, 2014), 83–86, 168–169.

6. Fred Kelly interview, Frank, ed., *Tap!*, 175; Kelly interview in Arthur Marx, "The Man Who Lived Dancing," *Parade Magazine*, Dec. 18, 1983; clipping, Robert Van Gelder, "Mr. Kelly, or Pal Joey," Box 6, Scrapbook 1, Gene Kelly Collection, BU; Conner, *Pittsburgh in Stages*, 112.

7. Clipping, Robert Van Gelder, "Mr. Kelly, or Pal Joey," Box 6, Scrapbook 1, Gene Kelly Collection, BU.

8. Hirschhorn, *Gene Kelly*, 27.

9. Toker, *Pittsburgh*, 83, 85.

10. Clipping, Robert Van Gelder, "Mr. Kelly, or Pal Joey," Box 6, Scrapbook 1, Gene Kelly Collection, BU.

11. Wintz, "Gene Kelly," 26.

12. Hirschhorn, *Gene Kelly*, 36.

13. "Reminiscences of Gene Curran Kelly: Oral History, 1958," 1, CU; Jack Howard, "Gene Kelly," Nov. 21, 1949, 4, Jack Hirshberg Papers, AMPAS; Fryxell, "The Dossier," 18.

14. Blair, *Memory*, 57.

15. Stieg, "Kelly Returns."

16. "Reminiscences of Gene Curran Kelly: Oral History, 1958," 1–2, CU; Jack Howard, "Gene Kelly," Nov. 21, 1949, 4, Jack Hirshberg Papers, AMPAS; Millar, *An Evening with Gene Kelly* [DVD].

17. Eleanor Ringel, "Gotta Dance: A Profile of Gene Kelly," *Atlanta Journal*, Aug. 16, 1980; "The Daughter of Rosie O'Grady" and "I Want to Be Happy," Box 27, Gene Kelly Collection, BU; Millar, *An Evening with Gene Kelly* [DVD]; Kelly on *The Tonight Show*, May 4, 1976.

18. Marilyn Hunt, "Gene Kelly Interview," NYPL, 12.

19. Hirschhorn, *Gene Kelly*, 26, 29.

20. Kelly quoted in Hirschhorn, 42–43.

21. Kelly quoted in Hirschhorn, 29–30, 43.

22. Kelly quoted in Hirschhorn, 30.

23. Fred Kelly interview, Frank, ed., *Tap!*, 175, 177; Alyn Shipton, *Hi-De-Ho: The Life of Cab Calloway* (New York: Oxford University Press, 2010), 56; Cab Calloway at the Sunset [website].

24. Fred Kelly interview, Frank, ed., *Tap!*, 177–178.

25. Fred Kelly interview, Frank, ed., 178.

26. Hirschhorn, *Gene Kelly*, 35; "Will You Remember?," Box 27, Gene Kelly Collection, BU.

27. Program, *Main Street to Broadway*, Box 8, Scrapbook 6, Gene Kelly Collection, BU; Hirschhorn, *Gene Kelly*, 33–34.

28. Jim Davidson, "Gene Kelly Dances at Downtown Rally," *Pittsburgh Press*, June 27, 1981; Hirschhorn, *Gene Kelly*, 33–34; *Jewish Criterion*, Apr. 8, 1932, CMUL.

29. Marilyn Hunt, "Gene Kelly Interview," NYPL, 14.

30. Hirschhorn, *Gene Kelly*, 30–32.

31. Hirschhorn, 32–33.

32. Hirschhorn, 36–37.

33. Hirschhorn, 34, 37.

34. Gene and Fred Kelly quoted in Hirschhorn, 24–25, 39.

35. Hirschhorn, 174; Millar, *An Evening with Gene Kelly* [DVD]; clipping, Robert Van Gelder, "Mr. Kelly, or Pal Joey," Box 6, Scrapbook 1, Gene Kelly Collection, BU; "Gene Kelly—June 3, 1954," File 1342, Hedda Hopper Collection, AMPAS.

36. "Reminiscences of Gene Curran Kelly: Oral History, 1958," 3, CU.

37. Hirschhorn, *Gene Kelly*, 38.

38. Marilyn Hunt, "Gene Kelly Interview," NYPL, 3; Kelly interview, Haver, "Kelly," 58; Hirschhorn, *Gene Kelly*, 43.

39. Clipping, Ernie Holmok and Stan Markey, "'Pickets, Please'!—The 31st," *Pitt Panther*, 1938, in Box 1, History Folder, Cap and Gown Club Records, UP.

40. Louis M. Fushan to Wesley Posver, Jan. 20, 1979, Box 1, Miscellaneous Correspondence Folder, Cap and Gown Club Records, UP; Conner, *Pittsburgh in Stages*, 71, 73.

41. *What's Up* Program, 7, 11, 13, 15, Box 1, Folder 22, and clipping, Florence Fisher Parry, "Pitt Cap and Gown Club In 'What's Up' at Nixon," and clipping, F.B., "Cap 'n' Gown 'What's Up' Scores Hit," Box 1, 1931 Folder, Cap and Gown Club Records, UP.

42. Reis amateur film of *The Silver Domino*, 1932, in G. Norman Reis Papers, UP; *The Silver Domino* Program, 5–6, 8–9, 14, Box 1, Folder 23, and clipping, "Sunny Weslager, a 'Natural' Is 'Silver Domino' Says Pitt Pourri of Extravaganza," *Pitt Weekly*, and clipping, Florence Fisher Parry, "On with the Show," Box 1, 1932 Folder, Cap and Gown Club Records, UP.

43. *The Silver Domino* Program, 5–6, 8–9, 14, Box 1, Folder 23, and Clipping, Florence Fisher Parry, "On With the Show," and clipping, "Sunny Weslager, A 'Natural' is 'Silver Domino' Says Pitt Pourri of Extravaganza," *Pitt Weekly*, and clipping, William J. Lewis, "'Silver Domino' Brought to Nixon By Cap and Gown," Box 1, 1932 Folder, and Horace J. Hubbard to Department of News and Publications, July 24, 1979, Box 1, Miscellaneous Correspondence Folder, Cap and Gown Club Records, UP.

44. *All to the Point* Program, 5, 9–10, Box 1, Folder 24, and clipping, Israel Goldberg, "'All to the Point' Greeted Downtown as Sparkling, Well-Rounded Production," Box 1, 1933 Folder, Cap and Gown Club Records, UP; Reis amateur film of *All to the Point*, 1933, G. Norman Reis Papers, UP.

45. Marilyn Hunt, "Gene Kelly Interview," NYPL, 26, 34–36; Kelly interview, Graham Fuller, "And Now, the Real Kicker: Gene Kelly," *Interview* 24, no. 5 (May 1994): 112;

Hirschhorn, *Gene Kelly*, 31, 42; Kelly interview, Howard Reich, "Hoofer of His Era, Kelly Really Wanted a Career in Ballet," *Pittsburgh Press*, Aug. 21, 1983.

46. Hirschhorn, *Gene Kelly*, 39.

47. "Reminiscences of Gene Curran Kelly: Oral History, 1958," 1, CU; Horace J. Hubbard to Department of News and Publications, July 24, 1979, Box 1, Miscellaneous Correspondence Folder, Cap and Gown Club Records, UP.

48. Clipping, Robert Van Gelder, "Mr. Kelly, or Pal Joey," Box 6, Scrapbook 1, Gene Kelly Collection, BU; Marilyn Hunt, "Gene Kelly Interview," NYPL, 25–26; Hirschhorn, *Gene Kelly*, 43–44.

49. Kelly quoted in Tony Thomas, *The Films of Gene Kelly: Song and Dance Man* (Secaucus, NJ: Citadel Press, 1974), 13; Kelly on *The Tonight Show*, Nov. 7, 1975.

50. Kelly interview, Haver, "Kelly," 58; "Gene Kelly—June 3, 1954," 4, File 1342, Hedda Hopper Collection, AMPAS; Kelly interview, Andrew Britton, ed., *Talking Films: The Best of* The Guardian *Film Lectures* (London: Fourth Estate, 1991), 200; Helen Dzhermolinska, "Yr. Pal Joey," *American Dancer* 14, no. 6 (Apr. 1941): 13, 26.

51. Marilyn Hunt, "Gene Kelly Interview," NYPL, 34.

Chapter 3. Dance Master of Pittsburgh, 1933–1938

1. Kelly interview, Haver, "Kelly," 58; Fred Kelly interview, Danny Daniels' History of American Tap, NYPL; Marilyn Hunt, "Gene Kelly Interview," NYPL, 26; "Reminiscences of Gene Curran Kelly: Oral History, 1958," 2, CU.

2. Hirschhorn, *Gene Kelly*, 46.

3. Marilyn Hunt, "Gene Kelly Interview," NYPL, 3–4; Kelly interview, Sheryl Flatow, "Through a Lens Brightly," *Ballet News* 6, no. 10 (Apr. 1985): 14–15; Kelly interview, Britton, ed., *Talking Films*, 198; Albin Krebs, "Gene Kelly, Dancer of Vigor and Grace, Dies," *New York Times*, Feb. 3, 1996.

4. Fred Kelly interview, Frank, ed., *Tap!*, 174–175.

5. Michael Kernan, "Grandpop Gene Kelly Still Active as He Nears Age 70," *Washington Post*, Apr. 18, 1982; clipping, "Pittsburgh Patter," June 29, 1935, Box 6, Scrapbook 1, Gene Kelly Collection, BU; Hirschhorn, *Gene Kelly*, 47–48; *Trenton Sunday Times Advertiser*, June 17, 1979.

6. Jeanne Coyne, "I Knew Him When" [website].

7. Christopher Rawson, "Pittsburghers Remember a Life of Amazing Grace," *Pittsburgh Post-Gazette*, Feb. 3, 1996.

8. Program, "Gene Kelly Studio Presents Its Annual Revue of the Dance," Spector Family Papers, HHC.

9. Jack Howard, "Gene Kelly," Nov. 21, 1949, 4, Jack Hirshberg Papers, AMPAS.

10. Ruth Portnoy to editor, *San Francisco Chronicle*, Feb. 7, 1996.

11. "Gene Kelly and the Jewish Community" [website].

12. "Gene Kelly and the Jewish Community" [website]; Gene Kelly Studio of the Dance ad in *Jewish Criterion*, Apr. 12, 1935, CMUL; Kelly telegram to Bobby Lazar, Nov. 21, 1938, Lazar Family Papers and Photographs, HHC; Portnoy to editor, *San Francisco Chronicle*, Feb. 7, 1996.

13. Gloria Elbling Gottlieb, oral history [website].

14. "Reminiscences of Gene Curran Kelly: Oral History, 1958," 3–4, CU; clipping, Stanley Markey, "Before The 'Trailer,'" *Pitt Panther*, 1937, in Box 1, History Folder, Cap and Gown Club Records, UP; Fryxell, "The Dossier," 18; clipping, Ben Baskin, "Gene Kelly Puts Cap, Gown Men Through Paces," Mar. 25, 1935, Box 6, Scrapbook 1, Gene Kelly Collection, BU.

15. Reis amateur film of *In the Soup*, 1935, G. Norman Reis Papers, UP; clipping, "Downtown," Box 6, Scrapbook 1, Gene Kelly Collection, BU.

16. "Reminiscences of Gene Curran Kelly: Oral History, 1958," 3–4, CU; Reis amateur film of *Out for the Count*, 1936, and *Trailer Ho!*, 1937, G. Norman Reis Papers, UP; clipping, "They Built the 'Trailer,'" *Pitt Panther*, 1937, Box 1, History Folder, Cap and Gown Club Records, UP.

17. Conner, *Pittsburgh in Stages*, 149.

18. "Reminiscences of Gene Curran Kelly: Oral History, 1958," 3, CU; Hirschhorn, *Gene Kelly*, 46–47; Kelly interview, Haver, "Kelly," 58.

19. Kelly quoted in Hirschhorn, *Gene Kelly*, 48–49.

20. Clipping, Robert Van Gelder, "Mr. Kelly, or Pal Joey," Box 6, Scrapbook 1, Gene Kelly Collection, BU; Millar, *An Evening with Gene Kelly* [DVD]; "Reminiscences of Gene Curran Kelly: Oral History, 1958," 4, CU; Hirschhorn, *Gene Kelly*, 49–50; Kelly interview, Haver, "Kelly," 58.

21. Thomas, *Films of Gene Kelly*, 13, 16.

22. Kelly meets Marlowe [website]; Helene Marlowe background [website]; Helene Marlowe obituary [website]; "Chorines Train Pitt Cap-and-Gowner," *Pittsburgh Post-Gazette*, Mar. 16, 1937, 4.

23. Kelly interview, Haver, "Kelly," 58; *Modern Screen* [website]; Hirschhorn, *Gene Kelly*, 50.

Chapter 4. Starting on Broadway, 1938–1940

1. Kelly quoted in Halsey and Record, "Gene Kelly," 15; Kelly interview, Haver, "Kelly," 58.

2. Hirschhorn, *Gene Kelly*, 50, 52–53.

3. Hirschhorn, 53–54; Brent Phillips, *Charles Walters: The Director Who Made Hollywood Dance* (Lexington: University Press of Kentucky, 2014), 29.

4. Thomas, *Films of Gene Kelly*, 18.

5. Charles Schwartz, *Cole Porter: A Biography* (New York: Da Capo Press, 1992), 192, 284; Mary Martin, *My Heart Belongs* (New York: William Morrow, 1976), 76; William McBrien, *Cole Porter: A Biography* (New York: Alfred A. Knopf, 1998), 220; Hirschhorn, *Gene Kelly*, 56; "Reminiscences of Gene Curran Kelly: Oral History, 1958," 7, CU. The authors have seen a Technicolor film of "My Heart Belongs to Daddy" at the Paley Center for Media, Museum of Television and Radio, Los Angeles. It is part of *You're the Top: The Cole Porter Story*, an episode of *American Masters* (1990). It is not possible to identify Gene Kelly among the chorus, which shows more than five men; most likely this was filmed after he left the show.

6. Marilyn Hunt, "Gene Kelly Interview," NYPL, 60; Hirschhorn, *Gene Kelly*, 54.

7. Marilyn Hunt, "Gene Kelly Interview," NYPL, 58–60; Hirschhorn, *Gene Kelly*, 56.

8. Kelly interview in *Exhibitors' Campaign Book*, for *Singin' in the Rain*, Ron Haver Papers, AMPAS.

9. Hess and Dabholkar, *Cinematic Voyage*, 71; Kelly interview, 3, 6, SMU/Ronald L. Davis Oral History Collection, AMPAS; Kelly quoted in Hirschhorn, *Gene Kelly*, 55.

10. Hirschhorn, *Gene Kelly*, 55–56.

11. Richard Watts Jr., "Ambassador Moore," *New York Herald Tribune*, Nov. 10, 1938; "Reminiscences of Gene Curran Kelly: Oral History, 1958," 8, CU; Hirschhorn, *Gene Kelly*, 57–58.

12. Kelly quoted in Knox, ed., *The Magic Factory: How MGM Made An American in Paris* (New York: Praeger, 1973), 166; Kelly quoted in Hirschhorn, *Gene Kelly*, 59–60.

13. Hugh Martin, *Hugh Martin: The Boy Next Door* (Encinitas, CA: Trolley Press, 2010), 85–87.

14. Martin, 88.

15. Hirschhorn, *Gene Kelly*, 58–59.

16. Hirschhorn, 60–62.

17. Earl J. Hess and Pratibha A. Dabholkar, *Singin' in the Rain: The Making of an American Masterpiece* (Lawrence: University Press of Kansas, 2009), 15.

18. Richard Somerset-Ward, *An American Theatre: The Story of Westport Country Playhouse, 1931–2005* (New Haven, CT: Yale University Press, 2005), 8.

19. Somerset-Ward, 67, 69; Hirschhorn, *Gene Kelly*, 63.

20. Somerset-Ward, *An American Theatre*, 71; Comden quoted in William Baer, "*Singin' in the Rain:* A Conversation with Betty Comden and Adolph Green," *Michigan Quarterly Review* 41, issue 1 (Winter 2002): 8; Green quoted in Hirschhorn, *Gene Kelly*, 63–64.

21. Hirschhorn, *Gene Kelly*, 64.

22. Wintz, "Gene Kelly," 26.

23. Marilyn Hunt, "Gene Kelly Interview," NYPL, 44–45; Blair, *Memory*, 12.

24. Marilyn Hunt, "Gene Kelly Interview," NYPL, 44; Hirschhorn, *Gene Kelly*, 64–65.

25. Kelly interview, Haver, "Kelly," 56; Kelly quoted in Hirschhorn, *Gene Kelly*, 58.

26. John Leggett, *A Daring Young Man: A Biography of William Saroyan* (New York: Alfred A. Knopf, 2002), 51, 63–64, 70, 73.

27. William E. Justice, ed., *He Flies Through the Air with the Greatest of Ease: A William Saroyan Reader* (Berkeley: Heyday Books, 2008), 321–322, 332–335.

28. Leggett, *Daring Young Man*, 71; Phillips, *Charles Walters*, 47; Hirschhorn, *Gene Kelly*, 65–66.

29. Ringel, "Gotta Dance"; Marilyn Hunt, "Gene Kelly Interview," NYPL, 6; Hirschhorn, *Gene Kelly*, 66.

30. Saroyan quoted in Hirschhorn, *Gene Kelly*, 66–67.

31. Leggett, *Daring Young Man*, 71–72; Kelly quoted in Hirschhorn, *Gene Kelly*, 67; Richard Watts Jr., "Barroom Talk," *New York Herald Tribune*, Oct. 26, 1939; Eleanor Roosevelt quoted in clipping, "Gene Kelly Popular Star in New York," Apr. 23, 1940, in Emerson Venable to Gene Kelly, July 25, 1989, Box 1, Folder 10, Emerson Venable Papers, HHC.

32. Richard Pleasant to Gene Kelly, Oct. 26, 1939, Box 10, Folder 830, American Ballet Theatre Records, NYPL.

33. Reminiscences of Gene Curran Kelly: Oral History, 1958," 8, CU.

34. Marilyn Hunt, "Gene Kelly Interview," NYPL, 89.

35. Hugh Fordin, *M-G-M's Greatest Musicals: The Arthur Freed Unit* (New York: Da Capo, 1996), ix, 26, 29.

36. Marilyn Hunt, "Gene Kelly Interview," NYPL, 89.

37. Kelly interview, Jerome Delamater, *Dance in the Hollywood Musical* (Ann Arbor: UMI Research Press, 1981), 213; Marilyn Hunt, "Gene Kelly Interview," NYPL, 24; Kelly interview, Britton, ed., *Talking Films*, 187–188.

38. Hirschhorn, *Gene Kelly*, 68–69.

39. Blair interview, Patrick McGilligan and Paul Buhle, eds., *Tender Comrades: A Backstory of the Hollywood Blacklist* (New York: St. Martin's Press, 1997), 541–542; Blair, *Memory*, 41, 64.

40. Blair interview, McGilligan and Buhle, eds., *Tender Comrades*, 542.

41. Blair, *Memory*, 8–9, 12.

42. Blair, 12–13, 15–16; Blair interview, McGilligan and Buhle, eds., *Tender Comrades*, 542; Hirschhorn, *Gene Kelly*, 70.

43. Kelly and Marlowe dating [website].

44. Blair, *Memory*, 16–17.

45. Hirschhorn, *Gene Kelly*, 56–57; Cynthia Brideson and Sara Brideson, *He's Got Rhythm: The Life and Career of Gene Kelly* (Lexington: University Press of Kentucky, 2017), 54.

46. Blair, *Memory*, 57–58.

47. Blair interview, McGilligan and Buhle, eds., *Tender Comrades*, 543.

48. McGilligan and Buhle, eds., *Tender Comrades*, 543; Blair, *Memory*, 20–21.

49. Somerset-Ward, *An American Theatre*, 71; *Two Weeks With Pay* [website]; clipping, Harold V. Cohen, "The Drama Desk," *Pittsburgh Post-Gazette*, Box 1, Folder 15, Gene Kelly Alumni Files, UP.

50. Somerset-Ward, *An American Theatre*, 73.

51. Somerset-Ward, 73–74, 263; *The Royal Roost* Information [website]; *The Royal Roost*, The New Yorker [website]; clipping, Harold V. Cohen, "The Drama Desk," *Pittsburgh Post-Gazette*, Box 1, Folder 15, Gene Kelly Alumni Files, UP.

52. Somerset-Ward, *An American Theatre*, 54, 66, 71, 74.

53. Marilyn Hunt, "Gene Kelly Interview," NYPL, 67.

54. Paul Robeson Jr., *The Undiscovered Paul Robeson: Quest for Freedom, 1939–1976* (Hoboken, NJ: John Wiley and Sons, 2010), 18.

55. Martin, *Hugh Martin*, 190.

56. Meryle Secrest, *Somewhere for Me: A Biography of Richard Rodgers* (New York: Alfred A. Knopf, 2001), 212; Stephen M. Silverman, *Dancing on the Ceiling: Stanley Donen and His Movies* (New York: Alfred A. Knopf, 1996), 19.

57. Phillips, *Charles Walters*, 46.

58. Hirschhorn, *Gene Kelly*, 72–73; "Blue Moon," Box 27, Gene Kelly Collection, BU.

59. Clipping, Robert Van Gelder, "Mr. Kelly, or Pal Joey," Box 6, Scrapbook 1, Gene Kelly Collection, BU; Hirschhorn, *Gene Kelly*, 70.

60. Clipping, Harold V. Cohen, "The Drama Desk," *Pittsburgh Post-Gazette*, Box 1, Folder 15, Gene Kelly Alumni Files, UP.

61. Clipping, Harold V. Cohen, "The Drama Desk," *Pittsburgh Post-Gazette*, Box 1, Folder 15, Gene Kelly Alumni Files, UP.

62. Richard Watts Jr., "Better Than Ever," *New York Herald Tribune*, Sept. 24, 1940; clipping, Harold V. Cohen, "The Drama Desk," *Pittsburgh Post-Gazette*, Box 1, Folder 15, Gene Kelly Alumni Files, UP.

Chapter 5. Triumph on Broadway, 1940–1941

1. Larry Billman, *Film Choreographers and Dance Directors: An Illustrated Biographical Encyclopedia, with a History and Filmographies, 1893 through 1995* (Jefferson, NC: McFarland, 1997), 204; "Reminiscences of Gene Curran Kelly: Oral History, 1958," 4, CU.

2. Marilyn Hunt, "Gene Kelly Interview," NYPL, 7, 53.

3. Kelly interview, Haver, "Kelly," 58–59; Thomas, *Films of Gene Kelly*, 18.

4. Hirschhorn, *Gene Kelly*, 74.

5. Secrest, *Somewhere For Me*, 212–213; Marilyn Hunt, "Gene Kelly Interview," NYPL, 56–57.

6. Marilyn Hunt, "Gene Kelly Interview," NYPL, 53–56; Kelly quoted in Ringel, "Gotta Dance."

7. Marilyn Hunt, "Gene Kelly Interview," NYPL, 57–58; clipping, Jack Holland, "Triple-Threat Kelly," Box 6, Scrapbook 2, Gene Kelly Collection, BU; "Reminiscences of Gene Curran Kelly: Oral History, 1958," 8, CU.

8. Sensenderfer, review of *Pal Joey*, *Philadelphia Evening Bulletin*, Dec. 12, 1940; Hirschhorn, *Gene Kelly*, 75.

9. Hirschhorn, *Gene Kelly*, 76–77.

10. Richard Watts Jr., "Night Club Portrait," *New York Herald Tribune*, Dec. 26, 1940.

11. Burns Mantle, "'Pal Joey' Smart and Novel," *New York Daily News*, Dec. 26, 1940; Walter Terry, review of *Pal Joey*, *New York Herald Tribune*, Mar. 23, 1941.

12. John Mason Brown, "'Pal Joey' Presented at the Ethel Barrymore," *New York Post*, Dec. 26, 1940; Richard Lockridge, "John O'Hara's 'Pal Joey' Is Offered at the Barrymore Theater," *New York Sun*, Dec. 26, 1940; Sidney B. Whipple, "Pal Joey Is a Bright Gay, Tuneful, Novel Work," *New York World-Telegram*, Dec. 26, 1940.

13. Brooks Atkinson, "Christmas Night Adds 'Pal Joey' to the Musical Stage," *New York Times*, Dec. 26, 1940.

14. Whipple, "Pal Joey."

15. Gerald Mast, *Can't Help Singin': The American Musical on Stage and Screen* (Woodstock, NY: Overlook Press, 1987), 181–182; Roy Hemming, *The Melody Lingers On: The Great Songwriters and Their Movie Musicals* (New York: Newmarket Press, 1986), 239.

16. Hermine Rich Isaacs, "Gene Kelly: Portrait of a Dancing Actor," *Theatre Arts* 30, no. 3 (Mar. 1946): 150.

17. Dzhermolinska, "Yr. Pal Joey," 13.

18. Kelly quoted in Dzhermolinska, 12–13.

19. Clipping, Robert Van Gelder, "Mr. Kelly, or Pal Joey," Box 6, Scrapbook 1, Gene Kelly Collection, BU; Marilyn Hunt, "Gene Kelly Interview," NYPL, 46.

20. Film of Gene Kelly in *Pal Joey*, *Anatomy of a Dancer* [DVD].

21. Halsey and Record, "Gene Kelly," 16; "Broadway Stars Taken Ill," *Los Angeles Times*, Jan. 18, 1941; "Bewitched (Bothered and Bewildered)," Box 27, Gene Kelly Collection, BU.

22. Silverman, *Dancing*, 28; Lockridge, "John O'Hara's 'Pal Joey.'"

23. Morgan Hudgins, "Directed by Kelly," *New York Times*, Aug. 14, 1949; clipping, Van Johnson, "I Saw A Future Dance Star," in exhibitors campaign book for *The Pirate*, Box 9, Scrapbook 8, Gene Kelly Collection, BU; Lockridge, "John O'Hara's 'Pal Joey.'"

24. Cole interview, Delamater, *Dance*, 197; Hirschhorn, *Gene Kelly*, 82.

25. Clipping, Robert Van Gelder, "Mr. Kelly, or Pal Joey," Box 6, Scrapbook 1, Gene Kelly Collection, BU.

26. Dzhermolinska, "Yr. Pal Joey," 12–13, 26.

27. Kelly quoted in Dzhermolinska, 26.

28. John Martin, "The Dance: Pal Kelly," *New York Times*, June 8, 1941.

29. Blair, *Memory*, 29–30, 34; Leggett, *Daring Young Man*, 82, 84; Hirschhorn, *Gene Kelly*, 71.

30. "Gene Kelly—June 3, 1954," 3, File 1342, Hedda Hopper Collection, AMPAS; "Reminiscences of Gene Curran Kelly: Oral History, 1958," 8, CU; Martin, *Hugh Martin*, 139.

31. Martin, *Hugh Martin*, 140–142.

32. Martin, 142–144.

33. Martin, 144–146.

34. Martin, 141, 148–149.

35. Coyne, "I Knew Him When" [website].

36. Coyne; Dzhermolinska, "Yr. Pal Joey," 26; Blair, *Memory*, 100.

37. Donen interview, 4, SMU/Ronald L. Davis Oral History Collection, AMPAS; Silverman, *Dancing*, 31.

38. Richard Watts Jr., "Youth! Youth!," *New York Herald Tribune*, Oct. 2, 1941; Brooks Atkinson, "The Play: George Abbott Opens the Musical Comedy Season with a Prep School Scuffle, 'Best Foot Forward,'" *New York Times*, Oct. 2, 1941.

39. Hirschhorn, *Gene Kelly*, 95–96.

40. Joe Pasternak, *Easy the Hard Way* (New York: G. P. Putnam's, 1956), 261; Kelly interview, Fuller, "And Now," 110; Fordin, *M-G-M's Greatest Musicals*, 61; Hirschhorn, *Gene Kelly*, 83.

41. Fordin, *M-G-M's Greatest Musicals*, 61; Hirschhorn, *Gene Kelly*, 83.

42. Fordin, *M-G-M's Greatest Musicals*, 63n.

43. Dzhermolinska, "Yr. Pal Joey," 26.

44. Kay Brown to Dan O'Shea, Jan. 28, 1941, Box 911, David O. Selznick Collection, UTA.

45. James Robert Parish and Ronald L. Bowers, *The MGM Stock Company: The Golden Era* (New Rochelle, NY: Arlington House, 1973), 796–797. But despite the financial success of *Gone with the Wind*, the film is a travesty supporting the negative ideology of the "lost cause." It appears in "20 Most Overrated Movies of All Time," a 2006 poll by *Premiere* magazine, where its racist tone is rightly criticized as follows: "Its depiction of a feudal, racist society" as a "victimized aristocracy" is "(at best) embarrassing."

46. Brown to O'Shea, Jan. 28, 1941, Box 911, David O. Selznick Collection, UTA.

47. Brown to O'Shea, copy to Selznick, Feb. 25, 1941, Box 1240, David O. Selznick Collection, UTA.

48. Martin, "The Dance: Pal Kelly."

49. Leland Hayward to Gene Kelly, July 16, 1941, Box 1240, David O. Selznick Collection, UTA.

50. Brown to Selznick, July 11, 1941, and Brown to O'Shea, July 11, 1941, and Selznick to O'Shea and Brown, July 15, 1941, Box 1240, David O. Selznick Collection, UTA; Leonard J. Leff, *Hitchcock and Selznick: The Rich and Strange Collaboration of Alfred Hitchcock and David O. Selznick in Hollywood* (Berkeley: University of California Press, 1987), 100–101.

51. Kelly interview, Fuller, "And Now," 110; Brown to O'Shea, July 15, 1941, Box 1240, David O. Selznick Collection, UTA.

52. Selznick to Mayer, July 15, 1941, Box 1240, David O. Selznick Collection, UTA.

53. Selznick to Mayer, July 15, 1941, and Hayward to Kelly, July 16, 1941, Box 1240, David O. Selznick Collection, UTA.

54. Hayward to Kelly, July 16, 1941, Box 1240, David O. Selznick Collection, UTA.

55. Hayward to Selznick, July 17, 1941, and Selznick to Mayer, July 17, 1941, Box 1240, David O. Selznick Collection, UTA.

56. Brown to O'Shea, July 21, 1941, Box 1240, David O. Selznick Collection, UTA.

57. Hayward to Kelly, July 16, 1941, Box 1240, David O. Selznick Collection, UTA.

58. Abstract of contract, July 17, 1941, Box 1240, David O. Selznick Collection, UTA.

59. Selznick to Whitney Bolton, July 16, 1941, and Selznick to O'Shea and Brown, July 19, 1941, and Brown to O'Shea, July 19 (9:55 A.M. and 1:25 P.M.) and July 21, 1941, and O'Shea to Darrow, July 28, 1941, and Selznick to Kelly, July 31, 1941, Box 1240, David O. Selznick Collection, UTA.

60. Selznick to Brown, copy to Hayward, no date, and Selznick to "Dear Dad," July 19, 1941, and Hayward to Kelly, Aug. 5, 1941, Box 1240, David Selznick Papers, UTA.

61. Selznick to John Houseman, copy to O'Shea, Aug. 5, 1941, Box 1240, and Eleanor Kennedy to Miss Rickman, Aug. 22, 1941, Box 911, David O Selznick Collection, UTA.

62. Selznick to Houseman, copy to O'Shea, Aug. 5, 1941, and Selznick to Brown, copy to O'Shea, Sept. 10, 1941, and Brown to Selznick, copy to O'Shea, Sept. 22, 1941, and Selznick to O'Shea, copies to Houseman and Mr. Klune, Sept. 30, 1941, Box 1240, David O. Selznick Collection, UTA.

63. Selznick to Brown, copy to O'Shea, Sept. 10, 1941, and Brown to Selznick, copy to O'Shea, Sept. 17, 1941, Box 1240, David O. Selznick Collection, UTA.

64. Brown to O'Shea, Oct. 1, 1941, Box 911, and Selznick to O'Shea, copy to Brown, Oct. 16, 1941, Box 1240, David O. Selznick Collection, UTA.

65. Selznick to Mayer, July 15, 1941, and Selznick to Brown, July 23, 1941, Box 1240, David O. Selznick Collection, UTA.

66. Helene Marlowe obituary [website].

67. Hirschhorn, *Gene Kelly*, 83.

68. Blair, *Memory*, 36–37; Blair interview, McGilligan and Buhle, eds., *Tender Comrades*, 544; Hirschhorn, *Gene Kelly*, 86.

69. Brown to Selznick, copy to O'Shea, Sept. 17, 1941, Box 1240, David O. Selznick Collection, UTA; Hirschhorn, *Gene Kelly*, 55.

70. "A Wedding Between Rehearsals," *Philadelphia Evening Bulletin*, Sept. 22, 1941; Blair interview, McGilligan and Buhle, eds., *Tender Comrades*, 544.

71. Brown to Selznick, Oct. 3, 1941, Box 1240, Brown to O'Shea, Oct. 1, 1941, and Brown

to Kelly, Oct. 3, 1941, and O'Shea to Ernest Scanlan, Feb. 27, 1942, Box 911, David O. Selznick Collection, UTA.

72. Blair, *Memory*, 82–84, 89.

73. Blair, 85.

74. Blair, 85, 88; Leggett, *Daring Young Man*, 74–76, 78.

75. Blair interview, McGilligan and Buhle, eds., *Tender Comrades*, 544.

Chapter 6. Taking on Hollywood, 1941–1944

1. Blair, *Memory*, 90–91; envelope postmarked Jan. 8, 1942, Box 1240, David O. Selznick Collection, UTA.

2. Aljean Harmetz, *On the Road to Tara: The Making of* Gone with the Wind (New York: Harry N. Abrams, 1996), 16, 24, 30, 208.

3. O'Shea to Selznick, Nov. 23, 1941, and Ray Klune to O'Shea, Nov. 27, 1941, and Brown to O'Shea, Dec. 1, 1941, Box 911, and Selznick to O'Shea, Dec. 16, 1941, Box 1240, David O. Selznick Collection, UTA; Leff, *Hitchcock and Selznick*, 100–101.

4. Selznick to O'Shea and Klune, copy to Miss Keon, Dec. 19, 1941, Box 1240, David O. Selznick Collection, UTA.

5. Brown to Mr. Lewton, Jan. 12, 1942, and Selznick to Brown, copy to O'Shea and Klune, Jan. 26, 1942, and Virginia Olds to Brown, Jan. 28, 1942, and Selznick to Klune, copy to Brown, Jan. 28, 1942, Box 1240, David O. Selznick Collection, UTA.

6. Publicity biography for Gene Kelly, and Olds to Selznick, Jan. 29, 1942, Box 1240, David O. Selznick Collection, UTA.

7. Hirschhorn, *Gene Kelly*, 92.

8. Selznick to Klune, copy to Brown, Jan. 28, 1942, and Brown to Selznick, Jan. 30, 1942, and Delivery Receipt, May 8, 19_8 (year obscured), Box 1240, David O. Selznick Collection, UTA.

9. Curtis Lee Hanson, "An Interview with Gene Kelly," *Cinema* 3, no. 4 (Dec. 1966): 27–28; Parish and Bowers, *MGM Stock Company*, 395.

10. Hanson, "An Interview with Gene Kelly," 27–28; Kelly interview, Delamater, *Dance*, 213.

11. Selznick to Brown, copy to O'Shea, Feb. 17, 1942, Box 1240, David O. Selznick Collection, UTA.

12. Ronald Mader to O'Shea, Feb. 26, 1942, and O'Shea to Ernest Scanlan, Feb. 27, 1942, and note concerning Kelly's contract, Oct. 20, 1942, Box 911, David O. Selznick Collection, UTA.

13. Kelly interview, Britton, ed., *Talking Films*, 188.

14. Blair, *Memory*, 92; Maxine Garrison, "Kelly's From Pittsburgh and He Is Almighty Proud of the Fact," *Pittsburgh Press*, Oct. 30, 1944; Blair interview, McGilligan and Buhle, eds., *Tender Comrades*, 546; 506-N-Alta-Drive Information [website]; Michael Frank, "Gene Kelly: Star of *An American in Paris* on Alta Drive," *Architectural Digest* 49, no. 4 (Apr. 1992): 188–189, 274.

15. Fordin, *M-G-M's Greatest Musicals*, 63.

16. "Production Information on the Films of Arthur Freed," *For Me and My Gal*, Arthur Freed Collection, USC.

17. Lorna Luft, *Me and My Shadows: A Family Memoir* (New York: Simon and Shuster,

1998), 26, 33, 36, 38; Assistant Director's Report, *For Me and My Gal*, Feb.–Apr., 1942, Arthur Freed Collection, USC.

18. Kelly quoted in John Fricke, *Judy Garland: A Portrait in Art & Anecdote* (Boston: Bulfinch Press, 2003), 113; Jeanine Basinger, *Gene Kelly* (New York: Pyramid, 1976), 30; Hirschhorn, *Gene Kelly*, 102.

19. George Murphy, "*Say . . . Didn't You Used to be George Murphy?*" (New York: Bartholomew House, 1970), 5, 162, 241.

20. Jeffrey Spivak, *Buzz: The Life and Art of Busby Berkeley* (Lexington: University Press of Kentucky, 2011), 192; Rex Reed, "Gene Kelly's Musical Memories," *Chicago Tribune*, Nov. 29, 1980.

21. "Production Information on the Films of Arthur Freed" and Assistant Director's Report, *For Me and My Gal*, Feb. 19–25, Mar. 11, 16, 21, Apr. 3, 1942, Arthur Freed Collection, USC.

22. Assistant Director's Report, *For Me and My Gal*, Apr. 4, 1942, Arthur Freed Collection, USC.

23. Assistant Director's Report, *For Me and My Gal*, May 23, 1942, Arthur Freed Collection, USC; Reed, "Gene Kelly's Musical Memories."

24. "Production Information on the Films of Arthur Freed," *For Me and My Gal*, Arthur Freed Collection, USC; Murphy, "*Say*," 242.

25. "Production Information on the Films of Arthur Freed" and Assistant Director's Report, *For Me and My Gal*, July 29, 1942, Arthur Freed Collection, USC; Murphy, "*Say*," 242–243.

26. Bosley Crowther, "'For Me and My Gal,' a Musical Moving Picture Concerned with Vaudeville, Makes Its Appearance at the Astor," *New York Times*, Oct. 22, 1942.

27. Foreword by Kelly, David Naylor, *Great American Movie Theaters* (Washington, DC: Preservation Press, 1987), 9; Kelly interview, Haver, "Pas de Deux," 25; Kelly interview, Delamater, *Dance*, 207–208.

28. John Updike, "Gotta Dance!," *The New Yorker* 70, no. 5 (Mar. 21, 1994): 168; Basinger, *Gene Kelly*, 29, 31; Pauline Kael, *5001 Nights at the Movies: A Guide from A to Z* (New York: Holt, Rinehart, and Winston, 1982), 193; John K. Newnham, "Tilly Losch in Hollywood's Most Costly Film: Dance Film Notes," *The Dancing Times* 36 (Dec. 1946): 135.

29. Fordin, *M-G-M's Greatest Musicals*, 66.

30. "Reminiscences of Gene Curran Kelly: Oral History, 1958," 13, CU; Irv Lichtman, "Song-and-Dance Man Gene Kelly Dies," *Billboard* 108, no. 7 (Feb. 17, 1996).

31. Dale Pollock, "Gene Kelly at 72," *Tampa Bay Times*, Aug. 4, 1984; Michele Willens, "Gene Kelly Opening Municipal Opera Season," *St. Louis Post-Dispatch*, July 1, 1974.

32. Philip K. Scheurer, "Gene Kelly's Real Life Symbolized by Dance," *Los Angeles Times*, Apr. 23, 1944; Saroyan to Kelly, May 23, 30, June 8, 1942, William Saroyan Papers, SU; Leggett, *Daring Young Man*, 93–99.

33. Thomas, *Films of Gene Kelly*, 34.

34. Blair, *Memory*, 110–111.

35. Kelly quoted in Hirschhorn, *Gene Kelly*, 102.

36. Dore Schary, *Heyday: An Autobiography* (Boston: Little, Brown and Company, 1979), 123; Thomas, *Films of Gene Kelly*, 36; Selznick to Kelly, Sept. 21, 1943, and Kelly to Selznick, Oct. 18, 1943, Box 1240, David O. Selznick Collection, UTA.

37. Kelly interview, Britton, ed., *Talking Films*, 189.

38. Billman, *Film Choreographers*, 316; Phillips, *Charles Walters*, 57; Walters interview, 18–19, SMU/Ronald L. Davis Oral History Collection, AMPAS; Walters interview, Fantle and Johnson, *Reel to Real*, 274.

39. Walters interview, Fantle and Johnson, *Reel to Real*, 274–275; Phillips, *Charles Walters*, 59–60.

40. Marilyn Hunt, "Gene Kelly Interview," NYPL, 94–96.

41. Blair, *Memory*, 96, 98; Frederick C. Othman, "Lucille Ball Discovers—12 Pounds of False Hair No Help While Dancing," *Tampa Bay Times*, Oct. 20, 1942; Edward Lawrence, "Kelly, Caught in the Draft," *New York Times*, Dec. 17, 1944; Olds to Joyce Allen, Oct. 19, 1942, Box 1240, David O. Selznick Collection, UTA.

42. Blair, *Memory*, 99, 105–106.

43. Blair, 10, 99–100.

44. Marilyn Hunt, "Gene Kelly Interview," NYPL, 96; Kelly interview, John Boorman and Walter Donohue, eds., *Projections 4: Film-Makers on Film-Making* (London: Faber and Faber, 1995), 280; Fordin, *M-G-M's Greatest Musicals*, 78.

45. Kelly interview, Delamater, *Dance*, 221; "Isobel Lennart Brilliantly Word-Paints the Real Gene Kelly" [website].

46. Pasternak, *Easy the Hard Way*, 7, 9, 50; Pasternak quoted in Hirschhorn, *Gene Kelly*, 149; Marilyn Hunt, "Gene Kelly Interview," NYPL, 97; Jane Feuer, *Hollywood Musical* (Bloomington: Indiana University Press, 1982), 5–6.

47. Marilyn Hunt, "Gene Kelly Interview," NYPL, 156.

48. James Agee, *Agee on Film: Reviews and Comments by James Agee* (New York: McDowell, Obolensky, 1958), 54; Thomas, *Films of Gene Kelly*, 43; John Russell Taylor and Arthur Jackson, *Hollywood Musical* (New York: McGraw-Hill, 1971), 61; Basinger, *Gene Kelly*, 34.

49. Blair, *Memory*, 93–94.

50. Blair, 105; Kelly interview, Fuller, "And Now," 112.

51. Clippings, Kay Proctor, "Hey, Irish!," *Photoplay*, May 1943, and Cynthia Miller, "Pal Genie," *Modern Screen*, June 1943, and "It's Like This—To be Mrs. Gene Kelly," *Photoplay*, June 1943, Box 6, Scrapbook 2, Gene Kelly Collection, BU; Blair, *Memory*, 108–109.

52. Maynard, "This Is About Gene Kelly" [website].

53. Blair, *Memory*, 113; Gene Kelly publicity photographs, Box 10, Folder 27, USO Camp Shows Publicity Records, 1941–1955, Billy Rose Theatre Division, NYPL.

54. Selznick to O'Shea, Mar. 12, 1942, and Selznick to Mayer, Apr. 13, 1942, Box 1240, David O. Selznick Collection, UTA.

55. Selznick to O'Shea, Nov. 18, 1942, Box 911, Olds to O'Shea, Oct. 6, 23, and Dec. 8, 1942, and Margaret McDonnell to Selznick, Dec. 7, 1942, Box 1240, David O. Selznick Collection, UTA.

56. Selznick to O'Shea, Nov. 23 and 30, 1942, and O'Shea to Selznick, Nov. 30, 1942, Box 1240, David O. Selznick Collection, UTA.

57. Selznick to O'Shea, Dec. 8, 1942, Box 911, and E. J. Mannix to O'Shea, Dec. 17, 1942, and Selznick to O'Shea, Dec. 18, 1942, Box 1240, David O. Selznick Collection, UTA.

58. O'Shea to Ben Thau, Dec. 30, 1942, and Jan. 20, 1943, Box 911, and Selznick to O'Shea, Dec. 19, 1942, and Jan. 4, 1943, Box 1240, David O. Selznick Collection, UTA.

59. Selznick to Mannix, Jan. 27, 1943, Box 1240, David O. Selznick Collection, UTA.

60. Olds to O'Shea, Feb. 3, 1943, Box 911, Mannix to O'Shea, Feb. 1, 1943, abstract of letter of agreement, Feb. 13, 1943, and Selznick to O'Shea, Mar. 9, 1944, Box 1240, David O. Selznick Collection, UTA.

61. Harmetz, *On the Road to Tara*, 208.

62. Agee, *Agee on Film*, 62; Kelly quoted in Hirschhorn, *Gene Kelly*, 106.

63. Fordin, *M-G-M's Greatest Musicals*, 81.

64. John Kobal, *Rita Hayworth: The Time, the Place, and the Woman* (New York: Norton, 1978), 85–87, 108; Kelly interview, 41, SMU/Ronald L. Davis Oral History Collection, AMPAS.

65. Kelly quoted in Hirschhorn, *Gene Kelly*, 111–112.

66. Reed, "Gene Kelly's Musical Memories"; Marilyn Hunt, "Gene Kelly Interview," NYPL, 104; Gene Kelly, "The Women in My Dancing Life," *National Women's Weekly*, July 17, 1952.

67. Phil Silvers, *This Laugh Is On Me: The Phil Silvers Story* (New York: W. H. Allen, 1974), 5, 15, 112, 122.

68. Saul Chaplin, *The Golden Age of Movie Musicals and Me* (Norman: University of Oklahoma Press, 1994), 47, 52.

69. Chaplin, 50–51.

70. Chaplin, 51.

71. Hirschhorn, *Gene Kelly*, 108.

72. Lichtman, "Song-and-Dance Man"; Kelly interview, 40–41, SMU/Ronald L. Davis Oral History Collection, AMPAS; Kelly interview with David Hartman, "Gene Kelly on 'Golden Age' Musicals," Sept. 30, 1980, MSU; Hemming, *Melody Lingers On*, 110.

73. Kelly interview, 33, 39, 41–42, SMU/Ronald L. Davis Oral History Collection, AMPAS; Marc Edward Houlihan, "An Analysis of Three Examples of the Technicolor Musicals," MA Thesis, University of California, Los Angeles, 1953, 96, 100.

74. Silvers, *This Laugh Is On Me*, 123; Kelly interview, 39, SMU/Ronald L. Davis Oral History Collection, AMPAS; Silverman, *Dancing*, 46, 48–49.

75. Blair, *Memory*, 82; Richard Dwenger background [website]; Richard Dwenger information [website].

76. "Make Way for Tomorrow," Box 27, Gene Kelly Collection, BU; Basinger, *Gene Kelly*, 39; Beth Genné, "'Dancin' in the Street': Street Dancing on Film and Video from Fred Astaire to Michael Jackson," in Alexandra Carter, ed., *Rethinking Dance History: A Reader* (London: Routledge, 2004), 133; Thomas, *Films of Gene Kelly*, 48–49.

77. Hanson, "An Interview with Gene Kelly," 25; Kelly interview, Haver, "Pas de Deux," 23; Houlihan, "Analysis," 154.

78. Blair, *Memory*, 114–116.

79. Silverman, *Dancing*, 58–60; Donen interview, 8, SMU/Ronald L. Davis Oral History Collection, AMPAS; Chaplin, *Golden Age*, 58.

80. Kelly interview, Delamater, *Dance*, 219; Donen interview, 8, SMU/Ronald L. Davis Oral History Collection, AMPAS; Houlihan, "Analysis," 156–157; Kelly interview, Fuller, "And Now," 112.

81. Chaplin, *Golden Age*, 58–59.

82. Marilyn Hunt, "Gene Kelly Interview," NYPL, 98–99; Kelly quoted in Thomas, *Films of Gene Kelly*, 53; Donen interview, 9, SMU/Ronald L. Davis Oral History Collection, AMPAS; Houlihan, "Analysis," 161.

83. Helen Hover, "Popping Questions at Gene Kelly," *Motion Picture* 68, No. 3 (Oct. 1944): 41; George Benjamin, "Kelly Is the Name!," *Modern Screen* (Aug. 1943): 121.

84. Scheurer, "Gene Kelly's Real Life"; Kelly quoted in Thomas, *Films of Gene Kelly*, 52–53; Chaplin, *Golden Age*, 58, 60.

85. Houlihan, "Analysis," 101, 123; Kobal, *Rita Hayworth*, 154; Chaplin, *Golden Age*, 61–63.

86. Jim O'Connor, "Present 'Cover Girl' on Musical Hall Screen," *New York Journal-American*, Mar. 31, 1944; Herb Stern, "Screen," *Rob Wagner's Script*, Apr. 15, 1955; Agee, *Agee on Film*, 87–88; Thomas, *Films of Gene Kelly*, 48, 53; Kobal, *Rita Hayworth*, 154–155; Hemming, *Melody Lingers On*, 109; Mary Jane Hungerford, "Dancing in Commercial Motion Pictures," PhD diss., Columbia University, 1946, 258.

87. Casey Charness, "Hollywood Cine-Dance: A Description of the Interrelationship of Camerawork and Choreography in Films by Stanley Donen and Gene Kelly," PhD diss., New York University, 1977, 44; Kelly interview, Haver, "Pas de Deux," 26; Kelly interview, Fuller, "And Now," 110; Marilyn Hunt, "Gene Kelly Interview," NYPL, 10.

88. Houlihan, "Analysis," 301–306.

89. Kelly interview, Delamater, *Dance*, 208, 213; Kelly quoted in Hirschhorn, *Gene Kelly*, 112.

Chapter 7. Dancing Sailor, 1944–1946

1. Kelly on *The Tonight Show*, May 4, 1976; Hirschhorn, *Gene Kelly*, 114.

2. Kelly interview, Knox, ed., *Magic Factory*, 18; Scheurer, "Gene Kelly's Real Life."

3. Chaplin, *Golden Age*, 65–66; Farley Granger, *Include Me Out: My Life from Goldwyn to Broadway* (New York: St. Martin's Press, 2007), 55.

4. Granger, *Include Me Out*, 55, 129–131.

5. Martin, *Hugh Martin*, 157, 178.

6. Martin, 178–179.

7. Garrison, "Kelly's From Pittsburgh."

8. Garrison.

9. "Reminiscences," [1992], 4, Sanford Baskind Papers, HHC.

10. Kelly to Robert Lazar, ca. Jan. 25, 1943, and Aug. 9, 1944, Lazar Family Papers and Photographs, HHC.

11. Garrison, "Kelly's From Pittsburgh."

12. Marcus Bright report, July 27, 1949, Gene Kelly FBI File.

13. D.M. Ladd memo to Director, Aug. 21, 1947, Gene Kelly FBI File; *Fourth Report*, 311.

14. Ladd memo to Director, Aug. 21, 1947, Gene Kelly FBI File.

15. Bright report, July 27, 1949, Gene Kelly FBI File.

16. Blair interview, McGilligan and Buhle, eds., *Tender Comrades*, 544–545; Pagán,

Murder at the Sleepy Lagoon: Zoot Suits, Race, and Riot in Wartime L.A. (Chapel Hill: University of North Carolina Press, 2003), 13–15, 77, 80–91, 133, 183; Ladd memo to Director, Aug. 21, 1947, Gene Kelly FBI File.

17. "Biography of Gene Kelly," Rogers and Cowan, Inc., Public Relations, Beverly Hills, 6, Box 1, Folder 10, Emerson Venable Papers, HHC.

18. "Gene Kelly Does a Job for Uncle Sam," *Screenland* (Sept. 1944): 71–73.

19. "Gene Kelly Does a Job for Uncle Sam," 73; Fordin, *M-G-M's Greatest Musicals*, 122.

20. Phillips, *Charles Walters*, 80; John Mueller, *Astaire Dancing: The Musical Films* (New York: Alfred A. Knopf, 1985), 247.

21. Thomas, *Films of Gene Kelly*, 2; Kelly interview, Delamater, *Dance*, 226.

22. Vincente Minnelli, *I Remember It Well* (New York: Samuel French, 1990), 111–112, 121, 129.

23. Scheurer, "Gene Kelly's Real Life"; "Kelly Notes," Feb. 19, 1981, Box 93, Folder 4, Joseph McBride Papers, WCFTR; Kelly quoted in Fordin, *M-G-M's Greatest Musicals*, 129–130; Minnelli interview, Fantle and Johnson, *Reel to Real*, 263; Marilyn Hunt, "Gene Kelly Interview," NYPL, 144.

24. Marilyn Hunt, "Gene Kelly Interview," NYPL, 145; Mueller, *Astaire Dancing*, 248.

25. Minnelli interview, Fantle and Johnson, *Reel to Real*, 263; Mueller, *Astaire Dancing*, 247, 250n; Fordin, *M-G-M's Greatest Musicals*, 128–129.

26. Mueller, *Astaire Dancing*, 248.

27. Mueller, 248.

28. Mueller, 248–249; Kelly quoted in Fordin, *M-G-M's Greatest Musicals*, 130; Smith interview, Delamater, *Dance*, 253.

29. Mueller, *Astaire Dancing*, 241, 248.

30. Fordin, *M-G-M's Greatest Musicals*, 143, 146; clipping, *Hollywood Reporter*, Aug. 14, 1945, Box 7, Scrapbook 3, Gene Kelly Collection, BU; Stanley Green and Burt Goldblatt, *Starring Fred Astaire* (New York: Doubleday, 1977), 277.

31. Basinger, *Gene Kelly*, 49; John Cutts, "Kelly: Dancer, Actor, Director," Pt. 1, *Films and Filming* 10, no. 11 (Aug. 1964): 40; Sheridan Morley and Ruth Leon, *Gene Kelly: A Celebration* (London: Pavilion Books, 1996), 68; Isaacs, "Gene Kelly," 156; Joseph Epstein, *Fred Astaire* (New Haven, CT: Yale University Press, 2008), 73; Peter J. Levinson, *Puttin' on the Ritz: Fred Astaire and the Fine Art of Panache* (New York: St. Martin's Press, 2009), 144; Green and Goldblatt, *Starring Fred Astaire*, 276.

32. Minnelli, *I Remember It Well*, 144; "Gene Kelly—June 3, 1954," 6, File 1342, Hedda Hopper Collection, AMPAS.

33. Kelly interview, Delamater, *Dance*, 226; Fred Astaire, *Steps in Time* (New York: Harper and Brothers, 1959), 266; Marilyn Hunt, "Gene Kelly Interview," NYPL, 146.

34. Clipping, *New York Journal-American*, Oct. 1942, Box 911, David O. Selznick Collection, UTA.

35. Kelly interview, Fuller, "And Now," 112; Hirschhorn, *Gene Kelly*, 148–149.

36. Thomas, *Films of Gene Kelly*, 61; Derek Jewell, *Frank Sinatra: A Celebration* (London: Pavilion Books, 1999), 21–23, 25, 34, 40, 46–48, 179–181.

37. Marilyn Hunt, "Gene Kelly Interview," NYPL, 105; Frank Sinatra foreword to Hirschhorn, *Gene Kelly*, 1.

38. Sinatra quoted in Hirschhorn, *Gene Kelly*, 123.

39. Charness, “Hollywood Cine-Dance,” 51–52, 54.

40. Kelly on *The Tonight Show*, May 4, 1976; “I Begged Her,” Box 27, Gene Kelly Collection, BU.

41. “Isobel Lennart Brilliantly Word-Paints the Real Gene Kelly” [website].

42. Marilyn Hunt, “Gene Kelly Interview,” NYPL, 125–126; Hirschhorn, *Gene Kelly*, 120.

43. Charness, “Hollywood Cine-Dance,” 59–60.

44. Marilyn Hunt, “Gene Kelly Interview,” NYPL, 138–140; Martin, “The Dance: Pal Kelly,” has a photograph of Kelly in his Spanish costume for *Pal Joey*, which looks exactly like what he wears in *Anchors Aweigh*.

45. Charness, “Hollywood Cine-Dance,” 62–63.

46. Hanson, “An Interview with Gene Kelly,” 25; Silverman, *Dancing*, 67; Joseph Andrew Casper, *Stanley Donen* (Metuchen, NJ: Scarecrow Press, 1983), 13; Donen interview, 13, SMU/Ronald L. Davis Oral History Collection, AMPAS.

47. Rudy Behlmer, “Gene Kelly Is One Dancer Who Can Also Act and Direct,” *Films in Review* 15, no. 1 (Jan. 1964): 10; Leonard Maltin, *Of Mice and Magic: A History of American Animated Cartoons* (New York: McGraw-Hill, 1980), 81–82; Hirschhorn, *Gene Kelly*, 143–144; “Reminiscences of Gene Curran Kelly: Oral History, 1958,” 10–11, CU; Donen interview, 16–17, SMU/Ronald L. Davis Oral History Collection, AMPAS; “Gene Kelly—June 3, 1954,” 8, File 1342, Hedda Hopper Collection, AMPAS.

48. Peter Hay, *MGM: When the Lion Roars* (Atlanta: Turner Publishing, 1991), 311; Maltin, *Of Mice and Magic*, 275, 277, 282–283; “Kenneth L. Muse Dies at 75: Animator for Major Studios,” *New York Times*, July 30, 1987; Silverman, *Dancing*, 72.

49. “Anchors Aweigh, Rough draft of cartoon sequence (pages 90–92a),” Aug. 10, 1944, Turner/MGM Scripts Collection, AMPAS.

50. Marilyn Hunt, “Gene Kelly Interview,” NYPL, 136–137; Charness, “Hollywood Cine-Dance,” 61–62; Anna Kisselgoff, “Just a Regular Joe Doing Ballet,” *New York Times*, Feb. 11, 1996; Isaacs, “Gene Kelly,” 155.

51. Maltin, *Of Mice and Magic*, 80, 293–294; Krebs, “Gene Kelly”; Kelly interview, Britton, ed., *Talking Films*, 197; Sidney interview, Fantle and Johnson, *Reel to Real*, 266–267.

52. Isaacs, “Gene Kelly,” 156; Barbera quoted in Silverman, *Dancing*, 72; Lawrence, “Kelly, Caught in the Draft”; Jim Hillier, “Interview with Stanley Donen,” *Movie* 24 (Spring 1977): 35; Ted Sennett, *The Art of Hanna-Barbera: Fifty Years of Creativity* (New York: Viking, 1989), 43; “Gene Kelly—June 3, 1954,” 8, File 1342, Hedda Hopper Collection, AMPAS.

53. Clipping, “Anchors Aweigh,” *Variety*, July 18, 1945, and clipping, John Maynard, “‘Anchors Aweigh’ is Voted Best of Screen Musicals,” Box 7, Scrapbook 2, Gene Kelly Collection, BU; Wanda Hale, “Delightful Musical at Capitol Theatre,” *Los Angeles Daily News*, July 20, 1945; Alton Cook, “Gene Kelly Can’t Anchor Dancing Feet with Sinatra,” *New York World Telegram*, July 19, 1945.

54. Hungerford, “Dancing,” 238–239; Maltin, *Of Mice and Magic*, 293–294; Kelly interview, Haver, “Pas de Deux,” 73; Marilyn Hunt, “Gene Kelly Interview,” NYPL, 137–138.

55. Spanish final dialogue script, July 11, 1946, and Spanish version trailer script, Aug. 15, 1946, and Spanish radio script for fifteen-minute broadcast, Oct. 1, 1946, Turner/MGM Scripts Collection, AMPAS.

56. Beth Genné, "'Freedom Incarnate': Jerome Robbins, Gene Kelly, and the Dancing Sailor as an Icon of American Values in World War II," *Dance Chronicle* 24, no. 1 (2001): 85, 87, 89, 94, 97.

57. Genné, 89.

58. Genné, 90.

59. George Q. Flynn, *The Mess in Washington: Manpower Mobilization in World War II* (Westport, CT: Greenwood Press, 1979), 201–203.

60. "Gives Advice on Ballot," *New York Times*, Oct. 14, 1944; Lawrence, "Kelly, Caught in the Draft."

61. Lawrence, "Kelly, Caught in the Draft."

62. Virginia McPherson, "Gene Kelly Dancing His Head Off," *Pittsburgh Post-Gazette*, Nov. 9, 1944; Lawrence, "Kelly, Caught in the Draft."

63. "Gene Kelly Is Inducted," *New York Times*, Nov. 21, 1944; Lawrence, "Kelly, Caught in the Draft"; Hirschhorn, *Gene Kelly*, 124.

64. James E. Wise Jr. and Anne Collier Rehill, *Stars in Blue: Movie Actors in America's Sea Services* (Annapolis, MD: Naval Institute Press, 1997), 185; Hirschhorn, *Gene Kelly*, 124; Blair, *Memory*, 121.

65. Blair, *Memory*, 123–124; Swanson, "Dance!" 30.

66. Blair, *Memory*, 124.

67. Wise and Rehill, *Stars in Blue*, 185; Hirschhorn, *Gene Kelly*, 124.

68. Wise and Rehill, *Stars In Blue*, 186.

69. Kelly interview, "Dialogue on Film," 35; Kelly interview, Michael Singer, *A Cut Above: 50 Film Directors Talk about Their Craft* (Los Angeles: Lone Eagle, 1998), 145.

70. Wise and Rehill, *Stars in Blue*, 186.

71. Wise and Rehill, 186–187; Kelly interview, "Dialogue on Film," 35; Hirschhorn, *Gene Kelly*, 127.

72. Wise and Rehill, *Stars in Blue*, 185; Hirschhorn, *Gene Kelly*, 125.

73. Wise and Rehill, *Stars in Blue*, 185–186.

74. Kelly quoted in Hirschhorn, *Gene Kelly*, 126; Wise and Rehill, *Stars in Blue*, 186.

75. Wise and Rehill, *Stars in Blue*, 186; Hirschhorn, *Gene Kelly*, 126–127.

76. Hirschhorn, *Gene Kelly*, 127.

77. Blair, *Memory*, 117, 123–124. Kelly's address can be found in [Salisbury] to Kelly, Jan. 19, 1946, Leah Jayne Salisbury Papers, CU.

78. "Branches Are Heart of Its Battle Against Jim Crow," *Ebony* 1, no. 9 (Aug. 1946): 37.

79. Kelly quoted in Hirschhorn, *Gene Kelly*, 128.

80. "President Hails 'Stream of Dimes,'" *New York Times*, Jan. 31, 1945; Emily W. Leider, *Myrna Loy: The Only Good Girl in Hollywood* (Berkeley: University of California Press, 2011), 237.

81. Ladd to Director, Aug. 21, 1947, Gene Kelly FBI File.

82. Ladd to Director, Aug. 21, 1947, Gene Kelly FBI File.

83. Ladd to Director, Aug. 21, 1947, Gene Kelly FBI File.

84. Ladd to Director, Aug. 21, 1947, Gene Kelly FBI File; "Biography of Gene Kelly," Rogers and Cowan, Inc., Public Relations, Beverly Hills, 6, Box 1, Folder 10, Emerson Venable Papers, HHC; Leider, *Myrna Loy*, 239.

85. *Dance News* 7, no. 4 (Dec. 1945): 1.

86. Halsey and Record, "Gene Kelly," 15; Marilyn Hunt, "Gene Kelly Interview," NYPL, 47; Forrestal to Kelly, Jan. 28, 1946, James V. Forrestal Papers, PU.

87. Isaacs, "Gene Kelly," 149–150.

88. Kelly to Cheyle Crawford, Aug. 17, 1945, and [Salisbury] to Kelly, Jan. 19, 1946, Leah Jayne Salisbury Papers, CU.

89. William Abbott to J. Edgar Hoover, Mar. 18, 1948, Gene Kelly FBI File; Wise and Rehill, *Stars in Blue*, 187; Fordin, *M-G-M's Greatest Musicals*, 203.

90. Marilyn Hunt, "Gene Kelly Interview," NYPL, 47–49.

91. Swanson, "Dance!," 30; Lois McClelland, "The Neighbors Are Talking," *Motion Picture Magazine* (Feb. 1950): 48, 73; Blair, *Memory*, 123–124.

92. Blair, *Memory*, 125.

Chapter 8. Restarting His Career, 1946–1948

1. Jack Howard, "Gene Kelly," Nov. 21, 1949, in Jack Hirshberg Papers, AMPAS.

2. Hanson, "An Interview with Gene Kelly," 27–28.

3. Hanson, 27.

4. Marilyn Hunt, "Gene Kelly Interview," NYPL, 156; Kelly interview, Boorman et al., *Projections 4*, 286.

5. Charness, "Hollywood Cine-Dance," 69; Ames interview, Delamater, *Dance*, 240; Donen interview, 18, SMU/Ronald L. Davis Oral History Collection, AMPAS.

6. Clipping, *Hollywood Reporter*, Oct. 14, 1947, and clipping, Virginia Wright review, Box 7, Scrapbook 3, Gene Kelly Collection, BU; Philip K. Scheurer, "Kelly's Luster as Dancer Undimmed by Absence," *Los Angeles Times*, Mar. 30, 1947; Marilyn Hunt, "Gene Kelly Interview," NYPL, 41–43.

7. McClelland, "Neighbors Are Talking," 73, 75.

8. McClelland, 73; Coyne, "I Knew Him When" [website].

9. McClelland, "Neighbors Are Talking," 73; *Los Angeles Times*, May 18, 1951.

10. Kelly to Balanchine, Dec. 30, 1946, George Balanchine Archive, HU.

11. Kelly interview, "Dialogue on Film," 38–39.

12. Saroyan to Kelly, Dec. 23, 1946, and June 21, 1948, William Saroyan Papers, SU; Leggett, *Daring Young Man*, 85–86.

13. Kelly to Saroyan, Dec. 17, 18, [1946], and Saroyan to Kelly, Dec. 23, 1946, William Saroyan Papers, SU; Leggett, *Daring Young Man*, 213, 220.

14. Newnham, "Tilly Losch," 134–135; John Martin, *The Dance: The Story of the Dance Told in Pictures and Text* (New York: Tudor, 1946), 153–154.

15. Johnstown Junior Chamber of Commerce Award [website].

16. Hess and Dabholkar, *Cinematic Voyage*, 3–49.

17. Kelly interview, Delamater, *Dance*, 214; Kelly interview, Haver, "Pas de Deux," 26; Ames interview, Delamater, *Dance*, 235–236.

18. Minnelli interview, Delamater, *Dance*, 267, 270; Minnelli interview, Fantle and Johnson, *Reel to Real*, 263.

19. Kelly interview, "Dialogue on Film," 36; "Reminiscences of Gene Curran Kelly: Oral History, 1958," 14–15, CU; Hess and Dabholkar, *Cinematic Voyage*, 58–61.

20. Kelly interview, Delamater, *Dance*, 214; Hess and Dabholkar, *Cinematic Voyage*, 63–66, 88–93.

21. Kelly interview, Delamater, *Dance*, 209; Kelly quoted in Hirschhorn, *Gene Kelly*, 137–138.

22. Fayard Nicholas interview, Fantle and Johnson, *Reel to Real*, 84; Hess and Dabholkar, *Cinematic Voyage*, 83–86, 217–218.

23. Smith interview, Delamater, *Dance*, 258; Hess and Dabholkar, *Cinematic Voyage*, 93–99.

24. Minnelli interview, Delamater, *Dance*, 269; Douglas McVay, "Minnelli and the Pirate," *The Velvet Light Trap*, issue 18 (Spring 1978): 37; Hess and Dabholkar, *Cinematic Voyage*, 119–124.

25. Smith Interview, Delamater, *Dance*, 259.

26. Minnelli interview, Delamater, *Dance*, 271; Hess and Dabholkar, *Cinematic Voyage*, 106–108.

27. Hess and Dabholkar, *Cinematic Voyage*, 133, 136–142.

28. Kelly quoted in Hirschhorn, *Gene Kelly*, 138.

29. David Vaughan, "Dance in the Cinema," *Sequence* 6 (Winter 1948–1949): 13; Joel Siegel, "The Pirate," *Film Heritage* 7, no. 1 (Fall 1971): 22, 27, 31–32; Beth Eliot Genné, "The Film Musicals of Vincente Minnelli and the Team of Gene Kelly and Stanley Donen: 1944–1958," PhD diss., University of Michigan, 1984), 239; McVay, "Minnelli and The Pirate," 36, 38; Hess and Dabholkar, *Cinematic Voyage*, xvi, 151–176.

30. Genné, "Film Musicals," 244.

31. Blair, *Memory*, 126; Dorothy O'Leary, "Always on His Toes!," *Silver Screen* 7, no. 6 (Apr. 1947): 79; Hudgins, "Directed by Kelly."

32. Swanson, "Dance!," 64; Blair, *Memory*, 126, 128, 130; McClelland, "Neighbors Are Talking," 73.

33. Blair *Memory*, 93, 128; Blair interview, McGilligan and Buhle, eds., *Tender Comrades*, 546–547.

34. Lena Horne and Richard Schickel, *Lena* (Garden City, NY: Doubleday, 1965), 127, 129, 222.

35. Swanson, "Dance!," 64; McClelland, "Neighbors Are Talking," 73–74.

36. Previn and Fosse quoted in Hirschhorn, *Gene Kelly*, 147–148, 172.

37. Arthur Laurents, *Original Story By: A Memoir of Broadway and Hollywood* (New York: Alfred A. Knopf, 2000), 26, 92, 94–95; Blair, *Memory*, 154.

38. Laurents, *Original Story*, 95.

39. Laurents, 95–96.

40. Marilyn Hunt, "Gene Kelly Interview," NYPL, 201; *Los Angeles Times*, Oct. 14, 1947; Michael Burrows, *Gene Kelly: Versatility Personified* (N.p.: Primestyle, 1972), 17; Fordin, *M-G-M's Greatest Musicals*, 226.

41. Gerald Clarke, *Get Happy: The Life of Judy Garland* (New York: Random House, 2000), 237–238.

42. "Play a Simple Melody," "Ragtime Violin," "Say It With Music," and "I Want to Go Back to Michigan," Box 27, Gene Kelly Collection, BU; Fordin, *M-G-M's Greatest Musicals*, 224.

43. F. A. Datig to Freed, Sept. 4, 15, 1947, Box 19, Folder 1 of 3, Arthur Freed Collection, USC; Fordin, *M-G-M's Greatest Musicals*, 225–226; Temporary complete screenplays, *Easter Parade*, Frances Goodrich and Albert Hackett, June 6, 1947–Sept. 17, 1947, and Sidney Sheldon, Oct. 20, 1947–Nov. 14, 1947, Turner-MGM Script Collection, AMPAS; Walters interview, 28–29, SMU/Ronald L. Davis Oral History Collection, AMPAS.

44. Marilyn Hunt, "Gene Kelly Interview," NYPL, 201–202; Smith interview, Delamater, *Dance*, 253; Astaire, *Steps in Time*, 282–284; clipping, Bob Thomas, "Fred Returns to Pictures," Box 7, Scrapbook 3, Gene Kelly Collection, BU.

45. Clipping, Bob Thomas, "Fred Returns to Pictures," Box 7, Scrapbook 3, Gene Kelly Collection, BU.

46. Clipping, Bob Thomas, "Fred Returns to Pictures," Box 7, Scrapbook 3, Gene Kelly Collection, BU; Astaire, *Steps in Time*, 290–291; Levinson, *Puttin' on the Ritz*, 155–157.

47. Louella Parsons, "Astaire to Replace Kelly in 'Parade,'" *New York Journal-American*, Oct. 16, 1947; Thomas F. Brady, "Astaire to Return to Acting in Films," *New York Times*, Oct. 16, 1947; O'Leary, "Always on His Toes!," 79.

48. Astaire, *Steps in Time*, 292; Astaire interview, 39, SMU/Ronald L. Davis Oral History Collection, AMPAS; Levinson, *Puttin' on the Ritz*, 158–159.

49. Kelly interview, Delamater, *Dance*, 226–227.

50. Walters quoted in Phillips, *Charles Walters*, 99; Mueller, *Astaire Dancing*, 277.

51. Temporary complete screenplay, *Easter Parade*, Frances Goodrich and Albert Hackett, June 6, 1947–Sept. 17, 1947, Turner-MGM Script Collection, AMPAS.

52. Mueller, *Astaire Dancing*, 278.

53. Fordin, *M-G-M's Greatest Musicals*, 537; Walters quoted in Phillips, *Charles Walters*, 105; Clarke, *Get Happy*, 239, 241.

54. Mueller, *Astaire Dancing*, 275.

55. "Kelly Notes," Feb. 19, 1981, Box 93, Folder 4, Joseph McBride Papers, WCFTR; Mueller, *Astaire Dancing*, 283; Gene Kelly quoted in Thomas, *Films of Gene Kelly*, 82.

Chapter 9. Red Scare—First Wave, 1946–1949

1. "Reminiscences of Gene Curran Kelly: Oral History, 1958," 20, CU.

2. Larry Ceplair and Steven Englund, *The Inquisition in Hollywood: Politics in the Film Community, 1930–1960* (Garden City, NY: Doubleday, 1980), 437–438; Murphy, "*Say,*" 283, 294.

3. "Branches Are Heart of Its Battle," 37.

4. "Actors to Discuss Citizenship," *New York Times*, Jan. 5, 1946.

5. "Gene Kelly Makes It Clear He's a Serious Young Fellow," *Brooklyn Daily Eagle*, May 5, 1946.

6. "Veterans' Rally Set," *New York Times*, May 11, 1946.

7. D. M. Ladd memo to Director, Aug. 21, 1947, Gene Kelly FBI File.

8. John Meroney, "Hollywood's Brewer" *National Review*, Sept. 19, 2006; Stephen Vaughn, *Ronald Reagan in Hollywood: Movies and Politics* (New York: Cambridge University Press, 1996), 133–135, 138–139, 142.

9. Vaughn, *Ronald Reagan*, 139, 142; Rogers St. Johns, *Photoplay* [website].

10. "Rival Screen Unions in Peace Move," *Los Angeles Times*, Oct. 25, 1946.

11. Jordan Goodman, *Paul Robeson: A Watched Man* (London: Verso, 2013), 172, 175–176; Ladd memo to Director, Aug. 21, 1947, Gene Kelly FBI File.

12. Ladd memo to Director, Aug. 21, 1947, Gene Kelly FBI File.

13. Marcus Bright report, July 27, 1949, Gene Kelly FBI File; "Film to Aid Brotherhood Drive" *New York Times*, February 3, 1947; "Brotherhood Week Backed by Truman," *New York Times*, Feb. 18, 1947; Ladd memo to Director, Aug. 21, 1947, Gene Kelly FBI File.

14. Bright report, July 27, 1949, Gene Kelly FBI File.

15. O'Leary, "Always on His Toes!," 78–79; *Movieland* [website].

16. David Caute, *Great Fear: The Anti-Communist Purge under Truman and Eisenhower* (New York: Simon and Shuster, 1978), 490–491.

17. Caute, 492–493.

18. Ceplair and Englund, *Inquisition*, 273–274; *Fourth Report of the Senate Fact-Finding Committee on Un-American Activities, 1948: Communist Front Organizations* (Sacramento: California Legislature, 1948), 357.

19. *Fourth Report*, 357, 393; Marcus Bright report, July 27, 1949, Gene Kelly FBI File.

20. Edward L. Barrett Jr., *The Tenney Committee: Legislative Investigation of Subversive Activities in California* (Ithaca: Cornell University Press, 1951), 362; Caute, *Great Fear*, 496–497.

21. Caute, *Great Fear*, 496; Bright report, July 27, 1949, Gene Kelly FBI File.

22. Blair interview, McGilligan and Buhle, eds., *Tender Comrades*, 549.

23. Ceplair and Englund, *Inquisition*, 290.

24. Billingsley, *Hollywood Party: How Communism Seduced the American Film Industry in the 1930s and 1940s* (Rocklin, CA: Prima, 1998), 191–192.

25. Kaspar Monahan, "Show Stops: Actors Denounce the 'Red' Probe," *Pittsburgh Press*, Oct. 28, 1947.

26. Ceplair and Englund, *Inquisition*, 288–289; Cogley, *Report on Blacklisting 1: Movies* (N.p.: Fund for the Republic, 1956), 5–6; Edward Dmytryk, *Odd Man Out: A Memoir of the Hollywood Ten* (Carbondale: Southern Illinois University Press, 1996), 71.

27. Ceplair and Englund, *Inquisition*, 288.

28. Cogley, *Report on Blacklisting*, 4–5; Gordon Kahn, *Hollywood on Trial: The Story of the 10 Who Were Indicted* (New York: Boni and Gaer, 1948), 140–141.

29. Gladwin Hill, "Stars Fly to Fight Inquiry into Films," *New York Times*, Oct. 27, 1947.

30. "Hollywood Fights Back," Nov. 2, 1947, Vincent Voice Library, MSU; Kahn, *Hollywood on Trial*, 222; Leider, *Myrna Loy*, 262–263; "Broadcast Attacks Inquiry," *New York Times*, Nov. 3, 1947.

31. Ceplair and Englund, *Inquisition*, 288; Caute, *Great Fear*, 496; Hunt interview, McGilligan and Buhle, eds., *Tender Comrades*, 317.

32. Vaughn, *Ronald Reagan*, 143; "Actors Elect Reagan," *New York Times*, Nov. 18, 1947.

33. "Actors Elect Reagan."

34. Vaughn, *Ronald Reagan*, 176–177.

35. Hunt interview, McGilligan and Buhle, eds., *Tender Comrades*, 306–307, 312.

36. Ceplair and Englund, *Inquisition*, 290–292.

37. Hunt and Blair interviews, McGilligan and Buhle, eds., *Tender Comrades*, 317, 549.

38. Hunt interview, McGilligan and Buhle, eds., 317; Ceplair and Englund, *Inquisition*, 290.

39. Blair interview, McGilligan and Buhle, eds., *Tender Comrades*, 550; *Fourth Report*, 356.

40. Blair, *Memory*, 154–156; Bright report, July 27, 1949, Gene Kelly FBI File.

41. Bright report, July 27, 1949, Gene Kelly FBI File; Hilary Mills, *Mailer: A Biography* (New York: Harper and Row, 1982), 109.

42. Granger, *Include Me Out*, 94–95.

43. Ceplair and Englund, *Inquisition*, 317; "Dinner Set By Hadassah," *Los Angeles Times*, Feb. 24, 1948.

44. Bright report, July 27, 1949, Gene Kelly FBI File.

45. Hoover to special agents, Los Angeles, May 20, 1949, and Bright report, July 27, 1949, and Hoover to director of Naval Intelligence, Sept. 2, 1949, Gene Kelly FBI File.

46. Hedda Hopper, "Just Plain Kelly," *Chicago Daily Tribune*, Oct. 9, 1949.

47. Barrett, *Tenney Committee*, 4–6.

48. Jack B. Tenney, comp., *Red Fascism* (New York: Arno Press, 1977), 78–80, 623, 625, 664; *Fourth Report*, 97.

49. Bright report, July 27, 1949, Gene Kelly FBI File; Barrett, *Tenney Committee*, 46, 67, 75, 315–317.

50. Kelly to Barrett, July 30, 1949, in Barrett, *Tenney Committee*, 364–365.

51. Kelly to Barrett, July 30, 1949, in Barrett, 365–366.

52. Kelly to Barrett, July 30, 1949, in Barrett, 367.

53. Blair interview, McGilligan and Buhle, eds., *Tender Comrades*, 547; Blair, *Memory*, 132–133; Billingsley, *Hollywood Party*, 63.

54. Blair in *Anatomy of a Dancer* [DVD].

55. Bright report, July 27, 1949, Gene Kelly FBI File.

56. Blair, *Memory*, 133; Lardner and Blair interviews, McGilligan and Buhle, eds., *Tender Comrades*, 412, 550; Ring Lardner, Jr., Notorious Offenders Files (NARA).

57. Wintz, "Gene Kelly," 24; Kelly interview, "Dialogue on Film," 36–37.

58. Kelly quoted in Hirschhorn, *Gene Kelly*, 112.

59. Wintz, "Gene Kelly," 24; Kenneth J. Heineman, "Catholics, Communists, and Conservatives: The Making of Cold War Democrats on the Pittsburgh Front," *U.S. Catholic Historian* 34, no. 4 (Fall 2016): 27.

60. Arthur S. Bennett report, Apr. 9, 1951, Gene Kelly FBI File.

61. Jack Howard, "Gene Kelly," Nov. 21, 1949, in Jack Hirshberg Papers, AMPAS.

62. Blair in *Anatomy of a Dancer* [DVD]; McClelland, "Neighbors Are Talking," 75.

Chapter 10. Surging to the Top, 1948–1949

1. Kelly interview, Haver, "Pas de Deux," 23; Hirschhorn, *Gene Kelly*, 140.

2. Hirschhorn, *Gene Kelly*, 139.

3. Kelly interview, 23, SMU/Ronald L. Davis Oral History Collection, AMPAS; Hirschhorn, *Gene Kelly*, 139–140.

4. Kelly interview, "Dialogue on Film," 40; color, home movies of filming the horses running on the beach sequence can be seen in the Gene Kelly Collection, Film and Television Archives, Archives Research and Study Center, UCLA.

5. Marilyn Hunt, "Gene Kelly Interview," NYPL, 162.

6. Schary, *Heyday*, 209.

7. Basinger, *Gene Kelly*, 56–57.

8. Marilyn Hunt, "Gene Kelly Interview," NYPL, 202; Burrows, *Gene Kelly*, 21; "Reminiscences of Gene Curran Kelly: Oral History, 1958," 14, CU.

9. Thomas, *Films of Gene Kelly*, 91.

10. David Soren et al., *Vera-Ellen: The Magic and the Mystery* (Baltimore: Luminary Press, 2003), 1–4, 8, 27, 30–31, 34, 41, 97.

11. Soren et al., 73; Kelly interview, Britton, ed., *Talking Films*, 194; Marilyn Hunt, "Gene Kelly Interview," NYPL, 203, 205.

12. Vera-Ellen quoted in Soren, *Vera-Ellen*, 73.

13. Marilyn Hunt, "Gene Kelly Interview," NYPL, 122; Beth Genné, *Dance Me a Song: Astaire, Balanchine, Kelly, and the American Film Musical* (New York: Oxford University Press, 2018), 84–87; Kelly interview, Boorman et al., *Projections 4*, 284; Thomas, *Films of Gene Kelly*, 92, 94.

14. Kelly interview, Boorman, et al., *Projections 4*, 282; Marilyn Hunt, "Gene Kelly Interview," NYPL, 123–124; Mark Knowles, *The Man Who Made the Jailhouse Rock: Alex Romero, Hollywood Choreographer* (Jefferson, NC: McFarland, 2013), 51.

15. "Reminiscences of Gene Curran Kelly: Oral History, 1958," 11, CU.

16. Smith interview, Delamater, *Dance*, 259–260; Marilyn Hunt, "Gene Kelly Interview," NYPL, 203–204.

17. Kelly interview, "Dialogue on Film," 39–40; Marilyn Hunt, "Gene Kelly Interview," NYPL, 204.

18. Soren, *Vera-Ellen*, 73–74; Fordin, *M-G-M's Greatest Musicals*, 239, 552; Sheaffer, "Star-Studded 'Words and Music,'" *Brooklyn Eagle*, Dec. 10, 1948; clipping, John K. Newnham, "Brilliant Film Ballet," *Dancing Times*, Aug. 1949, Box 8, Scrapbook 5, Gene Kelly Collection, BU.

19. Hemming, *Melody Lingers On*, 233; Basinger, *Gene Kelly*, 57, 59.

20. Bolger interview, Fantle and Johnson, *Reel to Real*, 59; Cutts, "Kelly," Pt. 1, 41; Taylor and Jackson, *Hollywood Musical*, 62; Soren, *Vera-Ellen*, 73; Basinger, *Gene Kelly*, 59.

21. O'Leary, "Always on His Toes!," 78; Kelly interview, in Britton, ed., *Talking Films*, 189–190.

22. Marilyn Hunt, "Gene Kelly Interview," NYPL, 211–212; Kelly interview, Delamater, *Dance*, 207; Kelly to Roy Myers, July 27, 1946, Turner/MGM Script Collection, AMPAS.

23. Gene Kelly and Stanley Donen, "Take Me Out to the Ball Game," Sept. 27, 1946, Turner/MGM Script Collection, AMPAS; Hirschhorn, *Gene Kelly*, 143.

24. Gene Kelly and Stanley Donen, "Take Me Out to the Ball Game," Sept. 27, 1946, 1–3, 6–7, Turner/MGM Script Collection, AMPAS.

25. "Production Information on the Films of Arthur Freed," *Take Me Out to the Ball Game*, Arthur Freed Collection, USC.

26. Thomas, *Films of Gene Kelly*, 95–96; Garrett interview, 29, SMU/Ronald L. Davis Oral History Collection, AMPAS; Hillier, "Interview with Stanley Donen," 28; Knowles, *Man Who Made*, 58.

27. "Production Information on the Films of Arthur Freed," *Take Me Out to the Ball Game*, Arthur Freed Collection, USC; Garrett interview, Delamater, *Dance*, 199; Marilyn Hunt, "Gene Kelly Interview," NYPL, 213; Esther Williams, *The Million Dollar Mermaid* (New York: Simon & Schuster, 1999), 168.

28. Williams, *Million Dollar Mermaid*, 162–163, 167–168.

29. Hover, "Popping Questions," 40; Marilyn Hunt, "Gene Kelly Interview," NYPL, 214–215; Williams, *Million Dollar Mermaid*, 167.

30. Williams, *Million Dollar Mermaid*, 168; Previn quoted in Hirschhorn, *Gene Kelly*, 147–148.

31. Williams, *Million Dollar Mermaid*, 168–169, 171.

32. Williams, 170–171.

33. Spivak, *Buzz*, 227–228; Williams, *Million Dollar Mermaid*, 171; Knowles, *Man Who Made*, 59.

34. Williams, *Million Dollar Mermaid*, 166, 187–188.

35. Garrett interview, 28, SMU/Ronald L. Davis Oral History Collection, AMPAS.

36. "Production Information on the Films of Arthur Freed," *Take Me Out to the Ball Game*, and Assistant Director's Report, *Take Me Out to the Ball Game*, Aug. 3–4, 6, 18, 27, 1948, Arthur Freed Collection, USC.

37. Assistant Director's Report, *Take Me Out to the Ball Game*, Sept. 23, 27–28, 1948, Arthur Freed Collection, USC.

38. Kelly quoted in Thomas, *Films of Gene Kelly*, 10; Basinger, *Gene Kelly*, 62; Richard Fehr and Frederick G. Vogel, *Lullabies of Hollywood: Movie Music and the Movie Musical, 1915–1992* (Jefferson, NC: McFarland, 1993), 213; Lew Sheaffer, "State's Tuneful 'Ball Game,' 'Alias Nick Beal' Unusual Fare," *Brooklyn Eagle*, Mar. 10, 1949.

39. "Strictly U.S.A.," Box 27, Gene Kelly Collection, BU; Charness, "Hollywood Cine-Dance," 73, 75.

40. Assistant Director's Report, *Take Me Out to the Ball Game*, Oct. 22, 25, Nov. 4, 1948, Arthur Freed Collection, USC; preview report, *Take Me Out to the Ball Game*, Box 24, Folder 2 of 2, and report of patrons comments, Box 24, Folder 1 of 2, Arthur Freed Collection, USC; Fordin, *M-G-M's Greatest Musicals*, 243.

41. Kelly interview, 51–52, SMU/Ronald L. Davis Oral History Collection, AMPAS; Kelly interview, Britton, ed., *Talking Films*, 190.

42. Otis L. Guernsey Jr., "On the Screen," *New York Herald-Tribune*, Mar. 10, 1949; Sheaffer, "State's Tuneful"; Kate Cameron, "A Lively Musical on Loew's State Screen," *New York Daily News*, Mar. 10, 1949.

43. Thomas, *Films of Gene Kelly*, 102; Jeff Kurtti, *The Great Movie Musical Trivia Book* (New York: Applause Books, 1996), 26.

44. Oliver Smith quoted in "On the Town: Projects Committee Introduces Its Landmark Series of Symposia," *Dramatist's Guild Quarterly* 18, no. 2 (Summer 1981): 20; Kelly interview, Singer, *A Cut Above*, 145; Kelly interview, Delamater, *Dance*, 227; Marilyn Hunt, "Gene Kelly Interview," NYPL, 216; Hirschhorn, *Gene Kelly*, 154.

45. Kelly interview, Singer, *A Cut Above*, 145.

46. Fordin, *M-G-M's Greatest Musicals*, 258.

47. Kelly quoted in Flatow, "Through a Lens," 14; "Reminiscences of Betty Comden and Adolph Green: Oral History, 1959," 25–26, CU; Marilyn Hunt, "Gene Kelly Interview," NYPL, 222; Kelly quoted in Norma McLain Stoop, "Gene Kelly: An American Dance Innovator Tells It Like It Was—And Is," *Dance Magazine* 50, no. 7 (July 1976): 71.

48. Kelly and Chaplin interviews, Haver, "Pas de Deux," 25; Fordin, *M-G-M's Greatest Musicals*, 259–260; Kelly quoted in Knox, *Magic Factory*, 173–174; Donen on *Musicals Great Musicals* [DVD]; Kelly interview, 46, SMU/Ronald L. Davis Oral History Collection, AMPAS.

49. Fordin, *M-G-M's Greatest Musicals*, 261; Garrett interview, Delamater, *Dance*, 200–201; Ann Miller, *Miller's High Life* (Garden City, NY: Doubleday, 1972), 29–31.

50. Soren, *Vera-Ellen*, 79; Kelly interview, Delamater, *Dance*, 224.

51. Kelly interview, Singer, *A Cut Above*, 145; Kelly interview, Flatow, "Through a Lens," 14.

52. Joanne D'Antonio, *Andrew Marton: A Directors Guild of America Oral History* (Metuchen, NJ: Scarecrow Press, 1991), 133; Assistant Director's Report, *On the Town*, Mar. 21, 25–26, 28, 30, 1949, Arthur Freed Collection, USC.

53. Assistant Director's Report, *On the Town*, May 4, 9–11, 1949, Arthur Freed Collection, USC.

54. Assistant Director's Report, *On the Town*, May 12–13, 16–18, 1949, Arthur Freed Collection, USC; Kelly interview, "Dialogue on Film," 35–36; Kelly interview, Singer, *A Cut Above*, 145; Betty Garrett and Ron Rapoport, *Betty Garrett and Other Songs: A Life on Stage and Screen* (Lanham, MD: Madison Books, 2000), 111.

55. Assistant Director's Report, *On the Town*, May 14, 22, 1949, Arthur Freed Collection, USC; Kelly interview, Flatow, "Through a Lens," 14; "Reminiscences of Betty Comden and Adolph Green: Oral History, 1959," 27, CU.

56. Assistant Director's Report, *On the Town*, June 28–29, 1949, Arthur Freed Collection, USC; Fordin, *M-G-M's Greatest Musicals*, 311; Billman, *Film Choreographers*, 485–486; Knowles, *Man Who Made*, 61–62.

57. Betty Comden and Adolph Green, *The New York Musicals of Comden & Green* (New York: Applause, 1997), 77; Marilyn Hunt, "Gene Kelly Interview," NYPL, 223; Stoop, "Gene Kelly," 71; Charness, "Hollywood Cine-Dance," 91.

58. Charness, "Hollywood Cine-Dance," 91, 95–96.

59. Kelly interview, Flatow, "Through a Lens," 15, 38; Kelly interview, "Dialogue on Film," 36.

60. Millar, *An Evening with Gene Kelly* [DVD]; Assistant Director's Report, *On the Town*, July 2, 1949, Arthur Freed Collection, USC.

61. Freed to Kelly and Donen, Apr. 13, 1949, Box 56, Folder 3, and preview report, Sept. 9, 1949, and Nov. 22, 1949, Box 56, Folder 2, and clipping, Milton Shulman, "Rub Your

Eyes! Here is a GOOD Musical," *Evening Standard*, Mar. 23, 1950, and clipping, Otis L. Guernsey Jr., "Three Sailors Back Again," New York *Herald Tribune*, Box 56, Folder 2, Arthur Freed Collection, USC; Fordin, *M-G-M's Greatest Musicals*, 267–268; Thomas Schatz, *The Genius of the System* (New York: Henry Holt, 1996), 449.

62. Clipping, Otis L. Guernsey Jr., "Three Sailors Back Again," *New York Herald Tribune*, Box 56, Folder 2, Arthur Freed Collection, USC; Thomas, *Films of Gene Kelly*, 102; Flatow, "Through a Lens," 11; Morley and Leon, *Gene Kelly*, 98, 102.

63. Donen quoted in James Clark, "Giving Life an Up-Beat," *Films and Filming* 4 (July 1958): 7; Silverman, *Dancing*, 106; Knowles, *Man Who Made*, 56.

64. Assistant Director's Report, Apr. 2, 1949, *On the Town*, Arthur Freed Collection, USC.

65. "Reminiscences of Gene Curran Kelly: Oral History, 1958," 17–19, CU; Taylor and Jackson, *Hollywood Musical*, 87; Kelly interview, Flatow, "Through a Lens," 11, 14; Basinger, *Gene Kelly*, 63; Genné, "Film Musicals," 293–294.

Chapter 11. Zenith, 1949–1952

1. Marilyn Hunt, "Gene Kelly Interview," NYPL, 84–85; Bosley Crowther, "'Black Hand,' with Gene Kelly and J. Carrol Naish in Main Roles, Opens at Capitol," *New York Times*, Mar. 13, 1950; *Toledo Blade*, Aug. 11, 1949.

2. Hopper, "Just Plain Kelly."

3. Marilyn Hunt, "Gene Kelly Interview," NYPL, 226; Walters interview, 32, SMU/Ronald L. Davis Oral History Collection, AMPAS; Walters interview, Fantle and Johnson, *Reel to Real*, 277; Clarke, *Get Happy*, 258–259.

4. Pasternak, *Easy the Hard Way*, 231–232; Silvers, *This Laugh is On Me*, 171; Chaplin, *Golden Age*, 125; Walters interview, 32, SMU/Ronald L. Davis Oral History Collection, AMPAS; Phillips, *Charles Walters*, 123.

5. Schary, *Heyday*, 214.

6. Marilyn Hunt, "Gene Kelly Interview," NYPL, 87, 231; Minnelli, *I Remember It Well*, 216; Kelly quoted in Joe Morella and Edward Z. Epstein, *Judy: The Films and Career of Judy Garland* (New York: Citadel Press, 1969), 32.

7. Billman, *Film Choreographers*, 254; Jennings quoted in Phillips, *Charles Walters*, 122.

8. Carpenter quoted in Phillips, *Charles Walters*, 122.

9. Chaplin, *Golden Age*, 126; Phillips, *Charles Walters*, 125–126.

10. Kelly interview, Britton, ed., *Talking Films*, 195–196; Marilyn Hunt, "Gene Kelly Interview," NYPL, 228–230; Millar, *An Evening with Gene Kelly* [DVD].

11. Kelly interview, Britton, ed., *Talking Films*, 195–196; Marilyn Hunt, "Gene Kelly Interview," NYPL, 230; Halsey and Record, "Gene Kelly," 15; Feuer, *Hollywood Musical*, 6.

12. Bosley Crowther review of *Summer Stock*, *New York Times*, Sept. 1, 1950, clipping in Box 8, Scrapbook 6, Gene Kelly Collection, BU; Kelly, "The Women in My Dancing Life"; Kelly interview, June 3, 1954, File 1342, Hedda Hopper Collection, AMPAS.

13. Freed interview, John Kobal, *People Will Talk* (New York: Alfred A. Knopf, 1985), 643; Minnelli, *I Remember It Well*, 229; Kelly interview, Knox, ed., *Magic Factory*, 47.

14. Antik and Minnelli interviews, Knox, ed., *Magic Factory*, 5, 60; Stephen Harvey,

Directed by Vincente Minnelli (New York: Harper and Row, 1989), 98; Sue Harris, *An American in Paris* (London: Palgrave, 2015), 46–47; Vanessa R. Schwartz, *It's So French! Hollywood, Paris, and the Making of Cosmopolitan Film Culture* (Chicago: University of Chicago Press, 2007), 22–23.

15. Harris, *An American in Paris*, 47; Ames, Antik, and Kelly interviews, Knox, ed., *Magic Factory*, 4–5, 32; Kelly interview, Haver, "Pas de Deux," 26.

16. Chaplin and Lerner interviews, Knox, ed., *Magic Factory*, 46, 48–49; Chaplin, *Golden Age*, 131; "Somebody Loves Me," "Soon," "Mine," "Tip-Toes," Box 27, Gene Kelly Collection, BU; "Musical Compositions Recorded in 'An American in Paris,'" Feb. 21, 1952, Turner/MGM Scripts Collection, AMPAS; Kelly interview, "Dialogue on Film," 39.

17. Ames interview, Delamater, *Dance*, 237; Leslie Caron, *Thank Heaven: A Memoir* (New York: Viking, 2009), 71.

18. Fordin, *M-G-M's Greatest Musicals*, 309; Freed and Schary interviews, Knox, ed., *Magic Factory*, 6, 39; Caron, *Thank Heaven*, 54–56.

19. Caron, *Thank Heaven*, 1, 6–7, 23, 25, 33–35, 42–46, 57; Caron quoted in Anna Kisselgoff, "The Ballerina in Leslie Caron, the Actress," *New York Times*, Mar. 12, 1995.

20. Freed and Minnelli interviews, Knox, ed., *Magic Factory*, 8; Caron, *Thank Heaven*, 54–55.

21. Fordin, *M-G-M's Greatest Musicals*, 311; Caron, *Thank Heaven*, 56–59, 62–63, 69–70.

22. Harvey, *Directed by Vincente Minnelli*, 99; Caron, *Thank Heaven*, 64, 70; Caron foreword, Morley and Leon, *Gene Kelly*, 7.

23. Caron foreword, Morley and Leon, *Gene Kelly*, 7.

24. Caron, *Thank Heaven*, 61.

25. Kelly, "The Women in My Dancing Life"; Caron, *Thank Heaven*, 61–62, 65; Caron foreword, Morley and Leon, *Gene Kelly*, 7.

26. Chaplin, *Golden Age*, 133; Oscar Levant, *The Memoirs of an Amnesiac* (Hollywood: Samuel French, 1989), 200–201.

27. Caron, Ames, Gilks, and Kelly interviews, Knox, ed., *Magic Factory*, 64–65, 105–106, 156–157.

28. Ames and Minnelli interviews, Knox, ed., *Magic Factory*, 49, 99; Minnelli, *I Remember It Well*, 232–233.

29. Chaplin interview, Knox, ed., *Magic Factory*, 50; Minnelli, *I Remember It Well*, 230–231; Levant, *Memoirs*, 201; Basinger, *Gene Kelly*, 75.

30. Kelly interview, Knox, ed., *Magic Factory*, 50–51; Minnelli interview, Delamater, *Dance*, 271; Levant, *Memoirs*, 201.

31. Kelly interview, Delamater, *Dance*, 225; Harvey, *Directed by Vincente Minnelli*, 99; Chaplin and Caron interviews, Knox, ed., *Magic Factory*, 130, 135–136; Caron, *Thank Heaven*, 71–72; Kelly interview, "Dialogue on Film," 36.

32. Kelly interview, Delamater, *Dance*, 221; Chaplin and Schary interviews, Knox, ed., *Magic Factory*, 44, 146; Minnelli, *I Remember It Well*, 235–237.

33. Foch and Minnelli interviews, Knox, ed., *Magic Factory*, 129, 138–139; Minnelli and Kelly, "*American in Paris*" *Ballet*, Sept. 9, 1950, Vincente Minnelli Collection, AMPAS;

Irene Sharaff, *Broadway & Hollywood: Costumes Designed by Irene Sharaff* (New York: Van Nostrand Reinhold, 1976), 76.

34. Kelly, Minnelli, Gleason, and Fazan interviews, Knox, ed., *Magic Factory*, 126–127, 139–140; Minnelli, *I Remember It Well*, 231; Fordin, *M-G-M's Greatest Musicals*, 319; Chaplin, *Golden Age*, 137–138; Marilyn Hunt, "Gene Kelly Interview," NYPL, 242–243.

35. Harvey, *Directed by Vincente Minnelli*, 99; Kelly interview, Britton, ed., *Talking Films*, 194; Kelly interview, Knox, ed., *Magic Factory*, 141.

36. Kelly interview, Boorman, et al., *Projections 4*, 282; Marilyn Hunt, "Gene Kelly Interview," NYPL, 243; Millar, *An Evening with Gene Kelly* [DVD]; Angela Dalle Vacche, *Cinema and Painting: How Art Is Used in Film* (Austin: University of Texas Press, 1996), 41.

37. Ames interview, Knox, ed., *Magic Factory*, 149–150.

38. Fordin, *M-G-M's Greatest Musicals*, 328; Thomas, *Films of Gene Kelly*, 123; Sharaff, *Broadway & Hollywood*, 76.

39. Wording of honorary award quoted in Knox, ed., *Magic Factory*, 182–184, 192; Fordin, *M-G-M's Greatest Musicals*, 328, 331; Thomas, *Films of Gene Kelly*, 130.

40. Knox, ed., *Magic Factory*, xv, 181–182, 187, 193; Lindsay Anderson, "Minnelli, Kelly and An American in Paris," *Sequence*, Issue 14 (1952): 38.

41. Harvey, *Directed by Vincente Minnelli*, 101; Schwartz, *It's So French!*, 19, 44–50; Thomas, *Films of Gene Kelly*, 120.

42. Kelly interview, Knox, ed., *Magic Factory*, 198; Thomas, *Films of Gene Kelly*, 123; Updike, "Gotta Dance!," 168–169; Anderson, "Minnelli, Kelly," 38.

43. Anderson, "Minnelli, Kelly," 38.

44. Harvey, *Directed by Vincente Minnelli*, 102; Foch interview, Knox, ed., *Magic Factory*, 175.

45. Harvey, *Directed by Vincente Minnelli*, 101.

46. James River Film Journal [website].

47. Caron and Foch interviews, Knox, ed., *Magic Factory*, 104, 195.

48. *Los Angeles Times*, May 18, 1951; Brideson and Brideson, *He's Got Rhythm*, 232.

49. Fordin, *M-G-M's Greatest Musicals*, 351; Baer, "Singin' in the Rain," 9; Irving Paul Lazar to Betty and Adolph, Mar. 14, 1951, Box 8, Folder 12, Comden and Green Papers, NYPL; Hess and Dabholkar, *Singin' in the Rain*, 13–17, 21–26.

50. Hess and Dabholkar, *Singin' in the Rain*, 43–48.

51. Hess and Dabholkar, 48–52.

52. Hess and Dabholkar, 52–54, 155–160.

53. Hess and Dabholkar, 17–20; Fordin, *M-G-M's Greatest Musicals*, 355; Kelly interview, Marion Meade/Buster Keaton Research Files, UI.

54. "Broadway Rhythm," "Fit as a Fiddle," and "Singin' in the Rain," Box 27, Gene Kelly Collection, BU.

55. Rita Moreno, *Rita Moreno: A Memoir* (New York: Penguin, 2013), 9, 96–97.

56. Hess and Dabholkar, *Singin' in the Rain*, 85, 101–103; Frank Phillips interview, Roy H. Wagner Facebook [website].

57. Hess and Dabholkar, *Singin' in the Rain*, 86–99, 103–106.

58. Kelly interview, Britton, ed., *Talking Films*, 192; Duell interview, Delamater, *Dance*,

245–246; Frank Phillips interview, Roy H. Wagner Facebook [website]; Kelly interview, "Dialogue on Film," 40; Hess and Dabholkar, *Singin' in the Rain*, 126–129.

59. Assistant Director's Report, July 18–19, 1951, *Singin' in the Rain*, Arthur Freed Collection, USC; Charness, "Hollywood Cine-Dance," 105–108; Hess and Dabholkar, *Singin' in the Rain*, 131–134.

60. Hess and Dabholkar, *Singin' in the Rain*, 123–126, 129–130; Idelson, O'Connor interview [website]; Moreno, *Rita Moreno*, 98.

61. Frank Phillips interview, Roy H. Wagner Facebook [website].

62. Hess and Dabholkar, *Singin' in the Rain*, 161–169, 180–182; Hanson, "An Interview with Gene Kelly," 24; Freed to Lela Simone, Sept. 9, 1952, Box 55, Folder 2, Arthur Freed Collection, USC.

63. Hess and Dabholkar, *Singin' in the Rain*, 179, 183–188, 212–217, 221; Walter Terry, "Kelly's Exhilarating Dance Tonic for April: 'Singin' in the Rain,'" *New York Herald Tribune*, Apr. 13, 1952.

Chapter 12. Turning Point, 1951–1953

1. Edwin Schallert, "In Movie Field, Gene Kelly Proves a Quintuple Threat," *Los Angeles Times*, Oct. 7, 1951.

2. Hirshchorn, *Gene Kelly*, 192–193; Thomas M. Pryor, "Gene Kelly Listed for Straight Role," *New York Times*, Dec. 31, 1951.

3. Charles Higham, *Merchant of Dreams: Louis B. Mayer, M.G.M., and the Secret Hollywood* (New York: Donald I. Fine, 1993), 258; Elstree and Borehamwood Official Guide [website]; Parish and Bowers, *MGM Stock Company*, 793; Hirschhorn, *Gene Kelly*, 192.

4. Kelly, "Invitation to the Dance," in A. H. Franks, ed., *Girl's Book of Ballet* (London: Burke, 1953), 110.

5. Tom Dancy, "At Home Abroad," *Modern Screen* (July 1953): 94; Hirschhorn, *Gene Kelly*, 192; Blair, *Memory*, 164; Blair, "I Married a Dynamo" [website].

6. Blair, *Memory*, 165–168.

7. Thomas M. Pryor, "Hollywood Dossier: Ban on Foreign, Communist-Made Films Is Sought by Labor Group—Addenda," *New York Times*, Aug. 31, 1952; Hirschhorn, *Gene Kelly*, 193–194.

8. Johnny Green to Kelly, Apr. 8, 1951 [1952], Box 55, Folder 2 of 2, Arthur Freed Collection, USC; McClelland quoted in *Motion Picture* [website].

9. Blair, *Memory*, 184; Fordin, *M-G-M's Greatest Musicals*, 374; Hirschhorn, *Gene Kelly*, 195, 206.

10. Kelly, "Invitation to the Dance," in Franks, *Girl's Book*, 108; Bob Thomas, "Kelly Finishing Dance Film With No Dialogue," Hollywood *Citizen-News*, Dec. 25, 1953; Millar, *An Evening with Gene Kelly* [DVD]; Thomas M. Pryor, "Gene Kelly Plans Own Metro Movie," *New York Times*, Nov. 27, 1951.

11. Fordin, *M-G-M's Greatest Musicals*, 376; "Notes Taken at Meeting Held in Conference Room on Thursday, 10th July, 1952," Box 14, Folder 3, Arthur Freed Collection, USC.

12. Lela Simone to Freed, July 17, 1952, Box 14, Folder 1, Arthur Freed Collection, USC; Rudy Behlmer, "An Oral History with Lela Simone," 311, AMPAS; costume descriptions,

Invitation to the Dance, Box 190, Folder 12, B. J. Simmons and Company Costume Design Records, UTA.

13. Simone Daily Report, Sept. 4, 1952, and Simone to Freed, Sept. 11, 1952, Box 55, Folder 2, and Sept. 22, 1952, Box 14, folder 4, and "Advice of Artistes' Engagements," Box 14, Folder 3, Arthur Freed Collection, USC; Marilyn Hunt, "Igor Youskevitch Interview," NYPL, 126.

14. Marilyn Hunt, "Igor Youskevitch Interview," NYPL, 125–126; Marilyn Hunt, "Gene Kelly Interview," NYPL, 178–179.

15. Ben Goetz to E. J. Mannix, Sept. 3, 1952, Box 14, Folder 2, and Freed to Simone, Sept. 2, 1952, and Simone to Freed, Sept. 4, 1952, Box 55, Folder 2, Arthur Freed Collection, USC.

16. Simone to Freed, Aug. 24 and Sept. 4, 1952, Box 55, Folder 2, and Goetz to Mannix, Sept. 9, 1952, Box 14, Folder 4, Arthur Freed Collection, USC.

17. Stephen Watts, "On Arranging Terpsichore for the Camera Eye," *New York Times*, Sept. 14, 1952; Capa photographs used in "Gene Kelly's Invitation to the Dance," *Look* Magazine Photograph Collection, LC.

18. Clause Bessy, email interview, Sept. 30, 2008.

19. Marilyn Hunt, "Gene Kelly Interview," NYPL, 180; Simone to Freed, Sept. 22, 1952, Box 14, Folder 4, Arthur Freed Collection, USC.

20. Kelly interview, Singer, *A Cut Above*, 147; Rudy Behlmer, "An Oral History with Lela Simone," 310, AMPAS.

21. Simone to Freed, Oct. 26, 30, 1952, Box 55, Folder 2, and Goetz to Mannix, Oct. 28, Nov. 25, 1952, Box 14, Folder 4, Arthur Freed Collection, USC.

22. Hirschhorn, *Gene Kelly*, 199; Simone to Freed, Feb. 17, 1953, Box 55, Folder 2, Arthur Freed Collection, USC; Fordin, *M-G-M's Greatest Musicals*, 389.

23. Freed to Kelly, Jan. 19, 1953, and Kelly to Freed, Jan. 20, 1953, Box 55, Folder 2, Arthur Freed Collection, USC.

24. Thomas M. Pryor, "Gene Kelly Steps into Officer Role," *New York Times*, Mar. 7, 1953; Thomas, *Films of Gene Kelly*, 153; Hirschhorn, *Gene Kelly*, 201–202; Marilyn Hunt, "Gene Kelly Interview," NYPL, 154.

25. Watts, "Arranging Terpsichore"; "Gene Kelly's Invitation to the Dance," *Look* 17 (Mar. 24, 1953): 88, 90, 94; Louis Berg, "Gene Kelly's Six-Way Stretch," *New York Herald Tribune*, Mar. 12, 1953; Kelly, "Invitation to the Dance," in Franks, *Girl's Book*, 109, 114.

26. Hirschhorn, *Gene Kelly*, 204; Joe Hyams, "Gene Kelly: All the World Loves to Dance," *Cue*, May 7, 1953; F. L. Hendrickson to Mannix, Nov. 24, 1952, Box 14, Folder 2, Arthur Freed Collection, USC; Kelly interview, Boorman, et al., *Projections 4*, 288.

27. Swanson, "Dance!" 64; Hirschhorn, *Gene Kelly*, 202, 204; Blair, *Memory*, 237–238.

28. Dancy, "At Home Abroad," 94; *New York Times*, Aug. 8, 1953; [Selznick] to Kelly, Aug. 11, 1953, and Kelly to Selznick, Sept. 10, 1953, Box 1240, David O. Selznick Collection, UTA; Hirschhorn, *Gene Kelly*, 204.

29. Kelly to Houlihan, May 27, 1953, Box 3, Folder 13, Gene Kelly Collection, BU; Kelly interview in Houlihan, "An Analysis," 115, 165.

30. "Invitation to the Dance, Cartoon Number, 'Sinbad the Sailor,' from Gene Kelly, 8–12–53," 1, Turner/MGM Scripts Collection, AMPAS.

31. Ruttenberg interview, Delamater, *Dance*, 277.

32. Kelly interview, June 3, 1954, File 1342, Hedda Hopper Collection, AMPAS; Marilyn Hunt, "Gene Kelly Interview," NYPL, 132; Assistant Director's Report, *Invitation to the Dance*, Oct. 13, 1953, Box 14, Folder 4, Arthur Freed Collection, USC.

33. Assistant Director's Report, *Invitation to the Dance*, Oct. 3, 1953, Box 14, Folder 4, Arthur Freed Collection, USC; David Kasday, email interview, Sept. 4, 6, 2008.

34. Sennett, *Art of Hanna-Barbera*, 44; Maltin, *Of Mice and Magic*, 294; Ruttenberg interview, Delamater, *Dance*, 277; Betsy Baytos, "Interview with Joe Barbera," NYPL, 1996, 7.

35. Assistant Director's Report, *Invitation to the Dance*, Oct. 12, 1953, Box 14, Folder 4, and Kelly to Freed, Jan. 20, 1953, and Green to Goetz, Sept. 21, 1954, Box 55, Folder, 2, and William Le Vanway to Goetz, Aug. 18, 1954, Box 14, Folder 2, and Kelly to Freed, July 28, Aug. 4, 1955, and Freed to Kelly, Aug. 12, 1955, Box 14, Folder 3, Arthur Freed Collection, USC; Fordin, *M-G-M's Greatest Musicals*, 396.

36. Thomas, "Kelly Finishing Dance Film"; "Analysis of Film Content," 4, and "Summary of Report," *Invitation to the Dance* Folder, MPAA Production Code Administration Records, AMPAS.

37. Thomas M. Pryor, "Uneasy Hollywood: Meeting of Labor Chiefs and Loew's Top Executive Disturbs Industry—Addenda," *New York Times*, June 22, 1952; "M-G-M Press Book," 10, *Invitation to the Dance* Production Files, Core Collection, AMPAS; Frank Whitbeck and Jack Atlas proposal for trailer, Apr. 13, 1955, and Howard Hertz to Howard Strickling, Sept. 20, 1955, Box 14, Folder 2, Arthur Freed Collection, USC.

38. Hertz to Strickling, Sept. 20, 1955, and Whitbeck to Howard Dietz, Nov. 13, 1954, and S. F. Seadler to Whitbeck, Mar. 23, 1955, and Whitbeck to Seadler, Nov. 24, 1954, and Apr. 7, 1955, Box 14, Folder 2, Arthur Freed Collection, USC.

39. William Saroyan to Kenneth McKenna, July 30, 1954, and Freed to McKenna, Aug. 2, 1954, Box 55, Folder 2, and Milton M. Beecher to Freed, Aug. 13, 1954, Box 14, Folder 2, Arthur Freed Collection, USC.

40. Clipping, Marjorie Trumbull, "Gene Kelly Talks With the Verve of a Dancer," Box 10, Scrapbook 9, Gene Kelly Collection, BU; Kelly to Freed, Aug. 12, 1955, Box 14, Folder 3, and Kelly to Freed, Jan. 20, 1953, Box 55, Folder 2, Arthur Freed Collection, USC; Kelly interview, Singer, *A Cut Above*, 146.

41. Thomas, "Kelly Finishing Dance Film"; clipping, Lloyd Shearer, "Gene Kelly: He Thinks on His Feet," 70, Box 10, Scrapbook 9, Gene Kelly Collection, BU.

42. Jack Guggenheim to E. Lapinère, Apr. 9, 1956, Box 14, Folder 5, and Jim Merrick to Freed, Dec. 17, 1956, Box 14, Folder 2, Arthur Freed Collection, USC; "Premiere of Film Will Help Ballet," *New York Times*, May 11, 1956; "'Invitation to the Dance' Wins at Berlin Film Fete," *New York Times*, July 4, 1956; "Biography of Gene Kelly," 7, Folder 10, Box 1, Emerson Venable Papers, HHC.

43. Fordin, *M-G-M's Greatest Musicals*, 396.

44. Clipping, Rose Pelswick, "All Dance, Pantomime; No Dialogue—Brilliant," Box 2, Folder 6, Gene Kelly Collection, BU; Aubrey B. Haines, "Gene Kelly," *Dance Digest* 7, no. 7 (July 1957): 259; Hazel Flynn, "Disappointing 'Invitation'!", Beverly Hills *Citizen*, Apr. 19, 1957.

45. Bosley Crowther, "Screen: Twinkle-Toes," *New York Times*, May 23, 1956, and "An 'A' for Effort," *New York Times*, May 27, 1956.

46. Marilyn Hunt, "Gene Kelly Interview," NYPL, 182; Kelly interview, Boorman, et al., *Projections 4*, 288; Gene Kelly interview, Singer, *A Cut Above*, 146–147; Kelly interview, Flatow, "Through a Lens," 38; Anna Kisselgoff, "Gene Kelly: Ballet Influenced His View of Dance," *New York Times*, Jan. 17, 1985; Blair, *Memory*, 192.

Chapter 13. Red Scare—Second Wave, 1950–1954

1. Billingsley, *Hollywood Party*, 233; Cogley, *Report on Blacklisting*, 159.

2. Cogley, *Report on Blacklisting*, 159; Peter Wollen, "Cine-dancer," *Sight and Sound* 6, Issue 3 (Mar. 1996): 3; Peter Wollen, *Singin' in the Rain* (London: British Film Institute, 1992), 43–48, 51; Morley and Leon, *Gene Kelly*, 120; Kelly interview, Boorman, et. al., *Projections 4*, 288.

3. D. M. Ladd to Director, Aug. 21, 1947, and Extract of Louis J. Budenz memorandum, June 20, 1950, Gene Kelly FBI File; Robert M. Lichtman, "Louis Budenz, the FBI, and the 'List of 400 Concealed Communists': An Extended Tale of McCarthy-Era Informing," *American Communist History* 3, no. 1 (2004): 26–27.

4. Jack Howard, "Gene Kelly," Nov. 21, 1949, in Jack Hirshberg Papers, AMPAS.

5. Ceplair and Englund, *Inquisition*, 292; Blair interview, McGilligan and Buhle, eds., *Tender Comrades*, 551–552.

6. Blair interview, McGilligan and Buhle, eds., *Tender Comrades*, 552–553; Blair, *Memory*, 207, 211.

7. Marcus M. Bright report, Jan. 27, 1951, Gene Kelly FBI File.

8. Lichtman, "Budenz," 26, 34–35, 37–38, 42–44, 52–53; SAC New York to Director, July 28, 1950, Gene Kelly FBI File.

9. Director to SAC Los Angeles, Nov. 2, 1950, and Bright report, Jan. 27, 1951, Gene Kelly FBI File.

10. Caute, *Great Fear*, 501.

11. J. B. Matthews [website]; J. B. Matthews, "Did the Movies Really Clean House?" *American Legion Magazine* (Dec. 1951): 50–51.

12. Bright report, Dec. 4, 1951, Gene Kelly FBI File.

13. Bright report, Dec. 4, 1951, and Administrative Page attached to Bright report, Jan. 27 and Dec. 4, 1951, and SAC Los Angeles to Director, Apr. 20 and Dec. 4, 1951, and Director to SAC, Los Angeles, Jan. 4, 1952, Gene Kelly FBI File.

14. SAC Los Angeles to Director, Mar. 3, 1952, Gene Kelly FBI File; *Hearings Before the Committee on Un-American Activities, House of Representatives, Eighty-Third Congress, First Session, March 23, 24, and 25, 1953* (Washington, DC: United States Government Printing Office, 1953), 355–357.

15. SAC Los Angeles to Director, Mar. 3, 1952. Gene Kelly FBI File; *Hearings Before the Committee*, 357–359.

16. Caute, *Great Fear*, 502–504; Cogley, *Report on Blacklisting*, 155–159.

17. Cogley, *Report on Blacklisting*, 159.

18. Billingsley, *Hollywood Party*, 237; Victor Riesel, "Inside Labor," *New York Mirror*, Apr. 6, 1953.

19. William Abbott to J. Edgar Hoover, Mar. 18, 1948, and Hoover to director of Naval

Intelligence, Sept. 2, 1949, and D. C. Hamberger to Hoover, Dec. 19, 1952, and Feb. 3, 1953, and Louis Budenz statement, Mar. 20, 1953, and SAC New York to Director, Mar. 31, 1953, and V. P. Keay to A. H. Belmont, Feb. 10, 1954, Gene Kelly FBI File.

20. Excerpts, Gene Kelly to Department of Naval Intelligence [website].

21. Excerpts, Gene Kelly to Department of Naval Intelligence [website].

22. Summary of Kelly case, written after 1954, and M. S. Schmidling to Hoover, Feb. 17, 1955, Gene Kelly FBI File.

23. Shaun Considine, *Mad As Hell: The Life and Work of Paddy Chayefsky* (New York: Random House, 1994), 74–75; Blair interview, McGilligan and Buhle, eds., *Tender Comrades*, 554.

24. Blair interview, McGilligan and Buhle, eds., *Tender Comrades*, 554; Blair, *Memory*, 146, 148.

25. Caute, *Great Fear*, 515–516, 519; SAC Los Angeles to Director, Oct. 14, 1960, Gene Kelly FBI File.

26. Blair, *Memory*, 133; Dassin interview, McGilligan and Buhle, eds., *Tender Comrades*, 200, 220.

27. "Reminiscences of Gene Curran Kelly: Oral History, 1958," 20, CU; Bill Drysdale, "Soundmatters," *Dancing Times* (Nov. 2001): 63; Pollock, "Gene Kelly at 72."

Chapter 14. Sunset of the Golden Age, 1953–1955

1. Pryor, "Uneasy Hollywood"; Mast, *Can't Help Singin'*, 267–268.

2. Pryor, "Gene Kelly Steps"; Kelly interview, June 3, 1954, File 1342, Hedda Hopper Collection, AMPAS; Fordin, *M-G-M's Greatest Musicals*, 422–423.

3. Kelly interview, 48–49, SMU/Ronald L. Davis Oral History Collection, AMPAS; Kelly quoted in Stoop, "Gene Kelly," 72; Kelly interview, Delamater, *Dance*, 217.

4. Kelly interview, Delamater, *Dance*, 217; Kelly interview, 49–50, SMU/Ronald L. Davis Oral History Collection, AMPAS; Alan Jay Lerner, *On the Street Where I Live* (New York: W. W. Norton, 1978), 140.

5. Alfred Gilks, "Some Highlights in the Filming of 'An American in Paris.'" *American Cinematographer* 33 (Jan. 1952): 18.

6. Ames interview, Delamater, *Dance*, 240–241.

7. Harvey, *Directed by Vincente Minnelli*, 129–131; Kelly and Ruttenberg interviews, Delamater, *Dance*, 217–218, 277; Fordin, *M-G-M's Greatest Musicals*, 425.

8. Minnelli, *I Remember It Well*, 281.

9. Howard Strickling, "First Preview, First Report," *Brigadoon*, Vincente Minnelli Collection, AMPAS; Harvey, *Directed by Vincente Minnelli*, 130.

10. *Dance News*, Sept. 1954, 11; Bosley Crowther, "The Screen in Review: 'Brigadoon,'" *New York Times*, Sept. 17, 1954; clipping, Harold V. Cohen review in *Pittsburgh Post-Gazette*, Oct. 23, 1954, Box 10 Scrapbook 9, Gene Kelly Collection, BU; McVay, "Magic of Minnelli," 34; Basinger, *Gene Kelly*, 100; Harvey, *Directed by Vincente Minnelli*, 130, 133.

11. Fred Kelly interview, Frank, ed., *Tap!*, 179; Marilyn Hunt, "Gene Kelly Interview," NYPL, 255–256.

12. Blair, *Memory*, 117; Fred Kelly to Mrs. L., Mr., youngsters and Grandmother, Feb.

28, and to Bob and Racelle, Apr. 19, 1942, Box 1, Folder 14, Lazar Family Papers and Photographs, HHC; "Born to Dance," *Pitt Magazine* (Mar. 15, 1994): 28–29; Fred Kelly interview, Frank, ed., *Tap!*, 170, 178; Fred Kelly interview, Danny Daniels' History of American Tap, NYPL; Kelly interview, June 3, 1954, File 1342, Hedda Hopper Collection, AMPAS.

13. Kelly interview, June 3, 1954, File 1342, Hedda Hopper Collection, AMPAS; Fred Kelly interview, Danny Daniels' History of American Tap, NYPL.

14. Thomas Brady, "Danny Kaye Signs for Role at Metro," *New York Times*, Jan. 18, 1951; Lerner, *Street Where I Live*, 140–141; Fordin, *M-G-M's Greatest Musicals*, 369; Schallert, "In Movie Field."

15. Dominic McHugh, ed., *Alan Jay Lerner: A Lyricist's Letters* (New York: Oxford University Press, 2014), 38–39, 43, 53; Rudy Behlmer, "An Oral History with Lela Simone," 318, AMPAS; Wollen, *Singin' in the Rain*, 50; Thomas M. Pryor, "Metro Will Film Twain Book in '59," *New York Times*, Oct. 28, 1958.

16. Thomas M. Pryor, "Porter's Music in Metro Plans," *New York Times*, Dec. 28, 1953; Kelly to Wilder, Dec. 30, 1953, Box 44, Folder 1166, Thornton Wilder Papers, YU.

17. Saroyan to Kelly, Oct. 16 and 20, 1954, and Kelly to Saroyan, Oct. 17, 1954, William Saroyan Papers, SU.

18. Kelly to Saroyan, Apr. 8, 1955, William Saroyan Papers, SU.

19. Kelly to Saroyan, Apr. 8, 1955, William Saroyan Papers, SU.

20. Saroyan to Kelly, May 3, 1955, William Saroyan Papers, SU.

21. Fordin, *M-G-M's Greatest Musicals*, 432–433.

22. Kelly interview, Haver, "Pas de Deux," 26; Hanson, "An Interview with Gene Kelly," 26; Kelly quoted in Fordin, *M-G-M's Greatest Musicals*, 436; Genné, "The Film Musicals," 406.

23. Kelly interview, Singer, *A Cut Above*, 147; Kelly interview, Delamater, *Dance*, 217.

24. Production Information on the Films of Arthur Freed," *It's Always Fair Weather*, Arthur Freed Collection, USC; Casper, *Stanley Donen*, 84; Silverman, *Dancing*, 212.

25. Assistant Director's Report, *It's Always Fair Weather*, Oct. 13, 20, 21, 28, Dec. 1, 1954, and Jan. 10–12, 31, Feb. 1, 1955, Arthur Freed Collection, USC; Dailey interview, 41, 64, SMU/Ronald L. Davis Oral History Collection, AMPAS.

26. Fordin, *M-G-M's Greatest Musicals*, 434–435; Michael Kidd, "Jack and the Space Giants," Folder 921, Turner/MGM Scripts Collection, AMPAS; Assistant Director's Report, *It's Always Fair Weather*, Dec. 30, 31, 1954, and Jan. 3, 1955, Arthur Freed Collevtion, USC.

27. Hanson, "An Interview with Gene Kelly," 26; Charness, "Hollywood Cine-Dance," 122–124.

28. Hillier, "Interview with Stanley Donen," 34; Rawson, "Pittsburghers Remember"; Comden in Anatomy of a Dancer [DVD]; Robert Trachtenberg interview [website].

29. Hemming, *Melody Lingers*, 65; Levinson, *Puttin' on the Ritz*, 98.

30. First Preview, *It's Always Fair Weather*, June 22, 1955, and "Production Information on the Films of Arthur Freed," *It's Always Fair Weather*, Arthur Freed Collection, USC; Harrison Carroll, "Gene Kelly's Roller-Skate Dance is 'Always Fair Weather' Standout," *Los Angeles Herald and Express*, Sept. 1, 1955; Mast, *Can't Help Singin'*, 288; Basinger, *Gene Kelly*, 105, 107; Michael Wood, *America in the Movies: Or, "Santa Maria, It Had Slipped My*

Mind" (New York: Columbia University Press, 1997), 160; Genné, "The Film Musicals," 403–404; Thomas, *Films of Gene Kelly*, 159, 162.

31. "Reminiscences of Betty Comden and Adolph Green: Oral History, 1959," 32–33, CU; Comden in *Anatomy of a Dancer* [DVD]; Hillier, "Interview with Stanley Donen," 34; Fordin, *M-G-M's Greatest Musicals*, 435–436; Kelly interview, Delamater, *Dance*, 219.

Chapter 15. New Directions, 1956–1960

1. Fordin, *M-G-M's Greatest Musicals*, 440, 442; Hirschhorn, *Gene Kelly*, 213; Thomas M. Pryor, "Gene Kelly Ends One Metro Pact," *New York Times*, Jan. 9, 1956.

2. Kelly interview, Singer, *A Cut Above*, 148–149.

3. Bosley Crowther, "The Screen: 'Happy Road' Arrives," *New York Times*, June 21, 1957; Hirschhorn, *Gene Kelly*, 216; Gene Kelly to Luce, June 10, 1957, Container 202, Folder 1957, Clare Booth Luce Collection, LC; "Biography of Gene Kelly," Rogers and Cowan, Box 1, Folder 10, Emerson Venable Papers, HHC; Fryxell, "The Dossier," 18.

4. Kelly interview, Singer, *A Cut Above*, 149; James Kelly Burial [website].

5. Blair, *Memory*, 223, 228, 231–233.

6. Hirschhorn, *Gene Kelly*, 214.

7. Blair, *Memory*, 234–235.

8. *Los Angeles Times*, Apr. 4, 1957.

9. Tony Martin and Cyd Charisse, *Two of Us* (New York: Mason-Charter, 1976), 211; Hirschhorn, *Gene Kelly*, 216–217.

10. Cole interview, Delamater, *Dance*, 193, 197; Billman, *Film Choreographers*, 268; Hirschhorn, *Gene Kelly*, 218–219.

11. Marilyn Hunt, "Gene Kelly Interview," NYPL, 256–258; Kelly interview, Singer, *A Cut Above*, 144.

12. Basinger, *Gene Kelly*, 115; Hirschhorn, *Gene Kelly*, 220; Thomas, *Films of Gene Kelly*, 180–181.

13. Kelly interview, Boorman, et al., *Projections 4*, 289; Bosley Crowther, "The Screen: 'Les Girls,'" *New York Times*, Oct. 4, 1957; Hemming, *Melody Lingers On*, 179.

14. Alex McNeil, *Total Television: A Comprehensive Guide to Programming from 1948 to 1980* (New York: Penguin Books, 1980), 615; Tim Brooks and Earle Marsh, *The Complete Directory to Prime Time Network and Cable TV Shows, 1946–Present*, 6th ed. (New York: Ballantine Books, 1995), 907–908; production still, Box 2, Binder 5, Image 51, General Still Photograph Collection, SYU.

15. Val Adams, "N.B.C. to Present Baseball Salute," *New York Times*, Mar. 12, 1957; McNeil, *Total Television*, 811.

16. Hirschhorn, *Gene Kelly*, 221.

17. "Reminiscences of Gene Curran Kelly: Oral History, 1958," 15–16, CU.

18. Transcript of interview, May 1968, Jack Hirshberg Papers, AMPAS; Marilyn Hunt, "Gene Kelly Interview," NYPL, 189; Kelly quoted in Hirschhorn, *Gene Kelly*, 222; Robert Wool, "Skiing in Klosters: The Stars Have Gone but the Glitter Remains," *New York Times*, Feb. 5, 1978.

19. Joe Hyams, "Do-It-Yourself Director," *Los Angeles Times*, Sept. 7, 1958.

20. Bosley Crowther, "Screen: 'Tunnel of Love,'" *New York Times*, Nov. 22, 1958.

21. Thomas M. Pryor, "Gene Kelly Buys Novel for Screen," *New York Times*, Sept. 12, 1957; Hedda Hopper, "Kelly to Star with Gina Lollabrigida," *Los Angeles Times*, May 17, 1958.

22. Hedda Hopper, "Gene Kelly Envisions 'Fancy Dancer' Self," *Los Angeles Times*, Oct. 4, 1957; A.H. Weiler, "Brand-New 'Scent' on the Todd Roster—Kelly's 'Gentleman'—Addenda," *New York Times*, Sept. 28, 1958; Hirschhorn, *Gene Kelly*, 226; Kelly to Balanchine, Feb. 13, 1959, George Balanchine Archive, HU.

23. Secrest, *Somewhere For Me*, 340.

24. Holis Alpert, "Old Friends in New Jobs," *Dance Magazine* 32, no. 12 (Dec. 1958): 53.

25. Hirschhorn, *Gene Kelly*, 223; Alpert, "Old Friends," 53, 55.

26. Secrest, *Somewhere For Me*, 340–341, 343; Richard Rodgers, *Musical Stages: An Autobiography* (New York: Random House, 1975), 295.

27. Brooks Atkinson, "Flower Song: Rodgers and Hammerstein Portray Chinese Traditions in America," *New York Times*, Dec. 7, 1958; Walter Kerr, "Flower Drum Song," *New York Herald Tribune*, Dec. 2, 1958; Secrest, *Somewhere For Me*, 343; Hirschhorn, *Gene Kelly*, 224.

28. Kelly quoted in Hirschhorn, *Gene Kelly*, 223; Kelly to Lee, Dec. 4, 1963, Box 2, Folder 24, C. Y. Lee Collection, BU.

29. Gene Kelly, "Musical Comedy is Serious Business," *Theatre Arts* 42, no. 12 (Dec. 1958): 19, 71–72.

30. "More Tape Shows on 'Playhouse 90,'" *New York Times*, June 30, 1958.

31. Notes and scripts for "Dancing: A Man's Game," Box 1, Folder 5, Gene Kelly Collection, BU.

32. Notes and scripts for "Dancing: A Man's Game," Box 1, Folder 5, Gene Kelly Collection, BU.

33. Murrow, *Person to Person* [DVD].

34. Murrow, *Person to Person* [DVD].

35. Script of "Dancing—A Man's Game," 1, 7, 10–11, 14–15, and "Studio Rehearsal Schedule," Box 3, Folder "DAMG," William A. Graham Collection of Television Scripts, YU.

36. Script of "Dancing—A Man's Game," 27–28, Box 3, Folder "DAMG," William A. Graham Collection of Television Scripts, YU.

37. Script of "Dancing—A Man's Game," 27–28, Box 3, Folder "DAMG," William A. Graham Collection of Television Scripts, YU.

38. Clippings, Donald Kirkley in Baltimore *Sun*, Dec. 23, 1958, and J. Walter Thompson in *Variety*, undated, and Bob Hull in *Herald Express*, Dec. 23, 1958, Box 1, Folder 5, Gene Kelly Collection, BU; Ann Barzel, "Dancing Is a Man's Game," *Dance Magazine* 33, no. 2 (Feb. 1959): 30; "Gene Kelly on TV," *Dance and Dancers* (Mar. 1959): 33; Irma Duncan (aka Mrs. Sherman Rogers) to Kelly, Dec. 22, 1958, Irma Duncan Papers, NYPL.

39. "Biography of Gene Kelly," Rogers and Cowan, Inc., Public Relations, Beverly Hills, 7, Box 1, Folder 10, Emerson Venable Papers, HHC; Richard Griffith, *The Cinema of Gene Kelly* (New York: Museum of Modern Art, 1962), 5; John Townsend Barrett, "A Descriptive Study of Selected Uses of Dance on Television: 1948–1958" (PhD diss., University of Michigan, 1968), 94; Basinger, *Gene Kelly*, 121; Marilyn Hunt, "Gene Kelly Interview," NYPL, 269–270.

40. Hirschhorn, *Gene Kelly*, 226–227; "Jet Averts Crash in Trip from Paris," *New York Times*, Feb. 4, 1959.

41. Fred Remington, "Kelly Comes to TV," *Pittsburgh Press*, Apr. 19, 1959.

42. Hirschhorn, *Gene Kelly*, 228; Minnelli, *I Remember It Well*, 338.

43. Minnelli, *I Remember It Well*, 338.

44. Claude Bessy, email interview, Sept. 30, 2008.

45. Clipping, Gross, "'Dancing Isn't Sissy'—Gene Kelly," February 1, 1959, Box 3, Folder 11, Gene Kelly Collection, BU; Peter Carlson, *K Blows Top: A Cold War Comic Interlude Starring Nikita Khrushchev, America's Most Unlikely Tourist* (New York: Public Affairs, 2009), 158.

46. Kelly to Susan M. Margulies, Sept. 21, 1959, Box 3, Folder 13, Gene Kelly Collection, BU; "Reminiscences of Gene Curran Kelly: Oral History, 1958," 13, CU.

47. Joe Finnigan, "Gene Kelly Calls Russ Dancing 'Behind Times,'" *Indianapolis Star*, Oct. 14, 1959.

48. Clipping, Edgar Penton, "'Dancing Is a Man's Game' Says Gene Kelly," *Showtime*, Nov. 14–15, 1959, Gene Kelly Biography File, Core Collection, AMPAS.

49. Burrows, *Gene Kelly*, 23; Kelly quoted in Hirschhorn, *Gene Kelly*, 229.

50. Bosley Crowther, "Intellect in Films," *New York Times*, Oct. 16, 1960, and "Screen: Triumphant Version of 'Inherit the Wind,'" *New York Times*, Oct. 13, 1960; Patricia Wilson, *Yesterday's Mashed Potatoes: The Fabulous Life of a Happy Has-Been* (Indianapolis: Dogear, 2009), 244.

Chapter 16. New Life, 1960–1969

1. Clipping, Naomi Barry, "Gene Kelly in Paris," Mar. 22, 1960, Box 3, Folder 11, Gene Kelly Collection, BU.

2. Clipping, Naomi Barry, "Gene Kelly in Paris," Mar. 22, 1960, Box 3, Folder 11, Gene Kelly Collection, BU; Claude Bessy, email interview, Sept. 30, 2008; Clive Barnes, "Gene Kelly & Co.," *Dance Magazine* 70, no. 4 (Apr. 1996): 126; *Pas de Dieux* [website].

3. Clipping, Naomi Barry, "Gene Kelly in Paris," Mar. 22, 1960, Box 3, Folder 11, Gene Kelly Collection, BU; Marilyn Hunt, "Gene Kelly Interview," NYPL, 69–71; Barnes, "Gene Kelly & Co.," 126; Flatow, "Through a Lens," 38.

4. Art Buchwald, "First Jazz Ballet Pas de Gene Kelly," *New York Herald Tribune*, June 19, 1960; "Ballet By Kelly Cheered in Paris," *New York Times*, July 7, 1960.

5. Buchwald, "First Jazz Ballet"; clipping, Hedda Hopper, "The Toast of Paris," Box 2, Folder 11, Gene Kelly Collection, BU; "Ballet By Kelly"; Marilyn Hunt, "Gene Kelly Interview," NYPL, 72; Flatow, "Through a Lens," 38; Barnes, "Gene Kelly & Co.," 126; Claude Bessy, email interview, Sept. 30, 2008.

6. Kelly interview, June 3, 1954, File 1342, Hedda Hopper Collection, AMPAS; Claude Bessy, email interview, Sept. 30, 2008; Kelly to Philip C. Ward, May 25, 1962, Agnes de Mille Collection, NYPL.

7. Kelly interview, June 3, 1954, File 1342, Hedda Hopper Collection, AMPAS; Hedda Hopper, "Gene Kelly, Assistant Married in Nevada," *Los Angeles Times*, Aug. 7, 1960; Hirschhorn, *Gene Kelly*, 235.

8. Hirschhorn, *Gene Kelly*, 236–237; Thomas, *Films of Gene Kelly*, 24.

9. William A. Henry III, *The Great One: The Life and Legend of Jackie Gleason* (New York: Doubleday, 1992), 207; James Bacon, *How Sweet It Is: The Jackie Gleason Story* (New York: St. Martin's, 1985), 154–155; Eugene Archer, "Focus on 'Gigot.' An Expensive 'Leg of Lamb,'" *New York Times*, July 2, 1961.

10. Archer, "Focus on 'Gigot.'"

11. Henry, *Great One*, 208; Bacon, *How Sweet It Is*, 155.

12. Henry, *Great One*, 207–209; Bosley Crowther, "Screen: Gleason's 'Gigot,'" *New York Times*, Sept. 28, 1962.

13. "Article for Bosley Crowther by Gene Kelly," Box 3, Folder 13, Gene Kelly Collection, BU; Behlmer, "Gene Kelly," 21.

14. John P. Shanley, "'Going My Way,'" *New York Times*, Sept. 30, 1962.

15. Hirschhorn, *Gene Kelly*, 239.

16. Fred Remington, "Two Decades of Stardom," *Pittsburgh Press*, Dec. 9, 1962.

17. Dick York, *The Seesaw Girl and Me: A Memoir* (Elizabeth, NJ: New Path Press, 2004), 15–16, 85–87.

18. Brooks and Marsh, *Complete Directory*, 403; Hirschhorn, *Gene Kelly*, 239; Edward L. Blank, "Gene Kelly: Hometown Hoofer Hosting 'The Funny Side,'" *Pittsburgh Press*, Oct. 26, 1971.

19. Eugene Archer, "Museums to Show Gene Kelly Films," *New York Times*, Aug. 10, 1962; "The Museum of Modern Art Presents a Gene Kelly Dance Film Festival," *Dance Magazine* 26, no. 9 (Sept. 1962): 36–37, 72; "Article for Bosley Crowther by Gene Kelly," Box 3, Folder 13, Gene Kelly Collection, BU; Griffith, *Cinema of Gene Kelly*, 37, 72; Marilyn Hunt, "Gene Kelly Interview," NYPL, 135, 166.

20. "Notes on Gene Kelly—Wednesday, August 3, 1960," File 1342, Hedda Hopper Collection, AMPAS; Hirschhorn, *Gene Kelly*, 239–240; "Kelly to Produce World War I Film," *New York Times*, June 17, 1965; Kelly quoted in Thomas, *Films of Gene Kelly*, 28.

21. "Frank Sinatra, Gene Kelly in *The New Yorkers* A New Musical Play for the Screen by Jerome Lawrence and Robert E. Lee," NYPL; Kelly to Raphaelson, Dec. 27, 1967, Samson Raphaelson Papers, CU; Kelly to Sam and Bella, Jan. 5, 1967, Samuel and Bella Spewack Papers, CU; transcript of interview, May 1968, Jack Hirshberg Papers, AMPAS.

22. Clipping, Sheilah Graham, "Gene Kelly Milliner's Dreams," May 22, 1965, Scrapbook, Gene Kelly Alumni Files, UP; Gene Kelly, "Some Notes for Young Dancers," *Dance Magazine* 39, no. 9 (Sept. 1965): 49; "Article for Bosley Crowther by Gene Kelly," Box 3, Folder 13, Gene Kelly Collection, BU.

23. Kelly introduction to John Springer, *They Sang! They Danced! They Romanced! A Pictorial History of the Movie Musical* (New York: Citadel Press, 1991), 8–9; Carol Lawson, "Lionizing M-G-M in Retrospect," *New York Times*, June 24, 1977; Kelly to Pierre Billard, Oct. 16, 1964, and draft of article for *Sound Stage*, Aug. 18, 1965, 2–4, 6–7, and Kelly to Selma Jeanne Cohen, Feb. 1, 1967, Box 3, Folder 13, Gene Kelly Collection, BU.

24. Kelly to Philip C. Ward, May 25, 1962, Box 14, Folder 1, Edward Weeks Papers, UTA; Kelly, "Some Notes," 49; Agnes de Mille, "Dance: We Deserve a Fair Showing," *New York Times*, Sept. 23, 1962: Kelly to Mrs. Kenneth A. Ives, Sept. 26, 1963, Box 10, Folder 830, American Ballet Theatre Records, NYPL.

25. Murray Schumach, "'Thinking' Actors in Vogue on Coast," *New York Times*, May 5, 1960; Murray Schumach, "Democrats Lead G.O.P. in Filmland," *New York Times*, Apr. 18, 1960; Murray Schumach, "Hollywood Wary over Rally Issue," *New York Times*, Apr. 12, 1962.

26. Betty Beale, "After Midnight—The 'Party' Really Rocked," *Tampa Bay Times*, Jan. 27, 1963; Michael Scanlon interview [website]; "$1,000-a-Plate Buffet Assists State's Democrats," *New York Times*, Dec. 15, 1965.

27. Kelly to Tony Thomas [website].

28. Clipping, Hedda Hopper, "The Toast of Paris," Box 3, Folder 11, Gene Kelly Collection, BU; Kelly interview, *Steve Allen Show*, Feb. 18, 1964, UCLA; Hirschhorn, *Gene Kelly*, 241; "Gene Kelly to Tour Africa under Cultural Exchange," *New York Times*, Dec. 21, 1963.

29. Joyce Brinkley, "On a Culture Safari," *New York Times*, Jan. 26, 1965; Kelly interview, 25, SMU/Ronald L. Davis Oral History Collection, AMPAS; Kelly quoted in Hirschhorn, *Gene Kelly*, 241.

30. Mark B. Lewis, "Gene Kelly, Ambassador," *Pittsburgh Post-Gazette*, Feb. 11, 1996.

31. Lewis, "Gene Kelly, Ambassador."

32. Hirschhorn, *Gene Kelly*, 242.

33. Marilyn Hunt, "Gene Kelly Interview," NYPL, 262.

34. Julia Atopol Hirsch, *The Sound of Music: The Making of America's Favorite Movie* (Chicago: Contemporary Books, 1993), 6, 8, 12–14, 51, 53.

35. Jack Gould, "TV: A Fetching Special," *New York Times*, Nov. 29, 1965.

36. "Dancing in the Dark," *Dance Magazine* 39, no. 12 (Dec. 1965): 103–104, 107.

37. Jack Gould, "TV: Tepid Melodic Tour," *New York Times*, Feb. 15, 1966.

38. Betsy Baytos, "Interview with Joe Barbera," NYPL, 1996, 5–6; Viola Hegyi Swisher, "Gene and Jack and the Beanstalk," *Dance Magazine* 31, no. 2 (Feb. 1967): 52.

39. Script and storyline, "Jack and the Beanstalk," and 4 by 6 cards, Box 5, Folder 18, Gene Kelly Collection, BU.

40. Bobby Riha, telephone interview, Aug. 31, 2008.

41. Kelly notes and marginal notes on music sheets, Box 5, Folder 18, Gene Kelly Collection, BU; Bobby Riha, telephone interview, Aug. 31, 2008.

42. Swisher, "Gene and Jack," 52.

43. Swisher, 53.

44. McNeil, *Total Television*, 827; Brooks and Marsh, *Complete Directory*, 1223.

45. John Kobal, *Gotta Sing, Gotta Dance: A History of Movie Musicals* (London: Spring Books 1983), 302; Hanson, "An Interview with Gene Kelly," 27.

46. Renata Adler, "Screen: Offbeat, Dreamlike Musical: Demy's 'Young Girls of Rochefort' Bows," *New York Times*, Apr. 12, 1968: Kobal, *Gotta Sing*, 330; Blank, "Gene Kelly: Hometown Hoofer"; Kelly quoted in Hirschhorn, *Gene Kelly*, 244.

47. Ruth Zekaria Levy, email interview, Mar. 16, 2014.

48. Ike Zekaria, email interview, Mar. 18, 2014.

49. Ruth Zekaria Levy, email interview, Mar. 16, 2014.

50. Tarloff interview, McGilligan and Buhle, eds., *Tender Comrades*, 653–654.

51. Tarloff interview, McGilligan and Buhle, eds., *Tender Comrades*, 655; McCarthy quoted in Hirschhorn, *Gene Kelly*, 248.

52. Matthau and McCarthy quoted in Hirschhorn, *Gene Kelly*, 248.

53. McCarthy quoted in Hirschhorn, 248–249.

54. Bosley Crowther, "Screen: 'Guide for the Married Man,'" *New York Times*, May 27, 1967; Raphaelson to Kelly, Dec. 21, 1967, Samson Raphaelson Papers, CU; Hirschhorn, *Gene Kelly*, 249.

55. Hirschhorn, *Gene Kelly*, 250–251.

56. Gene Kelly, "Directing Dolly," *Action* 4 (Mar.–Apr., 1969): 8; Matthew Kennedy, *Roadshow! The Fall of Film Musicals in the 1960s* (New York: Oxford University Press, 2014), 68.

57. Kelly, "Directing Dolly," 9; Final Shooting Schedule, Apr. 15–May 31, 1968, Box 27, Folder 4, Ernest Lehman Collection, UTA.

58. Richard F. Shepard, "Yonkers of 1890 Abuilding in Garrison," *New York Times*, May 29, 1968; Final Shooting Schedule, June 18–19, 1968, Box 27, Folder 4, and Lew Tate to Bob Daniels, Feb. 19, 1968, Box 25, Folder 1, Ernest Lehman Collection, UTA.

59. Laurents, *Original Story*, 246; James Spada, *Streisand: Her Life* (New York: Crown, 1995), 218–219; Randall Riese, *Her Name Is Barbra: An Intimate Portrait of the Real Barbra Streisand* (New York: Birch Lane Press, 1993), 274; Kelly, "Directing Dolly," 10.

60. Rob Edelman and Audrey Kupferberg, *Matthau: A Life* (Lanham, MD: Taylor Trade, 2002), 194–195; Riese, *Her Name Is Barbra*, 269–270, 273–278; Spada, *Streisand*, 213; Michael Crawford, *Parcel Arrived Safely, Tied With String: My Autobiography* (London: Century, 1999), 142–143.

61. Kelly, "Directing Dolly," 10; Lehman quoted in Spada, *Streisand*, 219.

62. Lehman quoted in Spada, *Streisand*, 218; Kelly, "Directing Dolly," 10.

63. Crawford, *Parcel Arrived Safely*, 136, 143, 278.

64. Fordin quoted in Kennedy, *Roadshow!*, 139–140; Laird quoted in Riese, *Her Name is Barbra*, 276; Crawford, *Parcel Arrived Safely*, 143; Matthau quoted in Edelman, *Matthau*, 193, 195.

65. Roy H. Wagner, email interview, June 2, 2009; Kelly interview, Delamater, *Dance*, 227; Kelly, "Directing Dolly," 10.

66. Production Budget, "Hello, Dolly!", Box 21, Folder 7, Ernest Lehman Collection, UTA; Kennedy, *Roadshow!*, 135, 140, 200–202, 205–206.

67. Canby, "On Screen, Barbra Streisand Displays a Detached Cool," *New York Times*, Dec. 18, 1969; Kirk Honeycutt, "Gene Kelly: Dancing on Film and Strolling Down Memory Lane," *New York Times*, June 1, 1980; Kennedy, *Roadshow!*, 203–204; Leo Braudy, *The World in a Frame: What We See in Films* (Garden City, NY: Anchor Press/Doubleday, 1976), 161.

68. Hirschhorn, *Gene Kelly*, 260–262.

69. Kennedy, *Roadshow!*, 204, 206.

Chapter 17. Kelly Resurgent, 1970–1979

1. Kelly quoted in Hirschhorn, *Gene Kelly*, 264; Roy Pickard, *Jimmy Stewart: A Life in Film* (New York: St. Martin's Press, 1993), 160–161; Michael Munn, *Jimmy Stewart: The Truth Behind the Legend* (Fort Lee, NJ: Barricade Books, 2006), 266–268.

2. Barrett quoted in Munn, *Jimmy Stewart*, 267–268.

3. Clipping, Win Fanning, "On the Air," Sept. 23, 1971, Box 1, Folder 17, Gene Kelly Alumni Files, UP; Blank, "Gene Kelly: Hometown Hoofer"; Brooks and Marsh, *Complete Directory*, 382.

4. Keith Garebian, *The Making of* Cabaret, 2nd ed. (New York: Oxford University Press, 2011), 3–4, 38–49, 133–134; Cy Feuer, *I Got the Show Right Here: The Amazing, True Story of How an Obscure Brooklyn Horn Player Became the Last Great Broadway Showman* (New York: Simon and Schuster, 2003), 242–243.

5. Kelly interview, "Dialogue on Film," 44; Feuer, *I Got the Show*, 243, 246–249, 252–253; Edward L. Blank, "Gene Kelly: Old Pro Is Still Dancing His Way into Our Hearts," *Pittsburgh Press*, Sept. 28, 1980.

6. Hirschhorn, *Gene Kelly*, 266, 269–270.

7. Dan Lewis, "Gene Kelly to Bugaloo for Scene in 'Forty Carats,'" *Pittsburgh Press*, Dec. 31, 1972; Hirschhorn, *Gene Kelly*, 270; Vincent Canby, "Liv Ullmann Portrays Heroine in '40 Carats,'" *New York Times*, June 29, 1973.

8. Hirschhorn, *Gene Kelly*, 267–269; Fryxell, "The Dossier," 18; Harriet Kelly Burial [website].

9. Clipping, "Jeanne Kelly," Box 1, Folder 17, Gene Kelly Alumni files, UP; Tim Kelly in *Anatomy of a Dancer* [DVD]; Land, "Magic Doesn't Age," 128; Louis Sweeney, "Gene Kelly's Dancing, Directing Life Rolls on No Matter What the Weather," Palatine, IL *Herald*, Dec. 7, 1977; Kelly interview, *Woman's Weekly* [website]; *People*, 1974 [website]; Arthur Marx, "The Man Who Lived Dancing," *Parade Magazine*, Dec. 18, 1983; Hirschhorn, *Gene Kelly*, 270–271; clipping, *Pittsburgh Press*, Nov. 29, 1970, Scrapbook, Gene Kelly Alumni Files, UP.

10. John Kander and Fred Ebb, *Colored Lights: Forty Years of Words and Music, Show Biz, Collaboration, and All That Jazz* (New York: Faber and Faber, 2003), 105–106.

11. Kander and Ebb, 107.

12. Marx, "The Man Who Lived Dancing."

13. Wilson, *Yesterday's Mashed Potatoes*, 75–76, 146, 165, 232–236.

14. Wilson, 236–237, 239; clipping, Aline Wilbur, "Gene Kelly Learning to Say 'No,'" Box 1, Folder 18, Gene Kelly Alumni Files, UP.

15. Wilson, *Yesterday's Mashed Potatoes*, 240–242; clipping, Aline Wilbur, "Gene Kelly Learning to Say 'No,'" Box 1, Folder 18, Gene Kelly Alumni Files, UP.

16. Willens, "Gene Kelly Opening Municipal Opera Season"; Wilson, *Yesterday's Mashed Potatoes*, 241, 244–245; clipping, George Anderson, "A Lot of People Here Saw Kelly," *Pittsburgh Post-Gazette*, and Nicklas to Kelly, July 23, 1974, Box 1, Folder 10, Gene Kelly Alumni Files, UP.

17. Wilson, *Yesterday's Mashed Potatoes*, 247–248.

18. Colleen Lester, "What One Person Learned from Gene Kelly," *Christian Science Monitor*, Mar. 29, 2007.

19. James Gregory and Edward Sigall, "Hollywood's Newest Romance: Gene Kelly & Columnist Joyce Haber," *National Enquirer*, May 6, 1975.

20. Drysdale, "Soundmatters," 63; Reed, "Gene Kelly's Musical Memories"; Burrows, *Gene Kelly*, 8, 35–36; Blank, "Gene Kelly: Hometown Hoofer."

21. Thomas, *Films of Gene Kelly*, passim; Hirschhorn, *Gene Kelly*, passim; Millar, *An Evening with Gene Kelly* [DVD].

22. Willens, "Gene Kelly."

23. Kelly interview, Delamater, *Dance*, passim.

24. Kelly interview, 53–55, SMU/Ronald L. Davis Oral History Collection, AMPAS.

25. Marilyn Hunt, "Gene Kelly Interview," NYPL, 80, 215, 234–235.

26. Fordin, *M-G-M's Greatest Musicals*, 524, 526.

27. Clipping, George Anderson, "A Lot of People Here Saw Kelly," *Pittsburgh Post-Gazette*, Box 1, Folder 10, Gene Kelly Alumni Files, UP.

28. Chaplin, *Golden Age*, 245–247; Levinson, *Puttin' on the Ritz*, 374–375.

29. Chaplin, *Golden Age*, 245–246; Bob Thomas, "Movie Musicals Should be Revived, Says Gene Kelly," *Pittsburgh Post-Gazette*, Dec. 12, 1975; Vernon Scott, "Pair of 'Entertainments' Renewing Kelly's Popularity," *Pittsburgh Press*, Aug. 20, 1976.

30. Astaire quoted in Levinson, *Puttin' on the Ritz*, 375.

31. Thomas, "Movie Musicals"; Vincent Canby, "'Entertainment'—An Eloquent Salute to Show Business," *New York Times*, May 30, 1976; Levinson, *Puttin' on the Ritz*, 377–378.

32. Scott, "Pair of 'Entertainments'"; Norma McLain Stoop, "That's Entertainment, Part 2: A Look at an American Art Form—the Movie Musical," *Dance Magazine* 50, no. 7 (July 1976): 70; Chaplin, *Golden Age*, 247–248; Robert Lindsey, "Astaire and Kelly in Spotlight Again," *New York Times*, May 10, 1976; Larry Billman, *Fred Astaire: A Bio-Bibliography* (Westport, CT: Greenwood Press, 1997), 212; Levinson, *Puttin' on the Ritz*, 376.

33. Vincent Canby, "Magical Sequel to 'That's Entertainment,'" *New York Times*, May 17, 1976; Updike, "Gotta Dance!" 166; Garrison quoted in Levinson, *Puttin' on the Ritz*, 375.

34. Siegel, "The Pirate," 27; Vincent Canby, "A Joyously Indestructible Movie Returns," *New York Times*, May 4, 1975; John Mariani, "Come on with the Rain," *Film Comment* 14, no. 3 (May–June 1978): 7–12.

35. Lawson, "Lionizing M-G-M"; Clive Barnes, "Movies Revisited: 'Invitation to Dance,'" *New York Times*, July 29, 1977; Sweeney, "Gene Kelly's Dancing."

36. Beebe Kline to Virginia Nicklas, Oct. 22, 1986, Box 1, Folder 1, Gene Kelly Alumni Files, UP.

37. Scott, "Pair of 'Entertainments'"; Fantle and Johnson, *Reel to Real*, 11–12; Kelly interview, Fantle and Johnson, *Reel to Real*, 69.

38. Burrows, *Gene Kelly*, 30, 34–35; clipping, Earl Wilson, "It Happened Last Night," [May 29, 1973], Box 1, Folder 17, Gene Kelly Alumni Files, UP; A. H. Weiler, "Kelly and Bricusse to Collaborate," *New York Times*, May 5, 1974; Thomas, "Movie Musicals"; Marilyn Hunt, "Gene Kelly Interview," NYPL, 271; Sweeney, "Gene Kelly's Dancing"; Kelly interview, "Dialogue on Film," 43–44; clipping, Aline Wilbur, "Gene Kelly Learning to Say 'No,'" Box 1, Folder 18, Gene Kelly Alumni Files, UP.

39. Kelly interview, "Dialogue on Film," 35; Stoop, "Gene Kelly," 73; Drysdale, "Soundmatters," 63; Tom Buckley, "At the Movies: Gene Kelly Taps Again in 'Xanadu,'" *New York Times*, Nov. 16, 1979.

40. Kelly to Tony Thomas [website]; Wallace Turner, "Movie Stars Take Old Political Roles," *New York Times*, July 26, 1970; Albin Krebs, "Young Dancer Named Reagan Shuns Spotlight," *New York Times*, June 27, 1980.

41. *The Spokesman Review* [website]; "Gene Kelly Leaves Hospital," *Los Angeles Times*, May 5, 1979; Fryxell, "The Dossier," 18; Rex Reed, "Gene Kelly's Musical Memories," *Chicago Tribune*, Nov. 29, 1980; Kelly interview, "Dialogue on Film," 44.

42. Thomas, "Movie Musicals"; Kelly interview, "Dialogue on Film," 44; McNeil, *Total Television*, 841.

43. Scott, "Pair of 'Entertainments.'"

44. Janet Maslin, "Knievel Evel, One Dares Say," *New York Times*, July 28, 1977.

45. John J. O'Connor, "Nice People on TV," *New York Times*, Mar. 13, 1978.

46. Clipping, Peter M. Garafola, "Gene Kelly Plays His Cards Right," Sept. 3, 1978, Box 1, Folder 17, Gene Kelly Alumni Files, UP; Knowles, *Man Who Made*, 135.

47. Brooks and Marsh, *Complete Directory*, 651–652.

48. "Reminiscences of Gene Curran Kelly: Oral History, 1958," 1, CU; Kline to Nicklas, Oct. 22, 1986, Box 1, Folder 1 and Kelly to Fred, Jan. 17, 1963, Box 1, Folder 9, Gene Kelly Alumni Files, UP; "Gene Kelly Awarded Degree," *New York Times*, Oct. 5, 1961; Fryxell, "The Dossier," 18.

49. Nicklas to Zacour, Dec. 15, 1970, and Nicklas to Koperek, Jan. 11, 1971, and Nicklas to Kelly, Feb. 15, 1971, and Bill to Bernie, Mar. 1, 1971, Box 1, Folder 10, Gene Kelly Alumni Files, UP.

50. Nicklas to Kelly, May 7, 1971, and Wesley W. Posvar to Kelly, May 7, 1971, and Lois McClelland to Nicklas, May 10, 1971, and Kelly to Posvar, May 13, 1971, and Nicklas to McClelland, June 21, 1971, Box 1, Folder 10, and photos of Kelly in Irish Room, Scrapbook, and clipping, *Alumni Times*, Aug. 1971, Box 1, Folder 3, Gene Kelly Alumni Files, UP; Toker, *Pittsburgh*, 86.

51. Nicklas to Paul Pugh, July 26, 1971, and Nicklas to Kelly, Sept. 21 and Oct. 14, 1971, Jan. 29 and Aug. 23, 1973, Jan. 24 and July 23, 1974, and Kelly to Nicklas, Feb. 9, 1973, Jan. 28, 1974, and Nicklas to Irving Leiber, May 23, 1973, Box 1, Folder 10, Gene Kelly Alumni Files, UP.

52. Clipping, George Anderson, "A Lot of People Here Saw Kelly," *Pittsburgh Post-Gazette*, Box 1, Folder 10, Gene Kelly Alumni Files, UP.

53. Bert O'Neal Pearson to Kelly, Jan. 30, 1979, and Kelly to Pearson, Feb. 3, 1979, and Kelly to Venable, Feb. 13, 1979, Box 1, Folder 10, Emerson Venable Papers, HHC.

54. Jeanette Blanco to Kelly, Apr. 12, 1979, and Kelly to Blanco, undated but received May 15, 1979, Box 1, Folder 10, Gene Kelly Alumni Files, UP.

55. Roberts, "Class of '29."

56. Kelly to Venable, June 26, 1979, Box 1, Folder 10, Emerson Venable Papers, HHC.

Chapter 18. Finale, 1980–1996

1. Ringel, "Gotta Dance"; Land, "Magic Doesn't Age," 56, 128; Honeycutt, "Gene Kelly"; Howard Reich, "Hoofer of His Era, Kelly Really Wanted a Career in Ballet," *Pittsburgh Press*, Aug. 21, 1983; Viola Hegyi Swisher, "Xanadu," *Dance Magazine* 54, no. 8 (Aug. 1980): 44.

2. Blank, "Gene Kelly: Old Pro Is Still Dancing"; "It's Not Hard to Believe in Magic of Fantasy 'Xanadu,'" *Pittsburgh Press*, Aug. 14, 1980; Morley and Leon, *Gene Kelly*, 159; Fehr and Vogel, *Lullabies of Hollywood*, 248–249; Kelly quoted in Hirschhorn, *Gene Kelly*, 272–273.

3. Blank, "Gene Kelly: Old Pro Is Still Dancing"; "Coppola Musicals: Gene Kelly As the Arthur Freed of the '80s," *Variety*, Oct. 1, 1980; Michael Goodwin and Naomi Wise, *On the Edge: The Life and Times of Francis Coppola* (New York: William Morrow, 1989), 296.

4. Kelly quoted in Hirschhorn, *Gene Kelly*, 273; Goodwin and Wise, *On the Edge*, 306–307, 311–317.

5. Goodwin and Wise, *On the Edge*, 333–336; Kelly letter to editor, *American Film*, 6.

6. Goodwin and Wise, *On the Edge*, 297–298.

7. John Corry, "Gene Kelly Puts Strut in 'Satchmo,'" *New York Times*, Aug. 24, 1981.

8. Kelly quoted in Hirschhorn, *Gene Kelly*, 274.

9. Wintz, "Gene Kelly," 24, 26.

10. Wintz, 20, 24, 26.

11. Clippings of ads for RCA videodiscs, Box 1, Folder 11, Gene Kelly Alumni Files, UP; Reich, "Hoofer of His Era"; Marx, "The Man Who Lived Dancing."

12. Eric Malnic, "Gene Kelly Saved from House Fire," *Los Angeles Times*, Dec. 23, 1983; "Gene Kelly Saved by Son As Fire Destroys His Home," *San Gabriel Valley Tribune*, Dec. 23, 1983; Peters, "Tim Kelly" [website].

13. Pollock, "Gene Kelly at 72"; Ruth Zekaria Levy, email interview, Mar. 16, 2014; Kelly family Christmas card, Box 1, Folder 14, Lazar Family Papers and Photographs, HHC.

14. Pat York, *Going Strong* (New York: Arcade, 1991), 160, 162–163.

15. Patricia Nolan, "Sins," *Globe*, Feb. 4, 1986.

16. Jack Pittman, "Kelly in London Tribute," *Variety*, June 4, 1980; Jack Anderson, "Innovative Dance Detail in a Gene Kelly Movie," *New York Times*, May 21, 1987.

17. Kelly interview, Haver, "Kelly," 56; Singer, *A Cut Above*, 143.

18. Corry, "Gene Kelly"; Marx, "The Man Who Lived Dancing"; Pollock, "Gene Kelly at 72."

19. Swisher, "Xanadu," 44–45; Kelly interview, Flatow, "Through a Lens," 38; clipping, Octavio Roca, "Hollywood Legend Gene Kelly Dies at 83," *San Francisco Chronicle*, no date, Box 1, Folder 11, Gene Kelly Alumni Files, UP.

20. Wintz, "Gene Kelly," 22, 24.

21. Land, "Magic Doesn't Age," 56; Kelly interview, Britton, ed., *Talking Films*, 196, 198–199; Kelly interview, Singer, *A Cut Above*, 148.

22. Clipping, *San Francisco Chronicle*, Mar. 9, 1985, Gene Kelly Biography, Core Collection, AMPAS; Honeycutt, "Gene Kelly"; Singer, *A Cut Above*, 150.

23. "Kelly Notes," Feb. 19, 1981, Box 93, Folder 4, Joseph McBride Papers, WCFTR; "Gene Kelly Saved by Son"; York, *Going Strong*, 162; Kelly interview, Singer, *A Cut Above*, 147.

24. Kelly interview, Haver, "Kelly," 56; Gene Kelly, "Foreword," Clive Hirschhorn, *The Hollywood Musical* (New York: Crown, 1981); Gene Kelly, "Foreword," Naylor, *Great American*; Kelly interview, Reich, "Hoofer of His Era"; Nolan, "Sins."

25. Nolan, "Sins"; Land, "Magic Doesn't Age," 128.

26. Kelly interview, Singer, *A Cut Above*, 149; George Anderson, "Life After Musicals," *Pittsburgh Post-Gazette*, Jan. 24, 1985; Nolan, "Sins"; Kelly interview, Haver, "Kelly," 56.

27. Kelly interview, Singer, *A Cut Above*, 149; Nolan, "Sins"; clipping, "Kelly Likes Break Dancing," Box 1, Folder 11, Gene Kelly Alumni Files, UP.

28. Kelly interview, Haver, "Kelly," 59; Irvin Molotsky, "Gene Kelly Brings Young Dancers to White House," *New York Times*, Mar. 29, 1982.

29. Irvin Molotsky, "Kennedy Center Honors 5 in the Arts," *New York Times*, Aug. 16, 1982.

30. Aljean Harmetz, "Film Institute Honors Gene Kelly," *New York Times*, Mar. 9, 1985; clipping, Sheilah Graham, "Gene Kelly Milliner's Dreams," May 22, 1965, Scrapbook, Gene Kelly Alumni Files, UP.

31. Kelly interview, Haver, "Kelly," 56; Martin A. David, "'That's Dancing!' That's Gene Kelly," *Dance Teacher Now* 7, no. 1 (Jan.–Feb. 1985): 32.

32. Marcia Pally, "Dancing for Their Lives," *Film Comment* 20, no. 6 (Dec. 1984): 51–52.

33. Noah James, "Making Sure the Seams Don't Show," *New York Times*, Nov. 3, 1985; Nolan, "Sins."

34. Blank, "Gene Kelly: Old Pro Is Still Dancing."

35. Clipping, Mar. 11, 1981, Box 1, Folder 18, Gene Kelly Alumni Files, UP; Davidson, "Gene Kelly."

36. Davidson, "Gene Kelly"; Nicklas to Kelly, July 8, 1981, and attached photograph, Box 1, Folder 4 and Kelly to Nicklas, Sept. 23, 1981, Box 1, Folder 11, Gene Kelly Alumni Files, UP.

37. Faires, "Immigrants and Industry," 18; Toker, *Pittsburgh*, 209.

38. Sherie R. Mershon and Joel A. Tarr, "Strategies for Clean Air: The Pittsburgh and Allegheny County Smoke Control Movements, 1940–1960," in *Devastation and Renewal: An Environmental History of Pittsburgh and Its Region*, ed. Joel A. Tarr (Pittsburgh: University of Pittsburgh Press, 2003), 145–147, 155, 162.

39. Clipping, *American Jewish Outlook*, Feb. 6, 1953, CMUL; "No One Believes"; Conner, *Pittsburgh in Stages*, 137.

40. Nicklas to Kelly, Jan. 14, 1987, Box 1, Folder 6, and Kelly to Nicklas, Feb. 1, 1987, Box 1, Folder 5, Gene Kelly Alumni Files, UP; clipping, *University Times*, Vertical File, Gene Kelly Alumni Files, UP; "Gene Kelly Days," *Pittsburgh Press*, June 23, 1987.

41. Clipping, Barbara Vancheri, "Kelly Saddened by Death of 'Immortal' Astaire," *Pittsburgh Post-Gazette*, and clipping, Margie Romero, "Singin' in the Square," Box 1, Folder 18, and Kelly to Nicklas, Sept. 23, 1981, and Oct. 2, 1987, and Kelly to Virgil Cantini, July 31, 1987, and Nicklas to Kelly, July 9 and Sept. 14, 1987, Box 1, Folder 11, Gene Kelly Alumni Files, UP.

42. Kelly to Venable, July 13, 24, 1989, Box 1, Folder 10, Emerson Venable Papers, HHC.

43. York, *Going Strong*, 162; Nolan, "Sins"; "Puddle Jumper," *People Weekly* 37, no. 23 (June 15, 1992), 86; Public Affairs Books [website]; clipping, *Pittsburgh Press*, Apr. 2, 1989, Box 1, Folder 10, Emerson Venable Papers, HHC; clipping, Leon Wagener, "Gene Kelly's Kids Furious Over His Will," Box 1, Folder 11, Gene Kelly Alumni Files, UP; *Pittsburgh Press*, Sept. 9, 1990.

44. "Puddle Jumper," 86.

45. Kelly to Venable, Apr. 17, 1990, and Mar. 4, 1991, Box 1, Folder 10, Emerson Venable Papers, HHC; Donald Rosenberg, "CLO's New Kellys to Honor Students," *Pittsburgh Press*, Feb. 26, 1991; Donald Rosenberg, "Woodland Hills' 'Guys and Dolls' Heads CLO's Gene Kelly Award List," *Pittsburgh Press*, May 20, 1991.

46. Nicklas to Kelly, Mar. 8, 1990, and Nicklas to Mark Cromie, Mar. 18, 1992, Box 1, Folder 12, and Patricia Kelly to Nicklas, Aug. 19, 1992, and Nicklas to Mr. and Mrs. Gene Kelly, Aug. 23 and Oct. 5, 1992, Box 1, Folder 8, Gene Kelly Alumni Files, UP.

47. Nicklas to David Raible, Jan. 6, 1993, Box 1, Folder 8, Gene Kelly Alumni Files, UP.

48. Kevin Thomas, "Gene Kelly Remembers Golden Age of Musicals," *Pittsburgh Post-Gazette*, May 3, 1993.

49. Kelly interview, Fantle and Johnson, *Reel to Real*, 73; Kelly interview, Fuller, "And Now," 110; Kelly to Charles Harmon, Mar. 11, 1991, Box 31, Folder 47, Leonard Bernstein Collection, LC; song sheets, Box 27, Gene Kelly Collection, BU.

50. Gregory Cerio et al., "No False Moves," *People Weekly* 45, no. 7 (Feb. 19, 1996): 36; Gregg Kilday, "Toeing the Lion: Gene Kelly of 'That's Entertainment! III,'" *Entertainment Weekly*, Number 222 (May 13, 1994): 41; *New York Times*, July 25, 1994, and Feb. 14, 1995; Krebs, "Gene Kelly."

51. Blair, *Memory*, 4–6.

52. Blair, 3, 6; Bob Hoover, "Betsy Blair Recalls her Hollywood Days with Gene Kelly," *Pittsburgh Post-Gazette*, Apr. 26, 2003.

53. Rawson, "Pittsburghers Remember."

54. Rawson.

55. "Puddle Jumper," 86; Michael Scanlon interview [website]; Kelly interview, Fantle and Johnson, *Reel to Real*, 71, 73; Hoover, "Betsy Blair"; *New York Post*, Sept. 12, 2002; Public Affairs Books [website].

Chapter 19. Renaissance Man

1. Don Alpert, "Gene Kelly: Guy without a Trade," *Los Angeles Times*, Sept. 13, 1964; Marilyn Hunt, "Gene Kelly Interview," NYPL, 36.

2. Delamater, *Dance*, 158, 161, 180; Land, "Magic Doesn't Age," 128.

3. Newnham, "Tilly Losch," 135; Youskevitch quoted in Hirschhorn, *Gene Kelly*, 201.

4. Gene Kelly, "Cine-Dance?" *Eleventh Annual San Francisco International Film Festival Magazine, October 20–29, 1966*: 38; Kelly interview, Fuller, "And Now," 112.

5. Kelly interview, Boorman, et al., *Projections 4*, 286; Reich, "Hoofer of His Era"; Marilyn Hunt, "Gene Kelly Interview," NYPL, 23.

6. Kelly interview, Boorman, et al., *Projections 4*, 277; Kisselgoff, "Just a Regular Joe."

7. Rick Altman, *The American Film Musical* (Bloomington: Indiana University Press, 1987), 54; Kisselgoff, "Gene Kelly"; Kelly interview, Britton, ed., *Talking Films*, 194; Kelly interview, Fantle and Johnson, *Reel to Real*, 72; York, *Going Strong*, 160; Kelly interview, June 3, 1954, File 1342, Hedda Hopper Collection, AMPAS.

8. Feuer, *Hollywood Musical*, 4–5; Mast, *Can't Help Singin'*, 248; Krebs, "Gene Kelly"; Kelly interview, Flatow, "Through a Lens," 14.

9. Jack Howard, "Gene Kelly," Nov. 21, 1949, in Jack Hirshberg Papers, AMPAS; Marilyn Hunt, "Gene Kelly Interview," NYPL, 40–41.

10. Land, "Magic Doesn't Age," 56.

11. Fred Kelly, Ryan, and Draper interviews, Frank, ed., *Tap!*, 171, 209–210, 235–236; Altman, *American Film Musical*, 54.

12. "Reminiscences of Gene Curran Kelly: Oral History, 1958," 8, CU; Alpert, "Gene Kelly"; Swisher, "Xanadu," 45.

13. "Reminiscences of Gene Curran Kelly: Oral History, 1958," 9, CU; York, *Going Strong*, 160; Delamater, *Dance*, 185.

14. Kelly, "Cine-Dance?," 38; Hanson, "An Interview with Gene Kelly," 24; Kelly interview, "Dialogue on Film," 37–38; Marilyn Hunt, "Gene Kelly Interview," NYPL, 114–115; transcript of interview, May 1968, Jack Hirshberg Papers, AMPAS.

15. Harvey, *Directed by Vincente Minnelli*, 133; Barnes, "Movies Revisited."

16. Delamater, *Dance*, 106–107, 139, 185; Beth Genné, "Dancin' in the Rain: Gene Kelly's Musical Films," in *Envisioning Dance on Film and Video*, ed. Judy Mitoma (New York: Routledge, 2002), 75; Basinger, *Gene Kelly*, 16; David Atkins, "Thank You Mr. Kelly," *Dance Australia*, no. 83 (Apr.–May 1996): 35.

17. Kelly interview, June 3, 1954, File 1342, Hedda Hopper Collection, AMPAS; Kelly quoted in Knox, [ed.,], *Magic Factory*, 108.

18. Kelly interview, 21, SMU/Ronald L. Davis Oral History Collection, AMPAS; Kelly quoted in Fricke, *Judy Garland*, 113; Kelly interview, Singer, *A Cut Above*, 148; Kelly interview, Britton, ed., *Talking Films*, 190.

19. "Reminiscences of Gene Curran Kelly: Oral History, 1958," 13–14, CU; Draft of "Type Casting!," Box 3, Folder 13, Gene Kelly Collection, BU.

20. Douglas Newton, "Poetry in Fast and Musical Motion," *Monthly Film Bulletin* 22, no. 1 (July–Sept. 1952): 35; Robert Trachtenberg interview [website]; Thomas, "Gene Kelly Remembers"; Kelly interview, Boorman, et al., *Projections* 4, 288–289.

21. Taylor and Jackson, *Hollywood Musical*, 60; Epstein, *Fred Astaire*, 73–74; Harvey, *Directed by Vincente Minnelli*, 101; Anderson, "Minnelli, Kelly," 37; Kelly interview, Britton, ed., *Talking Films*, 190; "Reminiscences of Gene Curran Kelly: Oral History, 1958," 14, CU.

22. Basinger, "Gene Kelly," 23.

23. *Nova* [website].

24. Fred Kelly interview, Frank, ed., *Tap!*, 171; Halsey and Record, "Gene Kelly," 15; Chaplin quoted in Knox, ed., *Magic Factory*, 54–55.

25. Transcript of interview, May 1968, Jack Hirshberg Papers, AMPAS, 20–21; Marilyn Hunt, "Gene Kelly Interview," NYPL, 62–63.

26. Marilyn Hunt, "Gene Kelly Interview," NYPL, 58–60; Kelly interview, Delamater, *Dance*, 223; Alyce Canfield, "Things I Wish I Knew 10 Years Ago," *Motion Picture Magazine* (Jan. 1945): 6–7.

27. Cerio, "No False Moves"; Marilyn Hunt, "Gene Kelly Interview," NYPL, 61; *Gene Kelly: Song & Dance Man*, Rodgers and Hammerstein Archives, NYPL.

28. Kelly interview, Singer, *A Cut Above*, 144; Hanson, "An Interview with Gene Kelly," 24.

29. Hudgins, "Directed by Kelly"; Delamater, *Dance*, 185; Beth Genné, "Dance in Film," in *The Living Dance: An Anthology of Essays on Movement and Culture*, ed. Judith Chazin-Bennahum (Dubuque, IA: Kendall/Hunt, 2003), 198; Barnes, "Movies Revisited."

30. Corry, "Gene Kelly"; Thomas, *Films of Gene Kelly*, 213, 227.

31. Claude Bessy, email interview, Sept. 30, 2008; Astaire quoted in Bob Thomas,

Astaire: The Man, The Dancer (New York: St. Martins, 1984), 285; O'Connor in *What a Glorious Feeling* [DVD].

32. Wheeler Winston Dixon, "An Interview with Wendy Toye," in *Re-viewing British Cinema, 1900–1992: Essays and Interviews*, Wheeler Winston Dixon, ed. (Albany: State University of New York Press, 1994), 133–135, 140.

33. Duell interview, Delamater, *Dance*, 246.

34. Kelly interview, Delamater, *Dance*, 212; Hungerford, "Dancing," 194; Roy H. Wagner, email interview, June 2, 2009; Kelly interview, Singer, *A Cut Above*, 148; Kelly interview, "Dialogue on Film," 40.

35. Kelly quoted in Knox, ed., *Magic Factory*, 170–171; Kelly interview, Singer, *A Cut Above*, 144, 148; Roy H. Wagner, email interview, June 2, 2009.

36. Transcript of interview, May 1968, Jack Hirshberg Papers, AMPAS; Kelly and Ruttenberg interviews, Delamater, *Dance*, 218–219, 278.

37. Sweeney, "Gene Kelly's Dancing"; Kelly, "Directing Dolly," 9.

38. Kelly interview, June 3, 1954, File 1342, Hedda Hopper Collection, AMPAS; "Reminiscences of Gene Curran Kelly: Oral History, 1958," 3, CU; Hedda Hopper, "Gene Kelly Would Rather Teach," *Los Angeles Times*, Oct. 4, 1957; Thomas, *Films of Gene Kelly*, 12.

39. Lois Elias, telephone interview, Oct. 3, 2006.

40. Marilyn Hunt, "Gene Kelly Interview," NYPL, 12–13.

41. Marilyn Hunt, "Gene Kelly Interview," NYPL, 127–128; clipping, "Kelly Would Like to Make Films for Kids," *Johnstown Tribune*, Box 8, Scrapbook 5, Gene Kelly Collection, BU; Howard Taubman, "Records: For the Children," *New York Times*, Nov. 17, 1946; Nicklas to Paul Pugh, July 26, 1971, Box 1, Folder 10, Gene Kelly Alumni Files, UP.

42. Eleanor Brooks Pasternak to Kelly, Nov. 11, 1946, and Robert Cornwall to Kelly, Oct. 2, 1954, and Frank Stauffacher to Kelly, Oct. 6, 1954, and George Savage to Kelly, Feb. 13, 1962, Box 2, Folder 10, and clipping, "Kelly Tells Historical Aspects of Dancing," May 1949, Box 8, Scrapbook 5, Gene Kelly Collection, BU.

43. Halsey and Record, "Gene Kelly," 14–15.

44. "Reminiscences of Gene Curran Kelly: Oral History, 1958," 16–17, CU; Kelly, "The Women in My Dancing Life"; Ellen quoted in Soren, *Vera-Ellen*, 134–135.

45. Lorraine Kriegel, "Interview with Luigi," 27–29, NYPL.

46. Blair, *Memory*, 116.

47. Stephen Harvey, "Stanley Donen," *Film Comment* 9, no. 4 (July–Aug. 1973): 7–9; Hess and Dabholkar, *Singin' in the Rain*, 205.

48. Kelly interview, Britton, ed., *Talking Films*, 194; Donen quoted in Hirschhorn, *Gene Kelly*, 73; Kelly interview, "Dialogue on Film," 37.

49. Hanson, "An Interview with Gene Kelly," 26; Delamater, *Dance*, 151–152, 155–156; Clark, "Giving Life," 7, 32; Casper, *Stanley Donen*, 5; Kelly interview, 51, SMU/Ronald L. Davis Oral History Collection, AMPAS; Kelly interview, "Dialogue on Film," 37; Kelly interview, Britton, ed., *Talking Films*, 195.

50. Clipping, Donen, "Some Guys are Never Satisfied," Box 10, Scrapbook 9, Gene Kelly Collection, BU; Duell interview, Delamater, *Dance*, 247; Chaplin, *Golden Age*, 59; Kelly interview, "Dialogue on Film," 37.

51. Kelly interview, Fuller, "And Now," 112; Blair, *Memory*, 114–115; Granger, *Include Me Out*, 55.

52. Silverman, *Dancing*, 75, 292–293, 312.

53. Casper, *Stanley Donen*, 46; Mast, *Can't Help Singin'*, 252.

54. Silverman, *Dancing*, passim.

55. Genné, "Dancin' in the Rain," 76n; Hess and Dabholkar, *Singin' in the Rain*, 200–207; Roy H. Wagner, email interview, June 2, 2009.

56. Hess and Dabholkar, *Cinematic Voyage*, 60–61, 147–148; Genné, "The Film Musicals," 234; Kelly interview, Delamater, *Dance*, 214–215.

57. Honeycutt, "Gene Kelly"; Strohm quoted in Knox, ed., *Magic Factory*, 109; Genné, "The Film Musicals," 107–108; Beth Genné, "Vincente Minnelli and the Film Ballet," in *Vincente Minnelli: The Art of Entertainment*, ed. Joe McElhaney (Detroit: Wayne State University Press, 2009), 244.

58. Isaacs, "Gene Kelly," 153; Hudgins, "Directed by Kelly"; Flatow, "Through a Lens," 14.

59. Epstein, *Fred Astaire*, 67; Levinson, *Puttin' on the Ritz*, 7, 10, 12, 22–24, 40, 53, 57, 59, 65, 223–224; Delamater, *Dance*, 109; Hungerford, "Dancing," 47–48, 220–221, 223; Astaire, *Steps in Time*, 325.

60. "Reminiscences of Gene Curran Kelly: Oral History, 1958," 5–7, CU; Levinson, *Puttin' on the Ritz*, 187.

61. Willens, "Gene Kelly"; Kelly interview, "Dialogue on Film," 43; "Kelly Notes," Feb. 19, 1981, Box 93, Folder 4, Joseph McBride Papers, WCFTR; Minnelli interview, Richard Schickel, *The Men Who Made the Movies: Interviews With Frank Capra, George Cukor, Howard Hawks, Alfred Hitchcock, Vincente Minnelli, King Vidor, Raoul Walsh, and William A. Wellman* (New York: Atheneum, 1975), 260; Stoop, "That's Entertainment, Part 2," 71; Levinson, *Puttin' on the Ritz*, 269; Fehr and Vogel, *Lullabies of Hollywood*, 213; Suzanne Carbonneau, "Interview with Doug Varone," 11, NYPL.

62. Mueller, *Astaire Dancing*, 26; Bill Adler, *Fred Astaire: A Wonderful Life* (New York: Carroll and Graf, 1987), 124; Levinson, *Puttin' on the Ritz*, 169, 185, 187; Delamater, *Dance*, 53, 133; Genné, "Dancin' in the Rain," 75.

63. Astaire interview, 6, 27, 45, SMU/Ronald L. Davis Oral History Collection, AMPAS; Levinson, *Puttin' on the Ritz*, 27, 33, 41, 378; Astaire, *Steps in Time*, 206.

64. Levinson, *Puttin' on the Ritz*, 154; Fordin, *M-G-M's Greatest Musicals*, 245.

65. Levinson, *Puttin' on the Ritz*, 91, 126, 135, 338–339.

66. Marilyn Hunt, "Gene Kelly Interview," NYPL, 146–147; David Lewin, "The Difference Between Astaire and Me," London *Daily Express*, Mar. 26, 1952; Kelly interview, June 3, 1954, File 1342, Hedda Hopper Collection, AMPAS; Levinson, *Puttin' on the Ritz*, 363, 375–376, 388, 398, 411, 413; Astaire, *Steps in Time*, 309; Adler, *Fred Astaire*, 172, 175.

67. Thomas, *Astaire*, 187; "Kelly Notes," Feb. 19, 1981, Box 93, Folder 4, Joseph McBride Papers, WCFTR; Levinson, *Puttin' on the Ritz*, 406.

68. Kelly interview, "Dialogue on Film," 42–43; transcript of interview, May 1968, Jack Hirshberg Papers, AMPAS; Behlmer, "Gene Kelly," 20.

69. Griffith, *Cinema of Gene Kelly*, 5.

70. Marilyn Hunt, "Gene Kelly Interview," NYPL, 269.

71. Kelly interview, "Dialogue on Film," 43; Lindsey, "Astaire and Kelly."

72. Ringel, "Gotta Dance"; Hemming, *Melody Lingers On*, 239; Martin, "The Dance: Pal Joey"; Richard Rodgers, "'Pal Joey': History of a 'Heel,'" *New York Times*, Dec. 30, 1951."

73. Thomas F. Brady, "Sequel on Jolson Planned by Metro," *New York Times*, Dec. 12, 1947; "My Mammy," Box 27, Gene Kelly Collection, BU.

74. Blair, *Memory*, 124.

75. Kelly interview, Haver, "Pas de Deux," 26, 73; Ringel, "Gotta Dance"; Hopper, "Just Plain Kelly."

76. "Reminiscences of Gene Curran Kelly: Oral History, 1958," 19–20, CU; Kelly quoted in Hirschhorn, *Gene Kelly*, 212; Ringel, "Gotta Dance."

77. Kelly quoted in Hirschhorn, *Gene Kelly*, 274.

78. Clipping, Gross, "'Dancing Isn't Sissy'—Gene Kelly," February 1, 1959, Box 3, Folder 11, Gene Kelly Collection, BU; draft of article for *Sports Illustrated*, Box 3, Folder 13, Gene Kelly Collection, BU.

79. Land, "Magic Doesn't Age," 128; Kelly interview, Britton, ed., *Talking Films*, 200; Astaire quoted in Parish and Bowers, *MGM Stock Company*, 30.

80. Kelly interview, June 3, 1954, File 1342, Hedda Hopper Collection, AMPAS; Ramsay Burt, *The Male Dancer: Bodies, Spectacle, Sexualities* (London: Routledge, 1995), 13–14, 21–22, 101–102.

81. Ted Shawn, *One Thousand and One Night Stands* (New York: Doubleday, 1960), 11, 240–247, 275; Walter Terry, *Ted Shawn, Father of American Dance: A Biography* (New York: Dial Press, 1976), 11, 84, 140; Burt, *The Male Dancer*, 102–103, 108–110; Maura Keefe, "Is Dance a Man's Sport Too? The Performance of Athletic-coded Masculinity on the Concert Dance Stage," in *When Men Dance: Choreographing Masculinities Across Borders*, ed. Jennifer Fisher and Anthony Shay (Oxford University Press, 2009), 95–98.

82. Wollen, *Singin' in the Rain*, 57; Flatow, "Through a Lens," 14; Basinger, *Gene Kelly*, 12.

83. David Anthony Gerstner, "Dancer from the Dance: Gene Kelly, Television, and the Beauty of Movement," *Velvet Light Trap*, no. 49 (Spring 2002): 57–59; Hess and Dabholkar, *Cinematic Voyage*, 173–175; Steven Cohan, "'Feminizing' the Song-and-Dance Man: Fred Astaire and the Spectacle of Masculinity in the Hollywood Musical," in *Screening the Male: Exploring Masculinities in Hollywood Cinema*, ed. Steven Cohan and Ian Rae Hark (London: Routledge, 1993), 46–47; Callahan, "Gene Kelly" [website].

84. Laurents, *Original Story*, 96; Brideson and Brideson, *He's Got Rhythm*, 144.

85. David Kasday, email interview, Sept. 4, 6, 2008; Keefe, "Is Dance," 92–95, 100, 103; Michael Gard, *Men Who Dance: Aesthetics, Athletics and the Art of Masculinity* (New York: Peter Lang, 2008), 4, 6, 8, 46–51; Doug Risner, "What We Know about Boys Who Dance: The Limitations of Contemporary Masculinity and Dance Education," in *When Men Dance*, ed. Fisher and Shay, 57–58, 60; Kelly to Smith, May 11, 1989, Box C16, Jack Smith Papers, HL; Marc, "Masculinity" [website].

86. Kelly interview, Haver, "Pas de Deux," 25; "Reminiscences of Gene Curran Kelly: Oral History, 1958," 9, CU.

87. Kelly interview, 20, SMU/Ronald L. Davis Oral History Collection, AMPAS; Hanson, "An Interview with Gene Kelly," 24; Kelly, "Cine-Dance?" 38.

88. Hanson, "An Interview with Gene Kelly," 24; Kelly interview, 32–34, SMU/Ronald L. Davis Oral History Collection, AMPAS.

89. Isaacs, "Gene Kelly," 155; Griffith, *Cinema of Gene Kelly*, 4.

90. Maya Deren, "Choreography for the Camera," in *Essential Deren: Collected Writings on Film by Maya Deren*, ed. Bruce R. McPherson (Kingston, NY: Documentext, 2005), 220–224; Martin, "The Dance," 154; Delamater, *Dance*, 185; Newnham, "Tilly Losch," 135; Gene Kelly, "Making a *Cine*ballet for 'American in Paris,'" *Dance Magazine* 25, no. 8 (Aug. 1951): 9, 24; "Reminiscences of Gene Curran Kelly: Oral History, 1958," 9–10, CU; Kelly interview, Boorman, et. al., *Projections 4*, 280.

91. Wollen, *Singin' in the Rain*, 34–35; Delamater, *Dance*, 103; Mueller, *Astaire Dancing*, 255.

92. Green and Goldblatt, *Starring Fred Astaire*, 177, 180, 274, 286; Atkinson, "Christmas Night."

93. "Reminiscences of Gene Curran Kelly: Oral History, 1958," 11, CU; Wollen, *Singin' in the Rain*, 40.

94. Marilyn Hunt, "Gene Kelly Interview," NYPL, 223–224; Mueller, *Astaire Dancing*, 255.

95. Marilyn Hunt, "Gene Kelly Interview," NYPL, 242–243; Kelly interview, Britton, ed., *Talking Films*, 194; Kelly interview, Flatow, "Through a Lens," 38.

96. Donen quoted in Casper, *Stanley Donen*, 34.

97. Mueller, *Astaire Dancing*, 35.

98. Thomas, "Gene Kelly"; Freed interview, Kobal, *Gotta Sing*, 201–202; Kelly quoted in Thomas, *Films of Gene Kelly*, 22; Kelly interview, Delamater, *Dance*, 213–214; Hanson, "An Interview with Gene Kelly," 26; Honeycutt, "Gene Kelly."

99. Kelly quoted in "Hollywood Dance Directors," *Dance Magazine* 21, no. 2 (Feb. 1947): 14–15.

100. Kelly interview, "Dialogue on Film," 42; Kelly quoted in Stoop, "Gene Kelly," 73; Kelly quoted in Morley and Leon, *Gene Kelly*, 126; Timothy E. Scheurer, "The Aesthetics of Form and Convention in the Movie Musical," *Journal of Popular Film* 3, no. 4 (Fall 1974): 307–309, 321.

101. Baer, "*Singin' in the Rain*," 18–19; Mueller, *Astaire Dancing*, 34; Chaplin, *Golden Age*, 251.

102. Kelly interview, Britton, ed., *Talking Films*, 191; Kelly interview, "Dialogue on Film," 37; Marilyn Hunt, "Gene Kelly Interview," NYPL, 173–174; Pam Cook, "British Cinema: Auteur and Studio," in *The Cinema Book*, 3rd ed., ed. Pam Cook (London: British Film Institute, 2007), 438–439.

103. Sarris, "Notes," 7–8; R.C. Dale, "René Clair in Hollywood: An Interview," *Film Quarterly* 24, no. 2 (Winter 1970–1971): 35–36; Satyajit Ray, *Our Films Their Films* (New York: Hyperion, 1994), 140.

104. James Naremore, *The Films of Vincente Minnelli* (New York: Cambridge University Press, 1993) 1; Delamater, *Dance*, 133.

105. Gillian Kelly, "Gene Kelly: The Performing Auteur—Manifestations of the Kelly Persona," *eSharp* (2010): 136–137, 141–150.

106. Robert Trachtenberg interview [website]; Mueller, *Astaire Dancing*, 388n.
107. Kelly interview, Delamater, *Dance*, 209.
108. Ames interview, Delamater, *Dance*, 238; "Gene Kelly's Invitation to the Dance," 90.
109. Hudgins, "Directed by Kelly"; Honeycutt, "Gene Kelly"; Burrows, *Gene Kelly*, 5.
110. Delamater, *Dance*, 166; Taylor and Jackson, *Hollywood Musical*, 63.

Bibliography

Archives

Academy of Motion Picture Arts and Sciences (AMPAS), Margaret Herrick Library
  Gene Kelly Biography File, Core Collection
  Hedda Hopper Collection, Special Collections
    "Gene Kelly—June 3, 1954," File 1342
    "Notes on Gene Kelly—Wednesday, August 3, 1960," File 1342
  Invitation to the Dance Production Files, Core Collection
  Jack Hirshberg Papers, Special Collections
  MPAA Production Code Administration Records
  "An Oral History with Lela Simone." Rudy Behlmer, Oral History Program
  Ron Haver Papers, Special Collections
  Southern Methodist University (SMU)/Ronald L. Davis Oral History Collection
    Fred Astaire Interview
    Dan Dailey Interview
    Stanley Donen Interview
    Betty Garrett Interview
    Gene Kelly Interview
    Charles Walters Interview
  Turner/MGM Script Collection
  Vincente Minnelli Collection, Special Collections
Boston University (BU), Howard Gotlieb Archival Research Center, Boston
  Gene Kelly Collection
  C. Y. Lee Collection
Carnegie Mellon University Libraries (CMUL), Digital Collections, Pittsburgh
  American Jewish Outlook Collection, Pittsburgh Jewish Newspaper Project
  Jewish Criterion Collection, Pittsburgh Jewish Newspaper Project
Columbia University (CU), Oral History Research Office, Popular Arts Project, New York
  "Reminiscences of Gene Curran Kelly: Oral History, 1958"
  "Reminiscences of Betty Comden and Adolph Green: Oral History, 1959"
Columbia University (CU), Rare Book and Manuscript Library, New York
  Samson Raphaelson Papers

Leah Jayne Salisbury Papers
Samuel and Bella Spewack Papers
Harvard University (HU), Houghton Library, Cambridge, MA
George Balanchine Archive
Heinz History Center (HHC), Pittsburgh
Sanford Baskin Papers, Rauh Jewish Archive
Lazar Family Papers and Photographs, Rauh Jewish Archive
Spector Family Papers, Rauh Jewish Archive
Emerson Venable Papers
Huntington Library (HL), San Marino, CA
Jack Smith Papers
Jimmy Carter Presidential Library (JCPL), Atlanta
Photograph Collection
Gene Kelly FBI File (various agencies of the US Government)
Kent State University (KSU), Special Collections and Archives, Kent, OH
Albert J. Flogge Performing Arts Collection
Library of Congress (LC), Manuscripts Division, Washington, DC
Leonard Bernstein Collection
Clare Booth Luce Collection
Library of Congress (LC), Prints and Photographs Division, Washington, DC
Look Magazine Photograph Collection
Michigan State University (MSU), Vincent Voice Library, Lansing
Gene Kelly interview with David Hartman, "Gene Kelly on 'Golden Age' Musicals," September 30, 1980
"Hollywood Fights Back." November 2, 1947
National Archives and Records Administration (NARA), College Park, MD
Ring Lardner Jr., 8016-CT.06/29/1950–12/30/1953, Notorious Offenders Files, RG129, Records of the Bureau of Prisons, 1870–2009.
New York Public Library (NYPL), Center for the Performing Arts, New York
American Ballet Theatre Records, Billy Rose Theatre Division
Betsy Baytos. "Interview with Joe Barbera." Oral History Program, Dance Division
Suzanne Carbonneau. "Interview with Doug Varone." Jerome Robbins Dance Division
Comden and Green Papers, Billy Rose Theatre Division
Danny Daniels History of American Tap, Performing Arts Research Collections—Dance, Jerome Robbins Dance Division
Agnes de Mille Collection, Jerome Robbins Dance Division
Irma Duncan Papers, Jerome Robbins Dance Division
"Frank Sinatra, Gene Kelly in *The New Yorkers*, A New Musical Play for the Screen by Jerome Lawrence and Robert E. Lee," Billy Rose Theatre Division
Marilyn Hunt. "Gene Kelly Interview." Oral History Program, Dance Division
Marilyn Hunt. "Igor Youskevitch Interview." Oral History Program, Dance Division
Gene Kelly: Song & Dance Man, Rodgers and Hammerstein Archives
Gene Kelly Publicity Photographs. USO Camp Shows Publicity Records, 1941–1955,

Billy Rose Theatre Division
Lorraine Kriegel. "Interview with Luigi," Jerome Robbins Dance Division
Paley Center for Media (PC), Museum of Television and Radio, Los Angeles
The Tonight Show, November 7, 1975, May 4, 1976, and January 24, 1985
You're the Top: The Cole Porter Story, American Masters (1990)
Princeton University (PU), Seeley G. Mudd Manuscript Library, Princeton
James V. Forrestal Papers
Stanford University (SU), Special Collections and University Archives, Stanford
William Saroyan Papers
Syracuse University (SYU), Special Collections Research Center, Syracuse, NY
General Still Photograph Collection, 1957–1958
Trent University (TU), Archives and Special Collections, Peterborough, Ontario
Gene Kelly Correspondence
University of California, Los Angeles (UCLA), Film and Television Archives, Archives Research and Study Center
"The American Film Institute Salute to Gene Kelly," 1985
"Dancing—A Man's Game," *Omnibus*
Gene Kelly: An American in Pasadena, 1977
Gene Kelly Collection
Gene Kelly Interview, *Steve Allen Show*, February 18, 1964
"The Gene Kelly Show," *Pontiac Star Parade*, April 24, 1959 and November 21, 1959
University of Iowa (UI), Special Collections, Iowa City
Marion Meade/Buster Keaton Research Files
University of Pittsburgh (UP), Archives and Special Collections, Pittsburgh
Cap and Gown Club Records
Gene Kelly Alumni Files
G. Norman Reis Papers
University of Southern California (USC), Archives of Performing Arts and Warner Bros. Archives, Los Angeles
Arthur Freed Collection
University of Texas (UTA), Harry Ransom Center, Austin
Ernest Lehman Collection
David O. Selznick Collection
B. J. Simmons and Company Costume Design Records
Edward Weeks Papers
Wisconsin Center for Film and Theater Research (WCFTR), Madison
Joseph McBride Papers
Yale University (YU), Beinecke Rare Book and Manuscript Library, New Haven, CT
William A. Graham Collection of Television Scripts
Thornton Wilder Papers
Yeshiva University (YeU), Archives and Special Collections, New York
Zionist Archives LP Collection ("Going Home," *Palestine Speaks!* Box 11)

Interviews

Claude Bessy, email interview, September 30, 2008.
Lois Elias, telephone interview, October 3, 2006.
David Kasday, email interview, September 4 and 6, 2008.
Ruth Zekaria Levy, email interview, March 16, 2014.
Bobby Riha, telephone interview, August 31, 2008.
Roy H. Wagner, email interview, June 2, 2009.
Ike Zekaria, email interview, March 18, 2014.

Magazines and Newspapers

Dance News
Indianapolis Star
Los Angeles Times
Modern Screen
Movieland
New York Daily News
New York Herald Tribune
New York Post
New York Sun
New York Times
New York World Telegram
Philadelphia Evening Bulletin
Pittsburgh Post-Gazette
Pittsburgh Press
Saturday Evening Post
Trenton Sunday Times Advertiser
Variety

DVDs

Anatomy of a Dancer. American Masters. PBS, 2002.
Edward R. Murrow, interview with Gene Kelly. *Person to Person*, December 19, 1958.
Gavin Millar, interview with Gene Kelly. *An Evening with Gene Kelly*. BBC Television, 1974.
Musicals Great Musicals: The Arthur Freed Unit at MGM. Great Performances. PBS, December 2, 1996.
What a Glorious Feeling, 2002.

Websites

506-N-Alta-Drive Information. https://www.zillow.com/homedetails/506-N-Alta-Dr-Beverly-Hills-CA-90210/20519217_zpid.

Babes in Toyland at St. Raphael. https://www.encyclopedia.com/humanities/encyclopedias-almanacs-transcripts-and-maps/kelly-eugene-curran-gene.

Blair, Betsy. "I Married a Dynamo," 1949. https://web.archive.org/web/20171002184927/https://www.freewebs.com/geneius/somebodyrootingforyou.htm.

Cab Calloway at the Sunset. http://www.thehidehoblog.com/blog/2017/08/august-12-1931-cab-calloway-at-the-sunset-altoona-pn.

Cadman, Sue. "Gene Kelly, Creative Genius." https://web.archive.org/web/20171002184243/http://www.freewebs.com/geneius/apps/faq/.

Callahan, Dan. "Gene Kelly Retro at Film Society." http://altscreen.com/07/13/2012/gene-kelly-at-film-society-thru-jul-26.

Coyne, Jeanne. "I Knew Him When," *Movieland*, November 1948. https://web.archive.org/web/20171002184927/http://www.freewebs.com/geneius/somebodyrootingforyou.htm.

Elstree and Borehamwood Official Guide. www.localauthoritypublishing.co.uk.

Excerpts, Gene Kelly to Department of Naval Intelligence, March 27, 1954. https://web.archive.org/web/20171002184954/http://www.freewebs.com/geneius/gooutandhavefun.htm.

Frank Phillips interview, Roy H. Wagner Facebook page. https://www.facebook.com/RoyHWagnerASC.

Franko, John. "St. Raphael School Alumni Look Back Fondly," October 23, 2015. http://www.pittsburghcatholic.org/News/St--Raphael-School-alumni-look-back-fondly-.

"Gene Kelly and the Jewish Community: 1931–1938." http://www.jewishfamilieshistory.org/exhibit/6398.

Gloria Elbling Gottlieb oral history interview in National Council of Jewish Women, Pittsburgh Section. http://www.jewishfamilieshistory.org/exhibit/6398.

Harriet Kelly Burial. https://www.findagrave.com/memorial/125882821/harriet-catherine-kelly.

Helene Marlowe background. https://forums.delphiforums.com/genescene/messages/?msg=1906.1, posted on May 17, 2013.

Helene Marlowe obituary. http://www.lawrencefuneralhome.com/obituary/Helene-Marlowe-Hall/Darien-CT/1542453.

Idelson, Karen. Donald O'Connor interview. www.dvdfile.com/news/special_report/ten_questions/oconnor_donald/singinintherain.

"Isobel Lennart Brilliantly Word-Paints the Real Gene Kelly," *Screen Stars*, February 1946. https://web.archive.org/web/20171002184625/http://www.freewebs.com/geneius/ohiknowyou.htm.

James Kelly Burial. https://www.findagrave.com/memorial/125882787/james-patrick_joseph-kelly.

James River Film Journal. https://jamesriverfilm.wordpress.com/2011/01/21.

J. B. Matthews. www.libraries.rutgers.edu/rul/libs/scua/consumers_research.

Johnstown Junior Chamber of Commerce Award, March 22, 1946. https://web.archive.org/web/20171002184906/http://www.freewebs.com/geneius/nocontest.htm.

Kelly and Marlowe dating. https://forums.delphiforums.com/genescene/messages/?msg=1906.1, posted on July 25, 2011.

Kelly interview, *Woman's Weekly*, 1976. https://web.archive.org/web/20190202060300/https://www.freewebs.com/geneius/. (This is the homepage; the specific webpage was not archived.)

Kelly meets Marlowe. http://www.jewishfamilieshistory.org/exhibit/6398.

Kelly to Tony Thomas, March 15, 1973. https://web.archive.org/web/20190202060300/https://www.freewebs.com/geneius/. (This is the homepage; the specific webpage was not archived.)

Marc. "Masculinity, Credibility, and Gene Kelly: A Scotsman's Quandary," August 12, 2011. https://medium.com/the-outtake/masculinity-credibility-and-gene-kelly-a-scotsman-s-quandary-61610d164985.

Maynard, John. "This Is About Gene Kelly, and That's All It's About," 1945, https://web.archive.org/web/20171002184600/http://www.freewebs.com/geneius/thelifetimesof.htm.

Michael Scanlon interview, *Irish America*, 1990. https:// web.archive.org/web/20190202060300/https://www.freewebs.com/geneius/. (This is the homepage; the specific webpage was not archived.)

Modern Screen, June 1943. https://web.archive.org/web/20171002184600/http://www.freewebs.com/geneius/thelifetimesof.htm.

Motion Picture, 1954. https://web.archive.org/web/20171002184906/http://www.freewebs.com/geneius/nocontest.htm.

Movieland, June 1947. Gene Kelly interview in untitled article, no author, [https://web.archive.org/web/20190202060300/https://www.freewebs.com/geneius/. (This is the homepage; the specific webpage was not archived.)

Nova, July 1972. https://web.archive.org/web/20190202060300/https://www.freewebs.com/geneius/. (This is the homepage; the specific webpage was not archived.)

Pas de Dieux. https://mainstreamspanking.wordpress.com/2015/05/04/pas-de-dieux.

People, 1974. https://web.archive.org/web/20190202060300/https://www.freewebs.com/geneius/. (This is the homepage; the specific webpage was not archived.)

Peters, Susan. "Tim Kelly Doesn't Have Gene's Magic Feet, but He Made Enough on an L.A. Dance Club to Become an American in Paris." https://people.com/archive/tim-kelly-doesnt-have-genes-magic-feet-but-he-made-enough-on-an-1-a-dance-club-to-become-an-american-in-paris-vol-21-no-24.

Pittsburgh Music History. https://sites.google.com/site/pittsburghmusichistory/pittsburgh-music-story/pop/gene-kelly.

PublicAffairs Books. www.publicaffairsbooks.com/uk/lif-seem.html.

Richard Dwenger background. https://web.archive.org/web/20171002184635/http://www.freewebs.com/geneius/duringthewar.htm.

Richard Dwenger information. www.maritimequest.com/warship_directory/us_navy_pages/destroyers/alpha_pages/b/buck_dd420_roll_c.

Robert Trachtenberg interview. www.pbs.org/wnet/americanmasters/database/kelly-g-interview.html.

Rogers St. Johns, Adela. Untitled article with Gene Kelly interview, in *Photoplay*, January 1947, [https://web.archive.org/web/20190202060300/https://www.freewebs.com/geneius/]. (This is the homepage; the specific webpage was not archived.)

The Royal Roost, Information. [https://web.archive.org/web/20171002184635/http://www.freewebs.com/geneius/duringthewar.htm].

The Royal Roost, New Yorker. archives.newyorker.com/default.aspx?iid=17612&startpage=page0000003.

The Spokesman Review, June 7, 1975. [https://web.archive.org/web/20190202060300/https://www.freewebs.com/geneius]. (This is the homepage; the specific webpage was not archived.)

Two Weeks with Pay. www.alhirschfeldfoundation.org/piece/two-weeks-pay.

Articles, Books, and Dissertations

"$1,000-a-Plate Buffet Assists State's Democrats." *New York Times*, December 15, 1965.

"Actors Elect Reagan." *New York Times*, November 18, 1947.

"Actors to Discuss Citizenship." *New York Times*, January 5, 1946.

Adams, Val. "N.B.C. to Present Baseball Salute." *New York Times*, March 12, 1957.

Adler, Bill. *Fred Astaire: A Wonderful Life*. New York: Carroll and Graf, 1987.

Adler, Renata. "Screen: Offbeat, Dreamlike Musical: Demy's 'Young Girls of Rochefort' Bows." *New York Times*, April 12, 1968.

Agee, James. *Agee on Film: Reviews and Comments by James Agee*. New York: McDowell, Obolensky, 1958.

Alpert, Don. "Gene Kelly: Guy without a Trade." *Los Angeles Times*, September 13, 1964.

Alpert, Hollis. "Old Friends in New Jobs." *Dance Magazine* 32, no. 12 (December 1958): 52–55.

Altman, Rick. *The American Film Musical*. Bloomington: Indiana University Press, 1987.

Anderson, George. "Life after Musicals." *Pittsburgh Post-Gazette*, January 24, 1985.

Anderson, Jack. "Innovative Dance Detail in a Gene Kelly Movie." *New York Times*, May 21, 1987.

Anderson, Lindsay. "Minnelli, Kelly and An American in Paris." *Sequence*. Issue 14 (1952): 36–38.

Archer, Eugene. "Focus on 'Gigot,' An Expensive 'Leg of Lamb.'" *New York Times*, July 2, 1961.

———. "Museum to Show Gene Kelly Films." *New York Times*, August 10, 1962.

Aronson, Michael. *Nickelodeon City: Pittsburgh at the Movies, 1905–1929*. Pittsburgh: University of Pittsburgh Press, 2008.

Astaire, Fred. *Steps in Time*. New York: Harper and Brothers, 1959.

Atkins, David. "Thank You Mr. Kelly." *Dance Australia*, no. 83 (April–May 1996): 34–35.

Atkinson, Brooks. "Christmas Night Adds 'Pal Joey' to the Musical Stage." *New York Times*, December 26, 1940.

———. "Flower Song: Rodgers and Hammerstein Portray Chinese Traditions in America." *New York Times*, December 7, 1958.

———. "The Play: George Abbott Opens the Musical Comedy Season with a Prep School Scuffle, 'Best Foot Forward.'" *New York Times*, October 2, 1941.

Bacon, James. *How Sweet It Is: The Jackie Gleason Story*. New York: St. Martin's, 1985.

Baer, William. "*Singin' in the Rain*: A Conversation with Betty Comden and Adolph Green." *Michigan Quarterly Review* 41, issue 1 (Winter 2002): 1–20.

"Ballet By Kelly Cheered in Paris." *New York Times*, July 7, 1960.
Barnes, Clive. "Gene Kelly & Co." *Dance Magazine* 70, no. 4 (April 1996): 126.
———. "Movies Revisited: 'Invitation to Dance.'" *New York Times*, July 29, 1977.
Barrett, Edward L. Jr. *The Tenney Committee: Legislative Investigation of Subversive Activities in California*. Ithaca, NY: Cornell University Press, 1951.
Barrett, John Townsend. "A Descriptive Study of Selected Uses of Dance on Television: 1948–1958." PhD diss., University of Michigan, 1968.
Barzel, Ann. "Dancing Is a Man's Game." *Dance Magazine* 33, no. 2 (February 1959): 30–33.
Basinger, Jeanine. *Gene Kelly*. New York: Pyramid, 1976.
———. "Gene Kelly: Who Could Ask for Anything More?" *American Film* 10, no. 5. (March 1985): 20–23.
Beale, Betty. "After Midnight—The 'Party' Really Rocked." *Tampa Bay Times*, January 27, 1963.
Behlmer, Rudy. "Gene Kelly Is One Dancer Who Can Also Act and Direct." *Films in Review* 15, no. 1 (January 1964): 6–22.
Benjamin, George. "Kelly Is the Name!" *Modern Screen* (August 1943): 40–41, 119–125.
Berg, Louis. "Gene Kelly's Six-Way Stretch." *New York Herald Tribune*, March 22, 1953.
Billingsley, Kenneth Lloyd. *Hollywood Party: How Communism Seduced the American Film Industry in the 1930s and 1940s*. Rocklin, CA: Prima, 1998.
Billman, Larry. *Film Choreographers and Dance Directors: An Illustrated Biographical Encyclopedia, With a History and Filmographies, 1893 through 1995*. Jefferson, NC: McFarland, 1997.
———. *Fred Astaire: A Bio-Bibliography*. Westport, CT: Greenwood Press, 1997.
Blair, Betsy. *The Memory of All That: Love and Politics in New York, Hollywood, and Paris*. New York: Alfred A. Knopf, 2003.
Blank, Edward L. "Gene Kelly: Hometown Hoofer Hosting 'The Funny Side.'" *Pittsburgh Press*, October 26, 1971.
———. "Gene Kelly: Old Pro Is Still Dancing His Way Into Our Hearts." *Pittsburgh Press*, September 28, 1980.
Bodnar, John, Roger Simon, and Michael P. Weber. *Lives of Their Own: Blacks, Italians, and Poles in Pittsburgh, 1900–1960*. Urbana: University of Illinois Press, 1982.
Boorman, John, and Walter Donohue, eds. *Projections 4: Film-Makers on Film-Making*. London: Faber and Faber, 1995.
"Born to Dance." *Pitt Magazine* (March 15, 1994): 28–29.
Brady, Thomas F. "Astaire to Return to Acting in Films." *New York Times*, October 16, 1947.
———. "Danny Kaye Signs for Role at Metro." *New York Times*, January 18, 1951.
———. "Sequel on Jolson Planned by Metro." *New York Times*, December 12, 1947.
"Branches Are Heart of Its Battle Against Jim Crow." *Ebony* 1, no. 9 (August 1946): 37.
Braudy, Leo. *The World in a Frame: What We See in Films*. Garden City, NY: Anchor Press/Doubleday, 1976.
Brideson, Cynthia, and Sara Brideson. *He's Got Rhythm: The Life and Career of Gene Kelly*. Lexington: University Press of Kentucky, 2017.
Brinkley, Joyce. "On a Culture Safari." *New York Times*, January 26, 1964.

Britton, Andrew, ed. *Talking Films: The Best of* The Guardian *Film Lectures*. London: Fourth Estate, 1991.

"Broadcast Attacks Inquiry." *New York Times*, November 3, 1947.

"Broadway Stars Taken Ill," *Los Angeles Times*, January 18, 1941.

Brooks, Tim, and Earle Marsh. *The Complete Directory to Prime Time Network and Cable TV Shows, 1946–Present.* 6th ed. New York: Ballantine Books, 1995.

"Brotherhood Week Backed by Truman." *New York Times*, February 18, 1947.

Brown, John Mason. "'Pal Joey' Presented at the Ethel Barrymore." *New York Post*, December 26, 1940.

Buchwald, Art. "First Jazz Ballet Pas de Gene Kelly." *New York Herald Tribune*, June 19, 1960.

Buckley, Tom. "At the Movies: Gene Kelly Taps Again in 'Xanadu.'" *New York Times*, November 16, 1979.

Burrows, Michael. *Gene Kelly—Versatility Personified*. N.p.: Primestyle, 1972.

Burt, Ramsay. *The Male Dancer: Bodies, Spectacle, Sexualities*. London: Routledge, 1995.

Cameron, Kate. "A Lively Musial on Loew's State Screen." *New York Daily News*, March 10, 1949.

Canby, Vincent. "'Entertainment'—An Eloquent Salute to Show Business." *New York Times*, May 30, 1976.

———. "A Joyously Indestructible Movie Returns." *New York Times*, May 4, 1975.

———. "Liv Ullmann Portrays Heroine in '40 Carats.'" *New York Times*, June 29, 1973.

———. "Magical Sequel to 'That's Entertainment.'" *New York Times*, May 17, 1976.

———. "On Screen, Barbra Streisand Displays a Detached Cool." *New York Times*, December 18, 1969.

Canfield, Alyce. "Things I Wish I Knew 10 Years Ago." *Motion Picture Magazine* (January 1945): 6–7.

Carlson, Peter. *K Blows Top: A Cold War Comic Interlude Starring Nikita Khrushchev, America's Most Unlikely Tourist*. New York: PublicAffairs, 2009.

Caron, Leslie. *Thank Heaven: A Memoir*. New York: Viking, 2009.

Carroll, Harrison. "Gene Kelly's Roller-Skate Dance is 'Always Fair Weather' Standout." *Los Angeles Herald and Express*, September 1, 1955.

Casper, Joseph Andrew. *Stanley Donen*. Metuchen, NJ: Scarecrow Press, 1983.

Caute, David. *The Great Fear: The Anti-Communist Purge under Truman and Eisenhower*. New York: Simon and Schuster, 1978.

Ceplair, Larry, and Steven Englund. *The Inquisition in Hollywood: Politics in the Film Community, 1930–1960*. Garden City, NY: Doubleday, 1980.

Cerio, Gregory, Anthony Duinan-Cabrera, Danielle Morton, Lynda Wright, and Tom Cunneff. "No False Moves." *People Weekly* 45, no. 7 (February 19, 1996): 36.

Chaplin, Saul. *The Golden Age of Movie Musicals and Me*. Norman: University of Oklahoma Press, 1994.

Charness, Casey. "Hollywood Cine-Dance: A Description of the Interrelationship of Camerawork and Choreography in Films by Stanley Donen and Gene Kelly." PhD diss., New York University, 1977.

"Chorines Train Pitt Cap-and-Gowner," *Pittsburgh Post-Gazette*, March 16, 1937, 4.
Clark, James. "Giving Life an Up-Beat." *Films and Filming* 4 (July 1958): 7, 32.
Clarke, Gerald. *Get Happy: The Life of Judy Garland*. New York: Random House, 2000.
Clotfelter, Charles L. "Patterns of Enrollment and Completion." In *Economic Challenges in Higher Education*, edited by Charles L. Clotfelter, Ronald G. Ehrenberg, Malcolm Getz, and John J. Siegfried, 28–58. Chicago: University of Chicago Press, 1991.
Cogley, John. *Report on Blacklisting: Vol. 1, Movies*. N.p.: Fund for the Republic, 1956.
Cohan, Steven. "'Feminizing' the Song-and-Dance Man: Fred Astaire and the Spectacle of Masculinity in the Hollywood Musical." In *Screening the Male: Exploring Masculinities in Hollywood Cinema*, edited by Steven Cohan and Ian Rae Hark, 46–69. London: Routledge, 1993.
Comden, Betty, and Adolph Green. *The New York Musicals of Comden & Green*. New York: Applause, 1997.
Conner, Lynne. *Pittsburgh in Stages: Two Hundred Years of Theater*. Pittsburgh: University of Pittsburgh Press, 2007.
Considine, Shaun. *Mad as Hell: The Life and Work of Paddy Chayefsky*. New York: Random House, 1994.
Cook, Alton. "Gene Kelly Can't Anchor Dancing Feet with Sinatra." *New York World Telegram*, July 19, 1945.
Cook, Pam. "British Cinema: Auteur and Studio." In *The Cinema Book*, edited by Pam Cook, 438–445. 3rd ed. London: British Film Institute, 2007.
"Coppola Musicals: Gene Kelly as the Arthur Freed of the '80s." *Variety*, October 1, 1980.
Corry, John. "Gene Kelly Puts Strut in 'Satchmo.'" *New York Times*, August 24, 1981.
Crawford, Michael. *Parcel Arrived Safely, Tied With String: My Autobiography*. London: Century, 1999.
Crowther, Bosley. "An 'A' for Effort." *New York Times*, May 27, 1956.
———. "'Black Hand,' with Gene Kelly and J. Carrol Naish in Main Roles, Opens at Capitol." *New York Times*, March 13, 1950.
———. "'For Me and My Gal,' a Musical Moving Picture Concerned with Vaudeville, Makes Its Appearance at the Astor." *New York Times*, October 22, 1942.
———. "Intellect in Films." *New York Times*, October 16, 1960.
———. "Screen: Gleason's 'Gigot.'" *New York Times*, September 28, 1962.
———. "Screen: 'Guide for the Married Man.'" *New York Times*, May 27, 1967.
———. "Screen: Triumphant Version of 'Inherit the Wind.'" *New York Times*, October 13, 1960.
———. "Screen: 'Tunnel of Love.'" *New York Times*, November 22, 1958.
———. "Screen: Twinkle-Toes." *New York Times*, May 23, 1956.
———. "The Screen: 'Happy Road' Arrives." *New York Times*, June 21, 1957.
———. "The Screen: 'Les Girls.'" *New York Times*, October 4, 1957.
———. "The Screen in Review: 'Brigadoon.'" *New York Times*, September 17, 1954.
Cutts, John. "Kelly: Dancer, Actor, Director." Pt. 1. *Films and Filming* 10, no. 11 (August 1964): 38–42.
Dale, R. C. "René Clair in Hollywood: An Interview." *Film Quarterly* 24, no. 2 (Winter 1970–1971): 34–40.

"Dancing in the Dark." *Dance Magazine* 39, no. 12 (December 1965): 103–107.

"Dancing in Rodgers & Hart Show Big Break for Kelly." *Pittsburgh Press*, December 16, 1948.

Dancy, Tom. "At Home Abroad." *Modern Screen* (July 1953): 48-49, 94–95.

D'Antonio, Joanne. *Andrew Marton: A Directors Guild of America Oral History*. Metuchen, NJ: Scarecrow Press, 1991.

David, Martin A. "'That's Dancing!' That's Gene Kelly." *Dance Teacher Now* 7, no. 1 (January–February 1985): 30–34.

Davidson, Jim. "Gene Kelly Dances at Downtown Rally." *Pittsburgh Press*, June 27, 1981.

Delamater, Jerome. *Dance in the Hollywood Musical*. Ann Arbor: UMI Research Press, 1981.

de Mille, Agnes. "Dance: 'We Deserve a Fair Showing.'" *New York Times*, September 23, 1962.

Deren, Maya. "Choreography for the Camera." In *Essential Deren: Collected Writings on Film by Maya Deren*, edited by Bruce R. McPherson, 220–224. Kingston, NY: Documentext, 2005.

"Dialogue on Film." *American Film* 4, no. 4 (February 1979): 33–44.

"Dinner Set by Hadassah." *Los Angeles Times*, February 24, 1948.

Dixon, Wheeler Winston. "An Interview with Wendy Toye." In *Re-viewing British Cinema, 1900–1992: Essays and Interviews*, edited by Wheeler Winston Dixon, 133–142. Albany: State University of New York Press, 1994.

Dmytryk, Edward. *Odd Man Out: A Memoir of the Hollywood Ten*. Carbondale: Southern Illinois University Press, 1996.

Drysdale, Bill. "Soundmatters." *Dancing Times* (November 2001): 63, 65, 67.

Duffus, R. L. "Is Pittsburgh Civilized?" *Harper's Magazine* (October 1930): 537–545.

Dzhermolinska, Helen. "Yr. Pal Joey." *American Dancer* 14, no. 6 (April 1941): 12–13, 26.

Edelman, Rob, and Audrey Kupferberg. *Matthau: A Life*. Lanham, MD: Taylor Trade, 2002.

Epstein, Joseph. *Fred Astaire*. New Haven, CT: Yale University Press, 2008.

Faires, Nora. "Immigrants and Industry: Peopling the 'Iron City.'" In *City at the Point: Essays on the Social History of Pittsburgh*, edited by Samuel P. Hays, 3–31. Pittsburgh: University of Pittsburgh Press, 1989.

Fantle, David, and Tom Johnson. *Reel to Real: 25 Years of Celebrity Interviews from Vaudeville to Movies to TV.* Oregon, WI: Badger Books/Waubesa Press, 2004.

Fehr, Richard, and Frederick G. Vogel. *Lullabies of Hollywood: Movie Music and the Movie Musical, 1915–1992*. Jefferson, NC: McFarland, 1993.

Feuer, Cy. *I Got the Show Right Here: The Amazing, True Story of How an Obscure Brooklyn Horn Player Became the Last Great Broadway Showman*. New York: Simon and Schuster, 2003.

Feuer, Jane. *The Hollywood Musical*. Bloomington: Indiana University Press, 1982.

"Film to Aid Brotherhood Drive." *New York Times*, February 3, 1947.

Finnigan, Joe. "Gene Kelly Calls Russ Dancing 'Behind Times.'" *Indianapolis Star*, October 14, 1959.

Flatow, Sheryl. "Through a Lens Brightly." *Ballet News* 6, no. 10 (April 1985): 11–15, 38.

Flynn, George Q. *The Mess in Washington: Manpower Mobilization in World War II*. Westport, CT: Greenwood Press, 1979.

Flynn, Hazel. “Disappointing ‘Invitation’!” Beverly Hills *Citizen*, April 19, 1957.
Fordin, Hugh. *M-G-M's Greatest Musicals: The Arthur Freed Unit*. New York: Da Capo, 1996.
Fourth Report of the Senate Fact-Finding Committee on Un-American Activities, 1948: Communist Front Organizations. Sacramento: California Legislature, 1948.
Frank, Michael. “Gene Kelly: Star of *An American in Paris* on Alta Drive.” *Architectural Digest* 49, no. 4 (April 1992): 188–189, 274.
Frank, Rusty E., ed. *Tap! The Greatest Tap Dance Stars and Their Stories, 1900–1955*. New York: William Morrow, 1990.
Franks, A. H. Ed. *Girl's Book of Ballet*. London: Burke, 1953.
Fricke, John. *Judy Garland: A Portrait in Art & Anecdote*. Boston: Bulfinch Press, 2003.
Fryxell, David A. “The Dossier on Pitt's Most Famous Graduate, Eugene E. Kelly, Class of ’33.” *Pitt Magazine* (March 1987): 18.
Fuller, Graham. “And Now, the Real Kicker: Gene Kelly.” *Interview* 24, no. 5 (May 1994): 110–113.
Gard, Michael. *Men Who Dance: Aesthetics, Athletics & the Art of Masculinity*. New York: Peter Lang, 2008.
Garebian, Keith. *The Making of* Cabaret. 2nd ed. New York: Oxford University Press, 2011.
Garrett, Betty, with Ron Rapoport. *Betty Garrett and Other Songs: A Life on Stage and Screen*. Lanham, MD: Madison Books, 2000.
Garrison, Maxine. “Kelly's From Pittsburgh and He Is Almighty Proud of the Fact,” *Pittsburgh Press*, October 30, 1944.
“Gene Kelly Awarded Degree.” *New York Times*, October 5, 1961.
“Gene Kelly Days.” *Pittsburgh Press*. June 23, 1987.
“Gene Kelly Does a Job for Uncle Sam.” *Screenland*. September 1944: 20, 71–73.
“Gene Kelly Is Inducted.” *New York Times*, November 21, 1944.
“Gene Kelly Leaves Hospital.” *Los Angeles Times*, May 5, 1979.
“Gene Kelly Makes It Clear He's a Serious Young Fellow.” *Brooklyn Daily Eagle*, May 5, 1946.
“Gene Kelly on TV.” *Dance and Dancers* (March 1959): 33.
“Gene Kelly Saved by Son As Fire Destroys His Home.” *San Gabriel Valley Tribune*, December 23, 1983.
“Gene Kelly's Invitation to the Dance.” *Look* 17 (March 24, 1953): 88, 90–94.
“Gene Kelly to Tour Africa under Cultural Exchange.” *New York Times*, December 21, 1963.
Genné, Beth. “Dance in Film.” In *The Living Dance: An Anthology of Essays on Movement and Culture*, edited by Judith Chazin-Bennahum, 192–206. Dubuque, IA: Kendall/Hunt, 2003.
———. *Dance Me a Song: Astaire, Balanchine, Kelly, and the American Film Musical*. New York: Oxford University Press, 2018.
———. “Dancin' in the Rain: Gene Kelly's Musical Films.” In *Envisioning Dance on Film and Video*, edited by Judy Mitoma, 71–77. New York: Routledge, 2002.
———. “‘Dancin' in the Street’: Street Dancing on Film and Video from Fred Astaire to Michael Jackson.” In *Rethinking Dance History: A Reader*, edited by Alexandra Carter, 132–142. London: Routledge, 2004.

———. "The Film Musicals of Vincente Minnelli and the Team of Gene Kelly and Stanley Donen: 1944–1958." PhD diss., University of Michigan, 1984.

———. "'Freedom Incarnate': Jerome Robbins, Gene Kelly, and the Dancing Sailor as an Icon of American Values in World War II." *Dance Chronicle* 24, no. 1 (2001): 83–103.

———. "Vincente Minnelli and the Film Ballet." In *Vincente Minnelli: The Art of Entertainment*, edited by Joe McElhaney, 229–251. Detroit: Wayne State University Press, 2009.

Gerstner, David Anthony. "Dancer from the Dance: Gene Kelly, Television, and the Beauty of Movement." *Velvet Light Trap*, no. 49 (Spring 2002): 48–66.

Gilks, Alfred. "Some Highlights in the Filming of 'An American in Paris.'" *American Cinematographer* 33 (January 1952): 18–19, 36–39.

"Gives Advice on Ballot." *New York Times*, October 14, 1944.

Goodman, Jordan. *Paul Robeson: A Watched Man*. London: Verso, 2013.

Goodwin, Michael, and Naomi Wise. *On the Edge: The Life and Times of Francis Coppola*. New York: William Morrow, 1989.

Gould, Jack. "TV: A Fetching Special." *New York Times*, November 29, 1965.

———. "TV: Tepid Melodic Tour." *New York Times*, February 15, 1966.

Granger, Farley. *Include Me Out: My Life from Goldwyn to Broadway*. New York: St. Martin's Press, 2007.

Green, Stanley, and Burt Goldblatt. *Starring Fred Astaire*. New York: Doubleday, 1977.

Gregory, James, and Edward Sigall. "Hollywood's Newest Romance: Gene Kelly & Columnist Joyce Haber." *National Enquirer*, May 6, 1975.

Griffith, Richard. *The Cinema of Gene Kelly*. New York: Museum of Modern Art, 1962.

Guernsey, Otis L. Jr. "On the Screen," *New York Herald-Tribune*, March 10, 1949.

Haines, Aubrey B. "Gene Kelly." *Dance Digest* 7, no. 7 (July 1957): 252–259.

Hale, Wanda. "Delightful Musical at Capitol Theatre." *Los Angeles Daily News*, July 20, 1945.

Halsey, Jan, and Tracy Record. "Gene Kelly on Campus." *Dance Teacher Now* 4, no. 6 (November–December 1982): 14–17.

Hanson, Curtis Lee. "An Interview with Gene Kelly." *Cinema* 3, no. 4 (December 1966): 24–29.

Harmetz, Aljean. "Film Institute Honors Gene Kelly." *New York Times*, March 9, 1985.

———. *On the Road to Tara: The Making of Gone With the Wind*. New York: Harry N. Abrams, 1996.

Harris, Sue. *An American in Paris*. London: Palgrave, 2015.

Harvey, Stephen. *Directed by Vincente Minnelli*. New York: Harper and Row, 1989.

———. "Stanley Donen." *Film Comment* 9, no. 4 (July–August 1973): 4–9.

Haver, Ron. "Kelly." *Film Comment* 20, no. 6 (December 1984): 56–59.

Haver, Ronald. "Pas de Deux with Saul Chaplin." *American Film* 10, no. 5. (March 1985): 23–26, 73.

Hay, Peter. *MGM: When the Lion Roars*. Atlanta: Turner Publishing, 1991.

Hearings Before the Committee on Un-American Activities, House of Representatives, Eighty-Third Congress, First Session, March 23, 24, and 25, 1953. Washington, DC: United States Government Printing Office, 1953.

Heineman, Kenneth J. "Catholics, Communists, and Conservatives: The Making of Cold War Democrats on the Pittsburgh Front." *US Catholic Historian* 34, no. 4 (Fall 2016): 25–54.

Hemming, Roy. *The Melody Lingers On: The Great Songwriters and Their Movie Musicals.* New York: Newmarket Press, 1986.

Henry, William A. III. *The Great One: The Life and Legend of Jackie Gleason.* New York: Doubleday, 1992.

Hess, Earl J., and Pratibha A. Dabholkar. *The Cinematic Voyage of The Pirate: Kelly, Garland, and Minnelli at Work.* Columbia: University of Missouri Press, 2014.

———. *Singin' in the Rain: The Making of an American Masterpiece.* Lawrence: University Press of Kansas, 2009.

Higham, Charles. *Merchant of Dreams: Louis B. Mayer, M.G.M., and the Secret Hollywood.* New York: Donald I. Fine, 1993.

Hill, Gladwin. "Stars Fly to Fight Inquiry into Films." *New York Times*, October 27, 1947.

Hillier, Jim. "Interview with Stanley Donen." *Movie* 24 (Spring 1977): 26–35.

Hirsch, Julia Antopol. *The Sound of Music: The Making of America's Favorite Movie.* Chicago: Contemporary Books, 1993.

Hirschhorn, Clive. *Gene Kelly: A Biography.* London: W. H. Allen, 1974; Chicago: Henry Regnery, 1975; New York: St. Martin's Press, 1984.

———. *The Hollywood Musical.* New York: Crown, 1981.

"Hollywood Dance Directors." *Dance Magazine* 21, no. 2 (February 1947): 9–15.

Honeycutt, Kirk. "Gene Kelly: Dancing on Film and Strolling Down Memory Lane." *New York Times*, June 1, 1980.

Hoover, Bob. "Betsy Blair Recalls Her Hollywood Days with Gene Kelly." *Pittsburgh Post-Gazette*, April 26, 2003.

Hopper, Hedda. "Gene Kelly, Assistant Married in Nevada." *Los Angeles Times*, August 7, 1960.

———. "Gene Kelly Envisions 'Fancy Dancer' Self." *Los Angeles Times*, October 4, 1957.

———. "Gene Kelly Would Rather Teach." *Los Angeles Times*, July 25, 1954.

———. "Just Plain Kelly." *Chicago Daily Tribune*, October 9, 1949.

———. "Kelly to Star with Gina Lollabrigida." *Los Angeles Times*, May 17, 1958.

———. "Looking at Hollywood." *Los Angeles Times*, April 3, 1948.

Horne, Lena, and Richard Schickel. *Lena.* Garden City, NY: Doubleday, 1965.

Houlihan, Marc Edmund. "An Analysis of Three Examples of the Technicolor Musicals." MA thesis, University of California, Los Angeles, 1953.

Hover, Helen. "Popping Questions at Gene Kelly." *Motion Picture* 68, no. 3 (October 1944): 40–41, 91–94.

Hudgins, Morgan. "Directed by Kelly." *New York Times*, August 14, 1949.

Hungerford, Mary Jane. "Dancing in Commercial Motion Pictures." PhD diss., Columbia University, 1946.

Hyams, Joe. "The Do-It-Yourself Director." *Los Angeles Times*, September 7, 1958.

———. "Gene Kelly: All the World Loves to Dance." *Cue*, May 7, 1953.

"'Invitation to the Dance' Wins at Berlin Film Fete." *New York Times*, July 4, 1956.

Isaacs, Hermine Rich. "Gene Kelly: Portrait of a Dancing Actor." *Theatre Arts* 30, no. 3 (March 1946): 149–156.

"It's Not Hard to Believe in Magic of Fantasy 'Xanadu.'" *Pittsburgh Press*, August 14, 1980.

James, Noah. "Making Sure the Seams Don't Show." *New York Times*, November 3, 1985.

"Jet Averts Crash in Trip From Paris." *New York Times*, February 4, 1959.

Jewell, Derek. *Frank Sinatra: A Celebration*. London: Pavilion Books, 1999.

Justice, William E., ed. *He Flies Through the Air with the Greatest of Ease: A William Saroyan Reader*. Berkeley: Heyday Books, 2008.

Kael, Pauline. *5001 Nights at the Movies: A Guide from A to Z*. New York: Holt, Rinehart, and Winston, 1982.

Kahn, Gordon. *Hollywood on Trial: The Story of the 10 Who Were Indicted*. New York: Boni and Gaer, 1948.

Kander, John, and Fred Ebb. *Colored Lights: Forty Years of Worlds and Music, Show Biz, Collaboration, and All That Jazz*. New York: Faber and Faber, 2003.

Keefe, Maura. "Is Dance a Man's Sport Too? The Performance of Athletic-coded Masculinity on the Concert Dance Stage." In *When Men Dance: Choreographing Masculinities across Borders*, edited by Jennifer Fisher and Anthony Shay, 91–106. New York: Oxford University Press, 2009.

Kelly, Gene. "Cine-Dance?" *Eleventh Annual San Francisco International Film Festival Magazine, October 20–29, 1966*: 38.

———. "Directing Dolly." *Action* 4 (March–April, 1969): 8–10.

———. Letter to Editor. *American Film* 7 (January 1982): 6.

———. "Making a *Cine*ballet for 'American in Paris.'" *Dance Magazine* 25, no. 8 (August 1951): 9, 24–25.

———. "Musical Comedy Is Serious Business." *Theatre Arts* 42, no. 12 (December 1958): 18–19, 71–72.

———. "Some Notes for Young Dancers." *Dance Magazine* 39, no. 9 (September 1965): 49.

———. "The Women in My Dancing Life." *National Women's Weekly*, July 17, 1952.

Kelly, Gillian. "Gene Kelly: The Performing Auteur—Manifestations of the Kelly Persona." *eSharp* (2010): 136–156.

"Kelly to Produce World War I Film." *New York Times*, June 17, 1965.

Kennedy, Matthew. *Roadshow! The Fall of Film Musicals in the 1960s*. New York: Oxford University Press, 2014.

"Kenneth L. Muse Dies at 75: Animator for Major Studios." *New York Times*, July 30, 1987.

Kernan, Michael. "Grandpop Gene Kelly Still Active as He Nears Age 70." *Washington Post*, April 18, 1982.

Kerr, Walter. "'Flower Drum Song.'" *New York Herald Tribune*, December 2, 1958.

Kilday, Gregg. "Toeing the Lion: Gene Kelly of 'That's Entertainment! III.'" *Entertainment Weekly*, no. 222 (May 13, 1994): 41.

Kisselgoff, Anna. "The Ballerina in Leslie Caron, the Actress." *New York Times*, March 12, 1995.

———. "Gene Kelly: Ballet Influenced His View of Dance." *New York Times*, January 17, 1985.

———. "Just a Regular Joe Doing Ballet." *New York Times*, February 11, 1996.

Knowles, Mark. *The Man Who Made the Jailhouse Rock: Alex Romero, Hollywood Choreographer*. Jefferson, NC: McFarland, 2013.

Knox, Donald, ed. *The Magic Factory: How MGM Made An American in Paris*. New York: Praeger, 1973.

Kobal, John. *Gotta Sing, Gotta Dance: A History of Movie Musicals*. London: Spring Books, 1983.

———. *People Will Talk*. New York: Alfred A. Knopf, 1985.

———. *Rita Hayworth: The Time, the Place, and the Woman*. New York; Norton, 1978.

Krebs, Albin. "Gene Kelly, Dancer of Vigor and Grace, Dies." *New York Times*, February 3, 1996.

———. "Young Dancer Named Reagan Shuns Spotlight." *New York Times*, June 27, 1980.

Kurtti, Jeff. *The Great Movie Musical Trivia Book*. New York: Applause Books, 1996.

Land, Jon. "Magic Doesn't Age." *Saturday Evening Post*, no. 252 (July–August 1980): 54–57, 128.

Laurents, Arthur. *Original Story By: A Memoir of Broadway and Hollywood*. New York: Alfred A. Knopf, 2000.

Lawrence, Edward. "Kelly Caught in the Draft." *New York Times*, December 17, 1944.

Lawson, Carol. "Lionizing M-G-M in Retrospect." *New York Times*, June 24, 1977.

Leff, Leonard J. *Hitchcock and Selznick: The Rich and Strange Collaboration of Alfred Hitchcock and David O. Selznick in Hollywood*. Berkeley: University of California Press, 1987.

Leggett, John. *A Daring Young Man: A Biography of William Saroyan*. New York: Alfred A. Knopf, 2002.

Leider, Emily W. *Myrna Loy: The Only Good Girl in Hollywood*. Berkeley: University of California Press, 2011.

Lerner, Alan Jay. *On the Street Where I Live*. New York: W. W. Norton, 1978.

Lester, Colleen. "What One Person Learned from Gene Kelly." *Christian Science Monitor*, March 29, 2007.

Levant, Oscar. *The Memoirs of an Amnesiac*. Hollywood, CA: Samuel French, 1989.

Levinson, Peter J. *Puttin' On the Ritz: Fred Astaire and the Fine Art of Panache*. New York: St. Martin's Press, 2009.

Lewin, David. "The Difference Between Astaire and Me." London *Daily Express*, March 26, 1952.

Lewis, Dan. "Gene Kelly to Bugaloo for Scene in 'Forty Carats.'" *Pittsburgh Press*, December 31, 1972.

Lewis, Mark B. "Gene Kelly, Ambassador." *Pittsburgh Post-Gazette*, February 11, 1996.

Lichtman, Irv. "Song-and-Dance Man Gene Kelly Dies." *Billboard* 108, no. 7 (February 17, 1996): 50.

Lichtman, Robert M. "Louis Budenz, the FBI, and the 'List of 400 Concealed Communists': An Extended Tale of McCarthy-Era Informing." *American Communist History* 3, no. 1 (2004): 25–54.

Lindsey, Robert. "Astaire and Kelly in Spotlight Again." *New York Times*, May 10, 1976.

Lockridge, Richard. "John O'Hara's 'Pal Joey' Is Offered at the Barrymore Theater." *New York Sun*, December 26, 1940.

Luft, Lorna. *Me and My Shadows: A Family Memoir*. New York: Simon and Schuster, 1998.

Malnic, Eric. "Gene Kelly Saved from House Fire." *Los Angeles Times*, December 23, 1983.

Maltin, Leonard. *Of Mice and Magic: A History of American Animated Cartoons*. New York: McGraw-Hill, 1980.

Mantle, Burns. "'Pal Joey' Smart and Novel." *New York Daily News*, December 26, 1940.

Mariani, John. "Come on with the Rain." *Film Comment* 14, no. 3 (May–June 1978): 7–12.

Martin, Hugh. *Hugh Martin: The Boy Next Door*. Encinitas, CA: Trolley Press, 2010.

Martin, John. *The Dance: The Story of the Dance Told in Pictures and Text*. New York: Tudor, 1946.

———. "The Dance: Debut." *New York Times*, April 25, 1954.

———. "The Dance: Pal Joey." *New York Times*, February 17, 1972.

———. "The Dance: Pal Kelly." *New York Times*, June 8, 1941.

Martin, Mary. *My Heart Belongs*. New York: William Morrow, 1976.

Martin, Tony, and Cyd Charisse. *The Two of Us*. New York: Mason-Charter, 1976.

Marx, Arthur. "The Man Who Lived Dancing." *Parade Magazine*, December 18, 1983.

Maslin, Janet. "Knievel Evel, One Dares Say." *New York Times*, July 28, 1977.

Mast, Gerald. *Can't Help Singin': The American Musical on Stage and Screen*. Woodstock, NY: Overlook Press, 1987.

Matthews, J. B. "Did the Movies Really Clean House?" *American Legion Magazine* (December 1951): 12–13, 49–52.

McBrien, William. *Cole Porter: A Biography*. New York: Alfred A. Knopf, 1998.

McClelland, Lois. "The Neighbors are Talking." *Motion Picture Magazine* (February 1950): 48, 73–75.

McGilligan, Patrick, and Paul Buhle, eds. *Tender Comrades: A Backstory of the Hollywood Blacklist*. New York: St. Martin's Press, 1997.

McHugh, Dominic, ed. *Alan Jay Lerner: A Lyricist's Letters*. New York: Oxford University Press, 2014.

McNeil, Alex. *Total Television: A Comprehensive Guide to Programming from 1948 to 1980*. New York: Penguin Books, 1980.

McPherson, Virginia. "Gene Kelly Dancing His Head Off." *Pittsburgh Post-Gazette*, November 9, 1944.

McVay, Douglas. "The Magic of Minnelli." *Films and Filming* 5 (June 1959): 11, 31, 34.

———. "Minnelli and the Pirate." *The Velvet Light Trap*, issue 18 (Spring 1978): 35–38.

Meroney, John. "Hollywood's Brewer," *National Review*, September 19, 2006.

Mershon, Sherie R., and Joel A. Tarr. "Strategies for Clean Air: The Pittsburgh and Allegheny County Smoke Control Movements, 1940–1960." In *Devastation and Renewal: An Environmental History of Pittsburgh and Its Region*, edited by Joel A. Tarr, 145–173. Pittsburgh: University of Pittsburgh Press, 2003.

Miller, Ann. *Miller's High Life*. Garden City, NY: Doubleday, 1972.

Mills, Hilary. *Mailer: A Biography*. New York: Harper and Row, 1982.

Minnelli, Vincente. *I Remember It Well*. New York: Samuel French, 1990.

Molotsky, Irvin. "Gene Kelly Brings Young Dancers to White House." *New York Times*, March 29, 1982.

———. "Kennedy Center Honors 5 in the Arts." *New York Times*, August 16, 1982.

Monahan, Kaspar. "Show Stops: Actors Denounce the 'Red' Probe." *Pittsburgh Press*, October 28, 1947.

Morella, Joe, and Edward Z. Epstein. *Judy: The Films and Career of Judy Garland*. New York: Citadel Press, 1969.

Moreno, Rita. *Rita Moreno: A Memoir*. New York: Penguin, 2013.

"More Tape Shows on 'Playhouse 90.'" *New York Times*, June 30, 1958.

Morley, Sheridan, and Ruth Leon. *Gene Kelly: A Celebration*. London: Pavilion Books, 1996.

Mueller, John. *Astaire Dancing: The Musical Films*. New York: Alfred A. Knopf, 1985.

Munn, Michael. *Jimmy Stewart: The Truth Behind the Legend*. Fort Lee, NJ: Barricade Books, 2006.

Murphy, George. *Say . . . Didn't You Used to Be George Murphy?* New York: Bartholomew House, 1970.

"The Museum of Modern Art Presents a Gene Kelly Dance Film Festival." *Dance Magazine* 36, no. 9 (September 1962): 36–37, 72.

Naremore, James. *The Films of Vincente Minnelli*. New York: Cambridge University Press, 1993.

Naylor, David. *Great American Movie Theaters*. Washington, DC: Preservation Press, 1987.

Newnham, John K. "Tilly Losch in Hollywood's Most Costly Film: Dance Film Notes." *The Dancing Times* 36 (December 1946): 134–135.

Newton, Douglas. "Poetry in Fast and Musical Motion." *Monthly Film Bulletin* 22, no. 1 (July–September 1952): 36–38.

Nolan, Patricia. "Sins." *Globe*, February 4, 1986.

"No One Believes Gene Kelly Was Her Dancing Mentor." *Trenton Sunday Times Advertiser*, June 17, 1979.

O'Connor, Jim. "Present 'Cover Girl' on Music Hall Screen." *New York Journal-American*, March 31, 1944.

O'Connor, John J. "Nice People on TV." *New York Times*, March 13, 1978.

O'Leary, Dorothy. "Always on His Toes!" *Silver Screen* 7, no. 6 (April 1947): 40, 78–80.

"On the Town: Projects Committee Introduces Its Landmark Series of Symposia." *Dramatist's Guild Quarterly* 18, no. 2 (Summer 1981): 11–24.

Othman, Frederick C. "Lucille Ball Discovers—12 Pounds of False Hair No Help While Dancing." *Tampa Bay Times*, October 20, 1942.

Pagán, Eduardo Obregón. *Murder at the Sleepy Lagoon: Zoot Suits, Race, and Riot in Wartime L.A.* Chapel Hill: University of North Carolina Press, 2003.

Pally, Marcia. "Dancing for Their Lives." *Film Comment* 20, no. 6 (December 1984): 51–55.

Parish, James Robert, and Ronald L. Bowers. *The MGM Stock Company: The Golden Era*. New Rochelle, NY: Arlington House, 1973.

Parsons, Louella. "Astaire to Replace Kelly in 'Parade.'" *New York Journal-American*, October 16, 1947.

Parton, James. "Pittsburgh." *Atlantic Monthly* 21, no. 123 (January 1868): 17–36.

Pasternak, Joe. *Easy the Hard Way*. New York: G. P. Putnam's, 1956.

Phillips, Brent. *Charles Walters: The Director Who Made Hollywood Dance*. Lexington: University Press of Kentucky, 2014.

Pickard, Roy. *Jimmy Stewart: A Life in Film*. New York: St. Martin's Press, 1993.

Pittman, Jack. "Kelly in London Tribute." *Variety*, June 4, 1980.

Pollock, Dale. "Gene Kelly at 72." *Tampa Bay Times*, August 4, 1984.
Portnoy, Ruth. To editor. *San Francisco Chronicle*, February 7, 1996.
"Premiere of Film Will Help Ballet." *New York Times*, May 11, 1956.
"President Hails 'Stream of Dimes.'" *New York Times*, January 31, 1945.
Pryor, Thomas M. "Gene Kelly Buys Novel for Screen." *New York Times*, September 12, 1957.
———. "Gene Kelly Ends One Metro Pact." *New York Times*, January 9, 1956.
———. "Gene Kelly Listed for Straight Role." *New York Times*, December 31, 1951.
———. "Gene Kelly Plans Own Metro Movie." *New York Times*, November 27, 1951.
———. "Gene Kelly Steps into Officer Role." *New York Times*, March 7, 1953.
———. "Hollywood Dossier: Ban on Foreign, Communist-Made Films Is Sought by Labor Group—Addenda.' *New York Times*, August 31, 1952.
———. "Metro Will Film Twain Book in '59." *New York Times*, October 28, 1958.
———. "Porter's Music in Metro Plans." *New York Times*, December 28, 1953.
———. "Uneasy Hollywood: Meeting of Labor Chiefs and Loew's Top Executive Disturbs Industry—Addenda." *New York Times*, June 22, 1952.
"Puddle Jumper." *People Weekly* 37, no. 23 (June 15, 1992): 86.
Rawson, Christopher. "Pittsburghers Remember a Life of Amazing Grace." *Pittsburgh Post Gazette*, February 3, 1996.
Ray, Satyajit. *Our Films Their Films*. New York: Hyperion, 1994.
Reed, Rex. "Gene Kelly's Musical Memories." *Chicago Tribune*, November 29, 1980.
Reich, Howard. "Hoofer of His Era, Kelly Really Wanted a Career in Ballet." *Pittsburgh Press*, August 21, 1983.
Remington, Fred. "Kelly Comes to TV." *Pittsburgh Press*, April 19, 1959.
———. "Two Decades of Stardom." *Pittsburgh Press*, December 9, 1962.
Rickey, Carrie. "A Dance Master Dies." *Pittsburgh Post-Gazette*, February 3, 1996.
Riese, Randall. *Her Name Is Barbra: An Intimate Portrait of the Real Barbra Streisand*. New York: Birch Lane Press, 1993.
Riesel, Victor. "Inside Labor." *New York Mirror*, April 6, 1953.
Ringel, Eleanor. "Gotta Dance: A Profile of Gene Kelly." *Atlanta Journal*, August 16, 1980.
Risner, Doug. "What We Know about Boys Who Dance: The Limitations of Contemporary Masculinity and Dance Education." In *When Men Dance: Choreographing Masculinities across Borders*, edited by Jennifer Fisher and Anthony Shay, 57–77. New York: Oxford University Press, 2009.
"Rival Screen Unions in Peace Move." *Los Angeles Times*, October 25, 1946.
Roberts, Chalmers M. "Class of '29." *Washington Post*, June 25, 1979.
———. *First Rough Draft: A Journalist's Journal of Our Times*. New York: Praeger, 1973.
Robeson, Paul Jr. *The Undiscovered Paul Robeson: Quest for Freedom, 1939–1976*. Hoboken, NJ: John Wiley and Sons, 2010.
Rodgers, Ann. "Louise, Last of Five Dancing Kellys, Dies." *Pittsburgh Post-Gazette*, February 24, 2008.
Rodgers, Richard. *Musical Stages: An Autobiography*. New York: Random House, 1975.
———. "'Pal Joey': History of a 'Heel.'" *New York Times*, December 30, 1951.
Rosenberg, Donald. "CLO's New Kellys to Honor Students." *Pittsburgh Press*, February 26, 1991.

———. "Woodland Hills' 'Guys and Dolls' Heads CLO's Gene Kelly Award List." *Pittsburgh Press*, May 20, 1991.

Sarris, Andrew. "Notes on the Auteur Theory in 1962." *Film Culture* 24 (Winter 1962): 1–8.

Schallert, Edwin. "In Movie Field, Gene Kelly Proves a Quintuple Threat." *Los Angeles Times*, October 7, 1951.

Schary, Dore. *Heyday: An Autobiography*. Boston: Little, Brown and Company, 1979.

Schatz, Thomas. *The Genius of the System*. New York: Henry Holt, 1996.

Scheurer, Philip K. "Gene Kelly's Real Life Symbolized by Dance." *Los Angeles Times*, April 23, 1944.

———. "Kelly's Luster as Dancer Undimmed by Absence," *Los Angeles Times*, March 30, 1947

Scheurer, Timothy E. "The Aesthetics of Form and Convention in the Movie Musical." *Journal of Popular Film* 3, no. 4 (Fall 1974): 307–324.

Schickel, Richard. *The Men Who Made the Movies: Interviews With Frank Capra, George Cukor, Howard Hawks, Alfred Hitchcock, Vincente Minnelli, King Vidor, Raoul Walsh, and William A. Wellman*. New York: Atheneum, 1975.

Schumach, Murray. "Democrats Lead G.O.P. in Filmland." *New York Times*, April 18, 1960.

———. "Hollywood Wary over Rally Issue." *New York Times*, April 12, 1962.

———. "'Thinking' Actors in Vogue on Coast." *New York Times*, May 5, 1960.

Schwartz, Charles. *Cole Porter: A Biography*. New York: Da Capo, 1992.

Schwartz, Vanessa R. *It's So French! Hollywood, Paris, and the Making of Cosmopolitan Film Culture*. Chicago: University of Chicago Press, 2007.

Scott, Vernon. "Pair of 'Entertainments' Renewing Kelly's Popularity." *Pittsburgh Press*, August 20, 1976.

Secrest, Meryle. *Somewhere for Me: A Biography of Richard Rodgers*. New York: Alfred A. Knopf, 2001.

Sennett, Ted. *The Art of Hanna-Barbera: Fifty Years of Creativity*. New York: Viking, 1989.

Sensenderfer, Robert. "Review of *Pal Joey*," *Philadelphia Evening Bulletin*, December 12, 1940.

Shanley, John P. "'Going My Way.'" *New York Times*, September 30, 1962.

Sharaff, Irene. *Broadway & Hollywood: Costumes Designed by Irene Sharaff*. New York: Van Nostrand Reinhold, 1976.

Shawn, Ted. *One Thousand and One Night Stands*. New York: Doubleday, 1960.

Sheaffer, Lew. "Star-Studded 'Words and Music.'" *Brooklyn Eagle*, December 10, 1948.

———. "State's Tuneful 'Ball Game,' 'Alias Nick Beal' Unusual Fare." *Brooklyn Eagle*, March 10, 1949.

Shepard, Richard F. "Yonkers of 1890 Abuilding in Garrison." *New York Times*, May 29, 1968.

Shipton, Alyn. *Hi-De-Ho: The Life of Cab Calloway*. New York: Oxford University Press, 2010.

Siegel, Joel. "The Pirate." *Film Heritage* 7, no. 1 (Fall 1971): 21–32.

Silverman, Stephen M. *Dancing on the Ceiling: Stanley Donen and His Movies*. New York: Alfred A. Knopf, 1996.

Silvers, Phil. *This Laugh Is On Me: The Phil Silvers Story*. New York: W. H. Allen, 1974.

Singer, Michael. *A Cut Above: 50 Film Directors Talk about Their Craft*. Los Angeles: Lone Eagle, 1998.

Somerset-Ward, Richard. *An American Theatre: The Story of Westport Country Playhouse, 1931–2005*. New Haven, CT: Yale University Press, 2005.

Soren, David, Meredith Banasiak, Bob Thomas, and Neill Johnston. *Vera-Ellen: The Magic and the Mystery*. Baltimore: Luminary Press, 2003.

Spada, James. *Streisand: Her Life*. New York: Crown, 1995.

Spivak, Jeffrey. *Buzz: The Life and Art of Busby Berkeley*. Lexington: University Press of Kentucky, 2011.

Springer, John. *They Sang! They Danced! They Romanced! A Pictorial History of the Movie Musical*. New York: Citadel Press, 1991.

Stern, Herb. "Screen." *Rob Wagner's Script*, April 15, 1955, 14.

Stieg, Bill. "Kelly Returns to Help CLO Frolic." *Pittsburgh Post Gazette*, June 27, 1981.

Stoop, Norma McLain. "Gene Kelly: An American Dance Innovator Tells it Like it Was—And Is." *Dance Magazine* 50, no. 7 (July 1976): 71–74.

———. "That's Entertainment, Part 2: A Look at an American Art Form—the Movie Musical." *Dance Magazine* 50, no. 7 (July 1976): 70–71.

Swanson, Pauline. "Dance!" *Motion Picture* (December 1953): 28–31, 64.

Sweeney, Louis. "Gene Kelly's Dancing, Directing Life Rolls on No Matter What the Weather." Palatine (Illinois) *Herald*. December 7, 1977.

Swisher, Viola Hegyi. "Gene and Jack and the Beanstalk." *Dance Magazine* 31, no. 2 (February 1967): 52–53.

———. "Xanadu." *Dance Magazine* 54, no. 8 (August 1980): 42–45.

Taubman, Howard. "Records: For the Children." *New York Times*, November 17, 1946.

Taylor, John Russel, and Arthur Jackson. *The Hollywood Musical*. New York: McGraw-Hill, 1971.

Tenney, Jack B. Comp. *Red Fascism*. New York: Arno Press, 1977.

Terry, Walter. "Kelly's Exhilarating Dance Tonic for April: 'Singin' in the Rain.'" *New York Herald Tribune*, April 13, 1952.

———. "Review of *Pal Joey*," *New York Herald Tribune*, March 23, 1941.

———. *Ted Shawn, Father of American Dance: A Biography*. New York: Dial Press, 1976.

Thomas, Bob. *Astaire: The Man, The Dancer*. New York: St. Martins, 1984.

———. "Kelly Finishing Dance Film with No Dialogue." Hollywood *Citizen-News*, December 25, 1953.

———. "Movie Musicals Should Be Revived, Says Gene Kelly." *Pittsburgh Post-Gazette*, December 12, 1975.

Thomas, Kevin. "Gene Kelly Remembers Golden Age of Musicals." *Pittsburgh Post-Gazette*, May 3, 1993.

Thomas, Tony. *The Films of Gene Kelly: Song and Dance Man*. Secaucus, NJ: Citadel Press, 1974.

Toker, Franklin. *Pittsburgh: An Urban Portrait*. University Park: Pennsylvania State University Press, 1986.

Turner, Wallace. "Movie Stars Take Old Political Roles." *New York Times*, July 26, 1970.

"TV Radio Mirror." *Pittsburgh Press*, December 9, 1962.
Updike, John. "Gotta Dance!" *The New Yorker* 70, no. 5 (March 21, 1994): 166–169.
Vacche, Angela Dalle. *Cinema and Painting: How Art Is Used in Film*. Austin: University of Texas Press, 1996.
Vaughan, David. "Dance in the Cinema." *Sequence* 6 (Winter 1948–1949): 6–13.
Vaughn, Stephen. *Ronald Reagan in Hollywood: Movies and Politics*. New York: Cambridge University Press, 1994.
"Veterans' Rally Set." *New York Times*, May 11, 1946.
Watts, Richard Jr. "Ambassador Moore." *New York Herald Tribune*. November 10, 1938.
———. "Barroom Talk." *New York Herald Tribune*, October 26, 1939.
———. "Better Than Ever." *New York Herald Tribune*, September 24, 1940.
———. "Night Club Portrait." *New York Herald Tribune*, December 26, 1940.
———. "Youth! Youth!" *New York Herald Tribune*, October 2, 1941.
Watts, Stephen. "On Arranging Terpsichore for the Camera Eye." *New York Times*, September 14, 1952.
"A Wedding Between Rehearsals." *Philadelphia Evening Bulletin*, September 22, 1941.
Weiler, A. H. "Brand-New 'Scent' on the Todd Roster—Kelly's 'Gentleman'—Addenda." *New York Times*, September 28, 1958.
———. "Kelly and Bricusse to Collaborate." *New York Times*, May 5, 1974.
Whipple, Sidney B. "Pal Joey Is a Bright Gay, Tuneful, Novel Work." *New York World-Telegram*, December 26, 1940.
Willens, Michele. "Gene Kelly Opening Municipal Opera Season." *St. Louis Post-Dispatch*, July 1, 1974.
Williams, Esther. *The Million Dollar Mermaid*. New York: Simon & Schuster, 1999.
Wilson, Patricia. *Yesterday's Mashed Potatoes: The Fabulous Life of a Happy Has-Been*. Indianapolis: Dogear, 2009.
Wintz, Jack. "Gene Kelly: Keeping That Singin'-in-the-Rain Spirit." *St. Anthony Messenger* 88, no. 3 (August 1980): 21–26.
Wise, James E. Jr., and Anne Collier Rehill. *Stars in Blue: Movie Actors in America's Sea Services*. Annapolis, MD: Naval Institute Press, 1997.
Wollen, Peter. "Cine-dancer." *Sight and Sound* 6, issue 3 (March 1996): 3.
———. *Singin' in the Rain*. London: British Film Institute, 1992.
Wood, Michael. *America in the Movies: Or, "Santa Maria, It Had Slipped My Mind."* New York: Columbia University Press, 1997.
Wool, Robert. "Skiing in Klosters: The Stars Have Gone but the Glitter Remains." *New York Times*, February 5, 1978.
York, Dick. *The Seesaw Girl and Me: A Memoir*. Elizabeth, NJ: New Path Press, 2004.
York, Pat. *Going Strong*. New York: Arcade, 1991.
Yudkoff, Alvin. *Gene Kelly: A Life of Dance and Dreams*. New York: Back Stage Books, 1999.

Index